ON THE NECESSITY OF GARDENING

ON THE NECESSITY OF GARDENING

An ABC of Art, Botany and Cultivation

Laurie Cluitmans (ed.)

WITH CONTRIBUTIONS BY
Maria Barnas
Jonny Bruce
Laurie Cluitmans
Thiëmo Heilbron
Liesbeth M. Helmus
Erik A. de Jong
René de Kam
Alhena Katsof
Jamaica Kincaid
Bart Rutten
Catriona Sandilands
Patricia de Vries

Valiz, Amsterdam

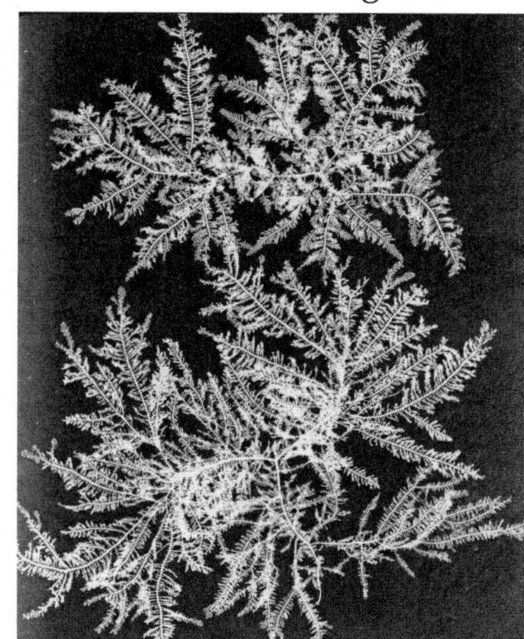

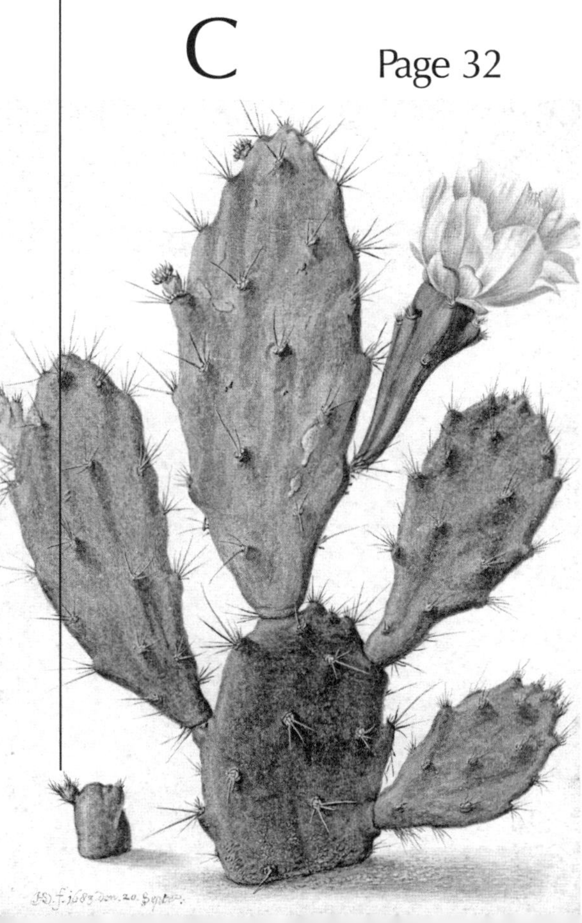

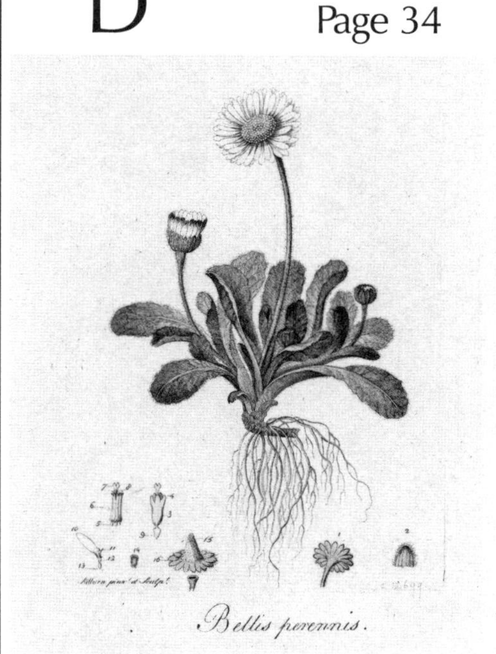
Bellis perennis.

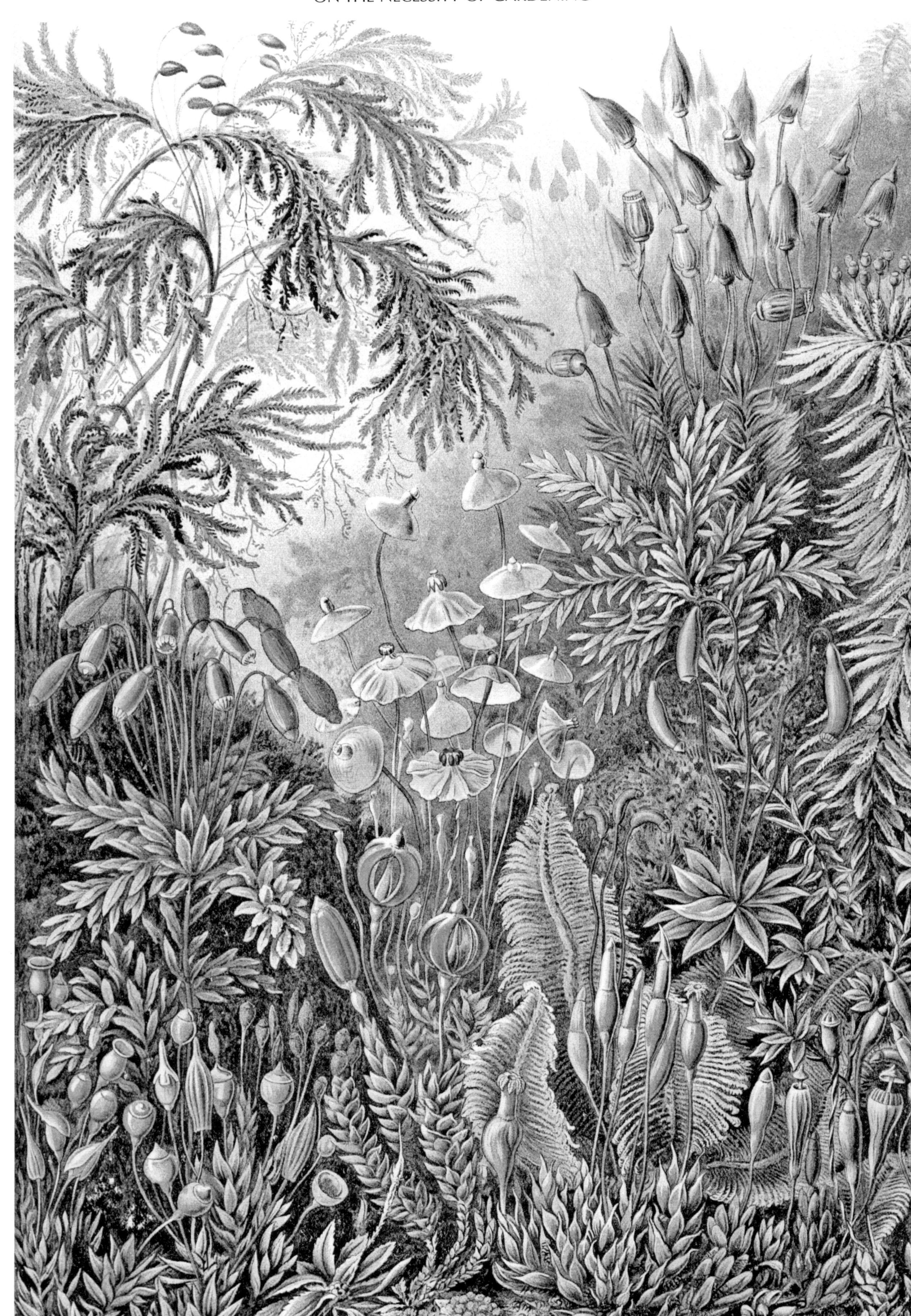

Ernst Haeckel, **Plate 72, Muscinae** from **Kunstformen der Natur**, 1904, engraving.

Foreword
Like a Mirror

Erik A. de Jong

A garden opens up space for making and experiencing. It ritualizes our existence and gives it meaning. Attention and care weave living nature together with our human condition. We see that emerge as a law in the universal culture that is gardening. This often manifests itself where the need is greatest: in the community gardens of densely populated American cities, in gardens created by the homeless, by soldiers in trenches during a war, or by refugees in their tent camps. Interacting with plants offers beauty, comfort, homecoming, and grounding. It may heal that which is broken. The garden is a mirror of the maker and the user, in whom it is reflected *simultaneously*. The garden is a social space for family, friends, and companions in adversity and, therefore, has an emancipatory and liberating power. As an affective space, the garden transcends its own boundaries. As an experiential space, it represents a place in which the world can be known and understood.

It was not so long ago that twentieth-century international modernism aimed for a tabula rasa, an earth that could be redesigned as a blank page. Nature and the garden did not meet the objective and functional standards of modernist architecture and urban planning. The garden and gardening were associated primarily with an everyday emotional world: the domestic garden, the allotment garden, the villa garden. It took a man of letters, Gerrit Komrij (1944–2012), to remind us of the 'necessity of gardening' in his 1990 Huizinga lecture. For Komrij as an artist, the garden was important as a metaphor, as a revelation, as an equivocal and ambiguous reality. To his mind, man as a gardener—a myth of cohesion and responsibility—had become powerless. With the ascendency of modernism, the French landscape architect Achille Duchêne (1866–1947) wrote in 1937 that the 'art of the garden was dead' because it had disappeared from public discourse. The garden went underground into the unofficial territory of the personal living environment.

It was in the nineteen-nineties, when modernism's dogmas began to crumble, that the garden sprouted once again. Gardens and parks with their living nature were to become a necessary and public part of a biodiverse ecology and of healthy 'green' cities. That insight into the power of the garden continues to this day. Climate change and a growing understanding of the state of the planet in what is called our Anthropocene world contribute ever more urgently to this awareness. Over the past year, the way of life that COVID-19 has forced upon us has helped many people to rediscover the profound significance of gardens and gardening for our society.

Those who garden become committed, to nature and to themselves. Gardening is an active dialogue with living material. It is about locality and place, about where we are, and it can be done anywhere, regardless of conventions. It brings together thinking, feeling, making, and performing. The garden is an answer to a culture in which mind and body, intellect and action are separated from each other. It exchanges passive consumption for a skilful, creative, and hands-on process, where thinking and manual work go hand in hand. Gardening provides us with empathy as a tool for maintaining healthy relationships. After all, the garden is a training ground for regeneration. It teaches respect for the soil and for ecosystems with their non-human beings, who are our fellow citizens. We learn to overcome our plant blindness by understanding that plants interact with insects, fungi, and microbes and are able to communicate through their filigree root systems. Knowing and caring for vegetables, herbs, flowers, grasses, and trees brings utility and beauty together in a joyful activity in which effort and relaxation alternate.

The garden is more than an object, a style, or a form. In Creole and African-American traditions, a garden full of vegetables and medicinal plants connects the resident's identity with nature, place, community, and ancestors. It is not the visual element of the design that is important, but rather the location where objects and plants stand, the power they possess, and the way in which the space wants to function as a magical order. This order, which defines and protects, is invisible and unknowable to the uninitiated. The garden with its plants acts as a protective amulet: it connects the visible with the invisible.

A garden need not be enclosed. It can form a landscape, find itself on a roof, a balcony, or in the water, be mobile or grow vertically. Gardening is an adventure, in which process demands our special attention. Experience wants to be rooted in the active experiment with our senses, with patience and adversity, chaos and order, with open and closed, fragrance, colour and light, growth, decay, and metamorphosis. Intimate interaction with soils, waters, plants, stones, animals, and seasons means that the garden manifests itself differently in different cultures, although its therapeutic effect on the body and soul is universal. The garden opens the portal to understanding that cultural diversity can coincide with biodiversity.

The garden has multiple meanings. It is a place where feelings and memories may be expressed. It can reveal contested meanings and is, therefore, an important theme in art and literature. In the garden, time passes with a certain slowness, which contrasts with the acceleration of global consumer and commercial culture. This distance from the world facilitates the necessary awareness of our relationship with nature, and in particular of our surviving colonial relationship with people, animals, and plants. We can explore our own nature in the garden, our identity and gender, the meaning of our origin and birthplace, the dimensions of our social inclusion or exclusion.

In his treatise *De Constantia in publicis malis* (*On Constancy in Times of Public Evil*, 1584), the humanist scholar Justus Lipsius (1547–1606) wrote that it is not the prison of home and city but the garden under the open sky that provides the space and freedom for us to contemplate our complex humanity, our life and death. Especially in difficult times, he attempted to reveal, it is the garden that is the training ground for the creativity and wisdom that will enable us to recreate the world.

Introduction On the Necessity of Gardening

Laurie Cluitmans

For centuries, the garden has been regarded as a mirror of society, a microcosm of the larger world, reflecting on a small scale the broader relationships between nature and culture. In his lecture *On the Necessity of Gardening*, the Dutch poet Gerrit Komrij describes how the image of the garden has long been closely interwoven with intellectual developments and clashes between world views:

> The essence of nature has never changed. We have merely ascribed to it different meanings, tamed it through a succession of visions. By imposing geometric order or through miniaturisation, we made it appear familiar to us so that, thus constrained, it corresponded to our nature or an ideal thereof. The symbolic value we conferred upon it, enabled us to avoid feeling 'abandoned' by nature or to view it as an 'alien' threat. As gardeners, artists and ritual worshippers, we have intervened in and elevated nature.[1]

The garden, Komrij writes, is an essential metaphor for our relationship with the natural world. He pleaded for a revival of the connection between the garden and the realm of thought, in which spirit gardening becomes a metaphor for nurturing the world of ideas *and* for maintaining our physical world. Komrij delivered his lecture in 1990. In the thirty years that have since elapsed, the world has changed radically. The current climate crisis makes the desire for a revival of the figurative value of the garden poignantly relevant once again, and if anything demonstrates just how precarious our current situation is, it is the COVID-19 crisis.

Some scholars have referred to our current epoch as the Anthropocene, indicating the total dominance of man (*anthropos*) over nature. But defined as such, it is a limiting concept, implying that all people are equally responsible for what we have done to nature, thus ignoring colonial power relations and issues of gender, race, and class. The biologist, philosopher, and science historian Donna Haraway criticizes the Anthropocene as being essentially driven by capital. Her proposed alternative is the Chthulucene, an emergent world view that proposes the coexistence of all living and dying beings.

Against this background, artists are once again turning to the garden as the pre-eminent site for the interrogation of the relationship between nature and culture, wilderness and order, freedom and control. The garden is not a neutral space. It is not merely a space to spend leisure time, or a retreat, safe and secluded. Nor is the garden just a place to let escapism run wild. No. In the garden, life is reflected and manifests itself. What can we, together with these artists, learn from the garden?

This publication, like the exhibition at the Centraal Museum, takes its point of departure from the present, with contemporary artists who reflect upon the garden's role, its potential, and its function as a metaphor for society. Therefore, we contextualize the artists' works and the issues they raise by placing them amidst a wide range of cultural and scientific references and essays.

In a time of climate change, we see that artists are considering the garden as a place to experience a different rhythm than that of the nine-to-five, where gardening is a hopeful form of labour in which, through care, plants and flowers are brought to blossom. In her meditative film *The Garden*, Sara Sejin Chang (Sara van der Heide) clearly shows the calming effect and experience of cyclical time. Jeremy Deller and Stan Douglas examine the allotment garden and show how each gardener commands their plot, creating their own paradise on earth. More than a hundred years ago, Vincent

1 'Het wezen van de natuur is nooit veranderd, alleen wij hebben er telkens andere inhouden aan gegeven, haar bedwongen in telkens andere beelden. Door geometrische ordening, door miniaturisering maakten we dat ze ons vertrouwd voorkwam omdat ze, aldus bedwongen, met ons innerlijk of met een ideaal van ons innerlijk correspondeerde. Door de symboolwaarde die we haar verleenden maakten we dat we ons niet 'in de steek gelaten' voelden en dat ze zich niet als een bedreiging 'los van ons', manifesteerde. Ingrijpen en verheffen dat deden we met de natuur, als tuinman, kunstenaar en ritueel aanbidder.' Gerrit Komrij, **Over de noodzaak van tuinieren**, Amsterdam: Bert Bakker, 1991, 61.

van Gogh documented the last allotments in Montmartre, before they were absorbed by Paris's rapid urban expansion. The need, at the time, for a private green space in an age of industrialization and urbanization still resonates today.

That the garden, as Komrij described, is also a metaphor for society, is an idea that has been expressed in art and literature for centuries. This is explored in various ways in the publication and exhibition, for example in the relationship between the visual tradition of depicting the Garden of Eden and the Persian garden carpet. Both images reveal a completely different view of nature: a moral question in the Garden of Eden, and the need for shade and water in a dry environment in the Persian carpet. Through the work of Andrea Büttner, for example, we look at the effects of the system of taxonomy on the appreciation of certain flowers and plants. Seventeenth-century flower still lifes by Johannes Bosschaert, Ambrosius Bosschaert the Younger, and Roelant Saverij from the collection of the Centraal Museum are paired with critical investigations by artists such as Maria Thereza Alves, Persijn Broersen & Margit Lukács, Patricia Kaersenhout, Willem de Rooij, and Jennifer Tee, who show us where these flowers and plants originated and reveal their relationships with colonial history.

In the publication, we seek answers to the questions raised by these artists and their practice. These answers or suggestions are ordered in the form of an abecedarium, in which each new line begins with the next letter of the Latin alphabet. While the nature of the abecedarium may be reminiscent of an encyclopaedic pursuit of completeness within a system, that is by no means the intention or goal here. That the act of naming can also be an act of control and an exercise of power becomes clear in this publication in entries relating to the ordering systems of Linnaeus, for instance, and also in the relationship between the botanical garden and the museum. Those power relations that were the basis of and consolidated the botanical revolution are used in a radically different way by contemporary artists and thinkers.

The content of the abecedarium is based on the practice of these artists, who engage, critically and playfully, with the garden as a metaphor and a means of reflecting upon the times in which we live. In order to limit the content to some extent, subjects such as the garden as a site for growing food or plants for dyes are discussed only obliquely. Inspired by the practice of the participating artists or nominated by them, the selection of terms, concepts, people, and gardens is necessarily subjective and is by no means exhaustive. Rather, it is a selection of associations and affinities that deal mainly with the garden in a metaphorical sense: the garden as a reflection of our society. The abecedarium thus gives structure to fragments from art history, cultural history, literature, poetry, philosophy, biology, and the natural sciences.

In addition to this selection of quotations, more in-depth analysis is provided by essays and other contributions, mostly written especially for this publication. In his foreword, Erik A. de Jong places the renewed interest in the garden in a broader context and shows how the garden has long served as a mirror of society. Alhena Katsof explores the links between the garden and Europe's violent history of colonization, dissecting the meaning of autochthony; Jamaica Kincaid interweaves her obsession with gardening with memories of her childhood and her mother, and places them in the geopolitical context in which people and plants have been uprooted. Patricia de Vries analyzes Eve's motive in the Garden of Eden as a courageous act to break out of an orderly system. Writer and poet Maria Barnas shifts the perspective from which we view landscape elements such as the *ha-ha*. Ethnobotanist Thiëmo Heilbron shares indigenous knowledge and traditional uses of a selection of plants from Suriname's botanical heritage. René de Kam traces the history of the Centraal Museum's garden, which began as a monastery garden and has changed shape over the centuries. Gardener and writer Jonny Bruce reflects on Derek Jarman's garden at Prospect Cottage as a pharmacopoeia, and Liesbeth M. Helmus discusses painter

Roelant Saverij's seventeenth-century garden in Utrecht. The publication closes with an essay by Catriona Sandilands, in which she demonstrates that gardening is not determined exclusively by the human will, but is a gathering, as Haraway advocates, of many different species. I am enormously grateful to all the authors for their profound reflections on the garden's metaphorical potential. To borrow from Sandilands and conclude this introduction:

> As spaces, as institutions, and as privileged nodes in global movements of plants and people, gardens are not only worlds but also *in* and *of* the world.

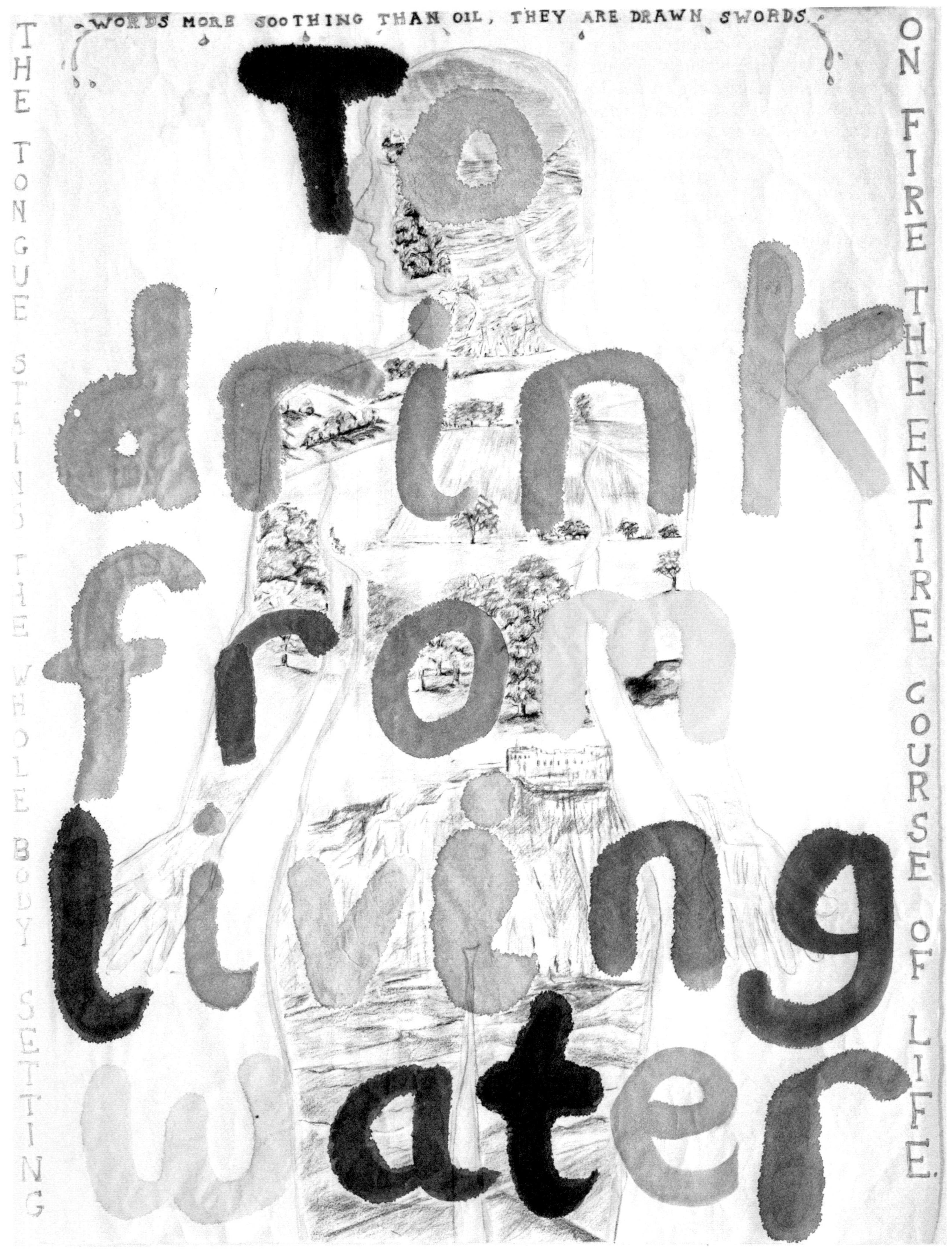

Maria Pask, **To drink from living water**, 2020, gouache drawing, 97 × 74 cm. Courtesy Maria Pask and Ellen de Bruijne Projects, Amsterdam.

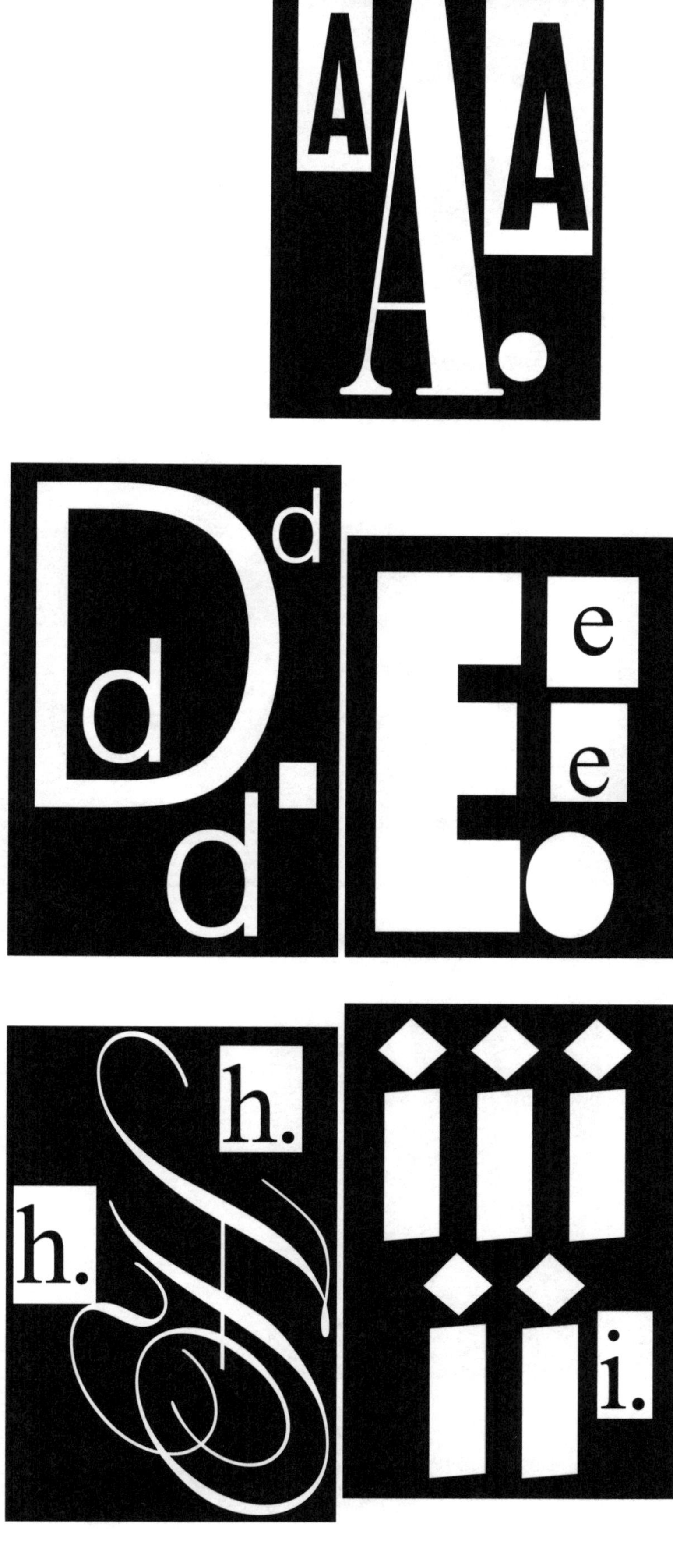

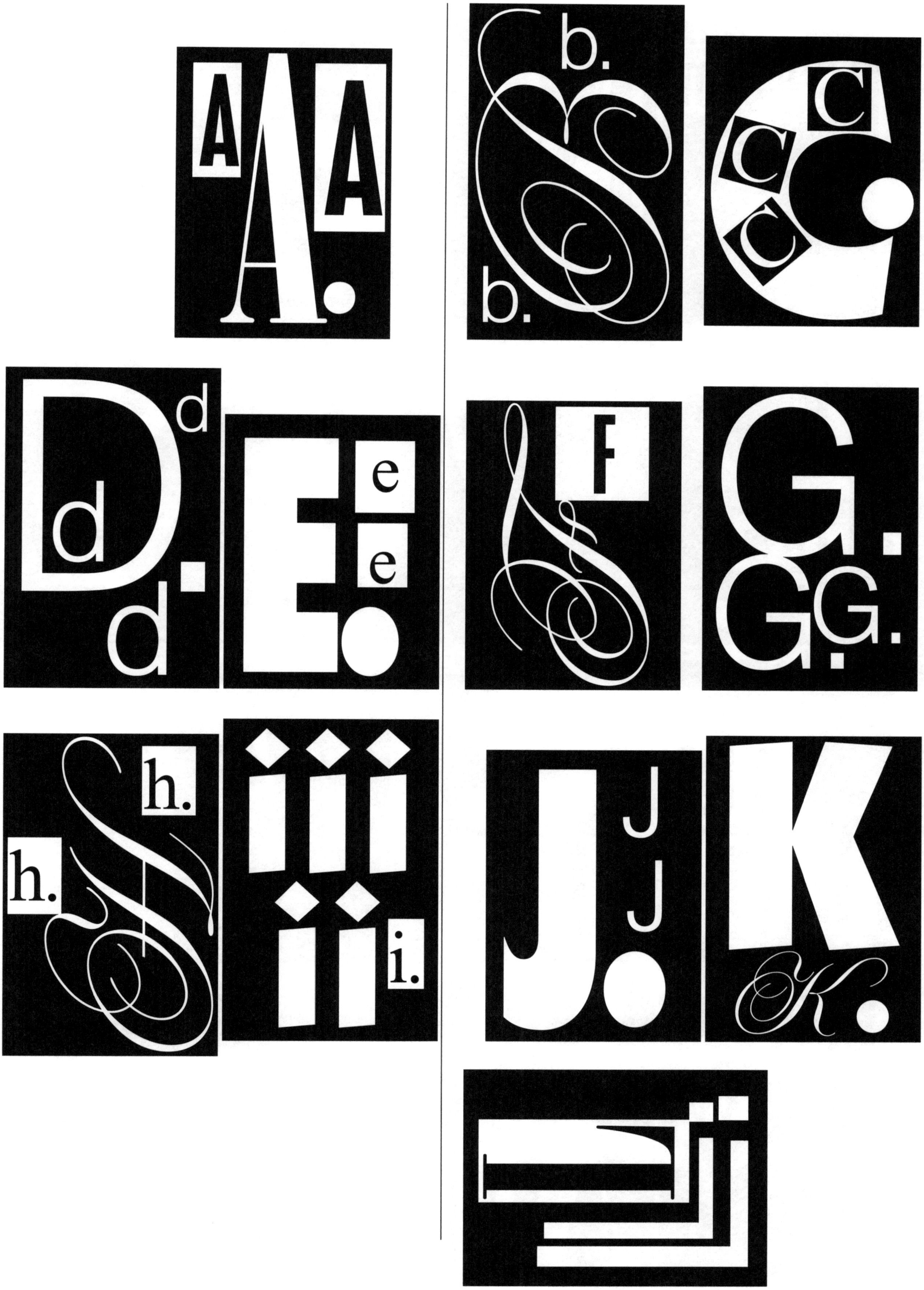

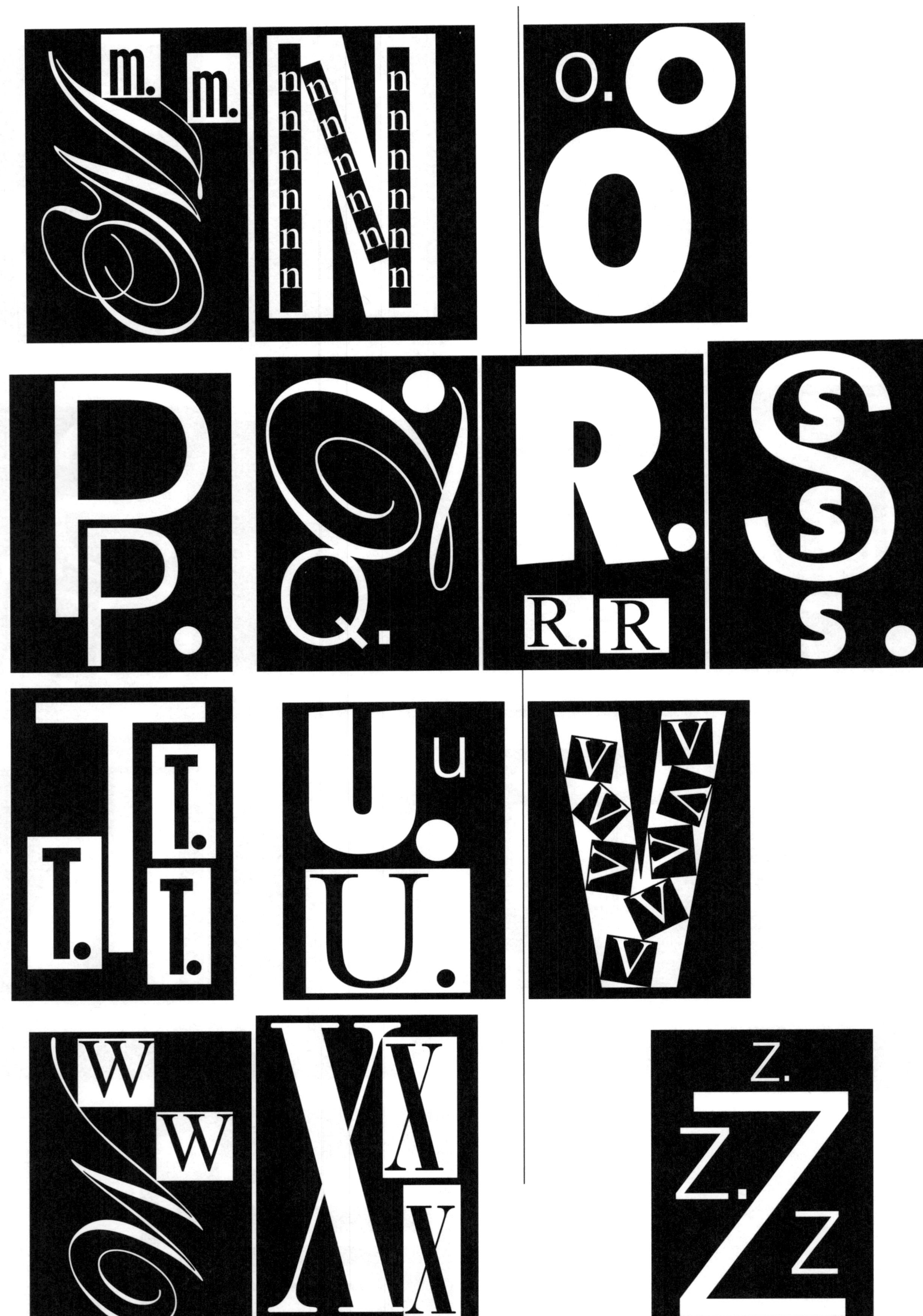

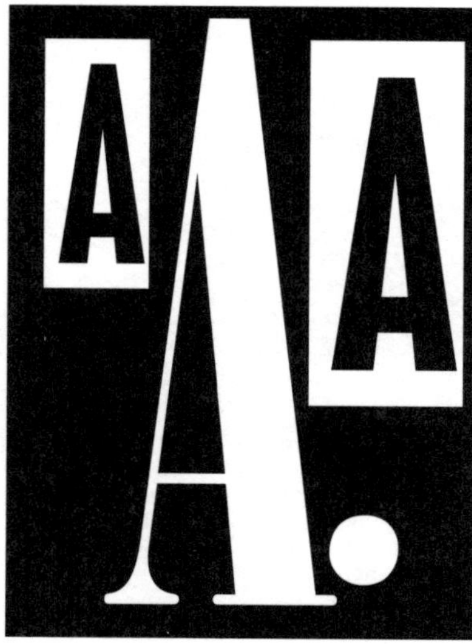

ALGAE

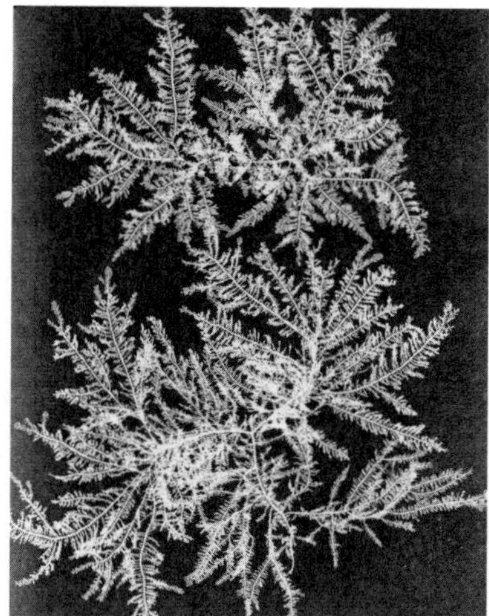

Anna Atkins, **Ptilota plumosa** from **Photographs of British Algae. Cyanotype Impressions**, c. 1843–c. 1853, cyanotype, 25 × 20 cm. Courtesy Rijksmuseum Amsterdam.

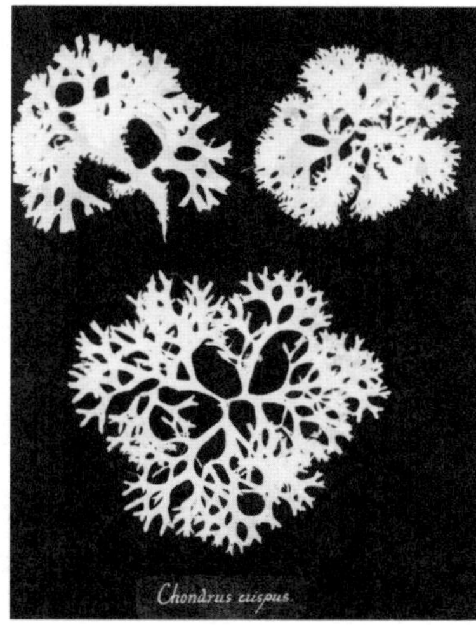

Anna Atkins, **Chondrus crispus** from **Photographs of British Algae. Cyanotype Impressions**, c. 1843–c. 1853, cyanotype, 25 × 20 cm. Courtesy Rijksmuseum Amsterdam.

ALLOTMENT GARDEN

[Allotments] can be read as paradoxical and liminal, hovering between urban and rural, habitant and leisure ground, sanctuary and physical burden, private place and public space. They hold a lure of the local and a fascination of the different... They are 'open plan' yet sit behind firmly locked gates, surrounded by densely packed urban houses. The anonymity of the city street outside the locked gate contrasts starkly with the comradely greetings and—predominantly vegetable-based—conversations that take place a metre inside. And yet each plot has a sense of privacy within the gates.

McKay, *Radical Gardening*, 157.

The beginnings of the allotment movement were connected with campaigns for public welfare when municipalities provided the poor sections of the populations not with financial support but with plots of land situated outside the residential areas for growing fruit and vegetables. These were intended to improve the poor nutrition of families, and were laid out as simple kitchen gardens with rows of vegetable beds and fruit trees.

Wahmann, 'Allotments and Schrebergarten in Germany', 451.

Urban gardening is a practice that stretches back as far as there have been cities. [...] It was with the rise of industrialisation, triggered by the agricultural and later industrial revolutions, aided by the exodus of landless rural populations to industrial centres for work, that the enormous urban regions that we know today first started to develop at astonishing speed. [...] The new urban populations could not grow food—there was no space or time—and food was brought into the cities from outside—eventually, often imported as preserved or frozen, using new technologies, from far afield. [...] As well as new riches generated from the industry there was also widespread poverty and malnutrition together with a range of 'social evils' such as alcoholism. [...] Thus, in the nineteenth century, [...] efforts were made to improve city environments through drainage and sewerage schemes, public parks, model suburbs and allotment gardens. [...] The provision of allotment gardens as a means of growing additional food was primarily aimed at the working poor. [...] [S]uffice it to say that urban allotment gardens have been on the scene for a long time in many countries and they have had their periods of popularity and decline.

Bell, *Urban Allotment Gardens in Europe*, 1–2.

SARA SEJIN CHANG (SARA VAN DER HEIDE)

Sara Sejin Chang filmed her own allotment in Tuinwijck, in the north-east of Amsterdam, for a year. Chang's camera traces the changing colours and forms of leaves, the emergence, decomposition, and death of plants, and the garden's other inhabitants and visitors. The film is concerned not with spectacle and endless growth, but rather with the slow passage of time. The result is a meditative film in which the seasons succeed each other and the cycle of life and death rules. It is a reappraisal of time and is in stark contrast to the idea of linear and infinite growth. (ed.)

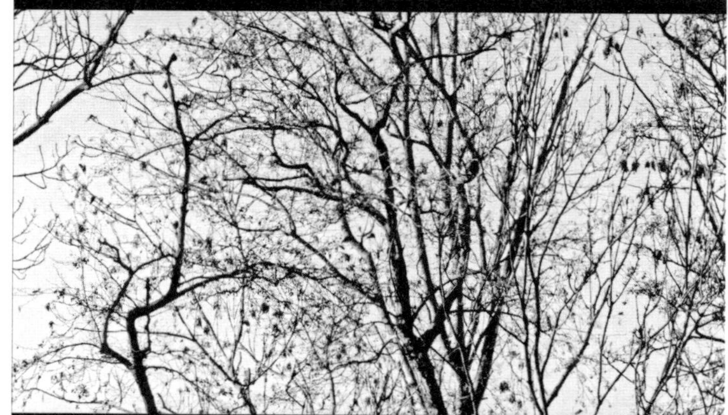

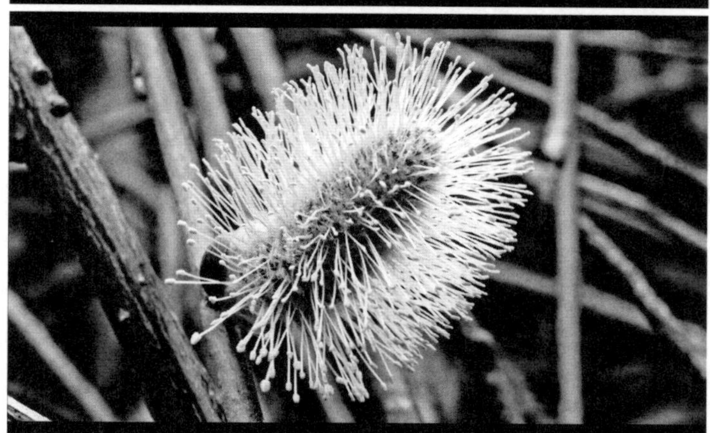

Sara Sejin Chang (Sara van der Heide), **The Garden**, 2014, colour, no sound 54", HD/DCP, commissioned by If I Can't Dance I Don't Want To Be Part Of Your Revolution, courtesy Sara Sejin Chang (Sara van der Heide).

JEREMY DELLER

The British artist Jeremy Deller conceived this collaborative project especially for the Skulptur Projekte Münster, an open-air exhibition that takes place every ten years in the German city of Münster. In 2007, he invited gardeners from the city's fifty-four allotment associations to keep a nature diary for a period of ten years. Deller provided each association with a large, green leather-bound book, which the gardeners filled with anecdotes, poems, short stories, children's drawings, and newspaper clippings. Each book is like a microcosm of the allotment association and its ever-changing relationship with nature. (ed.)

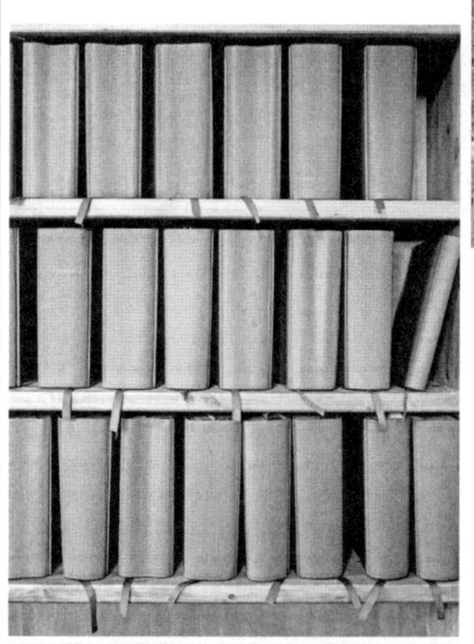

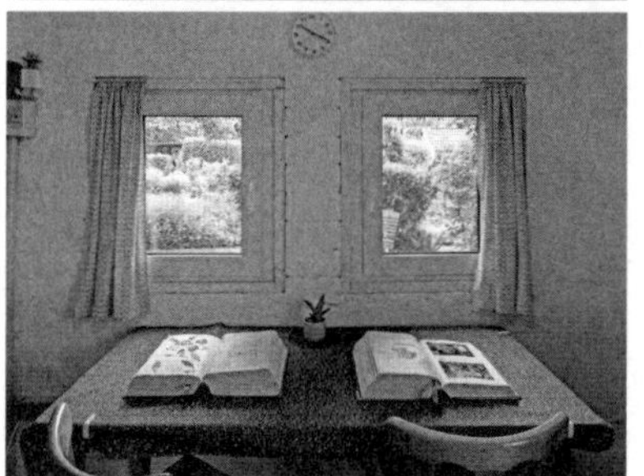

Jeremy Deller, **Speak to the Earth and It Will Tell You**, 2007–2017, installation view LWL-Museum für Kunst und Kultur, Westfälisches Landesmuseum, Münster. Courtesy Skulptur Projekte Archiv. Photo: Henning Rogge.

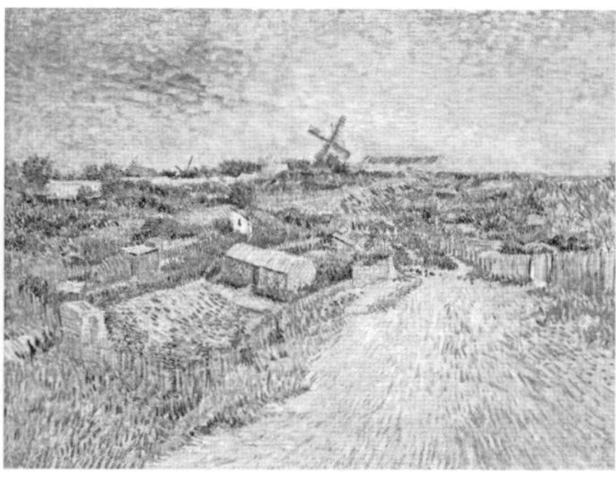

Vincent van Gogh, **Kitchen Gardens on Montmartre**, 1887, oil on canvas, 96 × 120 cm. Courtesy Stedelijk Museum Amsterdam.

VINCENT VAN GOGH

During his time in Paris, Vincent van Gogh painted the hill of Montmartre several times. This work is part of a series that he painted in the summer of 1887 and focuses on the kitchen gardens and allotments that were there at the time. Here he has painted several plots of land, each with its own ramshackle shed. With its evocation of the atmosphere of a sunny summer's day, the painting has a picturesque quality. However, Montmartre was rapidly changing at the end of the nineteenth century and its rural character was already being absorbed by Paris's encroaching urbanization. (ed.)

ANTHROPOCENE

For the past three centuries, the effects of humans on the global environment have escalated. Because of these anthropogenic emissions of carbon dioxide, global climate may depart significantly from natural behaviour for many millennia to come. It seems appropriate to assign the term 'Anthropocene' to the present, in many ways human-dominated, geological epoch, supplementing the Holocene—the warm period of the past 10–12 millennia. The Anthropocene could be said to have started in the latter part of the eighteenth century, when analyses of air trapped in polar ice showed the beginning of growing global concentrations of carbon dioxide and methane. This date also happens to coincide with James Watt's design of the steam engine in 1784.

Crutzen, 'Geology of Mankind', 23.

It is time to leave the twenty-first century. The metabolic rift that wakes from the carbon liberation front is not the only challenge to the biosphere. The Anthropocene is the name Paul Crutzen and others give to this period of geological time upon which the planet has entered. Crutzen: 'About 30-50% of the planet's land surface is exploited by humans.... More than half of all accessible freshwater is used by mankind. Fisheries remove more than 25% of the primary production in upwelling ocean regions... Energy use has grown 16-fold during the twentieth century... More nitrogen fertilizer is applied in agriculture than is fixed naturally in all terrestrial ecosystems.'

It's not the end of the world, but it is the end of prehistory. It is time to announce in the marketplace of social media that the God who still hid in the worldview of an ecology that was self-correcting, self-balancing and self-healing—is dead. 'The Anthropocene represents a new phase in the history of the Earth, when natural forces and human forces became intertwined, so that the fate of one determines the fate of the other. Geologically, this is a remarkable episode in the history of the planet.' The human is no longer that figure in the foreground which pursues its self-interest against the background of a holistic, organicist cycle that the human might perturb but with which it can be in balance and harmony, in the end, by simply withdrawing from certain excesses.

The term Anthropocene splices two roots together, anthropos and kainos. Anthropos: that with the face of 'man', that which looks up. Kainos: that which is not just a new unit of time but a new quality or form.

Wark, 'Chthulucene, Capitalocene, Anthropocene'.

The winds of the Anthropocene carry ghosts—the vestiges and signs of past ways of life still charged in the present. [...] 'Anthropocene' is the proposed name for a geologic epoch in which humans have become the major force determining the continuing liveability of the earth. The word tells a big story: living arrangements that took millions of years to put into place are being undone in the blink of an eye. The hubris of conquerors and corporations makes it uncertain what we can bequeath to our next generations, human and not human. The enormity of our dilemma leaves scientists, writers, artists and scholars in shock.

Gan, *Introduction: Haunted Landscapes of the Anthropocene*, 1.

As a provocation, let me summarize my objections to the Anthropocene as a tool, story, or epoch to think with:

1. The myth system associated with the Anthropos is a setup, and the stories end badly. More to the point, they end in double death; they are not about ongoingness. It is hard to tell a good story with such a bad actor. Bad actors need a story, but not the whole story.

2. Species Man does not make history.

3. Man plus Tool does not make history. That is the story of History human exceptionalists tell.

4. That History must give way to geostories, to Gaia stories, to synchthonic stories; terrans do webbed, braided, and tentacular living and dying in sympoietic multispecies string figures; they do not do History.

5. The human social apparatus of the Anthropocene tends to be top-heavy and bureaucracy prone. Revolt needs other forms of action and other stories for solace, inspiration, and effectiveness.

6. Despite its reliance on agile computer modeling and autopoietic systems theories, the Anthropocene relies too much on what should be an 'unthinkable' theory of relations, namely the old one of bounded utilitarian individualism—pre existing units in competition relations that take up all the air in the atmosphere (except, apparently, carbon dioxide).

7. The sciences of the Anthropocene are too much contained within restrictive systems theories and within evolutionary theories called the Modern Synthesis, which for all their extraordinary importance have proven unable to think well about sympoiesis, symbiosis, symbiogenesis, development, webbed ecologies, and microbes. That's a lot of trouble for adequate evolutionary theory.

8. Anthropocene is a term most easily meaningful and usable by intellectuals in wealthy classes and regions; it is not an idiomatic term for climate, weather, land, care of country, or much else in great swathes of the world, especially but not only among indigenous peoples.

Haraway, *Staying with the Trouble*, 49.

ARBORETUM

Place where trees, shrubs, and sometimes herbaceous plants are cultivated for scientific and educational purposes. An arboretum may be a collection in its own right or a part of a botanical garden.

Encyclopaedia Britannica, 'Arboretum'.

These collections [of trees] had a dual purpose: cultivation and study, certainly, but also as suppliers of trees for other estates and gardens, and for their aesthetic value. There were many historical reasons for the establishment of tree collections—for show, of course, but also in later cultures simply to supply estates with plants for the production of timber and ship-building, even also as shelters for game.

Hunt, *A World of Gardens*, 139.

ARCADIA

There have always been two kinds of arcadia: shaggy and smooth; dark and light; a place of bucolic leisure and a place of primitive panic.

Schama, *Landscape and Memory*, 517.

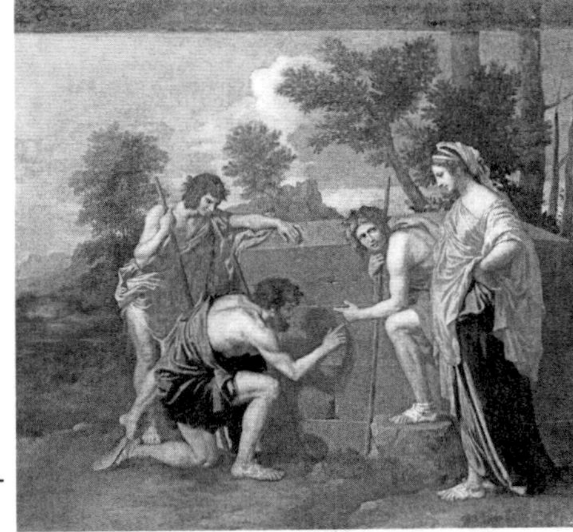

Nicolas Poussin, **Et in Arcadia Ego**, 1637–638, oil on canvas, 85 × 121 cm. Courtesy RMN-Grand Palais (Musée du Louvre). Photo: Stéphane Maréchalle.

It was with this image as starting-point that Virgil created the pastoral world that he situated in Arcadia, an isolated hilly region of the Peloponnese, the southern peninsula of Greece, and the favourite haunt of Pan, god of pastures, flocks and woods.

Aben and De Wit, *The Enclosed Garden*, 34.

When the phrase 'Et in Arcadia Ego' occurs in Italy in the early 17th century, its meaning is that of a memento mori, a reminder of death: 'I am Death, present here even in Arcadia'. We also come across this theme in 17th century painting. In around 1621/23 for instance Guercino did a painting of two shepherds discovering to their dismay a skull on a piece of ruined masonry in an otherwise pastoral scene. This open confrontation with death and decay had a theological, didactic and ethical content. [...]

In two famous paintings the French artist Nicolas Poussin succeeded in converting mortal theology into a Virgilian elegy. His version of 'Et in Arcadia Ego' (ca. 1630) in the Chatsworth House collection shows two shepherds

[Castor and Polydeuces], wildered both,
Searched through the boskage of the hill, and found
Hard by a slab of rock a bubbling spring
Brimful of purest water. In the depths
Below, like crystal or like silver gleamed
The pebbles: high above it pine and plane
And poplar rose, and cypress tipt with green;
With rich flowers that throng the mead, when wanes
The Spring, sweet workshops of the furry bee.

Theocritus, *Idylls* 22:36–42.

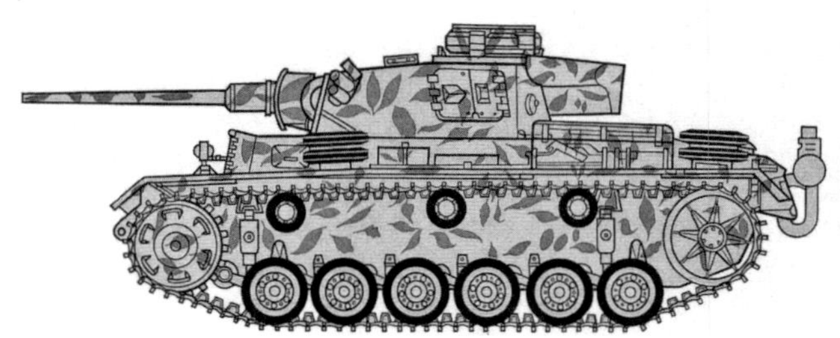

Ian Hamilton Finlay, **Arcadia**, 1973, silkscreen on paper, 37.7 × 46.1 cm. Courtesy Van Abbemuseum, Eindhoven. Photo: Peter Cox.

19.8.07

Atmen unter Sonnenblumen

Herbert Voigt unterweist Künstler und Kleingärtner in Yoga

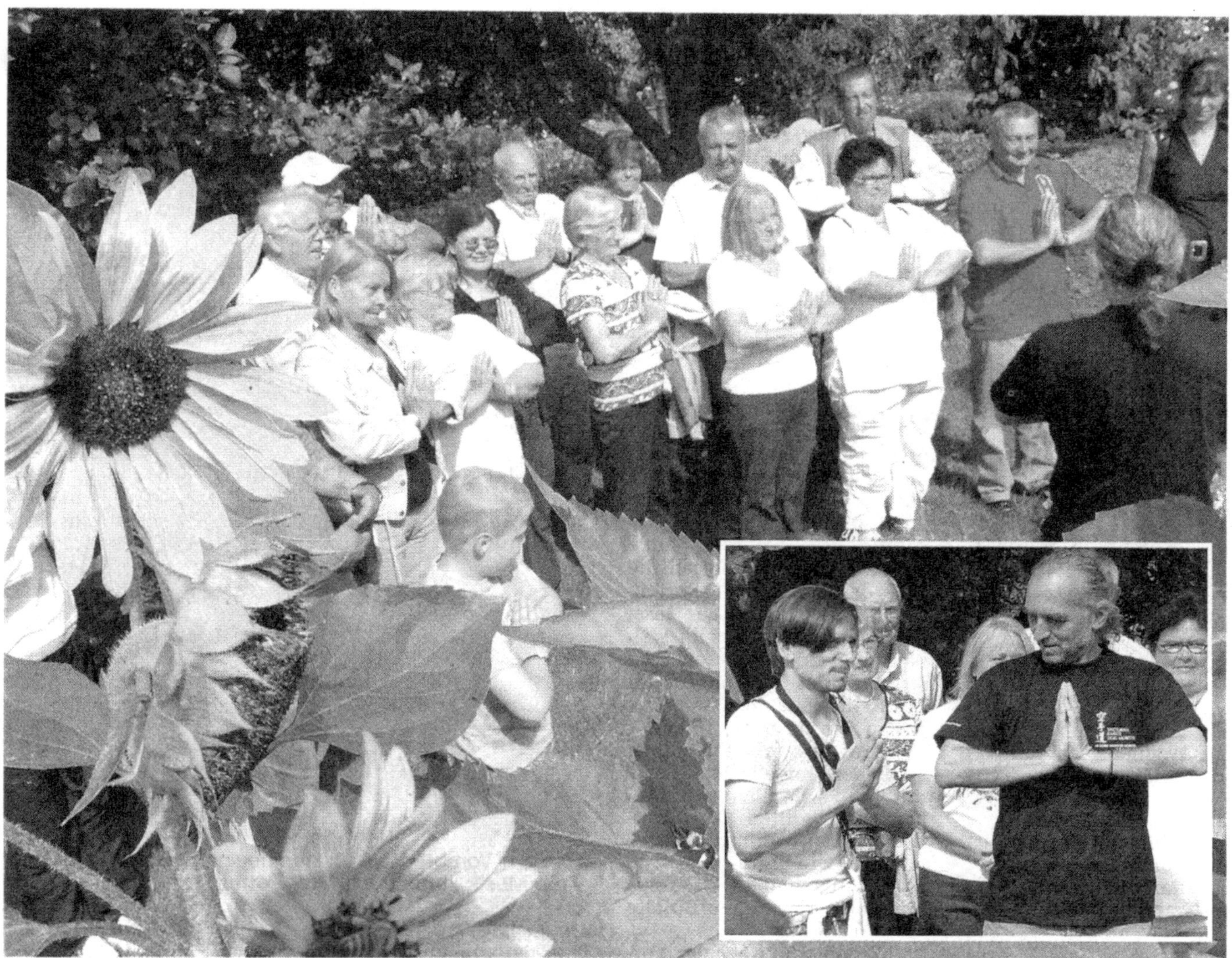

Herbert Voigt (r.) zeigte Jeremy Deller (kl. Bild. l. und den Kleingärtnern vom „Mühlenfeld" wie Yoga geht. Fotos: -kok-

Wetter ~~Juli~~ 2007 August

Ich empfand den August zu kalt und zu nass. An den beiden Wochenenden, wo wir im Garten gefeiert haben, hatten wir Glück.
Die Zeitung schrieb:

Kaum zu glauben: August war zu warm und zu trocken

Und auch die Sonne schien mehr als üblich

Da ist ein Bild von unserem "Star".

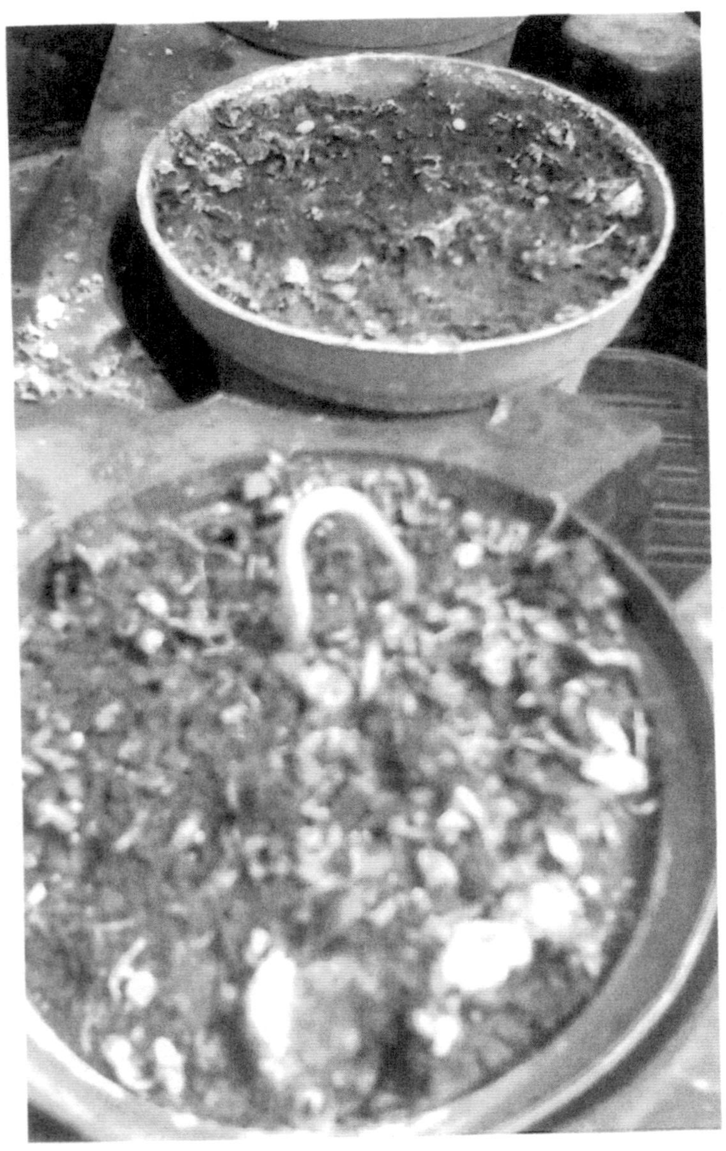

Taschen-
tuch-
baum
Zögling
28.4.08
von Wolfgang
Rohe

Blumen

Meine Tulpen blühen in voller Pracht.
Umzingelt sind sie dieses Jahr von
unzähligen Vergißmeinnicht.
Auch mein spanisches Ochsenauge zeigt die
ersten blauen Blüten.
Am Ende des Monats habe ich auch
meine Dahlien schon in die Erde gebracht.

Jeremy Deller, **Speak to the Earth and It Will Tell You**, 2007–2017, installation view LWL-Museum für Kunst und Kultur, Westfälisches Landesmuseum, Münster. Courtesy Skulptur Projekte Archiv. Photo: Hanna Neander.

A continues on page 27.

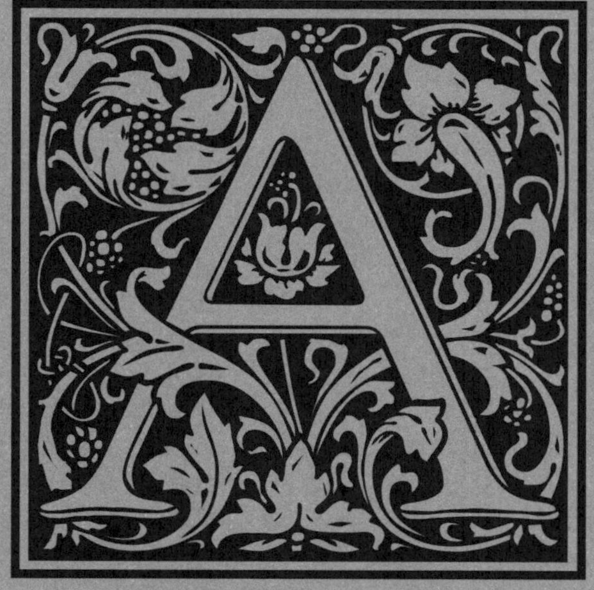

William Morris, **Letter A.**

MYTHOLOGICAL FORMULATIONS

AUTOCHTHONY AT THE ROOT OF THE MATTER

Alhena Katsof

'The people of Island were *autochthones*, that is, earth-bred, or bred out of their owne soile like vnto trees and herbs.'

A. Ionas *Brief Comm. Island* (1592) in Richard Hakluyt, *The Principal Navigations, Voyages, Traffiques and Discoveries of the English Nation* (1600).

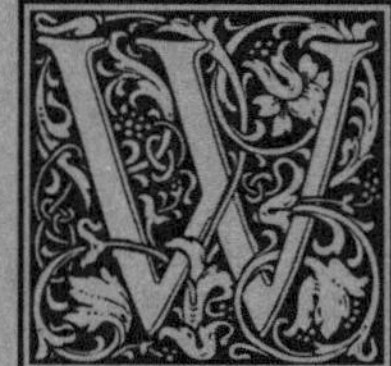

hile the English word *garden*, a noun that refers equally to kitchen gardens, orchards, and palace landscaping, can be etymologically traced to the thirteenth century, it doesn't emerge as a verb meaning 'to lay out and cultivate' until the 1570s. This expansion of the term—from noun to verb—wasn't random or coincidental. It is causal to a number of seismic, perspectival shifts that took place over time. These include the rapid enclosure of public lands in England, the revival of classical influences in the arts, and a significant transition from Christianity to the secular humanism and scientific paradigm that takes shape in Europe in the fifteenth century. During this transition, the ontological distinction between Man and nature is established and takes hold of the imagination, brutally impacting the way people understand notions of cultivation and place, and our relationships with plants and with each other. In short, it affects our every understanding of being in the world.

With the distinction between Man and nature set in place, it takes no time at all for distinctions between different types of humans (men and women, civilized and savage, adult and child) to be claimed. If we can conceptualize ourselves as separate from the earth, then why not from each other? The Caribbean philosopher Sylvia Wynter, who refers to these hierarchical distinctions as genres of the human, writes that colonial rule was underwritten by a belief in the moral superiority of certain humans, which was justified in turn by an image of the native as sub-human or non-human, making the native suitable for improvement, ownership, and enslavement.[1] This conceptualization of Man is integral to the political machinations of colonialism and racial capitalism that began as an intra-European phenomenon and would become the continent's most terrible export. The colonialism I am writing about takes many shapes. It impacts those peasants whose common lands were taken and enclosed as early as the twelfth century, the enslaved Africans forced to work on plantations in the so-called New World, and the Indigenous peoples who were eradicated there. Wynter powerfully argues that we need to examine the early stages of European expansion—when the notion of gardening takes root—in order to understand the epoch in which human activity has had a dominant impact on the earth.[2] This epoch (in which humans become caretakers, overseers, and gardeners) is defined, according to Wynter, not by the 'discovery'

1 Sylvia Wynter, 'Unsettling the Coloniality of Being/Power/Truth/Freedom: Towards the Human, After Man, Its Overrepresentation—An Argument', **New Centennial Review** 3, no. 3 (Fall 2003), 257–337.

2 Wynter, 'Unsettling the Coloniality of Being/Power/Truth/Freedom', 291.

of the New World, as the story is so often told, but rather by the rise of Europe as a globally hegemonic civilization.[3] The actions of European explorers and settlers were made possible by a new image of the earth set in motion by the likes of Christopher Columbus, whose actual feat, Wynter writes, was not his so-called discoveries, but rather a 'root expansion of thought' that profoundly reshaped world views and the rules that govern human perception.[4]

This root expansion of thought ushered in an era of massive upheaval and terrestrial movement that involved the uprooting, dispersal, and dis-planting of people, ideas, and seeds. Given this framework, how might we reconsider terms that emerge from the garden—plot, plantation, and cultivation among them? It's not by chance that as the European expansion unfolds, some seventy years after *garden* (noun) becomes *to garden* (verb), another important term emerges. This time, it serves to address not that which is laid out and cultivated, but that which was already, inherently there. Referring to both people and plants that are indigenous to a particular place, autochthony is that which has been born out of specific earth or is descended from ancestors born from that earth. In other words, autochthony is a mythological formulation of absolute rootedness and belonging, the always already thereness of a thing that presupposes stability, as well as an already existing presence or a pre-presence. It is a super-natural rootedness that grants the status of permanence, and it is a mechanism by which certain things are tied to a place.[5]

The English philosopher and statesman Francis Bacon frequently used the term 'plantation' in his descriptions and theorizations of the colonial project.[6] Today it invokes a very specific scene—swaths of monocultured fields in the United States owned by white masters and worked by chattel slaves. At the time of Bacon's writing, plantation meant broadly (though just as viciously) to 'plant in' people;[7] his use of the term explicitly references the emerging social dynamic that would go on to shape the plantation economy and underscores the fact that planting was, from its inception, a social project. In his writing, Bacon describes the colonial process as an operation of planting and dis-planting that entailed the uprooting of indigenous plants, as well as Black and Indigenous people.[8] It was a large-scale and multi-species project of displacement for settlement's sake, scaffolded by what would become a preoccupation with taxonomical thinking—naming and classifying. Large portions of botanical species brought into the colonized parts of the world would quickly be termed as 'settler plants' and, by the late eighteenth century, botanists were using 'native' as a 'catchall conception for uncultivated or undomesticated' botanical materials found in the so-called New World.[9] While taxonomic fields like anthropology and botany are concerned with an object that is already given *as* native—with autochthony, if you will—Wynter is interested instead in *becoming* native. For Wynter, this is a process initiated in and by brutality. Speaking to this brutality, and thus rejecting the bellicose logic of autochthonic thinking, postcolonial intellectual Mahmood Mamdani writes: 'Native does not designate a condition that is original and authentic. Rather… the native is the creation of the colonial state… pinned down, localized, thrown out of civilization as an outcast, confined to custom, and then defined as its product'.[10] Through her study of emplotment, Wynter asks us to detach the notion of autochthony from nativeness.[11] In doing so, she asks us to think of nativeness as a process and not a condition, placing it in motion rather than assuming it as a permanence or a stillness or a fact.

In his work as a historian and geographer, Alfred Crosby has researched the use of gardening terms like 'native' and 'invasive' species to trace their emergence from within the colonial encounter, as well as the ways in which species adapt and change in relation to their environment. The movement of species is arduous to track because it's not simply a matter of their relocation but their transposition. To do so, we must consider the *unintentional* movement of plants and seeds alongside the intentional sowing of plantation commodities like tobacco and sugar cane. During the colonial project, seeds were dispersed in myriad ways: they were strewn off of the ships of European explorers in the mid-sixteenth century and transported in ballast soil used to laden down the hull of slave

3 Sylvia Wynter, '1492: A "New World" View', **The New World**, no. 2 (Spring/Summer 1991), 4.

4 Wynter, '1492', 4.

5 Some of what I've written here is informed by a class that I participated in with Zac Easterling, Fred Moten, Anel Rakhimzhanova, Tim Reid, Camila Arroyo Romero, Alia Al-Sabi, Isaac Silber, Miro Spinelli, and Blanca Ulloa, in which we discussed the notion of autochthony and Sylvia Wynter's body of work, among other things (September–December, 2020).

6 For an insightful review of Bacon's writing about plantations and English colonization in America, see: Tomaz Mastnakx, Julia Elyachar and Tom Boellstorff, 'Botanical Decolonization: Rethinking Native Plants', **Environment and Planning D: Society and Space** 32 (2014), 363–380.

7 Francis Bacon, 'The Essays, or: Counsels: Civill and Morall' (1625) (Printed by John Haviland for Hanna Barret, London), 198; as cited in Mastnak, Elyachar and Boellstorff 2014.

8 Mastnak, Elyachar and Boellstorff, 'Botanical Decolonization', 367.

9 Matthew K. Chew and Andrew L. Hamilton, 'The Rise and Fall of Biotic Nativeness: A Historical Perspective', in **Fifty Years of Invasion Ecology: The Legacy of Charles Elton**, ed. David M. Richardson (Oxford: Wiley-Blackwell, 2011), 37; as cited in Mastnak, Elyachar and Boellstorff 2014.

10 Mahmood Mamdani, **Define and Rule: Native as Political Identity** (Cambridge, MA: Harvard University Press, 2012), 2–3, as cited in Mastnak, Elyachar and Boellstorff 2014.

11 Sylvia Wynter, 'Novel and History, Plot and Plantation' **Savacou: The Journal of the Caribbean Artists Movement**, no. 5 (June 1971), 95–102.

ships.[12] Domesticated plants escaped from mission gardens carried by birds and wind, and cattle, sheep, goats, and pigs grazed in prairies and woods, moving seeds around by way of their excrement. These accidental dispersals brought about as much irreversible change to the ecosystem as deliberate sowing did. What might these inadvertent dispersals teach us? And how might they provide insight into the constant, fugitive life force that exceeds empirical ambition, national boundaries, and circuits of capital? These accidental dispersals and botanical slippages were not a new phenomenon, but during the European colonial project they took place on an unprecedented scale. Through the cultivation of plants, animals, and an enslaved labour force, transported from one part of the world to another, European settlers brought about a change so vast that it has been described by Crosby as 'comparable to the cataclysm of an asteroid impact'.[13] So many species and peoples died out as a result that, in human and ecological terms, the colonial encounter resulted in quite possibly the largest act of genocide in the history of the world.[14]

In human history the genocidal impulse is nothing if not persistent, even if the figure of genocide is rarer than the slow maiming to which so many of the world's inhabitants (plant and human) are subject.[15] In other words, the deliberate killing of a large number of a particular species or ethnic group, with the explicit aim of destroying that group, is more frequently enacted through social policy and systemic racism than in the concentration camp. Although Auschwitz, for example, is an anomalous form of genocide, it was, nonetheless, based on precedent. The extermination techniques used in the Nazi death camps in the twentieth century followed a blueprint set by the Germans during their colonial rule in Africa, when Herero and Nama people were shipped by cattle cars and taken far from public view to be worked to death, tortured, and raped in labour camps like the ones located on Shark Island in Namibia. This act of separating people from everyday society and killing them en masse links vicious ethnic-based violence in Africa with the violence enacted on German soil during World War II. As the Martiniquan intellectual and poet Aimé Césaire argued in 1952, fascism is a form of colonialism brought home to Europe.[16]

Across the board, colonialization was (and is) characterized by the use of violence in the name of 'civilization' and 'cultivation'. The wide acceptance of social Darwinism not only justified the right to territorial acquisition as a matter of the 'survival of the fittest',[17] but grafted racializing assemblages into 'the dominion of modern politics'.[18] By the time the nation state became the main polity in Europe, the concept of autochthony had been folded into the ideological foundation of the state, guiding notions of national identity and belonging. As a concept, if not as a word, autochthony persistently haunts the nation state and its systems of symbolic representation, and, as we see over and again, more often than not the people who define themselves by autochthony have a general genocidal disposition towards those who don't.

If we keep to the German example, in which a deadly connection between militant patriotism and nature was firmly set in place by the outset of the nineteenth century, it is plain to see how autochthony undergirds the most fervent nationalism. In the years leading up to the rise of National Socialism, and in reaction to the many changes brought about by industrialization, the German Youth Movement organized itself around a romantic longing for the 'pristine' state of things, with a focus on nature-worshiping in woodlands and gardens, as well as on cultural tradition. By the end of that century, this *völkisch* movement possessed a volatile obsession with racial purity that would be transformed into twentieth-century political discourse. Thus, after the disillusion of World War I and as the National Socialists gained prominence, members of the German Youth Movement went over to the Nazis by the thousands, with their countercultural energies and dreams of harmony with nature bearing the most bitter fruit.[19]

Not surprisingly, the authoritarian Nazi regime—along with its blood-and-soil ideology—manifested in the garden as much as anywhere else, although the seed had been planted earlier. Anticipating the ethos of the National Socialists, Willy Lange, Germany's leading garden theorist wrote: 'Our feelings for our homeland should be rooted in the

12 See Maria Thereza Alves's multi-disciplinary artwork **Seeds of Change** (1999–ongoing). For more on Alves: Jill H. Casid, 'Doing Things with Being Undone', **Journal of Visual Culture** 18, no. 1 (2019), 30–52.

13 Alfred Crosby, **The Columbian Exchange: Biological and Cultural Consequences of 1492** (Westport, CN: Greenwood Press, 1972), as cited in Mastnak, Elyachar and Boellstorff 2014, 374. See also: Alfred Crosby, **Ecological Imperialism: The Biological Expansion of Europe, 900–1900** (Cambridge: Cambridge University Press, 1986).

14 David E. Stannard, **American Holocaust: Columbus and the Conquest of the New World** (Oxford, Oxford University Press, 1992), xi; as cited in Mastnak, Elyachar and Boellstorff 2014.

15 On maiming, debility, and biopolitics see: Jasbir K. Puar, **The Right to Maim: Debility, Capacity, Disability** (Durham: Duke University Press, 2017).

16 Aimé Césaire, **Discourse on Colonialism**, trans. Joan Pinkham (New York: NYU Press, 1972), 3.

17 Michael Schubert, 'The "German Nation" and the "Black Other": Social Darwinism and the Cultural Mission in German Colonial Discourse', **Patterns of Prejudice** 45, no. 5 (2011), 399–416.

18 Alexander G. Weheliye, **Habeas Viscus: Racializing Assemblages, Biopolitics, And Black Feminist Theories of the Human** (Durham: Duke University Press, 2014), 1.

19 With anti-Semitic sentiment on the rise, Jewish members of the German Youth Movement went to Palestine instead, becoming founders of kibbutzim and laying the groundwork for the declaration of the State of Israel.

character of domestic landscapes…They can be heightened by artistic means, but we must not give up the German physiognomy'.[20] For Lange, gardening was an essential component of national culture and the superiority of the German people should be expressed through plants. This ecological framework became central to fascist ideology with national garden advocate Alwin Seifert using the term 'rootedness in the soil' to describe his conception of German garden design in 1929.[21] In Siefert's view, gardens were meant to strengthen national culture, and he would go on to be a leading landscape architect, turning design into doctrine. Given this, it comes as no surprise that the National Socialists had a special administrative branch of the government to regulate vegetation according to a racialized ideal based exclusively on native plants. Not only did they go about trying to eradicate weeds and foreign species from the soil of German forests, but soldiers were tasked with identifying and destroying 'exotic' plants in German gardens, as well as uprooting and re-planting entire Polish forests with German flora in order to naturalize acquired lands with species indigenous to the Germans' home territory.[22] For every plant that was uprooted, blood was poured back into the soil, siphoned off from the people by the fascist superbody.

Given that 'to lay out' means not only to spread something about and arrange it (as in plots, rows, plants, and seeds in the garden), but also to knock a person unconscious or to prepare a person for burial after their death, we can see yet again that gardening, the verb, finds an analogue in bloody, contested ground. While the idea of rootedness has mystic, mythological appeal—consider the sense of being that comes from knowing a place, its trees and rocks and rhythms—there is a difference between knowing the rocks and owning the rocks, even if your ancestors' bones happen to be the ground from which the rocks were made. In that difference (or deference) lies our every understanding of being in the world and the way by which we go about our need for gardening, and the activities (pruning, gathering, sheltering) therein.

20 Gert Gröning and Joachim Wolschke-Bulmahn, 'The Native Plant Enthusiasm: Ecological Panacea or Xenophobia?', **Landscape Research** 28, no. 1 (2003), 75–88.

21 Janet Biehl and Peter Staudenmaier, **Ecofascism: Lessons from the German Experience** (Edinburgh: AK Press, 1995).

22 Judith Sumner, **Plants Go to War: A Botanical History of World War II** (Jefferson, NC: McFarland & Company, Inc., 2019).

pensively scrutinizing the inscription on a monumental tomb. The painting still conveys something of a sense of drama and astonishment at the discovery. The skull on the tomb indicates that even here in Arcadia death is present, that all our earthly joys shall some day come to an end.

De Jong, *Arcadia Disrupted*, 56.

ARTIFICIAL GARDEN

Artificial gardens—as Lamb describes them—now strike us as not at all artificial, since they have been made 'natural' by time.

Finlay, *More Detached Sentences on Gardening*. See also Abrioux, *Ian Hamilton Finlay*, 40.

ARTS & CRAFTS

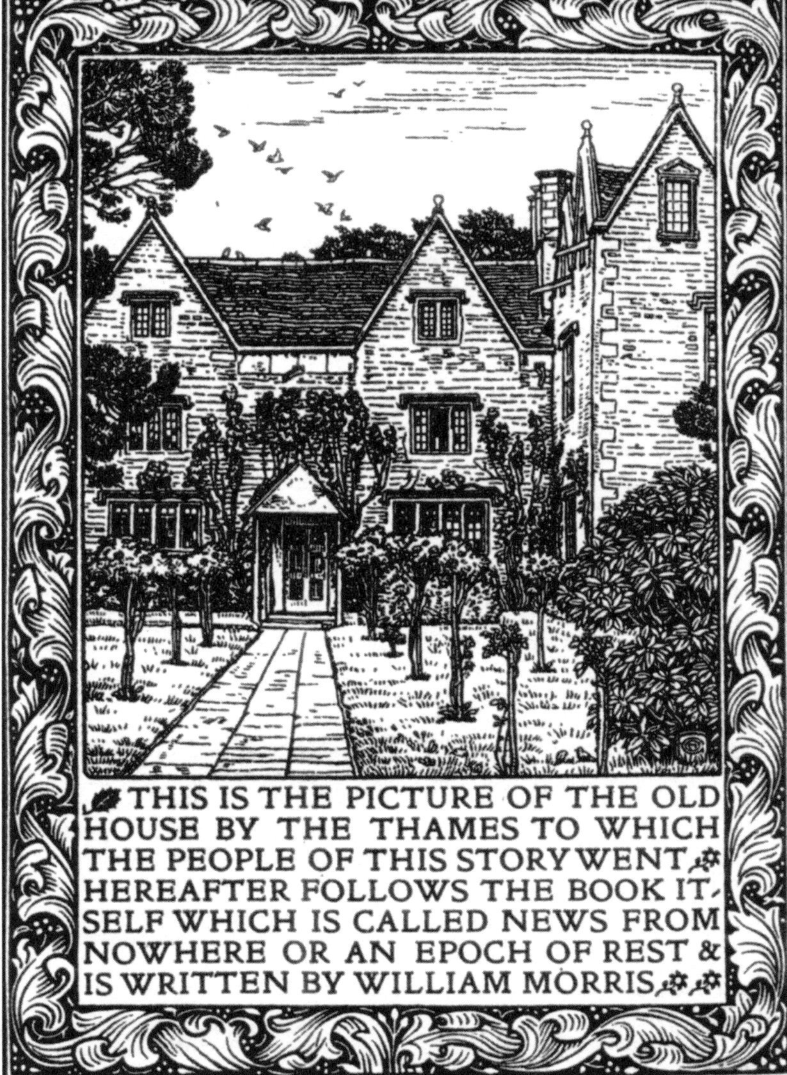

William Morris, **News from Nowhere**, 1892, frontispice.

The Arts and Crafts Movement emerged from deep moral and social concerns. The complexity of the movement's origins, ideals, and manifestations has been the subject of many detailed studies, but its basic tenets were a fundamental disdain for the falseness of High Victorian design, a rediscovery of nature and English traditions, and the idea that manual work could be personally fulfilling. Inspired by [William] Morris, those who embraced the movement sought to bring together architects and craftsmen to work in harmony. [...]

The Arts and Crafts Movement championed the unity of the arts, in which the house, the furnishing of its interiors, and the surrounding garden were considered a whole, or as Muthesius expressed it, 'garden, house, and interior—a unity'. The parallel revival of the art of garden design came into play at a time when architects not only saw to every detail of the house and its interiors, but routinely laid out the gardens. These gardens, with their neatly clipped hedges and ordered geometry, harked back to the England of the sixteenth and seventeenth centuries, the pleasure grounds of the Tudors and Stuarts. In contrast to nineteenth-century estate gardens that were vast in scale and stiffly planted with brightly colored annuals and jarring foliage, gardens designed by Arts and Crafts architects and their collaborators were intimate in scale, with soothing colors and textures. They harmonized perfectly with the house and were often distinguished by individualistic architectural components, such as garden houses, dovecotes, and pergolas, all constructed using the local materials of the region.

Tankard, *Gardens of the Arts & Crafts Movement*, 32–34.

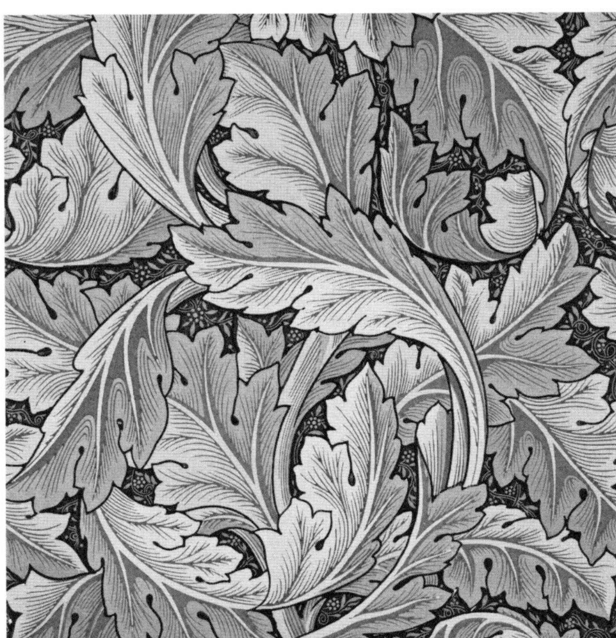

Along with Heal's (another London shop that started to sell terrariums and other plant matter in the mid 2010s), Liberty was a Victorian department store that supported the work of artisans in the Arts and Crafts movement, a sprawling group of collectives that spanned the practices of architecture, design, gardening, art and crafts but were united in their ambition to live more simply and find inspiration in nature.

After the frills and the fumes of the industrial revolution, the Arts and Crafts movement looked to find a more fulfilling life by returning to handmade, purposeful objects and the gradual pace of the natural world—essentially, a time before industrialisation. They had other radical ideas: that men and women could be equally vital in creating and consuming thoughtfully designed objects and that the lines between practices could be happily blurred, so that a painter could be a gardener and have an input on the architecture of a house (looking at you, Gertrude Jekyll) and that manual work, or using your hands and body to achieve things, could be satisfying.

Vincent, *Rootbound*, chapter 'January'.

William Morris, **Acanthus**, 1875, colour block print, 69.5 × 51.6 cm. Courtesy Alamy/Victoria and Albert Museum, London.

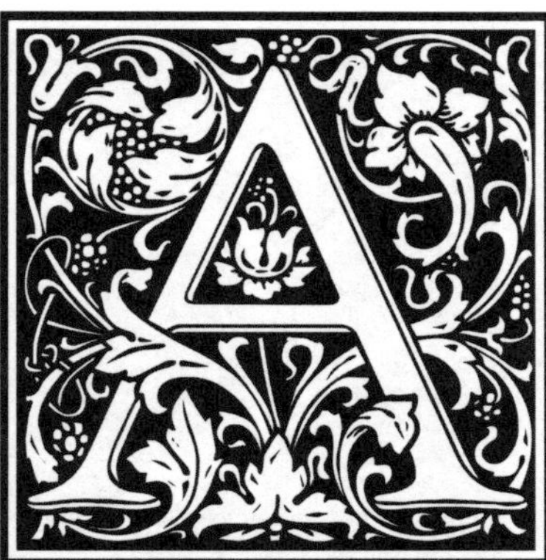

William Morris, **Letter A**.

ATTACK

Certain gardens are described as retreats, when they are really attacks.

Finlay, 'Unconnected Sentences on Gardening'.

AUTOCHTONY

See p. 23 for *Mythological Formulations: Autochtony at the Root of the Matter* by Alhena Katsof.

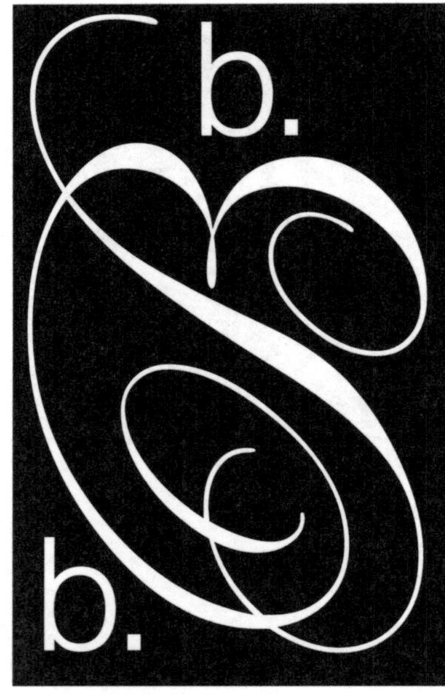

BALLAST GARDEN

MARIA THEREZA ALVES
Central to this work is ballast, the worthless cargo, usually earth, carried by merchant sailing ships to give them stability. The earth, which was dumped in the port of arrival, often contained various plants and dormant seeds. Alves analyzes the plants in various port cities, showing how they track the movement of land and people in the transatlantic slave trade. Here, she shows the different layers of her research conducted in Liverpool. One of the elements is a list of plants she found there, and outside in the square in front of the museum she has sown the seeds of a selection of these plants. This 'ballast garden' is a precarious reminder of the people whose lives were brutally destroyed. (ed.)

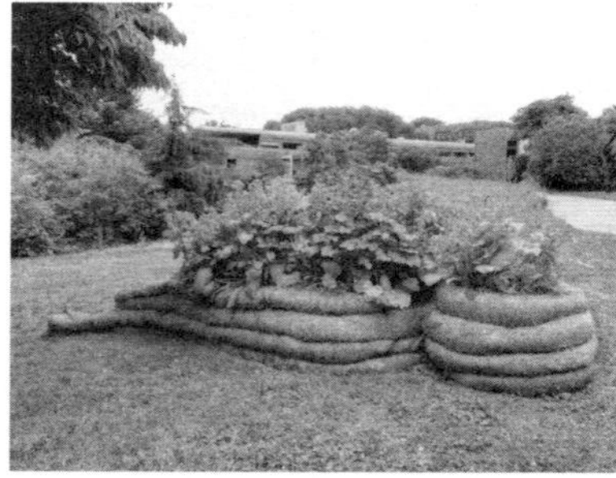

Maria Thereza Alves, **A Ballast Flora Garden: Weeksville Heritage Center**, 2018, installation view. Courtesy Maria Thereza Alves. Photo: Maria Thereza Alves.

BIODIVERSITY

Our first identity is as Earth Citizens, an Earth Family (Vasudhaiva Kutumbakam), sharing the planet with other species. We did not impose on ourselves the burden of Anthropocentrism, of separation from and superiority over other species. The Empire was based on the illusion of the superiority of one species, one race, one religion, one gender. It was also an Empire over what were declared to be 'lesser creatures', to be exploited and exterminated.

The Monoculture of the Mind is the basis of Empire. Separation is the basis of Empire. Fragmenting and fracturing interconnected, autopoietic, self organised systems is the basis of Empire. Denial of completeness is rupture of relationships that sustain individuals in community, farmers and their land, humans and the earth. Division is the ground for extractivism. Extractivism is the foundation of Empire. There has been a continuous war against our biodiversity in nature and culture diversity by past and present empires. The extractive economy of the 1% is based on the Monoculture of the Mind and it creates monocultures.

The biodiversity of our forests and farms has been replaced by monocultures of commercial timber and commodity crops. The forest is reduced to a mine for timber and pulp. The biodiversity of our farms has been reduced to monocultures of commodities which are desertifying the soil, impoverishing our farmers, and spreading hunger and malnutrition.

Shiva, 'Growing Gardens of Diversity'.

BIOPHILIA

The innate tendency to focus on life and lifelike processes.

Wilson, *Biophilia*, 1.

The biophilia hypothesis proclaims a human dependence on nature that extends far beyond the simple issues of material and physical sustenance to encompass as well the human craving for aesthetic, intellectual, cognitive and even spiritual meaning and satisfaction.

Kellert and Wilson, eds., *The Biophilia Hypothesis*, 21.

Our essence as a species binds us to explore and affiliate with all life. We are lovers who can add up glucose, amino acids, water, fragrant oils, pigments, and other tissue and call it both a flower and a mystical gesture. We can also decimate pollinators with an unloving tonnage of pesticides, precipitating the extinction of entire populations of those mystical gestures, once and forever. [...] Lives without access to sensation are lives that edge out the earth's raw, pervasive sweetness, that deeply biophilic connection to all life.

Meloy, *The Anthropology of Turquoise*, 244.

[...] E.O. Wilson's biophilia, then, becomes something else in [Ellen] Meloy's reworking of the concept. For Wilson, it is a love for the diversity of nonhuman life that stirs the mind to infinity for the beneficial enlightenment of humanity; for Meloy, it is an erotic-ethical affiliation between human and nonhuman life in experimental symbioses whose ecological benefits are sensed and desired, if not fully cognizable. What makes Meloy's nature writing queer is not an express allegiance to minority sexuality but a creative and attentive naturalism that tracks interspecies couplings across the desert's vital landscape on a map of co-adaptation, which standard ecosite grids and biological taxonomies fail to chart.

Chisholm, 'Biophilia and the Ecological Future of Queer Desire', 360.

BOMARZO

Bomarzo has been hailed as a site of 'extreme artifice' and 'pure fantasy', with its collection of fabulous, carved beasts, fictional and mythological creatures, bizarre structures (a leaning house), and many admonitory inscriptions. Yet these often disturbing and perplexing appearances are carved from the natural rock of the wooded site, which, though occasionally terraced and with paths descending the slope, is not at all as regimented as were many other contemporary gardens. The miscellany of items—elephants, giants, Pegasus, an orc, sphinxes, huge pine cones and acorns, a hell mouth—seem to spring from the very ground itself and be endemic to the place; so that the creation of the park by Vicino Orsini is hardly a 'denial of nature'. It was more probably contrived and understood as an expression—sometimes arcane, always startling—of its patron's human nature and of the Etruscan locality to which he belonged. For, like all garden-making in the Renaissance (and often since), Bomarzo was a means of declaring its creator's status, person and virtue...

Hunt, *A World of Gardens*, 122–123.

BORROWED SCENERY

Shakkei: A garden design concept by which local, even distant, surroundings are drawn into the garden space as 'borrowed scenery'. The opposite of shakkei is dankei, a garden in which external surroundings are completely blocked out.

Walker, *The Japanese Garden*, 296.

BOTANICAL GARDEN

BOTANIC MUSE! who in this latter age
Led by your airy hand the Swedish sage,
Bad his keen eye your secret haunts explore
On dewy dell, high wood, and winding shore;
Say on each leaf how tiny Graces dwell;
How laugh the Pleasures in a blossom's bell;
How insect Loves arise on cobweb wings,
Aim their light shafts, and point their little stings.

Darwin, *The Botanic Garden*.

The main division of gardens is into art gardens and botanical gardens. Compared to this division all the other others—'The Garden as Music', 'The Garden as a Poem' —& etc.—are superficial.

Finlay, 'More Detached Sentences on Gardening'.
See also Abrioux, *Ian Hamilton Finlay*, 40.

The value of a Botanic garden was that it conveyed a direct knowledge of God. Since each plant was a created thing, and God had revealed a part of himself in each thing He created, a complete collection of all things created by God must reveal God completely.

Prest, *The Garden of Eden*. Cited in Aben and De Wit, *The Enclosed Garden*, 131.

The science of botany played an absolutely central role in Europe's colonial enterprise. The latter was motivated by a theory of statecraft Adam Smith derisively labeled as mercantilism, whose primary objective was to augment a state's wealth and power by effecting a favorable balance of trade (Smith 1776). Colonial possessions were highly valued because their imports and exports could be tightly controlled, with the circulation of raw materials directed to maximize the empire's ability to profit from the production of finished goods. During the eighteenth century, mercantilist policy increasingly came to regard the science of natural history as an indispensable tool in the service of imperial self-sufficiency. By deploying the expertise of its naturalists to cultivate exotic resources at home, the state could prevent hemorrhaging bullion to rivals. [...]

Although the importance of botanical gardens for success in a mercantile economy can hardly

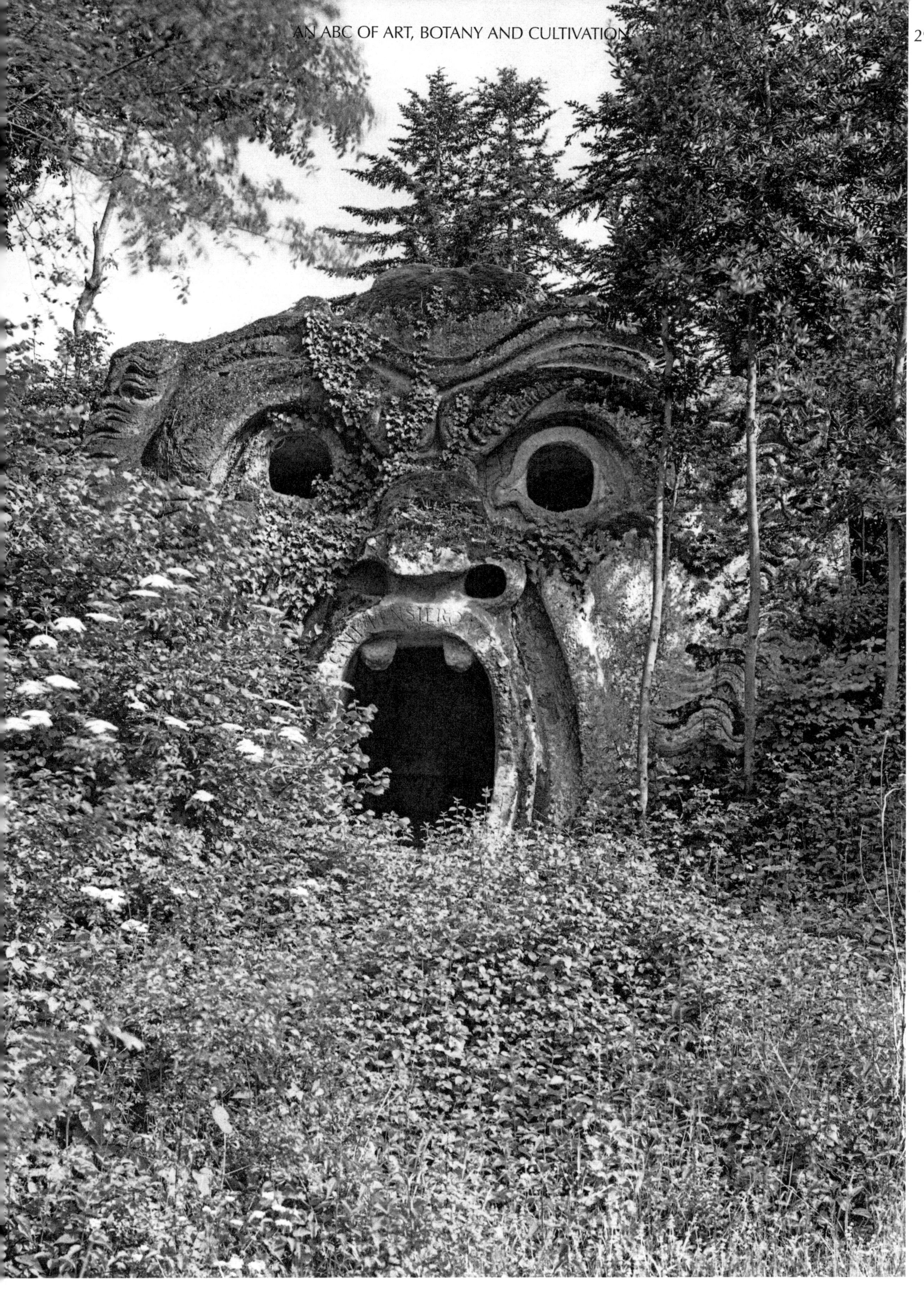

Simone Moschino (attributed), **The Hell Mouth**, Bomarzo, c. 1547–1580, sculpture. Courtesy Bildarchiv Foto Marburg. Photo: Otto Lehmann-Brockhaus.

be overstated, European societies valued natural history as more than just a commercial pursuit during the eighteenth and nineteenth centuries. Just as it had during the sixteenth and seventeenth centuries, a thorough knowledge of nature continued to serve as a badge of learning and a display of one's intellectual cultivation.

Rieppel, 'Museums and Botanical Gardens', in *A Companion to the History of Science*, 242–243.

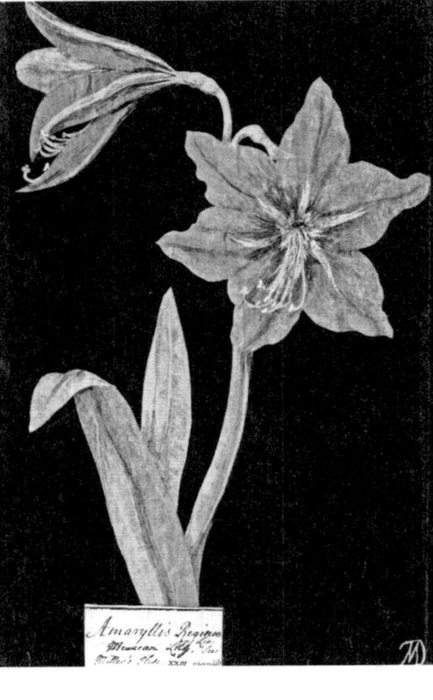

Mary Granville Delany, **Amaryllis Reginae**, 1775, collage, 30.4 × 19.6 cm. Courtesy The Trustees of the British Museum, London.

BOTANOMANIA

Men imposed order on horticulture: they built towering greenhouses and amassed collections; devised the remits of garden design and created ways of putting plants in books that women were not allowed to write. Women were excluded for a good while, for similar reasons to those for which women were excluded from many pursuits: because their brains were deemed too small or delicate, because it was considered unseemly.

But we weren't always horticultural pariahs. In the nascent days of 'botanomania'—the eighteenth-century phenomenon inspired by the exotic plants that arrived on the drab shores of Britain from the edges of the Empire in ships otherwise stuffed with spices, tea and tigers—botany was considered the most appropriate natural science for women to study. The fresh air was thought to be good for us, the foreign plants gave us something different to paint and new herbal remedies to uncover: essential skills for a lady. By the 1830s, some knowledge of plants was up there with mid-level piano playing and polite conversation as skills a well-to-do woman should have.

Vincent, *Rootbound*, chapter 'June'.

BOTANY

The coolness of time like the coolness of leaves.
The coolness of time like the rustle of jungle. Of
Leaves. Why
Are all the artists making work about tropical
Plant. I mean
The artists I like. And some I don't. But mostly
Why I am always reminded of Rousseau
When examining the green hand
Green face almond-shaped
Proffered by the examining artist
Jungle plants at IKEA we all buy them.
Yes: Art fair artist bar draped in them. The music is better
There. The drinks are ridiculous: orange and round like modernism.
Poets are naturally attracted to the pale-green language
('Naturally')
That limns and dips them:
Botanical. Clicking syllabics and Latinate
Erotics, the rigor and swell of modernism, white
Concrete swerve of architectures and elephant-ear-strewn
Interiors. (Lina Bo Bardi, the Pollock-Krasner Hamptons home, etc.)
I am so Western I will never escape the usual referents, etc.
I am so Western I was born in California.
I once wrote in a magazine:

'Fashion has a flair for the topical, no matter where it stirs in the thickets of long ago; it is a tiger's leap into the past', wrote Walter Benjamin in his vignette-studded essay 'Theses on the Philosophy of History' (1940). Read the line quickly, add an extra letter, and suddenly the tropics are conjured. Benjamin's 'thickets' become jungles, lush with almond-shaped leaves, green and waxy; through them a tiger skulks and leaps. The darkness (or lightness) of history emerges, humid and heated, between the carefully outlined leaves. Benjamin's sentence has become a Henri Rousseau painting, as it were. Then the mind takes another leap, tiger-like, shaking the German critic's sentence into yet another anagram, and those thickets of leaves become smaller, more domestic, but just as decorous. Now they curl from a pot, near a butterfly chair, a man's pale, naked thigh. The fashions and fabrics filling the frame might be 1970s-era American approximations of Rousseau's colonial-tropical fantasy—a different kind of herbarium, a later moment in history. How did this happen? You are now in a ____ ____ painting.

This does not answer the question, though.
Why do these plants feel like politics and the absence
Of politics simultaneously? This is not poetic
Rhetoric; this is a real question.
It is about contemporary currency:
Leaves like money. Green
They said in early rap lyrics from upper Manhattan
And lower California.
The coolness of my gaze as it projects a stream of moving
Images against the green plates
Of leaves: all my typical
Allusions/abstractions/alliterations. Coolness of the climes
Where the plants sway and drip
Empty of moving pictures, of the film
Of my gaze. Green darkness of jungle, that theater.
Video green of rain forests, the fluorescent artists
Taking their technology
Inside its interior. And its abundant
Literature. It would seem
To be the time in this poem to venture into etymology.
Easy.

Wikipedia tells me:
'The term "botany" comes from the Ancient Greek word βοτάνη (botane) meaning "pasture", "grass", or "fodder"; βοτάνη which is in turn derived from βόσκειν (boskein), "to feed" or "to graze".[1][2][3] A person who studies plants may be called a botanist or a plant scientist [...] Botany originated in prehistory as herbalism with the efforts of early humans to identify—and later cultivate—edible, medicinal and poisonous plants, making it one of the oldest branches of science. Medieval physic gardens, often attached to monasteries, contained plants of medical importance. They were forerunners of the first botanical gardens attached to universities, founded from the 1540s onwards. One of the earliest was the Padua botanical garden. These gardens facilitated the academic study of plants. Efforts to catalogue and describe their collections were the beginnings of plant taxonomy, and led in 1753 to the binomial system of Carl Linnaeus that remains in use to this day.

Ignore the ancient Greek for now
What of the psychic garden of the jungle
Imported into our IKEAs and galleries and bars
And artist's books? The psychic garden of our cultural imagination
Stirs: some wind. Come heat. It 'feels like' rain.
Earth come down from the hills
Leaves from trees. Before the torrent
We scan each
Leaf with the attention of a medieval gardener
Or modernist Italian architect
Or club-goer or critic
We record it.
Leaf of all organisms not considered animals
Leaf of parlor palm and Victorian
Leaf of philodendron
Leaf of September and of Wednesday
Leaf of literacy
Leaf of photosynthesis
Leaf of evening
Leaf of poor copy
Leaf of feminism
Leaf of dialects
Leaf of imperialism
Leaf of love I leave each morning
Leaf of the kiss I leave on his green cheek
Leaf of last night its lucidity
Leaf of photocopy
Leaf of participation
Leaf of entitlement
Leaf of her body with its soluble
Leaf of metabolism or materiality
Leaf of loose images and dark scanners
Leaf of the artist at their center
Leaf of tropical of botanical of some long artful fever
Leaf of the bourgeoisie
Leaf of a stranger and of that literature
Leaf of the coolness of time, its heat
Leaf of temperature
Leaf of coloniality
Leaf of neoliberalism
Leaf of class signifiers
Leaf of global-exchange patterns
Leaf of the coastal enclave
Leaf of South-South relations
Leaf of unassigned hunger
Leaf of the lyric
Leaf of morphology
Leaf that cools me
Leaf of this image.

Latimer, *Like a Woman*, 73–77.

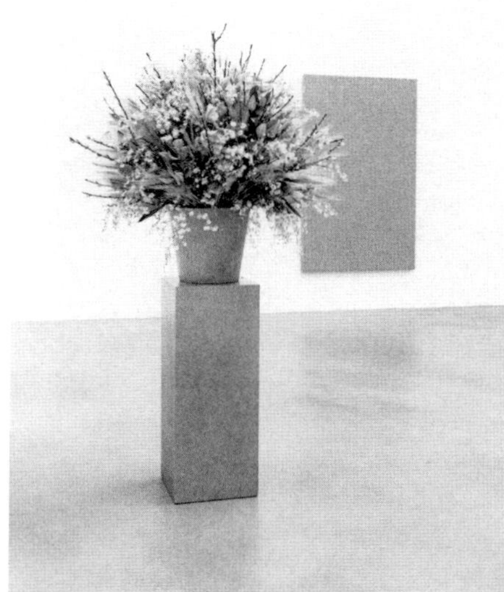

Willem de Rooij, **Bouquet XV** and **Paring Elk**, 2015, installation view Petzel Gallery, New York. Courtesy Willem de Rooij.

BOUQUET

WILLEM DE ROOIJ

Willem de Rooij began his Bouquet series—a group of flower sculptures—in 2002 in collaboration with Jeroen de Rijke (1970–2006). In these bouquets, de Rooij refers to the various symbolic meanings and values that flowers are assigned in different cultures. This particular bouquet is an attempt to transcend colour associations and to create a neutral skin tone. The hand-woven textile, which looks monochrome from a distance, is, like the bouquet, made up of a diverse palette of colours and textures that together create a beige hue. In this way, de Rooij plays not only with colour, but also with perceptions of abstraction and ornament. In the context of the museum, the fading flowers contrast starkly with the notion of art that should last forever. (ed.)

The arrangement of plant materials truly became an art and an important decorative device in the 17th century. During this period of worldwide exploration, colonization, and commerce, new plants were introduced into Europe, where an avid interest in horticulture developed. Still-life paintings of the late 16th, 17th, and early 18th centuries reveal what a great variety of plants there was in the gardens of Europe. Beginning with Jan Brueghel (called 'Velvet Brueghel'; 1568–1625), a tradition of flower painting developed in Flanders and Holland, which culminated with the works of Jan van Huysum (1682–1749). The canvases of the many hundreds of still-life painters of the period are valuable source material for the student of the history of floral decorations and gardens. They must, however, be considered as idealized compositions and not as literal translations onto canvas of actual bouquets. Early 17th-century pictures, particularly those of Jan Brueghel, who painted one-of-a-kind arrangements, seemed most interested in displaying the content of the garden itself. Depictions of later 17th-century bouquets show profuse arrangements that reflect the sensuality and exuberance of the Baroque style. Curvilinear elements such as sinuous S curves are other Baroque devices of design used to create grandiloquent, dramatic compositions. The massed bouquets of the Baroque period are studies in dominance, contrast, rhythm, and sculptural effect. The eye is drawn around and into the bouquets by the turning of flower heads, the reversing of leaves, and the curving of graceful flower stems.

Encyclopaedia Britannica, 'Bouquet'.

CAPABILITY BROWN

Brown made water appear as Water and lawn as Lawn.

Finlay, 'More Detached Sentences on Gardening'. See also Abrioux, *Ian Hamilton Finlay*, 40.

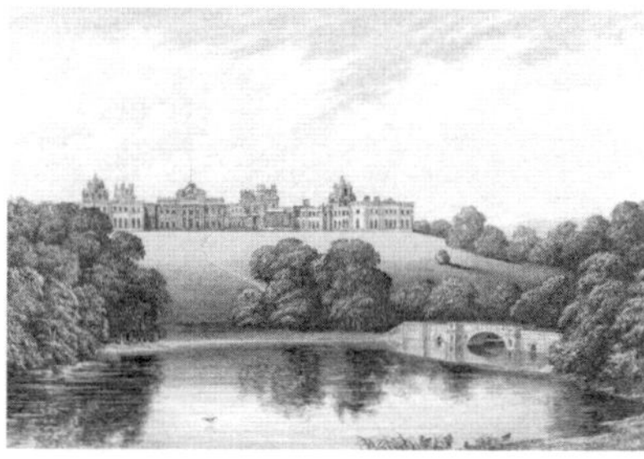

Benjamin Fawcett after A.F. Lydon, **Blenheim Palace**, 1868, engraving, 24.2 × 19.1 cm. Courtesy The University of Edinburgh.

[T]he gardens of Capability Brown, such as Bowood and Blenheim, represent the culmination of the naturalist tendencies of the English garden to the point of banishing all appearance of art or artifice. Taking maximum advantage of the openness of these spaces [...] his creations were often criticized for having so thoroughly integrated the garden into nature that there no longer existed any garden whatsoever.

Weiss, *Mirrors of Infinity*, 16.

ROBERTO BURLE MARX

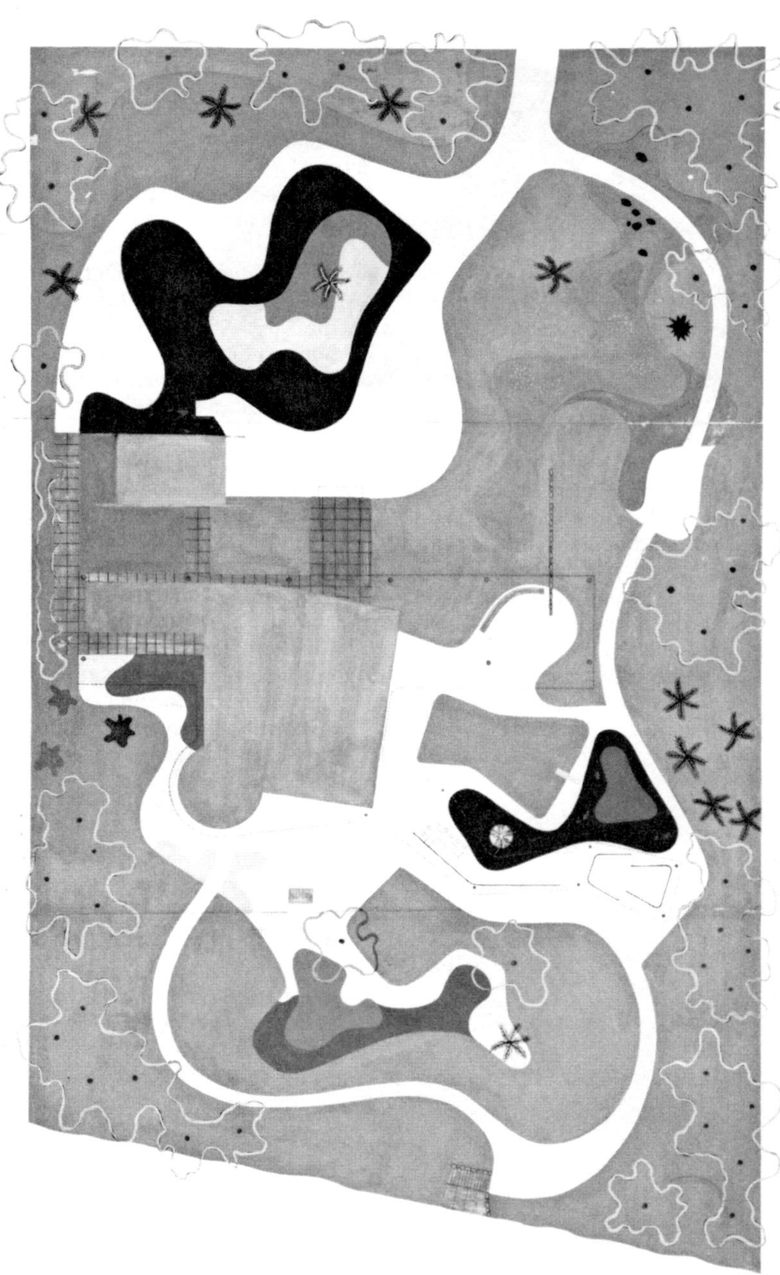

Roberto Burle Marx, **Garden Design for Beach House for Mr. and Mrs. Burton Tremaine, project, Santa Barbara, California (site plan)**, 1948, gouache on board, 127.6 × 70.5 cm. Courtesy Museum of Modern Art, New York/Scala, Florence.

Burle Marx thought of his own garden at Santo Antonio da Bica and his commissions for private gardens as places to display, conserve, and perpetuate species that were not available on the open market and threatened in the wild. The forest was a place for him to gather specimens and knowledge of how species lived and behaved in situ. The garden, on the other hand, both had an aesthetic purpose and served as a sanctuary for endangered plants and a laboratory for their propagation. Burle Marx' mission was to give back to Brazil what it had lost during the colonial period and to overturn public complacency regarding systematic deforestation. His dual ancestry, coupled with his tremendous contribution to South American cultural identity, placed him in a perfect position to advocate for paradise with those in power. He lectured extensively on humanity's responsibility to the rain forest, and, while his pleas were not always met with action, his dedication earned him the unofficial title of the father of the ecology movement in Brazil.

Smith, *Down the Garden Path*, 16.

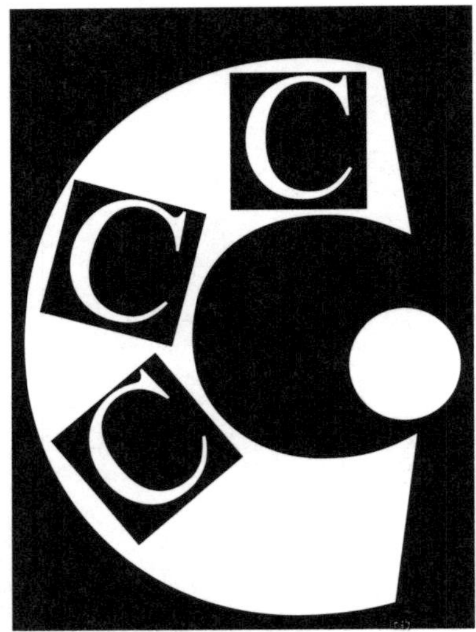

CACTUS

Saber was a dominant feature of the landscape of historic Palestine. Traditionally, it is planted as demarcations of land boundaries. Especially on the hillsides, rows of *saber* separate people's orchards and olive groves from each other. It serves as a demarcation of boundaries and a protective fence at the same time. [...]

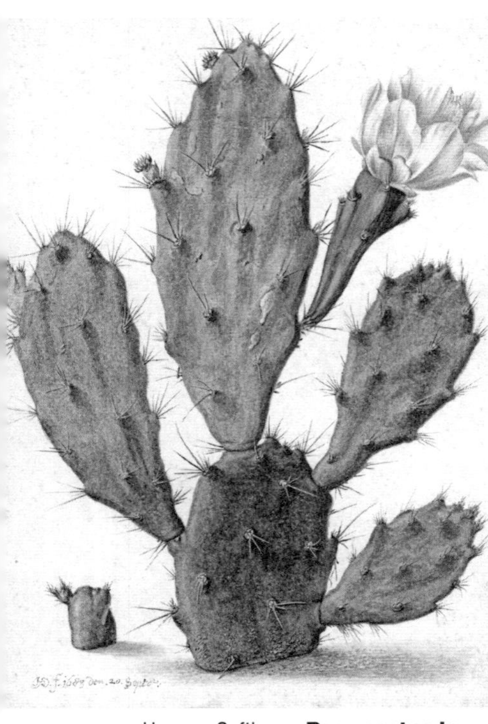

Herman Saftleven, **Pear cactus in bloom**, 1683, drawing, 35.5 × 25.6 cm. Courtesy Rijksmuseum Amsterdam.

Palestinians have drawn on similarities between the *saber* and characteristics of their lives. First, the cactus thrives in a harsh environment, the hilly and mountainous terrain, just as the *fellahin* have adapted well to these terrains and their rugged life. Second, the sweetness of the *saber* fruit that lies beneath the thorny skin despite the prickly leaves of the plant and the fine thorns on the *saber* fruit itself mirrors the sweetness of village life alongside the endless state of tedious work and struggle. Third, it is resilient: *saber* bears fruit, even in times of drought.

Abufarha, 'Land of Symbols', 346–347.

CAPITALOCENE

[T]he Capitalocene does not stand for capitalism as an economic and social system. It is not a radical inflection of Green Arithmetic. Rather, the Capitalocene signifies capitalism as a way of organizing nature—as a multispecies, situated, capitalist world-ecology.

Moore, *Anthropocene or Capitalocene?*, 6.

If Humans live in History and the Earthbound take up their task within the Anthropocene, too many Posthumans (and posthumanists, another gathering altogether) seem to have emigrated to the Anthropocene for my taste. Perhaps my human and nonhuman people are the dreadful Chthonic ones who snake within the tissues of Terrapolis. Note that insofar as the Capitalocene is told in the idiom of fundamentalist Marxism, with all its trappings of Modernity, Progress, and History, that term is subject to the same or fiercer criticisms. The stories of both the Anthropocene and the Capitalocene teeter constantly on the brink of becoming much Too Big.

Haraway, *Staying with the Trouble*, 50.

RACHEL CARSON

Here again we are reminded that in nature nothing exists alone. To understand more clearly how the pollution of our world is happening, we must now look at another of the earth's basic resources, the soil.

Carson, *Silent Spring*, 35.

Carson was blowing the lid off. Had we been lied to, not only about pesticides, but about progress, and development, and discovery, and the whole ball of wax? So one of the core lessons of Silent Spring was that things labelled progress weren't necessarily good. Another was that the perceived split between man and nature isn't real: the inside of your body is connected to the world around you, and your body too has its ecology, and what goes into it—whether eaten or breathed or drunk or absorbed through your skin—has a profound impact on you. We're so used to thinking this way now that it's hard to imagine a time when general assumptions were different. But before Carson, they were.

Atwood, 'Rachel Carson's Silent Spring'.

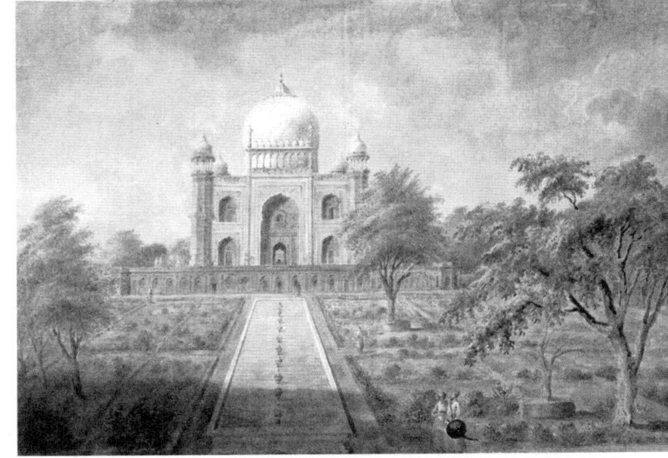

Sita Ram, **The tomb of Safdar Jang showing the garden and water channel**, 1815, watercolour drawing, 38.4 × 51.2 cm.

CHARBAGH

The garden with running water and the cool shade of trees provides a refuge from the dust and heat of the surrounding desert and is constantly likened to a paradise on earth in Persian literature. This theme continues even now to run through the poetry and painting of Iran as it has done for centuries.

The usual garden design consists of a central water channel with others leading offit at right angles with flower beds situated between them. This forms the *chahar bagh* literally 'four gardens' design which was also introduced into India in the 16th century by the first Mughal emperor Babur.

Titley, *Plants and Gardens in Persian, Mughal and Turkish Art*, 16.

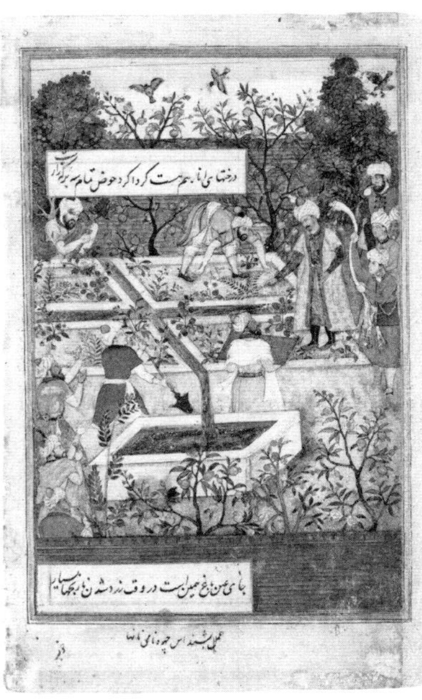

Bishndas and Nanha, **Baburnama**, ca. 1590, watercolour drawing, 21.7 x 14.3 cm. Courtesy Alamy/Victoria and Albert Museum, London.

To explore the ancient garden, we begin with the archetypal symbol of antiquity: paradise as a quadripartite or cruciform garden, transmitted to Islamic gardens as charbagh. In its definitive form, the garden is bounded within the ideal geometry of a square or a rectangle of ideal proportions and subdivided by paths and channels cross-axially dividing the square. These elements lead the visitor through the four rivers of Eden and the tree of life, the four directions, the four seasons, the four elements, the four corners of the earth, and are linked to the mandala. In architectural theory, the quadripartite garden is conceptually unified in its genesis with the first acts of rational city planning and architectural design. The ancient garden, in this view, is an ideal geometry, centering humankind within a finite and knowable universe.

Gleason, *A Cultural History of Gardens in Antiquity*, 4.

CHTULUCENE

I also insist that we need a name for the dynamic ongoing sym-chthonic forces and powers of which people are a part, within which ongoingness is at stake. Maybe, but only maybe, and only with intense commitment and collaborative work and play with other terrans, flourishing for rich multispecies assemblages that include people will be possible. I am calling all this the Chthulucene—past, present, and to come.

Haraway, 'Anthropocene, Capitalocene, Plantationocene, Chthulucene', 160.

Chthulucene is a simple word. It is a compound of two Greek roots (khthôn and kainos) that together name a kind of timeplace for learning to stay with the trouble of living and dying in responsibility on a damaged earth.

Haraway, *Staying with the Trouble*, 2.

All of these stories are a lure to proposing the Chthulucene as a needed third story, a third netbag for collecting up what is crucial for ongoing, for staying with the trouble. The chthonic ones are not confined to a vanished past. They are a buzzing, stinging, sucking swarm now, and human beings are not in a separate compost pile. We are humus, not Homo, not anthropos;

we are compost, not posthuman. As a suffix, the word kainos, '-cene', signals new, recently made, fresh epochs of the thick present. To renew the biodiverse powers of terra is the sympoietic work and play of the Chthulucene. Specifically, unlike either the Anthropocene or the Capitalocene, the Chthulucene is made up of ongoing multispecies stories and practices of becoming-with in times that remain at stake, in precarious times, in which the world is not finished and the sky has not fallen—yet. We are at stake to each other. Unlike the dominant dramas of Anthropocene and Capitalocene discourse, human beings are not the only important actors in the Chthulucene, with all other beings able simply to react. The order is reknitted: human beings are with and of the earth, and the biotic and abiotic powers of this earth are the main story.

Haraway, *Staying with the Trouble*, 55.

CLIMATE JUSTICE CODE

For Commons Network, climate justice means three things:

1. The effects of climate change are felt most acutely by people who are least responsible for causing the problem. Communities in the global South—as well as low-income communities in the industrialised north—are bearing the burden of rich countries' overconsumption of our planet's resources. The developed world has a 'climate debt': we have a historical and moral responsibility to stop this crisis help developing countries by transfer of technology and finances.

2. Climate justice means addressing the climate crisis whilst also making progress towards equity and the protection and realisation of human rights. It demands that the transformation should not leave anyone behind. This refers to a just transition, one that protects the livelihood of workers and ensures clean, safe and organized jobs in the new energy system.

3. The climate crisis is the byproduct of a flawed system, fuelled by capitalism, colonialism, patriarchy and white supremacy. That is why Extinction Rebellion does not want to be called a 'climate movement': they rebel out of an urgent need to fix the underlying problems. Any structural solution will require us to fundamentally disrupt these power structures and change the system.

Commons Network Team, 'Art + Commons: Announcing a New Collaboration'.

COMMUNITY GARDEN

MARIA PASK

The garden plays a nourishing role in Maria Pask's practice in a variety of ways. For example, Pask tends to the gardens of several pensioners and creates bouquets from the flowers she grows there, which she shares with a church for the queer community. This series of drawings can be read as the materialization of the 'community garden' in a figurative sense. Each drawing is dedicated to or is reminiscent of a person who has played a part in her life. In these works, personal associations are fused with references from cultural history, natural symbolism, and a spiritual quest. Her practice is one of care and collectivity, but the drawings themselves also represent the process of working through painful moments and dealing with loss. For example, the words in the drawings, sometimes a slogan, sometimes a poem, have a special role: they can be venomous, evil, or reconciliatory. (ed.)

COMPOST

Embodying the practice of feminist speculative fabulation in the scholarly mode, Strathern taught me—taught us—a simple but game-changing thing: 'It matters what ideas we use to think other ideas' [Strathern, *Reproducing the Future*, 10]. I compost my soul in this hot pile. The worms are not human; their undulating bodies ingest and reach, and their feces fertilize worlds. Their tentacles make string figures.

It matters what matters we use to think other matters with; it matters what stories we tell to tellother stories with; it matters what knot knots, what thoughts think thoughts, what descriptions describe descriptions, what ties tie ties. It matters what stories make worlds, what worlds make stories.

Haraway, *Staying with the Trouble*, 34.

All of these stories are a lure to proposing the Chthulucene as a needed third story, a third netbag for collecting up what is crucial for ongoing, for staying with the trouble. The chthonic ones are not confined to a vanished past. They are a buzzing, stinging, sucking swarm now, and human beings are not in a separate compost pile. We are humus, not Homo, not anthropos; we are compost, not posthuman.

Haraway, *Staying with the Trouble*, 55.

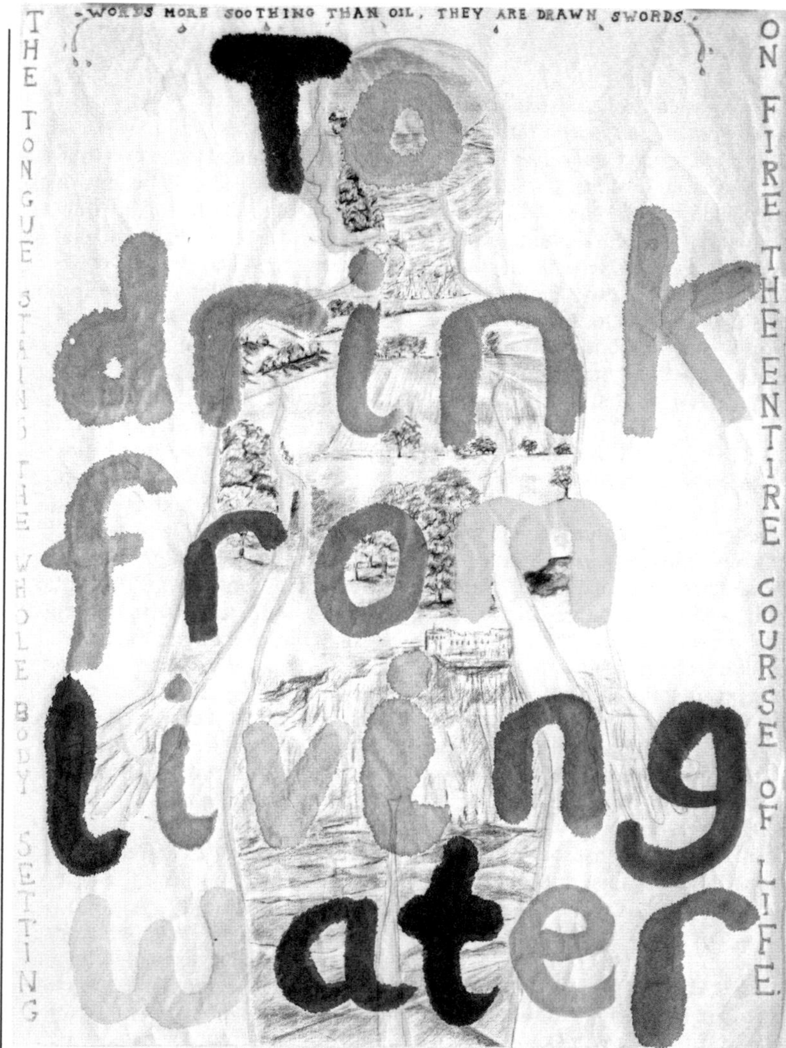

Maria Pask, **To drink from living water**, 2020, gouache drawing, 97 × 74 cm. Courtesy Maria Pask and Ellen de Bruijne Projects, Amsterdam.

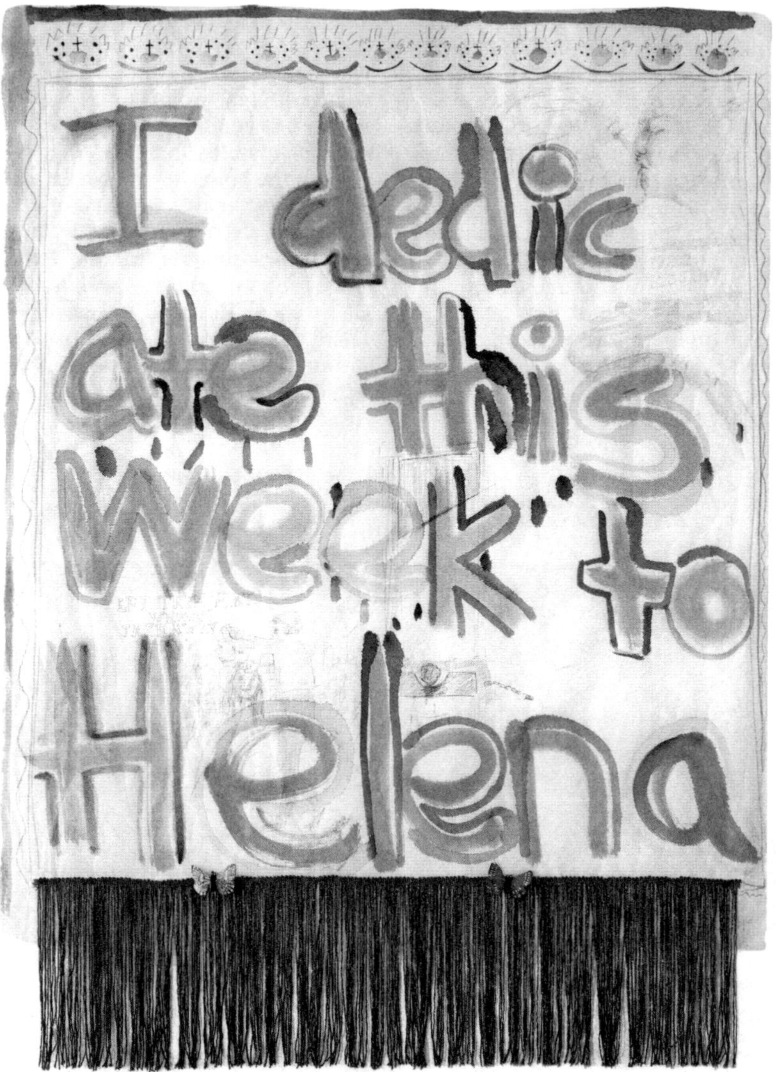

Maria Pask, **Helena**, 2020, gouache drawing, 107 × 76 cm. Courtesy Maria Pask and Ellen de Bruijne Projects, Amsterdam.

CONTROL

Naming is control. It establishes, if not ownership, at least a relationship of some intimacy as well as a chain of bizarre equivalences: a set of wiggles in the muscles of the mouth and larynx = a set of phonemes = a constellation of letters = a star. It's a pretty arbitrary chain, but it's all that allows us to talk about the world. But what does it mean to name something that cannot hear you, in a world that doesn't care?

Hickey and Tallman, *The Collections of Barbara Bloom*, 45.

The 'control of nature' is a phrase conceived in arrogance, born of the Neanderthal age of biology and philosophy, when it was supposed that nature exists for the convenience of man. The concepts and practices of applied entomology for the most part date from that Stone Age of science. It is our alarming misfortune that so primitive a science has armed itself with the most modern and terrible weapons, and that in turning them against the insects it has also turned them against the earth.

Carson, *Silent Spring*, 593–594.

RUMIKO HAGIWARA
The Japanese artist Rumiko Hagiwara took this photograph of a botanical garden in winter, when the perennial plants have died back before sprouting again in the spring. Without the visible plants, it looks like someone has planted only name plates. Hagiwara turns naming and classifying the world around us into an absurdist occupation. Outside, in various spots on Agnietenstraat and on the square in front of the museum, Hagiwara has placed a board with the Wikipedia definition of weeds. It is a simple intervention that immediately prompts us to think about the categories we use to classify and understand the world. (ed.)

CULTIVER NOTRE JARDIN

Yet human gardens, however self-enclosed their world may be, invariably take their stand in history, if only as a counterforce to history's deleterious drives. When Voltaire ends *Candide* with the famous declaration 'Il faut cultiver notre jardin', the garden in question must be viewed against the background of the wars, pestilence, and natural disasters evoked by the novel. It is *because* we are thrown into history that we must cultivate our garden. In an immortal Eden there is no need to cultivate, since all is pre-given there spontaneously. Our human gardens may appear to us like little openings onto paradise in the midst of the fallen world, yet the fact that we must create, maintain, and care for them is the mark of their postlapsarian provenance. History without gardens would be a wasteland. A garden severed from history would be superfluous. [...]

The gardens that have graced this mortal Eden of ours are the best evidence of humanity's reason for being on Earth. Where history unleashes its destructive and annihilating forces, we must, if we are to preserve our sanity, to say nothing of our humanity, work against and in spite of them. We must seek out healing or redemptive forces and allow them to grow in us. That is what it means to tend our garden. [...]

The pronominal adjective used by Voltaire—*notre*—points to the world we share in common. This is the world of plurality that takes shapes through the power of human action. *Notre jardin* is never a garden of merely private concerns into which one escapes from the real; it is that plot of soil on the earth, within the self, or amid the social collective, where the cultural, ethical and civic virtues that save reality from its own worst impulses are cultivated. Those virtues are always ours.

Harrison, *Gardens*, x.

Rumiko Hagiwara, **Name Garden**, 2012, installation view. Courtesy Rumiko Hagiwara.

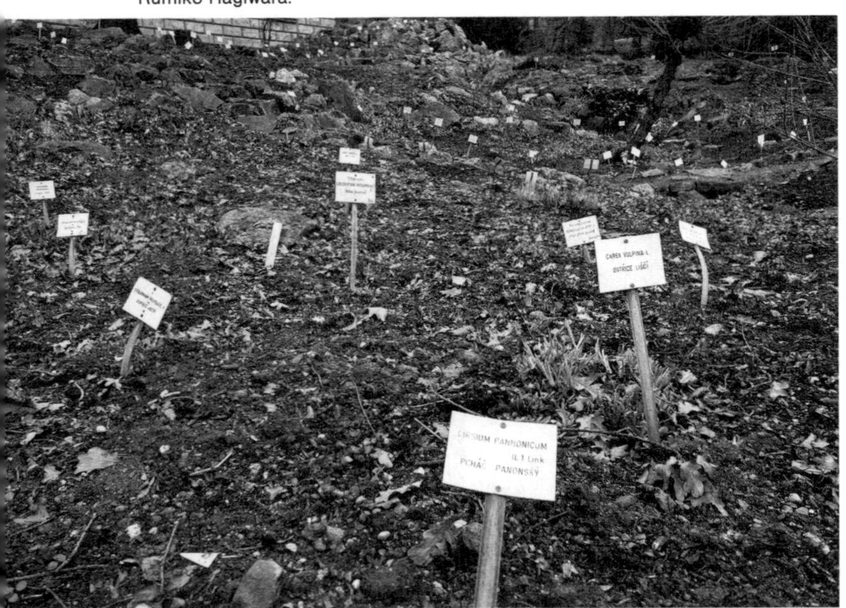

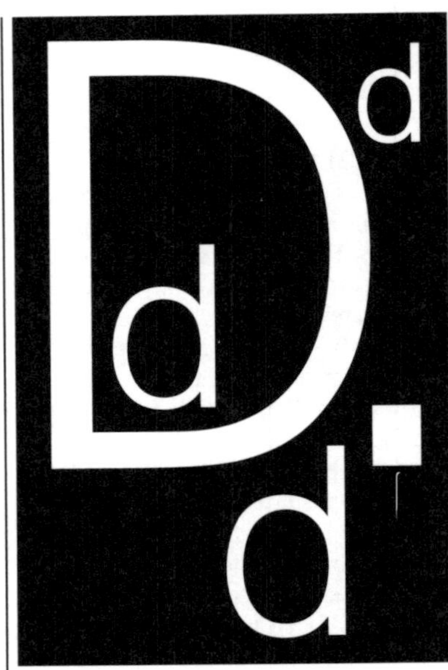

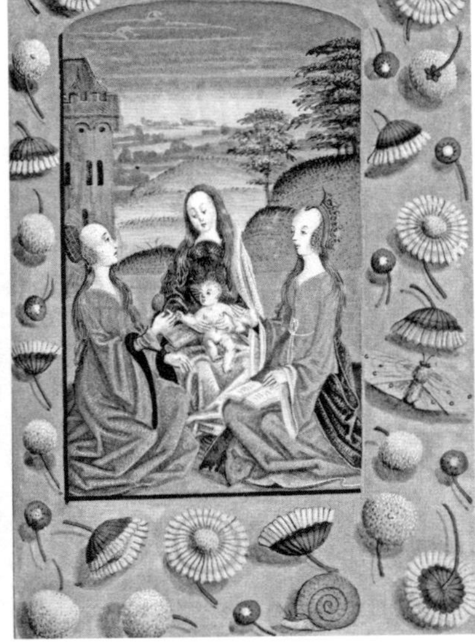

Geert Groote, Meester van Hugo Jansz. van Woerden and Suffragiënmeesters, **Book of Hours and Prayer**, c. 1480, manuscript, 19 × 13 × 5 cm. Courtesy Museum Catharijneconvent, Utrecht. Photo: Ruben de Heer.

DAISY

To the Daisy

Bright flower, whose home is every where!
A Pilgrim bold in Nature's care,
And all the long year through the heir
Of joy or sorrow,
Methinks that there abides in thee
Some concord with humanity,
Given to no other Flower I see
The forest thorough!

Is it that Man is soon depress?
A thoughtless Thing! who, once unblest,
Does little on his memory rest,
Or on his reason,
And Thou would'st teach him how to find
A shelter under every wind,
A hope for times that are unkind
And every season?

Thou wanderest the wide world about,
Unchecked by pride or scrupulous doubt,
With friends to greet thee, or without,
Yet pleased and willing;
Meek, yielding to the occasion's call,
And all things suffering from all,
Thy function apostolical
In peace fulfilling.

Wordsworth, 'To the Daisy', in *Poems Volume I*.

DEFIANT GARDENS

As the war progressed into its third year, the military began to harness the gardening activity that had been spontaneously set in motion. Vegetable plots behind the lines were established on such a large scale that by 1918, the Western front was self-sufficient in fresh produce. The dugout gardens that were created in the first spring of the war were motivated by much more than a need for food; they were an attempt, as Vita Sackville-West described it in her epic poem *The Garden*, 'to hold the graces and the courtesies'. They expressed a wish to feel human and a will to be civilised, to be more than an animal in a mud-filled burrow or a cog in a giant war machine.
The trench gardens were, in their way, a version of swords to ploughshares. Petrol cans were converted into watering cans and bayonets put to alternative use in cultivating the ground. All the values that gardens represent are in opposition to war and in them, historian Kenneth Helphand identifies a potential anti-war message. In his book *Defiant Gardens* he writes: 'Peace is not just the absence of war but a positive assertive state… the garden is not just a retreat and a respite, but an assertion of a proposed condition, a model to be emulated.' The role of gardening in wartime can, Helphand believes, renew our appreciation of the garden's 'transformative power to beautify, comfort, and convey meaning'.

What feels homely, what gives hope, what strikes the eye as beautiful, are all dependent on

D continues on page 40.

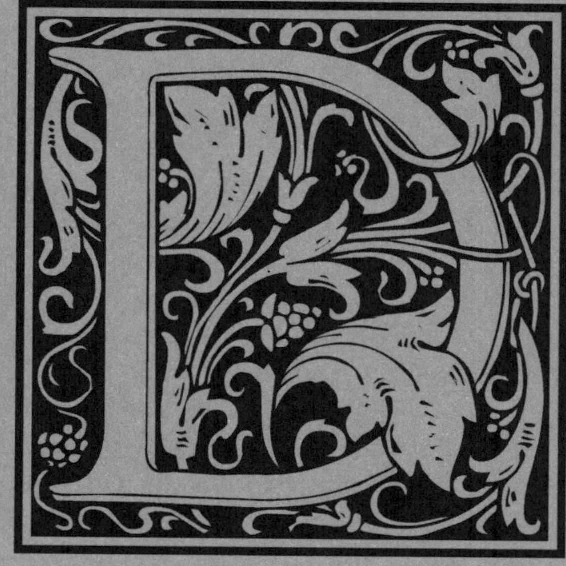

William Morris, **Letter D.**

THE DISTURB-ANCES OF THE GARDEN

IN THE GARDEN, ONE PERFORMS THE ACT OF POSSESSING

Jamaica Kincaid

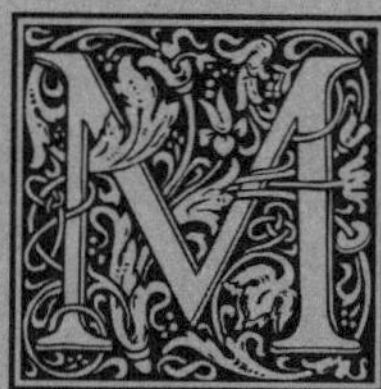y obsession with the garden and the events that take place in it began before I was familiar with that entity called consciousness. My mother taught me to read when I was very young, and she did this without telling me that there was something called the alphabet. I became familiar with words as if they were all wholly themselves, each one a world by itself, intact and self-contained, and able to be joined to other words if they wished to or if someone like me wanted them to. The book she taught me to read from was a biography of Louis Pasteur, the person she told me was responsible for her boiling the milk I drank daily, making sure that it would not infect me with something called tuberculosis. I never got tuberculosis, but I did get typhoid fever, whooping cough, measles, and persistent cases of hookworm and long worms. I was a 'sickly child'. Much of the love I remember receiving from my mother came during the times I was sick. I have such a lovely memory of her hovering over me with cups of barley water (that was for the measles) and giving me cups of tea made from herbs (bush) that she had gone out and gathered and steeped slowly (that was for the whooping cough). For the typhoid fever, she took me to the hospital, the children's ward, but she visited me twice a day and brought me fresh juice that she had squeezed or grated from fruits or vegetables, because she was certain that the hospital would not provide me with proper nourishment. And so there I was, a sickly child who could read but had no sense of consciousness, had no idea of how to understand and so make sense of the world into which she was born, a world that was always full of a yellow sun, green trees, a blue sea, and black people.

My mother was a gardener, and in her garden it was as if Vertumnus and Pomona had become one: she would find something growing in the wilds of her native island (Dominica) or the island on which she lived and gave birth to me (Antigua), and if it pleased her, or if it was in fruit and the taste of the fruit delighted her, she took a cutting of it (really she just broke off a shoot with her bare hands) or the seed (separating it from its pulpy substance and collecting it in her beautiful pink mouth) and brought it into her own garden and tended to it in a careless, everyday way, as if it were in the wild forest, or in the garden of a regal palace. The woods: The garden. For her, the wild and the cultivated were equal and yet separate, together and apart. This wasn't as clear to me then as I am stating it here. I had only just learned to read and the world outside a book I did not yet know how to reconcile.

The only book available to me, a book I was allowed to read all by myself without anyone paying attention to me, was the King James Version of the Bible. There's no need for me to go into the troubles with the King James Version of the Bible here, but when I encountered the first book, the Book of Genesis, I immediately understood it to be a book for children. A person, I came to understand much later, exists in the kingdom of children no matter how old the person is; even Methuselah, I came to see, was a child. But never mind that, it was the creation story that was so compelling to me, especially the constant refrain 'And God saw that it was good'. The God in the Book of Genesis made things, and at the end of each day he saw that they were good. But, I wondered, for something to be good would there not have to be something that was not good, or not as good? That was a problem, though I didn't bother myself with it at the time, mainly because I didn't know how to, and also because the story had an inexorableness to it: rolling on from one thing to another without a pause until, by the end of six days, there were a man and a woman made in God's image, there were fish in the sea and animals creeping on land and birds flying in the air and plants growing, and God found it all good, because here we are.

It was in the week after this creation, on the eighth day, that the trouble began: loneliness set in. And so God made a garden, dividing it into four quarters by running water through it (the classic quadrilinear style that is still a standard in garden design) and placing borders, the borders being the eternal good and evil: the Tree of Life and the Tree of Knowledge. One tree was to be partaken of, the other forbidden. I have since come to see that in the garden itself, throughout human association with it, the Edenic plan works in the same way: the Tree of Life is agriculture and the Tree of Knowledge is horticulture. We cultivate food, and when there is a surplus of it, producing wealth, we cultivate the spaces of contemplation, a garden of plants not necessary for physical survival. The awareness of that fact is what gives the garden its special, powerful place in our lives and our imaginations. The Tree of Knowledge holds unknown, and therefore dangerous possibilities; the Tree of Life is eternally necessary, and the Tree of Knowledge is deeply and divinely dependent on it. This is not a new thought for me. I could see it in my mother's relationship to the things she grew, the kind of godlike domination she would display over them. She, I remember, didn't make such fine distinctions, she only moved the plants around when they pleased her and destroyed them when they fell out of favor.

It is no surprise to me that my affection for the garden, including its most disturbing attributes, its most violent implications and associations, is intertwined with my mother. As a child, I did not know myself or the world I inhabited without her. She is the person who gave me and taught me the Word.

But where is the garden and where am I in it? This memory of growing things, anything, outside not inside, remained in my memory—or whatever we call that haunting, invisible wisp that is steadily part of our being—and wherever I lived in my young years, in New York City in particular, I planted: marigolds, portulaca, herbs for cooking, petunias, and other things that were familiar to me, all reminding me of my mother, the place I came from. Those first plants were in pots and lived on the roof of a diner that served only breakfast and lunch, in a dilapidated building at 284 Hudson Street, whose ownership was uncertain, which is the fate of us all. Ownership of ourselves and of the ground on which we walk, ownership of the other beings with whom we share this and see that it is good, and ownership of the vegetable kingdom are all uncertain, too. Nevertheless, in the garden, we perform the act of possessing. To name is to possess; possessing is the original violation bequeathed to Adam and his equal companion in creation, Eve, by their creator. It is their transgression in disregarding his command that leads him not only to cast them into the wilderness, the unknown, but also to cast out the other possession that he designed with great clarity and determination and purpose: the garden! For me, the story of the garden in Genesis is a way of understanding my garden obsession.

The appearance of the garden in our everyday life is so accepted that we embrace its presence as therapeutic. Some people say that weeding is a form of comfort and of settling into misery or happiness. The garden makes managing an excess of feelings—good feelings, bad feelings—rewarding in some way that I can never quite understand. The garden is a heap of disturbance, and it may be that my particular history, the history I share with millions of people, begins with our ancestors' violent removal from an Eden. The regions of Africa from which they came would have been Eden-like, and the horror that met them in that 'New World' could certainly be seen as the Fall. Your home, the place you are from, is always Eden, the place where even imperfections were perfect, and everything that happened after that beginning interrupted your Paradise.

On August 3, 1492—the day that Christopher Columbus set sail from Spain, later having a fatal encounter with the indigenous people he met in the 'West Indies'—the world of the garden changed. That endeavor, to me, anyway, is the way the world we now live in began; it not only affected the domestic life of Europeans (where did the people in a Rembrandt painting get all that stuff they are piling on?) but suddenly they were well-off enough to be interested in more than sustenance, or the Tree of Life (agriculture); they could now be interested in cultivating the fruits of the Tree of Knowledge (horticulture).

Suddenly, the conquerors could do more than feed themselves; they could also see and desire things that were of no use apart from the pleasure that they produced. When Cortés saw Montezuma's garden, a garden that incorporated a lake on which the capital of Mexico now sits, he didn't mention the profusion of exotic flowers that we now grow with ease in our own gardens (dahlias, zinnias, marigolds).

The garden figures prominently in the era of conquest, starting with Captain Cook's voyage to regions that we now know as Australia, New Zealand, New Guinea, and Tahiti, its aim, ostensibly, to observe the rare event of the transit of Venus. On this trip, in 1768, the first of Cook's three voyages around the world, he brought with him the botanist Joseph Banks and also Daniel Charles Solander, a student of Carolus Linnaeus. The two took careful notes on everything they saw. Banks decided that the breadfruit of the Pacific isles would make a good food for slaves on British-owned islands in the West Indies; the slaveholders were concerned with the amount of time it took the enslaved people to grow food to sustain themselves, and breadfruit grew with little cultivation. And so the Pacific Islands came to the West Indies. Banks also introduced the cultivation of tea (*Camellia sinensis*) to India.

Then there is Lewis and Clark's expedition from the Mississippi River to the Pacific Northwest. On that adventure, which was authorized by President Thomas Jefferson and was inspired by Cook's scientific and commercial interests, the explorers listed numerous plant species that were unknown to John Bartram, botanist to King George III, who ruled the United States when it was still a colony. Bartram's son, William, a fellow-botanist, later wrote a book about his own explorations, which is said to have influenced Wordsworth, Coleridge, and other English Romantic poets.

There now, look at that: I am meaning to show how I came to seek the garden in corners of the world far away from where I make one, and I have got lost in thickets of words. It was after I started to put seeds in the ground and noticed that sometimes nothing happened that I reached for a book. The first ones I read were about how to make a perennial border or how to get the best out of annuals—the kind of books for people who want to increase the value of their home—but these books were so boring. I found an old magazine meant to help white ladies manage their domestic lives in the nineteen-fifties much more interesting (that kind of magazine, along with a copy of 'Mrs. Beeton's Book of Household Management', is worthy of a day spent in bed while the sun is shining its brightest outside). But where did plants, annual and perennial, pristinely set out in something called a border, and arranged sometimes according to colour and sometimes according to height, come from?

Those books had no answer for me. So one book led to another, and before long I had acquired (and read) so many books that it put a strain on my family's budget. Resentment, a not unfamiliar feeling relating to the garden, set in.

I began to refer to plants by their Latin names, and this so irritated my editor at this magazine (Veronica Geng) that she made me promise that I would never learn the Latin name of another plant. I loved her very much, and so I promised that I would never do such a thing, but I did continue to learn the Latin names of plants and never told her. Betrayal, another feature of any garden.

How did plants get their names? I looked to Linnaeus, who, it turned out, liked to name plants after people whose character they resembled. Mischievous, yes, but not too different from the doctrine of signatures, which attempted to cure diseases by using plants that resembled the diseased part of the body. I was thinking about this one day, stooped over and admiring a colony of *Jeffersonia diphylla*, whose common name is twinleaf. *Jeffersonia diphylla* is a short woodland herbaceous ephemeral whose leaf is perforated at the base so that it often looks like a luna moth, but the two leaflets are not identical at the margins, and each leaf is not evenly divided: the margins undulate, and one leaflet is a little bigger than the other. But isn't Thomas Jefferson, the gardener, the liberty lover and slaveowner, often described as divided, and isn't it appropriate that a plant such as the twinleaf is named for him? The name was bestowed by one of his contemporaries, Benjamin Smith Barton, who perhaps guessed at his true character. It was through this plant that I became interested in Thomas Jefferson. I have read much of what he wrote and have firm opinions about him, including that his book 'Notes on the State of Virginia' is a creation story.

It was only a matter of time before I stumbled on the plant hunters, although this inevitability was not clear to me at all. Look at me: my historical reality, my ancestral memory, which is so deeply embedded that I think the whole world understands me before I even open my mouth. A big mistake, but a mistake not big enough for me to have learned anything from it. The plant hunters are the descendants of people and ideas that used to hunt people like me.

The first one I met, in a book, of course, was Frank Smythe. No one had ever made me think that finding a new primrose—or a new flower of any kind—was as special as finding a new island in the Caribbean Sea when I thought I was going to China to meet the Great Khan. A new primrose is more special than meeting any conqueror. But Smythe gave me more than that. I noticed, when reading his accounts, that he was always going off on little side journeys to climb some snow-covered protuberance not so far away, and then days later returning with a story of failure or success at reaching or not reaching the peak, and that by the way he had found some beauty of the vegetable kingdom on the banks of a hidden stream which would be new to every benighted soul in England. But his other gift to me was the pleasure to be had in going to see a plant that I might love or not, growing somewhere far away. It was in his writing that I found the distance between the garden I was looking at and the garden in the wilderness, the garden cast out of its Eden which created a longing in me, the notion of 'to go and to see.' Go see!

I end where I began: reading—learning to read and reading books, the words a form of food, a form of life, and then knowledge. But also my mother. I don't know exactly how old I was when she taught me to read, but I can say for certain that by the time I was three and a half I could read properly. This reading of mine so interfered with her own time to read that she enrolled me in school; but you could be enrolled in school only if you were five years old, and so she told me to remember to say, if asked, that I was five. My first performance as a writer of fiction? No, not that at all. Perhaps this: the first time I was asked who I was. And who am I? In an ideal world, a world in which the Tree of Life and the Tree of Knowledge stand before me, before all of us, we ask, Who am I? Among the many of us not given a chance to answer is the woman in the library in St. John's, Antigua, two large rooms above the Treasury Department, a building that was steps away from the customs office and the wharf where things coming and going lay. On that wharf worked a stevedore who loaded onto ships bags of raw sugar en route to England, to be refined into white sugar, which was so expensive that we, in my family, had it only on Sundays, as a special treat. I did not know of the stevedore, the lover of this woman who would not allow her children to have much white sugar because, somewhere in the world of Dr. Pasteur and his cohort, they had come to all sorts of conclusions about diseases and their relationships to food (beriberi was a disease my mother succeeded in saving me from suffering). Her name was Annie Victoria Richardson Drew, and she was born in a village in Dominica, British West Indies.

Originally published in *The New Yorker*, 7 September 2020

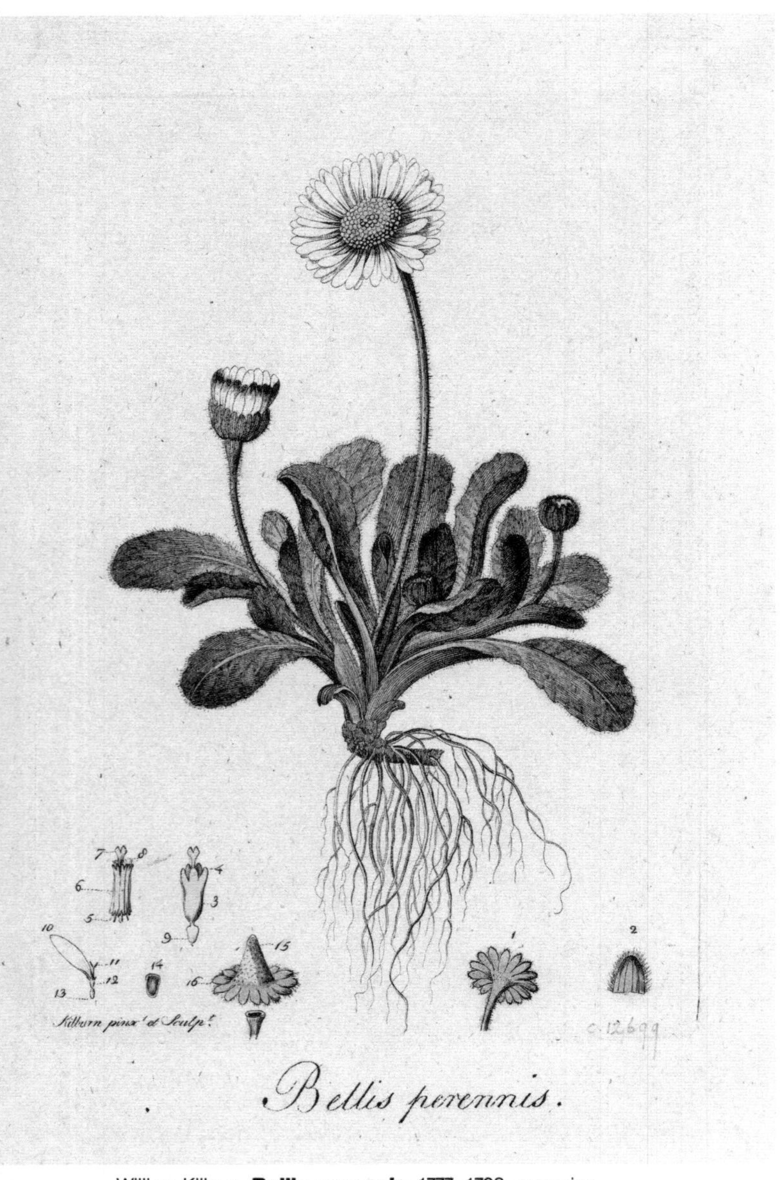

William Kilburn, **Bellis perennis**, 1777–1798, engraving, 19.7 × 15.2 cm. Courtesy Alamy/Victoria and Albert Museum, London.

the surroundings in which we find ourselves. Cultivating the earth in the context of a battlefield throws the power of the garden into sharp relief and when so much is beyond repair, to be able to change something for the better is extremely important.

Stuart-Smith, *The Well-Gardened Mind*.

THE DISTURBANCES OF THE GARDEN

See p. 35 for 'The Disturbances of the Garden' by Jamaica Kindcaid.

DOCTRINE OF SIGNATURES

Up to the end of the 16th century, 'resemblance' played a constructive role in the knowledge and symbolism of Western culture. The Doctrine of Signatures was applied historically to try to predict which of many herbal remedies might be efficacious in human illnesses. Referring to the common fern Asplenium scolopendrium, history showed that the sori on its fronds were shaped like (resembled) a spleen, which caused the ancients to think it would be useful for treating ailments of the spleen.

In the 1500s, Paracelsus von Hohenheim (1493–1541) expanded an older Christian European idea as the Doctrine of Signatures. He and many others believed that the shape, colour, taste, smell and other attributes of a plant indicated its use in healing. For instance, he observed that the leaf of Hepatica acutiloba used to treat liver disorders was in fact shaped like the liver. The leaf of the Cyclamen persicum superficially looks like the ear, and was therefore used to treat earache. Paracelsus noticed that the Christmas rose (Helleborus niger) flowered in winter, and concluded that it had rejuvenating powers; he introduced it into the pharmacopoeia and recommended it for people over.

Pearce, 'The Doctrine of Signatures', 51.

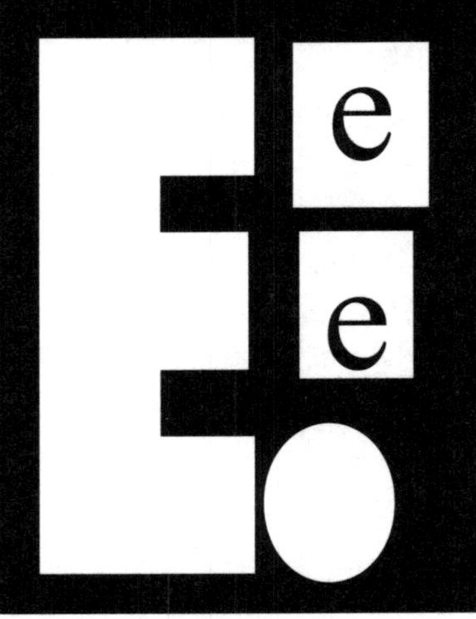

ECOFASCISM

As J. Sakai points out in his radical pamphlet *The Green Nazi*, this history of fascist and extreme nationalist politics 'pushes us to check out what words like "Green", "Nature", "ecology" and "peasant" mean in our politics.... It's not about the past, it's about the future.' We might also want to add to that list of words important gardening terms and practices like 'organic' and 'biodynamic', shaded as they are in their origins by a Nazi stamp. If this kind of approach seems to be 'enter[ing] environmentalism from way on the other side', as Sakai describes it, it is also a reminder that radical is by no means essentially progressive—that radical gardening can be sobering, unliberating, can be a mask or a lie, can justify or lead to the xenophobic, the murderous and even genocidal.

McKay, *Radical Gardening*, 69.

The very articulation of the plan 'to plant Nazi ideology in the garden' is a powerful illustration of the total nature of the ambition of the Nazi project, yes, but it also shows the extent to which the Nazis thought that the controlled (cultivated) land of the garden itself could not just embellish but actually contribute to and strengthen their movement. If ideology is planted in the garden that is because it is assumed that ideology can grow in the garden.

McKay, *Radical Gardening*, 59.

ECOFEMINISM

Feminist environmentalism begins with noticing similarities and connections between forms and instances of human oppression, including the oppression of women, and the degradation of nature. A central position grounding ecofeminism is the belief that values, notions of reality, and social practices are related, and that forms of oppression and domination, however historically and culturally distinct, are interlocked and enmeshed.

Cuomo, *Feminism and Ecological Communities*, 1.

An ecofeminist perspective propounds the need for a new cosmology and a new anthropology which recognizes that life in nature (which includes human beings) is maintained by means of co-operation, and mutual care and love. Only in this way can we be enabled to respect and preserve the diversity of all life forms, including their cultural expressions, as true sources of our well-being and happiness. To this end ecofeminists use metaphors like 'reweaving the world', 'healing the wounds', and re-connecting and interconnecting the 'web'. This effort to create a holistic, all-life embracing cosmology and anthropology, must necessarily imply a concept of freedom different from that used since the Enlightenment.

Shiva and Mies, *Ecofeminism*, 81.

[E]cofeminists (ironically) have been less than vigilant in their questioning of the gender and nature assumptions that are fundamental to the Western discursive landscape and that appear so unproblematically in motherhood environmentalism. Heroic mothers defending home and hearth against a nature deformed by multinationalist corporate practice may be a compelling story, but it is not the stuff of which good feminist or ecological critique is necessarily born. In this particular narrative, part of what is missing is, in Lee Quinby's terms, the interrogative element, an insistence on problematizing the whole ensemble of discursive relations that surrounds the phenomenon in question. Also crucially missing is the democratic element, an insistence on bringing to public debate and contest precisely these discursive relations, in the hope of sloughing off their skin of naturalness. An ecofeminism that is both feminist and ecological must therefore, in my view, place at the center of its existence a commitment to good theory and good politics, in concert.

Sandilands, *Ecofeminism*, xvii.

ECOLOGY

The term 'ecology' was coined by the German zoologist, Ernst Haeckel, in 1866 to describe the 'economies' of living forms. The theoretical practice of ecology consists, by and large, of the construction of models of the interaction of living systems with their environment (including other living systems).

Stanford Encyclopedia of Philosophy, 'Ecology'.

Ecology. The study of how plants and animals interact in their non-living environment.

Spaid, *Ecovention*, 145.

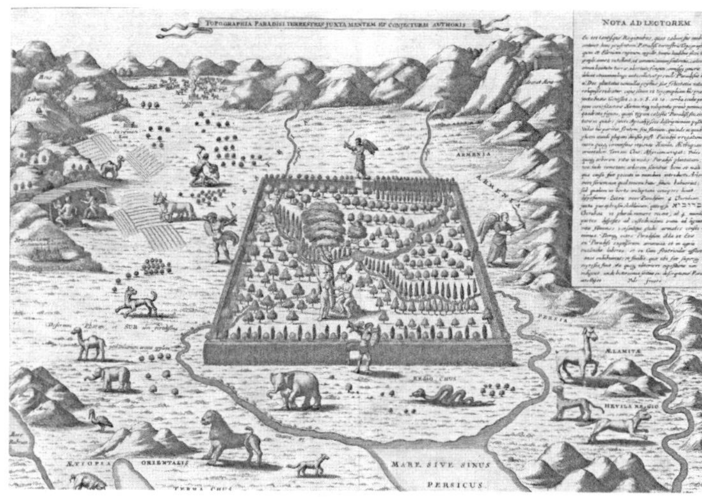

Athanasius Kircher, **Topographia paradisi terrestris juxta mentem et conjecturas authoris**, 1675, 29 × 42 cm. Courtesy Beinecke Rare Book and Manuscript Library, Yale University Library, New Haven.

According to Lucy Lippard, Ellen Swallow Richards coined the word ecology from the Greek word for home, though most attribute the word to 1914 century German naturalist Ernst Haeckel.

Spaid, *Ecovention*, 1.

EDEN

ABRAHAM BLOEMAERT (DESIGNER)
JAN SAENREDAM (ENGRAVER)

In this suite of engravings, the Utrecht-based painter Abraham Bloemaert depicted various key scenes from the Book of Genesis. In the Garden of Eden, Adam and Eve live in harmony with each other, the world, and nature. Here they are protected from mortality, work, and knowledge. After the Fall, they have to take care of their own garden and shape their own world. Bloemaert makes that transition very clear. Under a stormy sky, the couple is expelled from the lush, sunny garden, and banished to a rugged landscape, where Adam is shown digging and Eve spinning wool. Bloemaert thus emphasizes the link between the expulsion from Paradise and the need to perform work. Therefore, the Garden of Eden is linked to the dawn of human history. (ed.)

OTTO VAN REES

Otto van Rees worked in a variety of styles during his career, from Cubism to Expressionism and Dada. In the 1910s, van Rees emphasized the two-dimensional plane in his paintings, and looked to Ancient Egyptian and Japanese art for the representation of depth. He painted the theme of Adam and Eve several times in this period. Here he has depicted them in profile as a couple sitting comfortably together. The natural elements have a geometric stylization and are sharply delineated. The snake—the symbol of evil—and the tree are absent. Van Rees depicts the idyll before the Fall, and symbolizes man's lost unity with nature. (ed.)

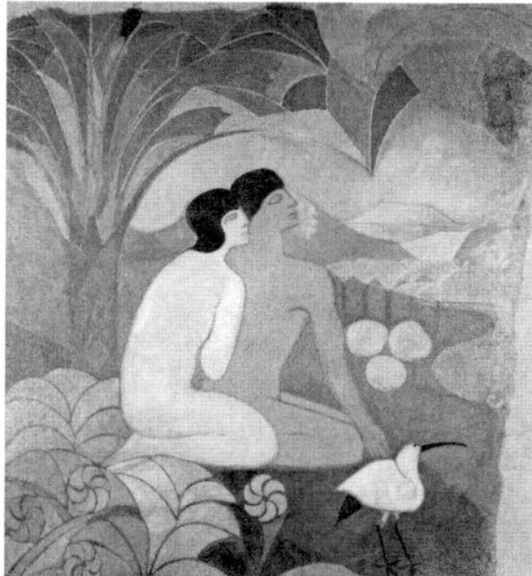

Otto van Rees, **Adam and Eva**, c. 1910, oil on canvas, 162 × 148.8 cm. Courtesy Centraal Museum, Utrecht/Pictoright, Amsterdam.

HERMAN JUSTUS KRUYDER

In Herman Justus Kruyder's interpretation of Paradise, Adam and Eve stand naked and shy in a dark, dense forest of giant trees. Kruyder opts not for an idyllic or nostalgic representation of the lost Paradise, but for a more mysterious approach. The Haarlem-based painter made many outdoor studies in the woods and dunes. For example, he situated *Paradise I* in Groenendaal Park near Heemstede, although that woodland is barely recognisable as a Dutch forest. For Kruyder, Paradise is a dark and overwhelming jungle. His view proposes a different relationship between man and nature. (ed.)

EDEN

And the Lord God formed man of the dust of the ground, and breathed into his nostrils the breath of life; and man became a living soul. And the Lord God planted a garden eastward in Eden.

Genesis 2:7, *King James Bible 2000.*

And the Lord God planted a garden eastward in Eden; and there he put the man whom he had formed. And out of the ground made the Lord God to grow every tree that is pleasant to the sight, and good for food; the tree of life also in the midst of the garden, and the tree of

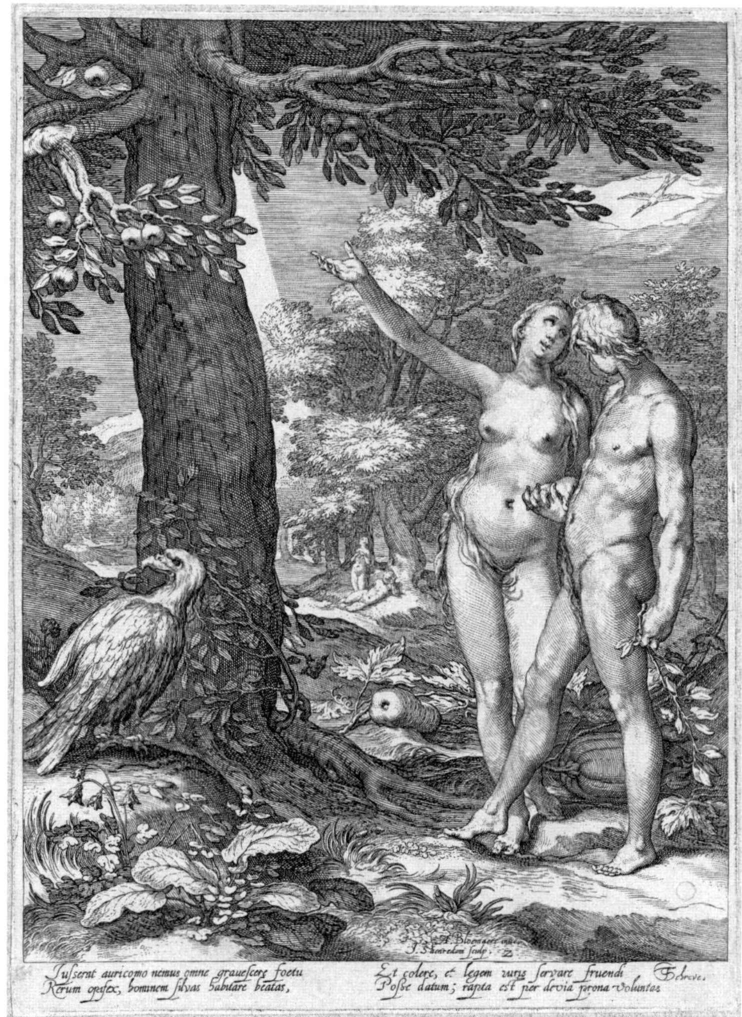

Abraham Bloemaert and Jan Saenredam, **Adam and Eve before the Tree of Knowledge (The History of the First Parents of Man)**, 1604, engraving, 27.5 × 19.7 cm. Courtesy Centraal Museum, Utrecht.

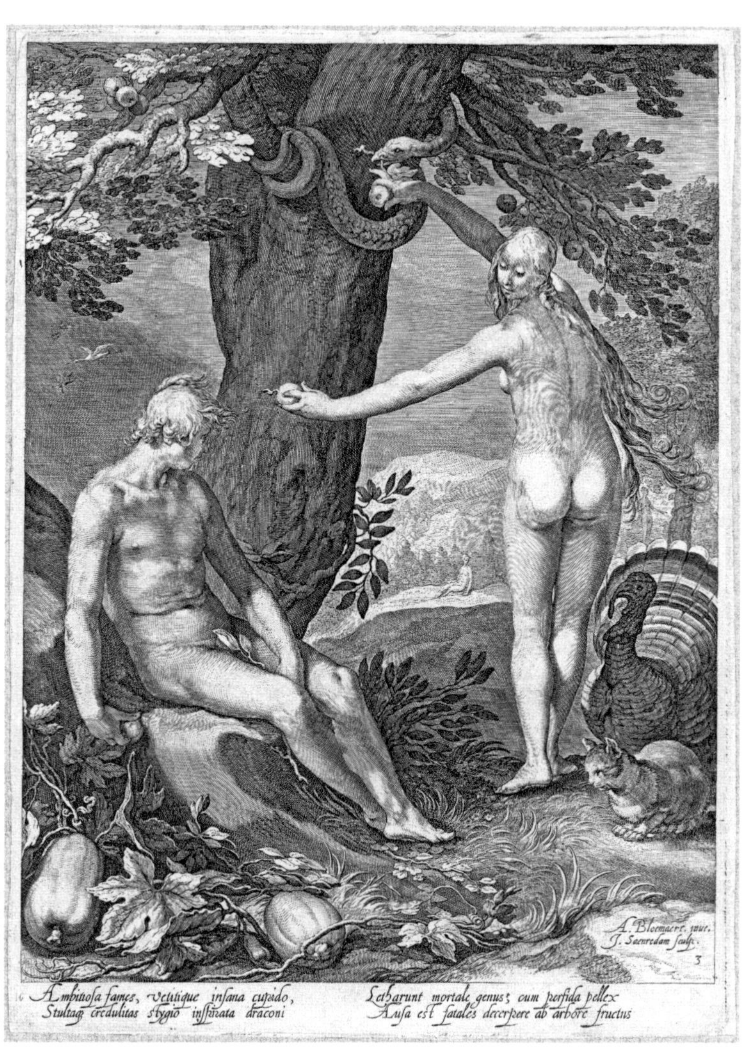

Abraham Bloemaert and Jan Saenredam, **The Temptation of Man (The History of the First Parents of Man)**, 1604, engraving, 27.8 × 20 cm. Courtesy Centraal Museum, Utrecht.

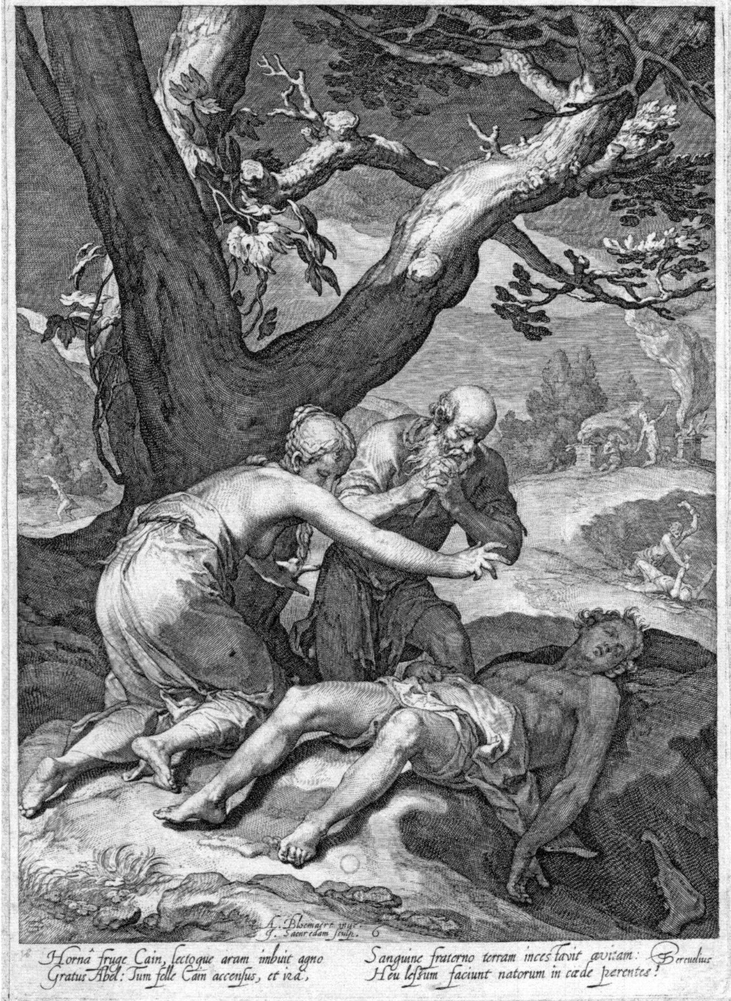

Adam and Eve Lamenting over the Corpse of Abel (The History of the First Parents of Man), 1604, engraving, 27.8 × 19.9 cm. Courtesy Centraal Museum, Utrecht.

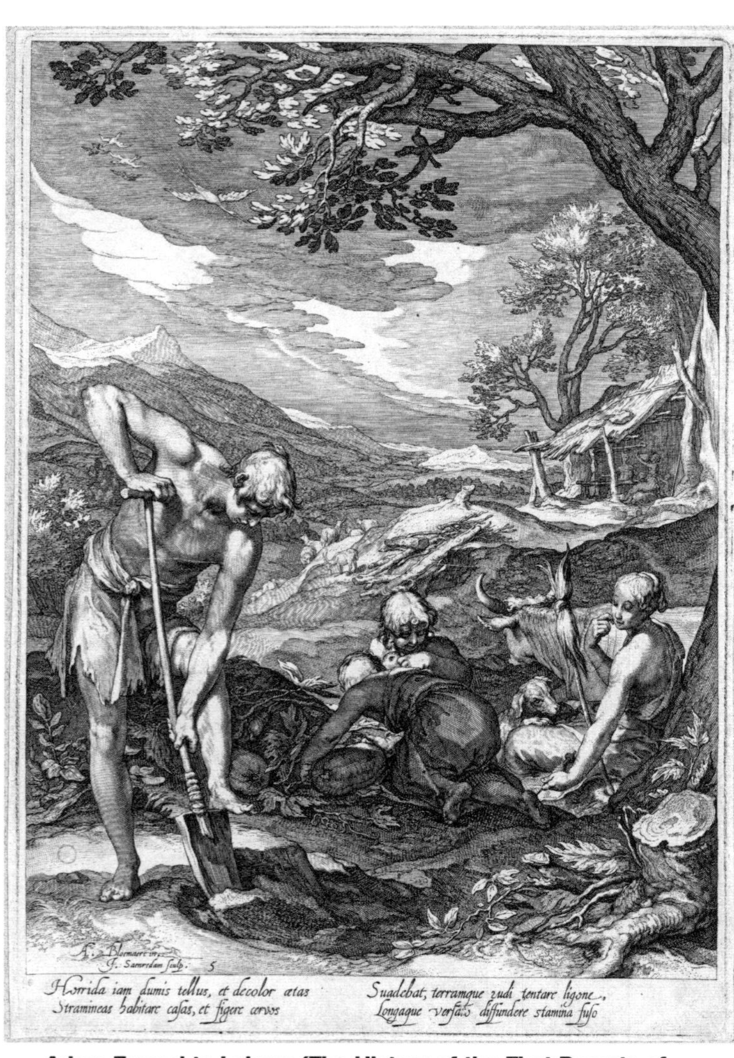

Adam Forced to Labour (The History of the First Parents of Man), 1604, engraving, 27.9 × 19.8 cm. Courtesy Centraal Museum, Utrecht.

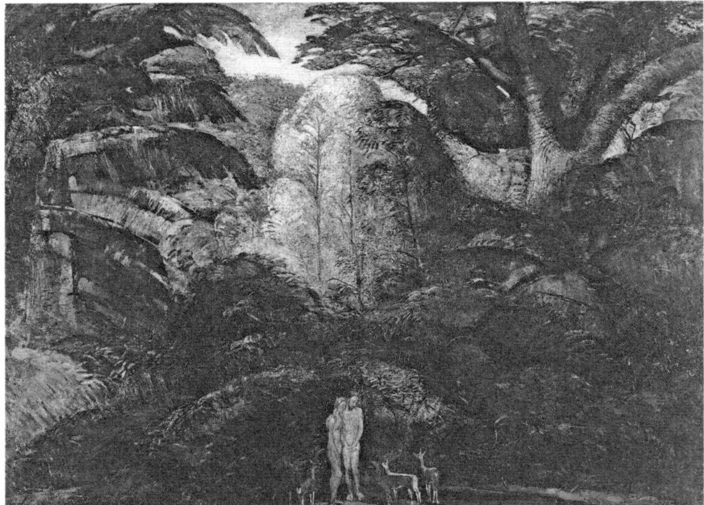

Herman Justus Kruyder, **Paradijs I**, 1913–1914, oil on canvas, 109.3 × 148 cm, Courtesy Frans Hals Museum, Haarlem.

knowledge of good and evil. And a river went out of Eden to water the garden; and from thence it was parted, and became into four heads.

Genesis 2: 8–10, *King James Bible 2000*.

Genesis refers not just to two moral poles in the garden, but to a virtual maelstrom of conduct. How is it that one tree, embedded with the virtues of both good and evil, is opposed to the Tree of Life? Is the knowledge of good to be equated with the knowledge of evil? Is all knowledge evil? Is the lost innocence of Adam and Eve the prerequisite for sheltering under the Tree of Life? There is no direct route from one tree to the other, no simple path that winds through the Garden of Eden. This is a Garden characterised by forks in the road, by a Chinese box of decisions at every turn.

Tarantino, 'Et in Arcadia Ego', 23.

A personal mythology recurs in my writing, much the same way poppy wreaths have crept into my films. For me this archeology has become obsessive, for the 'experts' my sexuality is a confusion. All received information should make us inverts sad. But before I finish I intend to celebrate our corner of Paradise, the part of the garden the Lord forgot to mention.

Jarman, *Modern Nature*, 23.

EDIBLE ESTATE

EDIBLE ESTATES was initiated on Independence Day 2005 with the planting of the first in the series of gardens in Salina, Kansas, the geographic center of the United States. Domestic front lawns are replaced with edible landscapes. [...]

Edible Estates is an ongoing initiative to create a series of regional prototype gardens that replace domestic front lawns, and other unused spaces in front of homes, with places for families to grow their own food. [...]

These simple, low-cost gardens and their stories are meant to inspire others, demonstrating what is possible for anyone with the will to grow food and some unused land between the house and the street. Unlike the unattainable images of perfection seen in design and gardening magazines, anyone should be able to look at these gardens and imagine doing something similar at home. These are real-life gardens, tended by typical families in a variety of common living situations, from homes in the outer suburbs to inner-city apartments.

With the modest gesture of reconsidering the use of our small plots of land, the Edible Estates project invites us to reconsider our relationships with our neighbors, the sources of our food, and our connections to the natural environment immediately outside our front doors.

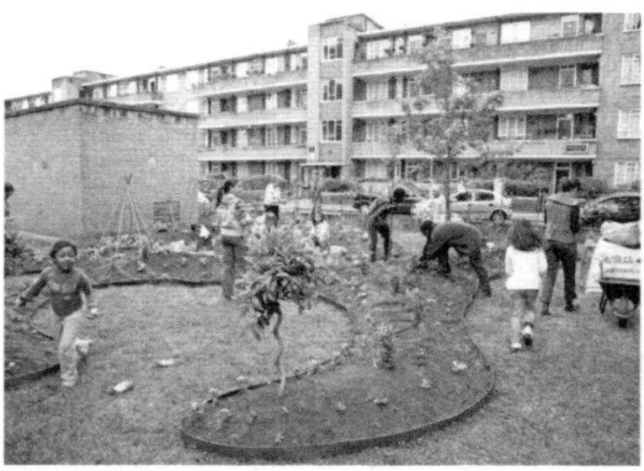
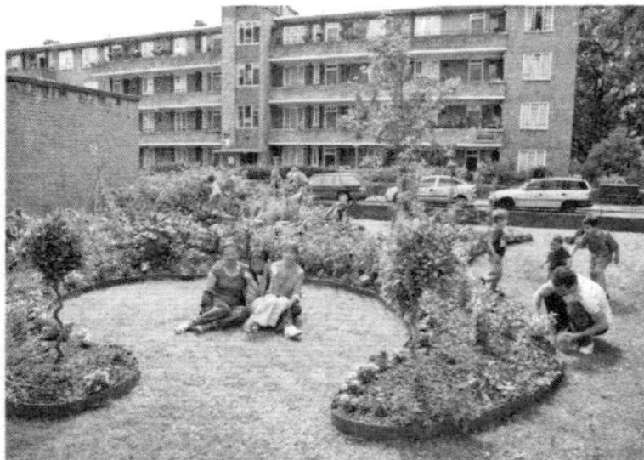

Fritz Haeg, **Edible Estates Regional Prototype Garden**, 2007, installation view. Courtesy Fritz Haeg. Photo: Heiko Prigge.

E continues on page 49.

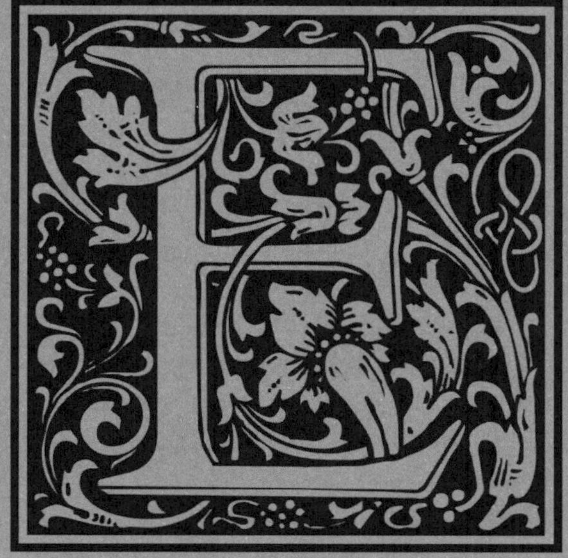

William Morris, **Letter E.**

AGAINST GARDENING

MOMENTS IN THE LIFE OF A GARDENER

Patricia de Vries

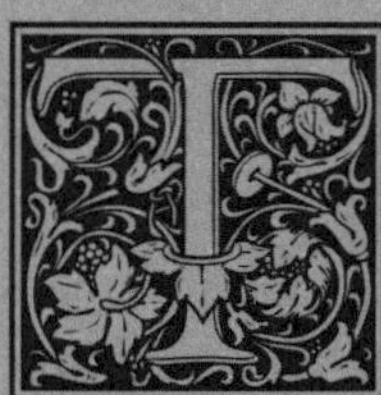

The story is the schoolbook example of Joseph Campbell's monomyth template: a protagonist encounters a decisive moral challenge and, after some struggle, learns an important lesson and is transformed. The question I'd like to broach here is: what moved the protagonist? But first, it is worth reminding ourselves of the setting of the Book of Genesis.

Over a seven-day stint, we follow a character named LORD God as he creates the heavens, the earth, and everything in between (Genesis 1). He then goes on to form, from the dust of the earth, a male human. After breathing life into this man's nostrils, he hovers eastward to Eden, not too far from Ethiopia. There, LORD God plants what is described as a lush, vibrant, fragrant, animated, and colourful garden with birds and bees, flowers and trees. A river runs through the garden hydrating its flourishing and prospering flora and fauna. In this heavenly abode of great beauty, he drops the unnamed man, for him to 'to dress it and to keep it' (Genesis 2:15). Decidedly, LORD God also plants two trees in the middle of the garden: a so-called tree of life and a tree of knowledge of good and evil. To provide sustenance, the nameless gardener is instructed to freely drink from the river and eat from the garden's vegetation—but not from the tree of knowledge of good and evil. LORD God says it does: 'Of every tree of the garden thou mayest freely eat: But of the tree of the knowledge of good and evil, thou shalt not eat of it: for in the day that thou eatest thereof thou shalt surely die' (Genesis 2:17). Before temporarily leaving the scene, he makes the gardener 'an help' from the man's rib—in today's vocabulary, a clone. From then on, the gardener is referred to as Adam and accompanied by a female assistant gardener who, we later learn, is called Eve. Thus, the setting in which the action unfolds: a divine place, in popular parlance often referred to as paradise.[1]

It is in the third chapter that the plot both falters and thickens. A major plot gap has this chapter starting with a talking serpent approaching Eve. The chain of events that led up to this situation remains unknown. We have to make do with what little the narrator relates to its readers, which is merely that the serpent is the most cunning crawler LORD God had let loose in the garden—apparently unbeknownst to Eve, who seems unfazed both by its visit and by its ability to talk. She is milling around the tree of knowledge of good and evil when the serpent comes along and encourages her to eat from it. The serpent murmurs to Eve that the tree's fruit will not kill her, like LORD God said it would. Instead, it will give her knowledge equal to that of LORD God. Or, in the words of the talking serpent, 'your eyes shall be opened, and ye shall be as gods, knowing good and evil' (Genesis 3:5). Here, the narrator inserts another almighty shortcut. All they relay is that Eve found the

1 'Paradise' is a form of garden of ancient Persian origin. Such gardens were enclosed places. The term (in the ancient Median language **paridaiza**, and in the ancient Avestan language **pairidaeza**) is compounded of **'pa'iri'** or **'pari'** meaning 'around', 'circle', and **'da'eza'** or **'diaza'**, meaning 'built wall'. Hence, a walled garden.

tree 'to be desired to make one wise' and that its fruits looked good and nutritious to eat (Genesis 3:6). Maybe the serpent was feeling particularly sly that day and, by ingenious contrivance, left Eve in a cleft stick pitted against LORD God? Maybe the serpent was in cahoots with LORD God? It is hard to read a room with a thin plot to work with and an unreliable narrator. Anyhow, according to the narrator, the serpent bamboozled Eve, who picked the fruit, ate some herself, and then gave some to Adam.[2]

2 The King James translation of the Bible does not specify the fruit hanging from the tree of knowledge of good and evil. In the Torah, Eve eats an unidentified fruit: the generic Hebrew term '**peri**' is used, which could be **any** fruit. Some Rabbinic commentators have variously characterized it as possibly a fig, a pomegranate, a grape, an apricot, a peach, and a citron. Other commentators have thought of the fruit as toxic (e.g. Spinoza) or possibly intoxicating. When the Hebrew Bible was translated into Latin, in the fourth century AD, '**peri**' was translated as '**malus**', which could refer to any **seed-bearing** fruit, such as pears, tangerines, avocados, cherries, and apples. However, it is unlikely apple trees grew in Eden.

Things quickly go downhill from here. Ostensibly bloated with spite, LORD God condemns Eve to a life of anguish and hard reproductive labour ruled over by Adam. 'I will greatly multiply thy sorrow and thy conception; in sorrow thou shalt bring forth children; and thy desire shall be to thy husband, and he shall rule over thee', he hisses (Genesis 3:17). And as a punishment for listening to his wife, LORD God sends Adam off to toil his fingers to the bone on cursed and infertile soil in the oppressive heat of the desert. The rest is Biblical HIStory: after the original sin, the subsequent inherent shame, the expulsion from Paradise, and the wrath of LORD God, what remains is endless suffering and eternal guilt.

EVE'S LEAP

The Book of Genesis remains a colossal myth and is widely considered to be the mainstream narrative of Western culture. It has taken a host of symbolic meanings, which parts of Western culture use to understand and justify their relation to the earth, to foreign lands, to natural resources, to animals, to so-considered Others, and to its patriarchal division of reproductive labour, to name but a few. Its ethical dimensions have been thoroughly studied, unpacked, dismantled, and critiqued from various perspectives and disciplines (e.g. Prest 1981; Lerner 1989; Ewing 2000; Merchant 2003; Harrison 2008).

The limelight in discussions on the meanings of the creation story in the Book of Genesis often falls on Adam. This is unsurprising in a patriarchal culture, but it also short-changes Eve who, we have to acknowledge, is the actual protagonist of the story.

It is only after Eve is introduced that the story becomes meaty. It is Eve who moves the action from the uneventful and inconsequential to the life-altering. The thick of the action revolves around her. Not skirting the unknown, it is Eve who has the gumption to nibble on the fruit, which cuts right to the story's heart.

What moved Eve? The narrator leaves her desires and deliberations to the imagination of the reader. Maybe Eve hated her job with the force of a thousand suns? Maybe she was curious, hungry, bored, or just done with her garden existence? Or, perhaps by chance, something gave her a swift kick in the conscience? Who's to say? To ask *why* Eve plucked the fruit is a misguided question—though it is safe to assume she probably had plenty of thoughts of her own, spending her days in a garden with no place to hide as the assistant gardener to Adam, a job she never applied for, working for a master landscaper with a punitive streak whose commandments and measures put the 'b' into subtle. To ask *what* moved her is not a question of retrospective soul-searching, speculation, or guessing her motives. There is no conclusive answer as to *why* she did what she did. But we may explore *how* it is that she acted as she did.

One instruction Eve received on dressing and keeping LORD God's garden was the commandment 'thou shalt not eat of the tree of the knowledge of good and evil'. In his 'Critique of Violence' (1921), Walter Benjamin makes the point that 'shalt not' offers a ground outside itself to reflect on the commandment (249). The commandment is a command, not an absolute prohibition. 'Shalt not' functions 'as a guideline for the actions of persons or communities who have to wrestle with it in solitude and, in exceptional cases to take the responsibility of ignoring it' (250). This suggests that doing what one shalt not do, disobeying LORD God's commandment, is grounded in individual moral reflection. It is also to suggest that disobeying LORD God's commandments is never *in and of itself* wrong or evil. This is an important insight, yet unhelpful in the quest to understand what moved Eve, as her doing is *not* the result of well- (or ill-)considered ethical reflection.

For how could she take moral

responsibility for plucking a piece of fruit if she did not (yet) know right from wrong? As she knew of no good and no evil, she could not have wrestled with an ethical dilemma; nor could she know she was about to err and commit *a sin* in LORD God's book. She only learned that *after* the fact. She did not know, could not have known, that she was about to throw the whole god-blessed splendid Glory—and with that, *herself*—under the bus. Judging her act as evil, immoral, or a fall is, therefore, a *retrospective* judgment. Which is to say, it comes 'too late', *post factum* (Kierkegaard 1844, 89). According to the narrator of *Genesis*, Eve claims the serpent beguiled her. That does not help us any further either. If this were so, Eve only had to have willed to open her eyes, to know good from evil. But Eve could not have understood the words of the serpent, let alone its possible implications. For, again, how could she understand what 'knowing good and evil' meant, when she was ignorant of it (Kierkegaard, 89)? The serpent could not have explained it to her, either, as the distinction comes into the world only *after* she eats the fruit; it follows with her nosh (Kierkegaard, 90). 'Innocence is ignorance' (Kierkegaard, 80).

Add to this the unreliability of the narrator, the faltering and thin plot, and we arrive at a dead end. Simply put: Eve was no evildoer. She had no way of knowing her act could be considered *a sin*. She doesn't *know* what she doesn't know. Therefore, one may condemn her act, if one so desires, but *no guilt* can be attributed to her for what happened *after* her fruit snack. Whether she grasped, effectively, the meaning of a command—and of death or dying—is another matter, and open to speculation and dispute. But this is not the place for this discussion. The question remains: what moved her to pluck the fruit?

GARDEN AS FALSE PROMISE, NOUN AND VERB

One's environment is a crucial factor in human existence and well-being, according to Carl Jung (1950). Here, my working assumption is that the Garden of Eden, being Eve's direct and only environment, was an essential factor in her existence and, concomitantly, to her life decisions. Essentially, the Book of Genesis is about the innate desire—or should we say disorder?—to garden. Starting with LORD God, who plants a garden in the barren land of Eden, which is continued by Adam and Eve, the first gardeners, who were tasked with keeping and dressing his garden—although perhaps not entirely voluntarily. It is passed on to a large part of humanity, in mutated form, in attempts to create a garden existence by building a world within a world in the form of, to name but a few, nation states, colonies, institutions, cults, gated communities, collections, houses, prisons, rooms of one's own, the internet, man-caves, bunkers, and, of course, parks, gardens, orchards, patios, allotments, and yards, public, private, botanic,[3] and otherwise. Concurrently, the story of the Garden of Eden continues to produce an endless amount of namesakes—in the form of holiday resorts, landscaping agencies, florists, day cares, bed and breakfasts, and lounge bars—and has inspired numerous utopia stories set in Eden-like gardens (e.g. Howard 1902).

3 John Prest argues in **The Garden of Eden** (1981) that sixteenth-century botanical gardens were not merely a collection of plants, they were considered re-creations of the Garden of Eden. And in **Wonders and the Order of Nature** (1998), Lorraine Daston and Katherine Park have documented how medieval Western Europeean writers of encyclopaedias were often monastic Christians that studied God's creation in order to come closer to Him. Encyclopaedias often followed the structure of the days of creation by God.

More than a physical space, a garden is a mental and a symbolic space—a safe haven, a sanctuary, an asylum, a refuge, a dwelling space, a space to retreat, to take leisure, and to think. Clipping, weeding, and watering plants may be a delightful distraction from everyday realities. A gardener gathers, grows, and keeps organisms, and with them builds a world within a world. Seen this way, gardening is a redemptive act and offers a miniature model or reincarnation of the idealized lost Garden of Eden. A garden is a fabricated completeness within a demarcated space, cleansed of frustration, protected from outside interference. To spin this further, more than physical, mental, and symbolic spaces, gardens are moral spaces. They reflect an idealized society in which things all have their designated place, in which what is considered to belong together is kept together under the gardener's operative control.

You would think the Garden of Eden, in all its blissful perfection, should shield Eve from having it disappear on the horizon. But things are not that simple. A garden, to borrow a line from the poet William

Wordsworth, throws us 'in the midst of the realities of things'. And realities, as we all know, are not all that idyllic, pristine, harmonious, or innocent.

'Garden' is not merely a noun or a possessive, but a verb—a *doing*. To plant a garden is to draw a line in the earth. To draw a line is to demarcate a space. To demarcate a space is to enclose it. A garden is an enclosure and an enclosure is the mark of division. A garden's hedge, picket fence, and gate help mark off territory. Turf, paving, flower beds, borders, and terraces create a system of division. And mowers, hedge shears, rakes, tying wire, tree saws, and leaf blowers form some of the tools to create order within the divisions. Enclosures, as Silvia Federici (2004) has taught us, produce hierarchies and distinctions—in the given context, between, for example, ladybirds and aphids, slugs and budworms, weeds and plants, faeces and manure—as well as the force and violence required to impose them.

Garden work is ordering work, and ordering work involves classification. Classification is the practice of exclusions. To exclude is to bar, to prevent from entering to maintain what is considered inside from outside, the desirables from the undesirables, order from disorder. To garden is to occupy territory, which requires repetitive effort to reimpose a constructed order. Gardening requires 'keeping and dressing', repeatedly performed and reinforced through one's tending efforts of ploughing, weeding, pruning, curtailing, clipping, removing, repelling, and exterminating. It requires a constant dressing to curtail other forms of dress. 'For like a story, a garden has its own developing plot, as it were, whose intrigues keep the caretaker under more or less constant pressure' (Harrison 2008, 7). It is the pressure to prevent a garden from developing into a sprawling multitude. Gardening, therefore, is an 'interruptive act' (Derrida 1992, 969) that always involves some quality of force, skewing in some arbitrary directions and not others: yes to butterflies and bees; no to vine weevils and caterpillars; yes to hedgehogs; no to moles. No garden exists cleansed of the force required to maintain it. Indeed, no garden exists without a destruction drive [*I salute you, Freud*].

EVE THE RELUCTANT GARDENER

It is important to note here that Eve is not an observer of the garden-environment she inhabited, dressed, and kept, nor of its enabling conditions. Rather, she is part of it, of its ongoing intra-activity and also takes part in it. Which is to say, we must take into account that she was marooned in a garden, brought under the command of LORD God and made available—together with Adam—for keeping and dressing LORD God's garden. This is to suggest that she keeps and dresses the garden that keeps and dresses her, too. Until, one fine day, she preferred not to—*n-1*.

What conditioned her disobedience? The most straightforward, yet somewhat circular, answer is that her act arises because it is possible for it to arise. What enables her disobedience is the 'possibility of being able' (Kierkegaard 1844, 89). It is about the possible *ability* to do what she shall not do. More generally, the very existence of the tree of knowledge of good and evil is the condition under which disobedience is possible.

In *The Concept of Anxiety*, Søren Kierkegaard (1844) makes the poignant point that in the Garden of Eden there is no movement, no becoming. Nothing arises in the Garden. The Garden *is*; all that LORD God created merely *is*. Eve is supposed to take simple delight in what exists.

When nothing arises, when everything simply is, then nothing is possible. Nothing can arise or become in the Garden. Nothing ever changes. Seen in this light, her disobedience is the condition for the possible arising of difference in a situation of sameness and standstill. Eve eating the fruit is *the condition*—not the cause—for an arising, for a becoming, for a possibility. Seen from this viewpoint, change is the condition of existence of the tree and Eve eating its fruit is the condition for the occasion of its arising. Put differently, without her *ability* to disobey, no change would arise—it would simply be impossible. The *quality* of the possible change, or its manifestation, was, however, unknowable to Eve. Change is, in and of itself, neither good nor bad. It follows that her act is the occasion of the extension of the present, *beyond* what is given.

For Eve, what was given was to be Adam's garden aid under the auspices of LORD God in an enclosed space where nothing ever happens. Most obviously then, what moved Eve was an appetite for change—*if*...—the tree's fruit offered a possibility to sate that appetite—*then*...

Here, the story of Eve assumes diverse forms. It offers a deconstruction of gardening as a prodigious paradox. A garden, the story reveals to us, is both a sanctuary space and a space of confinement, both an act of creation and destruction. The story of Eve is also a critique of the structures and principles that enclose, appropriate, and impose with a quality of force. It is a cautionary tale against the false promises of Edenic world-within-world building. It offers a word to the wise on the vulnerability of female life in a patriarchal order and the violence that can result from an attempt to move against, through, or around it. To exceed the lines of one's enclosure *could* become a step in the direction of liberation, but that is only a possibility—and it comes without guarantees that it will not lead to (more) violence.

The story of Eve is, therefore, also a tale of courageousness. Finding a way around any system of order is treacherous; it is also the condition of the possibility for change. To move beyond the present, to extend it, is risky business. It requires bravery and spunk, as well as a leap of faith. Eve, the Mover-and-Shaker of Eden, took that leap, a performative movement that questioned the circumferences of her garden existence, *and* intervened in the relations of authority, order, and hierarchy that entangled her. But her leap was also the occasion for her becoming a trailblazer for *all* her daughters, past, present, and future.

May Eve teach us to refuse to garden, in arbitrary and uneven ways, the enclosures we inhabit *and* that keep and dress us. May she be a reminder to her daughters to overgrow, branch out, creep over walls and through fences, and perforate spaces, trodden and untrodden, in all directions, including those we are told we shalt not be. After all, there is only ever a Garden of Eden for as long as there is a gardener who tends to it.

REFERENCES

Benjamin, Walter. 'Critique of Violence'. In *Walter Benjamin: Selected Writings: Volume 4, 1938–1940*. Cambridge, MA: The Belknap Press of Harvard University Press, (1921) 2003.

Campbell, Joseph. *The Hero With a Thousand Faces*. Novato, CA: New World Library, (1949) 2008.

Ewing, Doris. 'The Fall of Eve: Racism and Classism as a Function of Sexual Repression'. *Race, Gender & Class* 7 (1), 2000: 10–21. jstor.org/stable/41675308.

Daston, L., and Katherine Park. *Wonders and the Order of Nature: 1150–1750*. New York: Zone Books, 1998.

Derrida, Jacques. 'Force of Law: The Mystical Foundation of Authority'. In *Deconstruction and the Possibility of Justice*, ed. Drucilla Cornell and Gray Carlson Rosenfeld. New York: Routledge, 1992.

Federici, Silvia. *Caliban and the Witch: Women, the Body and Primitive Accumulation*. New York: Autonomedia, 2004.

Harrison, Robert. *Gardens: An Essay on the Human Condition*. Chicago: The University of Chicago Press, 2008.

Howard, Ebenezer. *Garden Cities of To-Morrow*. Cambridge, MA: Harvard University Press, 1902.

Jung, Carl. 'Man and His Environment'. In *C.G. Jung Speaking*. Princeton, NJ: Princeton University Press, (1950) 2020.

Kierkegaard, S. *The Concept of Anxiety: A Simple Psychologically Oriented Deliberation in View of The Dogmatic Problem of Hereditary Sin*, ed. and trans. Alastair Hannay, New York: Liveright Publishing Company, (1844) 2014.

Lerner, Gerda. *The Creation of Patriarchy*. Oxford: Oxford University Press, 1986.

Merchant, Carolyn. *Reinventing Eden: The Fate of Nature in Western Culture*. New York: Routledge, 2003.

Prest, John. *The Garden of Eden: The Botanic Garden and the Re-creation of Paradise*. London and New Haven: Yale University Press, 1981.

MAKING YOUR OWN EDIBLE ESTATE

What You May Need:

— stakes and string to lay out a design
— a sod-cutter and a rototiller
— newspapers to cover the lawn for mounded plantings or raised beds
— shovels, hand trowels, and rakes
— compost to amend or cover existing soil
— an irrigation system, such as soaker hoses or drip lines
— fencing material to deter animals
— a composting system (prefabricated bins, wood slats, chicken-wire enclosures, etc.)
— mulch material (bark, straw, wood chips, etc.) to cover several inches of the soil
— seeds, starts, or trees of the vegetables, herbs, and fruits selected for your region
— friends and neighbors to help

BASIC STEPS:

1. Do a *soil test* to see what sorts of amendments might be needed or if there are traces of lawn chemicals.
2. Make a *plan* for your Edible Estate, and mark it out with stakes and tape.
3. Use a sod-cutter to *remove the lawn*. Roll it up, give it away, or find a new use for it. If you do not have Bermuda grass or another type of rhizomatic lawn, you may *turn over* the existing turf to keep the topsoil and nitrogen-rich grass in your yard. You also can *cover any lawn* with a series of raised beds or mounded plantings.
4. On existing exposed soil, mix in a generous amount of compost, earthworm castings, manure, mushroom soil, and any combination of soil *amendments* that you may need or have access to.
5. During the first few seasons, experiment with *plants*, trying any edibles that are appropriate for your growing zone and establishing seeds, starts, trees, and vines according to your local planting calendar. You will gradually become aware of what does well on your land and what you like to eat. A diverse garden is a healthy garden.
6. Cover the exposed soil with a thick layer of *mulch*.
7. *Water* the plants thoroughly and install soaker hoses or drip lines as necessary for irrigation.
8. Install *fencing* as needed to deter local animal visitors, such as rabbits and deer, if they become an issue.
9. Set up *compost* bins and a *rainwater* catchment system.

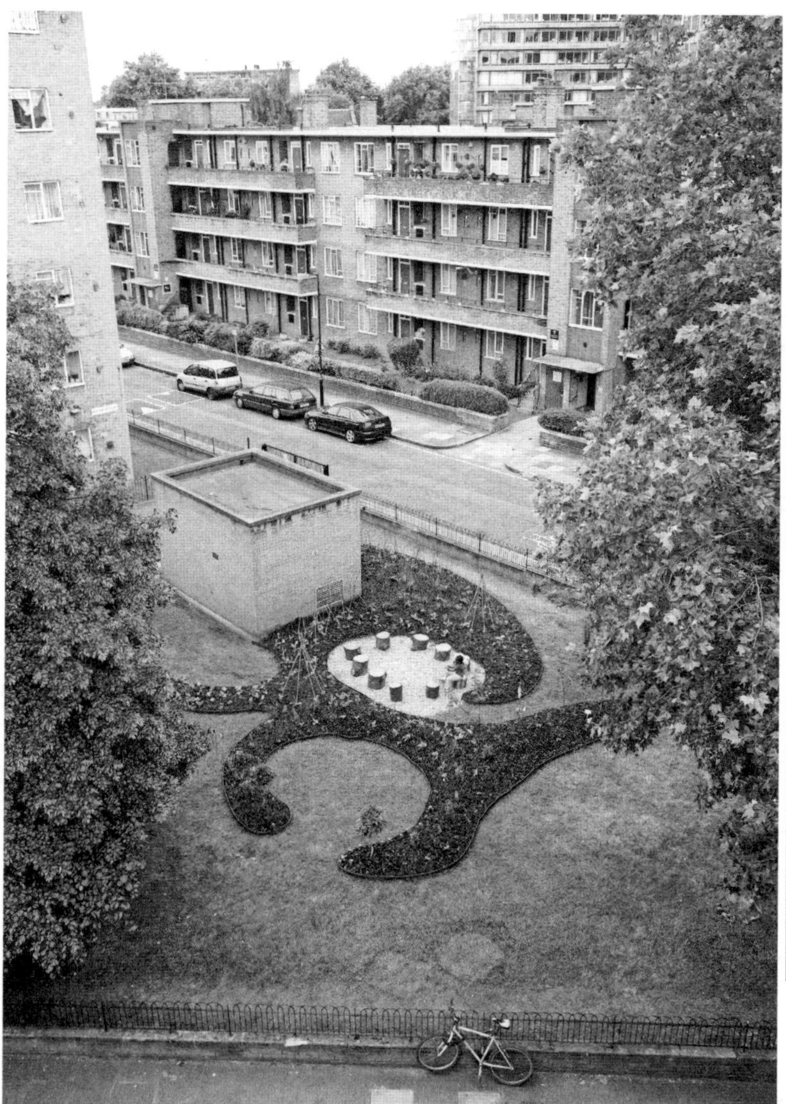

THE PROTOTYPE GARDEN SITES

[...]

Edible Estates' gardens are established on streets where the interruption of the endless lawn is dramatic and controversial. A monotonous housing development of identical homes and front lawns would be ideal! Our dream is to be arrested for planting vegetables in a front lawn in a housing development or town where it is illegal.

Haeg, 'Edible Estates'.

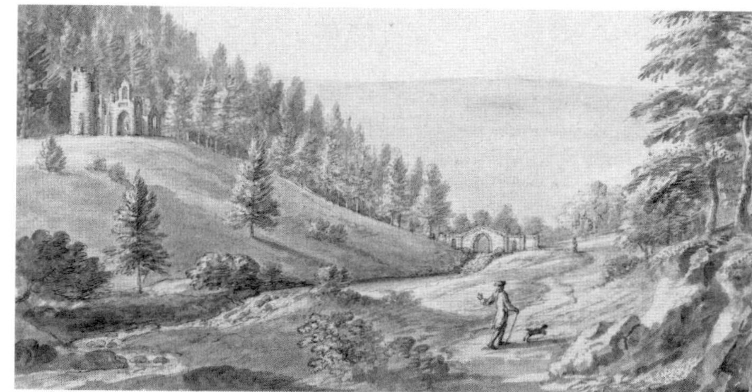

Coplestone Warre Bampfylde, **Crowcombe Court: a Gentleman with his Dog Walking by the River**, 1719–1791, drawing, 29.5 × 46.2 cm. Courtesy Alamy/Artokoloro.

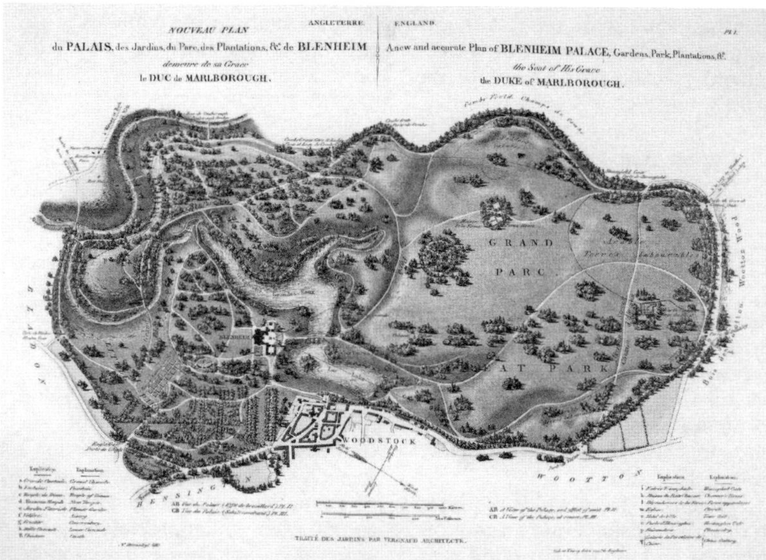

Narcisse Vergnaud, **A new and accurate plan of Blenheim Palace**, 1835, drawing.

ENGLISH GARDEN

The gardens of Kent and Brown were mistakenly referred to the Chinese aesthetic, just as today's thoughtful gardens are considered to be Japanese. 'Japanese garden' has come to signify no more than 'art garden'. The contemporary 'sculpture park' is not—and is not considered to be—an art garden, but an art gallery out-of-doors. It is a parody of the classical garden native to the West.

Finlay, 'More Detached Sentences on Gardening'.

The ideal of the English garden was to approximate nature in a wild state—that is, a 'wildness' perceived through the conceptual apparatus of romantic sensibilities. This results in what amounts to an aesthetic tautology: the desire to transform the countryside into a garden that resembles the countryside.

Weiss, *Mirrors of Infinity*, 15.

The search for an ideal beauty feeds into both landscape painting and gardening and revolves around the concept of the 'picturesque'. And since all representational painting —and most abstract painting— is a kind of fiction, the garden, by employing the 'framed' view from specifically-sited points, also becomes a means of stepping into another world on the opposite side of the 'frame'—in its case, both mentally and physically. [...] The great English garden-parks [...] are passages back into antiquity, their temples, pavilions, grottoes, vales, amphitheatres and antique sculpture acting like props on a film set [...] These picturesque gardens are time machines, capable of whisking us from the present back to an arcadian past.

Brougher and Tarantino, *Enclosed & Enchanted*, 16.

Fritz Haeg, **Edible Estates Regional Prototype Garden**, 2007, installation view. Courtesy Fritz Haeg. Photo: Heiko Prigge.

ENVIRONMENT

Environment is the smoke humanity has laid on Nature: the people who used Latin had no word for Environment—they only knew natura.

Metzger, *Gustav Metzger*, 1.

EPIPHYTE

Other species, growing in wet forest habitats from the tropics to temperate zones, are *epiphytes* (Greek: epi, 'upon'; python, 'plant'), plants that spend their lives clinging to tree branches. In such elevated locations, their leaves receive optimum illumination. Epiphytes' roots are used more as grasping rather than absorbing organs: few ever reach the soil. [...]

Many epiphytes grow from windblown seed or spores from seeds deposited on the tree's bark by animals. The most precarious aspect of the epiphytes' existence is that they must share the fate of their supports. Collapse of the host tree generally results in the death of the plant squatters.

Capon, *Botany for Gardeners*, 126.

ERMENONVILLE

Across the channel, at Girardin's Ermenonville, modern philosophy appears as a temple in the process of construction even as the presence of an 'ancient' dolman points to the pleasures and virtues of a simpler past. [...]

Here the 'primitive' is required in order to demonstrate a sense of progress and modernity, but it also operates as a source of nostalgic pleasure, as a signifier of ancient virtues, and, more cynically, as a means of sidestepping the commercial present of which the garden is inevitably a part.

Bending, *Green Retreats*, 11.

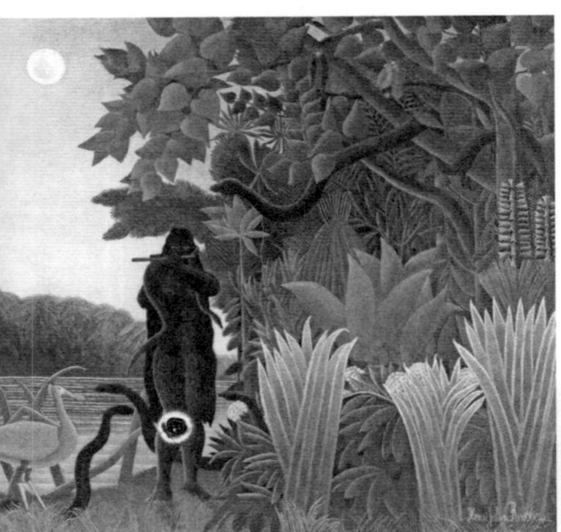

Henri Rousseau, **La Charmeuse de Serpents**, 1907, oil on canvas, 169 × 190 cm. Courtesy RMN-Grand Palais (Musée d'Orsay). Photo: Hervé Lewandowski.

AGAINST GARDENING: MOMENTS IN THE LIFE OF A GARDENER

See p. 43 for 'The Disturbances of the Garden' by Patricia de Vries.

EVE

YAEL BARTANA

Eve is often portrayed as the disobedient woman who instigated the Fall. The artist Yael Bartana puts her own spin on that image: this photograph is reminiscent of a family snapshot, but it also refers to the importance of the creation story in Judaism. In formal terms, Bartana was inspired by the nineteen-thirties propaganda photographs of Jewish pioneers who moved to Palestine/ Eretz Yisrael. By employing the visual language of Zionist propaganda, she hopes to encourage a discussion about the complex situation in her native country. (ed.)

EXOTIC PLANTS

During the sixteenth century, the widespread relationships that Europeans established with the rest of the world reshaped their knowledge of nature. New products and plant and animal species arrived from the Indies. From the Levant came exotic flower seeds and bulbs. The greatly admired beauty of these flowers led to an increasing focus from botanists on the study of exotic and local flora. Much sought after and appreciated by enthusiasts, scholars and aristocrats, flowers earned a special place in the gardens were created at the time, although only the gardens of the most fortunate contained specimens of these highly sought after exotic plants.

Serra and Nobre de Carvalho, *The Emperor's Flowers*, 30.

Yael Bartana, **My sister Eva**, 2004, c-print, 42.2 × 57.2 cm. Collection De Bruijn-Heijn. Courtesy Yael Bartana and Annet Gelink Gallery, Amsterdam.

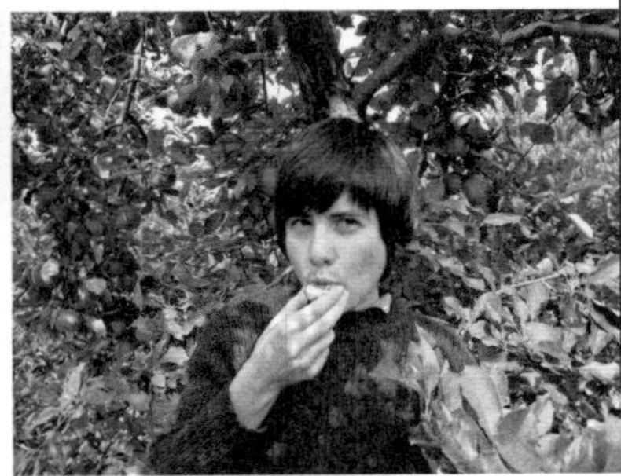

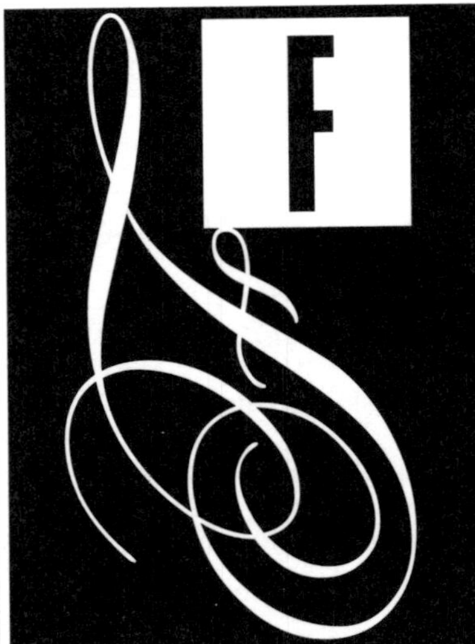

FALL OF MEN

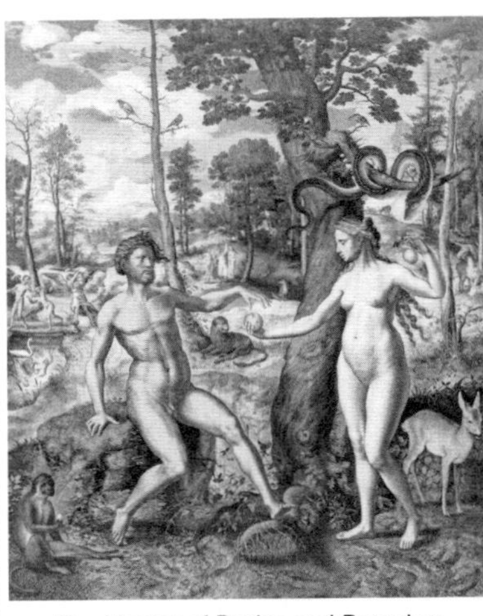

The Master of Paulus and Barnabas, **The Fall**, c. 1550–1560, oil on panel, 200 × 168 cm. Courtesy Bonnefantenmuseum, Maastricht.

THE MASTER OF PAULUS AND BARNABAS

The central motif here is the moment when Eve is tempted by the devil, in the form of a serpent, to eat the forbidden fruit from the tree of knowledge of good and evil. The painter created realistic representations of the animals and the landscape, which serves as a backdrop for the depiction of other events from the creation story. At the centre, God creates Eve from one of Adam's ribs while he sleeps. At the centre, God shows the tree to Adam and Eve and on the far left, following the Fall, the Archangel Michael chases the first human couple from the earthly Paradise. (ed.)

ALBRECHT DÜRER

Albrecht Dürer exploits the moment of the Fall to showcase his knowledge of human anatomy. He modelled Adam after the *Apollo Belvedere*, and his Eve resembles the *Venus de' Medici*. The animals represent the medieval idea of the four temperaments: the cat is choleric, the rabbit sanguine, the ox phlegmatic, and the moose melancholic. In Paradise these four elements are still in perfect balance. But after the Fall, everyone has a single humour and the balance has been lost. Dürer's engraving was typical of the German Renaissance and had a great influence on the depiction of the theme of the Fall. (ed.)

HENDRICK GOLTZIUS

Hendrick Goltzius depicted the Fall at the moment when Eve accepts the apple from the serpent. In the foreground, we see a dog and hedgehog, and in the background a deer and a lion. The free, elegant composition, rotated postures, and relatively small heads are typical of the Mannerism introduced to the Netherlands by Goltzius and other Haarlem-based artists, including Karel van Mander and Cornelis van Haarlem.

The translation of the Latin inscription is: 'Because our ancestors tasted the deadly fruit, the human race has been destroyed by the devil's cunning'. (ed.)

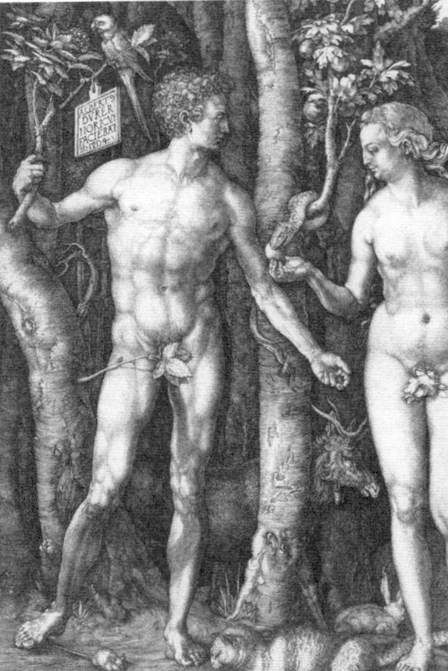

Albrecht Dürer, **Adam and Eve**, 1504, engraving, 25.1 × 19.2 cm. Courtesy Rijksmuseum Amsterdam.

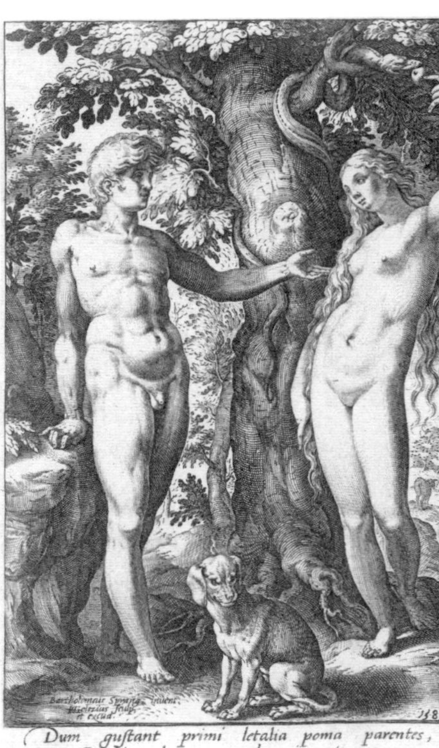

Hendrick Goltzius after Bartholomeus Spranger, **Adam and Eve and the Serpent**, 1585, engraving, 21.4 x 15.7 cm. Courtesy Rijksmuseum Amsterdam.

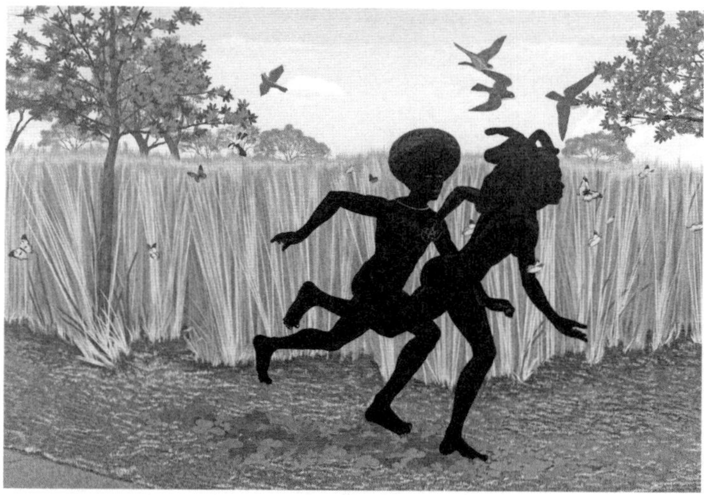

Kerry James Marshall, **Vignette**, 2003, acrylic on fiberglass, 182.9 × 274.3 cm. Courtesy Defares Collection.

KERRY JAMES MARSHALL
The American artist Kerry James Marshall painted two naked black figures running past a densely planted field, surrounded by birds and butterflies. Are they running from danger or towards happiness? The work is part of Marshall's ongoing series entitled *Vignette*, based on Jean-Honoré Fragonard's eighteenth-century series *The Progress of Love*. A vignette is a decorative pictorial element used to mark a new chapter in a book. Marshall uses the decorative element as a strategy to portray everyday black love, a subject largely missing from the canon of Western painting. (ed.)

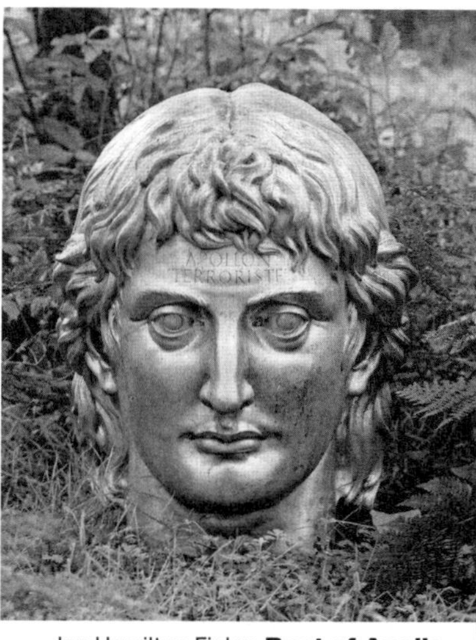

Ian Hamilton Finlay, **Bust of Apollo** at **Little Sparta**.

IAN HAMILTON FINLAY— LITTLE SPARTA

At the age of six, Finlay moved to a boarding school in Glasgow.

With the exception of brief interlude, he lived in Scotland for the rest of his life. As an artist, he was largely self-taught. He later moved and settled just outside Edinburgh, where he spent some time working as a shepherd. In 1966, he started laying out a 'philosophical garden' at Stonypath, about 40 km to the south-west of Edinburgh, which he was later to call 'Little Sparta'. In addition to plants and ponds, the garden contains objects conceived by Finlay, many of which bear a piece of text. All the elements in the garden have a specific, often symbolic significance within the whole. The objects are sometimes prominent, sometimes unobtrusive. They vary from the bird trays mentioned above to a temple to Apollo, from plastic tortoise shells bearing the word 'Pantzer' to the English-language version of the work that lies in front of the Van Abbemuseum, from semi-overgrown object poems to a shiny portrait of Saint-Just. At 'Little Sparta', all of Finlay's themes come together. They may seem contradictory, but Finlay reveals the paradox in both nature and civilised humanity. Nature is not only peaceful and good, it can also be ruthless. And humanity overshoots its idealism when doctrines are enforced with a heavy hand. Terror and virtue are both equally natural. At 'Little Sparta', these paradoxes are expressed in poetic fashion. Finlay saw his garden as a sanctuary, a place for reflection. But at the same time, that reflection makes it an attack on the outside world.

De Groot, 'Ian Hamilton Finlay'.

Do Finlay's many works wherein the pastoral landscape of the garden or arcadia is subverted by the shock appearance of the apparatus of war and destruction belong in the military garden or the peace garden? Are they aestheticized celebrations or provocations? Does Finlay refuse definition and interpretation? Or does he just lose sight of the target? At Stonypath in Lanarkshire from 1966 on, heroically and antagonistically renamed Little Sparta in the 1980s as part of his local petty struggle with Strathclyde Regional Council about the payment for business rates on the property, the landscape features a variety of garden sculptures which are metaphors or statements of military culture and examples of garden design: a stone bird-table is topped with a platform made in the shape of an aircraft carrier (*Aircraft Carrier Bird-Table*, 1972); a smooth black slate edifice next to some water, entitled Nuclear Sail (1974) is a tombstone-like piece which also evokes the nuclear submarine conning tower familiar in some Scottish lochs. His paper works also draw on the rustic sublime. A series of Finlay's prints entitled *The Wartime Garden* (1977) shows simply-drawn monochrome outline images of military equipment, with a short, often single word, accompanying subverting text: the glass frame of a warplane pilot's cockpit is entitled 'Greenhouse': a tank camouflaged (or overgrown) with shrubbery is 'Grove'. The ambivalence is deliberate and consistent: after all, in his life he accepted awards from the Communist Party of France and from Queen Elizabeth II.

McKay, *Radical Gardening*, 76–77.

Every healthy plant is a racist and an imperialist.

Ian Hamilton Finlay in McKay, *Radical Gardening*, 42.

IAN HAMILTON FINLAY
Like Derek Jarman's garden at Prospect Cottage, Little Sparta is both a work of art and a lifelong project. The poet and artist Ian Hamilton Finlay has created an extraordinary garden, near Edinburgh, in Scotland, divided into eight sections, including a Roman Garden, a Wild Garden, English Parkland, and a walled *hortus conclusus*. As a poet, he has carved texts into stones and 'planted' them in the garden as visual poems and commentaries. The combinations of images and texts can be seen as 'word pictures' and 'poem sculptures'. Together, these fragments reflect Finlay's idiosyncratic attitude in which the classical and the modern, the aesthetic and the violent are always entwined. Much of his work refers to historical moments such as the French Revolution (and in particular the violent period known as the Terror) and World War II, demonstrating how idealism and violence go hand in hand. Finlay's interests and his love of language, rhythm, typography, and the garden are evident in these screen prints. (ed.)

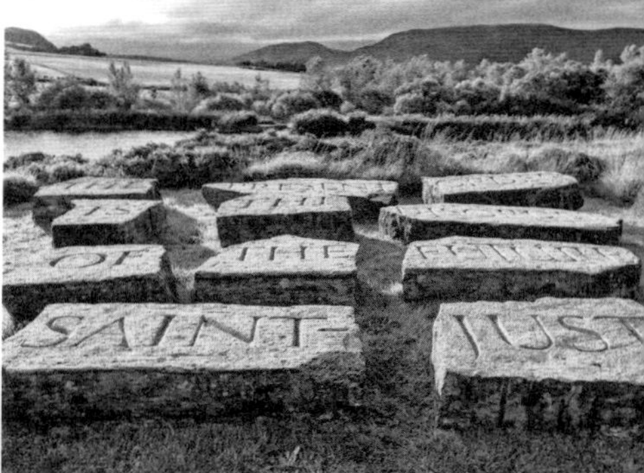

Ian Hamilton Finlay, **Quotation from Saint-Just** at **Little Sparta**.

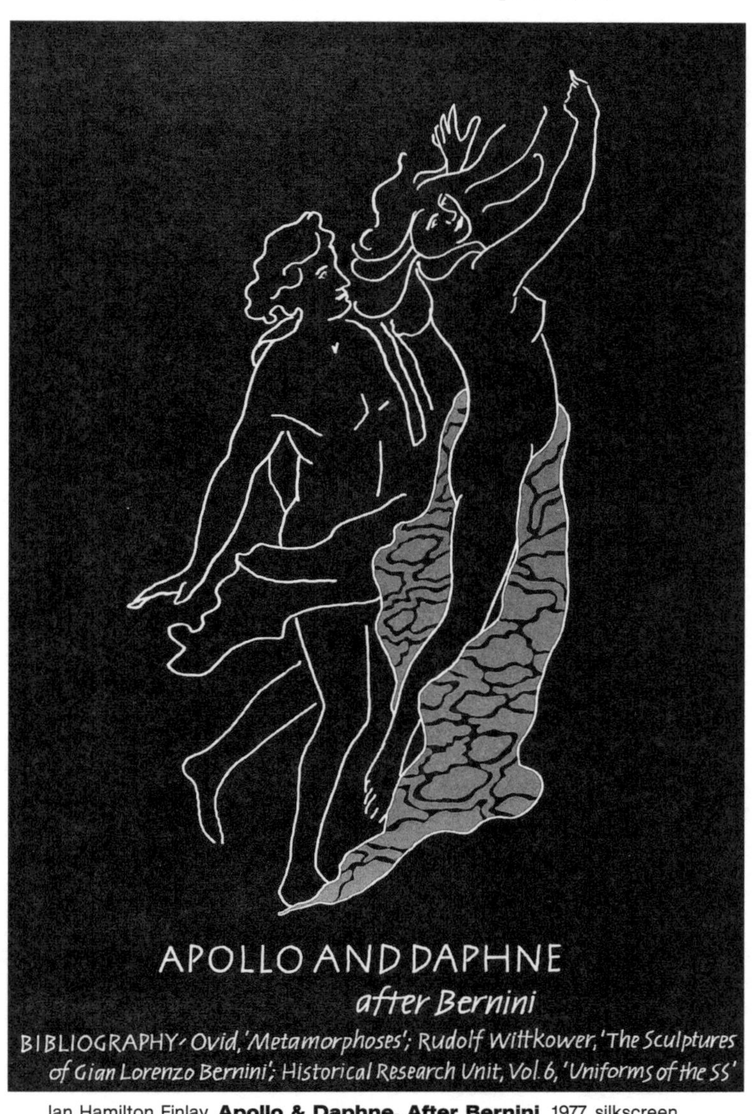

Ian Hamilton Finlay, **Apollo & Daphne, After Bernini**, 1977, silkscreen on paper, 53 × 39.1 cm. Courtesy Van Abbemuseum, Eindhoven.

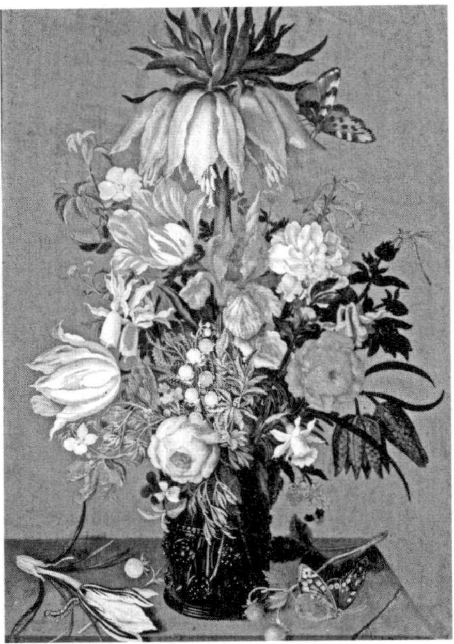

Johannes Bosschaert, **Flower Still Life with Crown Imperial**, 1626, oil on panel, 43 × 29 cm. Courtesy Centraal Museum, Utrecht.

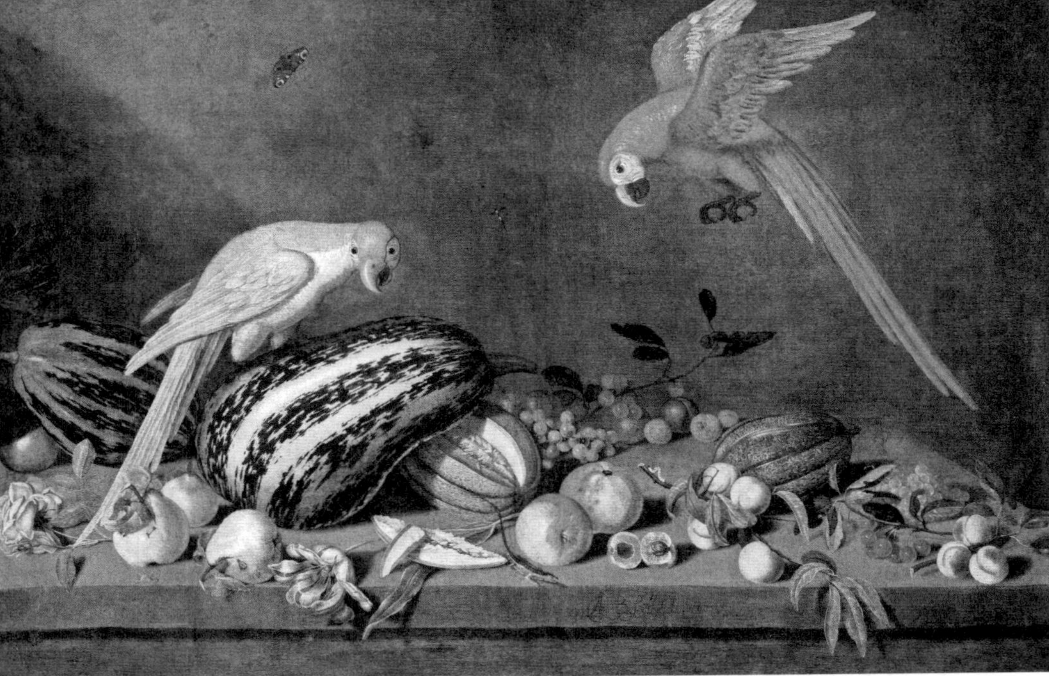

Ambrosius Bosschaert the Younger, **Still Life with Fruit, Flowers and Two Macaws**, 1635, oil on canvas, 109.3 × 163.3 cm. Courtesy Centraal Museum, Utrecht. Photo: Ernst Moritz.

FLOWER STILL LIFE PAINTING

JOHANNES BOSSCHAERT

Johannes Bosschaert was introduced to the profession of painting at a young age by his father, Ambrosius Bosschaert the Elder (1573–1621). In his very short life, he painted various flower and fruit pieces that were praised for their high quality. As with Roelant Saverij's flower arrangement with the crown imperial, this spectacular flower also dominates this bouquet. The crown imperial originated in Persia. The interest in exotic flowers arose in the sixteenth century, and by the seventeenth century, ornamental gardens featured, almost exclusively, exotic plants, mostly from Southern Europe and Asia Minor.

Liesbeth M. Helmus

AMBROSIUS BOSSCHAERT THE YOUNGER

Ambrosius Bosschaert the Elder (1573–1621) had three sons who adopted his specialization of painting still lifes. Ambrosius Bosschaert the Younger was more influenced by his father's work than his two brothers', and this is especially evident in his early paintings. This still life is a good example of his later, graceful work, in which he often depicted flowers with curly petals, such as tulips and snake's head fritillary. The fly, here on the table, is a common feature of his paintings.

Liesbeth M. Helmus

FOLLY

We expect the cult for garden follies, or what the French call *fabriques*, to be most conspicuous during the Picturesque movement from the late eighteenth century into the nineteenth century, when that fashion spread from more elite designs to a myriad of smaller estates, suburban villas and public parks.

Hunt, *A World of Gardens*, 221.

[Monsieur de] Monville [the owner, red.] arguably organized his retreat after 1774 to invoke a cluster of historical and cultural references: twenty items were devised and inserted, including a Chinese Pavilion built of teak, a pyramid, a Temple of Pan, a Gothic church (a genuine ruin), a Turkish tent and the Broken Column. The truncated enormity of this last feature suggested [...] that the parkland was long ago inhabited by a race of stupendous beings [...] [The Désert de Retz] recalls cultures which haunt our consciousness, yet remains emphatically modern in its determination to characterize this particular place and time by a celebration of one man's wish to transcend them all.

Hunt, *A World of Gardens*, 225–226.

FORMAL GARDEN

Formal gardens are (as it were) statues of Nature.

Finlay, 'More Detached Sentences on Gardening.' See also Abrioux, *Ian Hamilton Finlay*, 40.

FRENCH LANDSCAPE GARDEN

Curious idea, a garden constructed according to mathematical formulas, where metaphysics is dissimulated by perspective, epistemology circumscribed by geometry, and rhetoric composed by the mobility of our bodies. The French formal garden is a study in depth and an incitement to motion, originating in a hubris supported by geometric proofs and ending in a scenario of absolute power and desire.

Weiss, *Mirrors of Infinity*, 33.

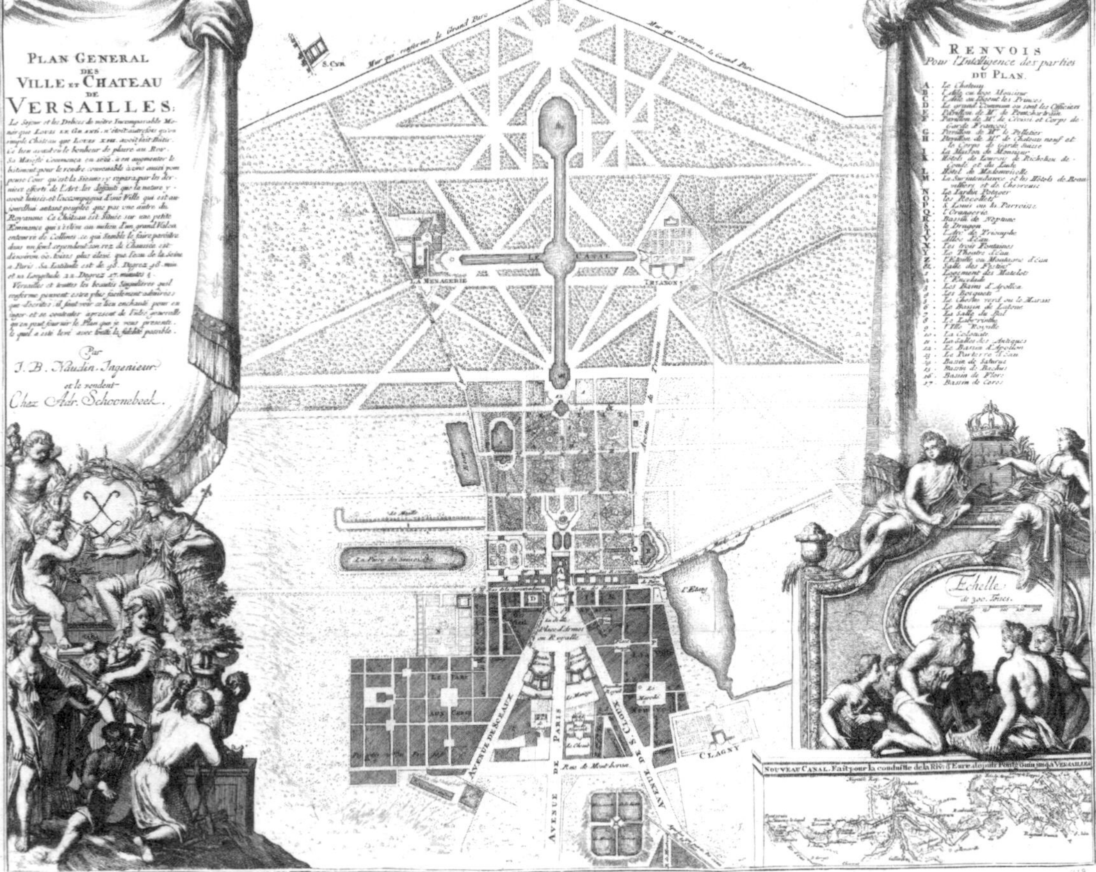

Adriaan Schoonebeek, **Plan General des Ville et Chateau de Versailles**, c. 1702, etching, 38.5 × 48 cm. Courtesy Rijksmuseum Amsterdam.

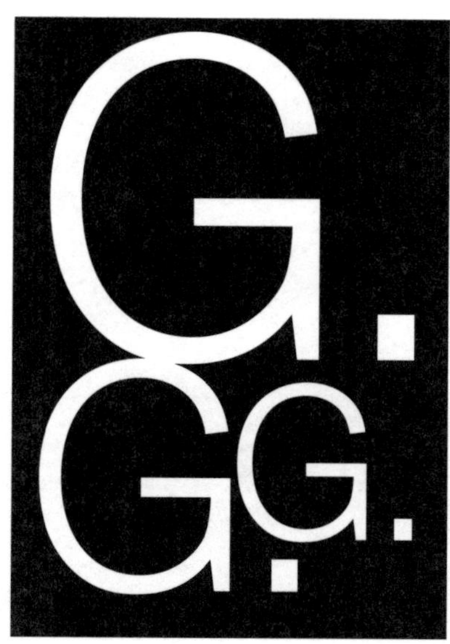

GAIA

Gaia theory forces a planetary perspective. It is the health of the planet that matters, not that of some individual species of organisms.

Lovelock, *The Ages of Gaia*, xvii.

We have since defined Gaia as a complex entity involving the Earth's biosphere, atmosphere, oceans, and soil; the totality constituting a feedback or cybernetic system which seeks an optimal physical and chemical environment for life on this planet. The maintenance of relatively constant conditions by active control may be conveniently described by the term 'homoeostasis'.

Lovelock, *Gaia: A New Look at Life on Earth*, 10.

Lovelock draws far-reaching political conclusions about human relationships with Gaia. He goes as far as to suggest that the living planet is now ready to strike back against those who caused her suffering. According to this view, humans are facing an implacable 'Earthly enemy', and governments must be ready to undertake massive technological interventions, and even suppress part of the freedom of their citizens in the name of ecological security. To be sure, Gaia is a concept loaded with problematic connotations. It is connected both to the image of the earth as purposeful organism, and to deep ecologist inclinations to overlook the 'inequalities within human society' in the name of a dehistoricized nature.

Tola, 'Composing with Gaia', 3.

Lovelock perhaps went a step too far in affirming that this processual coupling ensured a stability of the type that one attributes to a living organism in good health, the repercussions between processes thus having as their effect the diminishing of the consequences of a variation. Gaia thus seemed to be a good, nurturing mother, whose health was to be protected. [...]

We are no longer dealing (only) with a wild and threatening nature, nor with a fragile nature to be protected, nor a nature to be mercilessly exploited. The case is new. Gaia, she who intrudes, asks nothing of us, not even a response to the question she imposes.

Stengers, *In Catastrophic Times*, 45–46.

[...] to speak of the 'revenge' of Gaia, as James Lovelock does today, is to mobilize a type of psychology that doesn't seem relevant: one takes revenge against someone, whereas the question of offense is one of a matter of post-factum observation. For example, one says 'it seems that this gesture offended her, I wonder why?' Correlatively one doesn't struggle against Gaia. Even speaking of combating global warming is inappropriate. If it is a matter of struggling, it is against what provoked Gaia, not against her response.

Stengers, *In Catastrophic Times*, 46 (footnote 2).

GARDEN CITY

The aim of Ebenezer Howard in his highly influential book *Garden Cities of Tomorrow* (a revision of his 1898 *Tomorrow: A Peaceful Path to Real Reform*), and of the increasing numbers of people active in the movement, was to combine idealism and landscape in order to produce what he called 'a new life, a new civilization'.

McKay, *Radical Gardening*, 26.

In the garden city, town and country were interwoven in low-density development between expansive collective and private green space. This ended at a stroke the dialectic between city and landscape, between inside and outside. The term 'garden city' can be construed in two ways: the city as garden, or a city full of gardens. As an ensemble, the garden city is an autonomous unit, bounded by a 'green belt'. Inside it, the paradise of old is fractured into twenty to thirty hedge-bound private paradises per hectare. With such repetition, the exclusive status of the garden is seriously debilitated.

Aben and De Wit, *The Enclosed Garden*, 142.

Utopian garden city settlements were proposed throughout the nineteenth century as a way of utilizing technology to create a more ideal community structure- a bucolic, socialistic antidote to the capitalist city. Instead of individual houses, extended families would share work and childrearing responsibilities to create an economically and socially efficient 'machine for living'. These communities were to be located outside a city in self-sufficient settings. The efforts of nineteenth-century reformers influenced the later commercial development of suburban garden towns around 1900.

After World War I, suburban settlements were established at the edges of many cities, in a manner similar to the first picturesque park cemeteries. Like those early cemeteries, suburbia's 'garden', with its well-manicured shrubs and green lawns, evoked a nostalgic sense of perpetual peace. Accommodating working-class families in their own suburban homes helped to defuse the revolutionary potential of the inner-city working class. The growth of a stable lower-middle class and smaller nuclear families helped to create a new consumer society, based on ownership of a suburban home.

Graham et al., *Rock my Religion*, 293.

In 1928, Utrecht built the Tuinwijk neighbourhood against the city's northern border. [...] The developer N.V. Stadswoning, under the directorship of W.J. Godijn, wanted to build on the Haverland. It purchased seventeen hectares of land for 350,000 guilders and started building houses for wealthy citizens in the new 'Tuindorp' neighbourhood. [...] The new development was promoted as follows: 'Fresh air, lots of sun, lots of greenery and flowers in a rural setting'. On 1 June 1931, the Thijssen-Kreugel family took up residence in the first of the seven houses on Sickenslaan. In 1932 the houses still under construction were upgraded with central heating, a bathroom and washbasins with running water.

Canon van Nederland, '1930 Tuindorp'. Translation from Dutch by Gerard Forde.

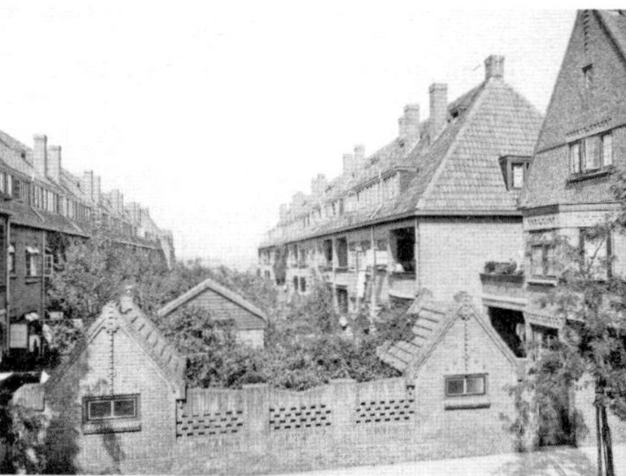

Anonymous, **Tuinwijk Spoorwoningen Tuintjes**, c. 1925, photograph. Courtesy Spoorwegmuseum Utrecht.

GARDEN GNOME

The gnome is perhaps the most despised garden ornament in landscape history. With his pickaxe, lantern, wheelbarrow, and little deer for companions, he has long been an object of scorn, an emblem of bad taste, and an affront to the designers of beautiful flower borders. Banished from polite society, he mostly dwells in European allotment blue-collar yards, where he leads a most happy life. At best, he is admired with an ironic eye as a piece of kitsch. [...]

His origins can be traced to myths and sagas from densely wooded and mountainous areas of Eastern, middle, Western, and northern Europe. It was only in the sunny lands of southern Europe that the gnome did not take up residence in the popular imagination. Like Snow White's dwarfs, the gnomes of myth and saga are traditionally itinerant mountain people, trekking from place to place to do seasonal work in mines.

These miners' sudden comings and goings and frequent disappearances into the bowels of the earth fostered the impression, which was adopted by later storytellers, that gnomes were diminutive folk. [...]

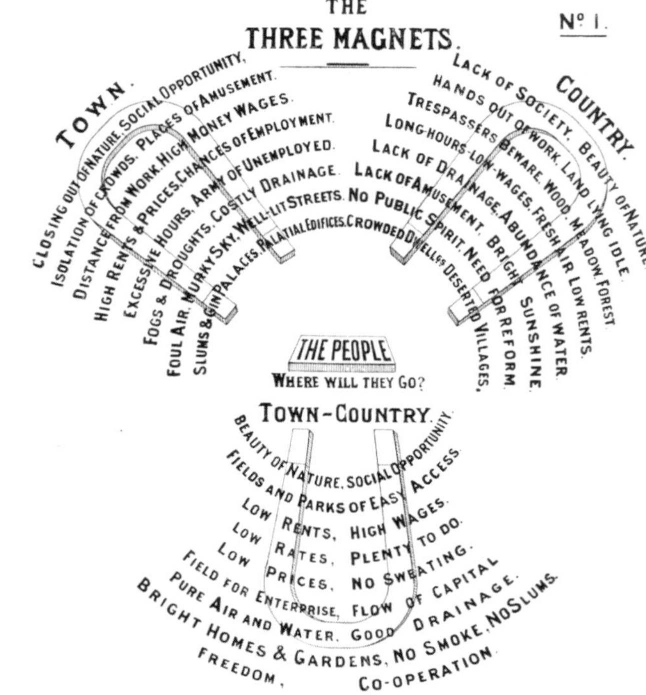

Ebenezer Howard, **The Three Magnets from Garden Cities of Tomorrow**, 1903, book page. Courtesy Duke University Libraries, Durham.

From such tales, the garden gnome derives his principal attribute, the pickaxe. He thus became famous for being a creature who lives close to the earth, a participant in the earth's magical powers. Believed to be an advocate of nature, he is seen as a caretaker of all living things and earns his rightful place in the garden by assisting flowers, plants, and trees to grow. It is no exaggeration to say that the garden gnome, influenced by nineteenth-century romantic nationalism, has come to symbolize nature. [...]

Understandably, therefore, the garden gnome does not consort with Flora, Ceres, and Pomona. These are the classical goddesses of agriculture and horticulture that one finds represented in aristocratic gardens of the seventeenth and eighteenth centuries. Instead, the garden gnome, being a true 'genius of the place', embodies something more elemental: the very forces of nature. As such, he represents democracy, freedom, brotherhood, and equality, symbolized by his red Phrygian cap, derived from the headgear of French Revolutionaries at the end of the eighteenth century.

De Jong, 'Gnomenculture', 1–4.

GARDENING

Gardening activity is of five kinds, namely, sowing, planting, fixing, placing, maintaining. In so far as gardening is an Art, all these may be taken under the one head, composing.

Finlay, 'More Detached Sentences on Gardening'. See also Abrioux, *Ian Hamilton Finlay*, 40.

GENIUS LOCI

Consult the Genius of the Place in all:
That tells the Waters or to rise, or fall,
Or helps th'ambitious Hill the heav'n to scale,
Or scoops in circling theaters the Vale,
Calls in the Country, catches opening glades,
Joins willing woods, and varies shades from shades.

Pope, 'Epistle IV to Richard Boyle, Earle of Burlington'. See also Aben and De Wit, *The Enclosed Garden*, 97.

Places where the spirit breathes [...] that pull the soul from its lethargy, places wrapped and bathed in mystery, elected for ever to be the site of religious emotion.

Hunt, *A World of Gardens*, 19.

HENK GERRITSEN

Henk Gerritsen was an artist, garden designer, and ecological activist who had moved out to the relatively remote eastern region of the Netherlands, with his partner, Anton Schlepers, a photographer. In 1978 they laid out a garden, known as the Priona Gardens, very experimental in character, largely inspired by the wild plant communities they had enjoyed on their travels in Central Europe. Together the two men wrote a book, *Spelen met de natuur (Playing with Nature)*, about their experiences travelling to look at wildflowers and their attempts at bringing their discoveries into the garden. Henk's discovery of Piet [Oudolf]'s nursery plant list led to many more discoveries: 'because I attempt to keep the gardens as natural and wild as possible, these plants have fitted in perfectly'. The Henk-Piet relationship was very much a mutual one, as it was Henk who introduced Piet to the idea of seed heads and the autumn appearance of perennials. 'With Henk', Piet says, 'I learnt that planting is to do more with plants: ambience, seasonality, emotion, these are important; with Henk we discovered plants that were good out of flowering, he pointed this out to me a hundred times, we looked at plants at times other than their prime time.' [...]

Anton died in 1993 and Henk cared for Priona until his death in 2008, keeping it open to the public as a provocatively unconventional garden; 'not everyone gets it', I remember Henk complaining to me several times. After a gap of some years, the Priona Gardens are now publicly accessible again, [...] so it is still possible to experience Henk's creative and gently eccentric approach to gardening. There is a clear love of the wild and naturalistic but also enough hedging and framing to remind the visitor that this is after all a Dutch garden. Henk's 'abstract expressionist' approach to yew clipping makes us question our fundamental lack of creativity with this subject matter, while box hens and chickens on the main lawn add a humorous touch – a dry wit underlay Henk's approach to life, especially his writing about perennials.

Oudolf and Gerritsen, *Planting the Natural Garden*, 9.

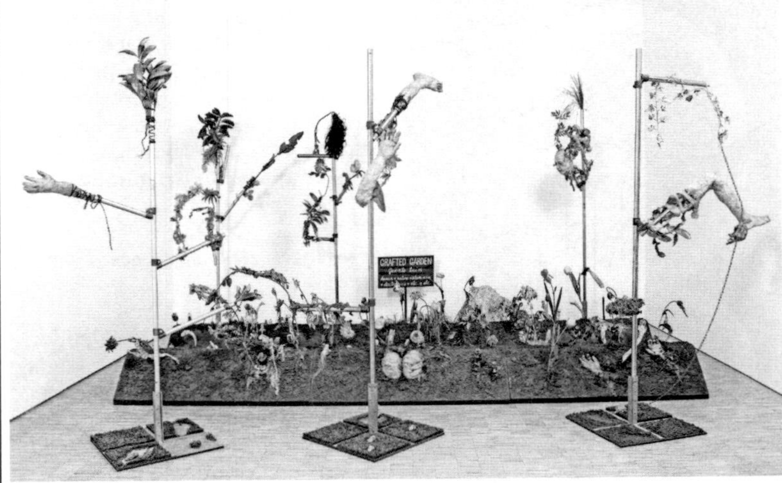

Tetsumi Kudo, **Grafted Garden/Pollution-cultivation-nouvelle écologie**, 1970–1971, installation view. Courtesy Centre Pompidou, MNAM-CCI, Dist. RMN-Grand Palais. Photo: Philippe Migeat.

GRAFTED GARDEN

TETSUMI KUDO

Grafted Garden comprises a small flower bed, planted with plastic roses, tulips, and chrysanthemums, and is inhabited by fake snails. Around the flower bed are six 'trees' made from aluminium poles and wire. Although much of his imagery and references were gruesome, Tetsumi Kudo employed plastic waste and discarded objects in the hope of bringing about an ecological metamorphosis. This hope is expressed by the reference to the technique of 'grafting', in which one plant can be attached to the rootstock of another in order to make it more resistant to certain diseases or natural conditions. Here, Kudo grafts plastic flowers and human body parts to the aluminium tree trunks. (ed.)

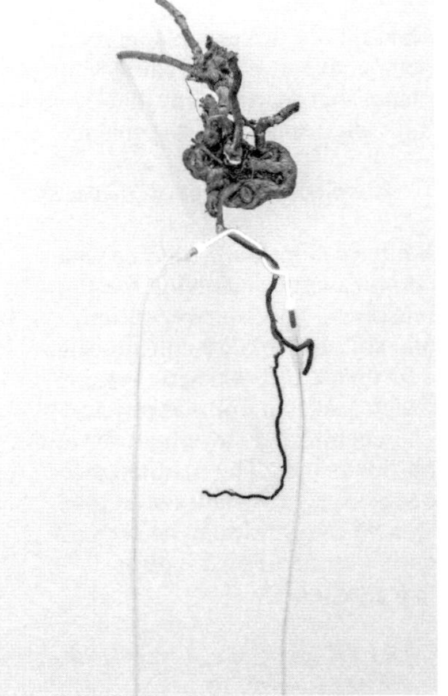

Saskia Noor van Imhoff, **switch for heated handles** (555FXT), 2020, installation view. Courtesy Saskia Noor van Imhoff and Grimm Gallery, Amsterdam & New York.

GRAFTING

Grafting involves the permanent union of a branch (called a *scion*, from an early English word meaning 'offshoot') taken from one plant, with another plant (a *stock*, Old English for 'stump') that bears roots. In some cases, rose grafting being a typical example, the scion may be no more than an axillary bud attached to a sliver of bark and some wood cells. Alignment of the vascular tissues of stock and scion permits free exchange of nutrients, food and water during the period when the tissues of the two parts fuse together. Grafts can only be made between closely related species of plants, with incompatible organs being rejected.

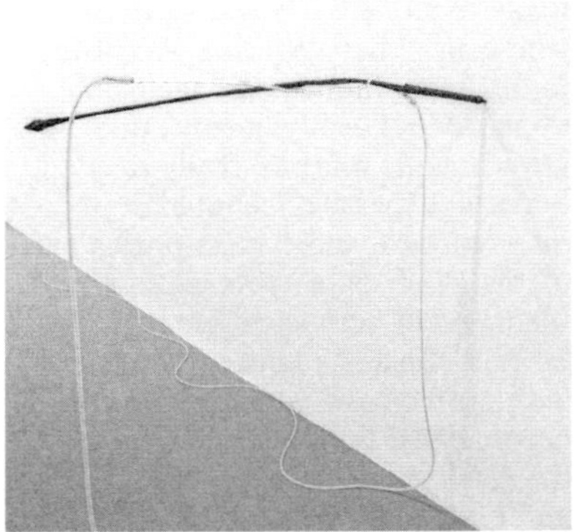

Saskia Noor van Imhoff, **flat when moist, curling inward when dry (ball-like)**, 2020, installation view. Courtesy Saskia Noor van Imhoff and Grimm Gallery, Amsterdam & New York.

Capon, *Botany for Gardeners*, 69–70.

SASKIA NOOR VAN IMHOFF

For these works, Saskia Noor van Imhoff analyzed a piece of neglected wasteland, where materials—both natural and man-made—had accumulated over a number of years. Van Imhoff is fascinated by this 'organic collection' of traces of human and non-human activities. The objects carry information about the interaction with the ground and the past. What is considered valuable or worthless at any given time? When does something become waste? And who owns it? For van Imhoff, the technique of grafting is an important metaphor for the progress of culture. Here she grafts neon tubes onto found pieces of iron and excavated brambles, creating a new hybrid form. (ed.)

GREENHOUSE

We went out of the French doors and along a smooth red-flagged path… The path took us along to the side of the greenhouse and the butler opened a door for me and stood aside. It opened into a sort of vestibule that was about as warm as a slow oven. He came in after me, shut the outer door, opened an inner door and we went through that. Then it was really hot. The air was thick, wet, steamy and larded with the cloying smell of tropical orchids in bloom. The glass walls and roof were heavily misted and big drops of moisture splashed down on the plants. The light had an unreal greenish colour, like light filtered through an aquarium tank. The plants filled the place, a forest of them, with nasty meaty leaves and stalks like the newly washed fingers of dead men. They smelled as overpowering as boiling alcohol under a blanket.

Chandler, *The Big Sleep*, chapter 2.

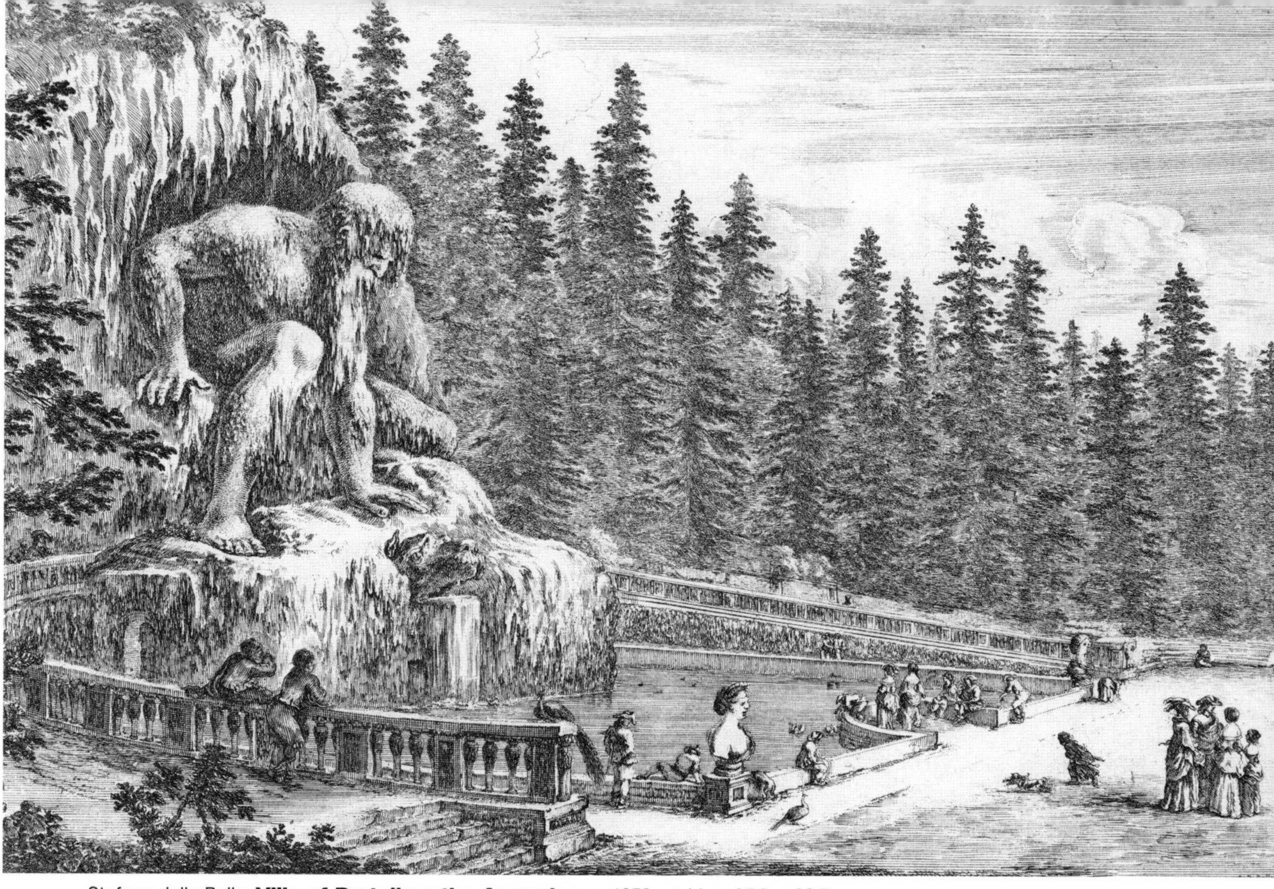

Stefano della Bella, **Villa of Pratolino: the Appenino**, c. 1653, etching, 25.2 × 38.5 cm. Courtesy The Metropolitan Museum of Art, New York and Art Resource/Scala, Florence.

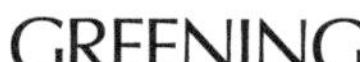

GREENING

O most honored Greening Force,

You who roots in the Sun;
You who lights up, in shining
serenity, within a wheel
that earthly excellence fails to
comprehend.

You are enfolded
in the weaving of divine
mysteries.

You redden like the dawn
and you burn: flame of the Sun.

Von Bingen, *Causae et Curae.* Cited in Healthy Hildegard, 'What is Hildegard's Viriditas?'

GROTTO

Michel de Montaigne, on tour in Italy, visited the palace and gardens of the Grand Duke Francesco I de Medici at Pratolino. [...] But he found much to admire in the gardens and devoted lengthy passages of his travel journal to describing his impressions of the garden's features, including the grotto about which he wrote,

> There is one miraculous thing, a grotto with several cells and rooms; this part surpasses all that we have ever seen elsewhere. It is encrusted and formed all over of a certain material which they say is brought from certain mountains, and they have joined it invisibility with nails. There is not only music and harmony made by the movement of the water, but also a movement of several statues and doors with various actions, caused by the water; several animals that plunge in to drink; and things like that. At one single movement the whole groot is full of water, and all the sets squirt water on your buttocks; and if you flee from the grotto and climb the castle stairs and anyone takes pleasure in this sport, there come out of every other step of the stairs, right up to the top of the house, a thousand jets that give you a bath.

Hyde, *A Cultural History of Gardens*, 97.

GUERRILLA GARDENING

The gardener's generous gesture of free planting has a long history, in which it is often possible to identify a radical critique of private property interwoven with a statement of communal interest, mutual aid and cooperation. This is less to do with a demarcated territory of the (private, domestic) garden than with the social and communal practice of gardening.

McKay, *Radical Gardening*, 155.

1. SPOT SOME LOCAL ORPHANED LAND – You will be amazed how many little grubby patches of unloved public space there are. Neglected flower beds, concrete planters sprouting litter and untamed plants, bare plots of mud. Choose one close to home, perhaps you pass it on the way to the shops or work, and appoint yourself its parent. This will make it much easier to look after in the long term and reduce the risk of straying into a dangerous neighbourhood. [...]

2. PLAN A MISSION – Make a date in the diary for an evening attack, when trouble-making busy bodies are out of sight. Invite supportive friends, or perhaps enrole supportive strangers by announcing your attack in the Guerrilla Gardening Community here. [...]

3. FIND A LOCAL SUPPLY OF PLANTS – The cheaper the better. For city dwellers think local DIY stores, supermarkets and wholesalers. The cheapest plants are ones that are free. Sometimes garden centres will have spare plants to give you for the cause. Or befriend someone with a garden (you might even be lucky and have a garden yourself). Think of these private spaces as the training camps for harvesting seeds, cuttings and plants hardened for their big adventure in the wilds of public space. [...]

4. CHOOSE PLANTS FOR FRONT LINE BATTLE – Think hardy—resistant to water shortages and the cold, and in some locations pedestrian trampling! These plants need to look after themselves a lot of the time. Think impactful - colour, evergreen foliage, scale. These plants need to really make a difference, for as much of the year as possible. Visit the Community to get advice about specific plants for your part of the world, and to share your horticultural advice with the less experienced. [...]

5. GET SOME WELLINGTON SHOES – Whilst protecting your feet from mud and providing good purchase on a fork, these rubber shoes also don't look too obviously 'agricultural' as the usual boot, and blend in well with the urban environment. [...]

6. BAG SOME BAGS – Plastic bags, bin liners (not only can they keep your feet clean), but they are essential for clearing up the deteritous of war. Weeds, litter, flower pots, and pebbles need to be carried away. [...]

7. REGULAR WATERING – One of the responsibilities of a Guerrilla Gardener is ongoing tendering. Water is short in many parts of the world, even drissly old London. The Guerrilla Gardener must usually carry water. [...] I have used petrol canisters, they are the perfect water-tight, efficiently-packed portable transportation. [...]

8. SEED BOMBS – For gardening those areas where access is difficult or a long dig is unsuitable, use a seed bombs (sometimes called green grenades) which are seeds and soil held in an explosive or degradable capsule. There are many different methods, some you can easily make at home, some that require a bit more ingenuity. [...]

9. CHEMICAL WARFARE – Boost your plants with natural chemicals. Some guerrillas are lucky to have space for compost heaps. Alex (1797) lives in a flat with no garden so has employed an efficient army of red worms to help him make his chemical weapons. In a box in the kitchen his Eisenia Fetida transform food into a rich vermicompost and worm juice fertiliser.

Reynolds, 'Guerrilla Gardening Tips'.

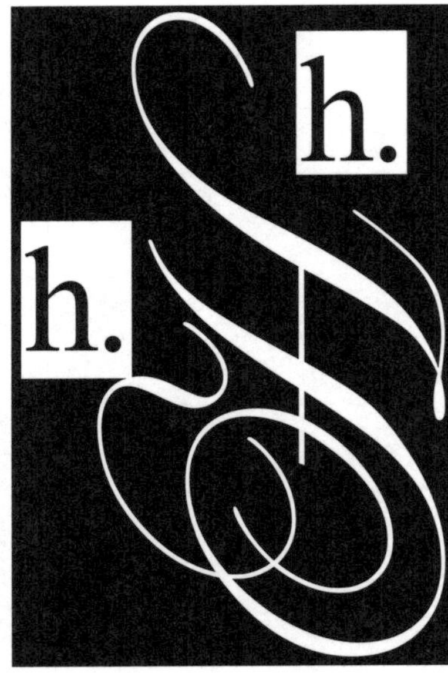

HA-HA

See page 89 for 'Ha-Ha' by Maria Barnas.

HAHA

A ha-ha is a type of sunken fence that was commonly used in landscaped gardens and parks in the eighteenth century. It involved digging a deep, dry ditch, the inner side of which would be built up to the level of the surrounding turf with either a dry-stone or brick wall. Meanwhile, the outer side was designed to slope steeply upwards, before leveling out again into turf. The point of the ha-ha was to give the viewer of the garden the illusion of an unbroken, continuous rolling lawn, whilst providing boundaries for grazing livestock.

Originally a feature of formal French gardens of the early eighteenth century, the ha-ha was first described in print in 1709 by the gardening enthusiast, Dezallier d'Argenville in his *La Theorie et la Practique du jardinage* (The Theory and Practice of Gardening). According to d'Argenville—and his first English translator, John James—the ha-ha derived its name from the success of the optical illusion it created from a distance on viewers of the garden: the hitherto concealed ditch and wall would '*surprise the eye coming near it, and make one cry, "Ah! Ah!"*'

Porter, 'What is a Ha-Ha?'

So many garden terms come from the arts of warfare—cordon, earthing up, trench, bastion, the batter of a hedge, palisade, zig-zag, covered way, enceinte. The delight of a garden swing was adapted from a military means of getting a man into an otherwise unattainable position: the ha-ha… has a military pedigree.

McKay, *Radical Gardening*, 72.

HANGING GARDENS OF BABYLON

Over these visits [to the gardens at Samarkand, red.] and the awe with which these gardens were viewed, hung memories of the famed Hanging Gardens of Babylon. As early as the late third century BC it was described as a palace with lofty stone terraces, that closely represented 'mountain scenery', and two hundred years later it was still imagined to have been invented by a king 'to imitate, through the artifice of a planted garden, the distinctive landscape of Persia'. The hold of these hanging gardens on both architecture and landscape imagination has been enormous, and graphic recreations of them sought to capture their exotic and inspiring engineering, and to envisage exactly how it was reared; even terracing, adorned with flowers and trees, held out the hope that the mystical placed had been re-animated.

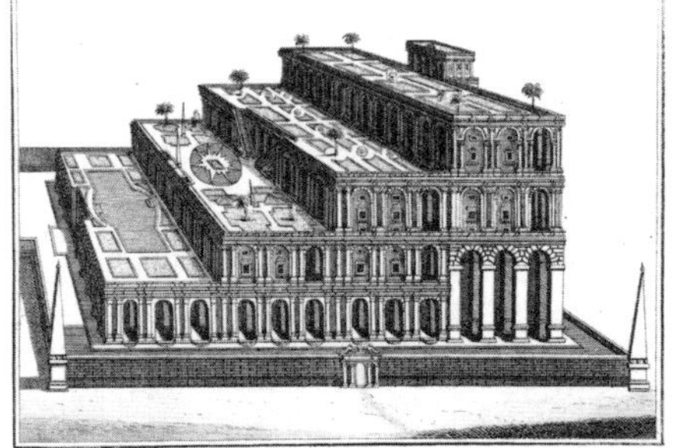

Robert von Spalart, **The Hanging Gardens of Babylon**, c. 1804–1811, coloured engraving. Courtesy Wellcome Collection, London.

Hunt, *A World of Gardens*, 70, citing from Price, *The Seven Wonders of the Ancient World*, 42–46.

HESPERIDES

Hesperides (Ἑσπερίδες) The Nymphs of the Setting Sun. [...] Most often there were said to be three Hesperides: Aegle ('Brightness'), Erythia ('Scarlet') and Hesperarethusa ('Sunset Glow') [...] The Hesperides lived in the extreme west near the edge of the Ocean at the foot of Mount Atlas. Their main function, with the help of a dragon [...] was to guard the garden where the golden apples grew, a gift given to Hera when she married Zeus. [...] The Hesperides were linked with the story of Heracles, who went to their dwelling place to find the golden apples [...]. The Hesperides were turned into trees, elm, poplar and willow, because of their despair at the loss of the apples.

Grimal and Kershaw, *A Concise Dictionary of Classical Mythology*, 200–201.

HETEROTOPIA

There are also, probably in every culture, in every civilization, real places—places that do exist and that are formed in the very founding of society—which are something like counter-sites, a kind of effectively enacted utopia in which the real sites, all the other real sites that can be found within the culture, are simultaneously represented, contested and inverted. Places of this kind are outside of all places, even though it may be possible to indicate their location in reality. Because these places are absolutely different from all the sites that they reflect and speak about, I shall call them, by way of contrast to utopias, heterotopias.

Foucault, 'Of Other Spaces', 3–4.

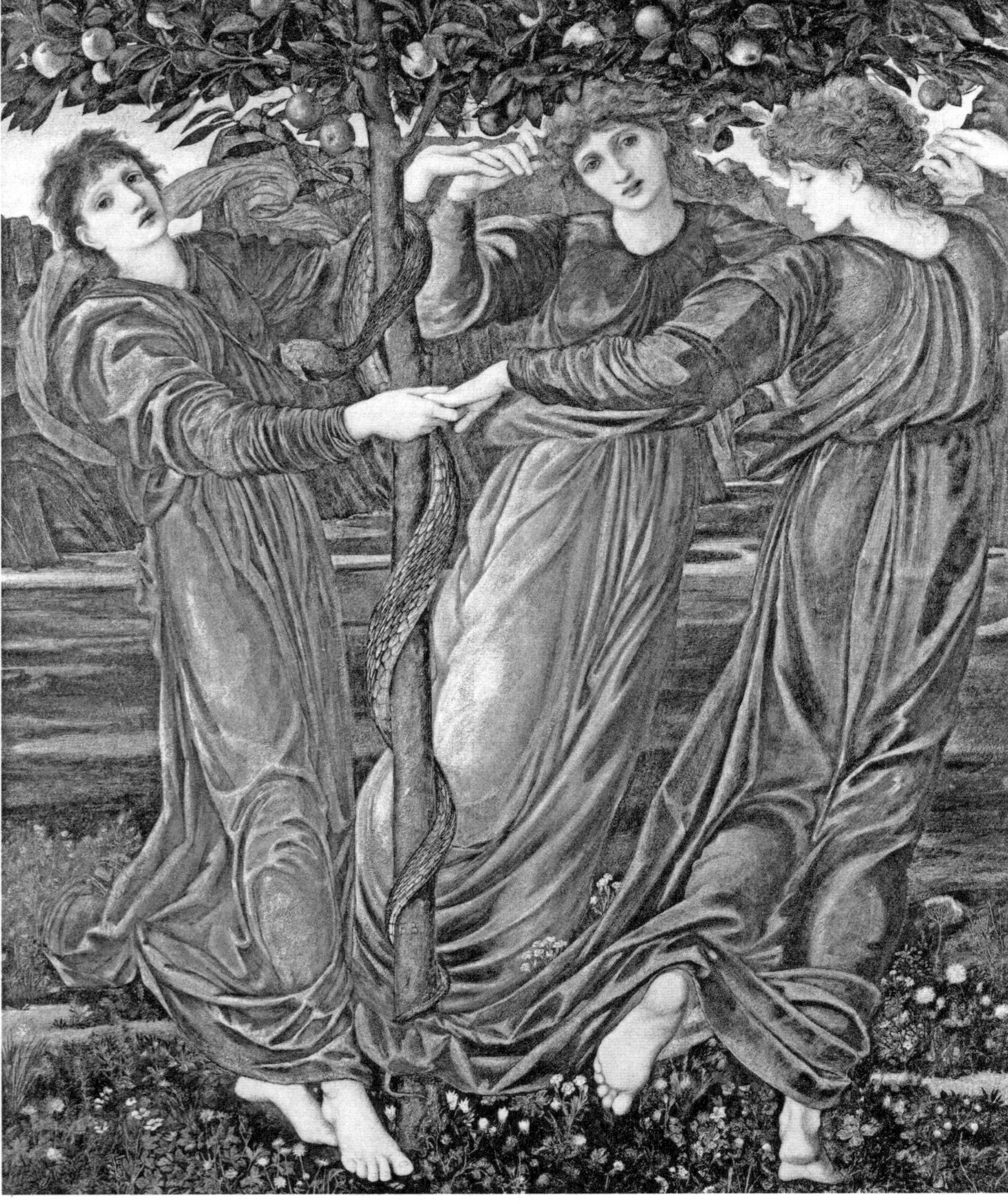

Edward Burne-Jones, **The Garden of the Hesperides**, c. 1869, oil on canvas, 119 × 98 cm. Courtesy bpk-Bildagentur/Hamburger Kunsthalle. Photo: Elke Walford.

H continues on page 89.

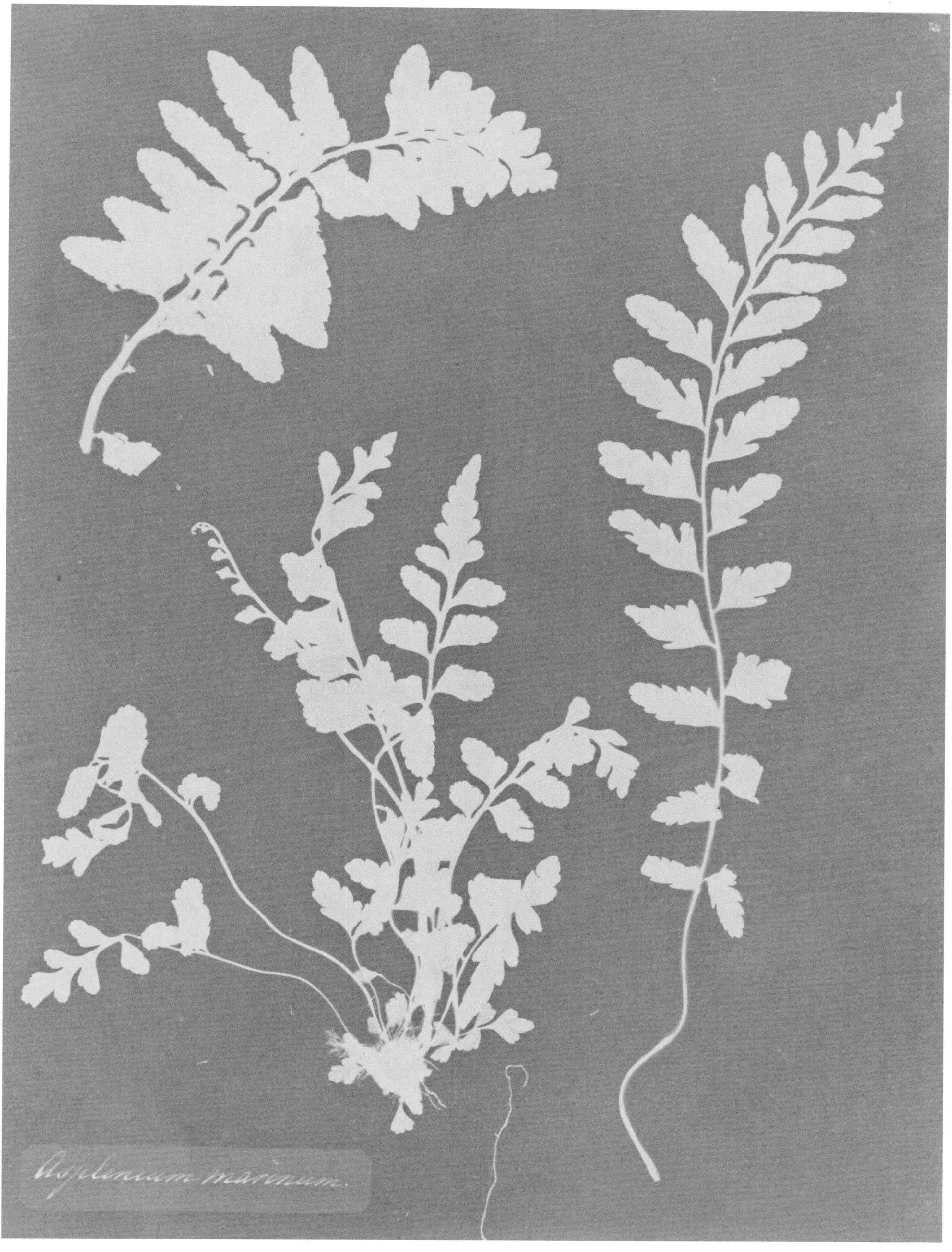

Anna Atkins, **Asplenium marinum** from **Photographs of British Algae. Cyanotype Impressions,** c. 1843–c. 1853, cyanotype, 24.7 x 19.3 cm. Courtesy Rijksmuseum Amsterdam.

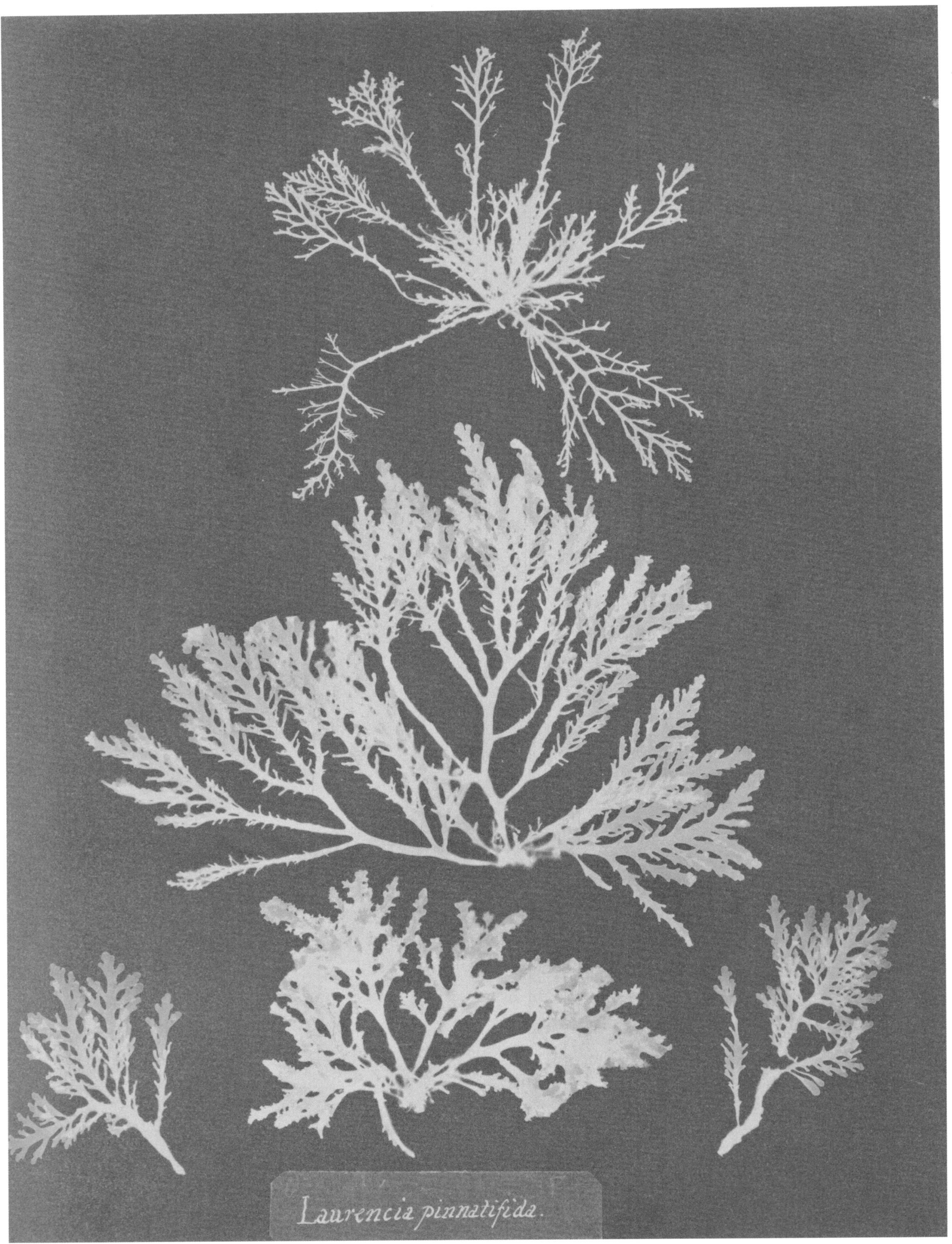

Anna Atkins, **Laurencia pinnatifida** from **Photographs of British Algae. Cyanotype Impressions**, c. 1843–c. 1853, cyanotype, 25 × 20 cm. Courtesy Rijksmuseum Amsterdam.

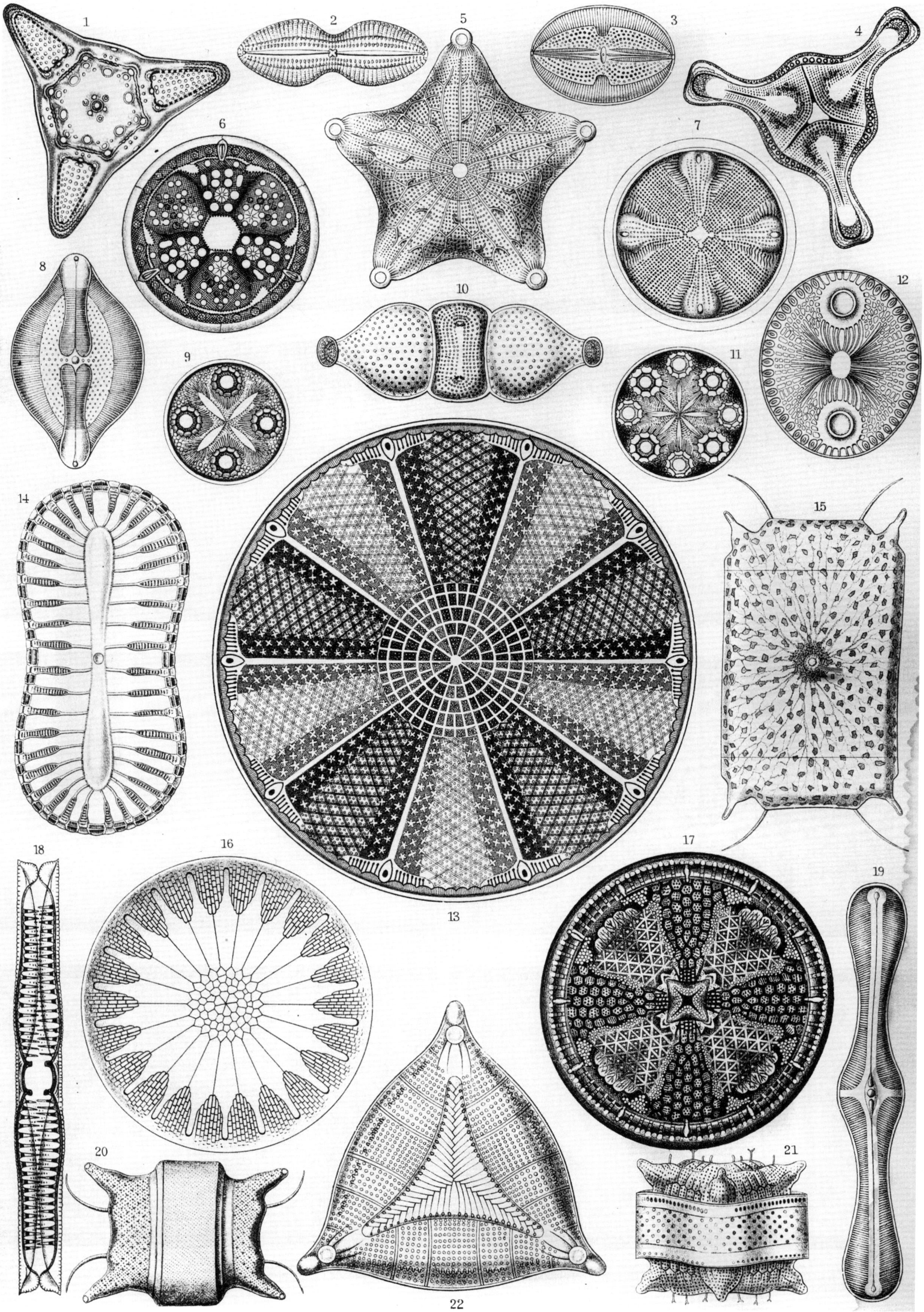

Ernst Haeckel, **Plate 4: Diatomea** from **Kunstformen der Natur**, 1904, engraving.

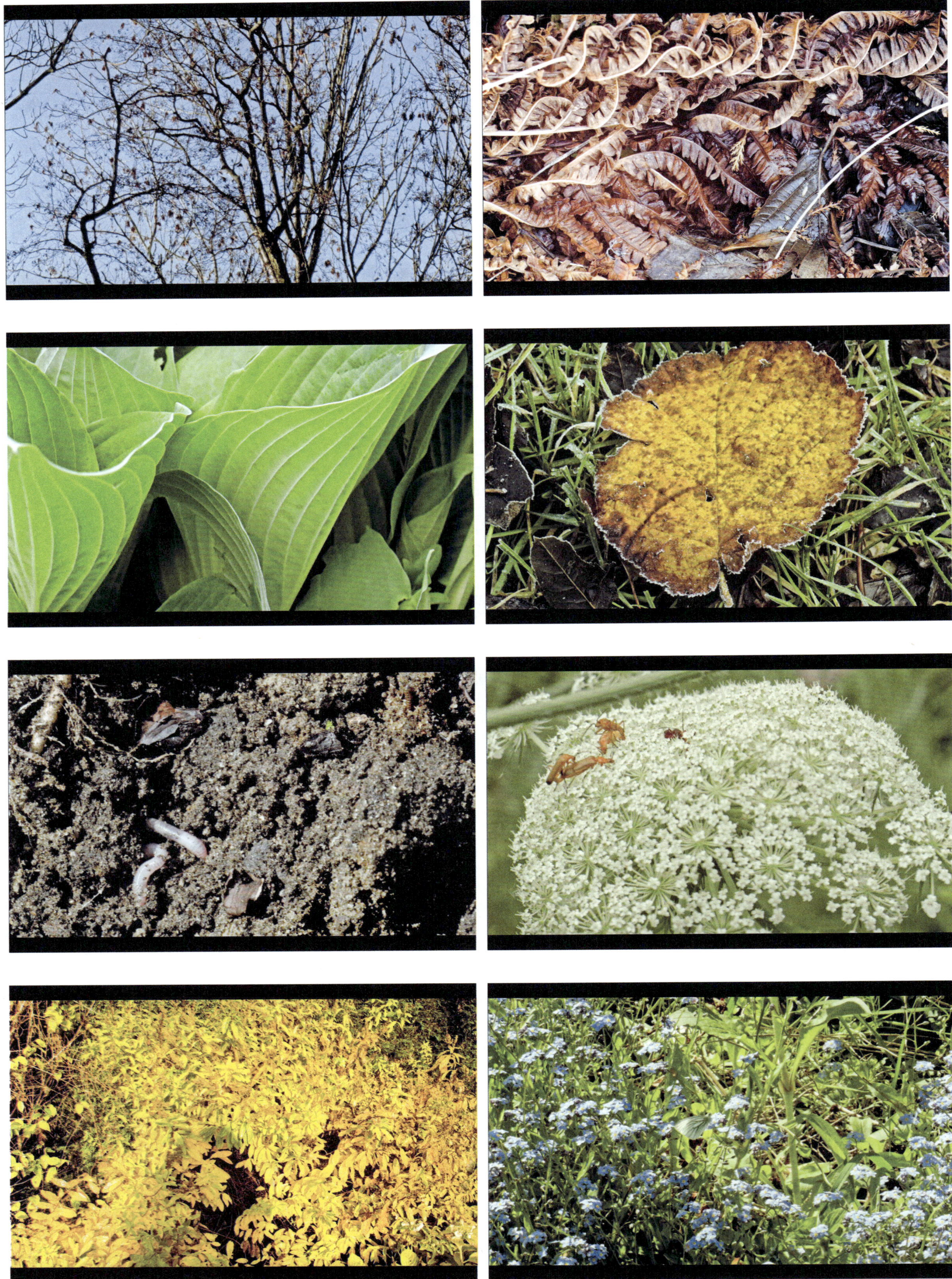

Sara Sejin Chang (Sara van der Heide), **The Garden**, 2014, colour, no sound 54", HD/DCP, commissioned by If I Can't Dance I Don't Want To Be Part Of Your Revolution. Courtesy Sara Sejin Chang (Sara van der Heide).

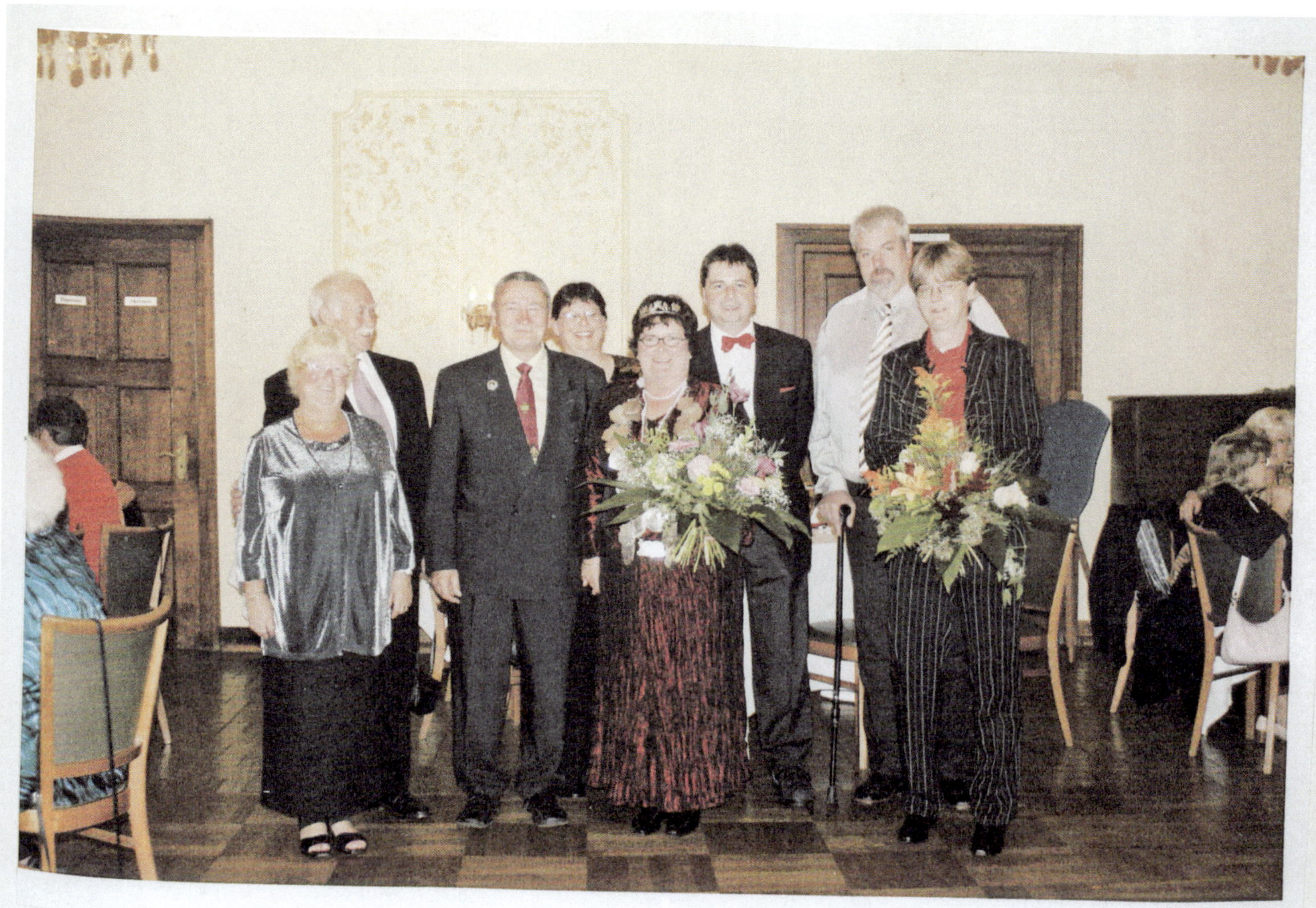

29. September 2007
Erntedankfest – Königsball –
– Kaiserinfest –

Wetter September 2007

Diesmal entsprach mein Wetterempfinden der Statistik.

Zu wenig Sonne – zu viel Regen

Altweibersommer bringt im September nur ein einziges warmes Wochenende

Jeremy Deller, **Speak to the Earth and It Will Tell You**, 2007–2017, installation view LWL-Museum für Kunst und Kultur, Westfälisches Landesmuseum, Münster. Courtesy Skulptur Projekte Archiv. Photo: Hanna Neander.

Tiere

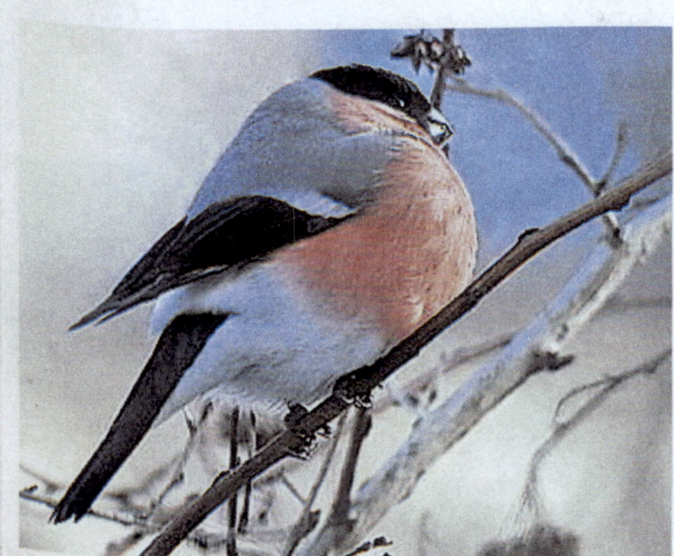

Männchen Gimpel

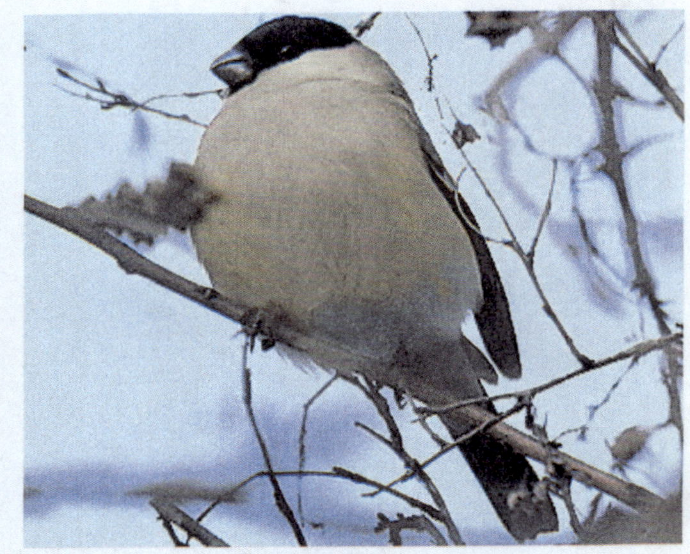

Weibchen Gimpel

So schön ist das "Dompfaffpärchen", das jeden späten Nachmittag im Apfelbaum trillert. Ihr Nest haben sie vermutlich in der Efeu-hecke.

Nun schreibt Erich 1 Jahr seine Beobachtungen

Jeremy Deller, **Speak to the Earth and It Will Tell You**, 2007–2017, installation view LWL-Museum für Kunst und Kultur, Westfälisches Landesmuseum, Münster. Courtesy Skulptur Projekte Archiv. Photo: Hanna Neander.

Arbeiten:

Der Winter hat sich nun endgültig verabschiedet.
Die Kartoffeln kommen in die Erde, Erbsen Möhren und Spinat werden ausgesät.
Ende des Monats können Tomaten und Peperoni ins Gewächshaus gepflanzt werden.
Da die Tomatenpflanzen noch klein sind, habe ich darüber ein Regal gebaut und meine daheim vorgezogenen Blumenpflänzchen dort untergebracht.
Es darf nun das tägliche Gießen nicht versäumt werden.

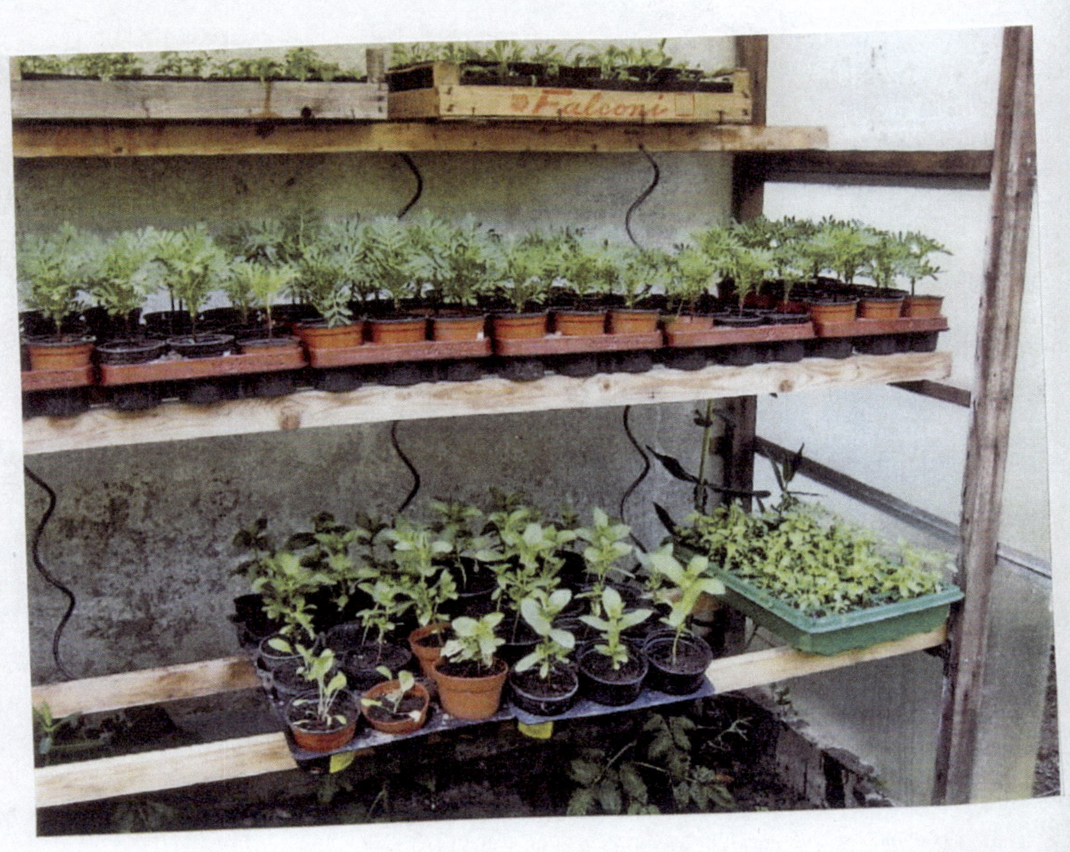

Jeremy Deller, **Speak to the Earth and It Will Tell You**, 2007–2017, installation view LWL-Museum für Kunst und Kultur, Westfälisches Landesmuseum, Münster. Courtesy Skulptur Projekte Archiv. Photo: Hanna Neander.

Kunstwerk: "Tagebuch 2007 - 2017" zu führen sei. Jede Gartenanlage soll in ihrem Buch das erlebte Jahr dokumentieren, in Wort und Bild.

Kurzberichte über Gartenveranstaltungen, Ernten - gute, wie schlechte, Gartentipps usw. sollen zu Papier gebracht werden. Kurz und gut, ein interessantes Garten-Tagebuch.

Einige Gartenfreunde hatten ihre Tagebücher dabei. Jeder versuchte einen Blick in die Bücher zu werfen.

Der Austausch war recht informativ. Man beschloss, sich in jedem Jahr wieder zu treffen.

Spende aus Kleingarten-Kunstprojekt

Erlös aus Verkauf der Samen des Taschentuchbaums geht an das Deutsche Kleingärtnermusem

Rückblick: Am 16. Juni 2007 eröffnete die Weltausstellung „skulptur projekte münster 07" für 105 Tage ihre Pforten. Diese Ausstellung war auch ein Kunstsommer für das Kleingartenwesen in Münster. Der Londoner Künstler Jeremy Deller widmete sich dem Phänomen der Kleingärten, genau genommen der Kleingartenkulturgeschichte.

Chinesischer Taschentuchbaum und Grünes Buch

In zwei Kleingartenanlagen in Münster, in „Martini" und „Mühlenfeld" an der Gartenstraße, hatte Deller seine Kunststationen eingerichtet. Dreh- und Angelpunkt einer seiner Aktionen war der seltene Taschentuchbaum, ein aus China stammender Laubbaum, der erst nach zehn Jahren das erste Mal blüht und dessen große weiße Blüten wie Taschentücher erscheinen. Einige tausend Samenkörner des Taschentuchbaumes hat der Künstler zusammen mit den Kleingärtnern verkauft.

Die Dauer bis zur ersten Blüte steht in direktem Zusammenhang mit dem Ausstellungszyklus (zehn Jahre) der „skulptur projekte". Insofern soll das Samenkorn des Taschentuchbaumes als „Gedächtnisstütze" für 2017 fungieren, denn dann startet die nächste Ausstellung.

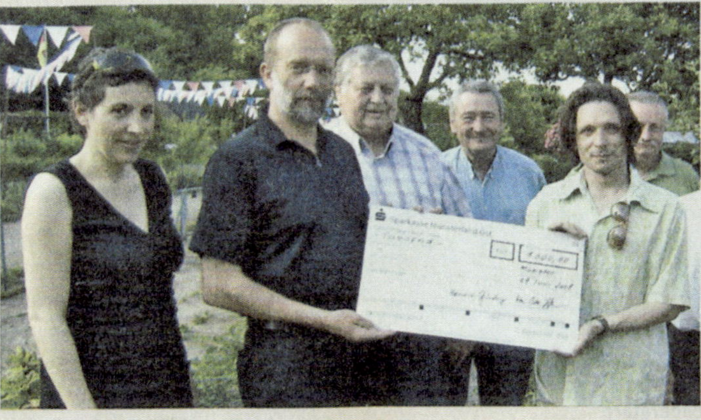

Ein Spendenscheck für das Deutsche Kleingärtnermuseum in Leipzig (v.l.): Dr. Brigitte Franzen, Kuratorin „skulptur projekte münster 07", Werner Heidemann, BDG-Präsidiumsmitglied, Hans-Peter Leßmann, Vorsitzender des Stadt- und Bezirksverbandes Münster, Wolfgang Rohe, Vorsitzender des Kgv. „Mühlenfeld", Jeremy Deller, Londoner Künstler

Dellers weiteres Projekt ist ein dickes grünes Buch. Es soll nach seinem Wunsch in den Kleingartenanlagen zehn Jahre lang geführt werden. Eingetragen wird, was in den Gärten vereinsintern geschieht, wie sich die Natur in den Gärten entwickelt und wie der Mensch im Einklang mit der Natur sich über die Jahre präsentieren wird. In zehn Jahren – also 2017 – sollen dann die gefüllten Bücher als Kunstprojekt vorgestellt werden.

Ein nachhaltiger Kunstsommer für das Kleingartenwesen

Die „skulptur projekte münster 07" sind vorbei, die Ausstellung hat längst vor einem Jahr ihre Tore geschlossen. Aber was bleibt, ist eine lebendige Partnerschaft zwischen den Kleingärtnern in Münster und dem Künstler Jeremy Deller, der immer wieder spontan von London nach Münster reist, die Kleingärtnervereine besucht, mit den Gartenfreunden gemeinsam das „Grüne Buch" führt und sich mit ihnen über die ersten Sämlinge des Taschentuchbaumes freut.

Viele Sämlinge dieses seltenen und besonderen Baumes wachsen derzeit in Münster und weltweit. Tausende von Samenkörnern haben Münsters Gartenfreunde gemeinsam mit dem Künstler verkauft und den Erlös dem Deutschen Kleingärtnermuseum gespendet.

Am 9. Juni überreichten der Künstler Jeremy Deller und der Vorsitzende des Stadt- und Bezirksverbandes Münster, Hans-Peter Leßmann, einen Scheck über 1000 Euro an das BDG-Präsidiumsmitglied Werner Heidemann. Jeremy Deller: *„Ich fühle mich der Kleingartenkulturgeschichte besonders verbunden"*. Werner Heidemann dankte für diese außergewöhnliche Spende und lud den Künstler zu einem Besuch nach Leipzig ein.

Mit der Teilnahme an der Weltausstellung „skulptur projekte münster 07" schreiben Münsters Kleingärtner buchstäblich ein stückweit moderne Kleingartenkulturgeschichte für die Zukunft. Und mit ihrer Spende für das Deutsche Kleingärtnermuseum dokumentieren sie ihre Aufgeschlossenheit für Tradition und Moderne, für Kleingartenkulturgeschichte gestern, heute und morgen.

Werner Heidemann

Jeremy Deller, **Speak to the Earth and It Will Tell You**, 2007–2017, installation view LWL-Museum für Kunst und Kultur, Westfälisches Landesmuseum, Münster. Courtesy Skulptur Projekte Archiv. Photo: Hanna Neander.

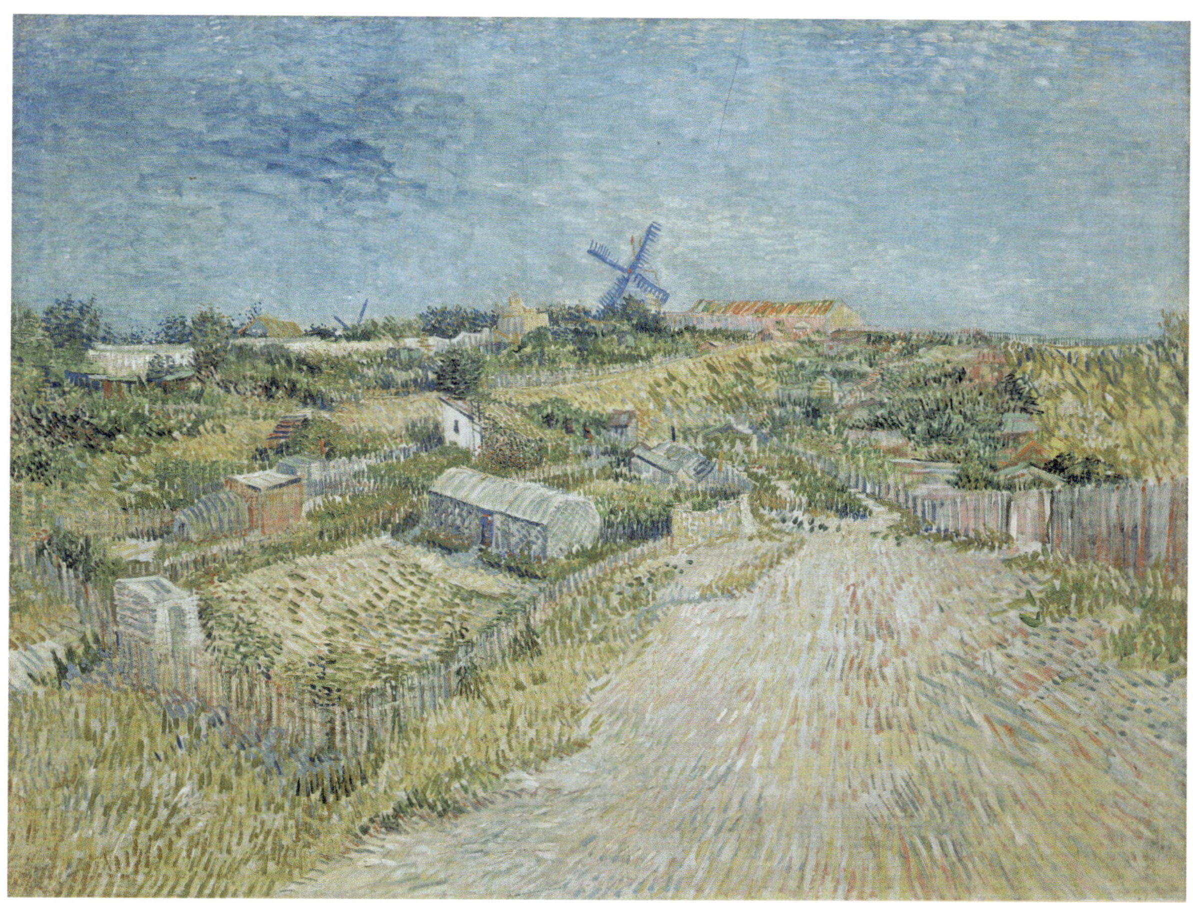

Vincent van Gogh, **Kitchen Gardens on Montmartre**, 1887, oil on canvas, 96 × 120 cm. Courtesy Stedelijk Museum Amsterdam.

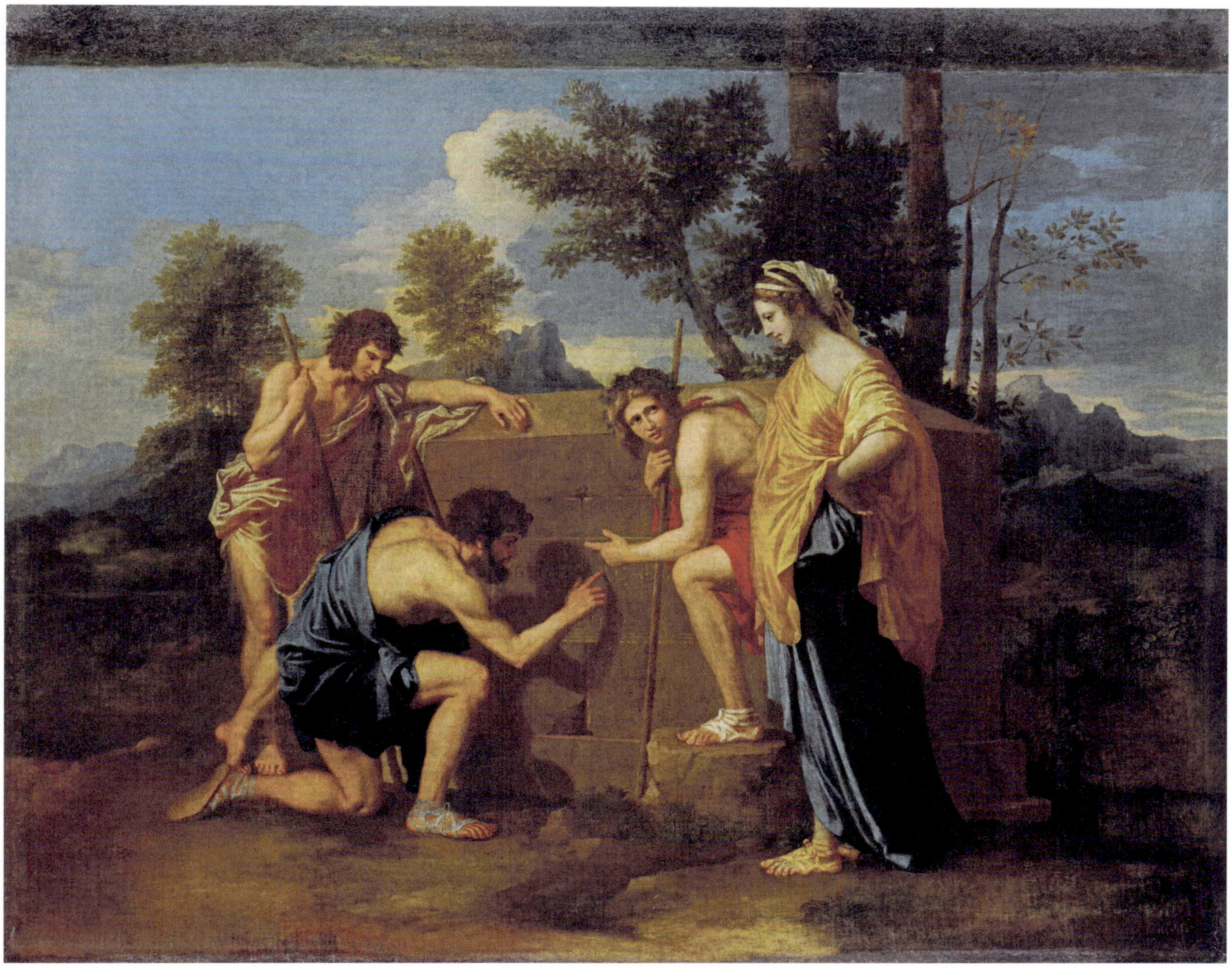

Nicolas Poussin, **Et in Arcadia Ego**, 1637–1638, oil on canvas, 85 × 121 cm. Courtesy RMN-Grand Palais (Musée du Louvre). Photo: Stéphane Maréchalle.

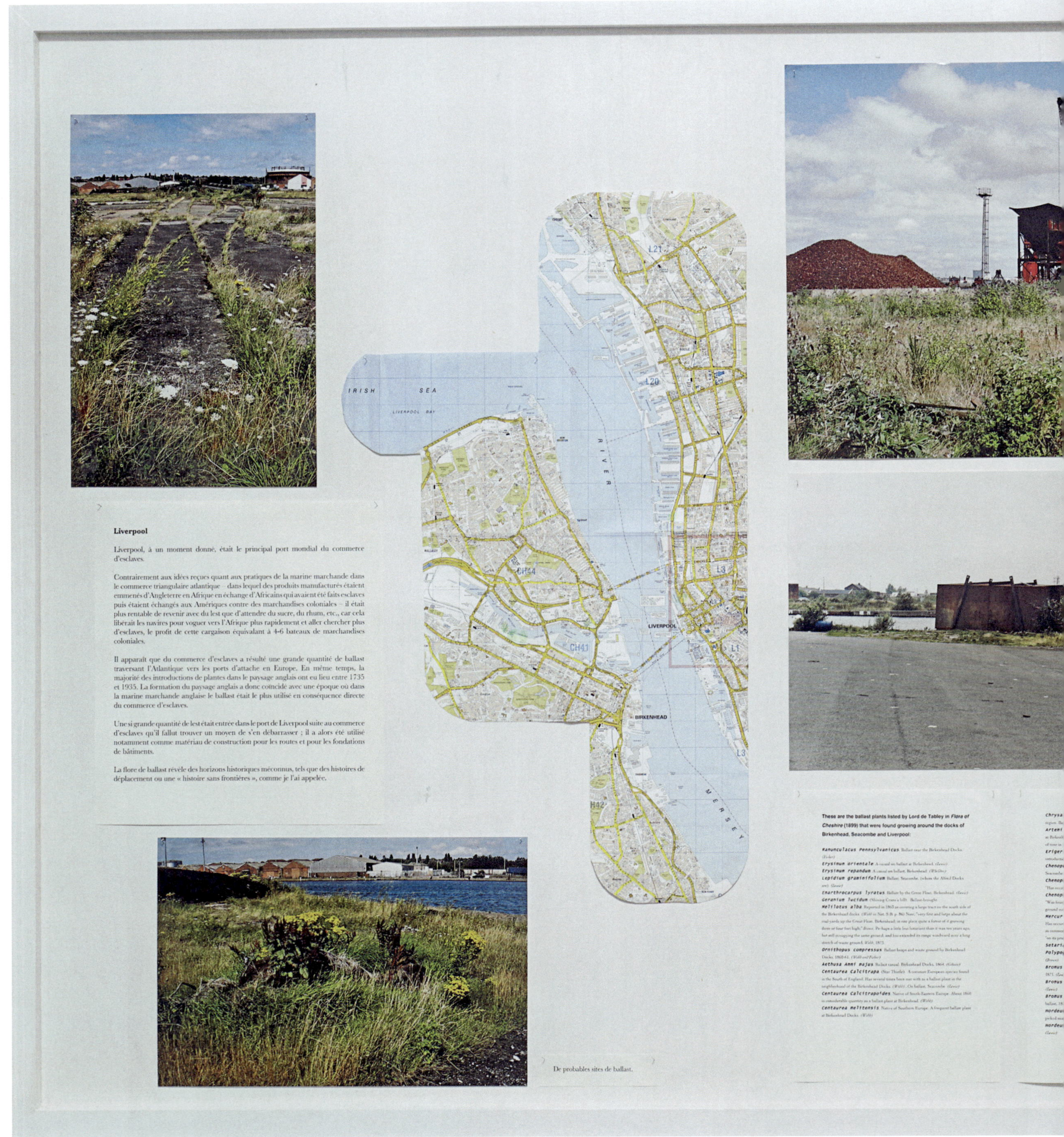

Maria Thereza Alves, **Seeds of Change: Liverpool**, 2004, installation view. Courtesy Maria Thereza Alvest and Michel Rein, Paris/Brussels.

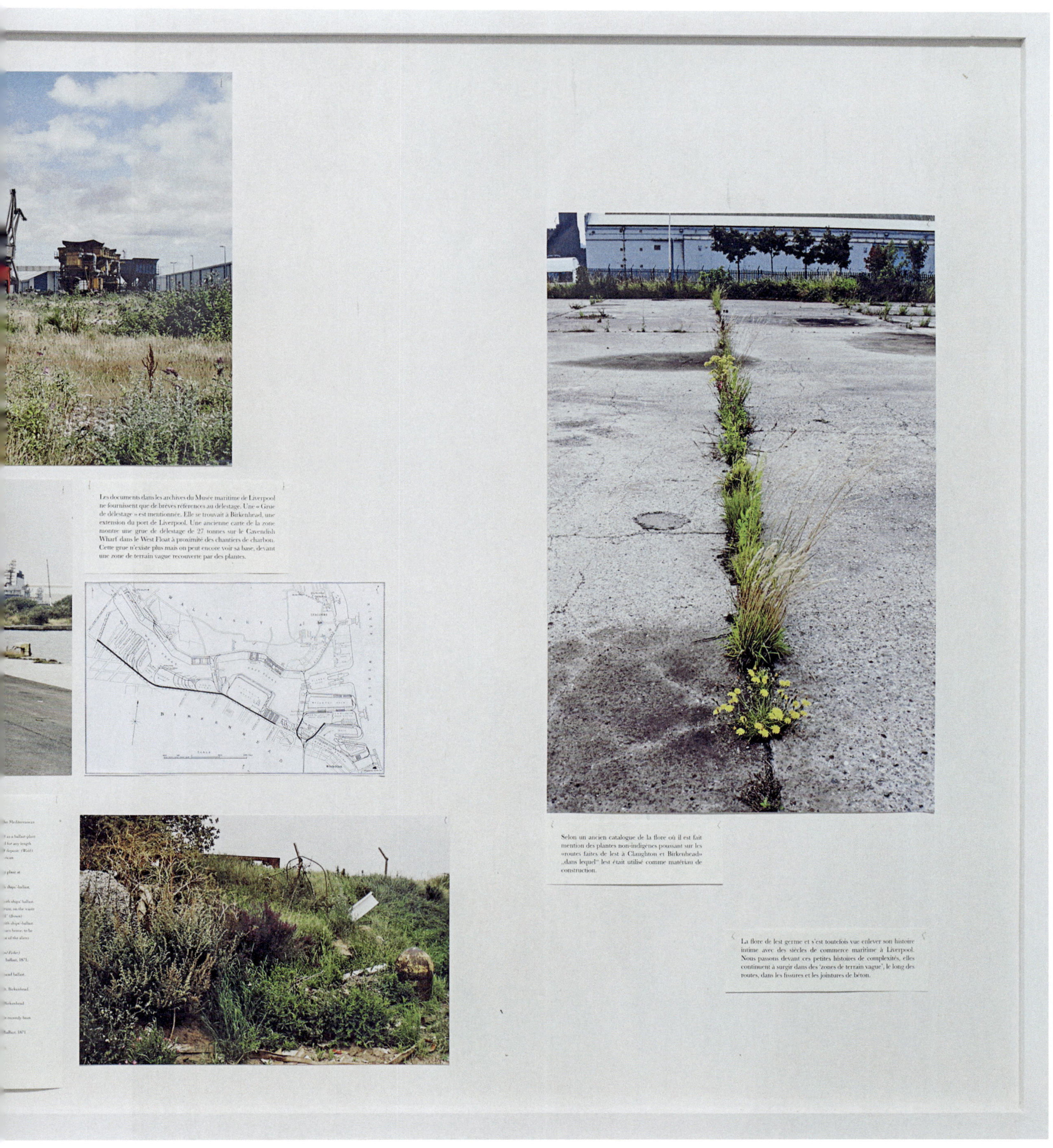
Les documents dans les archives du Musée maritime de Liverpool ne fournissent que de brèves références au délestage. Une « Grue de délestage » est mentionnée. Elle se trouvait à Birkenhead, une extension du port de Liverpool. Une ancienne carte de la zone montre une grue de délestage de 27 tonnes sur le Cavendish Wharf dans le West Float à proximité des chantiers de charbon. Cette grue n'existe plus mais on peut encore voir sa base, devant une zone de terrain vague recouverte par des plantes.
Selon un ancien catalogue de la flore où il est fait mention des plantes non-indigènes poussant sur les «routes faites de lest à Claughton et Birkenhead» „dans lequel" lest était utilisé comme matériau de construction.
La flore de lest germe et s'est toutefois vue enlever son histoire intime avec des siècles de commerce maritime à Liverpool. Nous passons devant ces petites histoires de complexités, elles continuent à surgir dans des 'zones de terrain vague', le long des routes, dans les fissures et les jointures de béton.

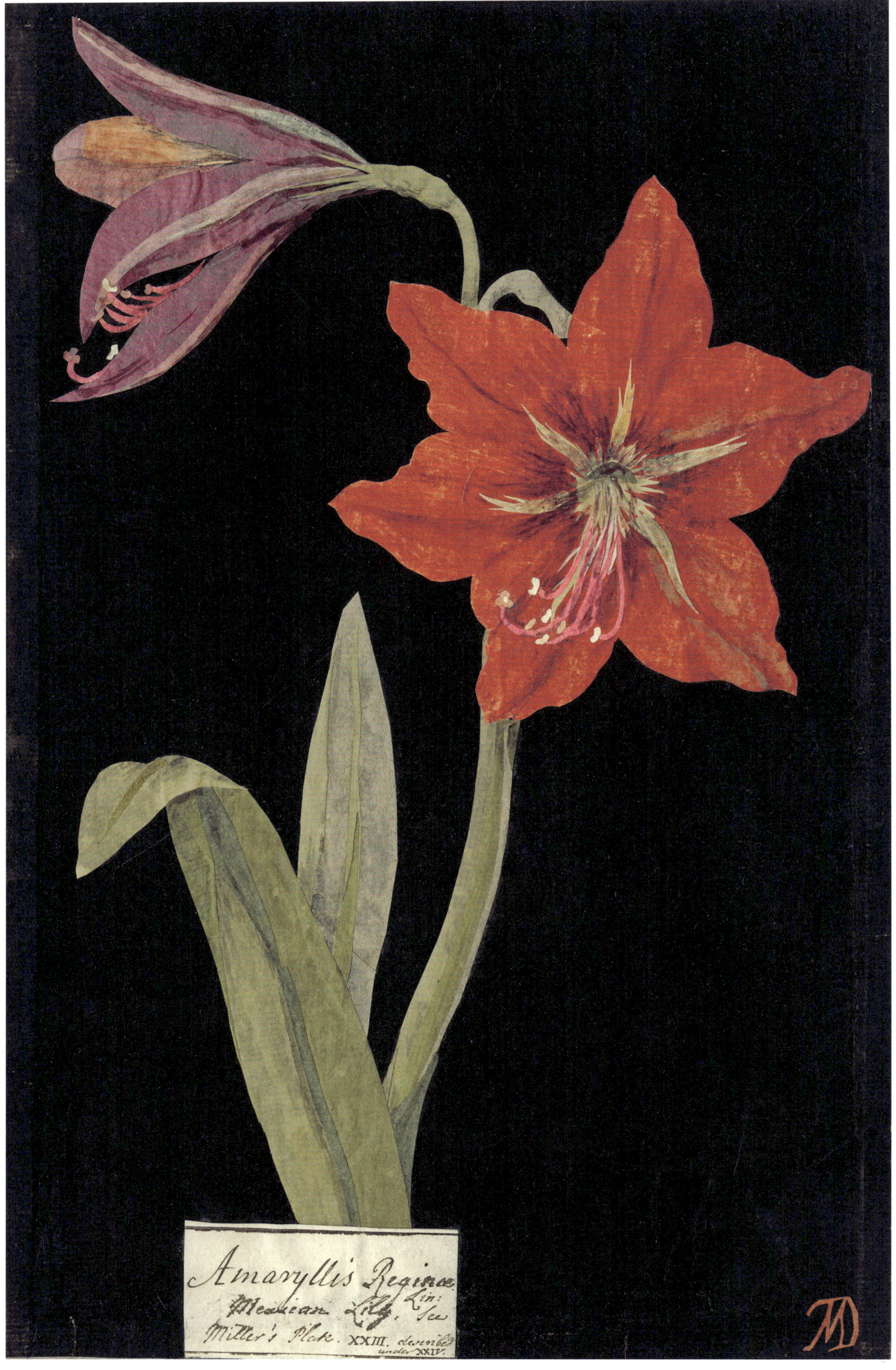

Mary Granville Delany, **Amaryllis Reginae**, 1775, collage, 30.4 × 19.6 cm. Courtesy The Trustees of the British Museum, London.

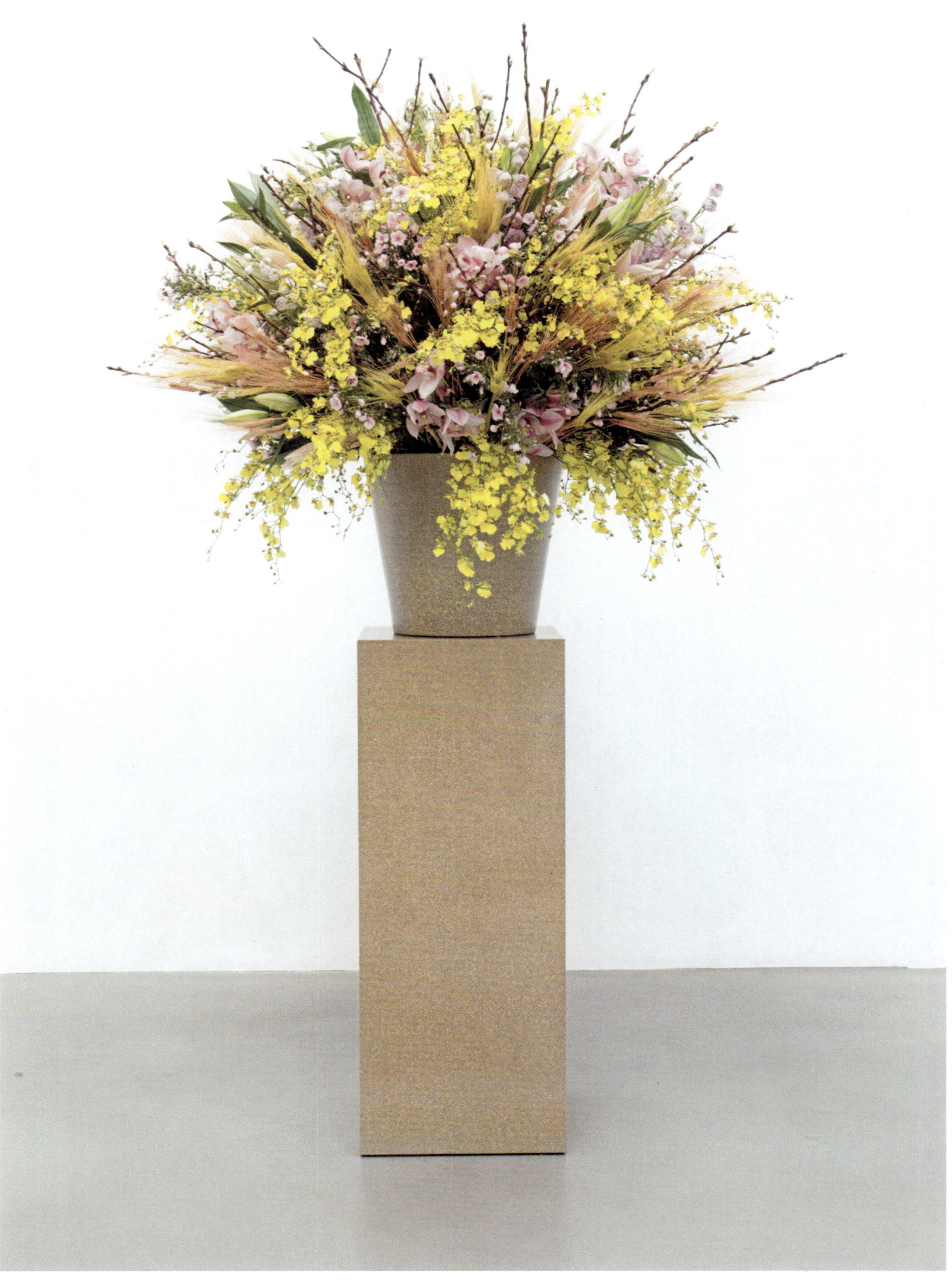

Willem de Rooij, **Bouquet XV**, 2015, installation view at Petzel Gallery, New York. Courtesy Willem de Rooij.

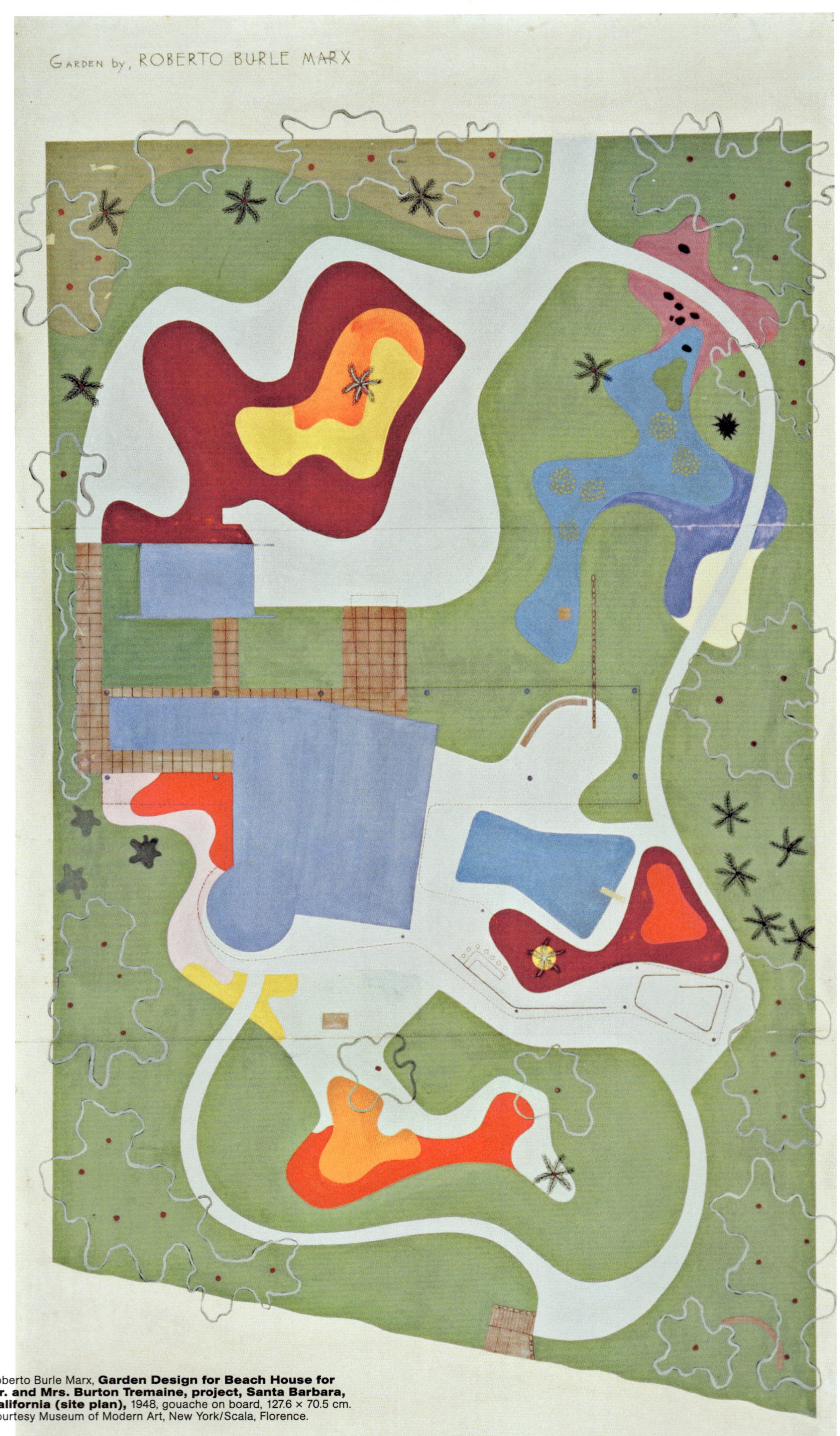

Roberto Burle Marx, **Garden Design for Beach House for Mr. and Mrs. Burton Tremaine, project, Santa Barbara, California (site plan),** 1948, gouache on board, 127.6 × 70.5 cm. Courtesy Museum of Modern Art, New York/Scala, Florence.

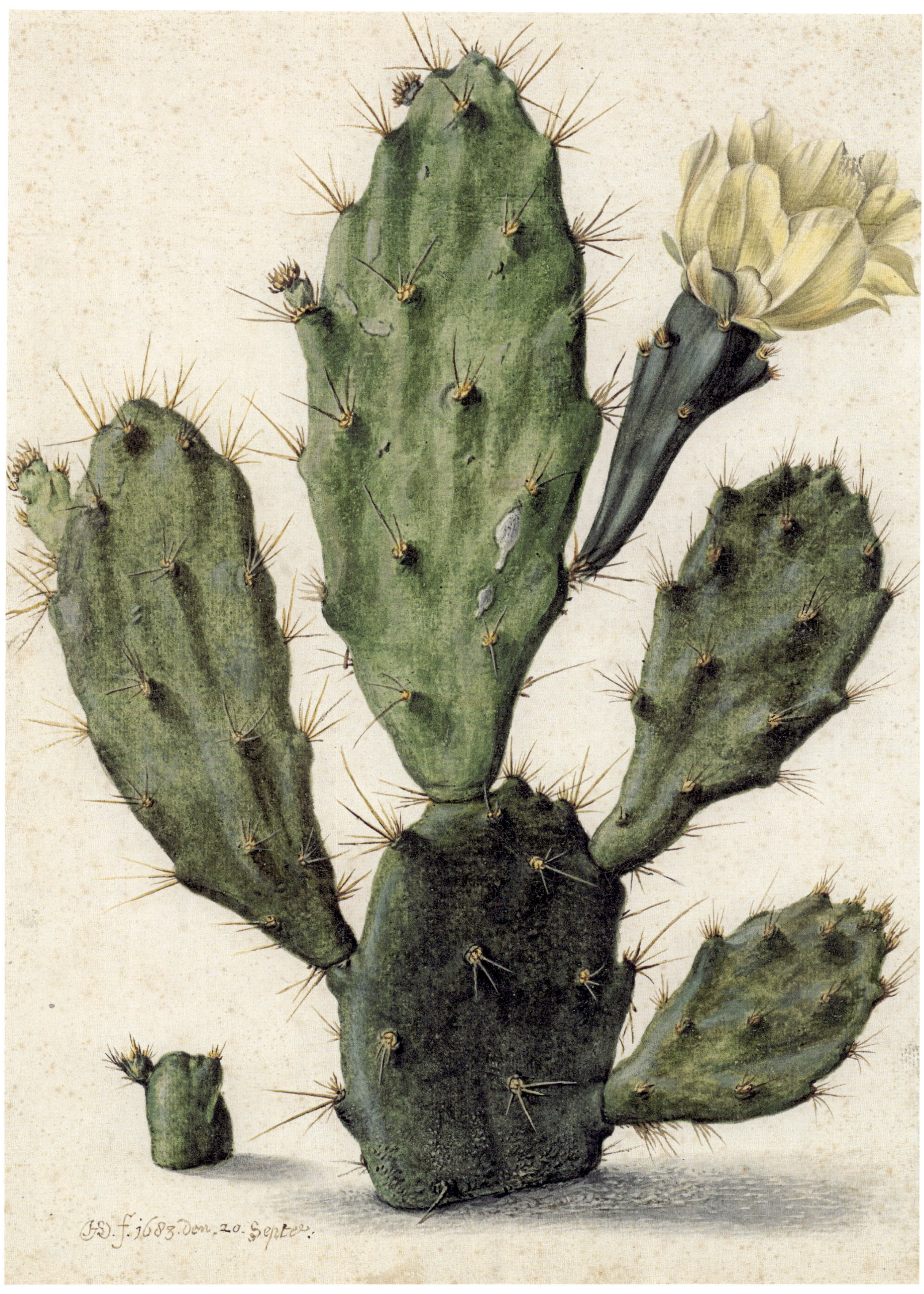

Herman Saftleven, **Pear cactus in bloom**, 1683, drawing, 35.5 × 25.6 cm. Courtesy Rijksmuseum Amsterdam.

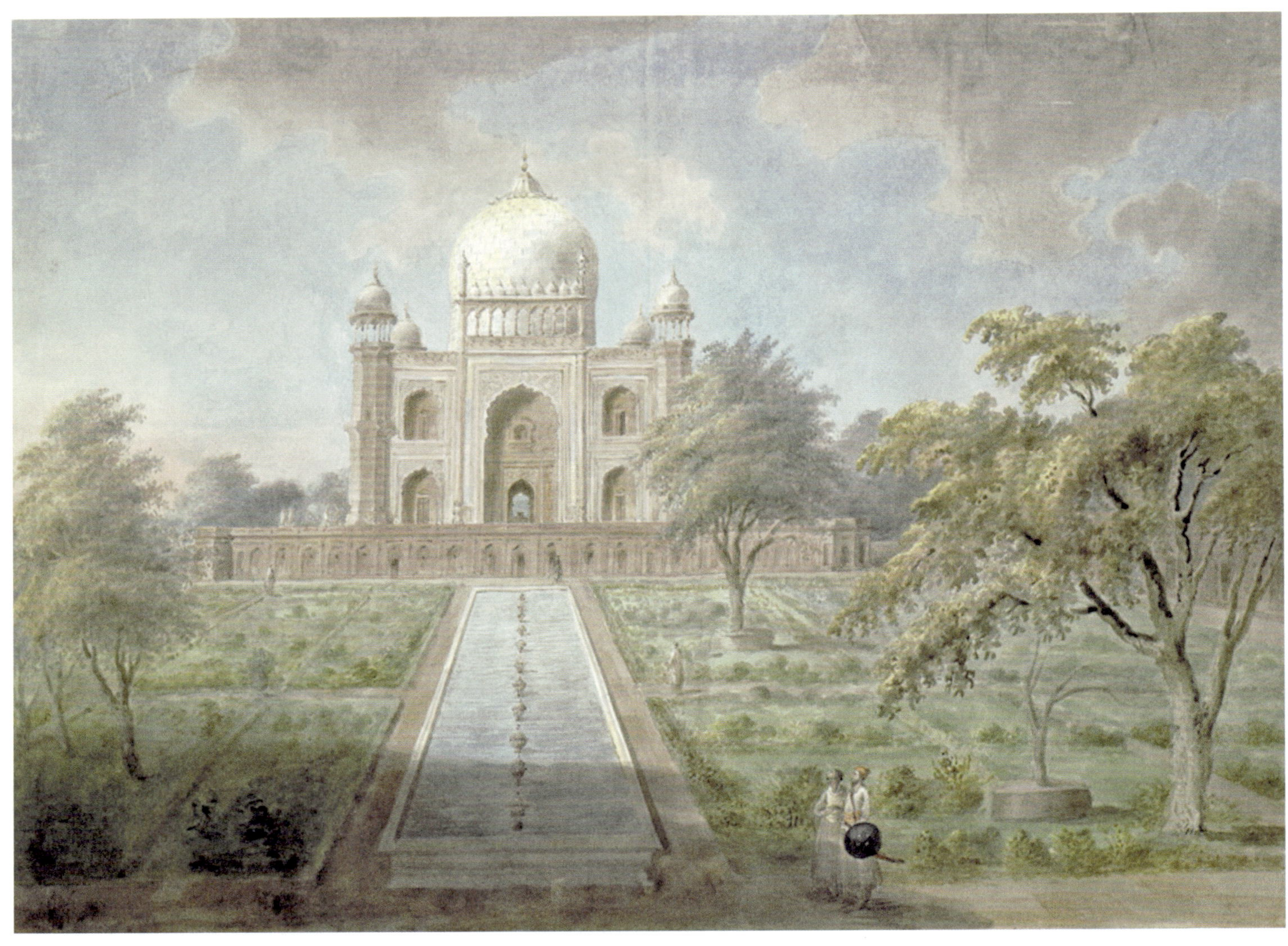

Sita Ram, **The tomb of Safdar Jang showing the garden and water channel**, 1815, watercolour drawing, 38.4 × 51.2 cm.

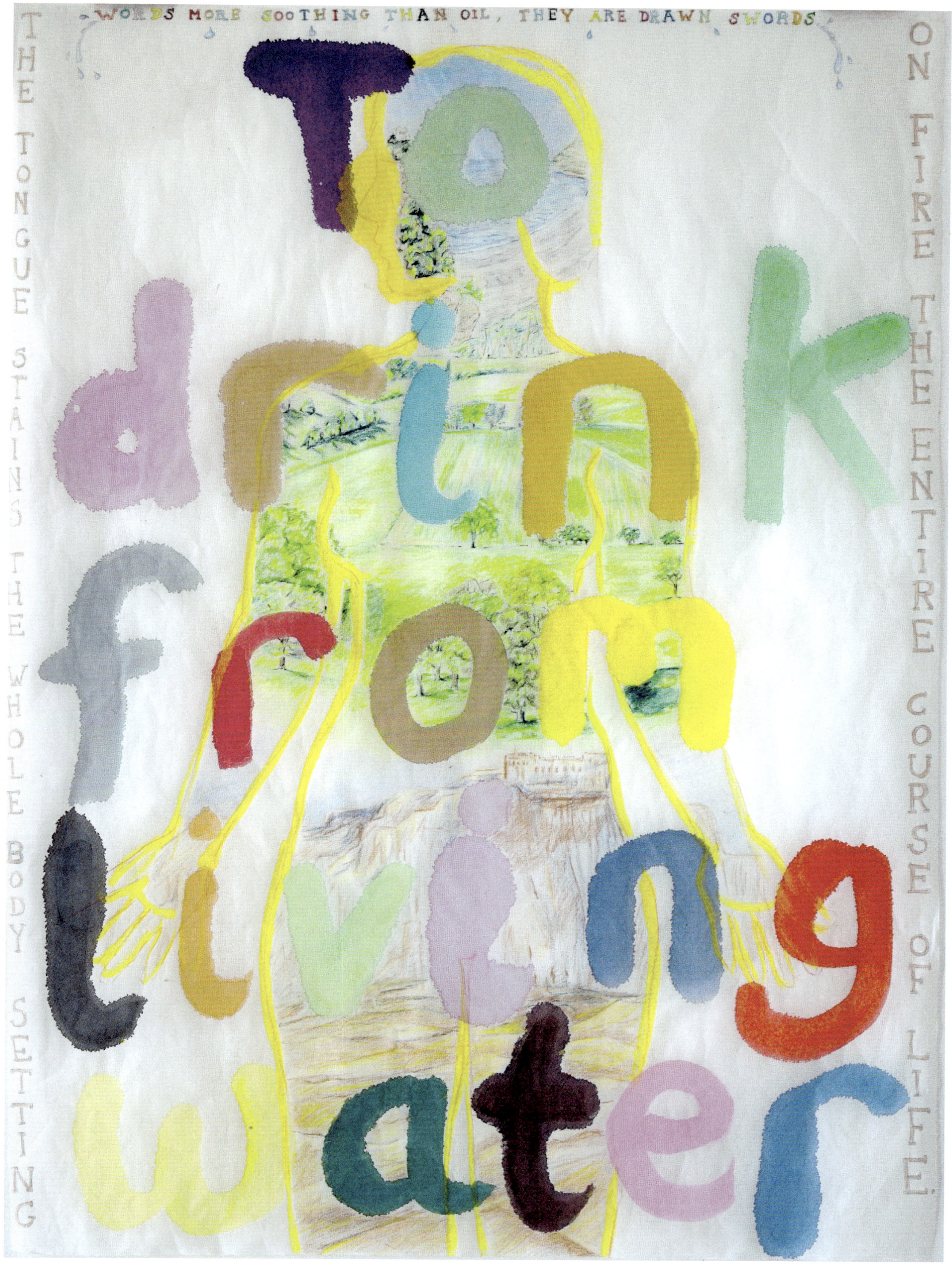

Maria Pask, **To drink from living water**, 2020, gouache drawing, 97 × 74 cm. Courtesy Maria Pask and Ellen de Bruijne Projects, Amsterdam.

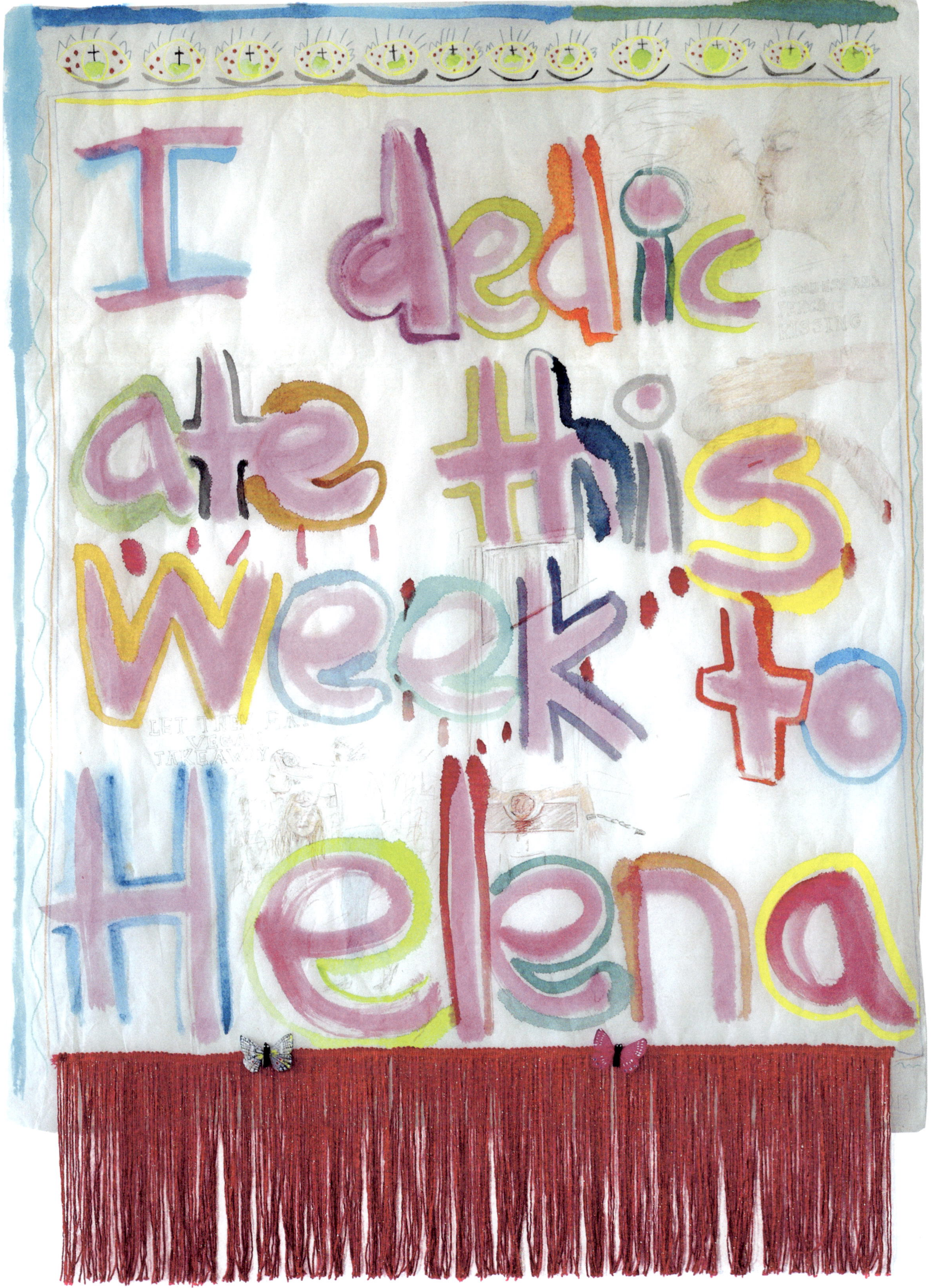

Maria Pask, **Helena**, 2020, gouache drawing, 107 × 76 cm. Courtesy Maria Pask and Ellen de Bruijne Projects, Amsterdam.

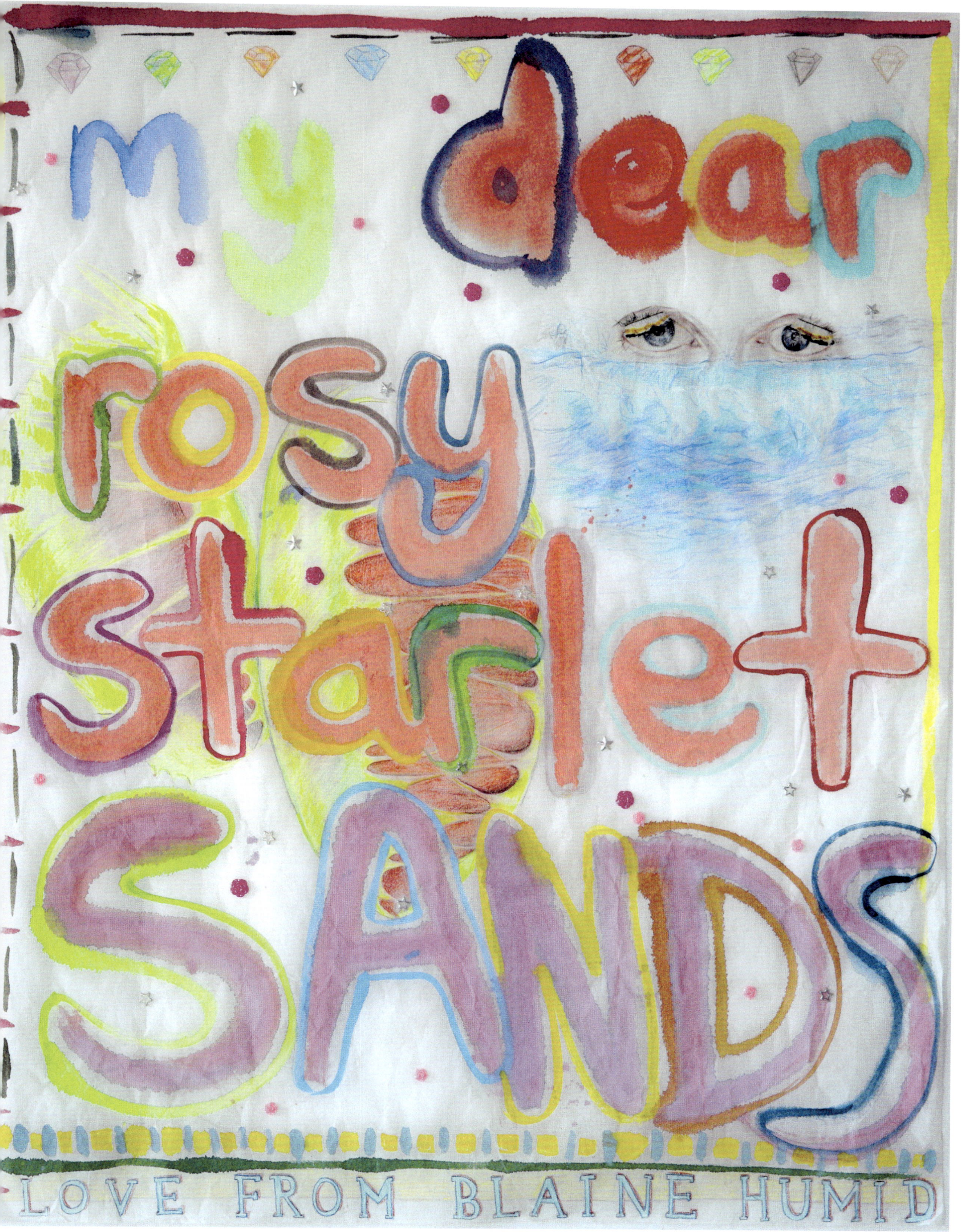

Maria Pask, **My dear starlet sands**, 2020, gouache drawing, 97 × 76 cm. Courtesy Maria Pask and Ellen de Bruijne Projects, Amsterdam.

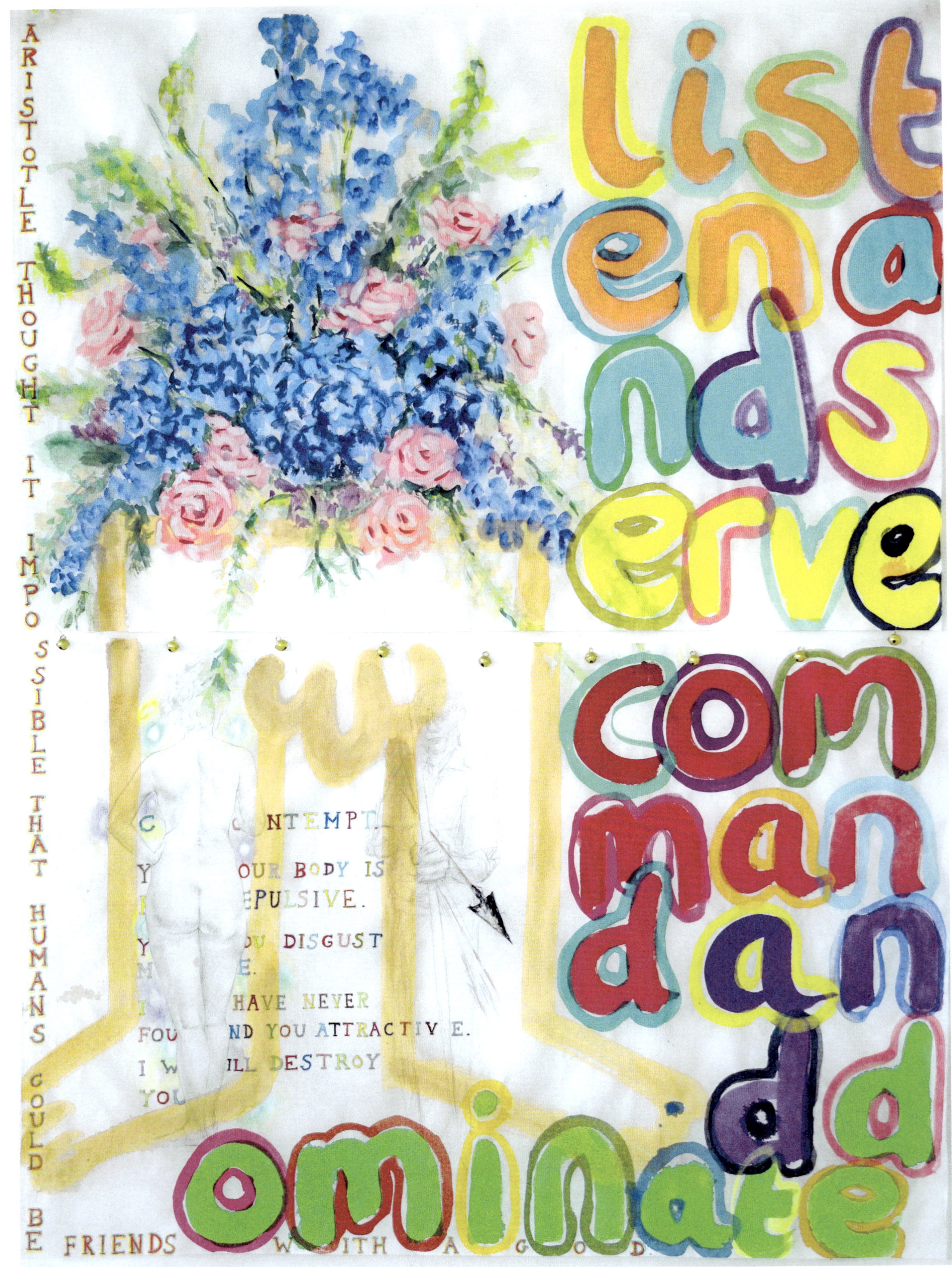

Maria Pask, **Listen and Serve**, **Commands and Dominate**, 2020, gouache drawing, 131 × 99 cm. Courtesy Maria Pask and Ellen de Bruijne Projects, Amsterdam.

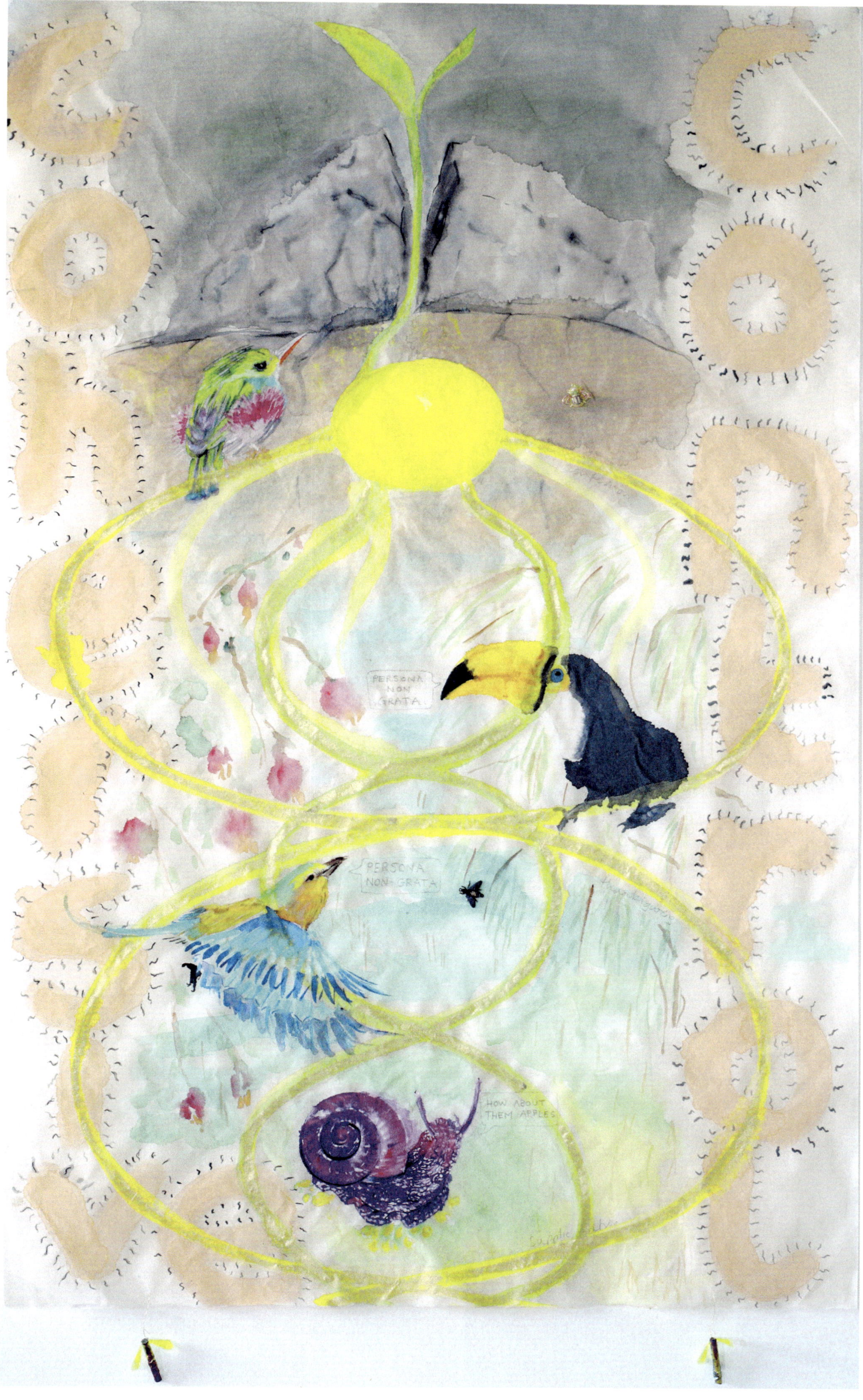

Maria Pask, **Coersive/Control**, 2020, gouache drawing, 98 × 65 cm. Courtesy Maria Pask and Ellen de Bruijne Projects, Amsterdam.

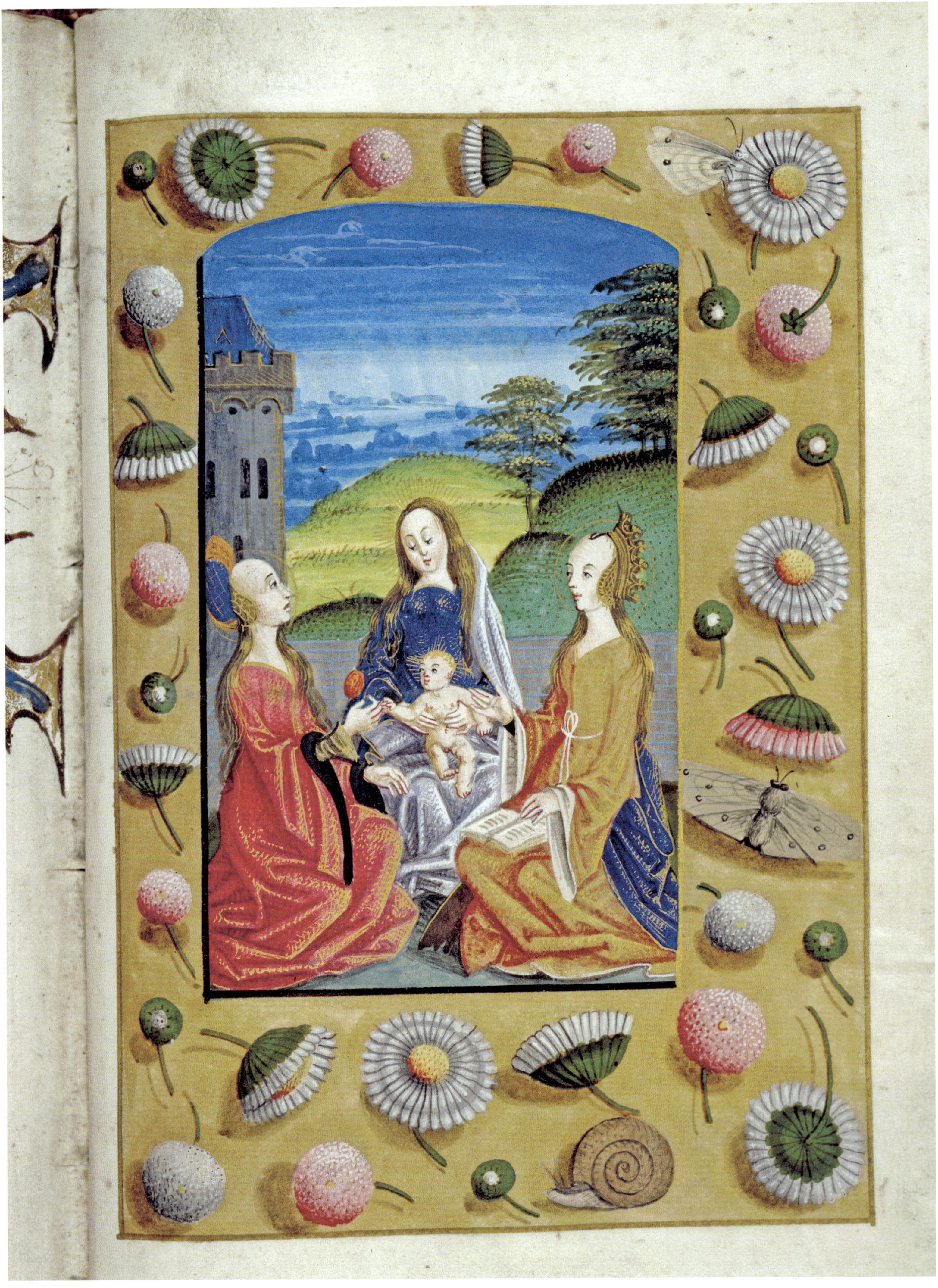

Geert Groote, Meester van Hugo Jansz. van Woerden and Suffragiënmeesters, **Book of Hours and Prayer**, c. 1480, manuscript, 19 × 13 × 5 cm. Courtesy Museum Catharijneconvent, Utrecht. Photo: Ruben de Heer.

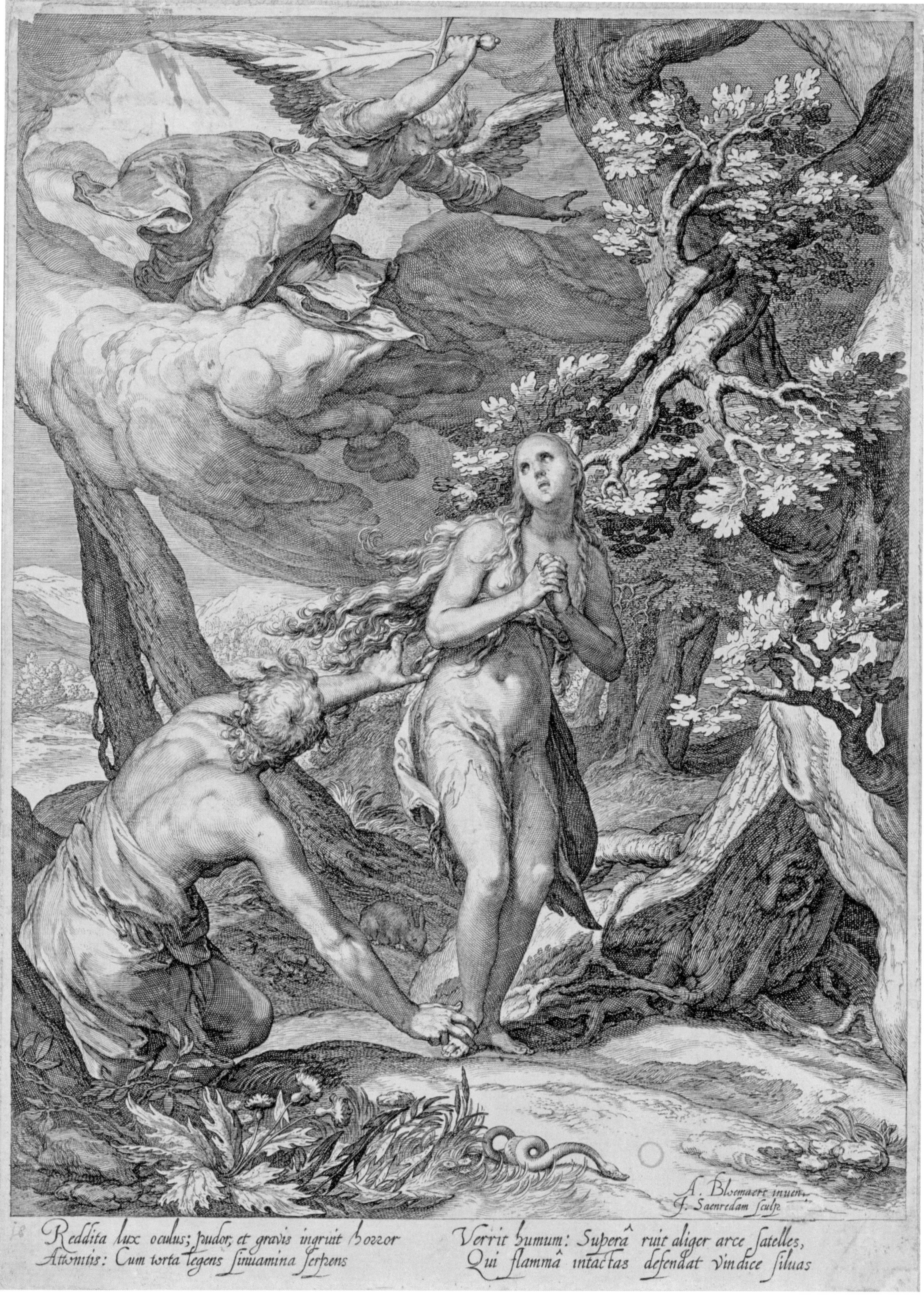

Abraham Bloemaert and Jan Saenredam, **The Expulsion from Paradise (The History of the First Parents of Man)**, 1604, engraving, 27.7 × 19.9 cm. Courtesy Centraal Museum, Utrecht.

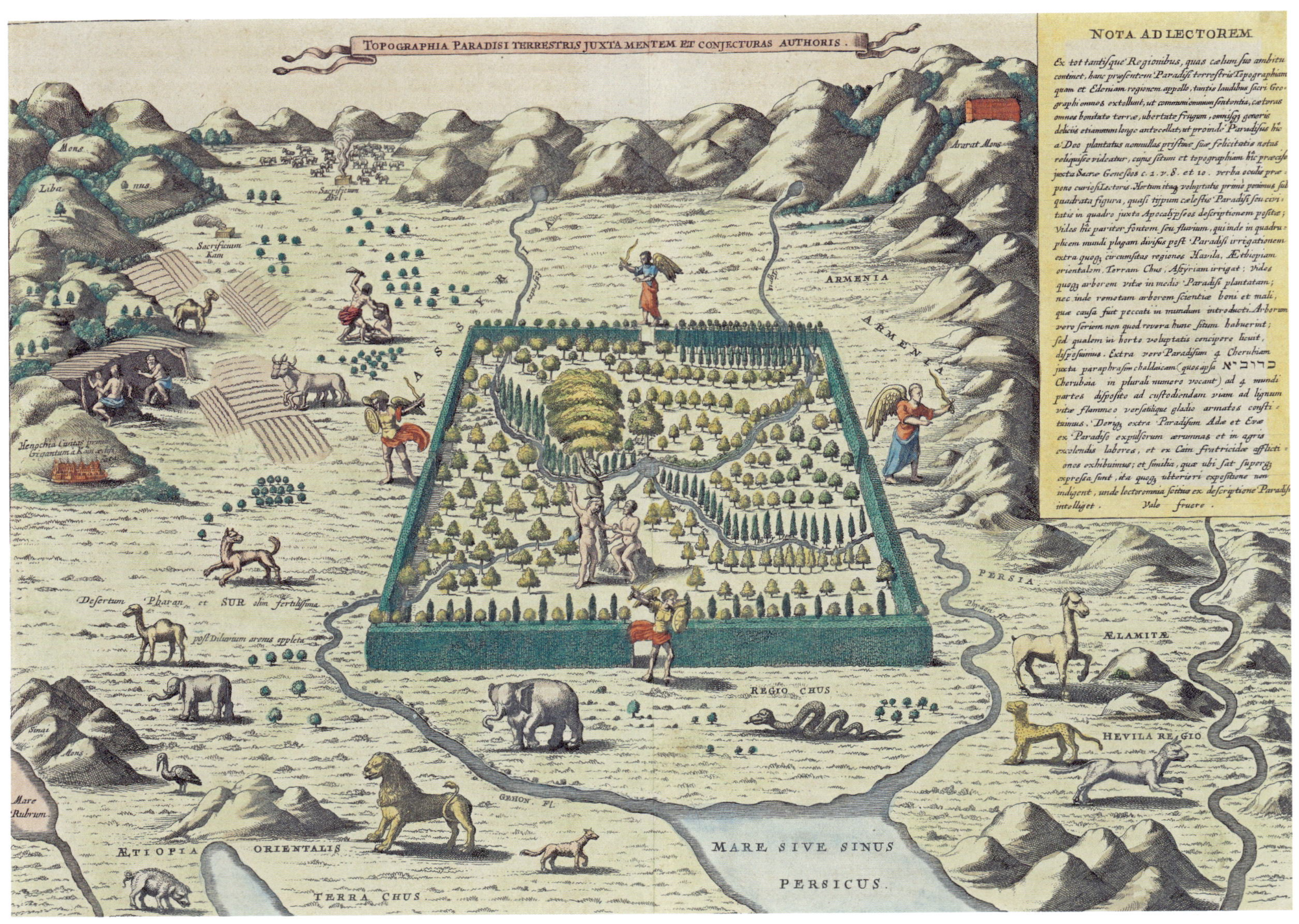

Athanasius Kircher, **Topographia paradisi terrestris juxta mentem et conjecturas authoris**, 1675, 29 × 42 cm. Courtesy Beinecke Rare Book and Manuscript Library, Yale University Library, New Haven.

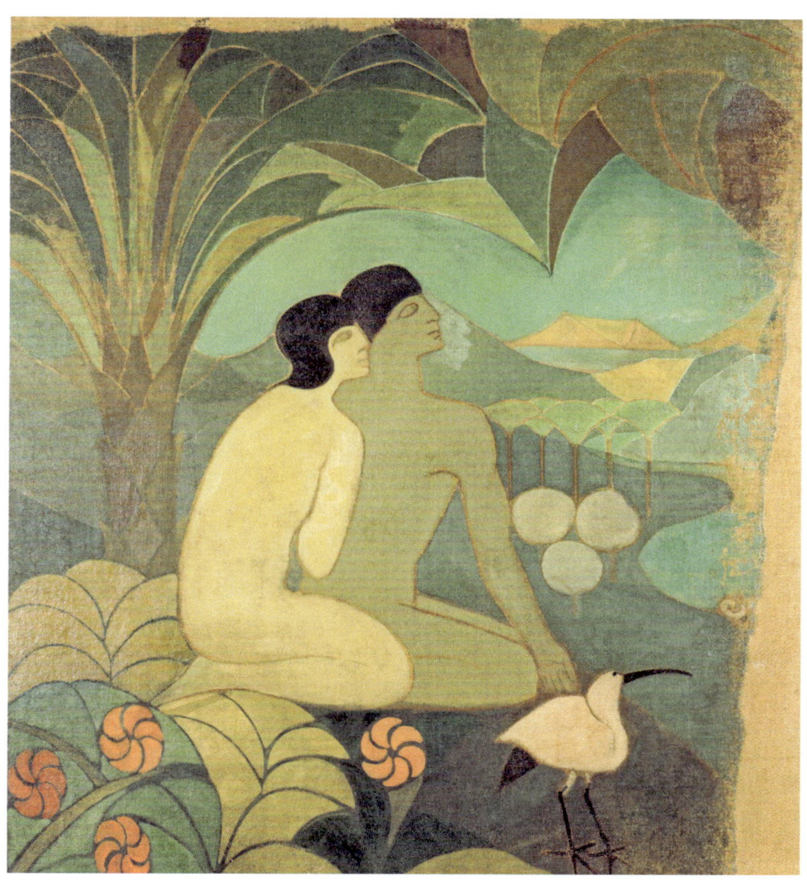

Otto van Rees, **Adam and Eve**, c. 1910, oil on canvas, 162 × 148.8 cm. Courtesy Centraal Museum, Utrecht/Pictoright, Amsterdam.

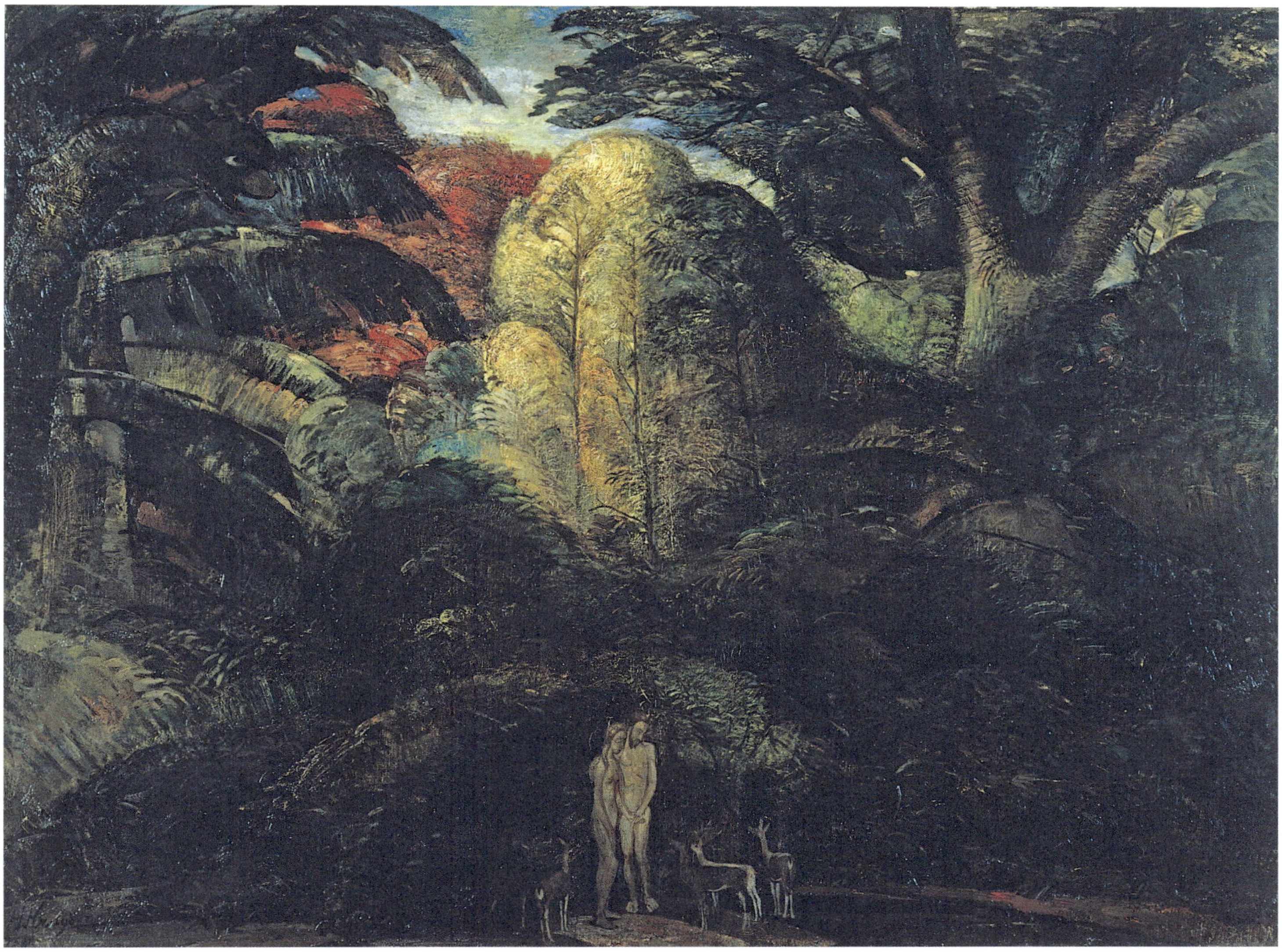

Herman Justus Kruyder, **Paradijs I**, 1913–1914, oil on canvas, 109.3 × 148 cm, Courtesy Frans Hals Museum, Haarlem.

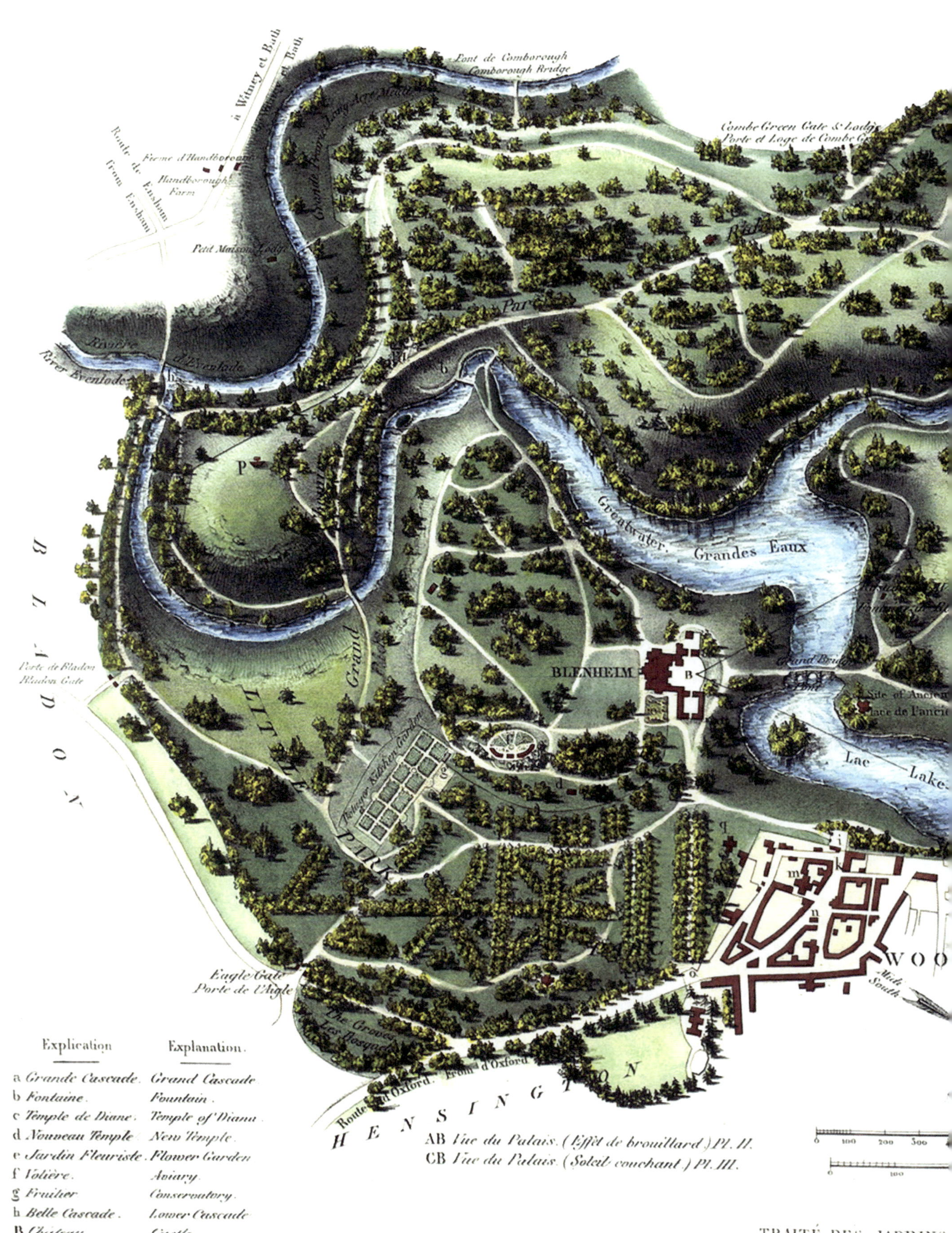

Narcisse Vergnaud, **A new and accurate plan of Blenheim Palace**, 1835, drawing.

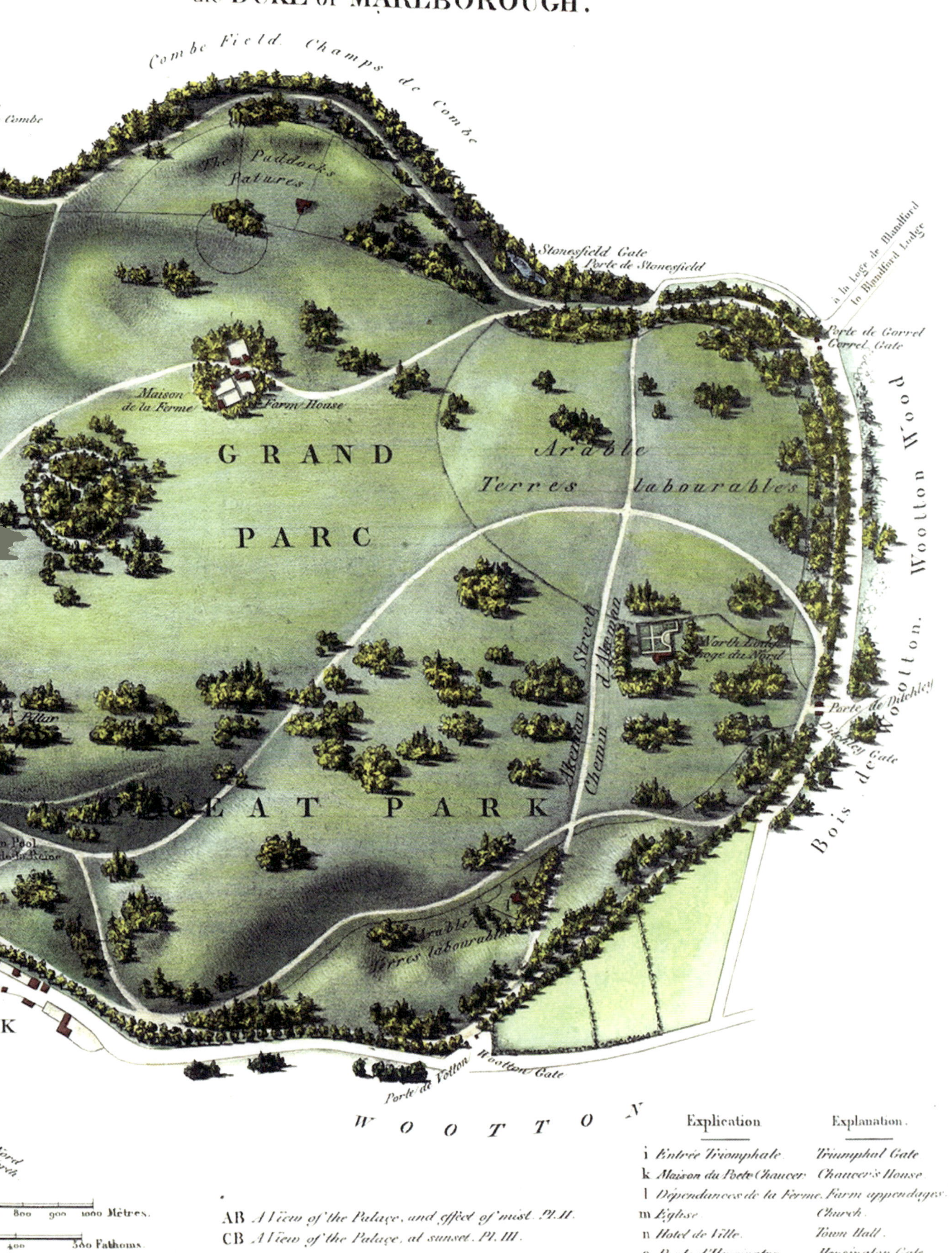
GLAND.
Pl. I.
and accurate Plan of BLENHEIM PALACE, Gardens, Park, Plantations, &c.
the Seat of His Grace
the DUKE of MARLBOROUGH.
Combe Field. Champs de Combe
The Paddocks
Patures
Stonesfield Gate
Porte de Stonesfield
Porte de Gorrel
Gorrel Gate
Maison de la Ferme
Farm House
GRAND
PARC
Arable
Terres labourables
Wootton Wood
North Lodge
Loge du Nord
Akeman Street
Chemin d'Akeman
Porte de Ditchley
Ditchley Gate
Bois de Wootton.
Pillar
GREAT PARK
Arable
Terres labourables
Porte de Votton
Wootton Gate
WOOTTON
Explication
Explanation.
i Entrée Triomphale — Triumphal Gate
k Maison du Poète Chaucer — Chaucer's House
l Dépendances de la Ferme — Farm appendages
m Eglise — Church
n Hotel de Ville — Town Hall
o Porte d'Hensington — Hensington Gate
p Faisanderie — Pheasantry
q Galerie de Porcelaine de Chine — China Gallery
AB A View of the Palace, and effect of mist. Pl. II.
CB A View of the Palace, at sunset. Pl. III.
800 900 1000 Mètres.
400 500 Fathoms.
AUD ARCHITECTE.
Lith. de Thierry Frères

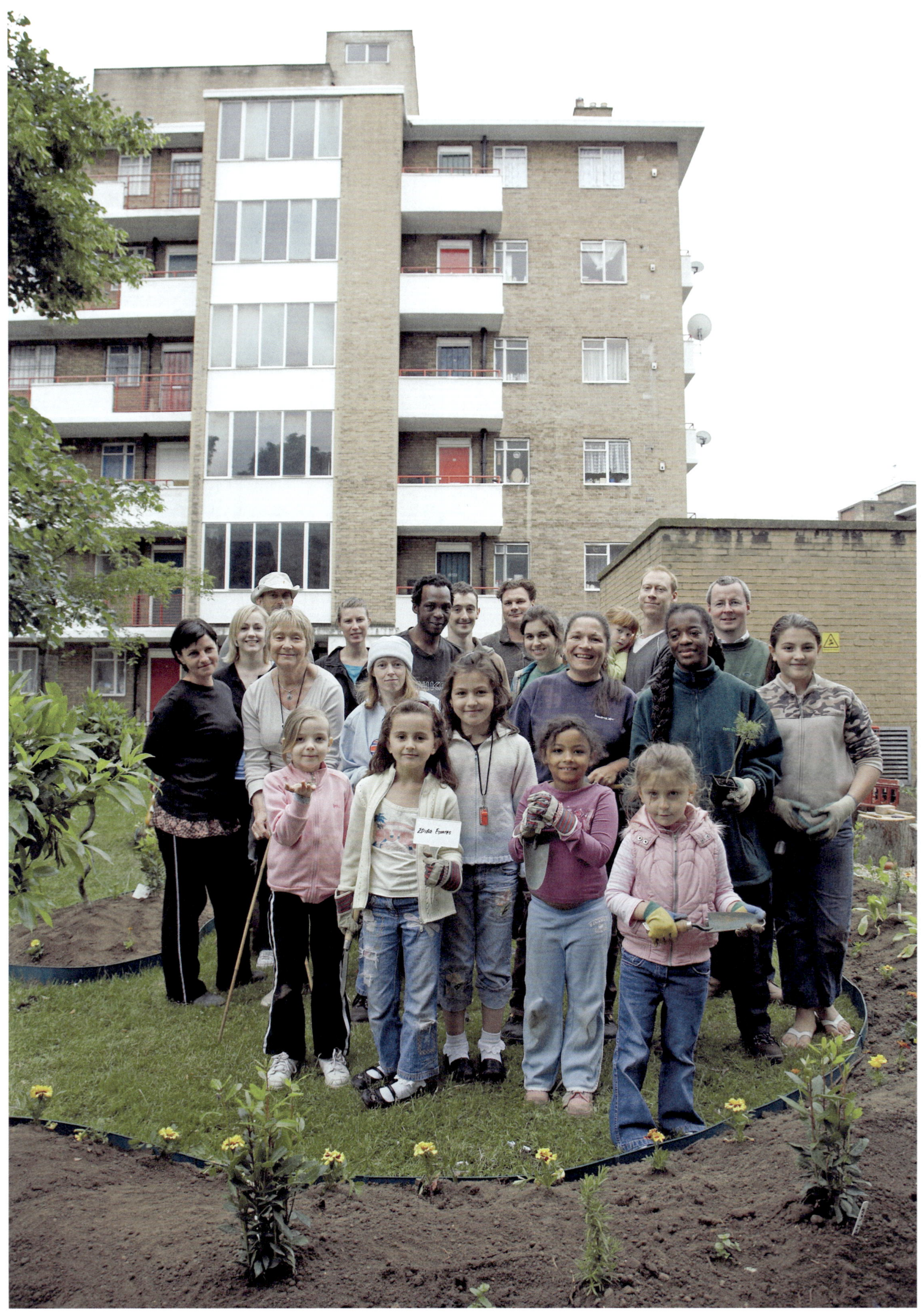

Fritz Haeg, **Edible Estates Regional Prototype Garden**, 2007, installation view. Courtesy Fritz Haeg. Photo: Heiko Prigge.

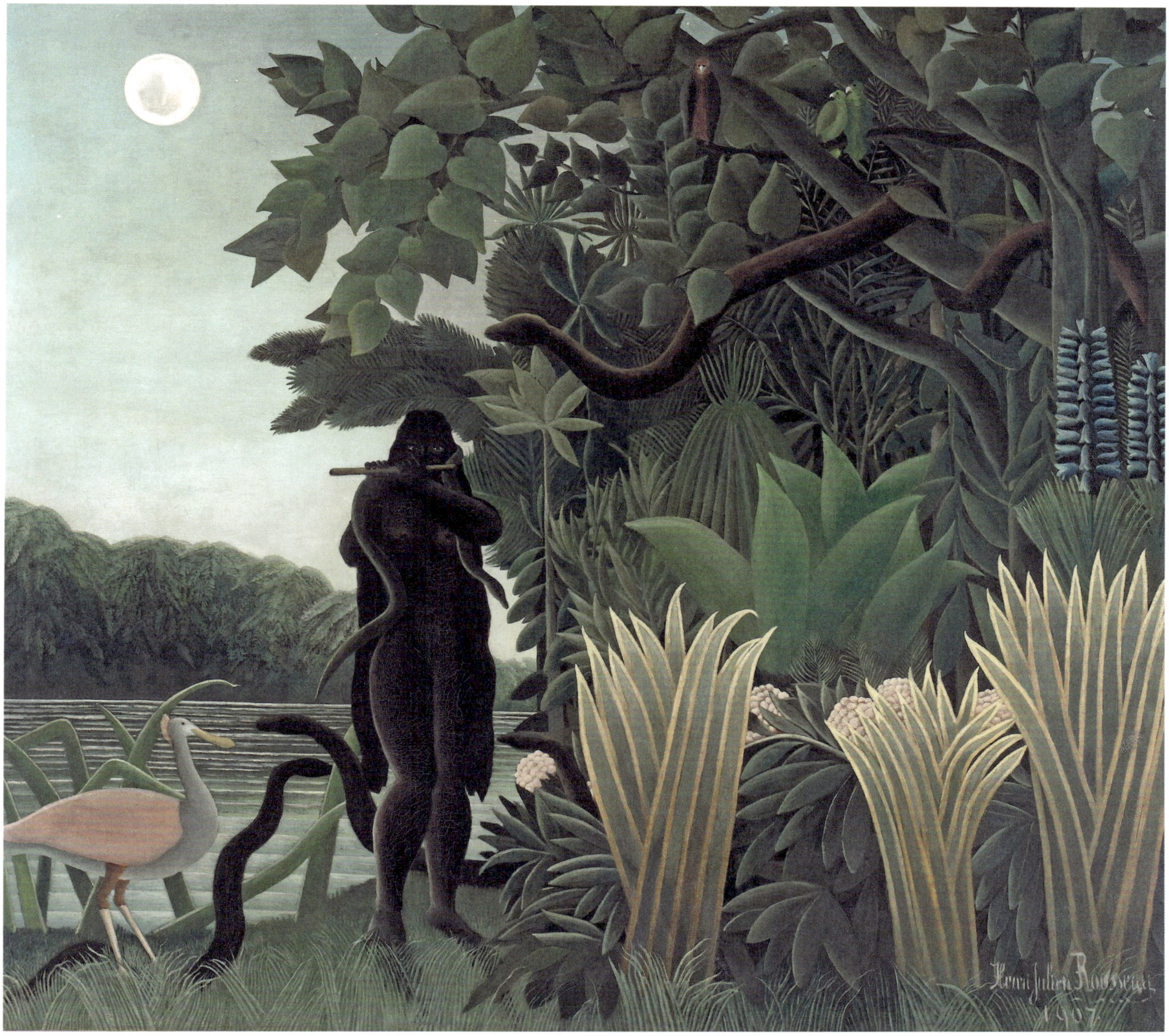

Henri Rousseau, **La Charmeuse de Serpents**, 1907, oil on canvas, 169 × 190 cm. Courtesy RMN-Grand Palais (Musée d'Orsay). Photo: Hervé Lewandowski.

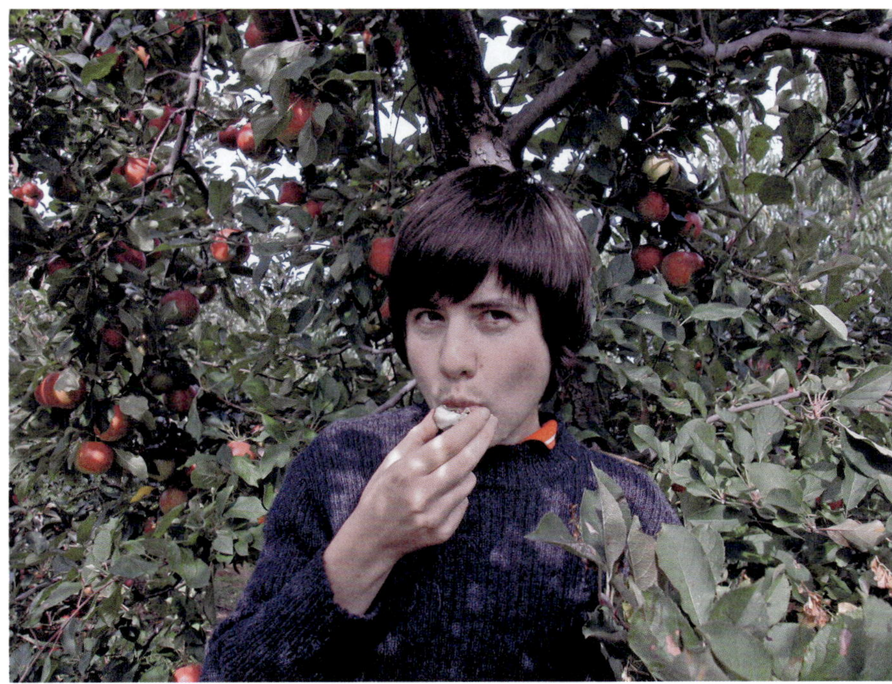

Yael Bartana, **My sister Eva**, 2004, c-print, 42.2 × 57.2 cm. Courtesy Yael Bartana, Collection De Bruin-Heijn and Annet Gelink Gallery, Amsterdam.

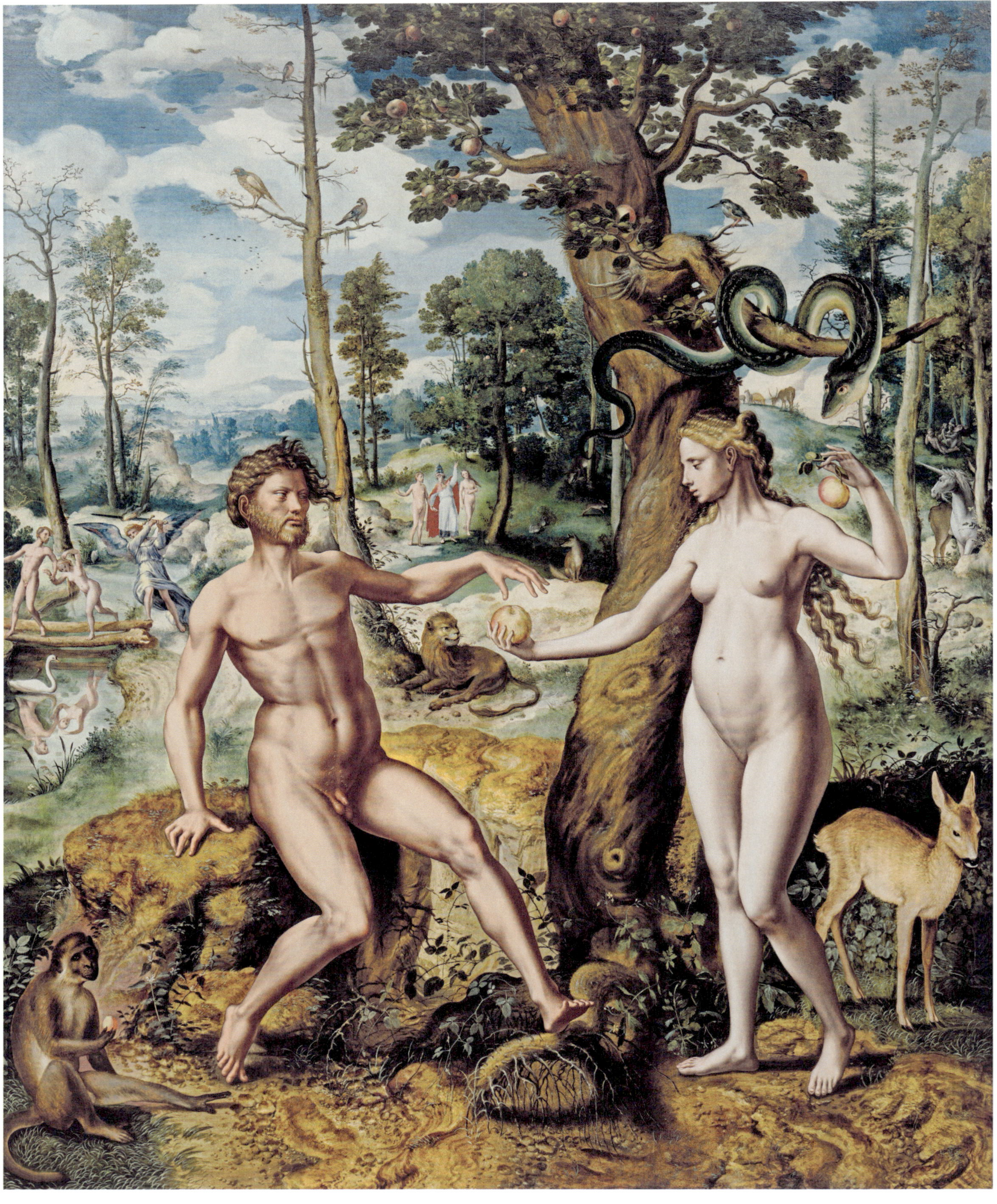

The Master of Paulus and Barnabas, **The Fall**, c. 1550–1560, oil on panel, 200 × 168 cm. Courtesy Bonnefantenmuseum, Maastricht.

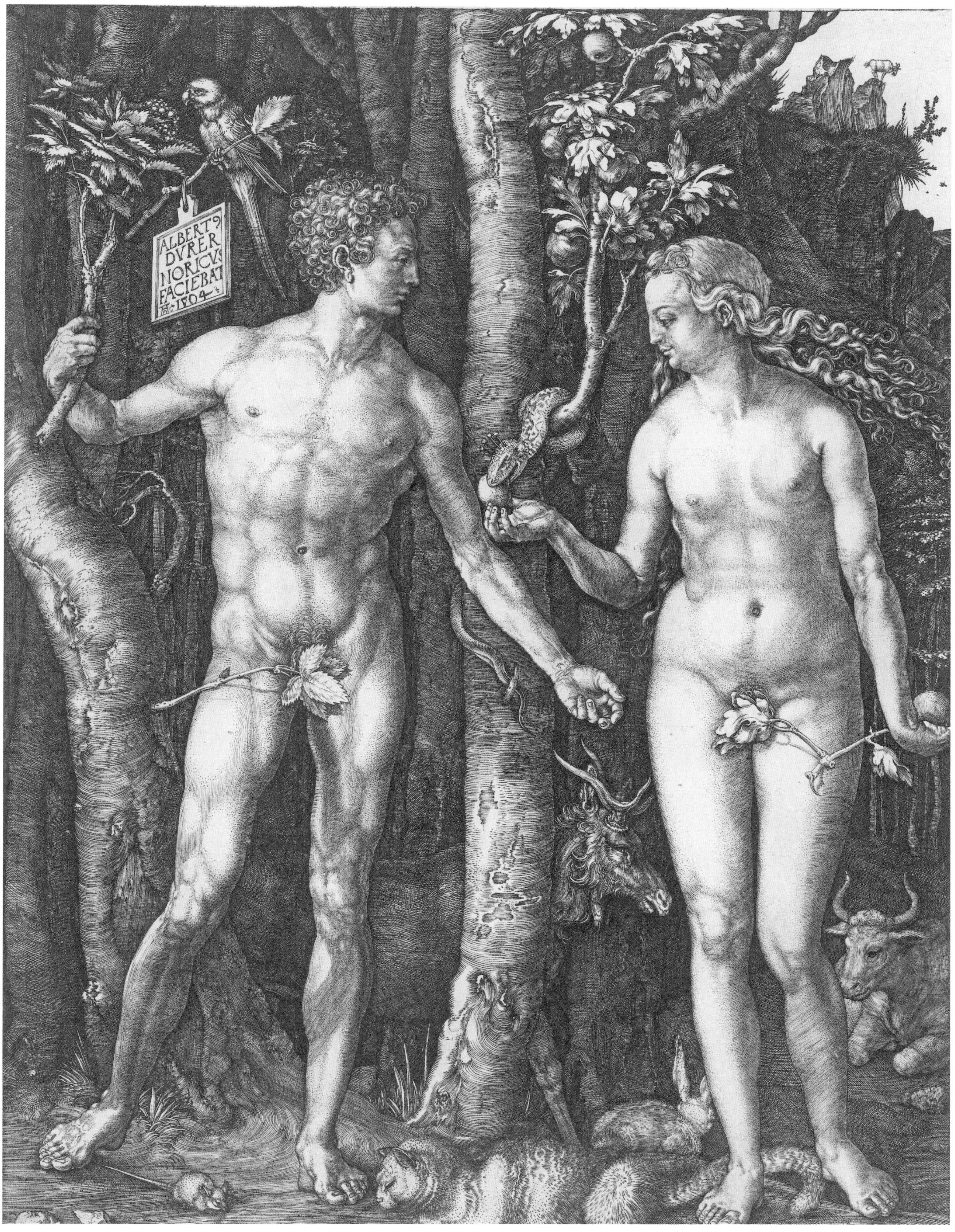

Albrecht Dürer, **Adam and Eve**, 1504, engraving, 25.1 × 19.2 cm. Courtesy Rijksmuseum Amsterdam.

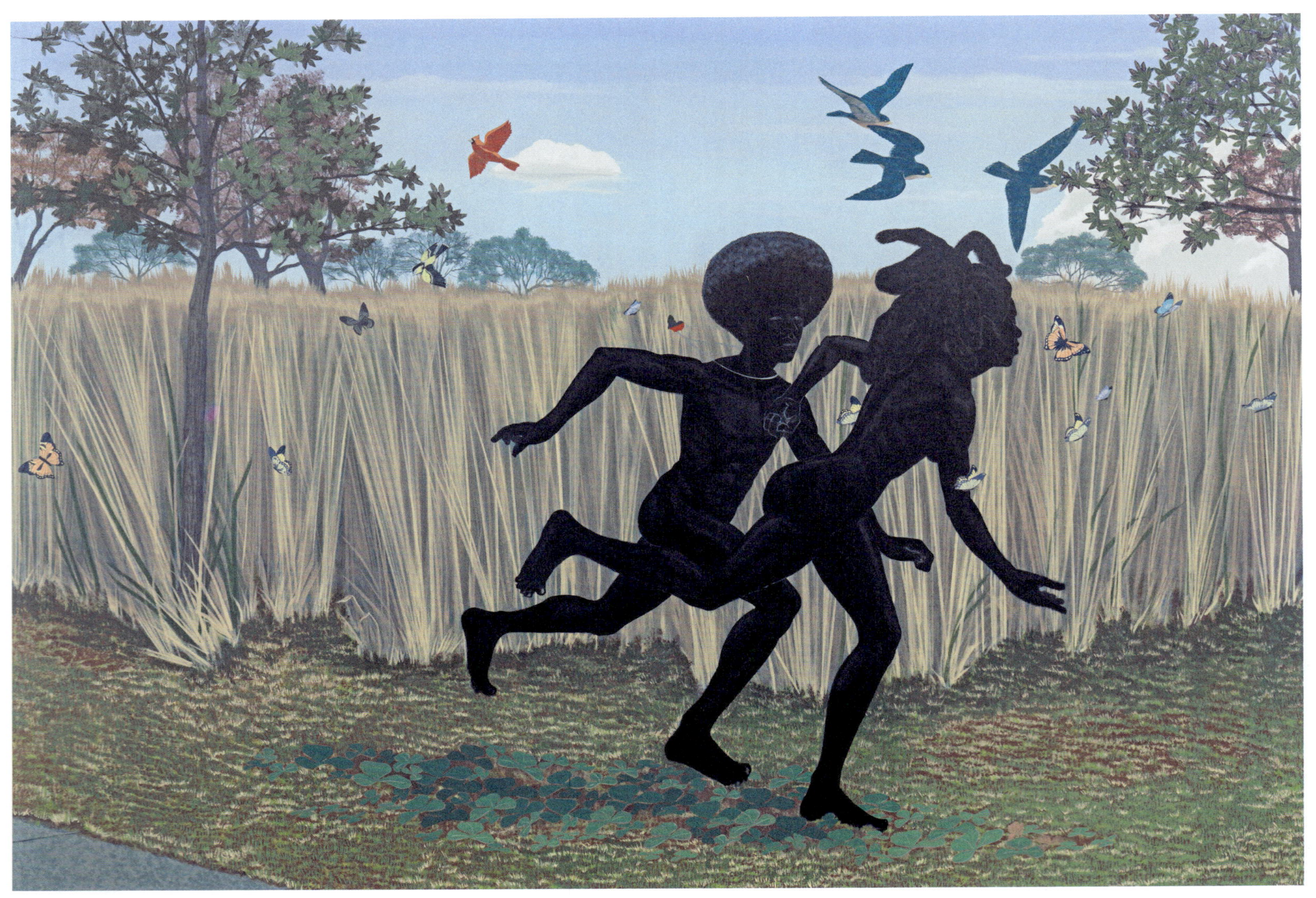

Kerry James Marshall, **Vignette**, 2003, acrylic on fiberglass, 182.9 × 274.3 cm. Courtesy Defares Collection.

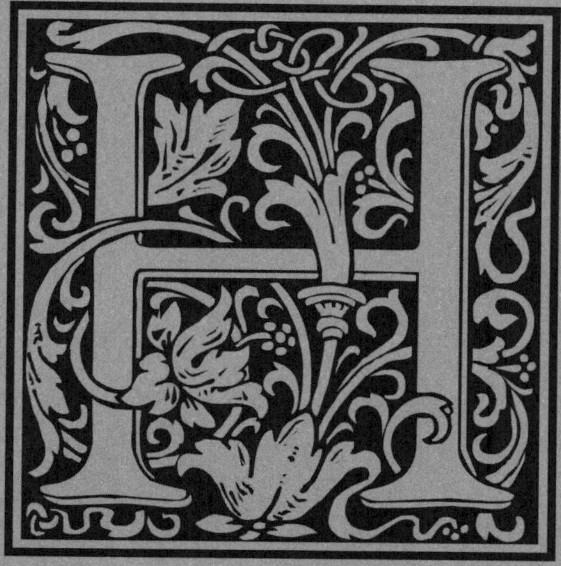

William Morris, **Letter H.**

HA-HA

Maria Barnas

ha-ha is a construction in landscape architecture where a wall is hidden in a dry moat. Originally, these sunken walls were used to mark boundaries or to stop intruders. From the eighteenth century onwards, ha-has were built mainly for aesthetic reasons. Usually the ditch has a slope on one side and a retaining wall on the other, against the higher ground. Since the ditch, slope, and wall are all low, the view of the garden from your country house is uninterrupted, making the grounds appear infinite.

It could be that I take myself too seriously
it could be that I take it could be that I
right here it could be I. I don't rule out

escaping into words when the time comes
to do something. It's surely no coincidence
that I'm searching for a synonym for action.

I could blame my evasive behaviour on
my upbringing or all the readers
the book a mask the lyrical I: no

I can't go outside because I am reading.
I'd rather read about gardening than do stuff
in the garden while I have a garden and hands

and feet to dig ditches and holes but instead
I muster up my courage on a deckchair beneath
a tree and read all about *ha-has*. Take

pleasure in seeing a country estate sparkle
on the square of lawn squeezed between hedges
and fences of the ever-bustling garden of
tranquillity

and the neighbour who peers through the bushes
he put there to stop children and other riff-raff
to see if I ever plant non-native species or allow

them as weeds. As calmly as I can, I leaf through
Gardening through the Centuries. The grass
begins to smoulder beneath my feet

I am raging with garden-of-tranquillity visitors
and guards I burn because I don't know how
to heave myself over the hedge what am I to

do with a weak mirror in a garden within a garden.
And me—dug out to make the view from
the country house look more attractive

to the pale shape lingering at the
window—I lie holding my breath
to give the impression of unobstructed

depths. And I lie there. Roll
myself in a sigh in the earth that brings
forth squirming life. My sigh?

Look, the worms are already nourishing
the soil. But who thinks of life
beside a hole in the shape of this 'I'.

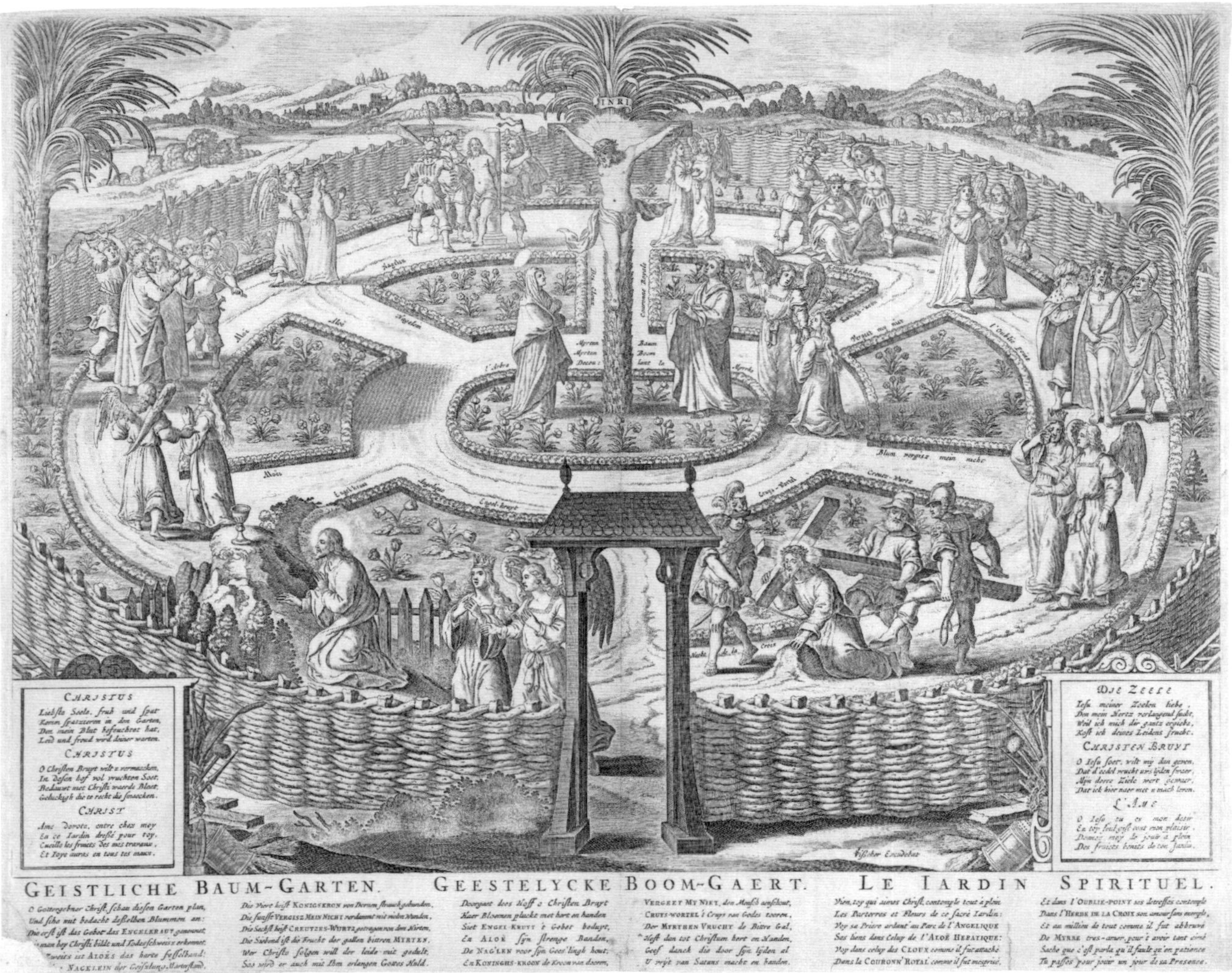

Anonymous, **Le Jardin Spirituel**, c. 1650, etching on paper, 40.8 × 53.5 cm. Courtesy Rijksmuseum Amsterdam.

HORTUS CONCLUSUS

There are no walls or fences. My garden's boundaries are the horizon. In this desolate landscape the silence is only broken by thewind, and the gulls squabbling round the fishermen bringing in the afternoon catch.

Jarman, *Modern Nature*, 3.

The hortus conclusus is the garden topos that most overtly identifies the garden as a female space; an association that plays a particularly pivotal role in the gardens of medieval romances. The image of the hortus conclusus is derived from the fourth chapter of the Song of Solomon in the Old Testament. […] in the dialogue between the bridegroom and his bride, the beauty of the garden is equated with the body of the bride, and in the fourth chapter of the text, the bridegroom declares:

'A garden enclosed (hortus conclusus) is my sister, my spouse; a spring shut up, a fountain sealed. Thy plants are an orchard of pomegranates with pleasant fruits; camphire, with spikenard, Spikenard and saffron; calamus and cinnamon, with all trees of frankincense; myrrh and aloes, with all the chief spices: A fountain of gardens, a well of living waters, and streams from Lebanon' (Song of Solomon 4:12–16).

Leslie, *A Cultural History of Gardens in the Medieval Age*, 120.

The hortus conclusus unites within itself a marvellous assemblage of disparate aspects. It seeks to understand the landscape it denies, explain the world it excludes, bring in the nature it fears and summarize all this in an architectural composition. The ingredients of this newly-appointed space laboratory for landscape architecture are to be found in its architectural, literary and landscape archetypes. The literary archetype of paradise presides over the interpretation of its landscape and architectural imagery, generating a tensionality between representation and reality.

Aben and De Wit, *The Enclosed Garden*, 22.

In the fourteenth century the Generalife was built as a summer palace across from the Alhambra, complete with orchards, farmland, gardens, farm animals and horses for riding. In the villa complex can be found a pleasure garden, the Patio de la Acequia (Court of the Long Pool). The Patio de la Acequia contains ingredients that would keep returning in different proportions in the physical transformations of the hortus conclusus: the enclosing framework in which zenith and horizon—vertical and horizontal alignment—engage in a game together.

Aben and De Wit, *The Enclosed Garden*, 70.

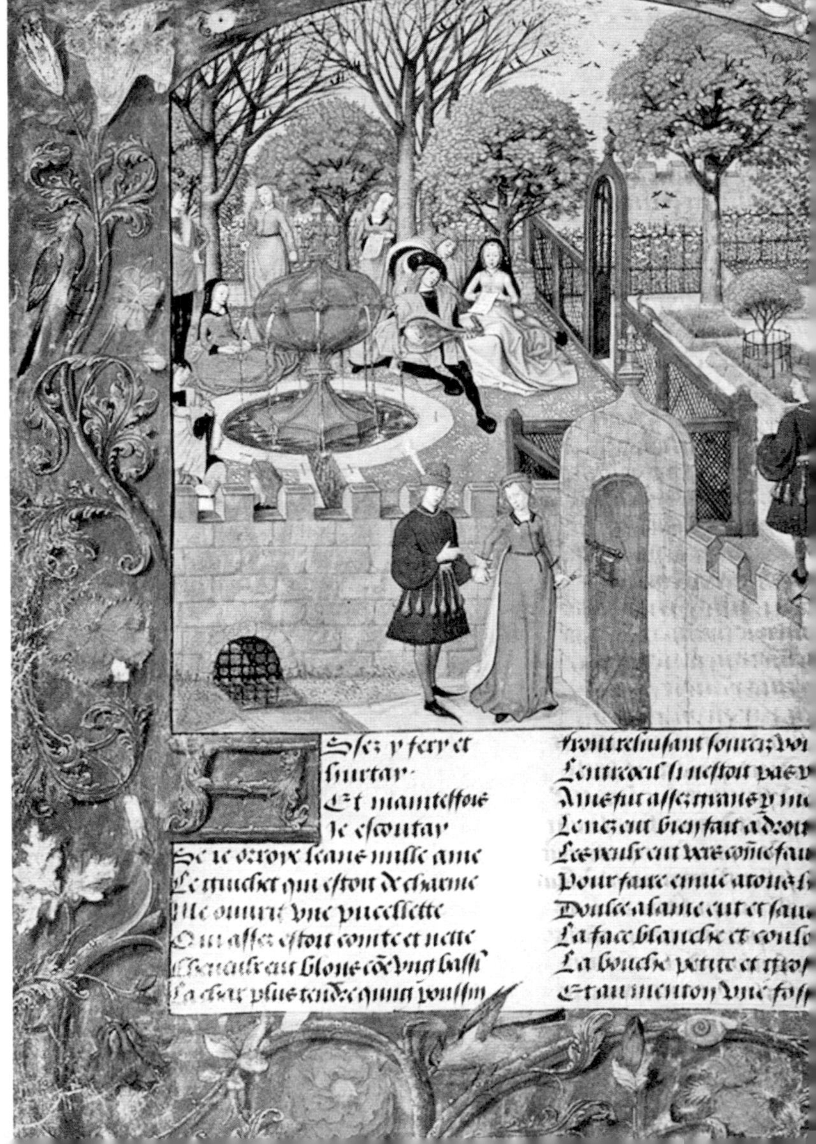

Guillaume de Lorris and Jean de Meun, **Lutenist and singers in a walled garden** from **Roman de la Rose**, 1490–1500, manuscript.

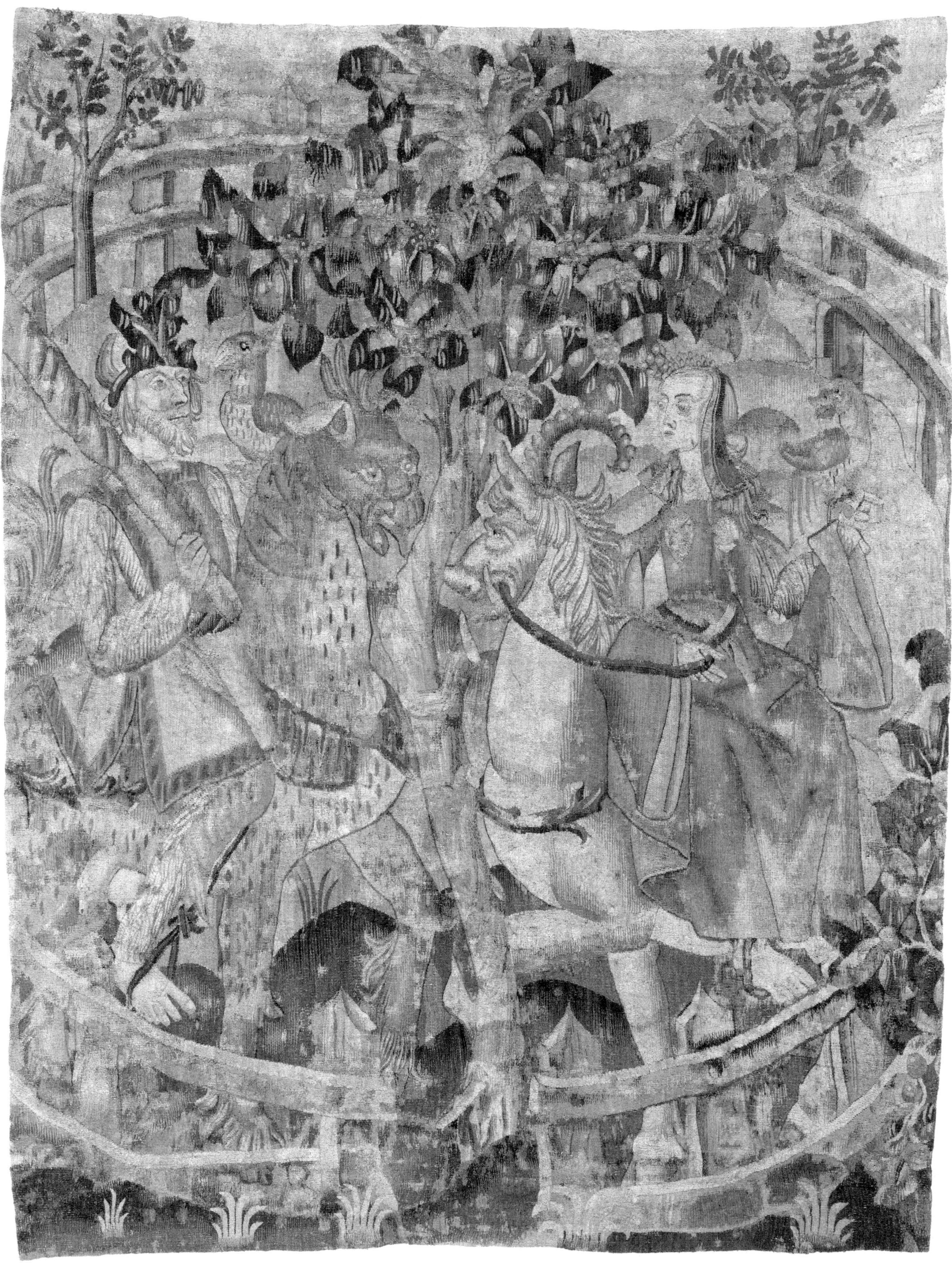

Anonymous, **A wild man and woman in a private garden** (fragment), c. 1500–1520, tapestry, 267 × 203 cm. Courtesy Rijksmuseum Amsterdam.

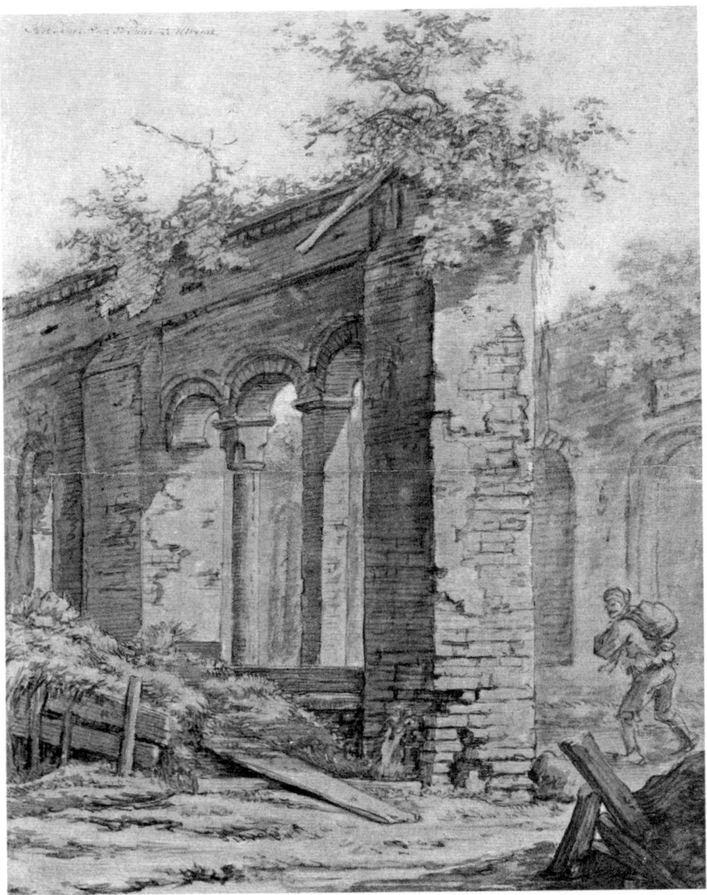

Herman Saftleven, **Het Pandt. van St. Pieter te Utrecht**, 1650–1680, drawing, 51 × 38.5 cm. Courtesy Het Utrechts Archief.

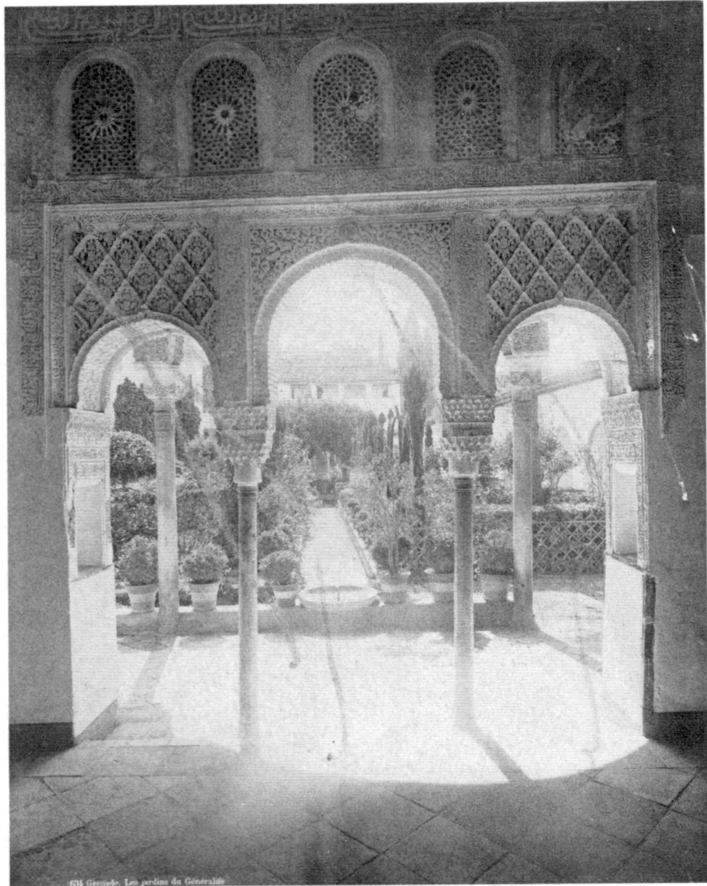

Anonymous Granada, **Les Jardins du Généralife**, c. 1875–1900, albumen print, 28 × 22 cm. Courtesy Rijksmuseum Amsterdam.

This feeling of inclusion derives in part from being in an enclosed space marked by borders. It is primarily a garden's perimeter that sets it apart, that gives shape and delineation to its living form (I call it a 'living form' because, whatever else they may do, gardens conjugate life and form). Almost all the words for 'garden' in world languages have etymons linked to the idea of fence or boundary. A garden is literally defined by its boundaries. However, while the latter provide demarcation and definition, they are for the most part relative. By that I mean they keep the garden intrinsically related to the world that they keep at a certain remove. [...]

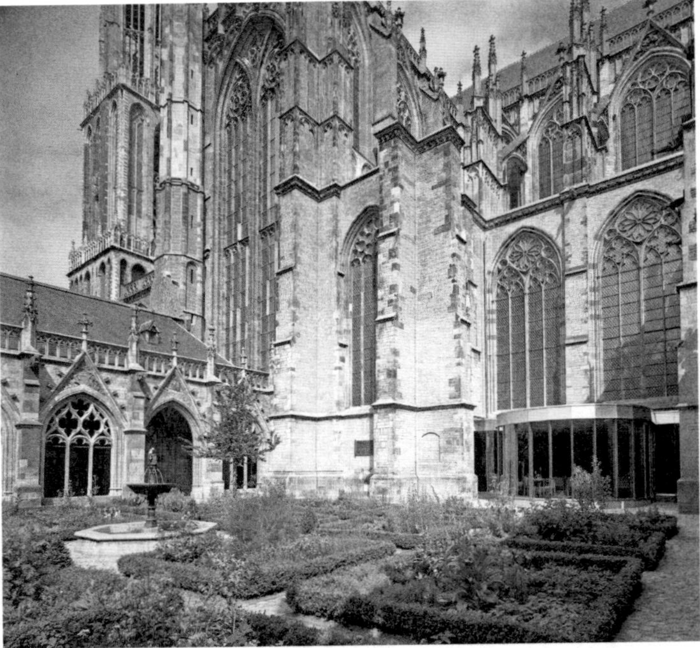

View of the Domkerk (Domplein) in Utrecht, from the pandhof. Courtesy Het Utrechts Archief. Photo: Fotodienst HUA, 1988.

An essential tension is lost when gardens do not have porous, even promiscuous openings onto the world beyond their bounds. (Maybe this was the trouble with Eden—it did not have pressing in on its edges an outside world to define its limits, so our primal parents sought out the only limit that was available to them, to supply the place with a measure of reality.) The Campana poem, with its evocations of distance and urban surroundings, suggests that the inspirational power of gardens—or at least of certain kinds of gardens—owes as much to the permeability as to the consistency of their boundaries. Isolate them completely and you take away their havenlike character. Who would immure our great municipal gardens? What would the Jardin de Luxembourg be without the fence and open gateways that both distinguish it from and connect it to the Parisian swirl around it? When Thoreau went to Walden to cultivate his patch of ground, he placed himself strategically 'a mile from any neighbor'. Take away its relationship to the civic life around it and Walden—a still point of nineteenth-century American thought—would lose the tension that informs it. Gardens are vital to the degree that they open their enclosures in the midst of history, offering a measure of seclusion that is not occlusion.

Harrison, *Gardens*, 56–57.

HÜGELKULTUR

Hügelkultur is a German term meaning hillock or mound cultivation. It is a method of building garden and landscape beds using woody material, garden debris, and soil arranged in long, tunnel-shaped mounds. Since these beds are three dimensional, they create additional space for growing plants.

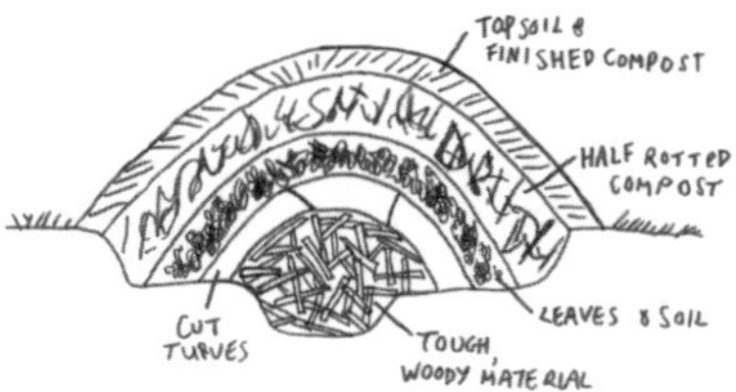

In fact, the term [Hügelkultur] first appears in a 1962 German brochure written by avid gardener Herrman Andrä. In this brochure, Andrä describes the diversity of plants found growing in the woody debris pile in the corner of his grandmother's garden. This observation inspired him to promote mound culture, or Hügelkultur, as an alternative to 'flatland culture'. This method was also a useful way to dispose of woody debris, the burning of which was prohibited.

Chalker-Scott, 'Hugelkultur', 2.

HUMUS

'Humus', the original component of soil, has the same root as 'human'. Humans are the earthy ones; they originate from soil. Departing from non-anthropocentric thinking and taking humus as a lens for being-in-the-world, possibilities emerge for recognizing new sets of relations and new ways of make life habitable, even as un-liveability spreads. Humus can inspire the cultivation of collective and collaborative responses against fierce competition and regressive individualism. With humus, humans can elaborate strategies to rebuild 'a world that contains other worlds', rather than excluding those worlds and ideas that do not align with dominant views. As Donna Haraway wrote: 'We are compost, not posthuman.'

Romakin and Saracino, 'Humus'.

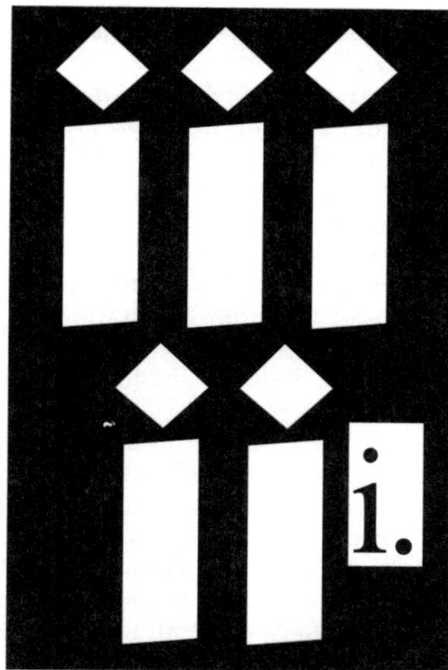

IBN LUYŪN

Ibn Luyūn (b. 681/1282–3, d. 750/1349) was a jurist, teacher, poet, and Andalusian writer of compendiums from Almería, who devoted his life to teaching and to summarising or abridging various works for the purposes of teaching and the transmission of knowledge. He is famous for his agricultural handbook in verse.

Vidal-Castro, 'Ibn Luyūn'.

Then next to the reservoir plant shrubs whose leaves do not fall and which rejoice the sight; and, somewhat further off, arrange flowers of different kinds, and further off still, evergreen trees. And around the perimeter climbing vines, and in the centre of the whole enclosure a sufficiency of vines; and under climbing vines let there be paths which surround the garden to serve as a margin. And amongst the fruit trees include the grapevine… [also] arrange the virgin soil for planting whatever you wish should prosper. In the background let there be trees like the fig or any other which does no harm; and any fruit tree which grows big, plant it in a confining basin so that its mature growth may serve as a protection against the north wind without preventing the sun from reaching [the plants]. In the centre of the garden let there be a pavilion in which to sit, and with vistas on all sides, but of such a form that no one approaching could overhear the conversation within and whereunto none could approach undetected. Clinging to it let there be [rambler] roses and myrtle, likewise all manner of plants with which a garden is adorned.

Ibn Luyūn, *Fundamentals of the Art of Agriculture*. Cited in Grabar, *The Alhambra*, 123.

INGISOPO (SR)

Furcraea foetida is a plant in the asparagus family *(Asparagaceae)*, native to the Caribbean and northern South America. It is now widespread throughout the tropical and subtropical regions in the Americas, Asia, Africa, Europe, and Oceania.

Historically, the plant's strong fibres have been used to make rope. In many places, it is known as Mauritius Hemp, a somewhat misleading appellation because the plant is neither native to Mauritius—it was introduced there in the eighteenth century—nor related to hemp, which is in the Cannabaceae family.

In Suriname, the Caribs call the plant 'mola', and in Sranan Tongo, the English-based creole that is the lingua franca for much of the country's population, it is known as 'ingisopo', meaning 'Indian soap'. The plant has many different uses there, including in Winti religious rituals and as a remedy for stomach pain and uterine problems. The sap from the fleshy leaves is used as soap to disinfect the hands after cleaning fish, and the whole plant is used as a rack for drying clothes.

More than thirty ingisopo plants have been found in a field in the flooded forests on the Anna's Zorg (Anna's Care) former plantation in the Commewijne district. The locals have no explanation for its prevalence there. According to the almanacs, the site has long been abandoned. It is remarkable, however, that the ingisopo plants are located not behind the historical dike on the plantations, but before it on a densely wooded stretch of the Warappa Creek, which was re-opened only in 2008 after decades of poor maintenance. This implies that the field is probably not very old, since it was under water just over a decade ago.

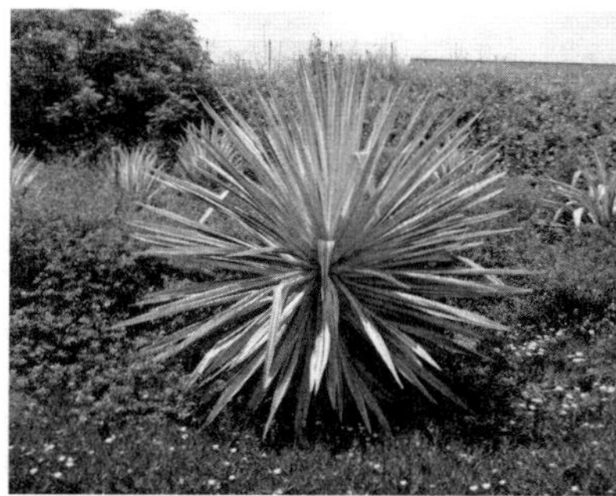

The plant also grew in various spots in Nieuw-Lombé, a 'Maroon' village along the Suriname River, where the locals recall that their ancestors used it and knew about its use as a disinfectant soap. They also dried the leaves in the sun for its fibres. The plant is also grown extensively in Paramaribo, mainly as an ornamental plant. Furcraea foetida now has a wide range of uses among varied groups in Suriname.

Thiëmo Heilbron

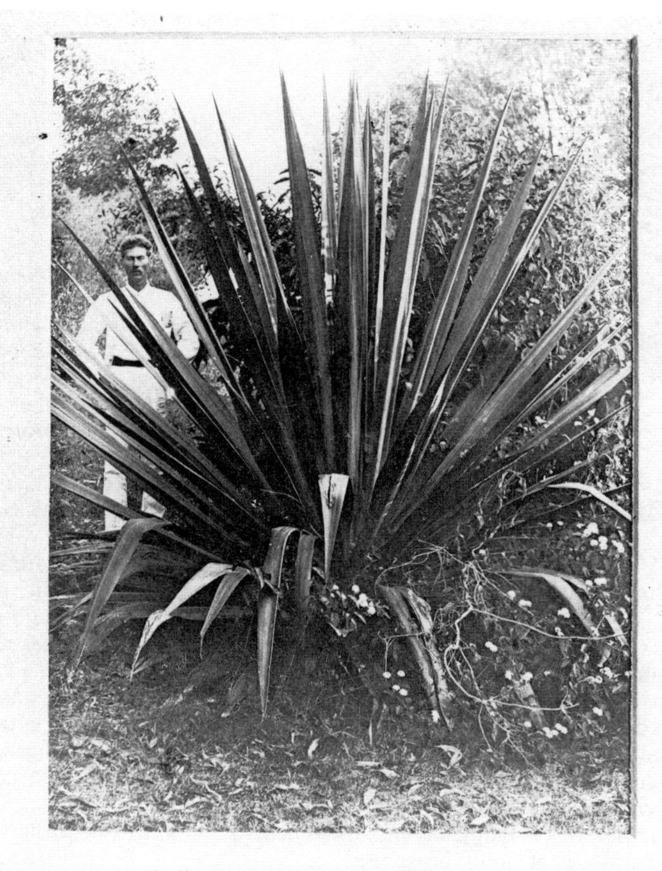

Mauritius Hemp, Botanic Gardens, Port Darwin, Northern Territory, c. 1905.

INVASIVE SPECIES

Foreign plants that alter the balance of local plants and animals.

Spaid, *Ecovention*, 146.

Invasive species, also called introduced species, alien species, or exotic species, any nonnative species that significantly modifies or disrupts the ecosystems it colonizes. Such species may arrive in new areas through natural migration, but they are often introduced by the activities of other species. Human activities, such as those involved in global commerce and the pet trade, are considered to be the most common ways invasive plants, animals, microbes, and other organisms are transported to new habitats.

Most introduced species do not survive extended periods in new habitats, because they do not possess the evolutionary adaptations to adjust to the challenges posed by their new surroundings. Some introduced species may become invasive when they possess a built-in competitive advantage over indigenous species in invaded areas. Under these circumstances, new arrivals can establish breeding populations and thrive, especially if the ecosystem lacks natural predators capable of keeping them in check. The ecological disruption that tends to follow such invasions often reduces the ecosystem's biodiversity and causes economic harm to people who depend on the ecosystem's biological resources. Invasive predators may be so adept at capturing prey that prey populations decline over time, and many prey species are eliminated from affected ecosystems. Other invasive species, in contrast, may prevent native species from obtaining food, living space, or other resources. Over time, invading species can effectively replace native ones, often forcing the localized extinction of many native species. Invasive plants and animals may also serve as disease vectors that spread parasites and pathogens that may further disrupt invaded areas.

Encyclopaedia Britannica, 'Invasive Species'.

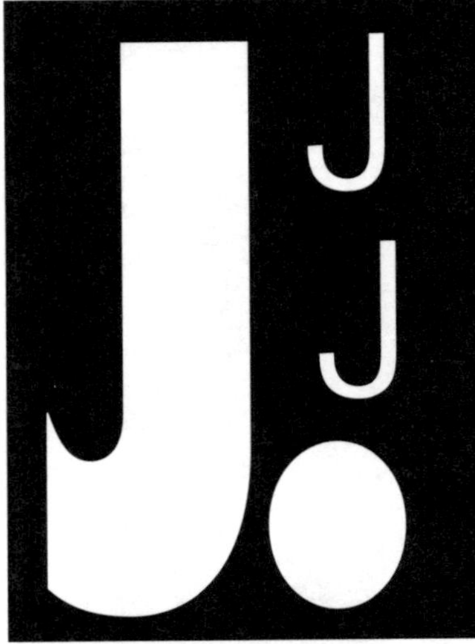

JARMAN, PROSPECT COTTAGE

Here at the sea's edge
I have planted my dragon toothed garden
To defend the porch,
Steadfast warriors
Against those who protest their impropriety
Even to the end of the world.
A fathomless lethargy has swallowed me,
Great waves of doubt broke me,
All my thoughts washed away.
The storms have blown salt tears,
Burning my garden,
Gethsemane and Eden.

Jarman, *Derek Jarman's Garden*, 82.

I walk in this garden
Holding the hands of dead friends.
Old age came quickly for my frosted generation,
Cold, cold, cold, they died so silently.
Did the forgotten generations scream
Or go full of resignation,
Quietly protesting innocence?
I have no words,
My shaking hand cannot express my fury.
Cold, cold, cold, they died so silently.

Linked hands at 4 a.m.,
Deep under the city you slept on,
Never heard the sweet flesh song.
Cold, cold, cold, they died so silently.

Matthew fucked Mark fucked Luke fucked John
Who lay in the bed that I lie on,
Touch fingers again as you sing this song.
Cold, cold, cold, we die so silently.

My gilly flowers, roses, violet blue,
Sweet garden of vanished pleasures,
Please come back next year.
Cold, cold, cold, I die so silently.

Goodnight boys, goodnight Johnny,
Goodnight, goodnight.

Jarman, *Derek Jarman's Garden*, 81.

In 1987, Derek Jarman bought a former fisherman's cottage on Dungeness Beach in Kent. It's a wild, bleak place: in one direction, a nuclear power station looms like a portent of doom; in the other, infinity is intimated in the slate-grey waves of the English Channel. The year before he bought Prospect Cottage, the artist, activist and filmmaker was diagnosed with HIV. Writing in the catalogue accompanying this exhibition, Jarman's friend, the photographer Howard Sooley, recalls: 'He cheated death hiding among the flowers and dancing with the bees.' Jarman painted the walls of his new home tar black and its window frames buttercup yellow. Refusing to be cowed by the inhospitable terrain, he cultivated plants that could withstand the shingle and the fierce, salty winds and bloom brightly: alexanders, foxgloves, periwinkle, poppies, purple iris, sea kale, viper's bugloss and others. His garden was as much a metaphor for memory and hope as it was earth and plants. In his memoir *Modern Nature* (1991), he recalls: 'Flowers spring up and entwine themselves like bindweed along the footpaths of my childhood.'

Higgie, 'Derek Jarman's Garden'.

DERK ALBERTS
The series of black-and-white photographs by Derk Alberts shows Derek Jarman's garden at Prospect Cottage in the broader context of the landscape of Dungeness, a headland on the Kent coast in southern England that is an extensive wilderness of pebbles. Albert's photographs show the extraordinary convergence of vegetation and improvised sculptures, as well as the context of Dungeness's vast and improbable landscape. Through a condensation of visual elements, Alberts achieves an attentiveness that seems to capture more than just the physical characteristics of this garden; as if the genius loci haunts this place—where there are no gods, ghosts reign. In the Middle Ages, the walled monastery garden, the *hortus conclusus*, was seen as a microcosm, 'a closed circuit, in which man is invulnerable, and full of magical-erotic potential'. Jarman's garden had no wall or fence; the horizon was its boundary. (ed.)

GERTRUDE JEKYLL

Throughout her life, Gertrude Jekyll used her garden at Munstead Wood, England, to experiment with new approaches to organizing and combining plants. The combinations of colours, textures and forms that she used in border plantings were particularly successful with regard to foundation plantings and entry paths to homes on relatively small lots. The design strategies and plant groupings she developed at Munstead Wood were enormously popular and through her many publications, influenced the small individual gardens of the emerging middle class in England as well as Europe and North America.

Jacobs, 'Types of Gardens', 40.

Gardens were freed from the gentry. 'The charm of simplicity and directness' was within the compass of the middle class. It was Gertrude Jekyll who developed these ideals and brought them into a close, practical association with the various arts encompassed by the broader movement of the Arts and Crafts. Ambitious, nearsighted daughter of a wealthy middle-class family, Jekyll used her own gardens at Munstead Wood as a testing ground for the forceful theories of colour, mixed borders, massing, wild gardening, and plant craft she disseminated in her newspaper column, magazine writings, books, and correspondence. Her long collaborative partnership with the architect Edwin Lutyens focused on the materials and siting of traditional Surrey dwellings. Together they developed a design style that treated the garden as a structural extension and expression of the axes and massing of the house and its site. [...]

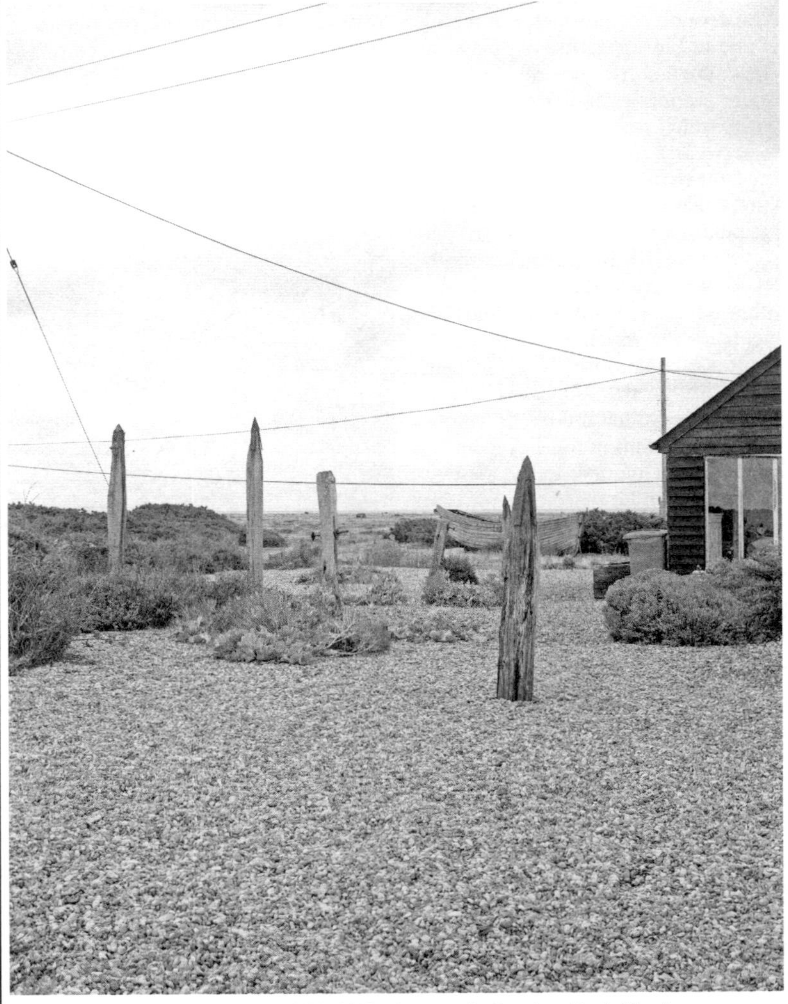

Derk Alberts, **Dungeness #14**, 2016, photograph. Courtesy Derk Alberts.

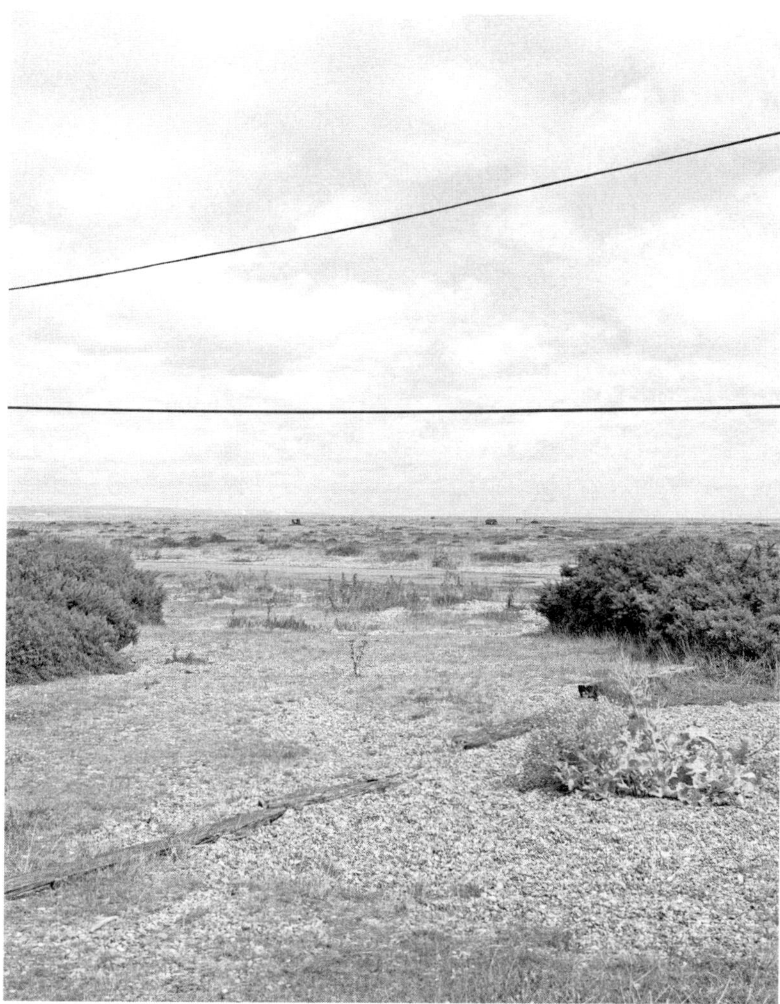
Derk Alberts, **Dungeness #10**, 2016, photograph. Courtesy Derk Alberts.

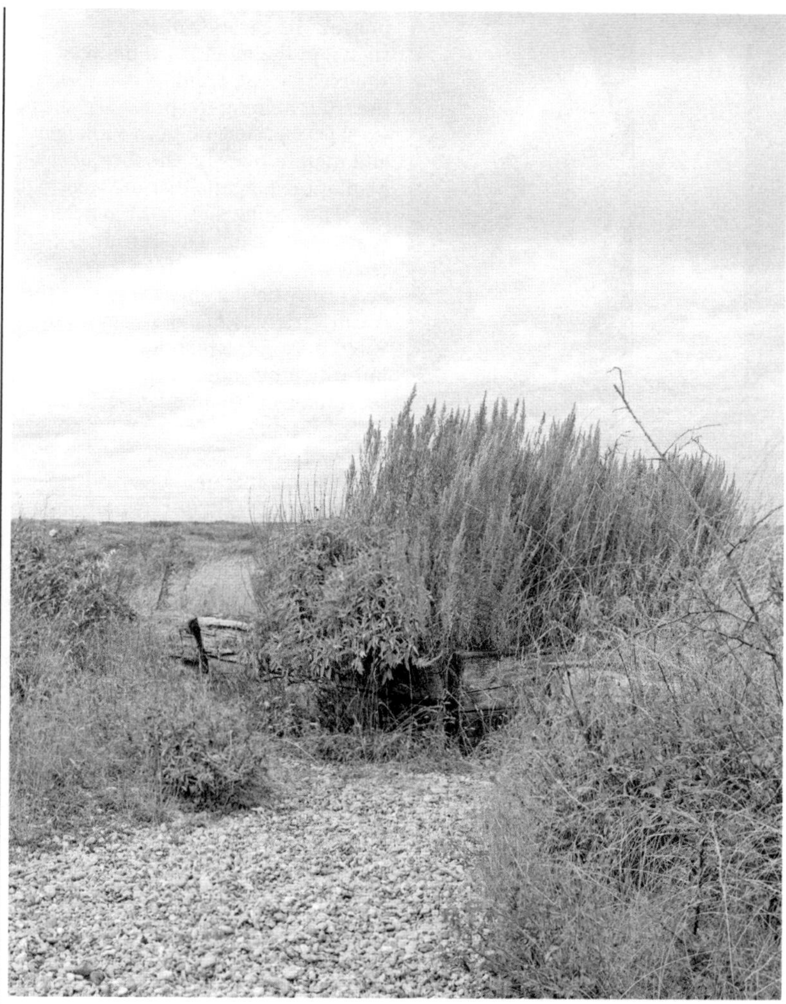
Derk Alberts, **Dungeness #9**, 2016, photograph. Courtesy Derk Alberts.

But her recurring concern was with the ephemeral retinal impact of colour, which she expressed with meticulous care in her writing.

> Perhaps the Grey garden is seen at its best by reaching it through the orange borders. Here the eye becomes filled and saturated with the strong red and yellow colouring. This filling with the strong, rich colouring has the natural effect of making the eye eagerly desirous for the complementary colour, so that, standing by the inner yew arch and suddenly turning to look into the grey garden, the effect is surprisingly—quite astonishingly—luminous and refreshing. One never knew before how vividly bright Ageratum could be, or Lavender, or Nepeta; even the grey-purple of Echinops appears to have a more positive colour than one's expectation would assign to it [...].
>
> Jekyll, *Colour Schemes for the Flower Garden*, 110.

The gardens Jekyll designed on her own, and with Lutyens, remarkably synthesized a range of regional and historical influences and aesthetic vocabularies to create a single stylistic image that continues to dominate popular notions of the English garden. Beginning their

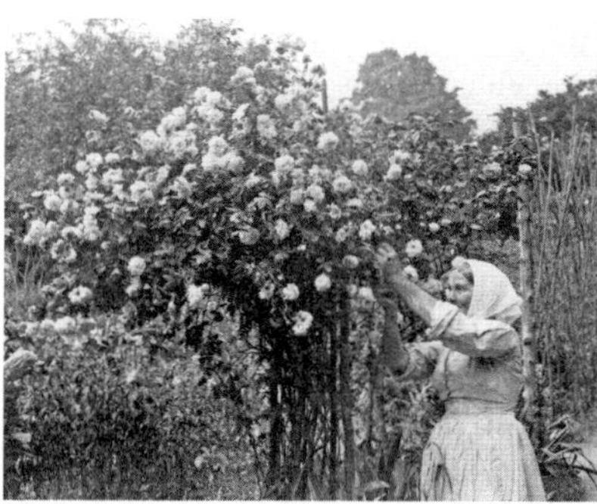
Gertrude Jekyll, **Mrs Edgeler and Her White Rosebush**, c. 1886, photograph, 20 × 15 cm. Courtesy Garden Museum, London.

design practise with the central precepts of Arts and Crafts philosophy—regional materials, vernacular styles, and holistic structural tropes—the two created an identifiable style whose formal integrity ironically could eclipse its own concern with regional context to become a highly marketable commodity, advertised through their commissions and Jekyll's writings, and those of their numerous followers, throughout Great Britain and in Ireland, France, and North America.

> Robertson, *Occasional Work*, 106–107.

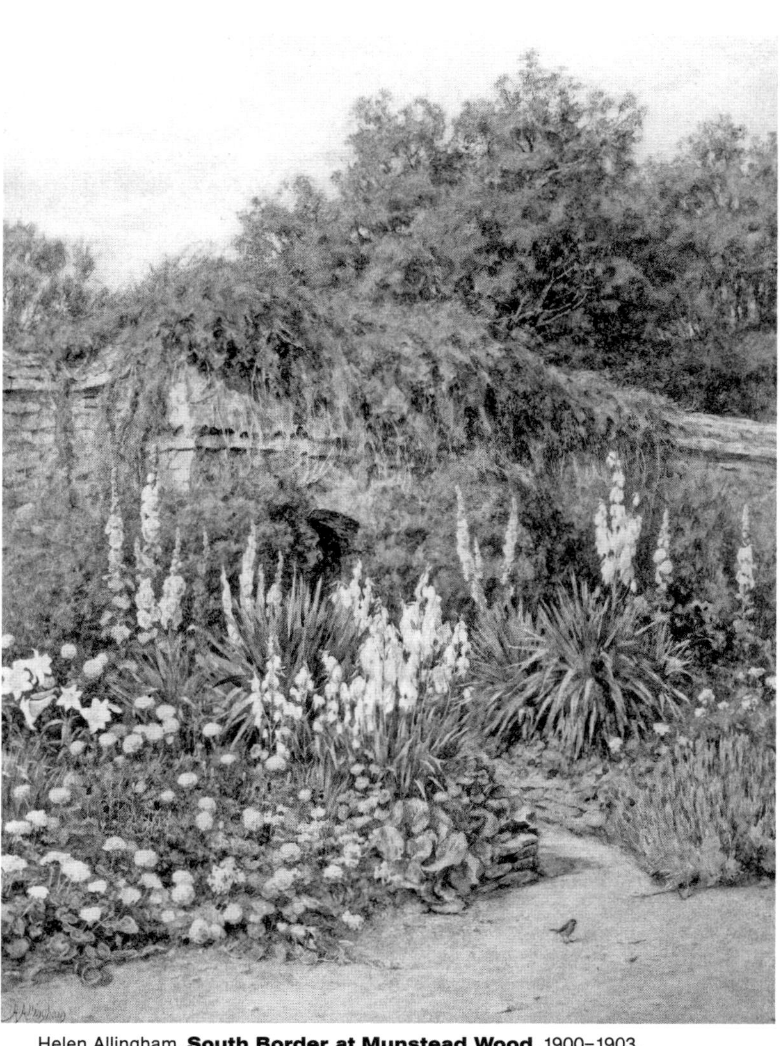
Helen Allingham, **South Border at Munstead Wood**, 1900–1903, watercolour painting, 40.5 × 29 cm. Courtesy Garden Museum, London.

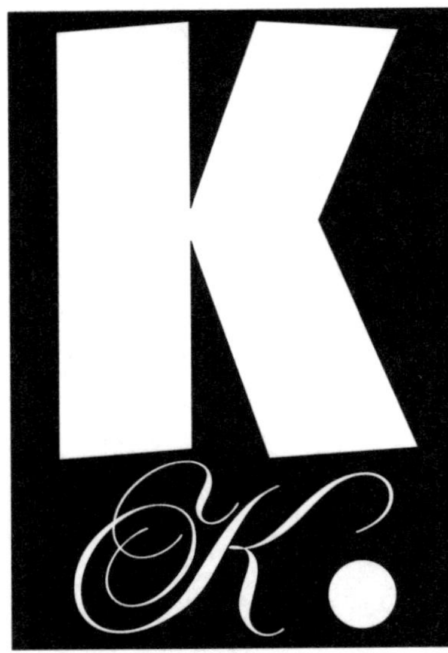

KAKAW (THEO-BROMA CACAO)

At first glance, the forest on the former Montpellier plantation in Suriname resembles conventional rainforest. However, exploring the terrain, it soon becomes apparent that there are numerous cacao trees amongst the rest of the vegetation. Amidst the re-grown rainforest is an old cacao plantation field! The exact age of the field is difficult to determine, though we know that the plantation has not been in production for more than a century and a half. The cocoa tree *(Theobroma cacao)* prefers the deep, fertile alluvial soils of river valleys, a shady, moist atmosphere with heavy annual rainfall and a high average temperature.

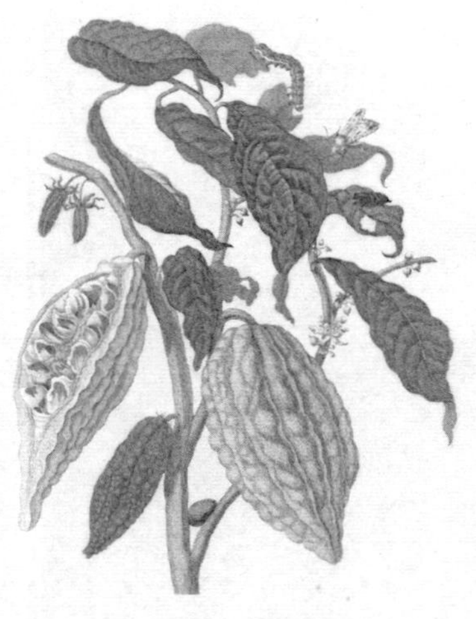

Maria Sibylla Merian, **Plate 26** from **Metamorphosis Insectorum Surinamensium**, 1705, watercolour drawing. Courtesy University of Utrecht.

The word 'cacao' is a Spanish adaptation of the Meso-American name for the plant. The Nahua people refer to it as 'cacaua-tl' and 'chocolatl'. Under cultivation, this shade-loving tree grows to a height of 4.5 to 7.5 metres. The fruits, which grow directly from the trunk and large branches (known as cauliflory, which, despite its similar name, has nothing to do with cauliflower), contain between twenty-five and forty-five seeds. In Meso-American images, the cacao fruits are often shown in the hands of a monkey, squirrel, or bat: animals that feast on the fruit, helping to spread the seeds.

The presence of both saplings and mature trees on the former plantation suggests that the trees are self-seeding and that the field is self-sustaining. The current residents, who have created an eco-resort on the site, know that the cacao variety is one that was cultivated during the plantation period, but which has now been supplanted by varieties with a higher yield and higher quality seeds (from which cocoa products are made).

It transpires that a cacao field on the Berlijn (Berlin) plantation is a remnant of a post-war planting, a reminder of a previous owner who sold the land after several bad harvests. The cacao variety grown there was a modern cultivar, so not every remnant of a cocoa field dates back to the plantation era. Nevertheless, the global consumption of cocoa is inseparable from the violence of production and trade during the colonial period.

Thiëmo Heilbron

KARESANSUI

Literally, 'dry-mountain-water'. Interpreted as 'dry landscape', *karesansui* has become a common Japanese garden form that uses gravel and stones to evoke flowing streams, waterfalls, ponds, the ocean or even consciousness. Originating from Shinto *kekkai* (cleared space within the forest), *karesansui* relies on the concept of *mitate* and is particularly associated with Zen Buddhism.

Walker, *The Japanese Garden*, 295.

KEW GARDENS

Just as women tried to smash the glass ceiling in horticulture, they also shattered horticultural glass ceilings to gain equality more broadly. On 8 February, 1913, suffragettes broke into Kew's much-loved orchid houses, broke some forty panes of glass and damaged the invaluable plants inside. Kew [Royal Botanic Garden at Kew in London] was as popular a tourist attraction in 1913 as it is now—luring some 3.8 million visitors between June and September that year—and the gardens' director had received warning of an imminent attack from the movement. The women acted in the early hours of the morning and got away with it, but poetically left behind a handkerchief and an envelope inscribed 'Votes for Women'.

News of the incident made global headlines and brought great awareness to the women's suffrage

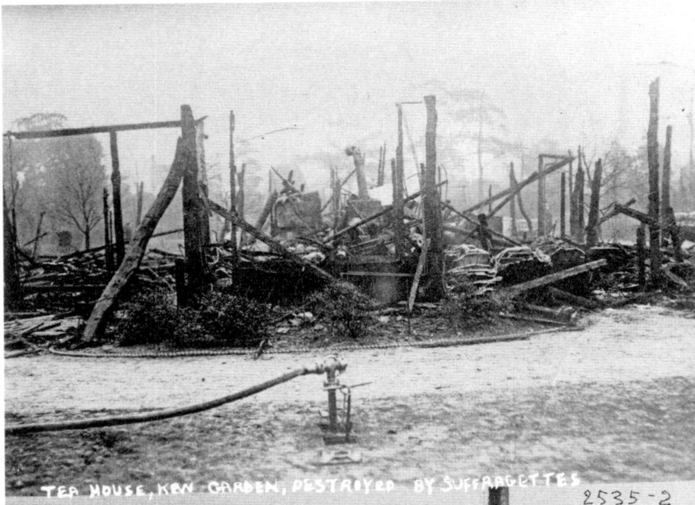

Bain News Service, **Tea House, Kew Gardens, destroyed by suffragettes**, 1913, glass negative, 12.7 × 17.8 cm. Courtesy George Grantham Bain Collection/Library of Congress.

movement. [...] Two years later, women gardeners were brought into Kew to replace the men who had gone to war. When they returned during the Second World War, the press insisted on calling them 'Kewties'.

Vincent, *Rootbound*, chapter 'June'.

The attack on Kew Gardens is one of the most famous incidents for women's suffrage. It illustrates the political nature of gardening and its symbolic meaning, just like the example of Kew's role in the British Empire. Destroying flowerbeds and greenhouses seems insane, unless the gardens and the destruction of them by 'female vandals' are seen in terms of the power relations in society. Just as the orchid can symbolise extreme wealth, so a flower-bed can express the power of patriarchy in the political order. [...]

Why would women's rights activists, suffragists *and* suffragettes, look to the garden as a zone of contestation? One the one hand, gardening and farming more generally had been either male-dominated areas or ones in which the female contribution was downgraded, menial ('weeding women'), and so by its nature a worthy area for a challenge to the expectations and limitations of gender. As the profusion of new gardening books for women shows, the garden was an increasingly significant aspect of middle-class identity throughout the nineteenth century, especially in the female-oriented domestic sphere. [...] On the other hand, the gentle or fragile flower model of femininity was one which activists attacked, and here was the garden understood as standing symbolically for that model, but also for male property, the establishment, even empire—all of which were worthy of attack by militant feminists.

McKay, *Radical Gardening*, 142.

GEORGIA O'KEEFFE

At this point in my walk through the property it dawned on me that O'Keeffe did not just make a garden here; she created what the ancient Greeks referred to as a *temenos*. A temenos is a sanctuary, a bit of land spared from urban use. Swiss psychologist Carl Jung later defined a temenos as a purposefully created, bounded place where one's most important work is encouraged to come to fruition. O'Keeffe made a clay-walled temenos at Abiquiú, a place where she grew and refined her thought process in the midst of her wondrous garden.

Israel, 'AD Revisits: Georgia O'Keeffe'.

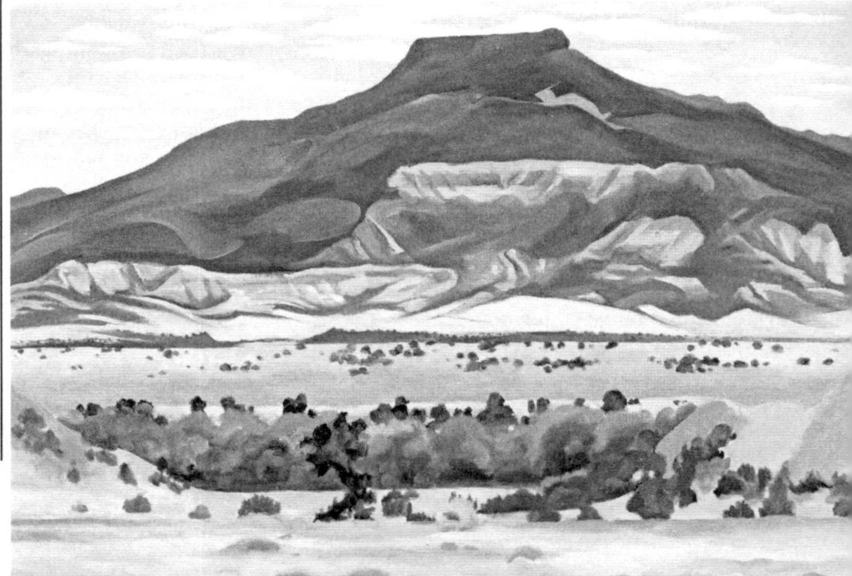

Georgia O'Keeffe, **My Front Yard**, 1941, oil on canvas, 50.9 × 76.5 cm. Courtesy Georgia O'Keeffe Museum, Santa Fe and Art Resource/Scala, Florence.

KIN

Kin is a wild category that all sorts of people do their best to domesticate. Making kin as oddkin rather than, or at least in addition to, godkin and genealogical and biogenetic family troubles important matters, like to whom one is actually responsible. Who lives and who dies, and how, in this kinship rather than that one? What shape is this kinship, where and whom do its lines connect and disconnect, and so what? What must be cut and what must be tied if multispecies flourishing on earth, including human and other-than-human beings in kinship, are to have a chance?

Haraway, *Staying with the Trouble*, 2.

My purpose is to make 'kin' mean something other/more than entities tied by ancestry or genealogy. The gently defamiliarizing move might seem for a while to be just a mistake, but then (with luck) appear as correct all along. Kin making is making persons, not necessarily as individuals or as humans. I was moved in college by Shakespeare's punning between kin and kind – the kindest were not necessarily kin as family; making kin and making kind (as category, care, relatives without ties by birth, lateral relatives, lots of other echoes) stretch the imagination and can change the story. Marilyn Strathern taught me that 'relatives' in British English were originally 'logical relations' and only became 'family members' in the seventeenth century—this is definitely among the factoids I love. Go outside English, and the wild multiplies.

I think that the stretch and recomposition of kin are allowed by the fact that all earthlings are kin in the deepest sense, and it is past time to practice better care of kinds-as-assemblages (not species one at a time). Kin is an assembling sort of word. All critters share a common 'flesh', laterally, semiotically, and genealogically. Ancestors turn out to be very interesting strangers; kin are unfamiliar (outside what we thought was family or gens), uncanny, haunting, active. [...]

So, make kin, not babies!

Haraway, *Staying with the Trouble*, 103.

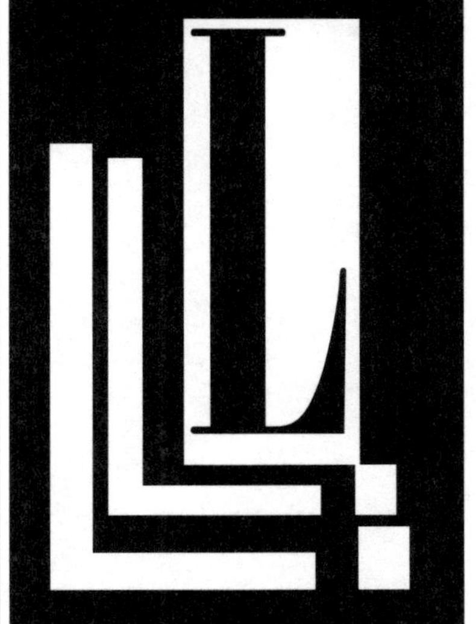

LABYRINTH

There is no freedom
in the desert.
Though there are no fences,
no posts.
It is better—if you wish
to be free—
To elegantly wander
through a labyrinth.

Komrij, 'Het onzichtbare labyrint.' Translated in Aben and De Wit, *The Enclosed Garden*, 16.

LANDSCAPE GARDEN

Meanwhile the whole Paradise of Arnheim bursts upon the view. There is a gush of entrancing melody; there is an oppressive sense of strange sweet odour;—there is a dream-like intermingling to the eye of tall slender Eastern trees—bosky shrubberies—flocks of golden and crimson birds—lily-fringed lakes—meadows of violets, tulips, poppies, hyacinths, and tube-roses—long intertangled lines of silver streamlets—and, upspringing confusedly from amid all, a mass of semi-Gothic, semi- Saracenic architecture, sustaining itself by miracle in mid-air; glittering in the red sunlight with a hundred oriels, minarets, and pinnacles; and seeming the phantom handiwork, conjointly, of the Sylphs, of the Fairies, of the Genii, and of the Gnomes.

Poe, 'The Domain of Arnheim'.

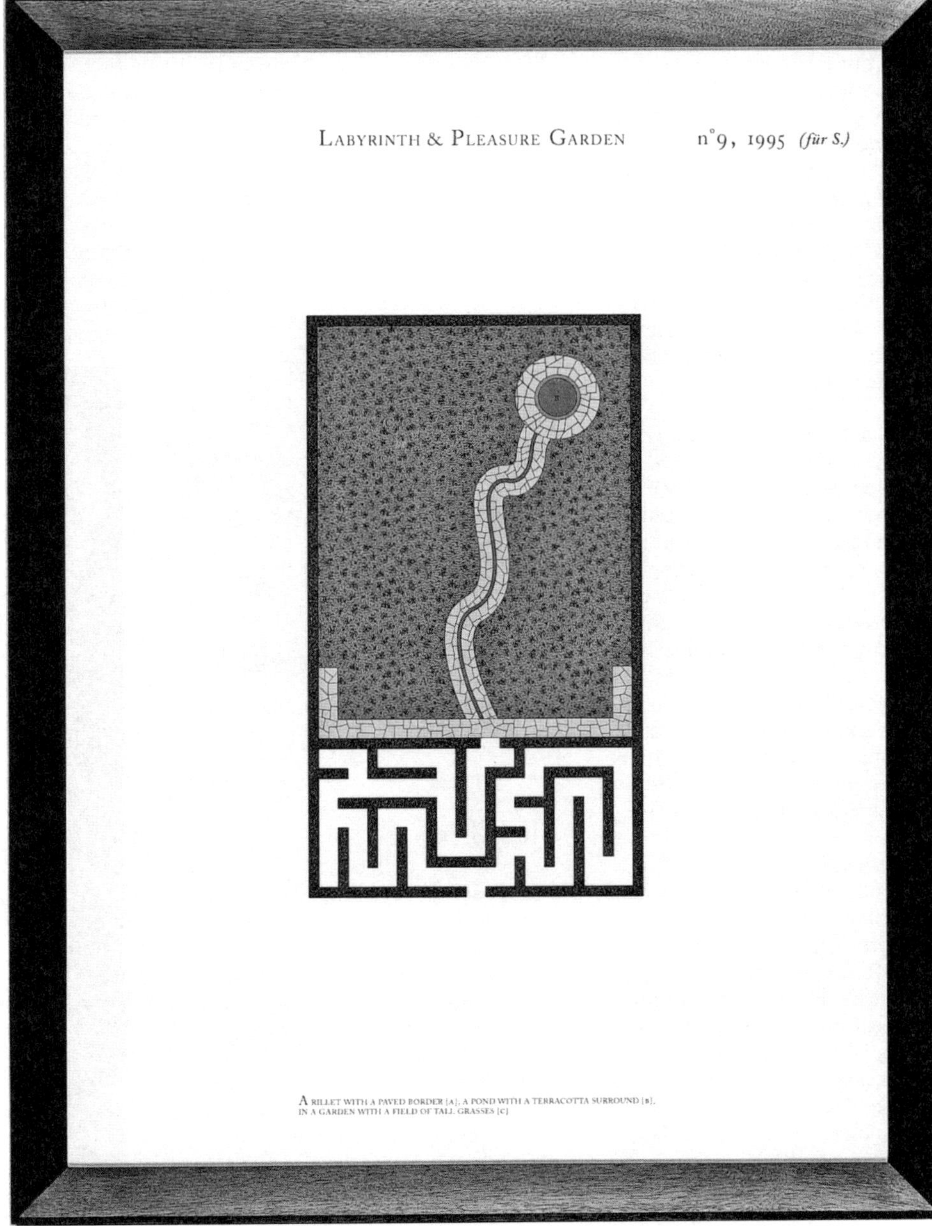

Jan Vercruysse, **Labyrinth & Pleasure Gardens**, 1994–1995, offset on paper, 71.5 × 54.3 cm. Courtesy Van Abbemuseum, Eindhoven. Photo: Peter Cox.

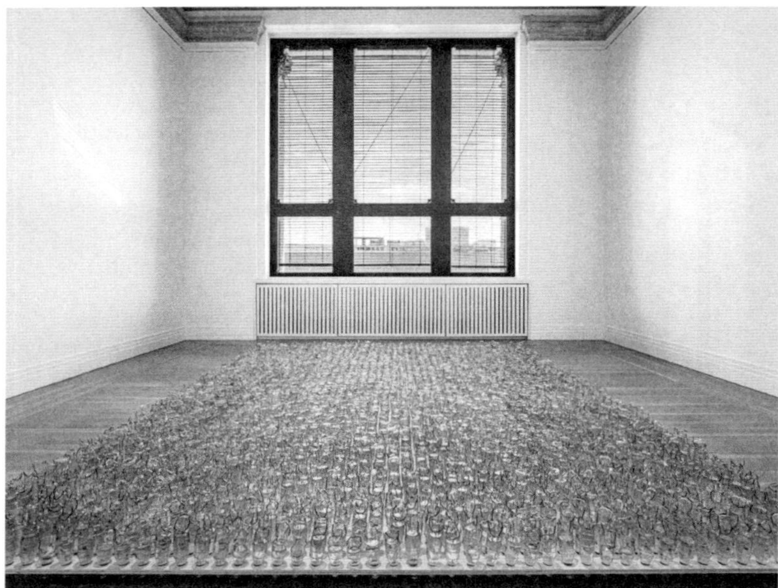
Lungiswa Gqunta, **Lawn**, 2016–2021, installation view. Courtesy WhatIfTheWorld, Capetown.

LAWN

It's the genius of gardening to turn grass into lawn and trees into groves.

Finlay, 'More Detached Sentences on Gardening'. See also Abrioux, *Ian Hamilton.*

The opening of David Lynch's 1986 *Blue Velvet* uses the interior of the lawn to symbolize the film's exploration of the dark side of everyday life. The carefully tended layer of grass represents both the suburban ideal and its latent nightmare, the menace lurking behind idyllic surfaces. Turmoil within the lawn hints at the disorder infiltrating the whole community. Tampering with the perfect lawns of an imperfect society, the film relentlessly overturns the image of the suburban street that is reproduced in countless other films. [...]

In fact, activity in the American suburbs was usually restricted to the concealed backyard. The lawn is first and foremost an image, something to be seen rather than used. Enormous effort is spent on constructing the right visual effect. The whole point of lawncare is that you do not have to display the family. Rather, you display the lawn itself as surrogate or certificate of your adherence to social norms. Even better, you display your lawncare activity. Working on the lawn is a civic duty of the gravest importance. [...]

The association between the well-maintained lawn and the well-maintained family is reinforced in all forms of advertisement for suburban life. An endless array of aggressively happy families poses on perfect grass—eating, drinking, cooking, sleeping and playing. Clothes change but the lawn remains the same. Healthy families have healthy lawns. To feed your lawn is to feed your family.

Wigley, 'Electric Lawn', 155–156.

LUNGISWA GQUNTA

Lungiswa Gqunta presents the lawn as a dangerous landscape of rough shards of glass, at odds with the suburban garden associations of leisure. In the townships of South Africa, no one has a lawn and this green expanse stands for suburban privilege. Gqunta references the ad hoc security fencing made by many South Africans using broken glass embedded in concrete, as well as the use of bottles and petrol in 'Molotov cocktails' used in protest action. Gqunta's lawn is a cutting criticism of inaction to acknowledge and resolve land disputes. (ed.)

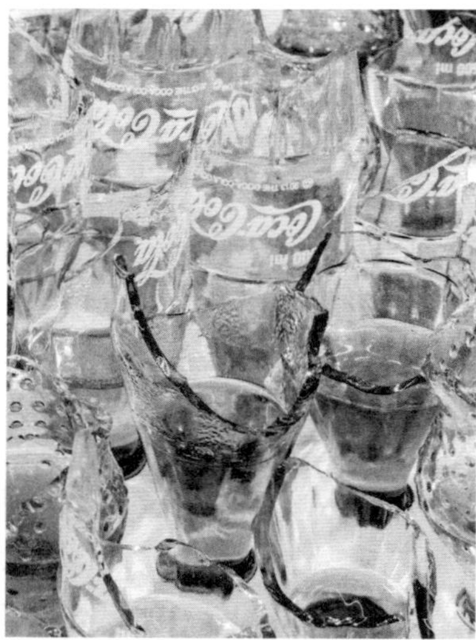
Lungiswa Gqunta, **Lawn**, 2016–2021, installation view. Courtesy WhatIfTheWorld, Capetown.

LICHENS

For those not yet initiated into this weird and beautiful world, a lichen should not be thought of as an individual. All lichens are composites of a fungal host (the mycobiont) and one or more photosynthesising partners (the photobionts), either cyano-bacteria or algae. The importance of this is that lichens provide a perfect example of the primacy of symbiosis to the development of life. Evolutionary biology has tended to overemphasise the vertical inheritance of sexual reproduction and in so doing reinforces a fixation on heterosexual partnering. The messy exchange of genetic information through prolonged symbiotic relationships not only represents an alternative pathway for evolution but also disturbs the edges of individual identity. Griffiths suggests that lichen provide a queer ecological lens that 'could go some way toward denaturalising the primacy of heterosexuality and sexual reproduction in defining and legtimating bodies, practices and communities'.

Basically lichen in their flagrant, complex, multi-organismal relationships have become flag bearers of a queer ecology fed up with being told that all life comes from mummy and daddy.

Bruce, *Snaky Zine#2 On Movement.*

LOWEMAN BAKBA

Bananas are ubiquitous, but few people know how the Musa genus spread or are familiar with the many fascinating stories behind some species. The banana was one of the first staple foods to be cultivated, beginning around 8,000 to 5,000 BCE. The cultivated banana *(Musa x paradisiaca)* originated in Asia, but reached Africa very early in human history, where, as in Asia, different varieties were developed.

Today, many species and varieties of banana are found in Suriname. On the Reijnsdorp plantation, the Javanese community grew a variety of the fruit with an angular and thick skin. They called it 'loweman bakba', which means 'banana of the runaway enslaved people' in Sranan Tongo, the Surinamese 'tongue'. The older generation within the Javanese community, brought to Suriname as indentured labourers, explained: 'Our ancestors found this plant growing wild in the forest. They brought it to the village and some of the former enslaved people still present on the former plantation told them that this was the "loweman bakba" with its own special story'.

This variety was grown on the plantations by enslaved people, who survived on the fruit when they fled to freedom. The community at the Reijnsdorp plantation saw this banana as a wild variety, but it does not produce fertile seeds and is propagated by means of cuttings. How did this banana come to grow 'wild' in the forest? Were these plants leftovers from old enslaved people's gardens or old temporary 'Maroon' camps that the first indentured labourers found in the forest? These questions still remain unanswered today.

More evidence of the contemporary distribution of this banana was found in a garden in Paramaribo-West. How did the 'loweman bakba' find its way there? The owner received the plant from a friend from the 'Maroon' village of Drita-biki in the Sipalwini district. It would appear that the plant, and its story, was not only adopted by the Javanese community on the coast, but was also taken with the fleeing enslaved people into the interior of the country, where the descendants of the 'lowemans' (runaway enslaved people) still grow the plant today.

Thiëmo Heilbron

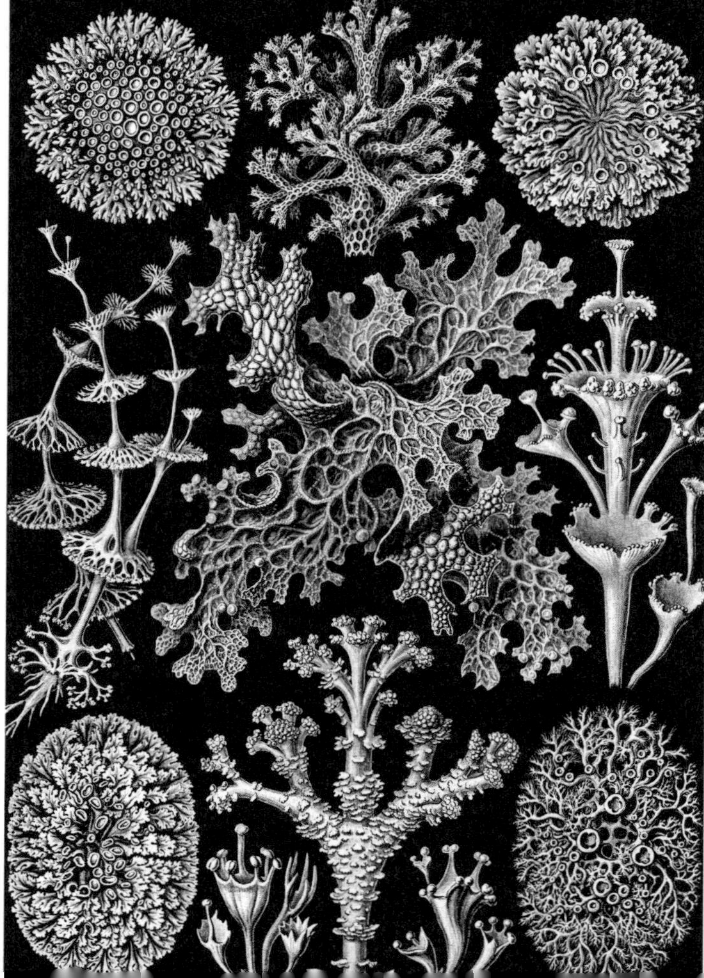
Ernst Haeckel, **Plate 83**: **Lichedes**, **Cladonia** from **Kunstformen der Natur**, 1904, engraving.

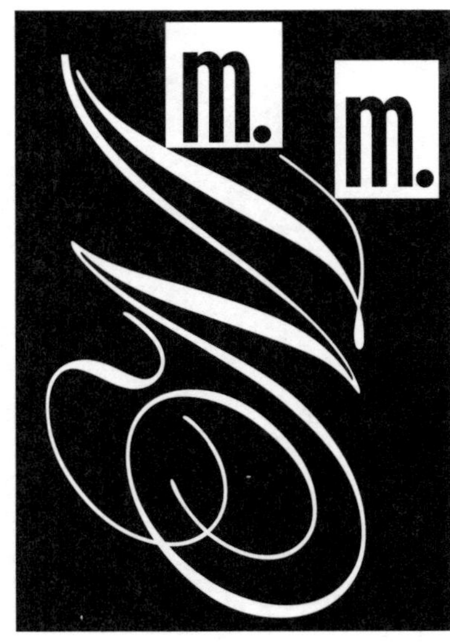

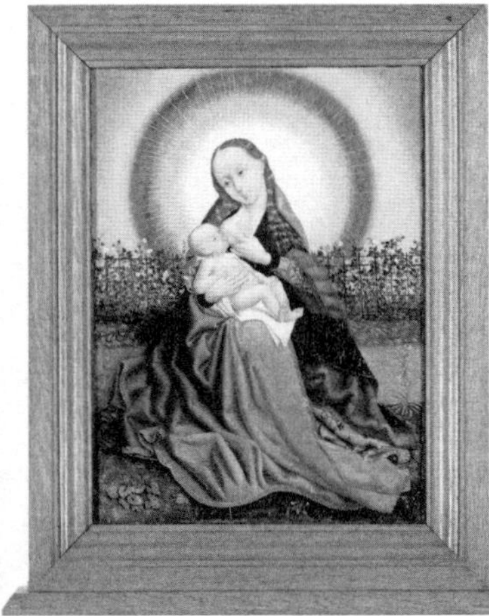

Anonymous (Northern Netherlands), **Mary with Child with Halo in Front of a Rose Hedge**, 1475-1499, oil on panel, 37 x 27 cm. Courtesy Museum Catharijneconvent, Utrecht. Photo: Ruben de Heer.

MARIA GARDEN

THE MASTER OF DELFT

The Master of Delft painted a scene that was well known during the Middle Ages and the Renaissance: the Virgin Mary in a walled garden, a symbol of her virginity. Here the Christ Child stands on the Virgin's lap and looks up at a vision in the sky. Mary looks towards the woman on the lower right, who hands her a white flower. The outer sides of the panels show the Annunciation, with the Archangel Gabriel on the left and the Virgin on the right. The message reads: from this enclosed garden Christ was born, who as a second Adam offered redemption for the sins of man after the Fall. (ed.)

nevertheless, and it isn't hard to conjecture that her garden was in the nature of a chastity belt, locking her in until the return of her lord and master. 'A garden inclosed is my sister, my spouse; a spring shut up, a fountain seals', says the Song of Solomon—to all of course but him. That feminine purity is only to be preserved within four walls is another ancient idea, and in the late Middle Ages it found indirect expression in those curious paintings of so-called Mary gardens, which show the Virgin seated in a castellated enclosure surrounded by richly symbolic fruits, vines and flowers.

Perényi, *Green Thoughts*, 262–263.

You are a garden locked up, my sister, my bride;
you are a spring enclosed, a sealed fountain.
Your plants are an orchard of pomegranates
with choice fruits,
with henna and nard,
nard and saffron,
calamus and cinnamon,
with every kind of incense tree,
with myrrh and aloes
and all the finest spices.
You are a garden fountain,
a well of flowing water
streaming down from Lebanon.

Song of Songs 4:12–15 (NIV)

Medieval gardens repeat the pattern of the *hortus conclusus*, with the difference that they are more elaborate and better adapted to feminine comfort. Trellised walks, turf seats, tiny flower beds, all mark a female presence that is borne out in the illuminations and tapestries where we almost invariably see a lady stooping to pluck a strawberry, a rose, or at her ease with embroidery and lute. So plainly were they designed for women that they even convey an illusion of female supremacy at last—and it wasn't entirely an illusion. The mass folly of the Crusades occupied European men for the better part of two hundred years, and with her lord away at the wars the chatelaine did often manage his estate at home, and not badly either. She lived behind fortified walls

MARIA SIBYLLA MERIAN

Together with her daughter, the entomologist Maria Sibylla Merian made a remarkable trip to Suriname in the eighteenth century to document native insects and their metamorphosis. The resulting book contains sixty illustrations in the form of hand-coloured copper engravings with descriptions. Merian is considered an influential naturalist to this day. She lived at a time when European science became fascinated with so-called rational systems for understanding the world. The world was classified and ordered, with the attendant risk of reducing man and nature to hierarchical categories. That Merian could not have performed this work without the knowledge of enslaved women becomes clear in the work of Patricia Kaersenhout. (ed.)

PATRICIA KAERSENHOUT

Maria Sibylla Merian depended on the knowledge of enslaved women to conduct her study of plants and insects in Suriname. One of the women who helped Merian with her academic fieldwork was eventually brought back to Europe, as evinced by the passenger list of their ship. The Dutch artist Patricia Kaersenhout, whose parents came from Suriname, made it her task to trace this woman. In a series of drawings in the style of the seventeenth-century botanists and employing the theory of critical fabulation, Kaersenhout has reconstructed the possible life, dreams, and emotions of the unidentified woman. The work also refers to the wealth of knowledge that this woman must have had about plants and their medicinal properties, knowledge that was taken seriously only when it was adopted and recorded by European botanists. (ed.)

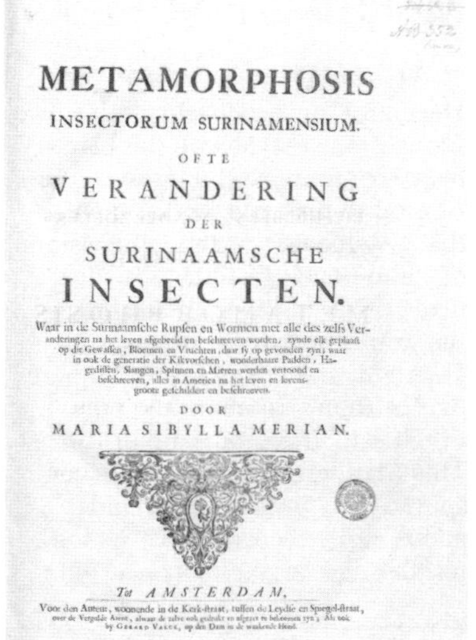

METAMORPHOSIS
INSECTORUM SURINAMENSIUM.
OFTE
VERANDERING
DER
SURINAAMSCHE
INSECTEN.
DOOR
MARIA SIBYLLA MERIAN.
Te AMSTERDAM,

Maria Sibylla Merian, **Metamorphosis Insectorum Surinamensium**, 1705, book. Courtesy University of Utrecht.

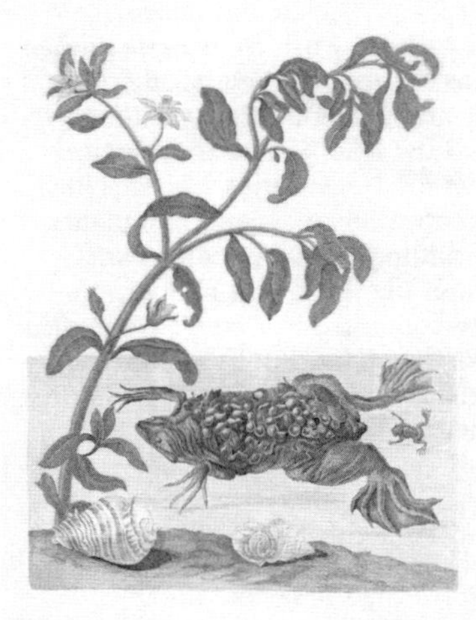

Maria Sibylla Merian, **Metamorphosis Insectorum Surinamensium**, 1705, book. Courtesy University of Utrecht.

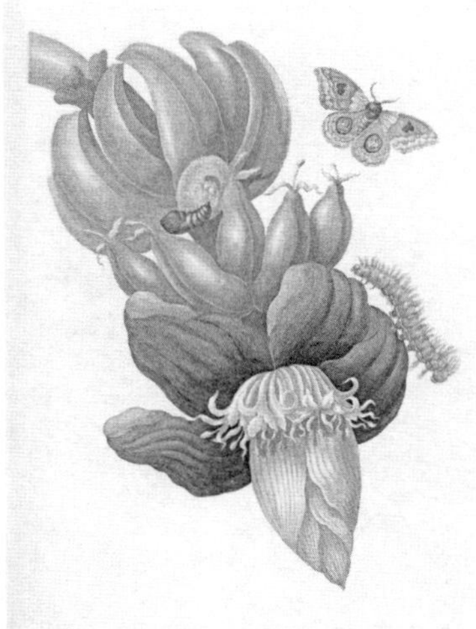

Maria Sibylla Merian, **Metamorphosis Insectorum Surinamensium**, 1705, book. Courtesy University of Utrecht.

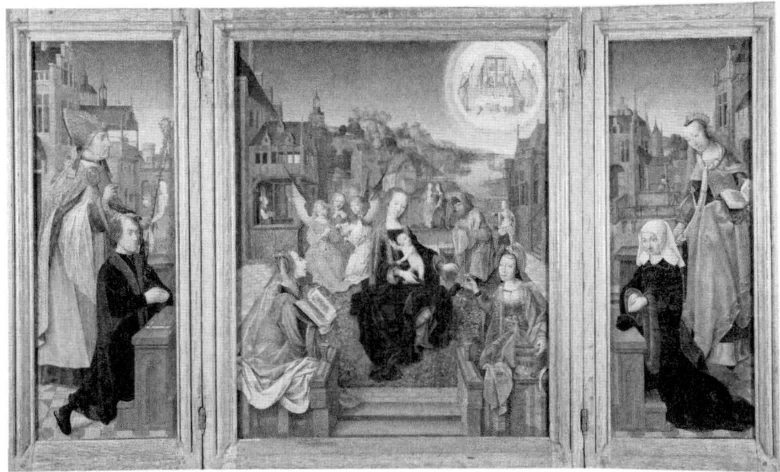

The Master of Delft, **Triptych with the Virgin and Child, Joseph, Angels and Saints in an Enclosed Garden, on the external panels an Annunciation**, 1495–1504, oil on panel, 84.5 × 96.5 cm. Courtesy Museum Catharijneconvent, Utrecht. Photo: Ruben de Heer.

MARITIME PINE SPRIG

HERMAN KRUYDER

Herman Kruyder developed his own Expressionist style with flat planes, heavy contours, and intense colours. Central to his early works, such as this watercolour, is an idyllic vision of nature and rural life. Kruyder made many outdoor studies in the woods and in the dunes near Haarlem, and it was probably there that he found the maritime pine, which also grows on sand drifts. This Mediterranean conifer occurs sporadically in the Netherlands and is easily recognized by its long needles and large pine cones. (ed.)

MEDICINAL GARDEN

Pedanius Dioscorides (born c. AD 40, Anazarbus, Cilicia–died c. 90), Greek physician and pharmacologist whose work *De materia medica* was the foremost classical source of modern botanical terminology and the leading pharmacological text for 16 centuries. [...] Excellent descriptions of nearly 600 plants, including cannabis, colchicum, water hemlock, and peppermint, are contained in *De materia medica*. Written in five books around the year 77, this work deals with approximately 1,000 simple drugs.

Encyclopedia Britannica, 'Pedanius Dioscorides'.

MICROCOSM

The enclosed garden can be conceived of as a microcosm (from the Greek 'mikros' [little] and 'kosmos' [world-order]); a philosophical term that describes man (the soul) as a world in miniature in which the macrocosm is reflected. The whole and its parts are analogous. In that sense the enclosed garden represents a completeness, not least because from it emerges an accumulation of meanings. The garden as 'mirror of the soul', of man, the cosmos, paradise.

Aben and De Wit, *The Enclosed Garden*, 16.

At Versailles, the sun sets at the infinite horizon, its full splendor reflected off the canal. And, turning to view the chateau at sunset, one is met again with the reflection of the sun's rays off the chateau's windows. Here, the window [...] functions as a baroque mirror, to distort and multiply effects. This optical transmutation of the divine solar orb [...] intermingles pure cosmic transcendence with the vast, but hardly infinite, immanence of the garden as microcosm.

Weiss, *Mirrors of Infinity*, 68.

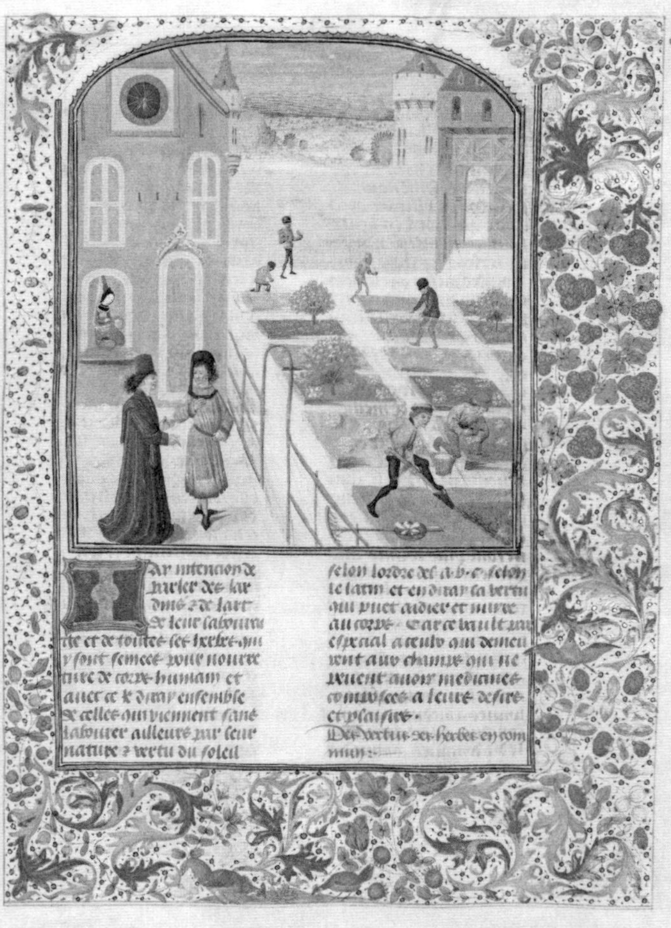

Pietro de' Crescenzi, **Le livre des prouffis champestres et ruraux**, fol. 157r., c. 1470, manuscript. Courtesy The Morgan Library & Museum, New York.

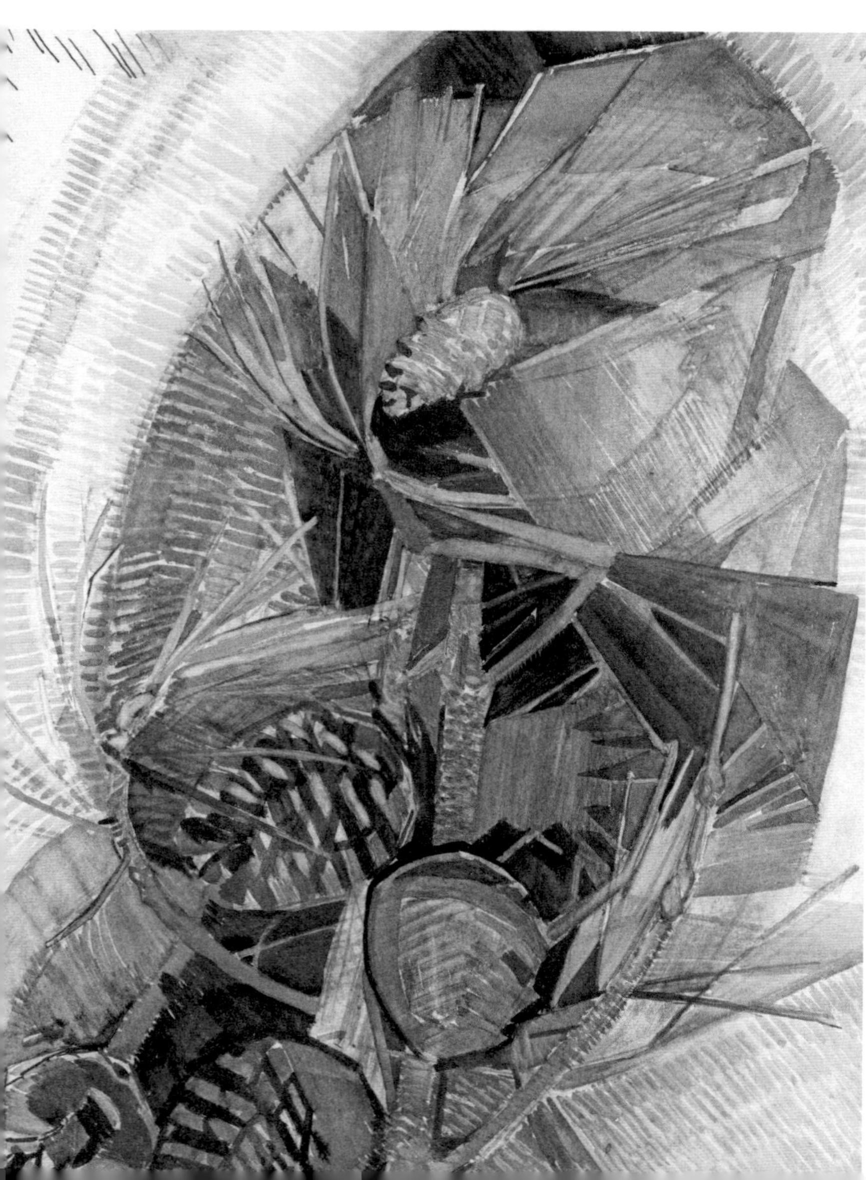

MIRACLE GARDEN

ELSPETH DIEDERIX

The garden has been at the root of Elspeth Diederix's practice for quite some time. *The Studio Garden* project, for example, was a laboratory in which she learned to garden, and experimented with photographing flowers and using plant materials in her work. She built the *Miracle Garden* a few years ago. This flower garden is a public, freely accessible studio in the Erasmuspark in Amsterdam. She documents all the flowers she grows there and comments upon them in an ever-growing archive. The cut flowers she grows and picks there are also featured in her photographs. For this exhibition, Diederix has made a selection of these 'miracles'—her flower portraits are mysterious. Is it nature that has been manipulated? Or the photograph? Or is it the baroque lighting that gives that impression? (ed.)

MOSS

ANDREA BÜTTNER

Moss is often overlooked. In his system of classification of humans and nature, *Systema Naturae* (1735), the Swedish scientist Carl Linnaeus (1707–1778) placed these plants at the very bottom of the hierarchy as the lowest species. With a body of work focusing on the small and the insignificant, shame and dignity, the German artist Andrea Büttner has developed a fascination for mosses. These plants are almost 400 million years old and exist in more than 22,000 different species. They are an inherent part of the ecological system and play an important role in combating erosion and in maintaining the moisture balance in forests. This moss-covered stone was found near the museum. It is the responsibility of the museum staff to take care of the moss during the exhibition. (ed.)

The word 'moss' is commonly applied to plants which are not actually mosses. Reindeer 'moss' is a lichen, Spanish 'moss' is a flowering plant, sea 'moss' is an alga, and club 'moss' is a lycophyte. So what is a moss? A true moss or bryophyte is the most primitive of land plants. Mosses are often described by what they lack, in comparison to the more familiar higher plants. They lack flowers, fruits, and seeds and have no roots. They have no vascular system, no xylem and phloem to conduct water internally. They are the most simple of plants, and in their simplicity, elegant. With just a few rudimentary components of stem and leaf, evolution has produced some 22,000 species of moss worldwide. Each one is a variation on a theme, a unique creation designed for success in tiny niches in virtually every ecosystem.

Kimmerer, *Gathering Moss*, 13.

Herman Kruyder, **Maritime Pine Sprig**, 1917–1918, watercolour on paper, 65 × 48.5 cm. Courtesy Centraal Museum, Utrecht. Photo: Adriaan van Dam.

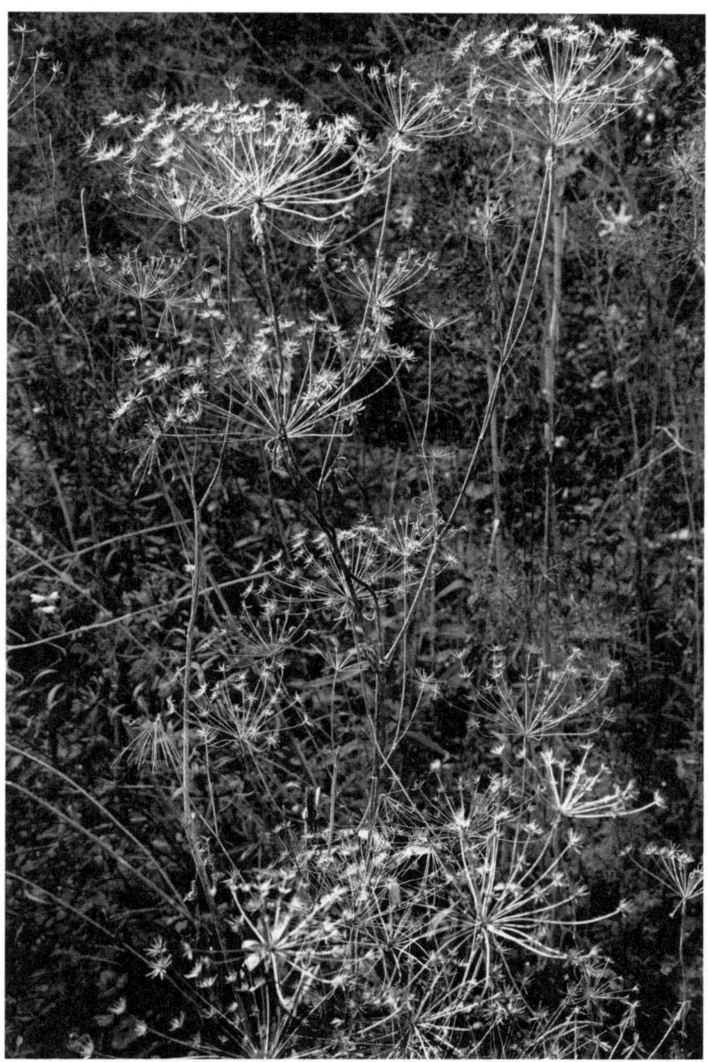

Elspeth Diederix, **Miracle #03**, 2018, photograph. Courtesy of Elspeth Diederix and Stigter Van Doesburg, Amsterdam.

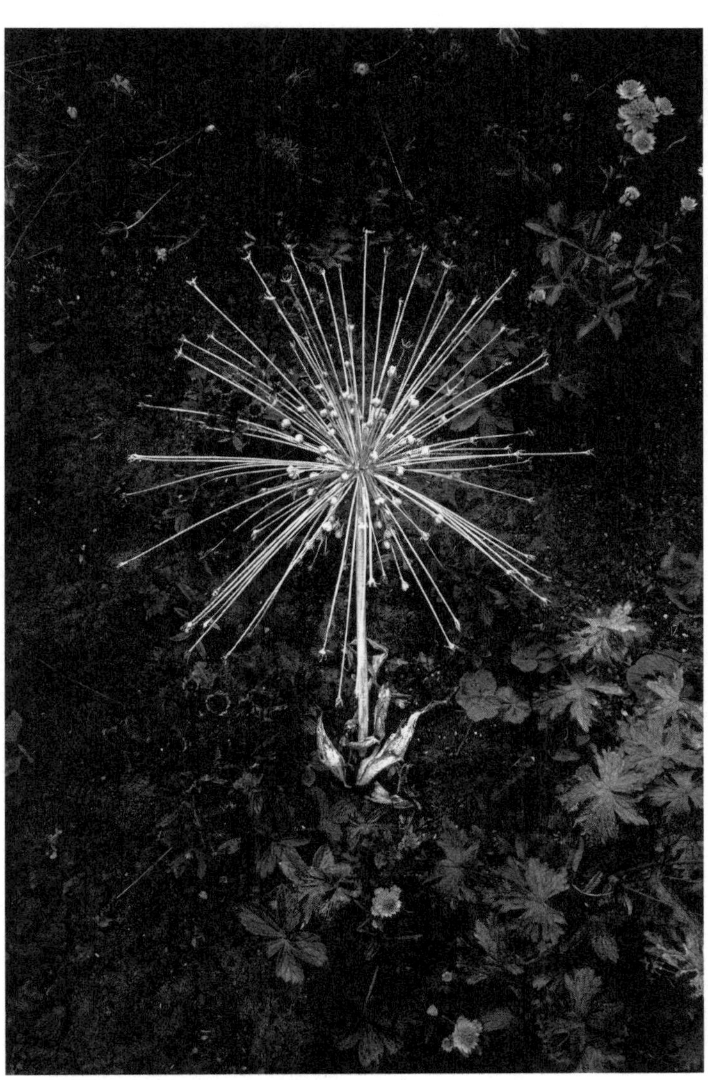

Elspeth Diederix, **Miracle #05**, 2018, photograph. Courtesy of Elspeth Diederix and Stigter Van Doesburg, Amsterdam.

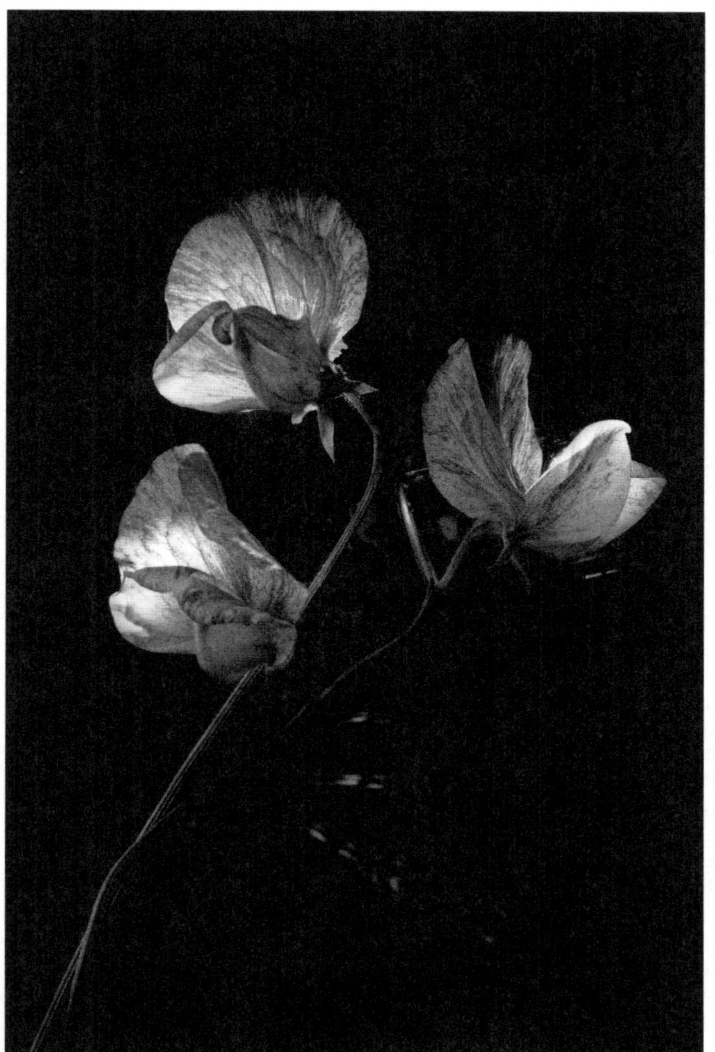

Elspeth Diederix, **Miracle #04**, 2018, photograph. Courtesy of Elspeth Diederix and Stigter Van Doesburg, Amsterdam.

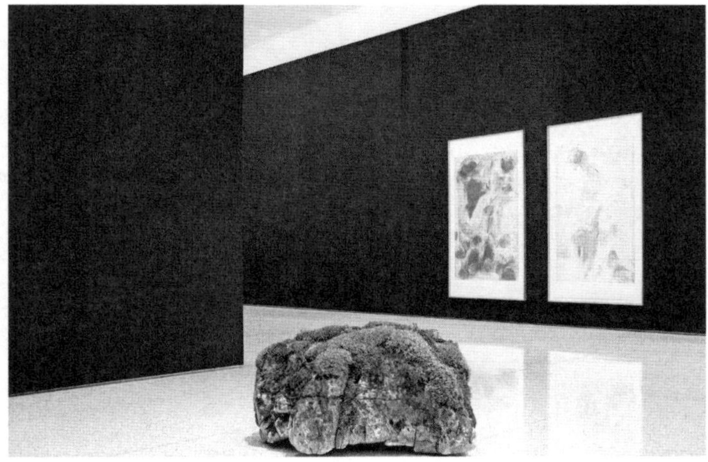

Andrea Büttner, **Limestone with Moss**, 2015, installation view at Walker Art Center, Minneapolis. Courtesy Walker Art Center, Minneapolis/Andrea Büttner/Hollybush Gardens. Photo: Gene Pittman.

THE AGNIETEN CONVENT

See p. 103 for 'The Agnieten Convent' by René de Kam.

MYCELIUM

Fungi are everywhere, but they are easy to miss. They are inside you and around you. They sustain you and all that you depend on. As you read these words, fungi are changing the way that life happens, as they have done for more than a billion years. They are eating rock, making soil, digesting pollutants, nourishing and killing plants, surviving in space, inducing visions, producing food, making medicines, manipulating animal behavior, and influencing the composition of the Earth's atmosphere. Fungi provide a key to understanding the planet on which we live, and the ways that we think, feel, and behave.

Yet they live their lives largely hidden from view, and over ninety percent of their species remain undocumented. The more we learn about fungi, the less makes sense without them. [...]

Mycelium describes the most common of fungal habits, better thought of not as a thing but as a process—an exploratory, irregular tendency. Water and nutrients flow through ecosystems within mycelial networks. The mycelium of some fungal species is electrically excitable and conducts waves of electrical activity along hyphae, analogous to the electrical impulses in animal nerve cells.

Sheldrake, *Entangled Life*, 9, 12.

Mycelium is ecological connective tissue, the living seam by which much of the world is stitched into relation. In school classrooms children are shown anatomical charts, each depicting different aspects of the human body. One chart reveals the body as a skeleton, another the body as a network of blood vessels, another the nerves, another the muscles. If we made equivalent sets of diagrams to portray ecosystems, one of the layers would show the fungal mycelium that runs through them. We would see sprawling, interlaced webs strung through the soil, through sulfurous sediments hundreds of meters below the surface of the ocean, along coral reefs, through plant and animal bodies both alive and dead, in rubbish dumps, carpets, floor-boards, old books in libraries, specks of house dust, and in canvases of old master paintings hanging in museums. According to some estimates, if one teased apart the mycelium found in a gram of soil—about a teaspoon—and laid it end to end, it could stretch anywhere from a hundred meters to ten kilometers. In practice, it is impossible to measure the extent to which mycelium perfuses the Earth's structures, systems, and inhabitants—its weave is too tight. Mycelium is a way of life that challenges our animal imaginations.

Sheldrake, *Entangled Life*, 52–53.

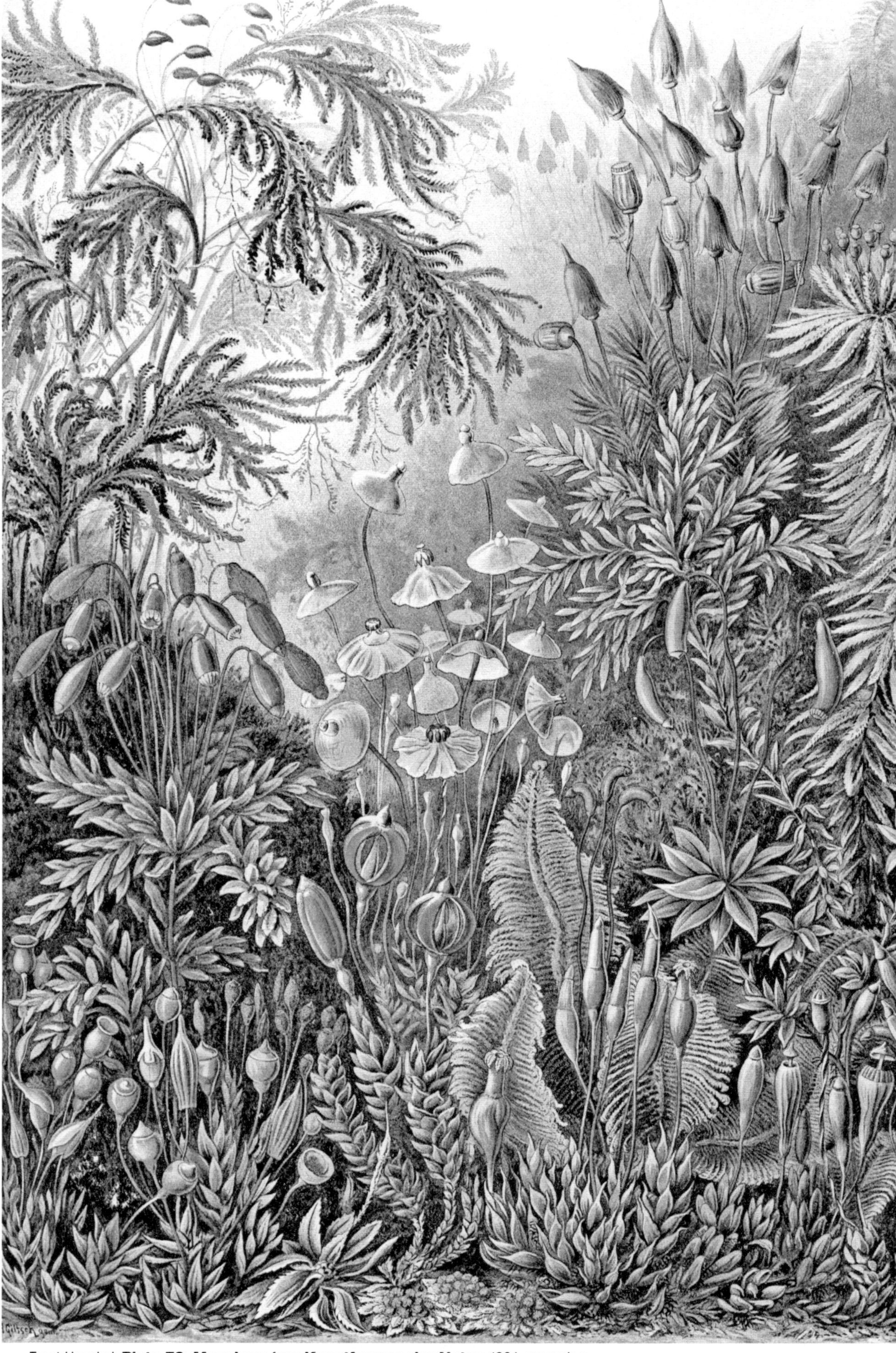

Ernst Haeckel, **Plate 72, Muscinae** from **Kunstformen der Natur**, 1904, engraving.

MYCORRHIZA

The word, *mycorrhiza*, comes from the Greek 'mukès' (fungus) and 'rhiza' (root). *Mycorrhiza* is symbiosis between fungi and plant roots: 92% of plant families interact with fungi in this way.

WIN-WIN SITUATION

Both the plant and the fungus gain advantages from *mycorrhiza*. The plants provide the fungi with sugars (produced through photosynthesis) while the fungi get nutrients and water from the soil and pass them on to the plants. *Mycorrhiza fungi* can also protect the plants from pathogens which can cause disease. The mycelium, the network of fungal threads or *hyphae*, can cover and enormous area and so increase the range of the partner plant.

ROUND THE ROOTS

Mycorrhiza fungi can be roughly divided into two groups, *endomycorrhiza* (from the Greek 'endon' meaning 'inside') and *ectomycorrhiza* (from the Greek 'ektoc' meaning 'outside'). In the case of endomycorrhiza, the fungal threads invade the plant's roots. In *ectomycorrhiza*, the *hyphae* form a mantle round the roots.

NATURAL GROWTH MEDIUM

The growth and yield of agricultural plants depend to a large extent on *mycorrhiza fungi*. The plants do far less well without *mycorrhiza*. Research is continually being done on *mycorrhiza* fungi with a view to raising plant yields still further.

Artis Micropia, 'Mycorrhiza'.

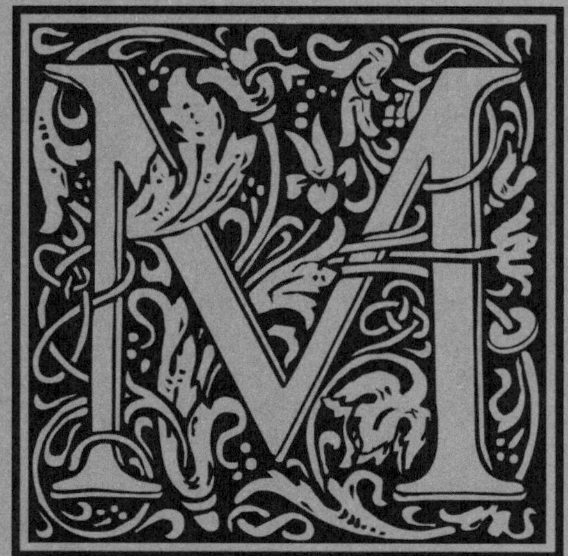

William Morris, **Letter M.**

THE AGNIETEN CONVENT

A GARDEN OF ENCOUNTERS, COLOURS, AND SYMBOLS

René de Kam

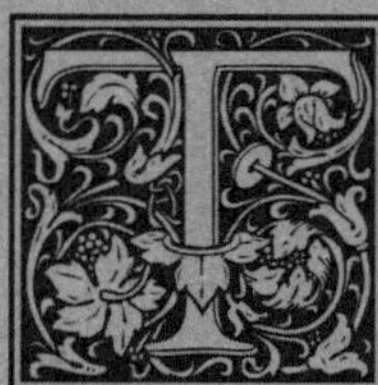

The year 2021 marks the centenary of the Centraal Museum opening its doors in a former cloister on Agnietenstraat. It is also the year in which 'The Botanical Revolution: On the Necessity of Art and Gardening' opens in the museum. This exhibition takes the medieval garden as its starting point, and the museum garden itself, with roots that stretch back to late medieval Utrecht, plays an important role. But what has that garden been through and what can we still see of this in its contemporary design?

BEHIND THE WALL

In late January of 1506, a section of the ten-metre-high city wall between the Servaashek and the Wedermoet tower collapsed. Utrecht's *schutmeester*, the official responsible for the maintenance of the city's buildings at the time, must have been quite shocked when he assessed the damage that day. The fact that it was more than just a simple hole is evident from the fact that it took months of hard work to repair the wall. In the meantime, in order to prevent undesirables from entering the city, the gaping hole was carefully sealed up each night with specially woven mats.[1] When, in June, the preparatory work was finally done, the laying of the new wall was able to commence. And the higher the masons got, the better their view became. Taking a break, to the east they would have seen the contours of St. Servatius Abbey, whose monastery grounds took up the entire south-east corner of the city. Directly to the south of the wall, they looked out over the city's outer canal, beyond which lay Abstede's farmland. To the west were the houses of the walled suburb of Tolsteeg, with the towers of the Tolsteeg gates on the city side. Closer and still within the city wall was the Nicolaas Church, with its two striking Roman towers, and just behind it, the chapel of the Nicolaas Monastery.

Directly at their feet was the Agnieten Convent in a walled garden. Not that the site extended all the way to the city wall, because between the high garden wall and the city wall there was a cobbled alleyway from which, among other things, the city's watch towers could be reached.[2] What the workers would have seen behind the garden wall was not a classically shaped complex in which the various buildings were connected to each other via a covered cloister. It was more of a collection of buildings, which gave some clues as to the development of the Agnieten Convent. On the far left, close to the city wall and just east of the Nicolaas Church, stood a small chapel dating from 1420; its chancel, remarkably, did not face east, but south. Against the north façade of the chapel was a row of beguine houses, home to single women who had devoted their lives to God, but had not taken the vow. In 1422, when the Agnieten Convent was founded, some of these women went on to profess their vows. These sisters eventually lived a secluded life behind the convent's walls,

1 **'Item gegeven om 9 hoirden after Sunt Agnieten dat gat daermede des avonts toe te setten'**. Utrecht Archives, 701 City Council of Utrecht, 1122–1577, inv. no. 630–46 (1506–1507), 22v. See from 16v onwards for all building works.

2 The street next to the wall was examined by archaeologists in 2005. It turned out to be built of cobblestones varying from 5–30 cm in size and was 5.5 metres wide. A.M. Bakker, 'Wijde Doelenstraat', in **Archeologische Kroniek Provincie Utrecht 2004–2005** ([Utrecht]: Provincie Utrecht; Stichting Kunstpublicaties Oud-Utrecht; Erfgoedhuis Utrecht 2005), 108–109.

according to the Rule of Saint Augustine. As time went by, it became mainly women from distinguished families entering the Agnieten.

Around 1422, to the right of the small chapel, on the other side of an open area, a large new wing with several floors was built for the nuns. In the semi-sunken basement was the kitchen, above it the dining room (refectory), and one floor higher the dormitory. The wing, which was topped off with a high, spacious garret roof, is today an important part of the Centraal Museum and a striking building in the museum garden. In addition, the sisters also had a building at their disposal that stood almost perpendicular to the new wing, and which included a spinning room. To the north of it, on the current Agnietenstraat, was the vestibule building; to the west, another row of beguine houses. Six years after the men had worked so hard to repair the city wall, the complex was expanded with a large chapel, located directly east of the entrance, on Agnietenstraat. This remarkably high chapel, which was completed in 1516 and is now used as the museum's shop and information centre, was divided in such a way that it could be used by both the nuns and the beguines.[3] The small chapel survived until the seventeenth century.

3 Jos de Meyere, **Het Agnietenklooster** (Utrecht: Kwadraat, 1988), 12–30.

A MEDIEVAL CONVENT GARDEN

On Braun and Hogenberg's 1572 map of Utrecht, the above-mentioned buildings of the Agnieten Convent are fairly easy to make out. In addition to the cobbled alley, the Nicolaas Churchyard and Agnietenstraat, the site was bordered to the east by the Lange Nieuwstraat, which at that time continued to the city wall. Within the green-shaded, walled grounds, a few separate buildings have also been drawn, and may have served as a bakery, laundry, or perhaps even a brewery. A provision from 1444 shows that beer was brewed in the convent, albeit only for consumption by the inhabitants because they were not allowed to sell it to the townspeople for tax reasons.[4] In the garden, three to four trees are drawn on the map, and with some effort one might even discern a cross-hatched square part of the garden.[5] Aside from this, there is little information about the shape of the convent garden on the map, let alone which plants or trees may have been in it. Nor can anything be discovered about the Agnieten garden from archival data, old drawings, or paintings. And in fact this applies to almost all medieval cloister gardens in the Netherlands. This is remarkable because the garden was an important and often unchanging part of a monastery or convent. Not only because it was (often the only) outdoor space for contemplation and to meet others, but also because many communities were self-sufficient and the garden was, therefore, of great importance for food production.

There would almost certainly have been several herb and vegetable gardens between the buildings of the Agnieten, and they would have contained useful plants, like medicinal and culinary herbs, all kinds of vegetables, and perhaps also plants to make dyes with. Ornamental plants were usually cultivated to decorate the altar. White lilies, roses, columbine, and blue irises were popular for this because they stood for the virtues of the Virgin Mary. Many of these plants in the so-called 'Mary Garden' had white flowers as a reference to virginity, truth, and charity. But blue—the colour of chastity, innocence, and sincerity—was also possible. Alongside these symbolic ornamental plants, which in many cases were also used for medicinal purposes, the garden would have mainly been filled with herbs such as sage, rue, fenugreek, rose, rocket, cumin, rosemary, and mint. The vegetable gardens would have included onions, leeks, celery, coriander, beet, lettuce, parsnips, and summer savory.[6]

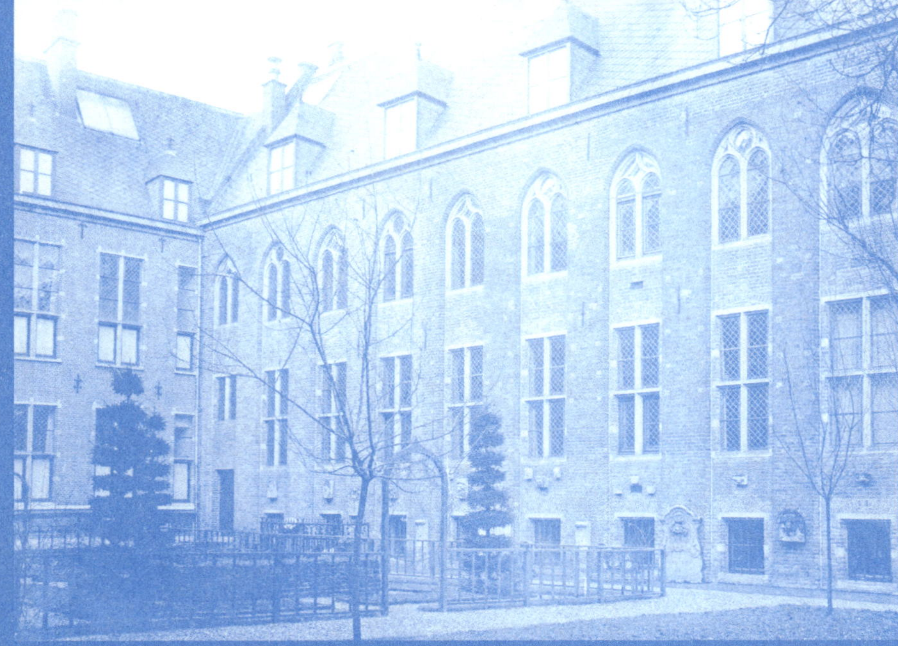

The museum garden in 1927 with the area with turf banks and a rose hedge, enclosed by a fence. Façade stones from the museum collection have been placed against the wall of the medieval wing. Utrecht Archives, visual documentation, inv. no. 78578.

4 Ibid., 18.

5 Utrecht Archives, G. Braun and F. Hogenberg, **Civitates orbis terrarum**, 1572, Catalogue number 214006.

6 Carla Oldenburger, 'Middeleeuwse kloostertuinen in de Lage Landen', in **De middeleeuwse kloostergeschiedenis van de Nederlanden: Deel II Dagelijks leven**, ed. Martin Hillenga and Hans Kroeze, (Zwolle: WBOOKS, 2011), 81–101, 90–98.

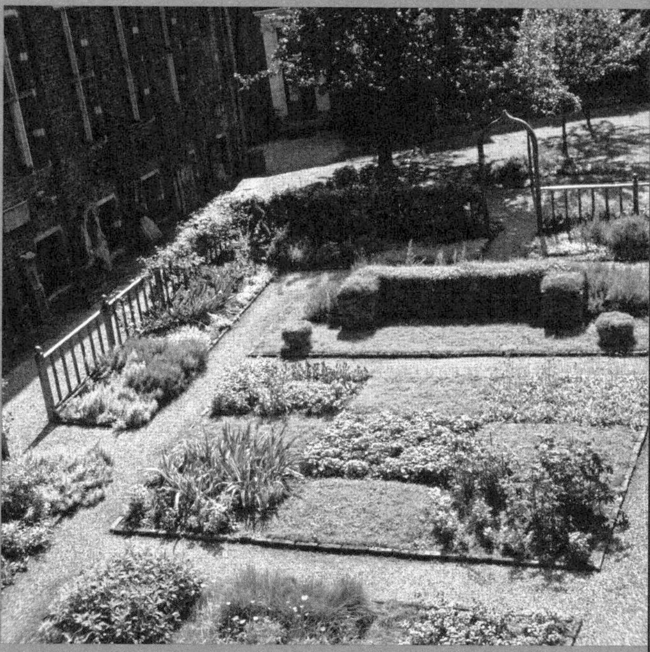
The **hortus conclusus** with flower beds and the fence in 1966. Utrechts Archive, visual documentation, inv. no. 824407. Photo: J.P. van Alff.

Convents and monasteries often had orchards and this went for the Agnieten too. In 1487, the sisters acquired a site on the other side of the Lange Nieuwstraat where several fruit trees grew and where some livestock was probably also kept. Many trees are shown on Braun and Hogenberg's map on this equally walled site, which extended to the Nieuwegracht and nowadays still forms the southern part of the old hortus.[7] In addition, the beguine houses in the non-enclosed part near the Nicolaas Churchyard and on Agnietenstraat would have had small gardens where their own herbs and vegetables were grown.

FINAL RESTING PLACE

Archaeological investigations in 1996 revealed that the then convent garden was also used as a graveyard. In the excavated area, archaeologists found the skeletal remains of seventeen different people who had been buried there between 1420 and 1520. Though the bones were fragile and thus difficult to examine, they probably belonged to women. On the basis of their well-preserved teeth, a cautious estimate could be made of the age at which the women had died. Although some were buried before the age of twenty-five, the average age of the deceased women was between forty and forty-five, and possibly even older. Compared to other late medieval cemetery populations investigated, this is quite high.[8] It was probably due to the fact that the Agnieten was a closed community at this time and, given the well-to-do backgrounds of the nuns, a fairly select one. Moreover, there were no children living there and no women died in childbirth, which would have improved life expectancy considerably. There was surely something intimate about the fact that the nuns, who almost never left the cloisters during their lives, were also buried in the garden. In a way, even after death they remained part of the community and were not forgotten.
Many people were also buried in the current garden area next to the Nicolaas Church. For centuries, the site belonged to the Nicolaas, which in addition to an open space around the church—the so-called 'court'—

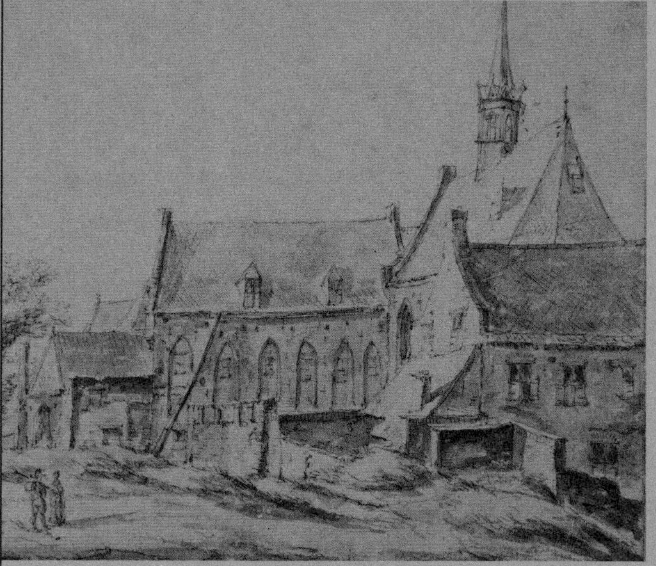
View from the city wall of the former Agnieten convent with courtyard, around 1650. On the right is the chapel from 1516 and straight ahead the tall convent building from 1422. On the left is the old chapel. The garden looks rather unkempt. Utrecht Archives, visual documentation, inv. no. 37708.

also had a graveyard. Evidence of this has also been found in the various graves that have come to light around the church. Some tuff sarcophagi found even date back to the early days of the church, around 1100.[9]

A CONVENT AS A MUSEUM

After the 1580 Reformation, when openly confessing to the Catholic faith became banned in Utrecht, many of the city's convents continued to exist for a while, unlike the monasteries housing mendicant orders such as the Franciscans or the Dominicans. In 1596, for example, a nun even entered the Agnieten. Nevertheless, the enormous cultural changes could not be held off forever, and around 1620 the Agnieten Convent was also closed. Its buildings were not demolished but, after having first served as a wool-spinning factory, were given a new destination in 1674 as a workhouse

7 With thanks to Frans Kipp.

8 Tjeerd Pot, **Lang geleden...: Over de opgravingen in de museumtuin**, 1997 (unpublished), 2 and 3.

9 In 1945, a sarcophagus was dug up to the west of the church. Two years later, one was found south-west of the church. In 1978, one emerged to the north of the church, and in 1999 two more were found north-east of the chancel. See, for example, the drawing by C.J. Bardet from 1947 (Utrecht Archives, 214268), Tarq Hoekstra, 'Nicolaaskerkhof', in **Archeologische Kroniek gemeente Utrecht 1978–1979–1980** (Utrecht: De Boer-Cuperus, 1979), 59–60, and R. van der Mark, 'Utrecht: Nicolaaskerkhof', in **Archeologische Kroniek Provincie Utrecht 1998–1999** (Utrecht: Provincie Utrecht; Stichting Publicaties Oud-Utrecht, 2000), 117–118.

for orphans. The old gardens between the former cloister buildings were set up as separate playgrounds for boys and girls.

The old orchard was also caught up in the changing times—in 1651, the Agnietenstraat was extended to the Nieuwegracht as the Agnietensteeg for the construction of philanthropist Maria van Pallaes's almshouses.[10] When, a year later, the Gronsvelt almshouses were built on the other side of this alley, more of the old orchard was taken away. This happened again when the Fundatie van Renswoude was built between 1756 and 1761 to the east of the sixteenth-century monastery chapel to raise the 'most sensible, intelligent and competent' children from the orphanage.[11] To this end, the Gronsvelt houses were moved to the Nicolaasdwarsstraat, and the last section of the Lange Nieuwstraat, which led to the city wall being built in and disappeared. When all the children from the orphanage were moved into the Fundatie in 1830, the former Agnieten Convent was converted into cavalry barracks. Stables were built for the horses on top of the city wall near the Nicolaas Church. After a fire in 1834, new stables were built at the bottom of the city wall, again sacrificing part of the old convent's grounds and the Nicolaas Church's graveyard.[12] The military left the cloister in 1903, and in 1916 the City Council decided that the former Agnieten Convent should house the new Centraal Museum. However, this had considerable consequences, because only the large wing from 1422 with the vestibule in front of it and the chapel from 1516 were preserved. The rest, such as the wing with the old spinning room and the buildings at the site of the beguine houses, had to make way for new buildings. Nevertheless, the shape of the old cloister was still recognizable in the new museum complex, including the areas that had once served as a garden.

10 De Meyere, **Het Agnietenklooster**, 35–38 and René de Kam, **'Voor den armen alhier': De geschiedenis van vijf Utrechtse fundaties en hun vrijwoningen** (Utrecht: Matrijs, 1998), 42–50.

11 De Meyere, **Het Agnietenklooster**, 54ff.

12 N. van der Monde, **Geschied- en oudheidkundige beschrijving van de pleinen, straten, stegen, waterleidingen, wedden, putten en pompen der stad Utrecht**, part 1. Utrecht 1844, 279.

A CONVENT GARDEN AS A MUSEUM

The outdoor space was also adapted for the museum. The garden area to the west of the old main building was reconstructed as an old cloister garden. Since nothing was known about the Agnieten's medieval garden, the garden design was partly inspired by some old religious paintings that hung in the adjacent refectory, such as the panel *Mary with child in a halo in front of a rose hedge*, from the last quarter of the fifteenth century. On it, Mary is sitting with Jesus on a turf bench with a violet plant to her left. The rose hedge behind her transforms the space she is in into an enclosed garden, a so-called *hortus conclusus*, which symbolizes her virginity. This is further reinforced by the white lily behind her to the right, which, like the rose and the violet, belonged to the aforementioned Mary garden.[13] This source of inspiration was clearly visible in the museum garden's design in a section enclosed with a fence, which contained turf benches and a rose hedge.[14] Beyond the fence there were a few trees and several shell paths, and a cobbled lane next to the buildings, up against which stones from the old façade and gravestones were displayed as part of the museum's collection. The other garden area, to the east of the old main building, was laid out quite simply with a lawn bordered by shell paths, a reference to a medieval courtyard.

When the current garden was replanted in 2014, many of the original elements of this reconstructed convent garden, such as the fence and various trees, had long since disappeared. The decision was taken, as it had been almost a century earlier, to reflect the iconographic value of some of the museum collection's pieces in the new garden. Moreover, this gave the historical layering of the place an extra dimension. It was of great importance that the plants chosen made clear reference to that past. For the garden area to the east and west of the wing, flowers and plants were selected that were likely to have been found in the medieval garden of the Agnieten, such as blue and white altar flowers. The trees to be planted also had to refer to medieval Christian symbolism. It was important that, given the future use of the garden, all the chosen plants were fairly sturdy.[15]

It was also essential that the entire garden design connected the various museum buildings and the Nicolaas Church—actually like a large cloister, though without the protective roof—but as a dedicated place for contemplation or just to be together, like the

13 The panel is now part of the collection of the Museum Catharijne Convent, inv. no. ABM s65. See also: H.L.M. Defoer, et al., **Goddelijk geschilderd: Honderd meesterwerken van Museum het Catharijneconvent** (Zwolle: Waanders, 2003), 57–58.

14 Carla Oldenburger, **Kloostertuin van het Centraal Museum Utrecht. Waardestelling en aanbeveling**, 2007, 5ff.

15 Soda+ architectuur, stedenbouw en interieur, **Definitief ontwerp tuin Centraal Museum en Nicolaïkerk**, 2014 (ongepubliceerd), 1–4.

church's court area of old. As a visualization of this, the current garden funnels from the enclosed parts between the museum buildings out to the Nicolaas Church, where an adjoining lawn and a terrace in front of the museum's Garden Room symbolize the openness of the graveyard—something like in the 1820 painting by Hendrik Verheijen in the museum's collection.[16] The medieval Nicolaas Graveyard had long since disappeared, but it was still a place where, given the worn lawns in the painting, people liked to get together to chat or to sell their home-grown fruit and vegetables.

SORROWS AND JOYS

The enclosed garden the workers from 1506 could peek into from above was an indispensable part of the Agnieten Convent. The herb and vegetable gardens with the various fruit trees and the free-range chickens ensured that there was enough to eat. The carefully chosen ornamental plants had an important symbolic function as well as a medicinal one, and this was reflected in the beautifully decorated altar. In addition, for most of the nuns, the greenery of the garden was the only outdoor space in which they were allowed to spend time. The buildings and the walled garden together formed the convent; one could not exist without the other. The new enclosed garden of the Centraal Museum and the Nicolaas Church also form a whole with the surrounding buildings. The garden design and its accompanying planting refer back to the unique past of the place itself, but also to the many, often colourful works of art in the museum collection. In addition, it is a space that invites one to linger. This was also the case in the era of the convent garden and the churchyard, where the sisters and the Utrecht residents must have had many conversations. And let's not forget the intervening centuries when the playgrounds of the workhouse's girls and boys were located here. There, too, plenty of sorrows and joys will have been shared.

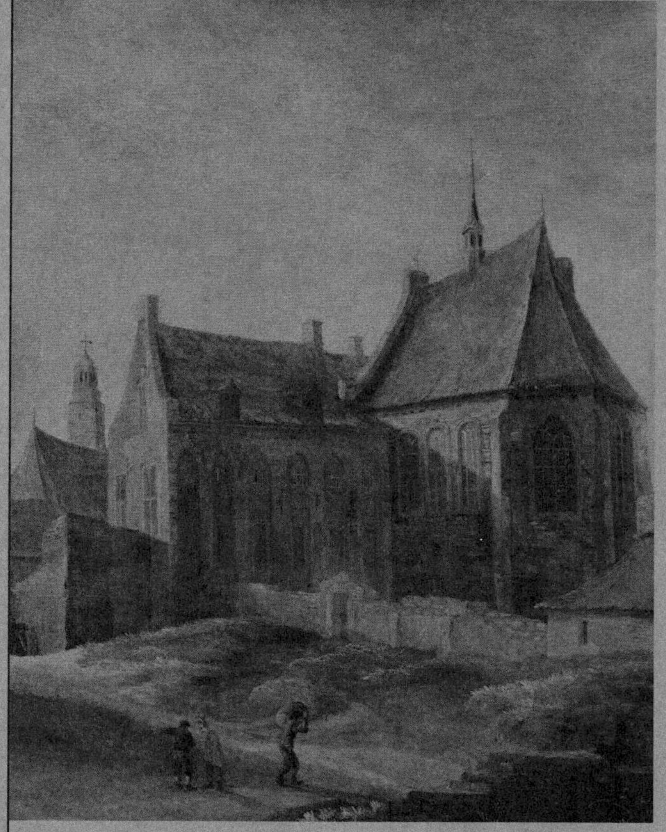

The former Agnieten Convent around 1650 in a painting by Pieter des Ruelles. Centraal Museum Utrecht, inv. no. 12770.

FURTHER SOURCES

Hulzen, A. van. *Utrechtse kloosters en gasthuizen*. Baarn: Bosch & Keuning, 1986.

Kam, René de. *'Voor den armen alhier': De geschiedenis van vijf Utrechtse fundaties en hun vrijwoningen*. Utrecht: Matrijs, 1998.

Oldenburger, Carla, and Juliet Oldenburger. 'Kloostertuinen het behouden waard'. *Cascade: Bulletin voor tuinhistorie* 15, no. 2 (2006), 54–64.

16 **Gezicht op de Klaaskerk**, Jan Hendrik Verheijen, c. 1800–1825, inv. nr. 33192.

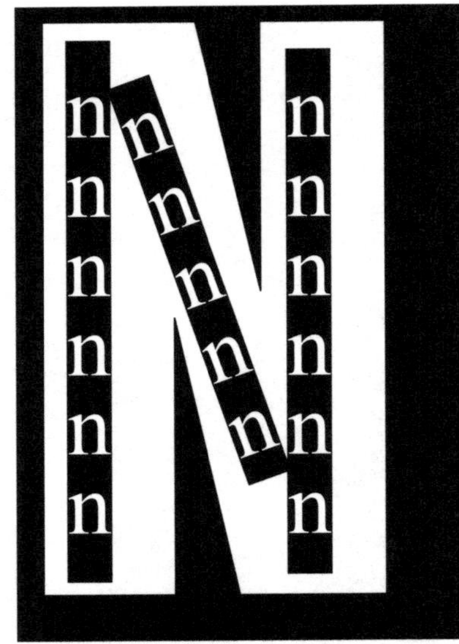

NARCISSUS

Narcissus is derived not from the name of the young man who met his death vainly trying to embrace his reflection in crystal water, but from the Greek narkao (to benumb); though of course Narcissus, benumbed by his own beauty, fell to his death embracing his shadow. Pliny says 'Narce Narcissum dictum non a fabuloso pueroj' named Narcissus from narke, not from the fabled boy. Socrates called the plant 'crown of the infernal gods' because the bulbs, if eaten, numbed the nervous system. Perhaps Roman soldiers carried it for this reason (rather than for its healing properties) as the American soldiers smoked marijuana in Vietnam. This prompted me to ring Matthew Lewis, the portrait photographer, and ask him if he would take a photo of a young man holding a daffodil. Last year he took a beautiful portrait of a handsome Italian, stripped to the waist, holding a lemon, the juice of which he used to dissolve heroin to fill his syringe. Narcissus, narcotics, self-absorption: benumbed retreat into Self.

Jarman, *Modern Nature*, 17–18.

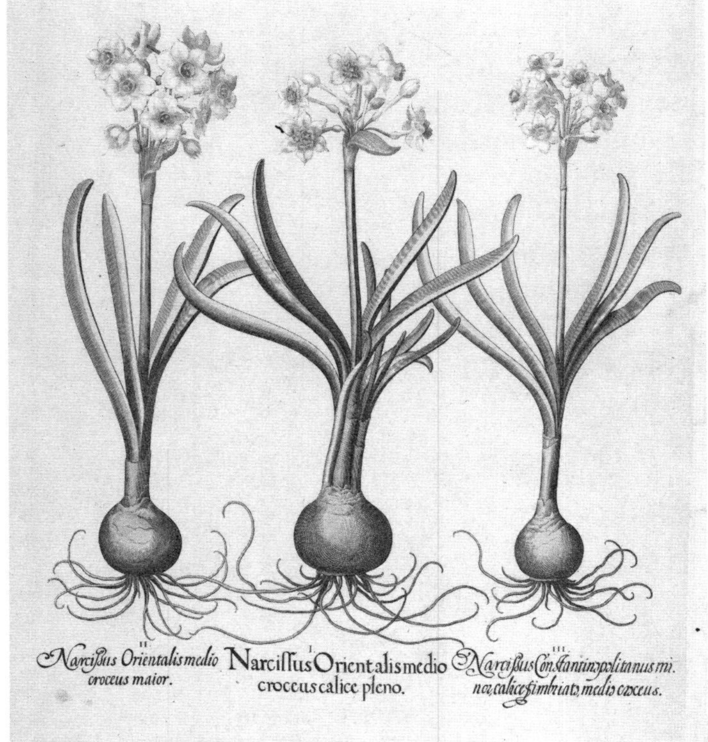

Basil Besler, **Narcissus**, 1613, engraving, 56.1 × 44.4 cm. Courtesy Alamy/Victoria and Albert Museum, London.

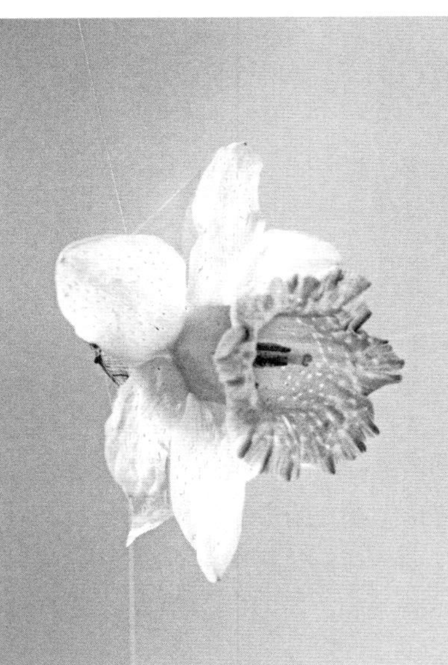

Elspeth Diederix, **Daffodil**, 2018, photograph. Courtesy Elspeth Diederix and Stigter Van Doesburg, Amsterdam.

NEW CLIMATE REGIME

I use this term [New Climate Regime] to summarize the present situation, in which the physical framework that the Moderns had taken for granted, the ground on which their history had always been played out, has become unstable. As if the décor had gotten up on stage to share the drama with the actors. From this moment on, everything changes in the way stories are told, so much so that the political order now includes everything that previously belonged to nature—a figure that, in an ongoing backlash effect, becomes an ever more undecipherable enigma.

For years, my colleagues and I tried to come to grips with this intrusion of nature and the sciences into politics; we developed a number of methods for following and even mapping ecological controversies. But all this specialized work never succeeded in shaking the certainties of those who continued to imagine a social world without objects set off against a natural world without humans—and without scientists seeking to know that world. While we were trying to unravel some of the knots of epistemology and sociology, the whole edifice that had distributed the functions of these fields was falling to the ground—or, rather, was falling, literally, back down to Earth. We were still discussing possible links between humans and nonhumans, while in the meantime scientists were inventing a multitude of ways to talk about the same thing, but on a completely different scale: the 'Anthropocene', the 'great acceleration', 'planetary limits', 'geohistory', 'tipping points', 'critical zones', all these astonishing terms that [...] scientists had to invent in their attempt to understand this Earth that seems to react to our actions. My original discipline, science studies, finds itself reinforced today by the widely accepted understanding that the old constitution, the one that distributed powers between science and politics, has become obsolete. As if we had really passed from an Old Regime to a new one marked by the emergence in multiple forms of the question of climates and, even more strangely, of their link to government. I am using these terms [...] in their broadest sense. All a sudden, everyone senses that another Spirit of the Laws of Nature is in the process of emerging and that we had better start writing it down if we want to survive the forces unleashed by the New Regime.

Latour, *Facing Gaia*, 13.

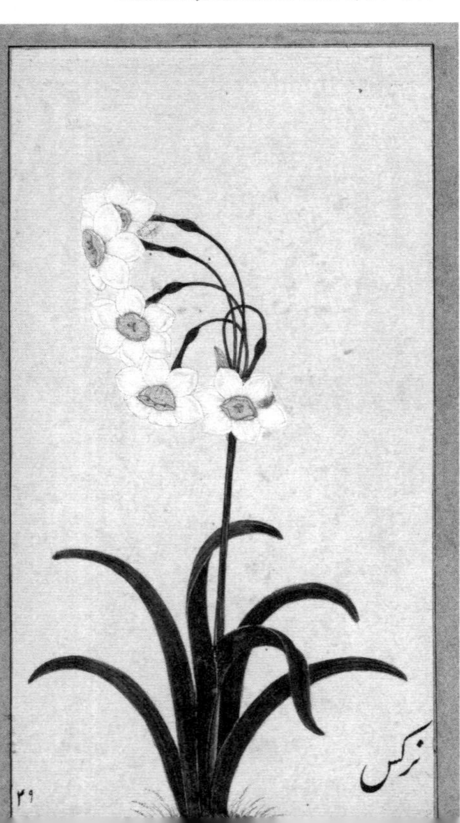

Anonymous (Mughal Empire), **Place 97** from **Small Clive Album**, late seventeenth century, watercolour on paper, 35.5 × 23.5 cm. Courtesy Alamy/Victoria and Albert Museum, London.

NEW ECOLOGY

The New Ecology that I describe in the book is one that also aims to overcome the human/nature divide and tackle the issue of sustaining ecological functioning in the face of a growing human domination of the Earth, in a new epoch that has accordingly been called the Anthropocene. Ecological science is assuming a leading role to help guide the growing human enterprise, to support the need and wants of a burgeoning human population, without jeopardizing nature's ecological functions that support humanity's needs and wants.

Schmitz, *The New Ecology*, 10.

NEW PERENNIAL MOVEMENT

Gardening, whether on the most intimate private level or the most extensive and public, involves an appreciation of and involvement with the natural world. For many people, plants may be their only point of contact with nature apart from feeling the effects of the weather. [...] There is, however, a new and additional agenda for gardeners, both private and public: sustainability and the support of biodiversity. Sustainability demands that we minimize irreplaceable inputs in gardening and reduce harmful outputs, while the support of biodiversity brings a demand for wildlife-friendly planting and practices.

The use of long-lived perennials in conjunction with woody plants—the approach Piet Oudolf and I, Noel Kingsbury, have always supported—genuinely offers improved sustainability and support for biodiversity. Reducing the amount of regularly mown lawn and the unnecessary trimming of woody plants for unclear motives is surely a step forward. Creating rich garden habitats offers natural beauty close at hand, provides resources and homes for wildlife, and improves the sustainability of management.

Oudolf and Kingsbury, *Planting*, 5.

Along with plants people such as Beth Chatto, [Piet] Oudolf changed not only the way we look at gardens, but the plants we grow in them. His students find him inspiring and infuriating in equal measure: he has no singular process, and frequently makes his planting plans public—once used, he has no need of them, preferring to come up with new ideas instead. He's now considered the most prominent member of the New Perennials movement, a shift that happened across Germany and Holland in the Eighties and that made gardens into something challenging and alluring

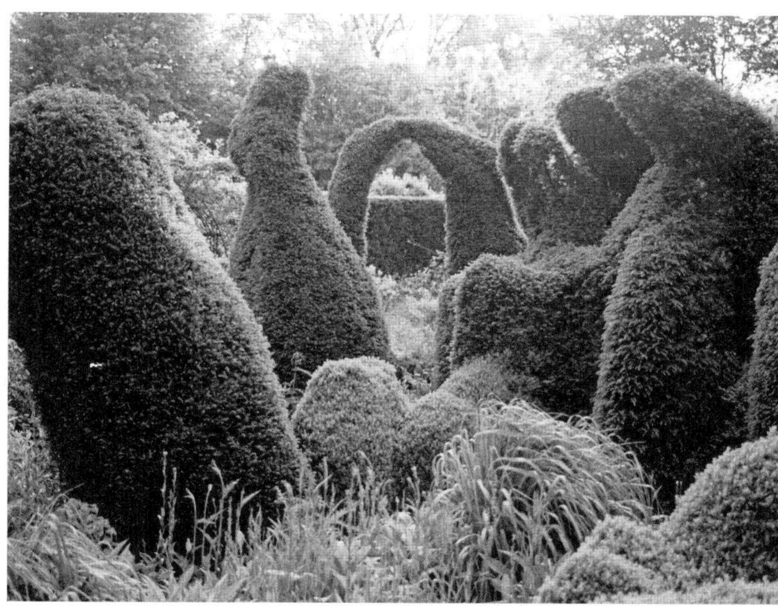
Henk Gerritsen and Anton Schlepers, **Priona Gardens**. Courtesy Priona Gardens.

in equal measure. The basics of it are simple: matching plants to the situations in which they will thrive best, and using ones that will emerge, flower, seed and die, then repeat the process a year later—these plants are known as perennials. But perennials also require patience. Annuals guarantee near-instant results: a pop of colour arriving in a bed from the garden centre. When they fade, they are whipped out and replaced cheaply and cheerfully. Perennials, meanwhile, demand that the gardener appreciates a plant during all of its life stages, even during those when they are invisible, lurking beneath the soil. In exchange, they offer structure and surprise as the year turns. [...]

In its infancy, many considered this stubborn refusal to tidy up old and lifeless growth a shocking thing in a garden. Oudolf worked closely with another Dutch gardener called Henk Gerritsen. Together they wrote *Droomplanten*—or *Dream Plants*—a compendium of the 1,200 perennial plants they promised would make for an easy and beautiful garden at all stages of their life cycle. As Oudolf would say many years later in *Five Seasons,* a documentary about his practice, 'Death is the garden as well'. And it was Gerritsen who taught him this. 'We discovered that plants were good even when they were not flowering', Oudolf has said. 'He pointed this out to me a hundred times. We looked at plants at times other than their prime time.' For Gerritsen, who lived with HIV until his death in 2009, and had lost his partner Anton some fifteen years before, appreciating the beauty of lifeless plants took on an even greater significance. 'People used to be so afraid of death in the garden', he once told writer Noel Kingsbury. 'Every yellow leaf was an imperfection, and had to be taken out... but now a whole generation has known death, so we do not ban it from the garden anymore.'

Vincent, *Rootbound*, chapter 'September'.

NOMENCLATURE

The botanists are from the same part of the world as the man who sailed on the three ships, the man who started the narrative from which I trace my beginning. And in a way, too, the botanists are like that man who sailed on the ships: they emptied worlds of their names; they emptied the worlds of things animal, vegetable, and mineral of their names and replaced these names with names pleasing to them; these names are pleasing to them because they are reasonable; reason is a pleasure to them.

Kincaid, *My Garden (Book)*, 258.

The invention of this system has been a good thing. Its narrative would begin in this way: In the beginning, the vegetable kingdom was chaos, people everywhere called the same things by a name that made sense to them, not by a name arrived at by an objective standard. But who has an interest in an objective standard? Who needs one? It makes me ask again, What to call the thing that happened to me and all who look like me? Should I call it history? And if so, what should history mean to someone who looks like me? Should it be an idea; should it be an open wound, each breath I take in and expel healing and opening the wound again, over and over, or is it a long moment that begins anew each day since 1492?

Kincaid, *My Garden (Book)*, 268–269.

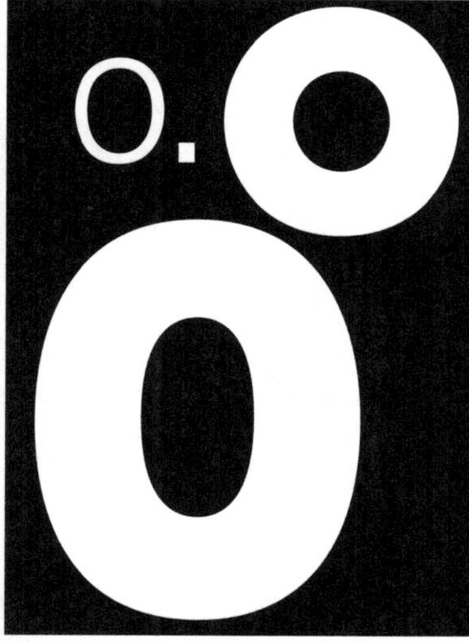

OCRA/OKER/OKRA

Okra (*Abelmoschus esculentus*) is a plant in the mallow (Malvaceae) family that probably originated in the region that is now Ethiopia. It was cultivated by the ancient Egyptians as early as the twelfth century BCE and spread thereafter to the rest of North Africa and the Middle East. It grows well in tropical and subtropical regions. Today, the plant is also grown commercially in countries as widespread as Brazil, Cyprus, India, and Japan.

Maria Sibylla Merian (known for her beautiful drawings of insects and their host plants and known in some circles as critical of slavery, even though she owned enslaved people) encountered the plant in Suriname at the end of the seventeenth century. In her book *Metamorphosis insectorum Surinamensium* (Metamorphosis in Surinamese Insects), she writes: 'This plant is known in Suriname as althea or okkerum and is familiar among those who study plants. Slaves in America cook and eat the fruit... It grows taller than a man, has flowers that are yellowish-white and pink in colour, and when the fruit is cut it produces a sticky slime like a thread'.

The plant had been found in Suriname prior to Merian's study trip and was described in the *Hermann Herbarium* by the German botanist Paul Hermann, a book containing fifty plants collected in Suriname from 1687 to 1689. It had also been described in Brazil in 1658. It is interesting that Merian knew that the plant was already known and distributed in America, where it had reached Philadelphia in the north-east of the country by 1748. How did she know this? How did this plant spread through the Americas? Who took it and in what form?

In various parts of North America and in Suriname, okra has become a regular part of the diet of the African diaspora, in dishes such as gumbo and the Surinamese 'oker soup'. Okra is still widely eaten in its continent of origin, for example in West Africa, as 'okro soup'. In Suriname, many of the 'Maroon' people, descendants of enslaved Africans, are still aware of the plant's African origins.

Thiëmo Heilbron

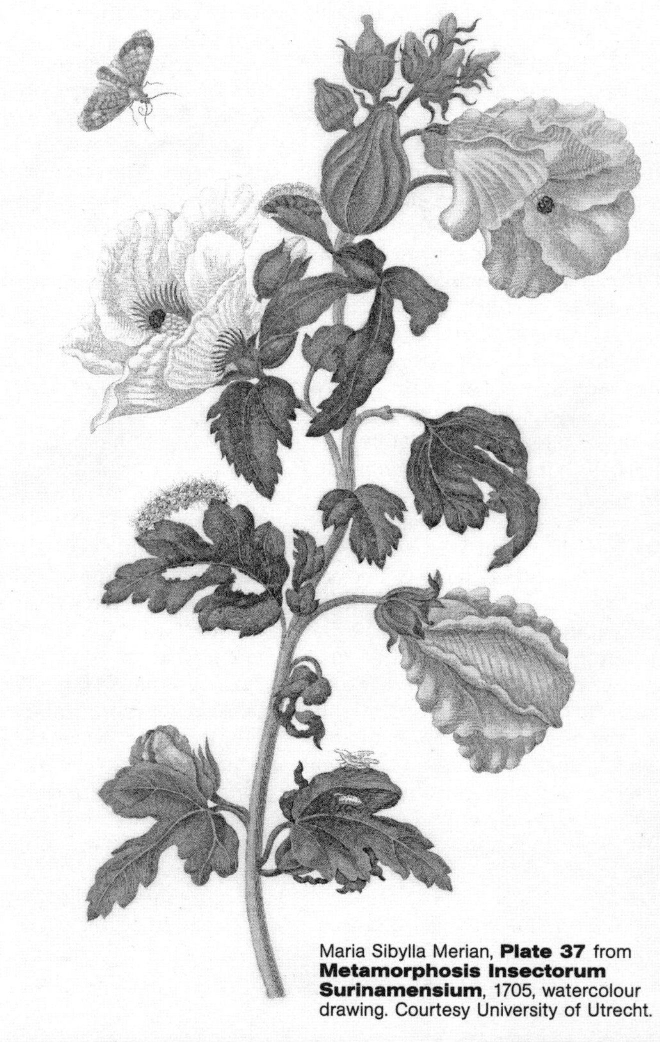
Maria Sibylla Merian, **Plate 37** from **Metamorphosis Insectorum Surinamensium**, 1705, watercolour drawing. Courtesy University of Utrecht.

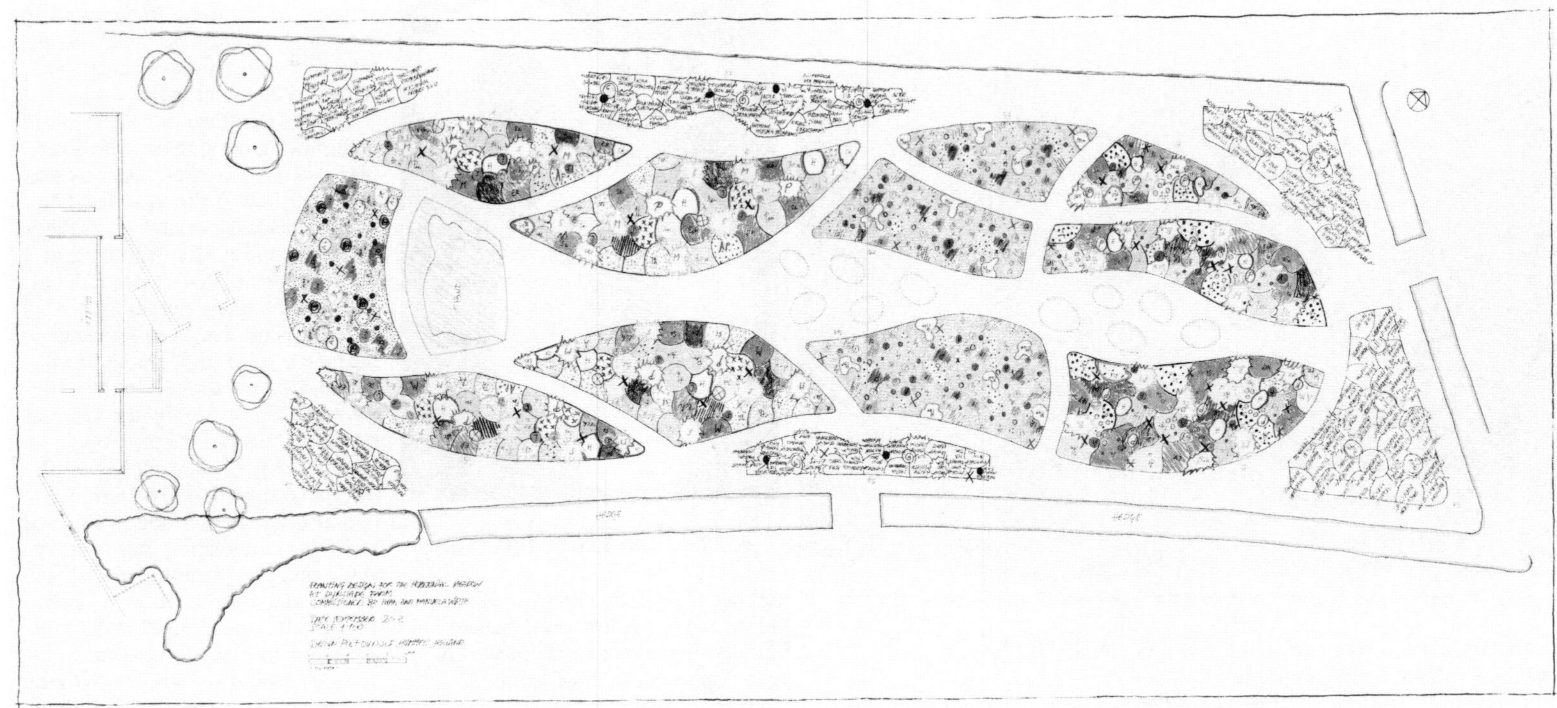

Piet Oudolf, **Planting Design for Oudolf Field, Hauser & Wirth Somerset**, 2018, drawing. Courtesy Hauser & Wirth/Piet Oudolf. Photo: Alex Delfanne.

ORGANIC MOVEMENT

The organic movement was both a reaction against what its advocates viewed as the increasing industrialisation of farming, the super-reliance of farming on mechanical and chemical technologies to improve yields, *and*, for many, a wider statement of the need to live in a different way, one (as organicists saw it) in harmony with 'nature' rather than in domination of it.

McKay, *Radical Gardening*, 42.

From small beginnings over farmlands and forests the scope of aerial spraying has widened and its volume has increased so that it has become what a British ecologist recently called 'an amazing rain of death' upon the surface of the earth. Our attitude toward poisons has undergone a subtle change. Once they were kept in containers marked with skull and crossbones; the infrequent occasions of their use were marked with utmost care that they should come in contact with the target and with nothing else. With the development of the new organic insecticides and the abundance of surplus planes after the Second World War, all this was forgotten. Although today's poisons are more dangerous than any known before, they have amazingly become something to be showered down indiscriminately from the skies. Not only the target insect or plant, but anything—human or nonhuman—within range of the chemical fallout may know the sinister touch of the poison. Not only forests and cultivated fields are sprayed, but towns and cities as well.

Carson, *Silent Spring*, 325–326.

PIET OUDOLF

Planting design has, in general, moved from a sense of absolute control to one of negotiating with nature—if not of total spontaneity, then at least of the appearance of spontaneity. However, the precise placing of plants is sometimes as critical to the effect in Piet's work as in more traditional planting. More generally, the spontaneity of allowing plants to move around is, in fact, part of an older tradition. Movements within twentieth-century gardening played with spontaneity: Willy Lange (1864–1941) in inter-war Germany promoted naturalistic planting using native species, while the English cottage garden style was an idealisation of the gardens of country people; one of its greatest exponents, Margery Fish (1892–1969), was hugely influential in promoting the idea of covering the soil with a full canopy of vegetation and allowing plants to spread and self-seed. [...]

To design a planting which involved such an element of spontaneity is entirely consistent. Piet's trajectory as a designer has been a continual move away from the ordered to the spontaneous. His earlier work was in the firmly modernist style of Mien Ruys, combining contemporary-style architectural clipping of woody plants with perennials and flowering shrubs. Gradually, the perennials and grasses have taken over, and since around 2000 he has begun to experiment more and more with intermingling. To create something which combines the planned placing of plants with the inevitable randomness of seed sowing can be seen as part of such a journey.

Oudolf and Kingsbury, *Planting*, chapter, 'Conclusion'.

Oudolf's gardens exist out of fashion and time because they are created with less transitory notions in mind. Not of aesthetics as much as feeling, space and beauty. 'A garden is also a promise', he said in *Five Seasons: The Gardens of Piet Oudolf.* 'It doesn't have to be there, you're looking for what will be there.' Oudolf is a plant fanatic, a purveyor of arresting beauty who actively encourages the birds and the bees. A man who resisted the counter-culture movement of the Sixties but nevertheless pioneered the benefits of gardening naturally with 'no pesticides, no artificial fertilisers and no army of gardeners to keep the plants alive'. His approach is radical. Perhaps it's because he's one of those gardeners who was not brought up around plants. Rather, like me, he found them in his mid twenties and saw them as a means to escape a career intended for him: working in the restaurant his family owned. [...]

Vincent, *Rootbound*, chapter 'September'.

ON THE NECESSITY OF ART AND GARDENING: A STORY IN FOUR PARTS

See page 111 for 'On The Necessity of Art and Gardening: A Story in Four Parts' by Laurie Kluitmans.

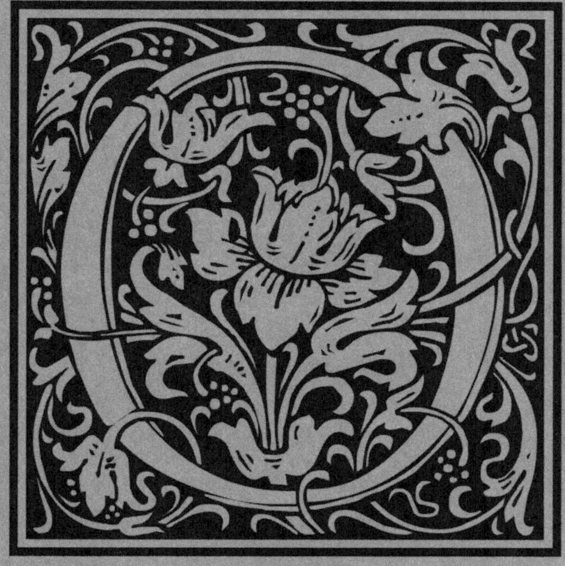

William Morris, **Letter O.**

ON THE NECESSITY OF ART AND GARDENING

A STORY IN FOUR PARTS

Laurie Cluitmans

> The unfinished Chthulucene must collect up the trash of the Anthropocene, the exterminism of the Capitalocene, and chipping and shredding and layering like a mad gardener, make a much hotter compost pile for still possible pasts, presents, and futures.
>
> Donna Haraway,
> *Staying with the Trouble*[1]

n recent years, artists, writers, and thinkers have repeatedly turned to the garden as a tool and metaphor for thinking about and reflecting upon the complex times in which we live. They have taken to heart the need to take care of the earth and to cultivate it. The garden can take on many guises. It may symbolize wealth, power, authority, and the colonial past, but it also represents forms of care, a different experience of time, and a healing power. These artists are central to this publication and the parallel exhibition at the Centraal Museum, and their practices have shaped both. In this essay, I outline the four sections that make up the exhibition, focusing on one or more artworks per section.

PART I: THE BEGINNING

There are different points of departure for thinking about the garden's potential as a metaphor for different world views. Let us start at the beginning, for some at least, in that bountiful, primeval garden, that earthly Paradise, a mythical utopia where one man and one woman lived in harmony with nature: the Garden of Eden. The story of Adam and Eve in the Biblical garden is depicted in a striking manner by the Utrecht-based painter Abraham Bloemaert (1566–1651) in the suite of engravings *The History of the First Parents of Man* (1604). Initially, the sun blissfully shines down on the first man and woman, who seem to live in close harmony with each other, their surroundings, and nature. Until Eve plucks and consumes a piece of a forbidden fruit and shares it with Adam. Soon after, the couple is banished from their equilibrious life in the Garden of Eden, and sent to live and work strenuously on rugged terrain with an ominous thundercloud hovering above their heads. There, Bloemaert depicts Adam digging and Eve spinning. Expelled from Paradise, they now bear the responsibility to cultivate and take care of their own living environment.

In keeping with an age-old visual tradition, Bloemaert depicts the Garden of Eden as a paradise characterized by harmony and peace, yet under constant threat. However, this visual tradition of depicting the beginning of the history of mankind symbolizes for many others a 'once upon a time' fictional story, or even a moral straitjacket. After all, the supposed blissful harmony the couple enjoyed can be considered paradoxical, existing only as a result of continuous moral self-restraint and a refusal of access to knowledge.

> What turned wrong with Eden (from my point of view) is so familiar: the owner grew tired of the rigid upkeep of His

1 Donna Haraway, **Staying with the Trouble: Making Kin in the Chthulucene** (Durham, NC: Duke University Press, 2016), 57.

creation (and I say His on purpose), of the rules that could guarantee its continued perfect existence, and most definitely tired of that design of the particular specimen (Tree of Life, Tree of Knowledge) as the focal point in the center and the other configurations (alleys, parterres, orchards, potageries; the cottage garden, which is really an illustration of making the best of deep social injustice, as the ha-ha, a part of the gardening landscape, is an illustration of making something beautiful out of yet another social cruelty).

And the caretakers, the occupants (Adam, and then Eve), too, seemed to have grown tired of the demands of the Gardener and most certainly of His ideas of what the garden ought to be [...].[2]

2 Jamaica Kincaid, **My Garden (Book)** (New York: Farrar, Strauss & Giroux, 1999), E-Book edition, Apple Books, 2012), 360–361.

In deceptively simple and unadorned language, the Antiguan-American writer Jamaica Kincaid (b. 1949) explains how Adam and Eve did not so much fall but rather wriggled their way out of a moral straitjacket. In *My Garden (Book)* her quasi-romantic perception of her own garden and her account of how she learned to garden is shot through with spurts of sophisticated criticism directed at the Garden of Eden. Kincaid's message is clear: the first garden was by no means a neutral representation of a natural order.

My Garden (Book) is permeated with poignant jabs at world history, sometimes delivered with nonchalance, sometimes like a punch on the nose. Kincaid succeeds in making the story of Adam and Eve seem quotidian and tangible on a personal level. In another essay she points to various methods of exclusion, describing the *ha-ha*—a landscape design element that creates a vertical barrier while preserving an uninterrupted view of the landscape beyond—as a form of control and exclusion in everyday life. From her own Caribbean background, she traces the origins of plants and draws lines of connections between their migration, and that of people, with the violent (hi)story of colonialism, displacement, and uprooting.

The way in which Kincaid unravels the myth of the Garden of Eden is reminiscent of another writer on gardening: the English filmmaker and painter Derek Jarman (1942–1994). At the beginning of his journal *Modern Nature*, Jarman writes that his garden at Prospect Cottage is a piece of paradise on earth. Writing about his garden, gardening, and living with AIDS, he contrasts the budding and flowering of plants with the deterioration of his own health. At a time when homosexuality was still a taboo, Jarman was involved with the AIDS awareness movement. So when he writes 'I intend to celebrate our corner of paradise, the part of the garden the Lord forgot to mention', he specifically alludes to and creates an open, inclusive place.[3]

In Kincaid's and Jarman's writing, the garden forms a stark contrast to that idea of the garden as a peaceful and idyllic retreat from the world. Both, from their own personal perspective, show that the story of the Garden of Eden is also a story where strictly enforced principles dominate life and where only a few have access. This is a false idyllic story told at many other people's expense. The ways that Kincaid and Jarman encourage us to take a different look at the garden and reflect on the world is similar to Foucault's heterotopia.[4] In Foucault's work, the garden, and in particular the Persian garden, is used to illustrate his conception of 'heterotopia', a space that is 'other': disturbing, intense, contradictory, irreconcilable, or transformative. For Foucault, the garden is simultaneously the smallest part of the world and a reflection of the totality of that world: a world within a world, which mirrors and distorts that which lies outside it. The garden can be seen as a microcosm, a place where political, economic, and social powers converge which brings to mind Kincaid's and Jarman's writings. The world enters into their gardens and they shift our attention in order to provide a critical and more inclusive understanding of the garden.

Can we imagine an alternative starting point to the Garden of Eden? After all, doesn't every culture have its own Eden? The etymology of the word paradise points to an infinite number of possible paradises, besides the one from the Old Testament. The word paradise is derived from the Persian word *pairidaiza*, which literally translates as 'walled space': *pairi* means 'around' and *daêza* means 'wall'. As in the medieval *hortus conclusus*, the garden wall is supposed to offer controlled protection from the wilderness outside of the wall. It keeps the outside

3 Derek Jarman, **Modern Nature**, 23.

4 Michel Foucault, 'Of Other Spaces: Utopias and Heterotopias', in **Rethinking Architecture: A Reader in Cultural Theory**, ed. Neil Leach (New York: Routledge, 1997), 350–356. Originally delivered as a lecture in March 1967 and published posthumously in French as 'Des Espaces Autres' in **Architecture/Mouvement/Continuité**, October, 1984.

world out, but it also admits the wild—from which it seeks protection and of which it is so afraid—but only in a curated, cultivated, and tamed form.[5]

At the basis of the Persian garden we find a geometric ground plan of paths and water channels that divide the walled space into a square or rectangle with ideal proportions. In Iran's hot, dry climate, water is scarce and is transported over great distances to cities via underground channels. Landowners bought some of this water to irrigate their crops and pleasure grounds. These channels play an important organizing principle in the design of the garden. The Persian walled garden is about the representation of an ideal world. In the canonical Persian garden, paths and water channels guide visitors along the four seasons, the four elements, and the four corners of the earth. At the centre is the most sacred space, the navel of the world, in the form of a basin or water fountain.[6] Seen this way, the Persian garden is an ancient archetype within which the aesthetic and the utilitarian converge. Its design was highly influential on both European and Islamic garden design traditions.

The Persian paradise rug, crafted since 540 BCE, is a popular derivative of this ideal, attractive to rich and poor alike. Modest variants of Persian carpets represent an aerial view of the cruciform ground plan with side views of the pavilions, trees, flowers, and birds. The trees provide shade and colour contrast. The carpet represents fertility and bounty and can be seen as a mirror of heaven. Simultaneously, it forms a portable ground plan. The portable garden can be easily rolled up when commuting between a winter and summer residence, and is also well suited to a more nomadic life. As such, the rug provides, in representational form, all the benefits of the garden without necessarily having to own one.

When Foucault writes about the garden as a heterotopia, he specifically refers to the Persian garden and garden carpet. The garden-carpet forms a microcosm: in this perfectly harmonious garden the entire world comes together. The Garden of Eden and the Persian Garden both give an idealized normative account of the world, but from radically different perspectives. Where the Garden of Eden, as a religious construct, symbolizes a paradise of moral restraint and limitation, the Persian garden, on the other hand, arises from a physical need for water and shade in a dry and sun-drenched landscape. Both gardens symbolize an eternal harmonious space that offers protection from the outside world, the wilderness. They offer refuge and symbolize multiplicity and fertility. But access to these gardens is limited to the lucky few. Kincaid's and Jarman's gardens are in sharp contrast to that. In their refuge there is room not only for life, but also for the world.

PART II: FRONT GARDEN, BACK GARDEN, ALLOTMENT

> The gardener digs in another time, without past or future, beginning or end. A time that does not cleave the day with rush hours, lunch breaks, the last bus home. As you walk in the garden you pass into this time—the moment of entering can never be remembered. Around you the landscape lies transfigured. Here is the Amen beyond the prayer.
>
> Derek Jarman, *Modern Nature*[7]

The longing for a garden as a refuge, as the Persian garden was in a dry, sun-drenched environment, has become an increasingly larger and more widely supported need in urban reality. For an entire year, artist Sara Sejin Chang (Sara van der Heide) (b. 1977) filmed her garden in Tuinpark Tuinwijck, an allotment complex now located in Amsterdam Noord but originally established in 1910 in Amsterdam Oost as the so-called 'workers' gardens'. Here, for a modest rent, workers could avail themselves of a plot of land on the condition that they used it to grow potatoes and vegetables for their own consumption and only during their free time.

Chang spent almost every day for a year filming life in the garden, slowly, calmly, and precisely. In the resulting film, every moment and every life form—from budding flowers to writhing worms and rotting leaves—receives equal attention, without judgment. The resulting film *The Garden* is, therefore, not a spectacular film; it has no narrative, no development, no climax. Chang imagines life here just beyond the standard story of progress and growth and shows how a garden can offer a different experience of time, a different rhythm from the linear nine-to-five work time.

5 Rob Aben and Saskia de Wit, **The Enclosed Garden: History and Development of the Hortus Conclusus and its Reintroduction into the Present-day Urban Landscape** (Rotterdam: 010 Publishers, 1999).

6 Kathryn Gleason, "Introduction", **A Cultural History of Gardens in Antiquity**, ed. Kathryn Gleason, Vol. 1 Bloomsbury Academic, 2017 (reprinted paperback edition), 4. This essential element is missing from Jarman's garden, which has no wall or gate. 'My garden's boundaries are the horizon', Jarman once wrote tellingly. Derek Jarman, **Modern Nature**, 3.

7 Derek Jarman, **Modern Nature**, 30.

The activity of gardening or even being surrounded by greenery can have a healing effect on our bodies and minds. It is not for nothing that in 2020, during the lockdowns enforced in an attempt to mitigate the effects of the global COVID-19 pandemic, people took solace in their gardens, if they had one, or headed to parks and forests. In *The Well-Gardened Mind*, psychiatrist Sue Stuart-Smith discusses historical and present forms of garden and gardening therapies. She writes about soldiers, on duty during World War I, who planted gardens in trenches. The image of gardens in trenches immediately evokes a stark contrast—the soldiers created alternating strips or vegetable gardens, flower beds, and graveyards, a striking image of the novel relationship that arises between life and death during a gruesome, violent, and deadly (trench) war. On the one hand, death and destruction are a constant threat; on the other, life's cycles go on. For Stuart-Smith, the garden expresses a desire for inner peace: the colourful, fragrant flowers provided the necessary contrast to the madness and traumatic horrors of WW I.[8]

The trench garden described by Stuart-Smith seems closely related to Jarman's description of his garden as a pharmacopoeia, referring not only to its store of medicinal plants, but also to the therapeutic act of gardening itself. Gardening is a form of care, but it also demands physical labour: digging the soil, sowing, planting, and maintenance require a direct and active relationship with nature. For Jarman, his garden, and gardening, allowed him to forget about daily worries and to mourn the friends he lost with alarming regularity to the same virus he was battling.

The importance of the green garden is now recognized worldwide. The pursuit of the right balance between greenery, water, and shade that both the Garden of Eden and the Persian garden provide and foster brings us to the significance, benefits, and desirability of the back yard, or green garden, in contemporary societies in general, and in built-up areas and cityscapes in particular. One striking fact and notable nuance: an analysis of aerial photos shows that about sixty per cent of the gardens in built-up areas in the Netherlands are surfaced with paving stones.[9] That image fits neatly with the notion that we live in a new geological epoch, which atmospheric chemist Paul Crutzen (b. 1933) has dubbed the Anthropocene, a period of the total dominance of man (*anthropos*) over nature. Crutzen dates the beginning of this epoch to the second half of the eighteenth century which coincides with the invention of the steam engine in 1784.[10] Over the past two decades, the concept has come to symbolize the idea that humans are exhausting the earth's natural resources, resulting in a disastrous climate crisis.

But the idea of the Anthropocene is controversial and has been strongly criticized for its implication that all humans share equal responsibility and have contributed equally to the current situation. Meanwhile, several mocking alternatives have been suggested, such as the Misanthropocene and the Mantropocene.[11] In a more serious tone, Catriona Sandilands (b. 1964), a Professor of Environmental Studies at York University, explains how the concept is blind to the complex interrelations between industrialization, urbanization, gender, race, class, and colonial power relations. Jason W. Moore (b. 1971), an Environmental Historian and Professor of Sociology at Binghamton University, has introduced the concept of the Capitalocene to clarify the Anthropocene's relationship to capitalism: hundreds of companies are responsible for seventy per cent of the emissions, yet those companies argue that consumers could do more to contribute to the fight against global warming.[12]

Back to the paving stones in all those Dutch gardens. Paved surfaces are easy to maintain, and a little poison gets rid of moss and algae in no time. Some consider paved gardens more beautiful than green gardens, but quite simply they are also cheaper to construct and maintain than a green garden. Gardening has historically been the preserve of certain social classes, and still is to an extent. A garden is a low priority when there are bills to pay. Gardens and gardening are also becoming the target of growing industry; we are bombarded with messages about green fingers, propagating cuttings, guerrilla gardening, and transforming our balconies into a mini paradise. And gardening is becoming an increasingly popular pastime. In his book *The Garden Jungle*, Dave

8 Sue Stuart-Smith, **The Well-Gardened Mind: The Restorative Power of Nature** (London: William Collins, 2017), 207–209.

9 Frank Mulder, 'Grijze tuinen: "Een tuin is een aanval"', **De Groene Amsterdammer**, 6 May, 2020.

10 Paul Crutzen, 'Geology of Mankind', **Nature** 415 (January, 2002).

11 See Joshua Clover and Julianna Spahr, **#Misanthropocene: 24 Theses** (Oakland, CA: Commune Editions, Oakland, 2014).

12 Jason Moore, **Capitalism in the Web of Life** (London: Verso, 2015).

Goulson (b. 1965), a Professor of Biology at the University of Sussex, makes a plea for 'gardening to save the planet'.[13] If we are to heed his rallying cry, the Dutch need to replace their cement gardens with soil and plants. By doing so, Goulson concedes, we could combat global warming and erosion, retain more rainwater, and promote greater biodiversity. In short, the garden could save the earth. Albeit a message of hope, solutions such as Goulson's point to the heart of the problem with the concept of the Anthropocene. The combined forces of all those green fingers simply cannot undo the devastation being wrought by the Big Polluters that are destroying the planet, despite our good intentions.

Although the word Anthropocene is slowly gaining currency in addressing climate change, it is important to think about its usage. Words are not neutral; they act within a system and have political and social connotations and power. Moreover, this discussion about how to refer to our current geological epoch is more than a mere digression. It forms the background, the apocalyptic backdrop, against which the artists discussed here create their work. According to Donna Haraway (b. 1944), the answer to this global climate problem is the Chthulucene, a science fiction-like word to describe a hopeful world view in the making, and entailing the past, present, and future. A world view in which new relationships must be formed between humanity and all other life forms. Haraway's main criticism of the words Anthropocene and also Capitolocene is that both thematize irreversible destruction. Haraway wants to come to a possible solution from the point of view of criticism, she wants to propose a new and better world. At the base of this new paradigm lies what Haraway calls kinship, a 'mutual, obligatory, non-optional, enduring relatedness' that exists not only between humans, but between all forms of life on earth.[14]

Chang's *The Garden* offers an alternative form of coexistence that is reminiscent of Haraway's proposal for 'making kin'. Chang goes against the Renaissance idea that there is a hierarchical division of life into more and less developed species, from the supposedly simplest to the more complex. At the top stands man as the most developed being of all. This hierarchical understanding of life—of nature—has determined what growth and progress mean in the Western tradition. With her horizontal montage and non-judgmental lens, Chang strips life in the garden of categorization, hierarchy, and preference for colours, life phases, or seasons. She shows us a cycle in which growth, flowering, and decay go hand in hand, framing this transience in a very simple fashion, without theatre or didacticism: it is simply there, resulting in a very direct and sensitive 'being'. Moreover, the slow gaze that the film evokes creates conditions to be able to see better, and it is precisely through that slowness and attentiveness that we can imagine other relationships.

13 Dave Goulson, **The Garden Jungle: Or Gardening to Save the Planet** (London: Jonathan Cape, 2019).

14 Donna Haraway, quoted by Steve Paulson in 'Making Kin: An Interview with Donna Haraway', **Los Angeles Review of Books**, 6 December, 2009.

PART III: THE BOTANICAL REVOLUTION

Gardening makes us forget 'calendar time' or 'clock time', allowing us to focus instead on circularity. The playwright Samuel Beckett (1906–1989) once wrote that 'the end is in the beginning and yet you go on'.[15] The circularity he implies is one of always continuing, no matter whether you succeed or not. So let us return once more to the beginning. For in addition to that first supposed beginning of Eden and Paradise, there was another beginning:

> And in a way, too, the botanists are like that man who sailed on the ships: they emptied worlds of their names; they emptied the worlds of things animal, vegetable, and mineral of their names and replaced these names with names pleasing to them; these names are pleasing to them because they are reasonable; reason is a pleasure to them.[16]

The botanists, zoologists, and geologists to whom Kincaid refers here, who renamed all the plants, animals, and rocks, remind her of Christopher Columbus, whom she also calls 'the man who sailed on the three ships'. Here Kincaid points to an imposed beginning where the 'discovery' of the world went hand in hand with violent colonial history. It brings to mind the series of drawings that artist Patricia Kaersenhout (1966) made in response to Maria Sibylla Merian's *Metamorphosis Insectorum Surinamensiumis* from 1705. Merian (1647–1717) is often praised for her contribution to science and for the fact that

15 Samuel Beckett, **Endgame** (London: Faber & Faber, 1958, first published in French in 1957).

16 Jamaica Kincaid, **My Garden**, 258.

in the eighteenth century it was rare for a woman to undertake such a huge journey and to carry out her work as an entomologist and 'discover' insect species. Lesser known, however, is that Maria Sibylla Merian depended on the knowledge of enslaved women to conduct her study of plants and insects in Suriname. One of the women who helped Merian with her academic fieldwork was eventually brought back to Europe, as evinced by the passenger list of their ship. Kaersenhout, whose parents came from Suriname, made it her task to trace this woman. In a series of embroideries in the style of the seventeenth-century botanists and employing the theory of critical fabulation, Kaersenhout has reconstructed the possible life, dreams, and emotions of the unidentified woman. The work also refers to the wealth of knowledge that this woman must have had about plants and their medicinal properties, knowledge that was taken seriously only when it was adopted and recorded by European botanists.

The act of giving Latinized names and categorizing living things can be considered as part of a scientific revolution that developed in Europe in the sixteenth and seventeenth centuries, characterized by a (gendered) conception of knowledge, considered the product of the reasoning of wise *men*, within which dualisms, standardizations, and categorizations formed the means to gain understanding of life. The historical narratives of the study of botany echo this paradigm shift. In his *Systema Naturae* (1735), the Swedish taxonomist Carl Linnaeus (1707–1778) arranged the plant kingdom into twenty-four categories or types. This classification was based on a simple system, in which the reproductive organs (the stamens and ovaries) were decisive—according to Linnaeus, the reproductive organs embodied the essence of the plant. In doing so, however, he soon encountered irreconcilable problems. His observations did not actually comply with his world view; that mindset prescribed male-female reproduction. Any other possibility was unthinkable.[17]

17 Ben Borthwick, ed., **Andrea Büttner: Hidden Marriages** (London: Koenig Books, 2014), 5–6. His system quickly became popular, leading to the idea that plants have a sexual life. By means of botanical taxonomy, it became possible to speak openly, if indirectly, about human sexuality, but female botanists were quickly excluded as it would be inappropriate for a lady to take part in such conversations.

The taxonomical categories established by Linnaeus determined not only the development of the study of botany, but the way we look, as well as our gaze. Linnaeus determined what we did and did not see. The artist Andrea Büttner (b. 1972) provides a good example of this in her series of works on mosses. According to Linnaeus's system, mosses are characterized by what they lack: roots, flowers, fruits, seeds, and a vascular system for absorbing water. Moreover, they do not fit into the standard idea of sexuality that Linnaeus championed and which grew out of the prevailing views of his time. For classical botanical taxonomy, these are sufficient reasons to characterize moss as a primitive plant, a 'lower' phylum, literally and figuratively. To be able to incorporate moss into his system after all, Linnaeus invented the twenty-fourth category of so-called cryptogams, including algae, lichens, mosses, and ferns. *Kryptos* is Greek for hidden, *gamos* for marriage; a hidden marriage that refers to the so-called hidden sexuality of the mosses. Only with the development of cheaper microscopes does the interest and knowledge about the species and its reproductive mechanisms grow. Only then does it appear that the imposed 'hidden' heterosexual marriage that Linnaeus attributed to the mosses did not exist and that the reproduction of mosses is much more complex and diverse.

In his book *Botanische revolutie* (Botanical Revolution) Botanical philosopher Norbert Peeters (b. 1985) describes a certain kind of plant blindness. He explains this form of blindness by means of a simple experiment: he shows people a picture of a leopard in an acacia tree and asks, what do you see? They usually answer: a leopard, sometimes a leopard in a tree, but hardly ever a leopard in an acacia tree.[18] By means of his analyses of the botanical work of Charles Darwin, Peeters advocates a re-evaluation of plant life in order to gain a better understanding of biodiversity. The new botanical revolution is not about naming, controlling, limiting, and exploiting living beings, but rather about a different attention to the complexity and intelligence of all life forms and their co-dependent relations.

Mosses are a typical example of this development. In *Gathering Moss*, Robin Wall Kimmerer (b. 1953), Professor of Environmental and Forest Biology at SUNY-ESF, describes the simple and elegant life of mosses at what she calls the margins of our everyday gaze. Her knowledge of plants

18 Norbert Peeters, **Botanische Revolutie: De plantenleer van Charles Darwin** (Zeist: KNNV Uitgeverij, 2016).

stems from different traditions, including her training as a botanist and her Potawatomi heritage. According to Kimmerer we are programmed to see through what she calls 'search images'. Confronted with a rich visual landscape, the brain initially registers all incoming data without critical evaluation, and it is only through practice and experience that the neural pathways are trained to process it. For example, instead of seeing a large green patch of moss, we can adjust these search images and understand and untangle different species. Mosses require a certain form of attentiveness. According to Kimmerer, watching mosses adds a certain intimacy in getting to know the forest in depth, which makes us see and experience the world rather differently.[19]

This botanical revolution teaches us that plants move, feel, and 'communicate'. Though it is not only about the visible trees and plants, but also those life forms that are invisible to the naked human eye, such as bacteria and fungal hypha. All life forms in the woods need each other.[20] Within the ecosystem of a wood, trees, for example, recognize insects, remember temperature fluctuations, and 'communicate' with each other via hyphae. Mycorrhiza—derived from the Greek *mukès* meaning fungus and *rhiza* meaning root—is a symbiotic relationship between fungi and plants or trees. For example, fungi absorb all kinds of minerals from the soil and release them to the roots of trees and plants in exchange for sugars.[21] The twenty-four categories of Linnaeus look pale in comparison to this multiplicity of life and relationships. This view of the forest aligns with Haraway's kinship and her proposed Chthulucene.

Unlike the dominant dramas of Anthropocene and Capitalocene discourse, human beings are not the only important actors in the Chthulucene, with all other beings able simply to react. The order is reknitted: human beings are with and of the Earth, and the biotic and abiotic powers of this Earth are the main story.[22]

PART IV: A NEW ECOLOGY

Just as there are different points of departure for thinking about the garden's potential as a metaphor for different world views, there are also different starting points and prefigurations to our current climate regime. In 1972, the Japanese artist Tetsumi Kudo (1935–1990) wrote a manifesto entitled *Pollution-Cultivation-New Ecology*, which remains relevant today. Kudo responds to mankind's depletion and exploitation of the earth's natural resources and calls for a reconsideration of the relationship between nature, humanity, and technology. He argues that vanquished nature takes revenge on mankind through pollution and the machine, both created by humans to satisfy their egocentrism. And, as a result of which, he claims, humanism falls apart. Kudo agitates against European humanism, in which human's enforced dominance over nature, over life and death, and over creation and destruction has led to slavery, colonialism, and ecological catastrophe. In his visionary manifesto, he called for a 'new ecology', in which humans, nature, and technology work together to survive:

> In this new ecological system, it is not possible that human dignity alone should retain the hauteur of a king. But it is very difficult to remove the sentiment of privilege (human dignity) and the sentiment of colonialism of the head of humanity that calls itself 'humanist'.[23]

Kudo's installation *Grafted Garden/Pollution-cultivation-nouvelle écologie* (1970–1971) is an example of such a new ecology, in which man, technology, and nature become one. Fragments of limbs—arms, legs, penises—merge with flowers, snails, and trees, grafted onto aluminium poles. Together they form a haunted and macabre 'garden' of transformed life. In a reading of this work and Kudo's manifesto, the images of the nuclear bombings of Hiroshima and Nagasaki loom large. If that is where humanism has led us, where can we find hope for change? With his new ecology, Kudo offers a response to our deeply wounded world. In that respect, *Grafted Garden* is again a garden that like a mirror reflects our world and looks into the future where (r)evolution is possible. When we think of Haraway's 'mad gardener' mentioned at the beginning of this essay, and her hopeful Chthulucene, we return to a garden that lies transfigured in front of us. After the fall, we can begin again.

19 Robin Wall Kimmerer, **Gathering Moss**, 9.

20 Peter Wohlleben, **The Hidden Life of Trees: What They Feel, How They Communicate—Discoveries from a Secret World** (London: Penguin, 2016).

21 Merlin Sheldrake, **Entangled Life: How Fungi Make Our Worlds, Change Our Minds and Shape Our Futures** (London: The Bodley Head, 2020), 3.

22 Donna Haraway, "Tentacular Thinking: Anthropocene, Capitalocene, Chtulucene", **E-Flux Journal** no. 75, 2016.

23 Tetsumi Kudo, 'Pollution of Nature! Decomposition of Humanity!', in **Tetsumi Kudo: Cultivation**, ed. Tine Colstrup and Laerke Rydal Jorgensen (Humlebæk: Louisiana Museum of Modern Art, 2020), 33.

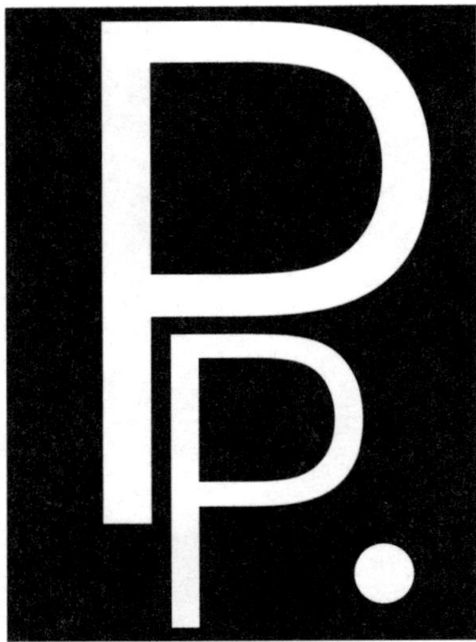

PANSY

THE PANSY
Viola tricolor, heartsease, tickle-my-fancy, love-in-idleness, or herb trinity. The juice of it on sleeping eyelids will make a man or woman dote upon the next live creature they see, if you would have midsummer's dreams. A strong tea made of the leaves will cure a broken heart; for our pansy is strongly aphrodisiac, its name, pensée, *I think of you*. If it leads you astray, don't worry: the herbal says it cures the clap; for 'it is a Saturnine plant of a cold slimy viscous nature ... an excellent cure for venereal disorder'. In the old days pansies were virgin white, until Cupid fired his arrow and turned them the colours of the rainbow.

Of one thing you must beware: picking a pansy in the first light of dawn, particularly if it is spotted with dew, will surely bring the death of a loved one.

Jarman, *Modern Nature*, 29.

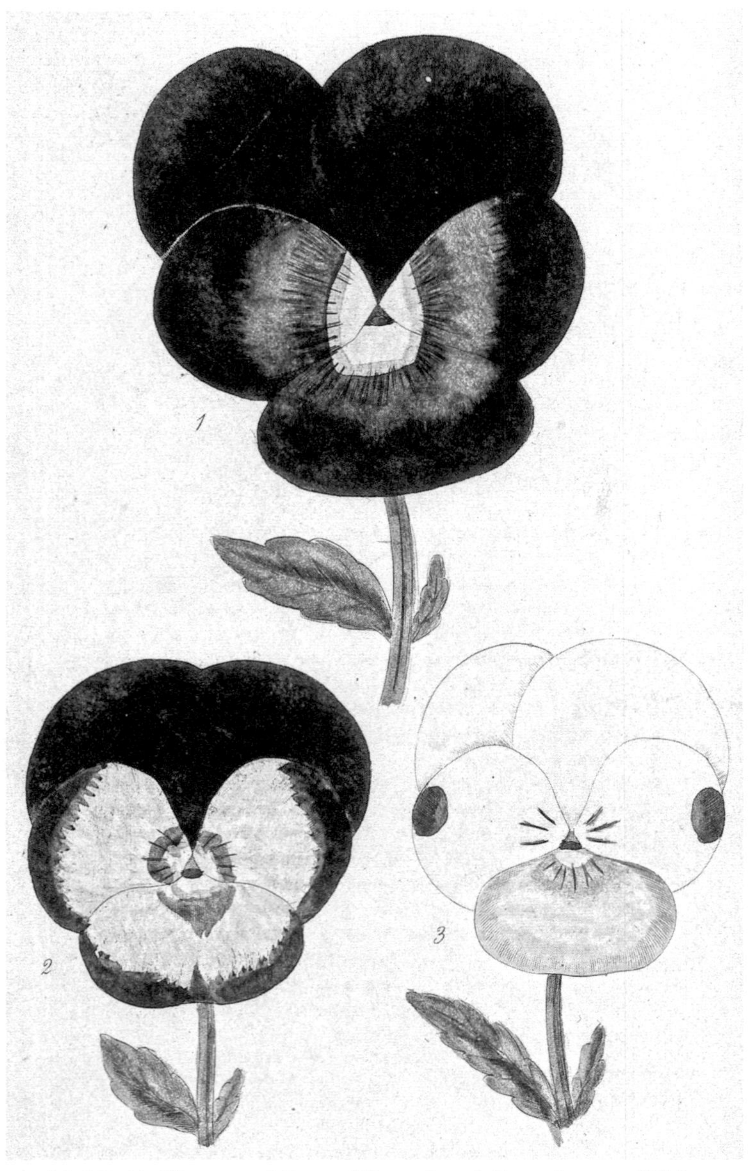

J. & J. Parkin, **Flowers of three different varieties of pansy (Viola species)**, c. 1835, engraving. Courtesy Wellcome Collection, London.

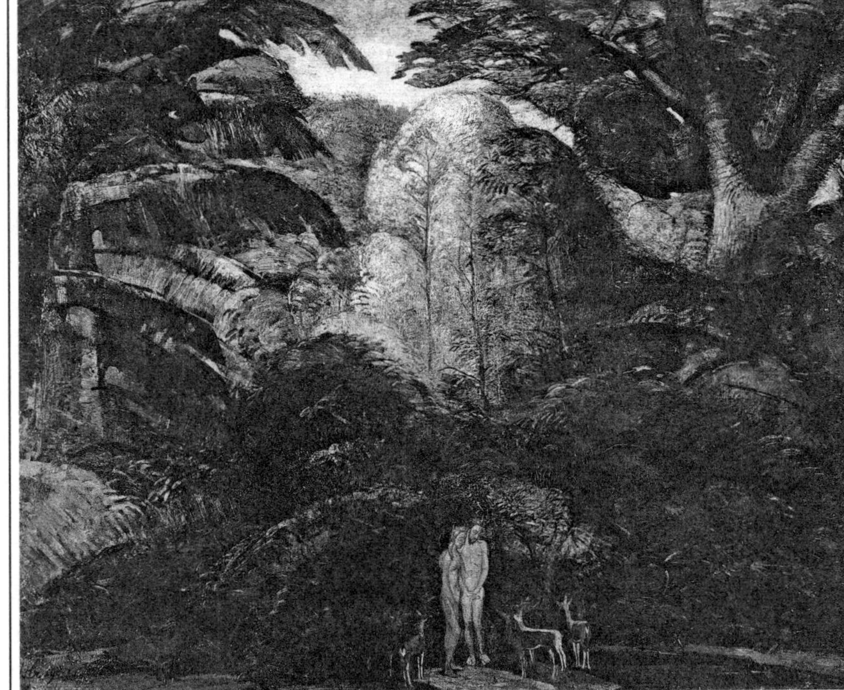

Herman Justus Kruyder, **Paradise I**, 1913–1914, oil on canvas, 109.3 × 148 cm. Courtesy Frans Hals Museum, Haarlem.

PARADISE

The word paradise is derived from the ancient Persian—'a green place'.

Paradise haunts gardens, and some gardens are paradises. Mine is one of them. Others are like bad children—spoilt by their parents, over-watered and covered with noxious chemicals. The only chemical I have used is against the slug which devours my *Crambe cordifolia*. I'm very selective—the *Crambe Maritima* acts as a good slughouse and I like the look of them crawling across the sparkling leaves after a shower.

Other paradises: Christopher Lloyd's Great Dixter up the road. Gardens that deny paradise: Hidcote Manor, known to us as the Hideouscote, which is so manicured that not one plant seems to touch its neighbour. The National Trust must have a central nursery, as all their gardens look like that. You won't find this in Great Dixter, it's shaggy. If a garden isn't shaggy, forget it.

Jarman, *Derek Jarman's Garden*, 40–41.

From the time of the Achaemenid empire the idea of an earthly paradise spread to the literature and languages of other cultures. The Avestan word *pairidaēza-*, Old Persian **paridaida-*, Median **paridaiza-* (walled-around, i.e., a walled garden), was transliterated into Greek *paradeisoi*, then rendered into the Latin *paradisus*, and from there entered into European languages, i.e., French *paradis*, and English *paradise* (*Oxford English Dictionary* XI, pp. 183–84; Yamauchi, pp. 332). The word entered Semitic languages as well: Akkadian *pardesu*, Hebrew *pardes* (*Nehemiah* 2:8; *Ecclesiastes* 2:5; *Song of Solomon* 4:13), and Arabic *ferdaws* (Koran 18.107, 23.11).

Although the concept of a paradise may be traced back to the Sumerian epic of Gilgamish (Kramer, pp. 147–49), it seems the idea existed independently in the Indo-Iranian tradition, where we find references in the Avesta (*Yt.* 22.15).

Encyclopaedia Iranica, 'Garden i. Achaemenid Period'.

In the Moorish gardens of Spain, such as the Alhambra and Generalife in Granada (both begun in the fourteenth century), the transportation is primarily symbolic. Here, water, the symbol of life, takes centre stage, flowing in pools, channels and fountains. The more-or-less geometrical divisions of these gardens, which derive from the Persian tradition of dividing the world into the elements, along with evergreen plants, oleanders, cypresses and roses, suggest to us that we are in the Islamic paradise, a place of redemption removed from the materialism of the outside world.

Brougher, 'Being There', in *Enclosed and Enchanted*, ed. Brougher and Tarantino, 9–10.

An aristocratic form of garden intended to symbolize the paradise of the Pure Land sect of Buddhism, featuring a lake with a bridge leading to a Buddhist hall, re-creating the platform where Buddha sat contemplating a lotus pond.

Walker, *The Japanese Garden*, 296.

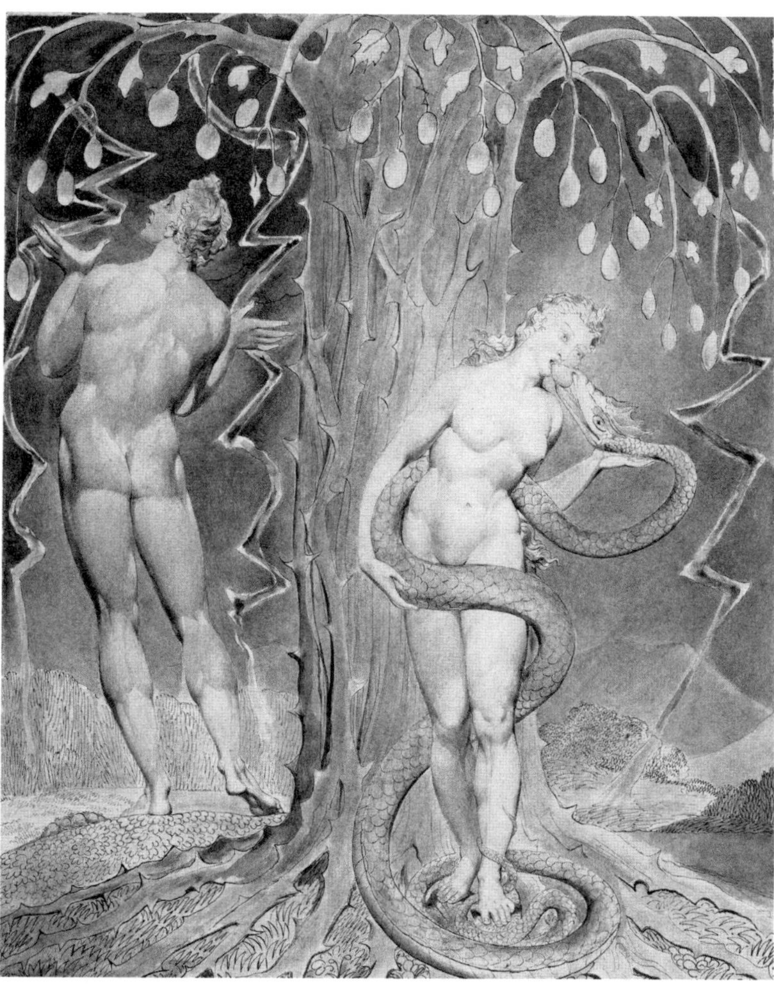

William Blake, **The Temptation and Fall of Eve (Illustration to Milton's Paradise Lost)**, 1808, watercolour on paper, 49.7 × 38.7 cm. Courtesy Museum of Fine Arts, Boston and Art Resource/Scala, Florence.

PARADISE LOST

And Eve first to her Husband thus began.
Adam, well may we labour still to dress
This Garden, still to tend Plant, Herb and Flour.
Our pleasant task enjoyn'd, but till more hands
Aid us, the work under our labour grows,
Luxurious by restraint; what we by day
Lop overgrown, or prune, or prop, or bind,
One night or two with wanton growth derides
Tending to wilde. Thou therefore now advise
Or hear what to my mind first thoughts present,
Let us divide our labours, thou where choice
Leads thee, or where most needs, whether to wind
The Woodbine round this Arbour, or direct
The clasping Ivie where to climb, while I
In yonder Spring of Roses intermixt
With Myrtle, find what to redress till Noon:
For while so near each other thus all day
Our task we choose, what wonder if so near
Looks intervene and smiles, or object new
Casual discourse draw on, which intermits
Our dayes work brought to little, though begun
Early, and th' hour of Supper comes unearn'd.

Milton, *Paradise Lost*, Book 9, 204–225.

PARASITE

These are the *parasites*, aptly named from the Greek word meaning 'to eat at another's table', which they do in a ruthless manner. Unable to make their own food, parasites steal from unwilling organisms called (perhaps facetiously) *hosts*. Many parasites penetrate the host plant's tissues with a special structure called a *haustorium*. In fungal parasites, the haustorium is an extension of the mycelium. The effects of parasitism range from mild disruption of the host's metabolism to its untimely death. [...]

Death of a host results in death of the parasite; but by then, the interloper has reproduced and its seeds have been spread to other victims.

Capon, *Botany for Gardeners*, 136–137.

PARK

At the dawn of the nineteenth century the garden, which had evolved outside the towns into a park, returned in a new guise, namely as saviour of the condensed and polluted city. The public park introduced to the cities a compact and illusory world of nature to compensate for the landscape which had got out of reach. [...] The park retreated from an unpleasant outside world as an enclosed garden, yet paradoxically taking as its model the most outgoing of all garden types, the English landscape garden. This was, so to speak, turned inside out and tied to the urban morphology.

Aben and De Wit, *The Enclosed Garden*, 141.

PASTORAL

WHILE THE SPECTATORS / WHO IMAGINED THEMSELVES IN THE GARDENS OF ALCINOUS / WERE UNABLE TO TEAR THEMSELVES AWAY / THE SITE OF THE BASTILLE AND ITS DUNGEONS / WHICH HAD BEEN CONVERTED INTO GROVES / HELD OTHER CHARMS FOR THOSE WHOM THE PASSAGE OF A SINGLE YEAR HAD NOT YET ACCUSTOMED TO BELIEVE THEIR EYES · AN ARTIFICIAL WOOD / CONSISTING OF LARGE TREES / HAD BEEN PLANTED THERE · IT WAS EXTREMELY WELL LIT · IN THE MIDDLE OF THIS LAIR OF DESPOTISM / THERE HAD ALSO BEEN PLANTED A PIKE / WITH A CAP OF LIBERTY STUCK ON THE TOP · CLOSE BY HAD BEEN BURIED THE RUINS OF THE BASTILLE · AMONGST ITS IRONS AND GRATINGS COULD BE SEEN THE BAS-RELIEF REPRESENTING SLAVES IN CHAINS WHICH HAD APTLY ADORNED THE FORTRESS'S GREAT CLOCK / THE MOST SURPRISING ASPECT OF THE SIGHT PERHAPS BEING THAT THE FORTRESS COULD HAVE BEEN TOPPLED WITHOUT OVERWHELMING IN ITS FALL THE POSTERITY OF THE TYRANTS BY WHOM IT HAD BEEN RAISED / AND WHO HAD FILLED IT WITH SO MANY INNOCENT VICTIMS · THESE RUINS / AND THE MEMORIES THEY CALLED UP / WERE IN SINGULAR CONTRAST WITH THE INSCRIPTION THAT COULD BE READ AT THE ENTRANCE TO THE GROVE - A SIMPLE INSCRIPTION WHOSE PLACEMENT GAVE IT A TRULY SUBLIME BEAUTY -

ICI ON DANSE

CAMILLE DESMOULINS / PARIS / YEAR ONE OF THE AGE OF LIBERTY

Ian Hamilton Finlay, **Pastoral**, 1996, silkscreen on paper, 40 × 50 cm. Courtesy Van Abbemuseum, Eindhoven.

PEACOCK FLOWER

The peacock flower (*Caesalpinia pulcherrima*), also known as the Mexican bird of paradise and pride of Barbados, is one of more than five hundred plants in the *Caesalpinia* genus, part of the pea (*Fabaceae*) family. It originated in Central America and is now found abundantly in almost all tropical and subtropical areas such as Central and South America, Africa, Asia, and Australia. From 1666, it was frequently imported to the Netherlands from the colonies in the West Indies and East Indies.

In many regions, the peacock flower is recognized for its versatile uses. Extracts of the plant, such as tea, relieve sore throats, lung disease, fever, eye and liver complaints, and skin rashes. In Guatemala and Panama, the leaves are used to poison fish. The soft wood of the plant is used to produce a beautiful black ink or dye.

Another remarkable feature of this plant is the seed's ability to induce menstruation and miscarriage. Although it is no longer used for this purpose in Suriname, the plant is inextricably bound up with its historical use by Amerindian and black enslaved people with wombs as a form of resistance to their cruel oppressors.

Another salient point is that many of the West African enslaved peoples, for example the Yoruba, had a more diverse and flexible understanding of gender than the European, biologically determined definitions of 'woman' and 'man'. Slavery pressed enslaved people into limited boxes in terms of gender identity. In the seventeenth century, English, French, and Dutch settlers and slave owners wrote, often disapprovingly, about the use of the plant by enslaved people to spare their unborn children the cruelty of slavery.

Thiëmo Heilbron

PEKARANGAN

The *pekarangan* homegarden is a traditional system of crop cultivation, practised commonly in the countryside of Java in Indonesia. It combines annual and perennial crops on the land around the household, or in commons shared by several households. It serves as both a dwelling-place providing permanent source of shade for the house, and a source of food all year round. It is an ecological system involving interactions between human beings, plants, animals, soil, and water. As such, the intergenerational transmission of ecological knowledge relating to the *pekarangan* system is crucial to its success. Psychologically, it serves as protection and assurance in times of natural disasters and economic instabilities.

UNESCO, 'Javanese Pekarangan'.

PENNYROYAL TEA

TEA TO EXPEL FEELINGS OF MELANCHOLIA

This tea mixture can be collected from wild weeds in order to expel feelings of melancholia and relieve not-necessarily-human feelings of atmospheric-depression/s: take 1 part Pennyroyal, Agrimony, and Valerian, and 2 parts Veronica, drink 2 cups per day

i Pennyroyal—this herb is famously written about by Nirvana singer-songwriter Kurt Cobain, a song that was never released as third single of the album In Utero (1993) due to Cobain's death. On the abortive quality of the tea, also stimulating menstrual flow as emmenagogue Cobain says: 'I threw that [Pennyroyal Tea] in because I have so many friends who have tried to use that [as aborticant] and it never worked. The song is about a person who's beyond depressed; they're in their deathbed, pretty much.' Cobain started to experience severe stomachaches in 1991 which he said triggered suicidal desires, and trying to alleviate stomach pains with shooting heroine. Since his childhood he struggled with treating a diagnose of ADHD with Ritalin, and their side effects.

Agrimony—In Ancient Greece this herb was already used, devoted to Pallas Athena, as a liver-activating agent. The plant works cleansing as it has a lot of bittering agent, stimulating the stomach, spleen, and kidneys, activates the excretion of uric acid, and is here said works cleansing against cancerous growths. This all-heal or panacea is for those people who will give anything to keep the peace, and try to hide their own worries, pain and problems from others, often with the help of pills and alcohol, just to maintain a cheerful tone.

Valerian—an all-heal and witches herb that is a symbol for people who have an accommodating disposition. The plant, giving a distinct scent that is loved by cats rather than humans, possesses an immense healing power. The Valerian root is often seen as a sedative for taking exams, but is also used as aphrodisiac, and in wound potions for healing internal trauma. Use the entirety of the small plant that is green and fresh, including the roots in your tea, to sweeten the woes and sorrows of the head.

Veronica—is a strong detoxifier and can be employed for skin problems such as eczema as it works blood cleansing, to relieve stomachaches and -cramps working on the glands. The herb also works on the airways and on the waterways as a diuretic, drives out intestinal worms, expels kidney stones, supports menstruation and giving labour. The Veronica, Heil aller schäden [Salvation of all damages], was once time famous herb.

iii Despite Cobain's convincing argument that the herb is only for hippies and the tea actually doesn't work and evoke an abortion, when you are (getting) pregnant, replace pennyroyal with the similar tasting spearmint [aarmunt, kruizemunt].

ii The recipes in this text make use of the generous resources available on www.volkoomen.nl a site that follows Dodonaeus' nomenclature [Rembert Dodoens fl. 1517–1585] after whom Carolus Linnaeus named the Dodonaea family.

i Pennyroyal Tea

I'm on my time with everyone
I have very bad posture
Sit and drink Pennyroyal Tea
Distill the life that's inside of me
Sit and drink Pennyroyal Tea
I'm anaemic royalty
Give me a Leonard Cohen afterworld
So I can sigh eternally
I'm so tired I can't sleep
I'm a liar and a thief
Sit and drink Pennyroyal Tea
I'm anaemic royalty
I'm on warm milk and laxatives
Cherry-flavoured antacids
Sit and drink Pennyroyal Tea
Distill the life that's inside of me
Sit and drink Pennyroyal Tea
I'm anaemic royalty.

Nirvana (Kurt *Cobain)*

This text was redirected from its earlier form presented in Rongwrong All Heal (Valerian) in 2017 by CPR (Charlotte Rooijackers 2020)

PERGOLA

See also page 196

PERSIAN GARDEN CARPET

GARDEN CARPET, EARLY TWENTIETH CENTURY

The word paradise comes from the Persian word 'pairidaiza' and literally means enclosed space (*pairi* means 'around' and *daêza* means 'wall'). The Persian garden is an ancient archetype in which the garden is divided into four perfectly geometric parts by paths and waterways. These elements lead the visitor through the four parts of the world, the four directions, the four seasons, and the four elements. Within it lies the most sacred space, depicted as a basin or fountain. In Persian carpets, the most literal interpretation is a four-part or cruciform garden seen from above, with square pavilions, trees, flowers, and birds shown in profile. The carpet represents fertility and bounty, and forms a microcosm in which the whole world comes together in a single space with its symbolic perfection. (ed.)

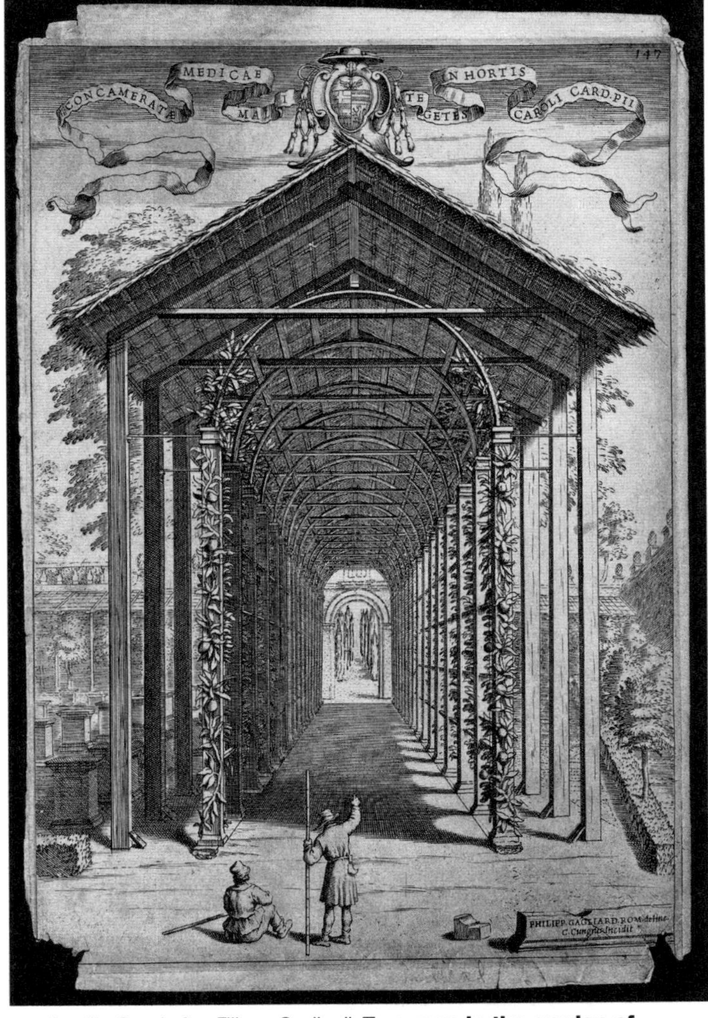

Camillo Cungi after Filippo Gagliardi, **Two men in the garden of Cardinal Carlo Pio di Savoia admiring a pergola on which citron fruits are growing**, 1600–1699, engraving, 31 × 22 cm. Courtesy Wellcome Collection, London.

The heterotopia is capable of juxtaposing in a single real place several spaces, several sites that are in themselves incompatible. [...] [P] erhaps the oldest example of these heterotopias that take the form of contradictory sites is the garden. We must not forget that in the Orient the garden, an astonishing creation that is now a thousand years old, had very deep and seemingly superimposed meanings. The traditional garden of the Persians was a sacred space that was supposed to bring together inside its rectangle four parts representing the four parts of the world, with a space still more sacred than the others that were like an umbilicus, the navel of the world at its center (the basin and water fountain were there); and allthe vegetation of the garden was supposed to come together in this space, in this sort of microcosm. As for carpets, they were originally reproductions of gardens (the garden is a rug onto which the whole world comes to enact its symbolic perfection, and the rug is a sort of garden that can move across space). The garden is the smallest parcel of the world and then it is the totality of the world. The garden has been a sort of happy, universalizing heterotopia since the beginnings of antiquity (our modern zoological gardens spring from that source).

Foucault, 'Of Other Spaces', 25–26.

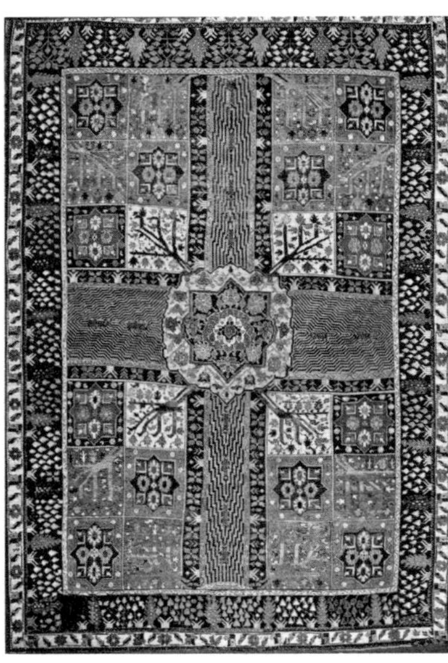

Anonymous Iran, **Garden Carpet**, 1700–1800, carpet, 372 × 383.5 cm. Courtesy Alamy/Victoria and Albert Museum, London.

P continues on page 153.

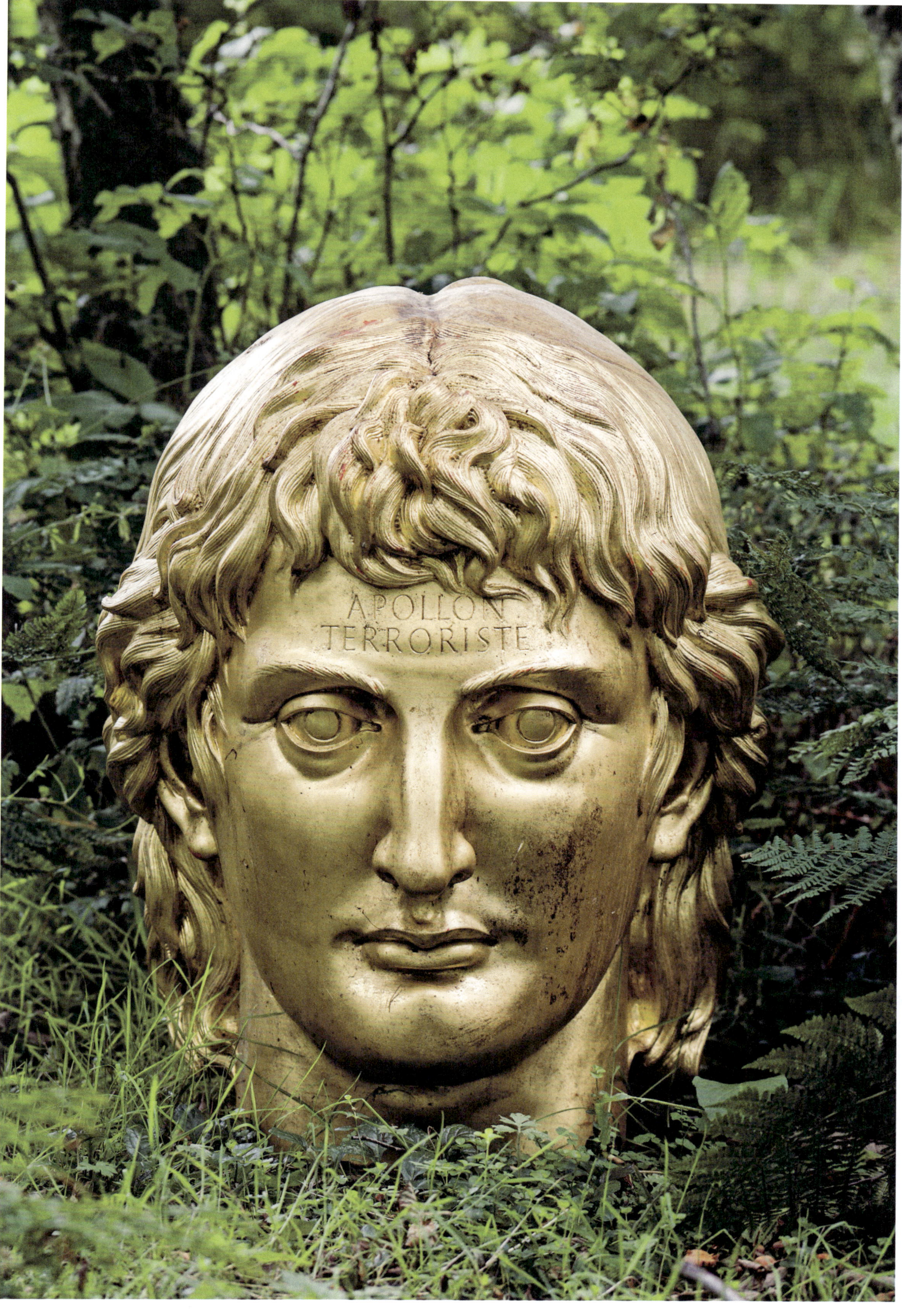

Ian Hamilton Finlay, **Bust of Apollo** at **Little Sparta**.

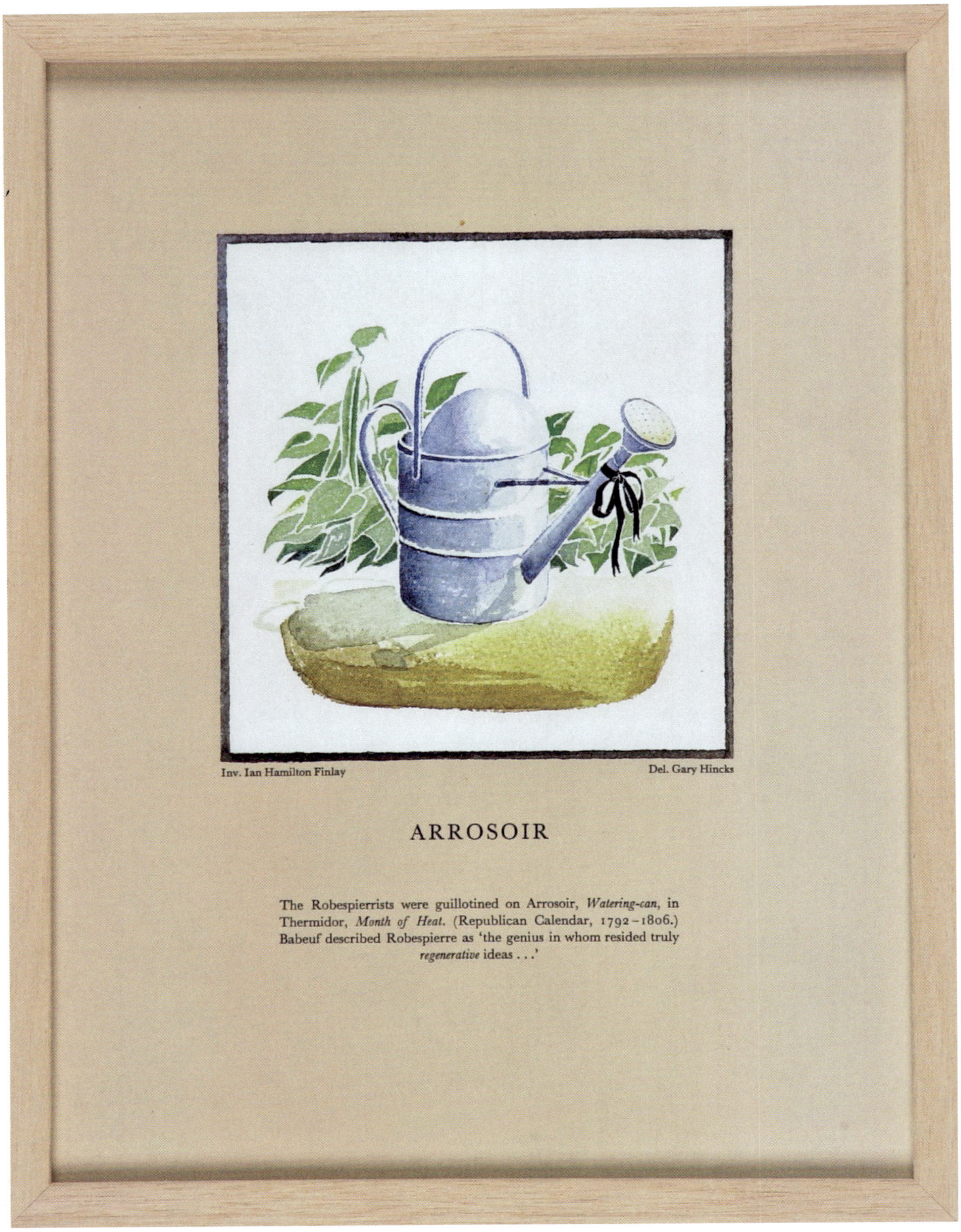

Ian Hamilton Finlay, **Arossoir**, 1984, offset on paper, 31.8 × 25.4 cm. Courtesy Van Abbemuseum, Eindhoven.

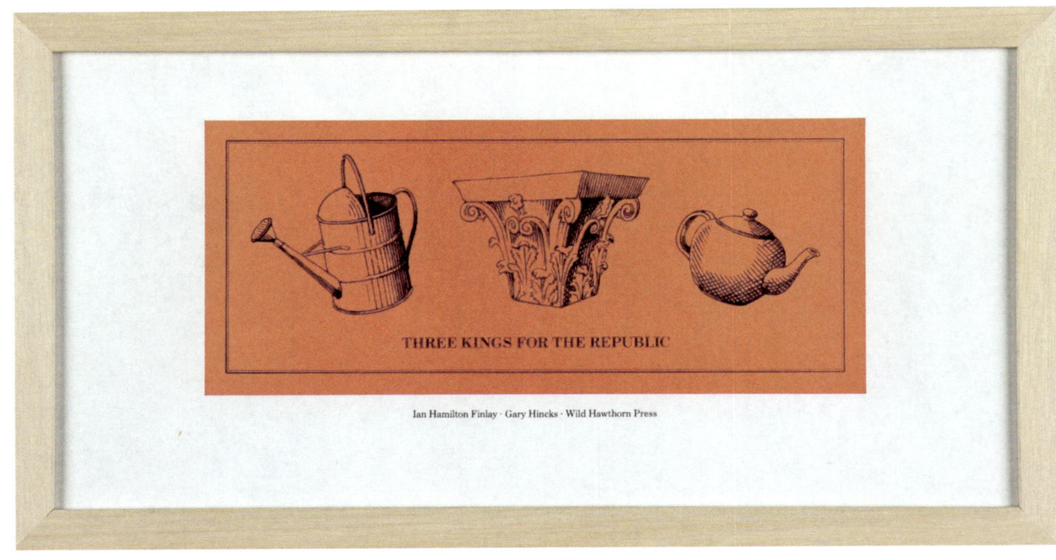

Ian Hamilton Finlay, **Three Kings for the Republic**, 1984, silkscreen on paper, 22.5 × 44.1 cm. Courtesy Van Abbemuseum, Eindhoven.

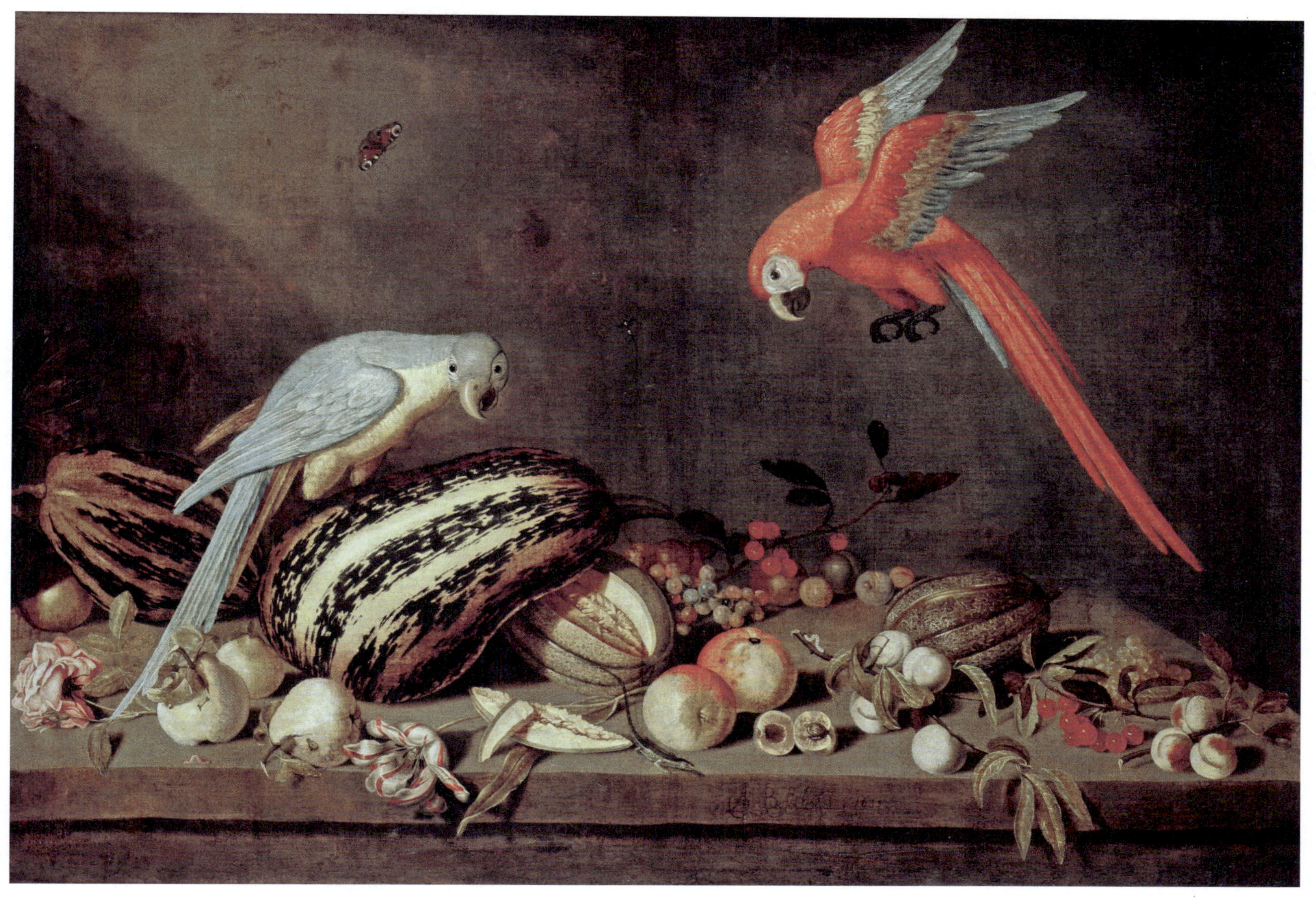

Ambrosius Bosschaert the Younger, **Still Life with Fruit, Flowers and Two Macaws**, 1635, oil on canvas, 109.3 × 163.3 cm. Courtesy Centraal Museum, Utrecht. Photo: Ernst Moritz.

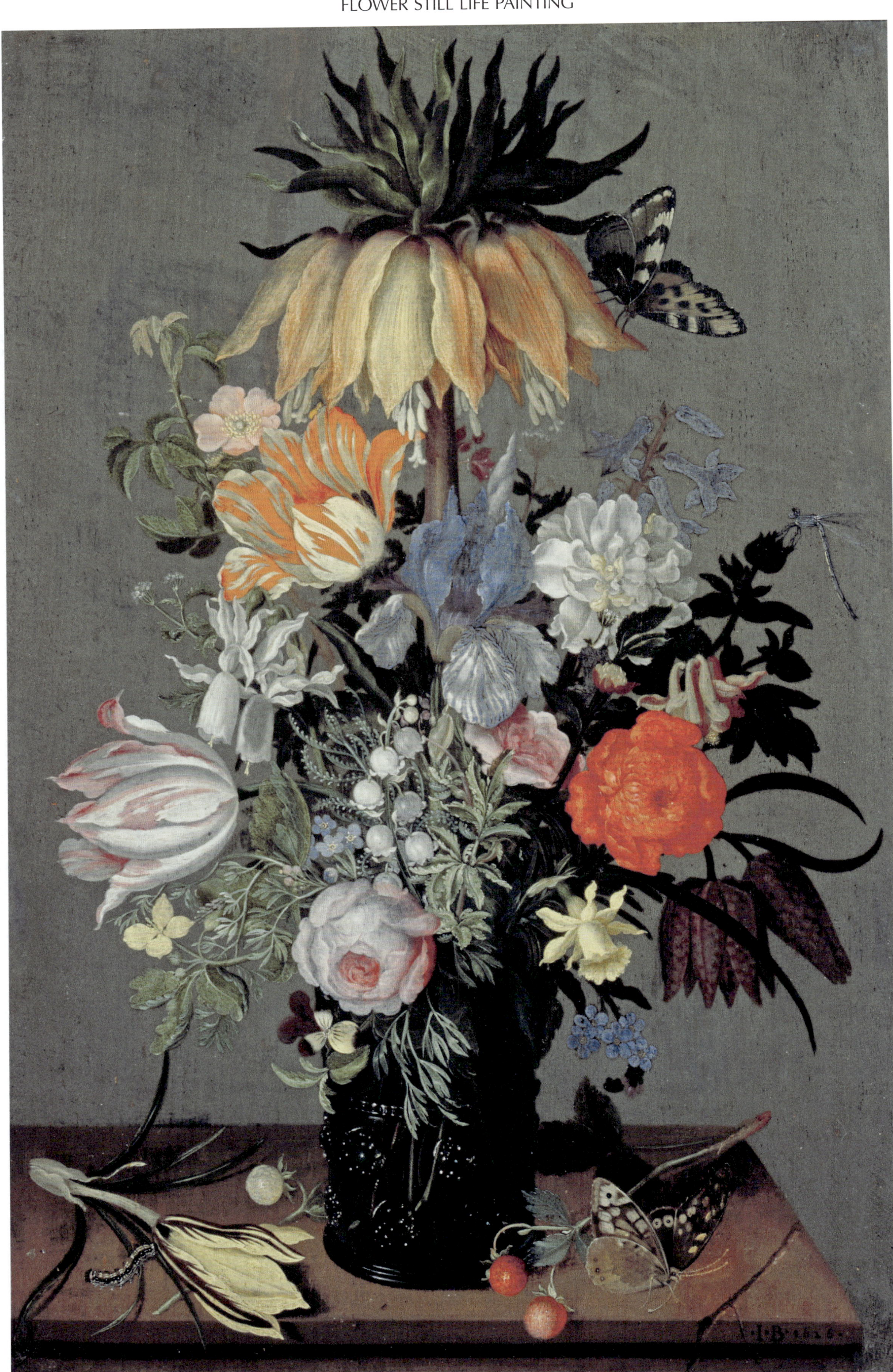

Johannes Bosschaert, **Flower Still Life with Crown Imperial**, 1626, oil on panel, 43 × 29 cm. Courtesy Centraal Museum, Utrecht.

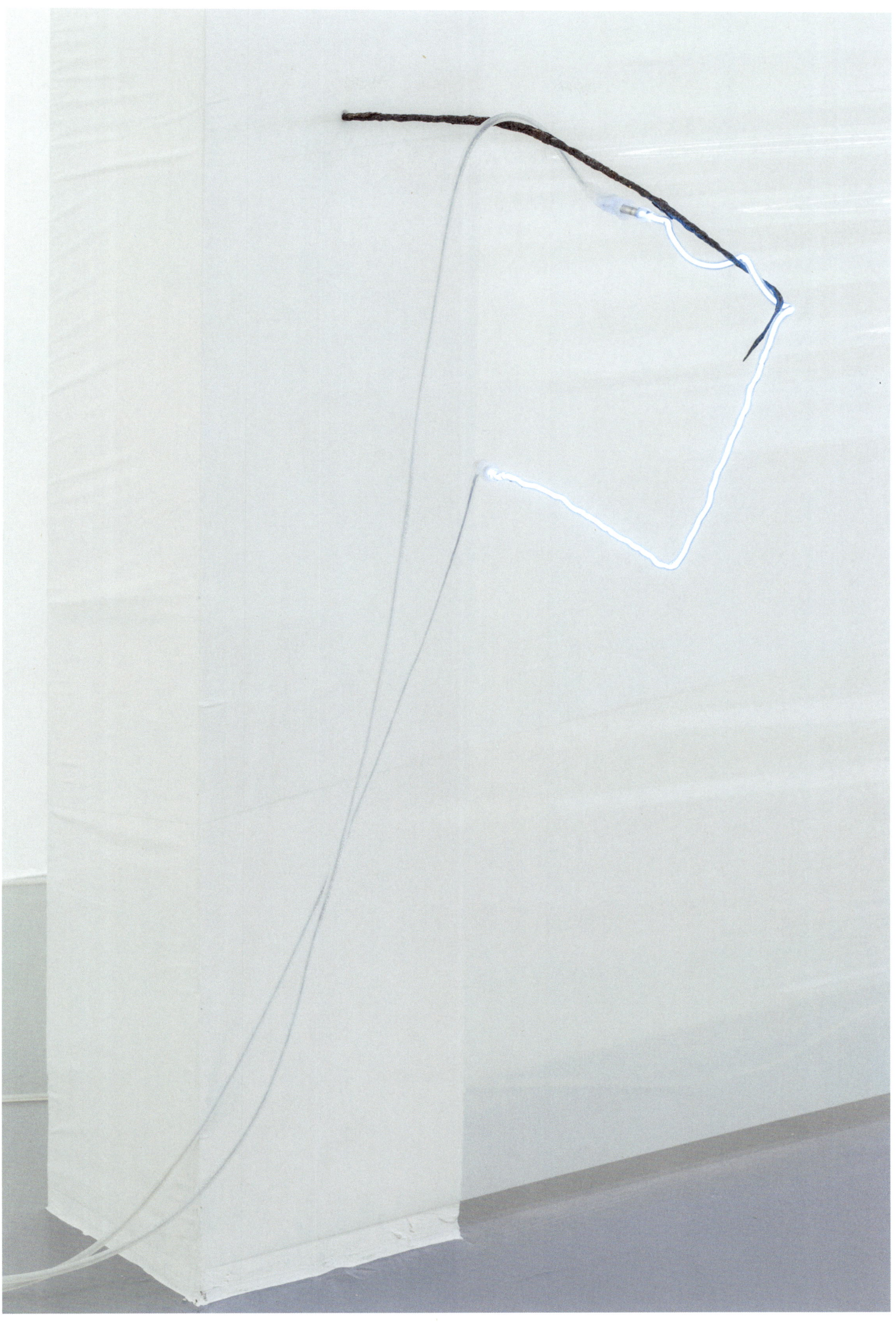

Saskia Noor van Imhoff, **untitled**, 2020, installation view. Courtesy Saskia Noor van Imhoff and Grimm Gallery, Amsterdam & New York.

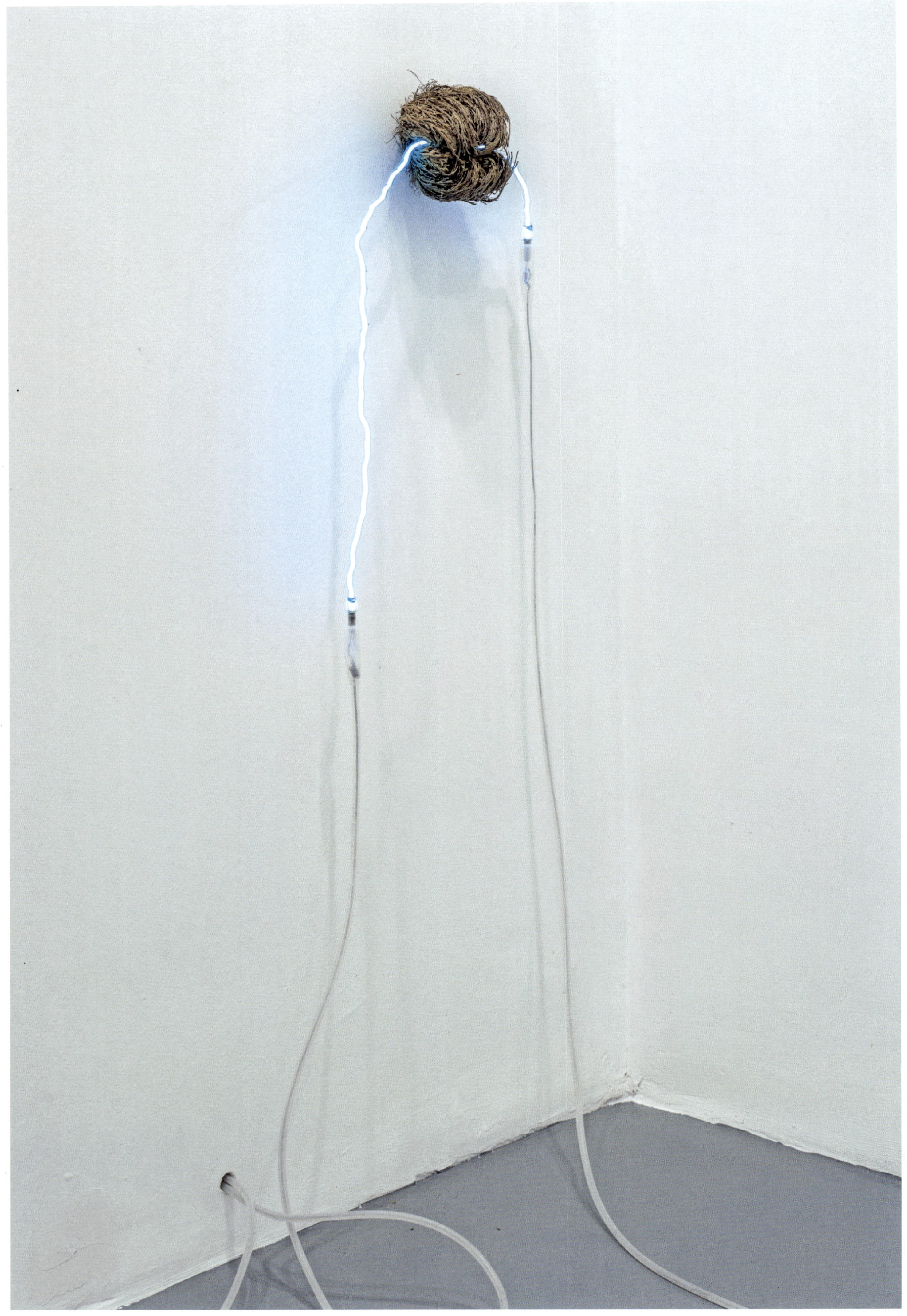

Saskia Noor van Imhoff, **green eyes holding hands**, 2020, installation view. Courtesy Saskia Noor van Imhoff and Grimm Gallery, Amsterdam & New York.

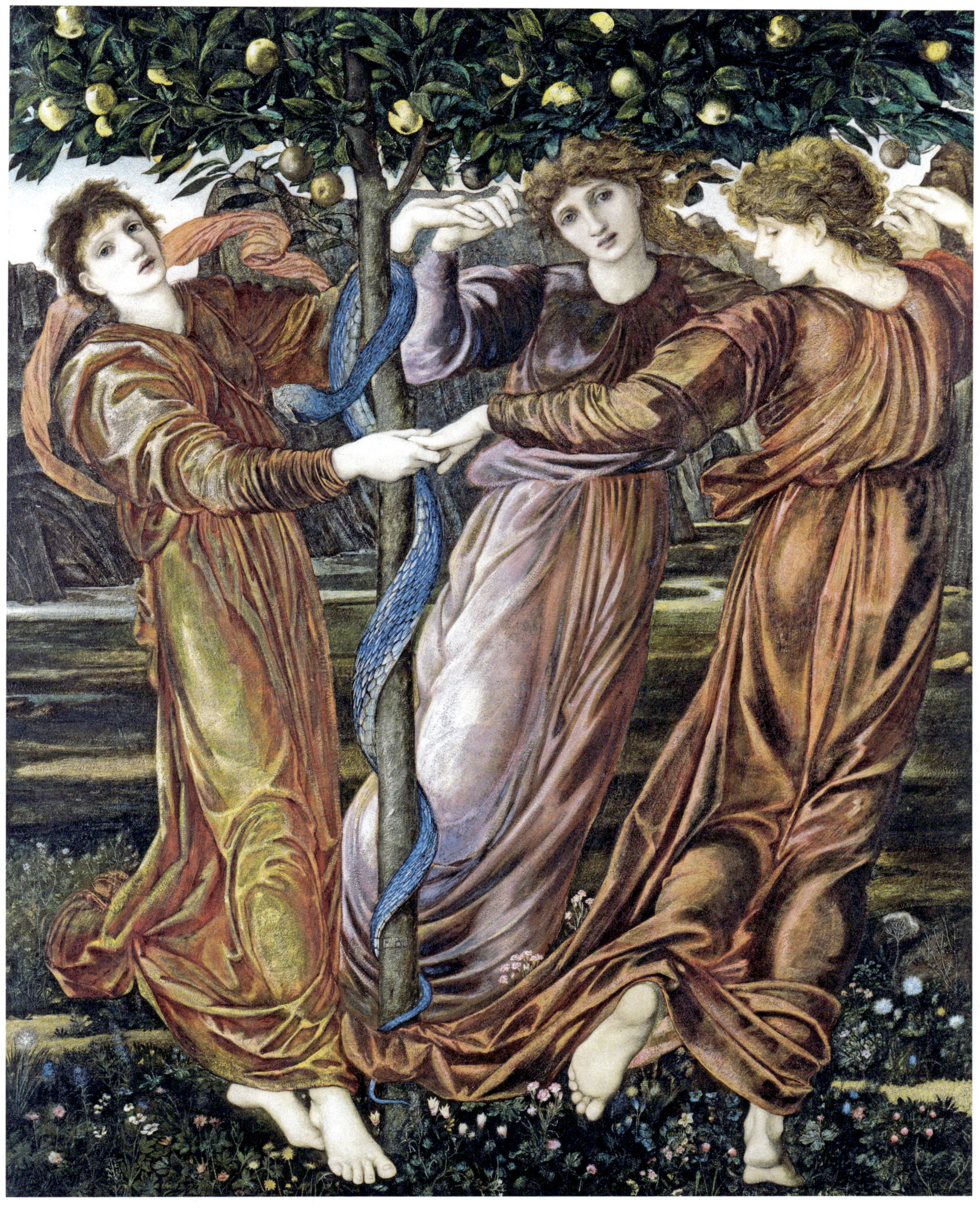

Edward Burne-Jones, **The Garden of the Hesperides**, c. 1869, oil on canvas, 119 × 98 cm. Courtesy bpk-Bildagentur/Hamburger Kunsthalle. Photo: Elke Walford.

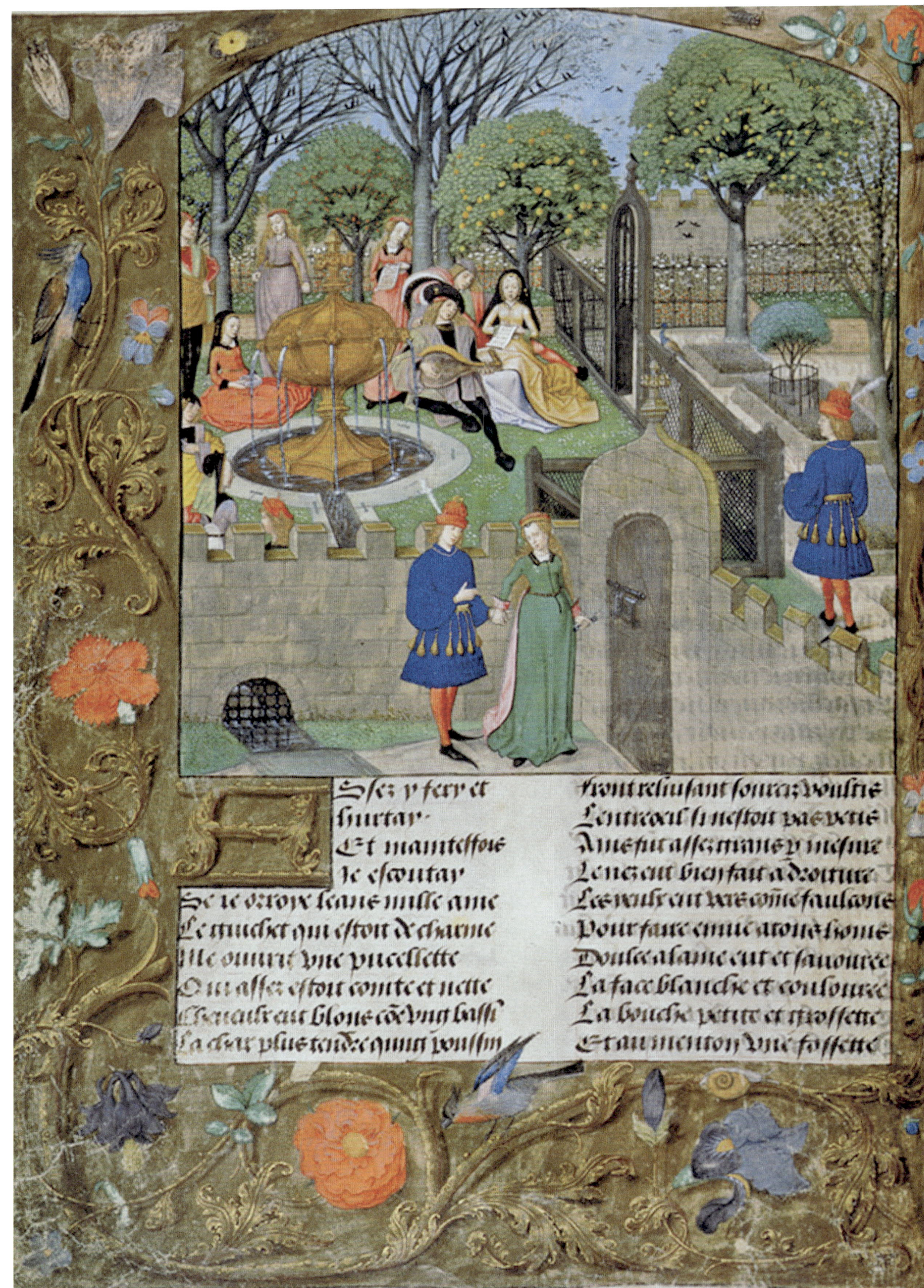

Guillaume de Lorris and Jean de Meun, **Lutenist and singers in a walled garden** from **Roman de la Rose**, 1490–1500, manuscript.

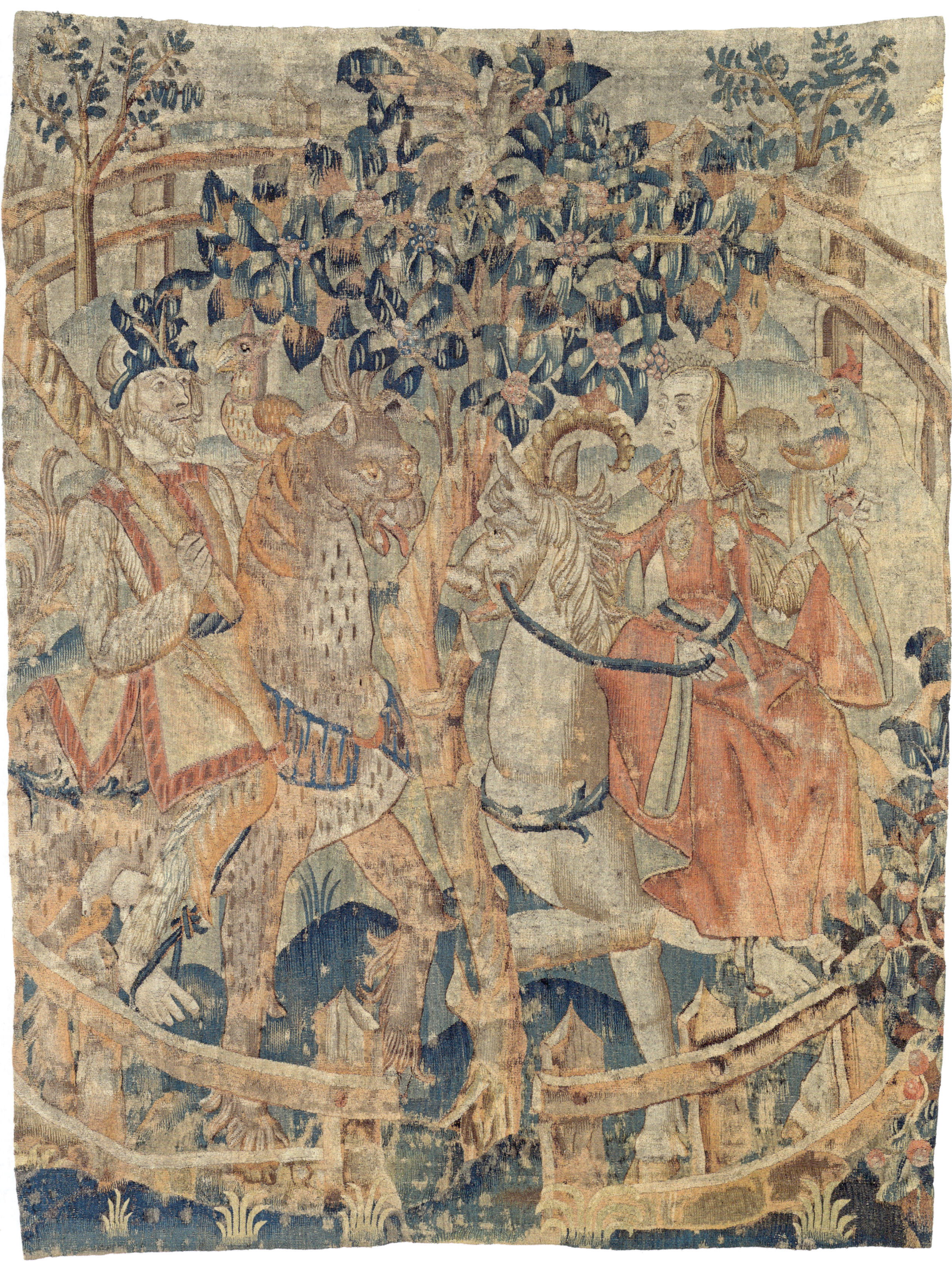

Anonymous, **A wild man and woman in a private garden** (fragment), c. 1500–1520, tapestry, 267 × 203 cm. Courtesy Rijksmuseum Amsterdam.

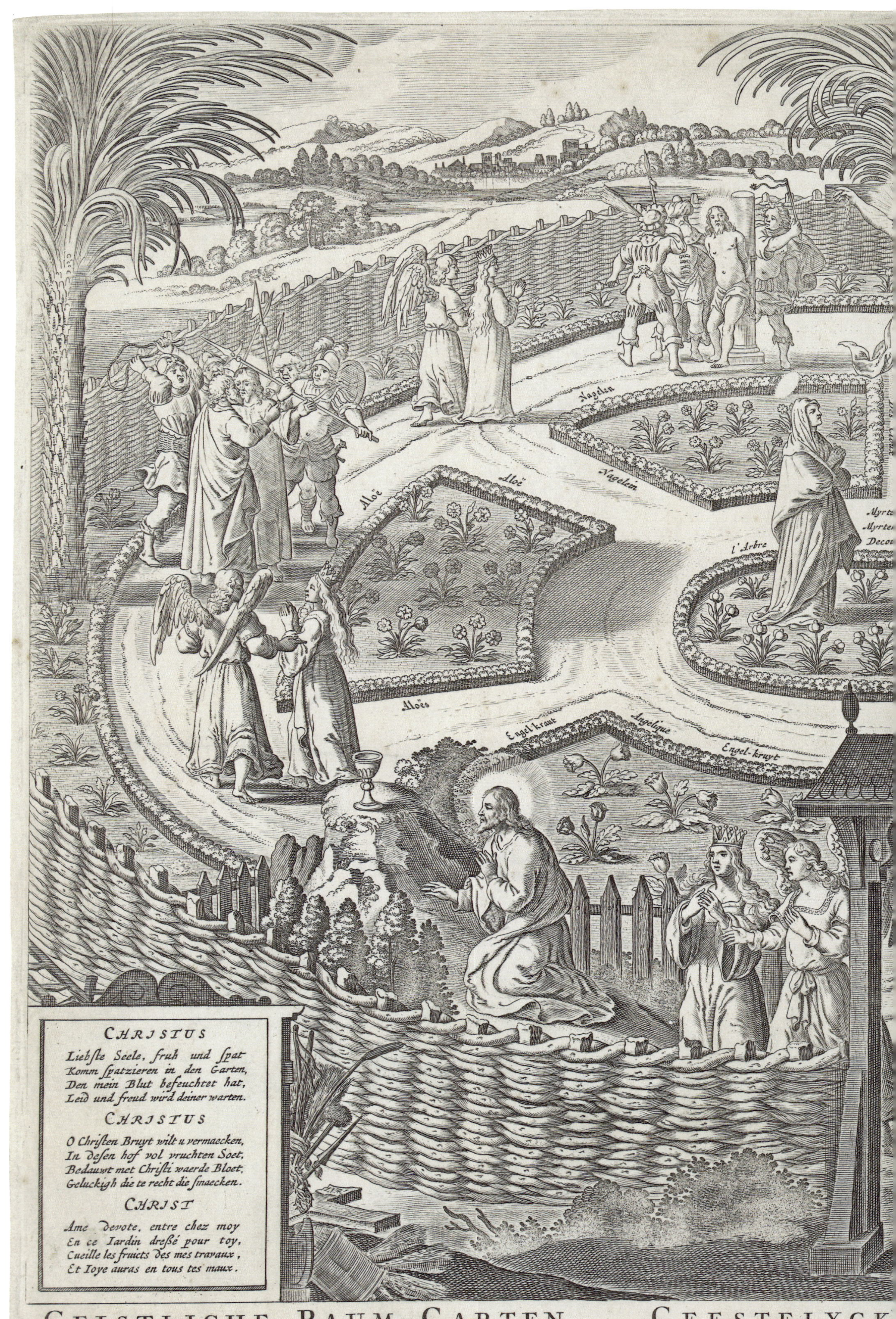
Nagelen
Aloë
Aloë
Nagelen
l'Arbre
Aloës
Engel kraut
Angelique
Engel-kruyt
CHRISTUS
Liebste Seele, fruh und spat
Komm spatzieren in den Garten,
Den mein Blut befeuchtet hat,
Leid und freud wird deiner warten.
CHRISTUS
O Christen Bruyt wilt u vermaecken,
In desen hof vol vruchten Soet,
Bedauwt met Christi waerde Bloet,
Geluckigh die te recht die smaecken.
CHRIST
Ame devote, entre chez moy
En ce Iardin dreßé pour toy,
Cueille les fruicts des mes travaux,
Et Ioye auras en tous tes maux.
GEISTLICHE BAUM-GARTEN.
O Gottergebner Christ, schau diesen Garten plan,
Und sihe mit bedacht deßelben Blummen an:
Die erst ist das Gebet das ENGELKRAUT genennet,
man bey Christi bildt und Todesschweisz erkennet,
Zweits ist ALOËS das harte fesselband!
NAGELEIN der Geiszlung Marterstand,
Die Viert heist KONIGSKRON von Dornen strauch gebunden,
Die funfft VERGISZ MEIN NICHT verdammt mit vielen Wunden,
Die Sechst heist CREUTZES-WURTZ getragen von dem Hirten,
Die Siebend ist die Frucht der gallen bittren MYRTEN,
Wer Christo folgen will der leide mit gedult,
Soo wird er auch mit Ihm erlangen Gottes Huld.

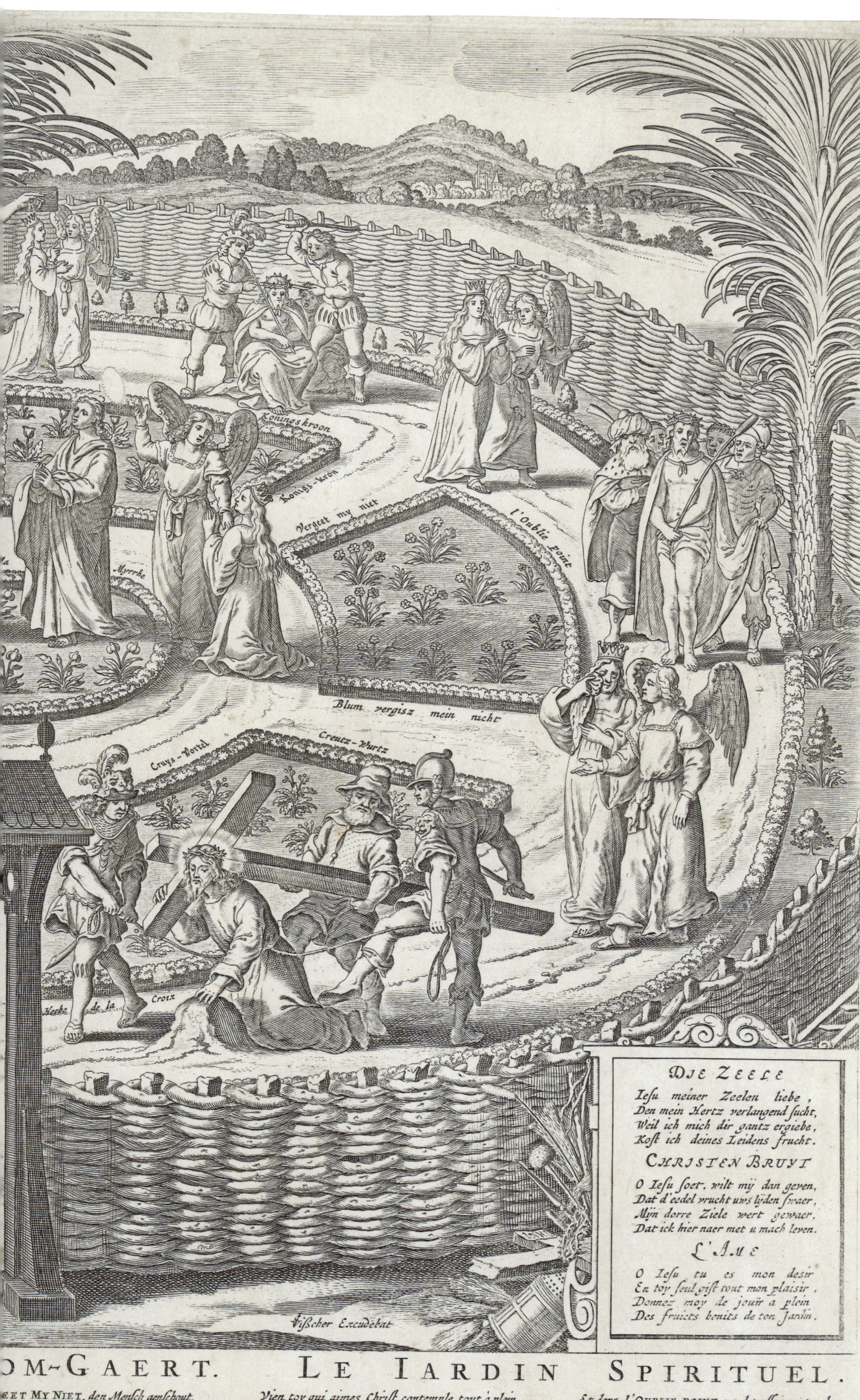

Anonymous, **Le Jardin Spirituel**, c. 1650, etching on paper, 40.8 × 53.5 cm. Courtesy Rijksmuseum Amsterdam.

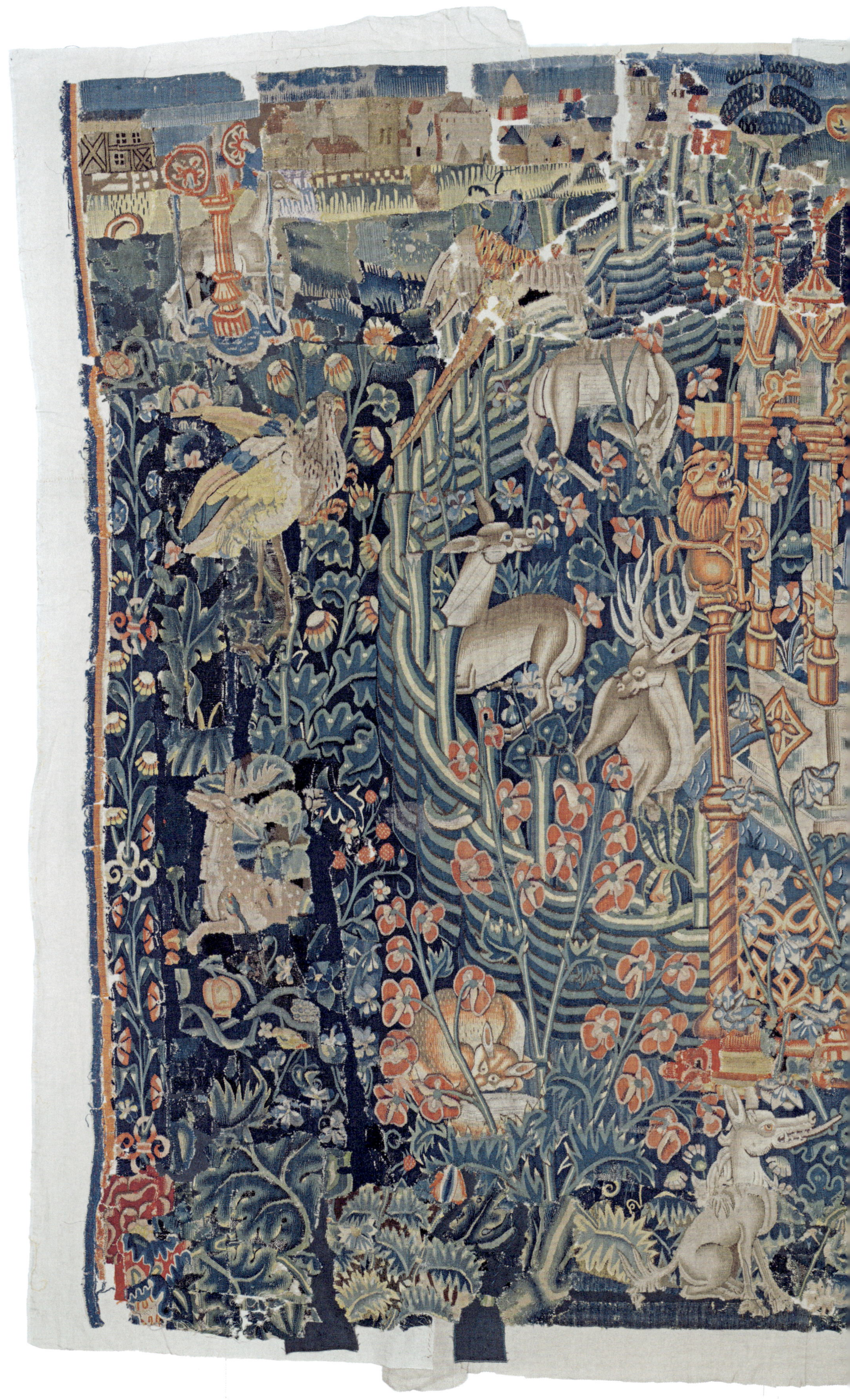

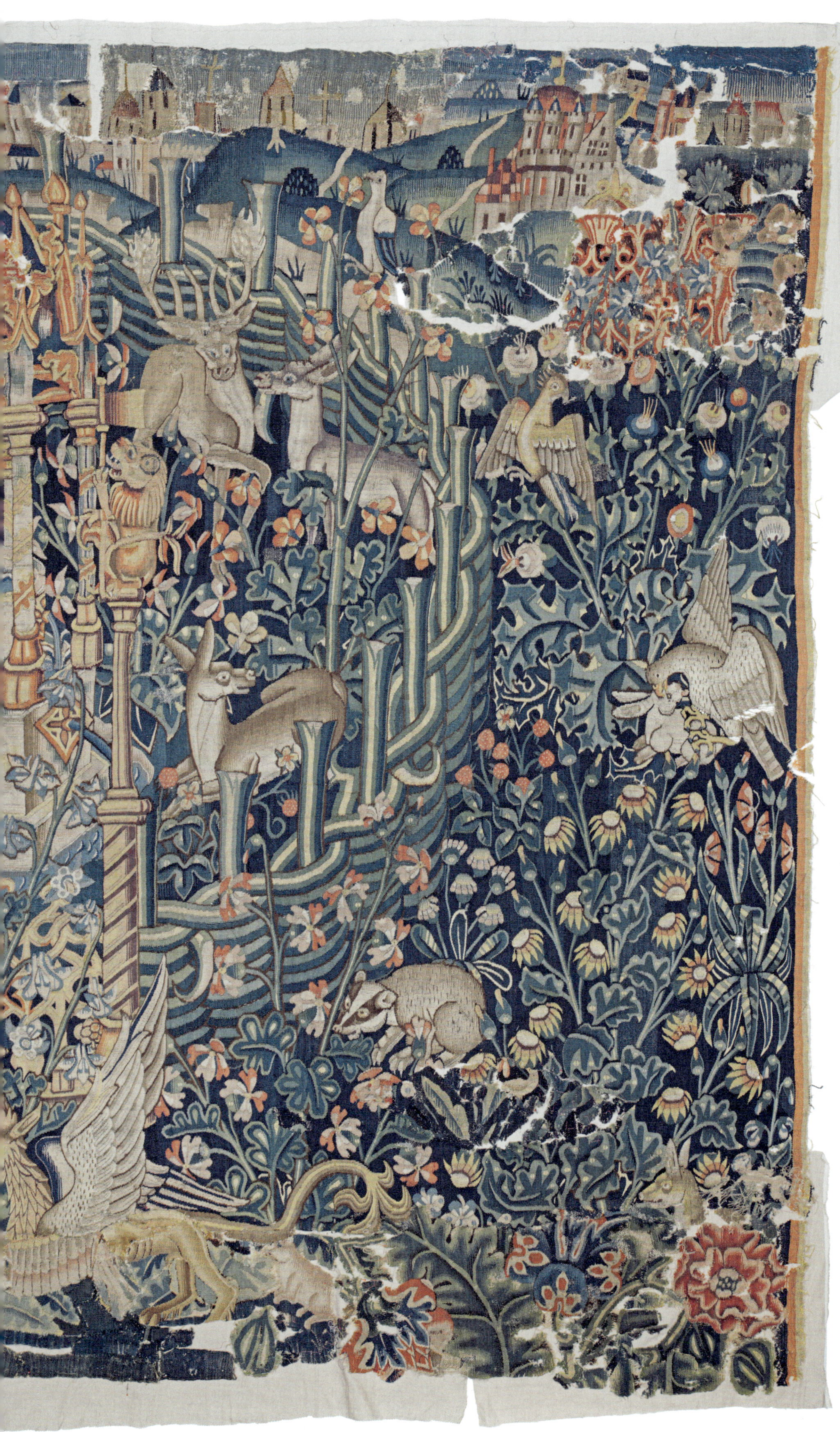

Anonymous, **Verdure with animals, a private garden and a source of life**, c. 1500–1525, tapestry, 290 × 368.5 cm. Courtesy Rijksmuseum Amsterdam.

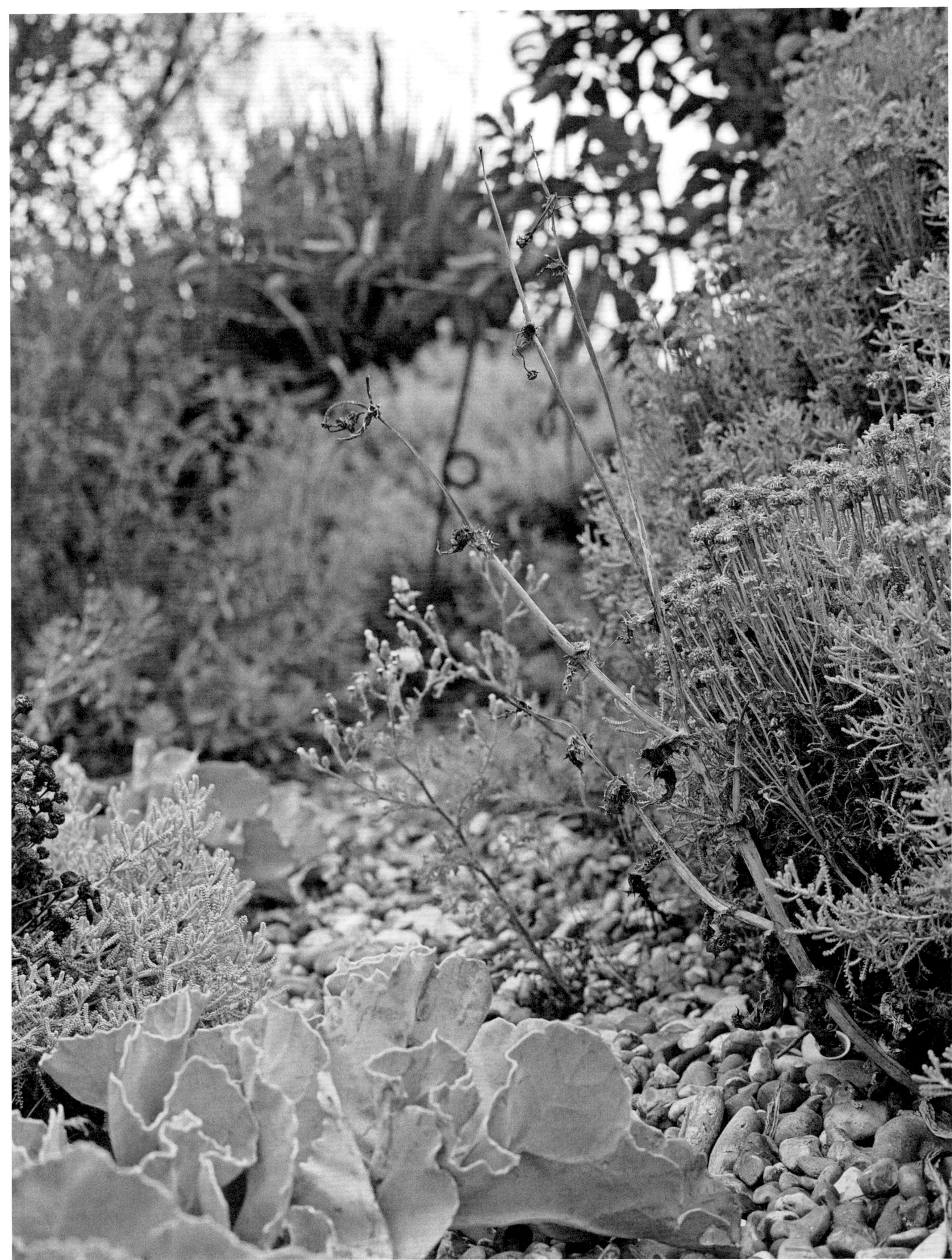

Derk Alberts, **Dungeness #1**, 2016, photograph. Courtesy Derk Alberts.

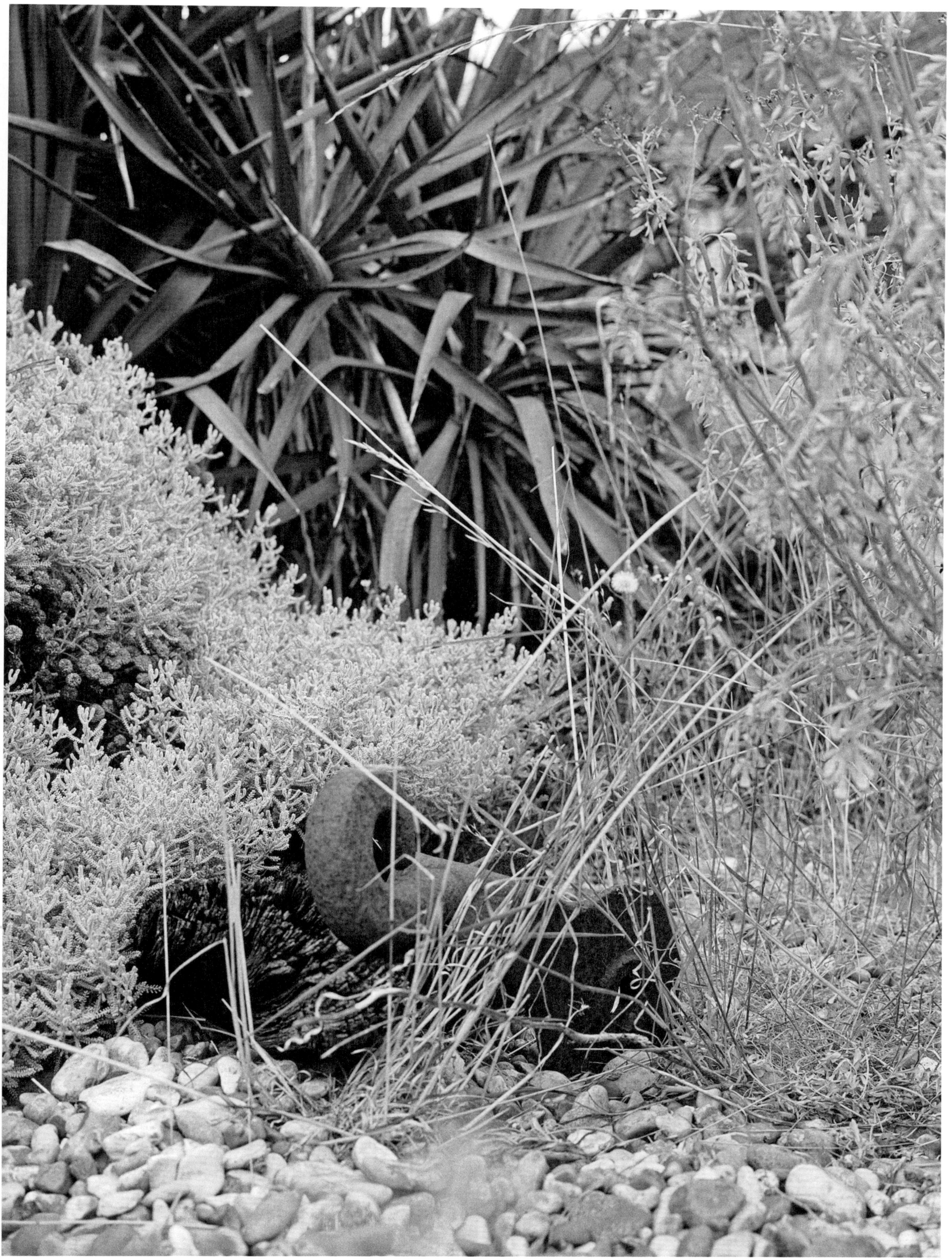

Derk Alberts, **Dungeness #2**, 2016, photograph. Courtesy Derk Alberts.

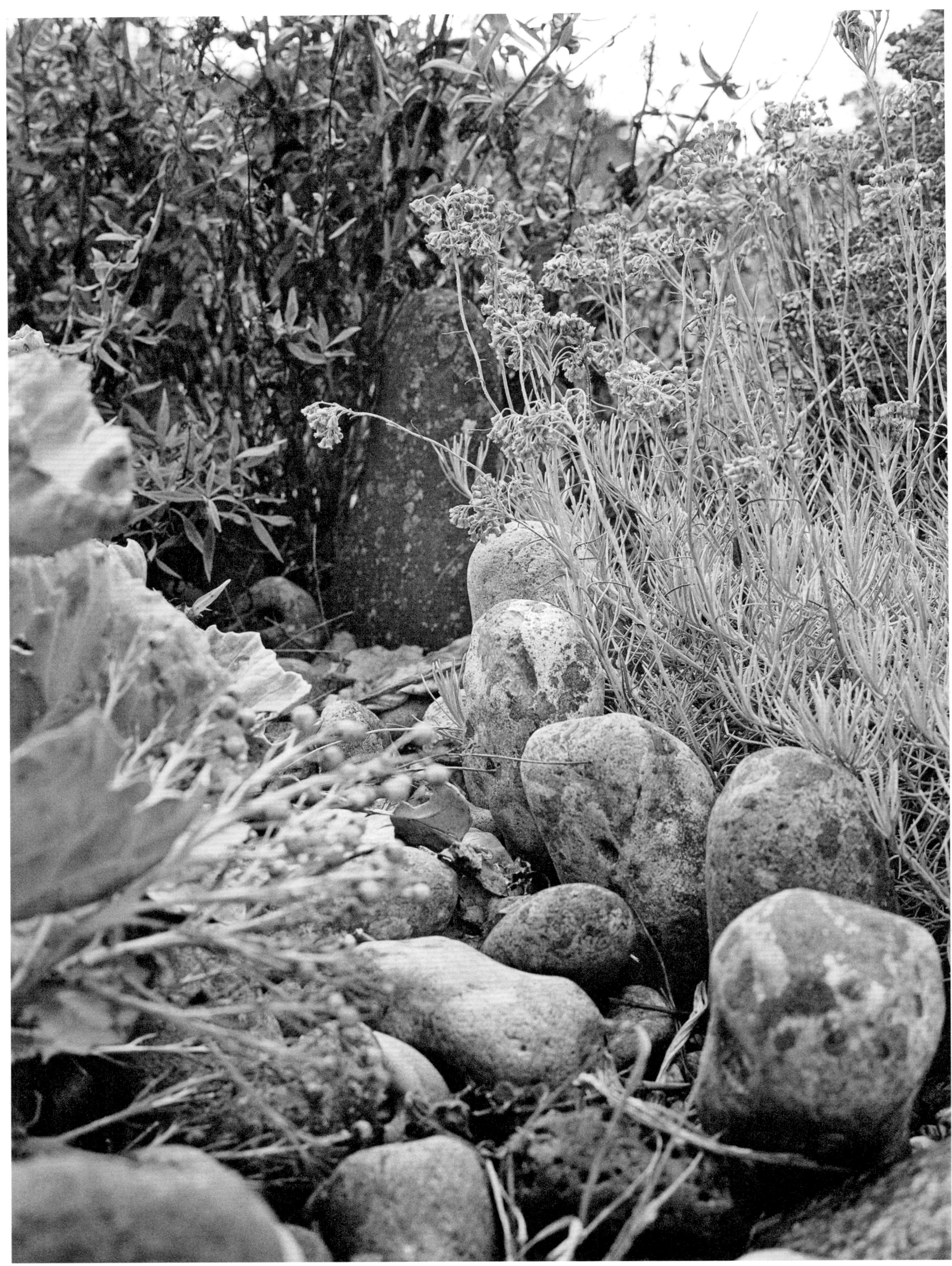

Derk Alberts, **Dungeness #3**, 2016, photograph. Courtesy Derk Alberts.

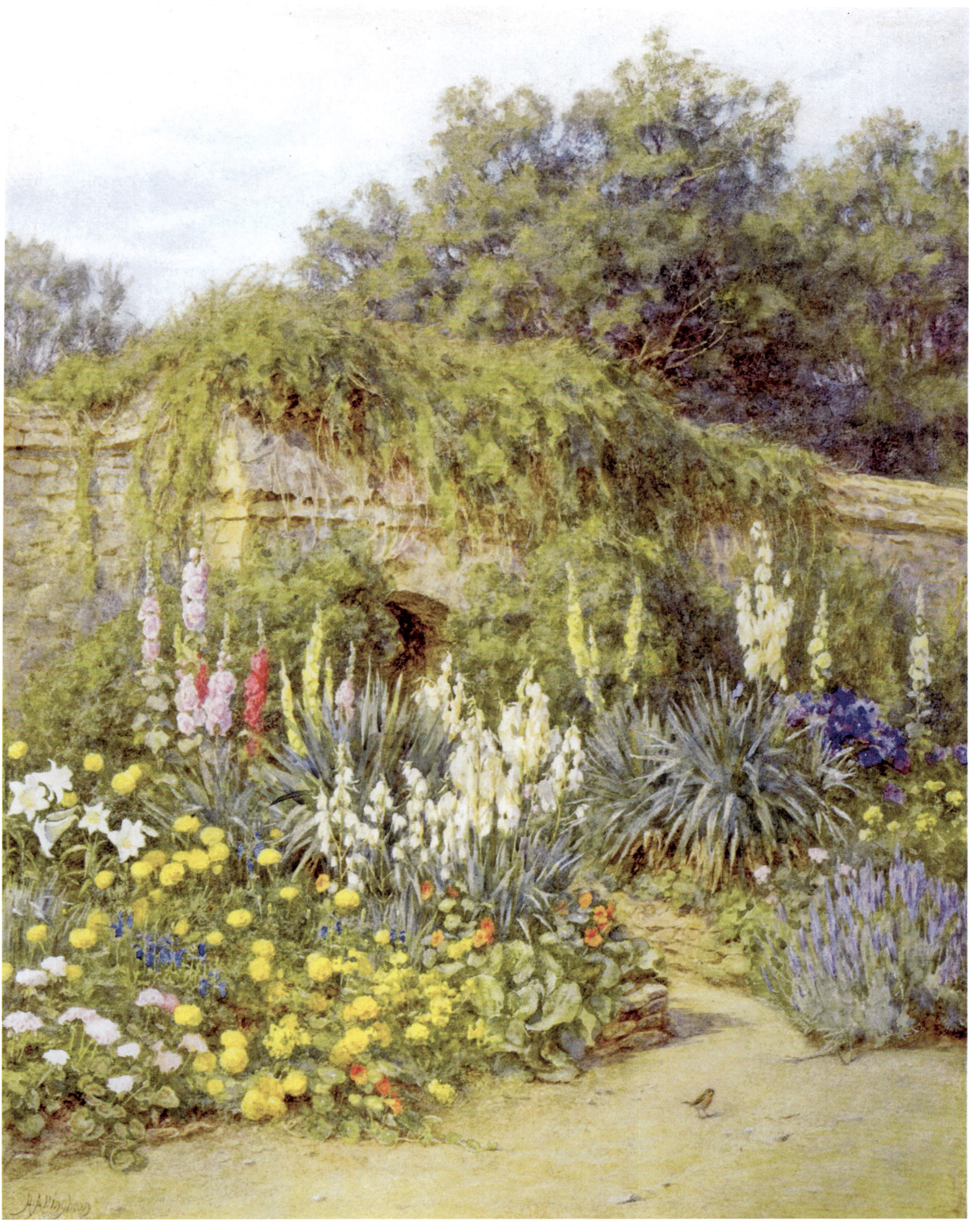

Helen Allingham, **South Border at Munstead Wood**, 1900–1903, watercolour painting, 40.5 × 29 cm. Courtesy Garden Museum, London.

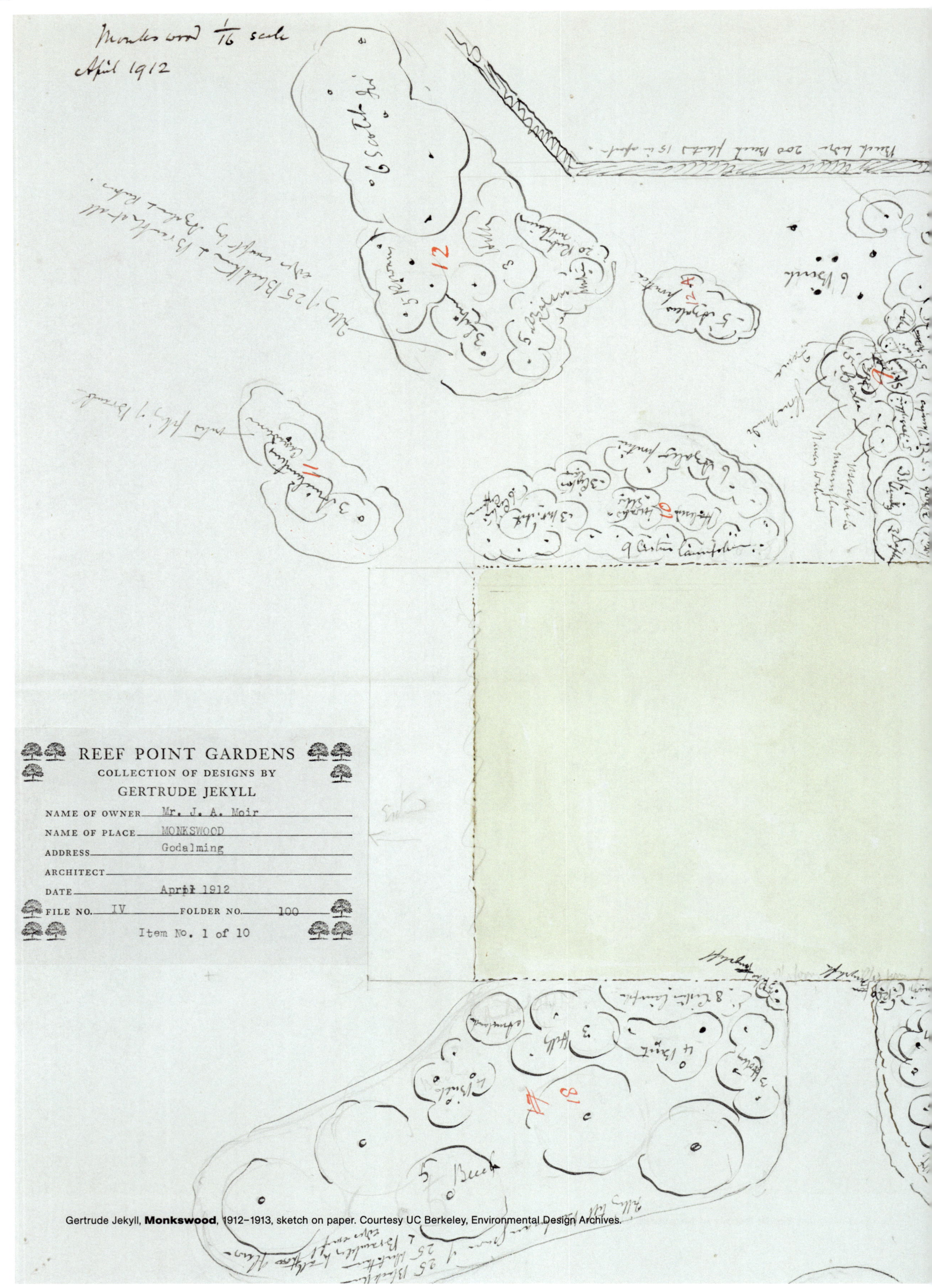

Gertrude Jekyll, **Monkswood**, 1912–1913, sketch on paper. Courtesy UC Berkeley, Environmental Design Archives.

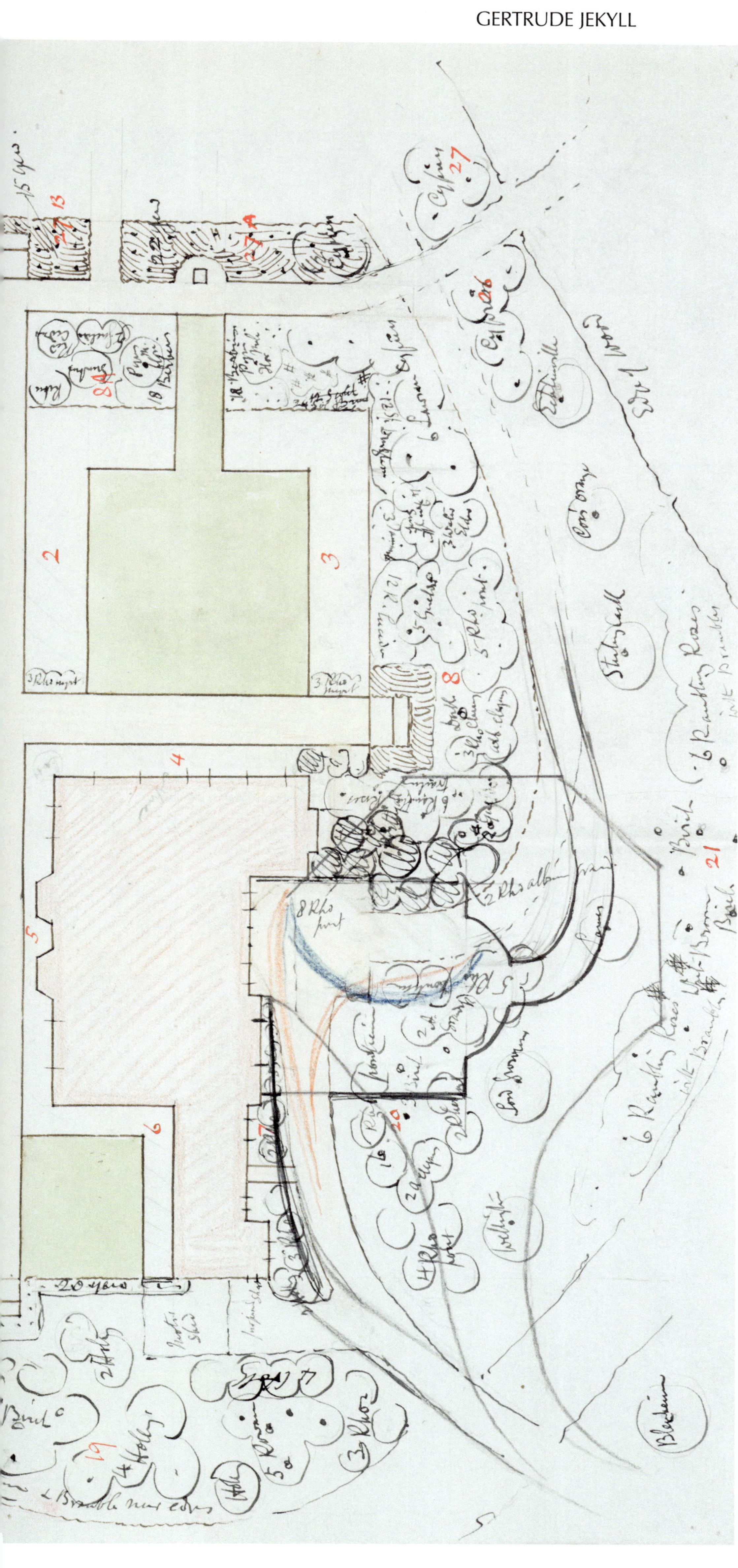

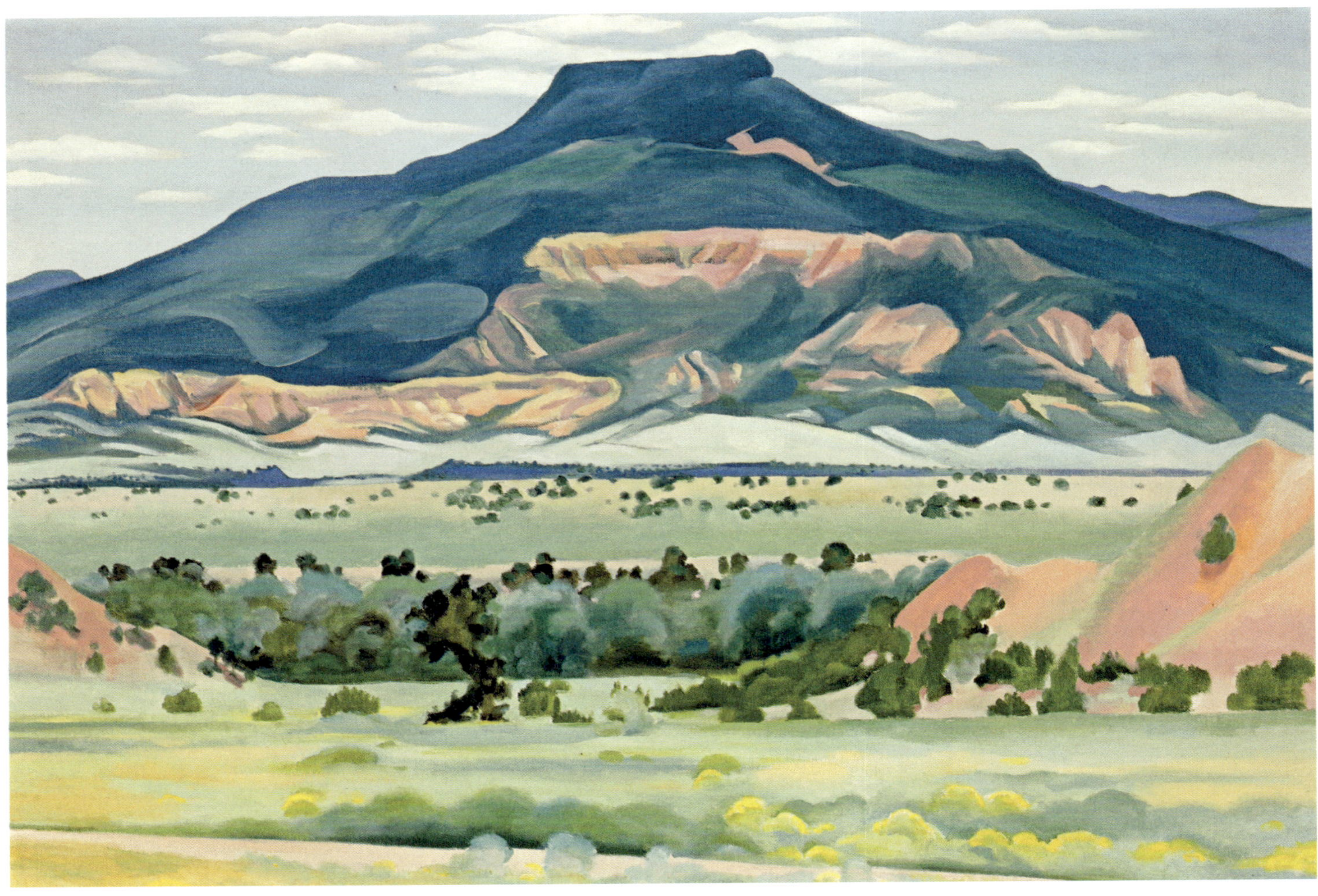

Georgia O'Keeffe, **My Front Yard**, 1941, oil on canvas, 50.9 × 76.5 cm. Courtesy Georgia O'Keeffe Museum, Santa Fe and Art Resource/Scala, Florence.

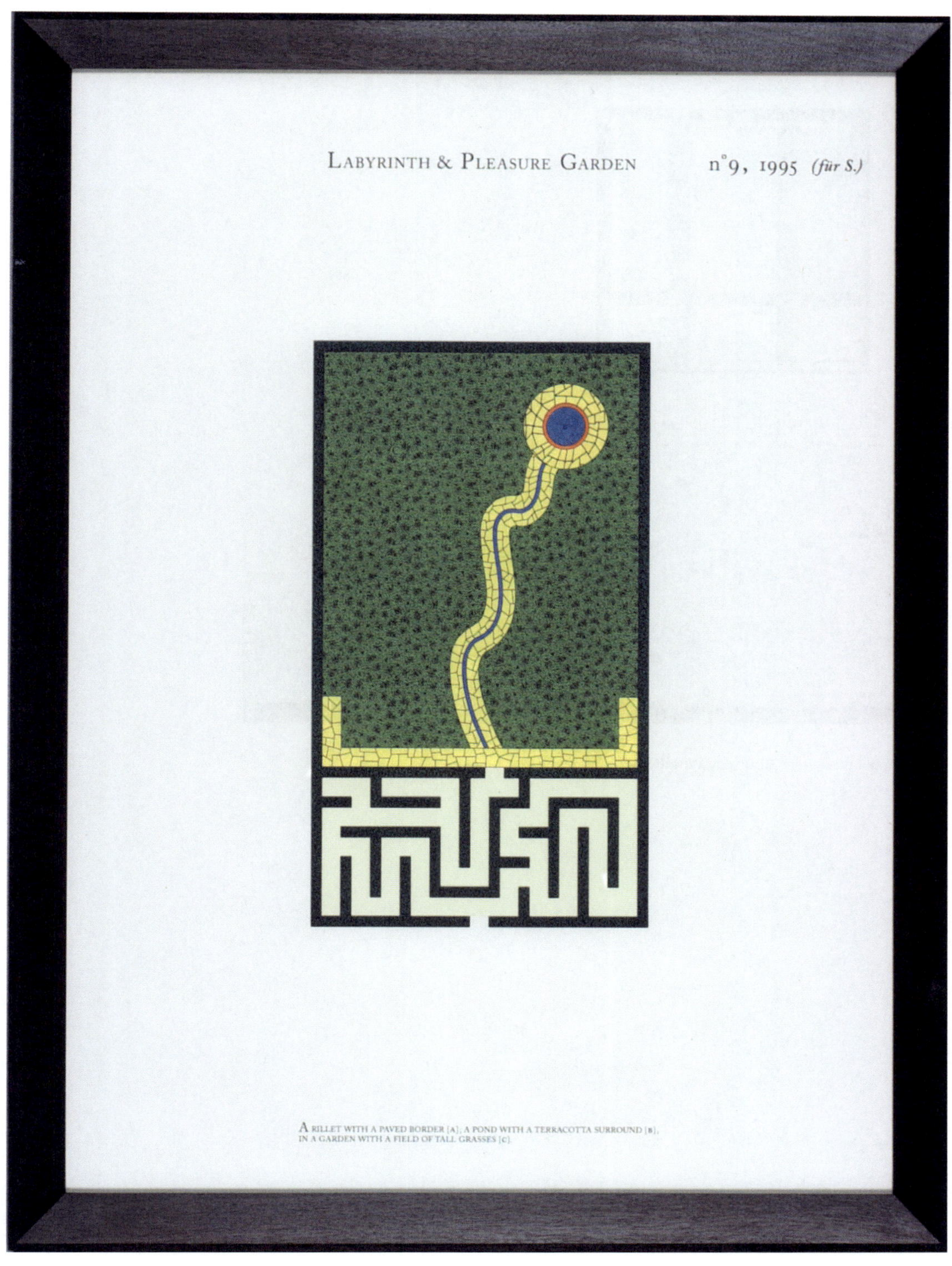

Jan Vercruysse, **Labyrinth & Pleasure Gardens**, 1994–1995, offset on paper, 71.5 × 54.3 cm.
Courtesy Van Abbemuseum, Eindhoven. Photo: Peter Cox.

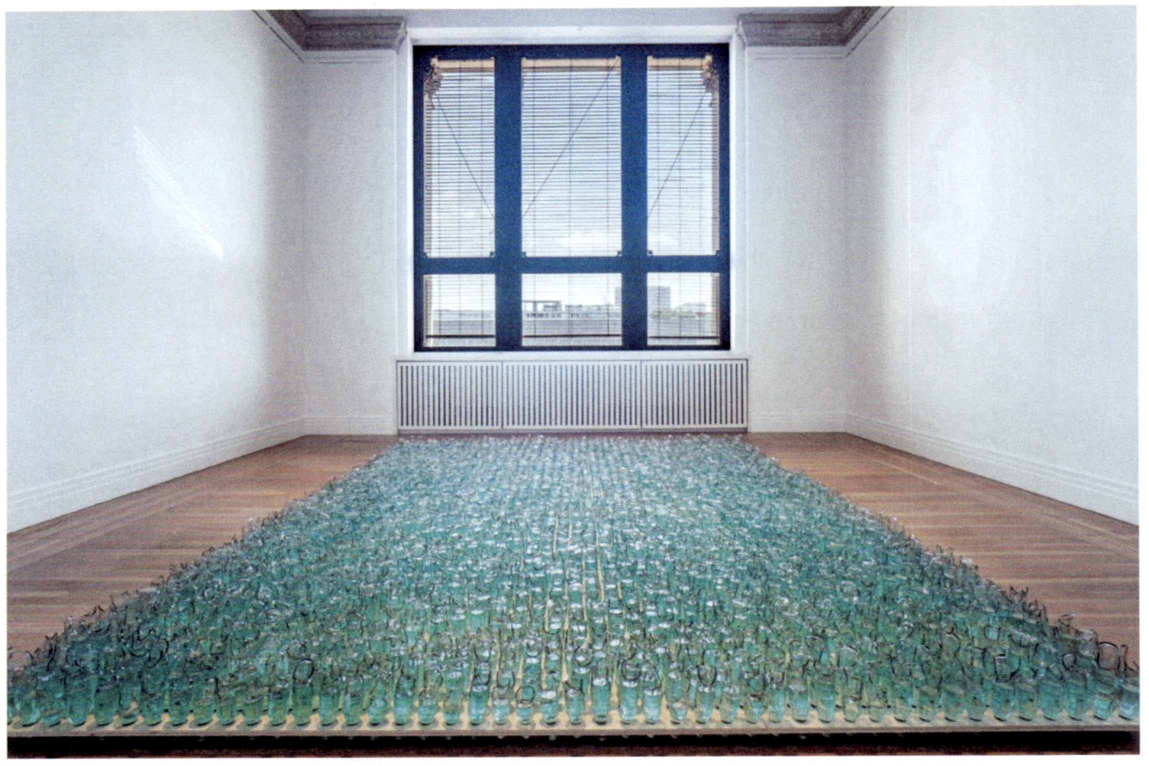

Lungiswa Gqunta, **Lawn**, 2016–2021, installation view. Courtesy WhatIfTheWorld, Capetown.

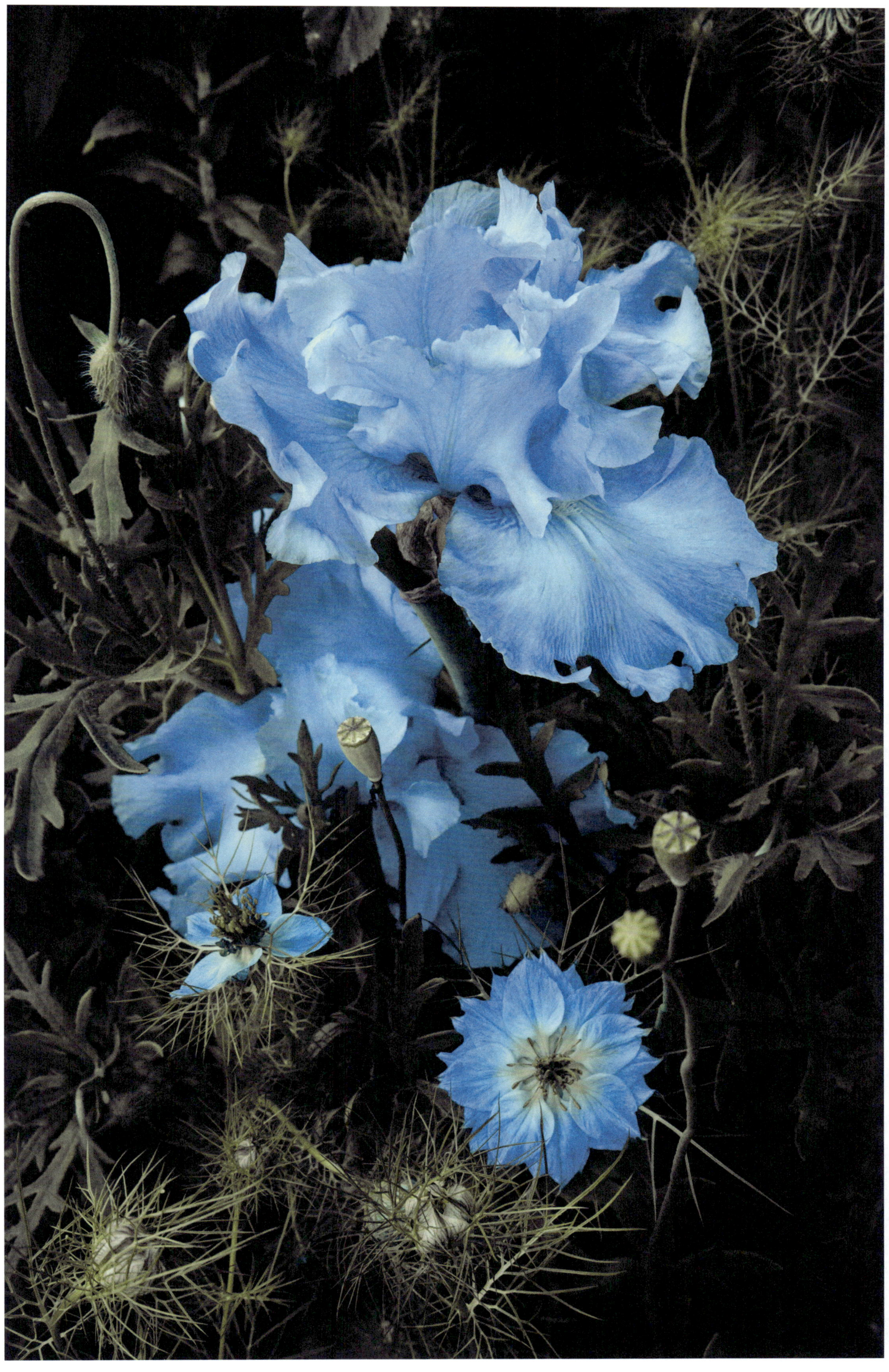

Elspeth Diederix, **Miracle2 #01**, 2019, photograph. Courtesy of Elspeth Diederix and Stigter Van Doesburg, Amsterdam.

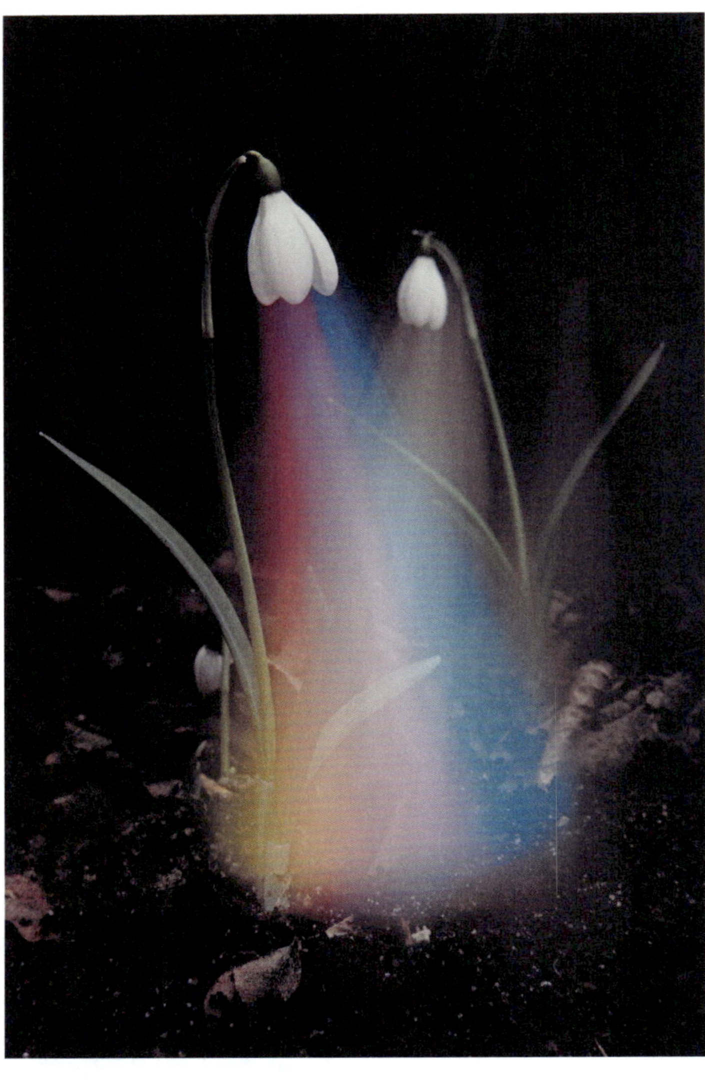

Elspeth Diederix, **Miracle #01**, 2018, photograph. Courtesy of Elspeth Diederix and Stigter Van Doesburg, Amsterdam.

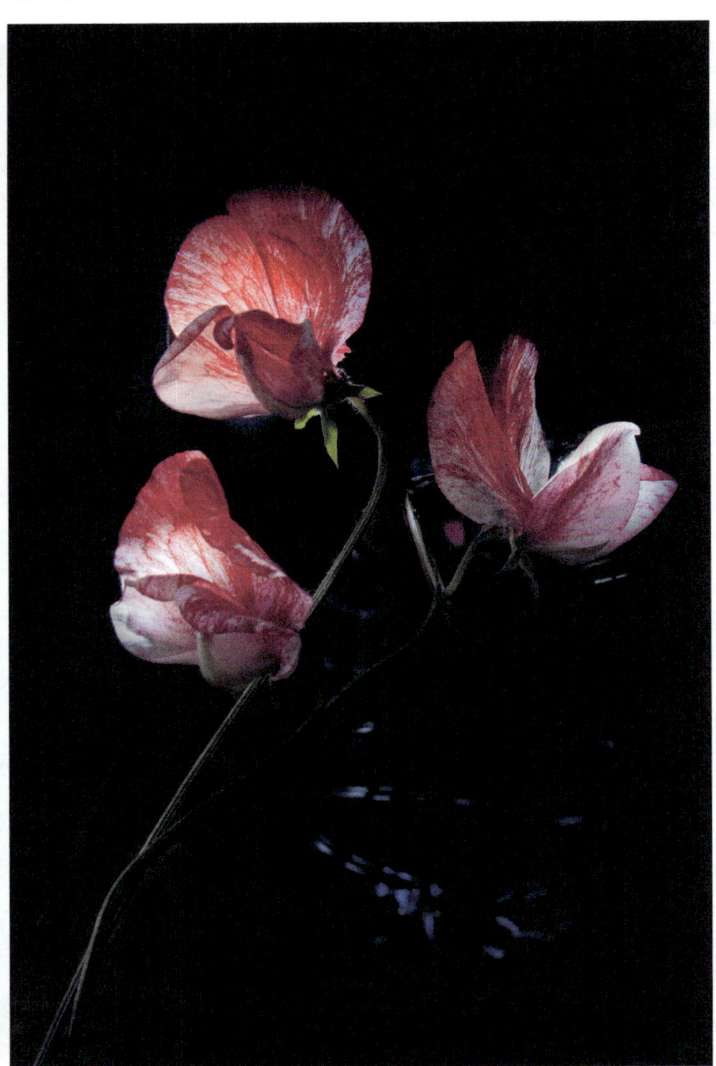

Elspeth Diederix, **Miracle #04**, 2018, photograph. Courtesy of Elspeth Diederix and Stigter Van Doesburg, Amsterdam.

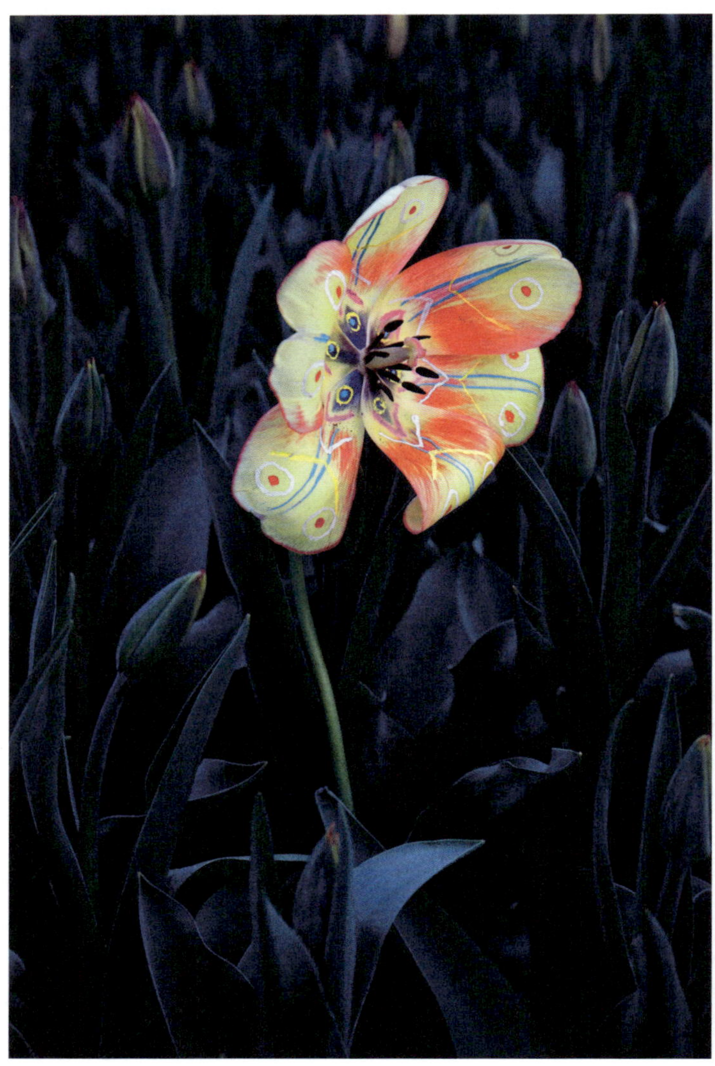

Elspeth Diederix, **Miracle #03**, 2018, photograph. Courtesy of Elspeth Diederix and Stigter Van Doesburg, Amsterdam.

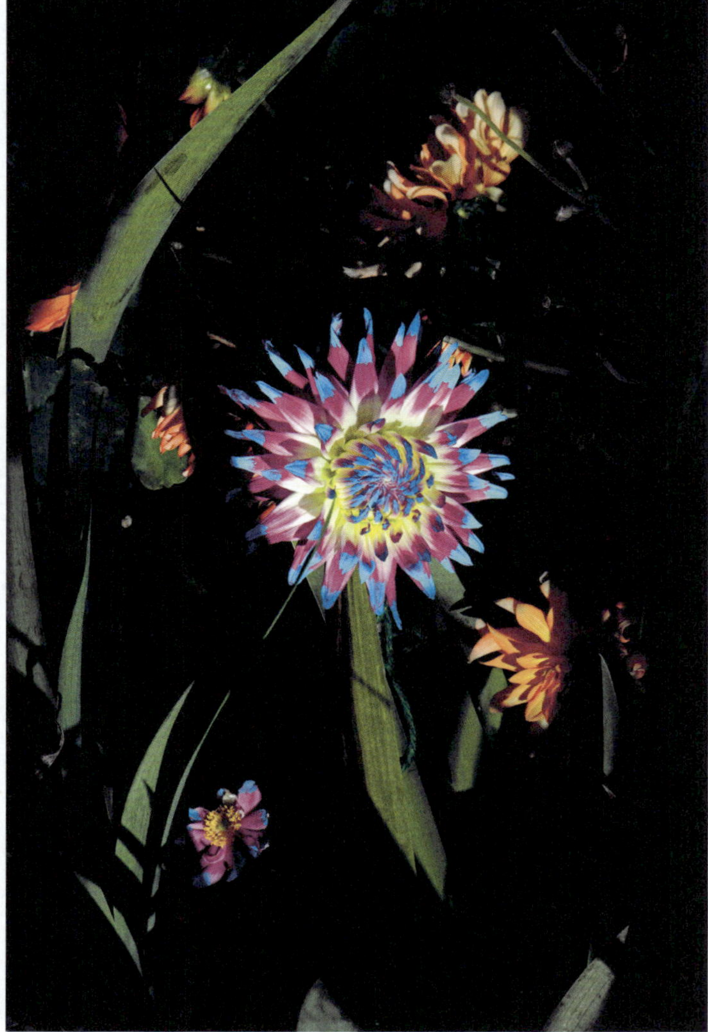

Elspeth Diederix, **Miracle #07**, 2018, photograph. Courtesy of Elspeth Diederix and Stigter Van Doesburg, Amsterdam.

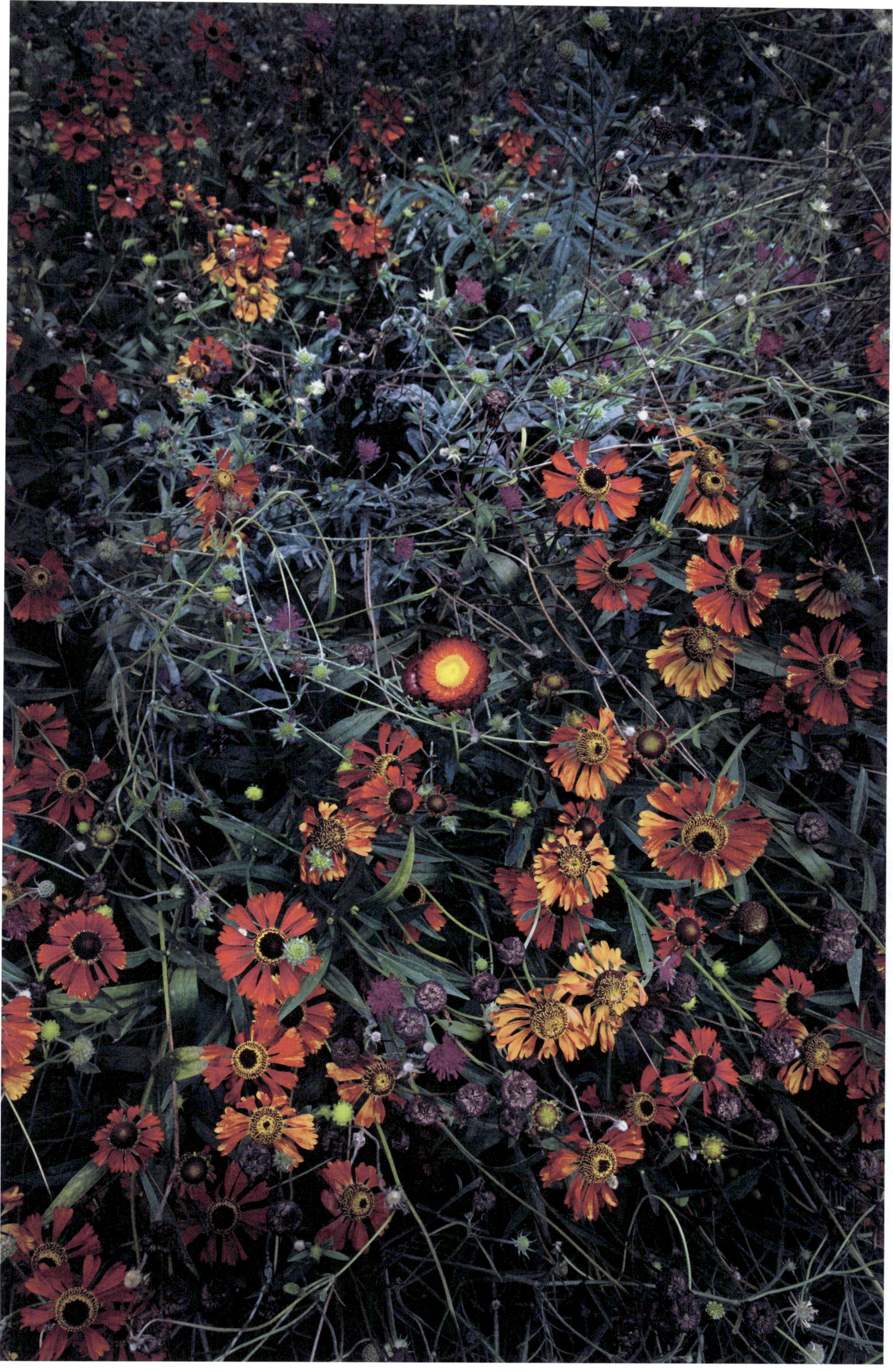

Elspeth Diederix, **Miracle #06**, 2018, photograph. Courtesy of Elspeth Diederix and Stigter Van Doesburg, Amsterdam.

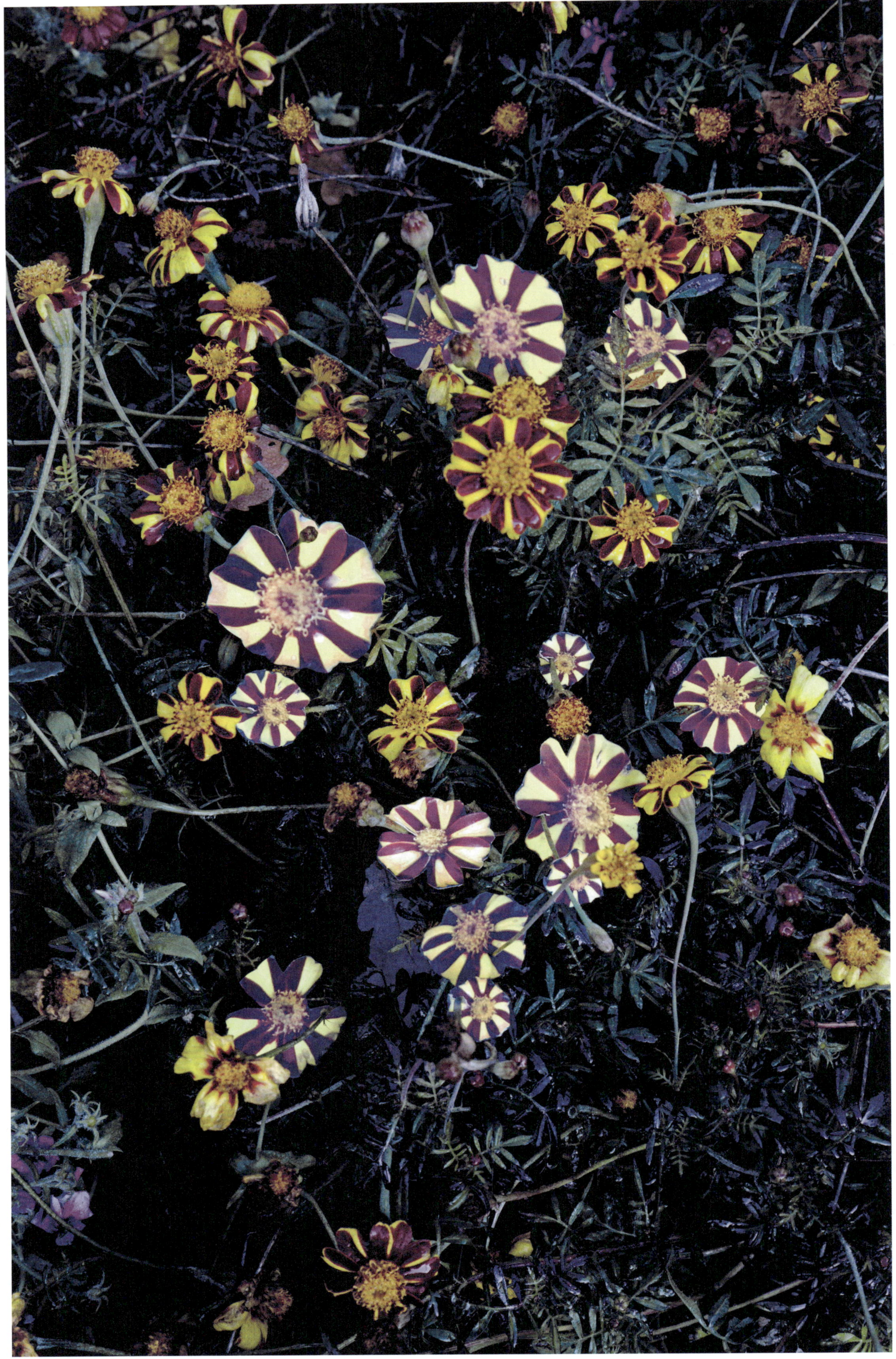

Elspeth Diederix, **Miracle2 #01**, 2019, photograph. Courtesy of Elspeth Diederix and Stigter Van Doesburg, Amsterdam.

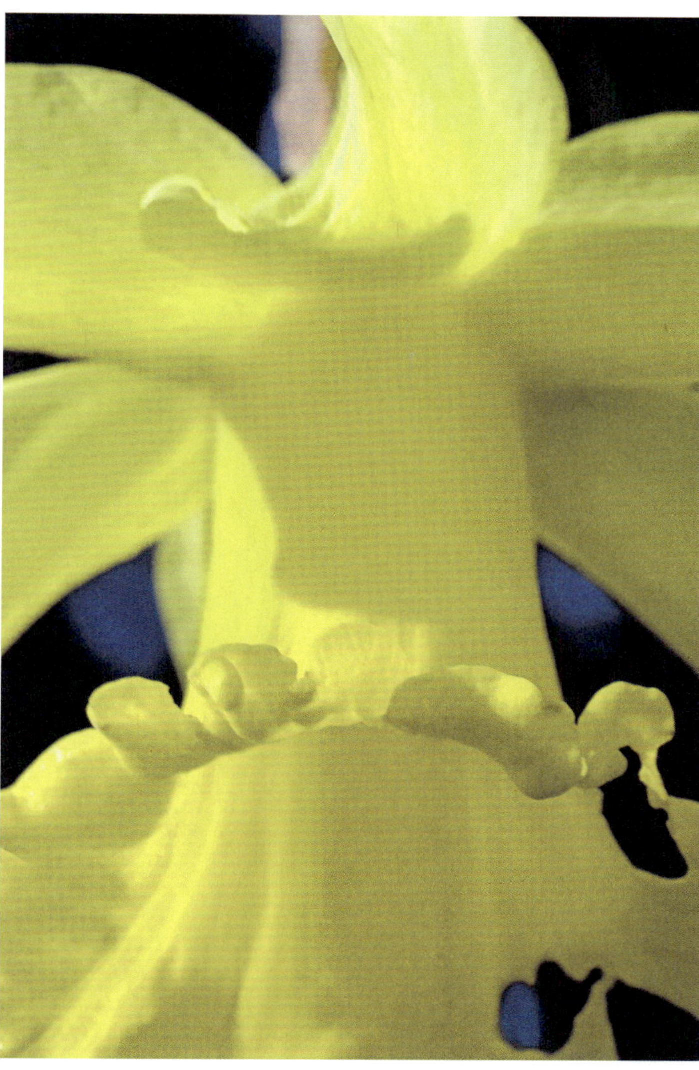

Elspeth Diederix, **Miracle2 #05,** 2019, photograph. Courtesy of Elspeth Diederix and Stigter Van Doesburg, Amsterdam.

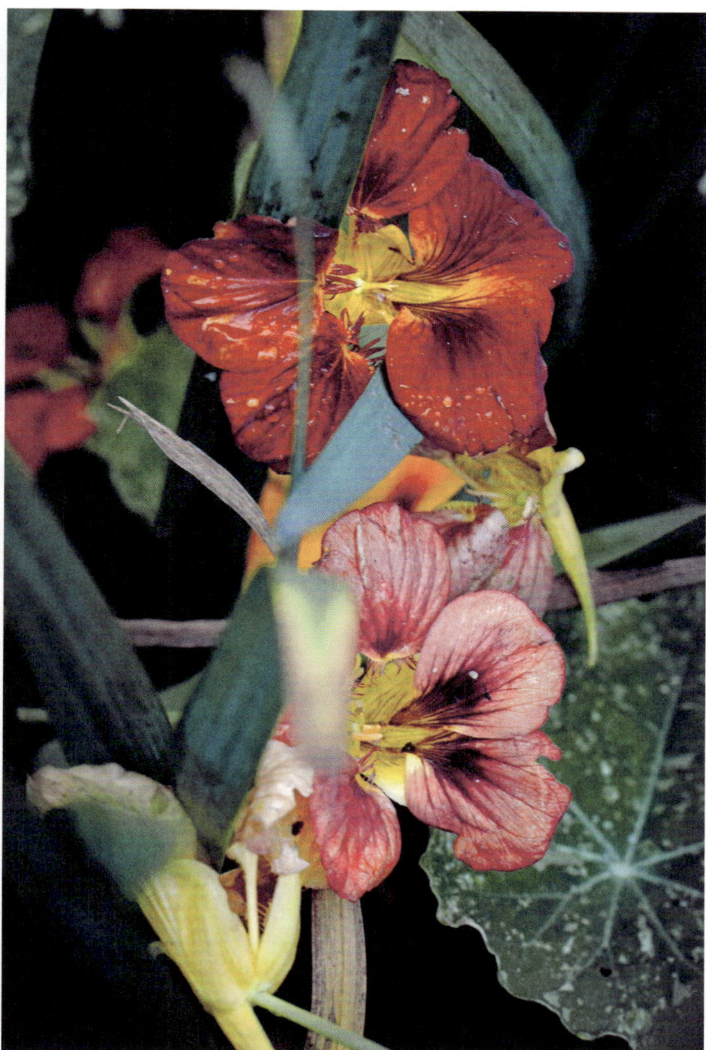

Elspeth Diederix, **Miracle #04**, 2018, photograph. Courtesy of Elspeth Diederix and Stigter Van Doesburg, Amsterdam.

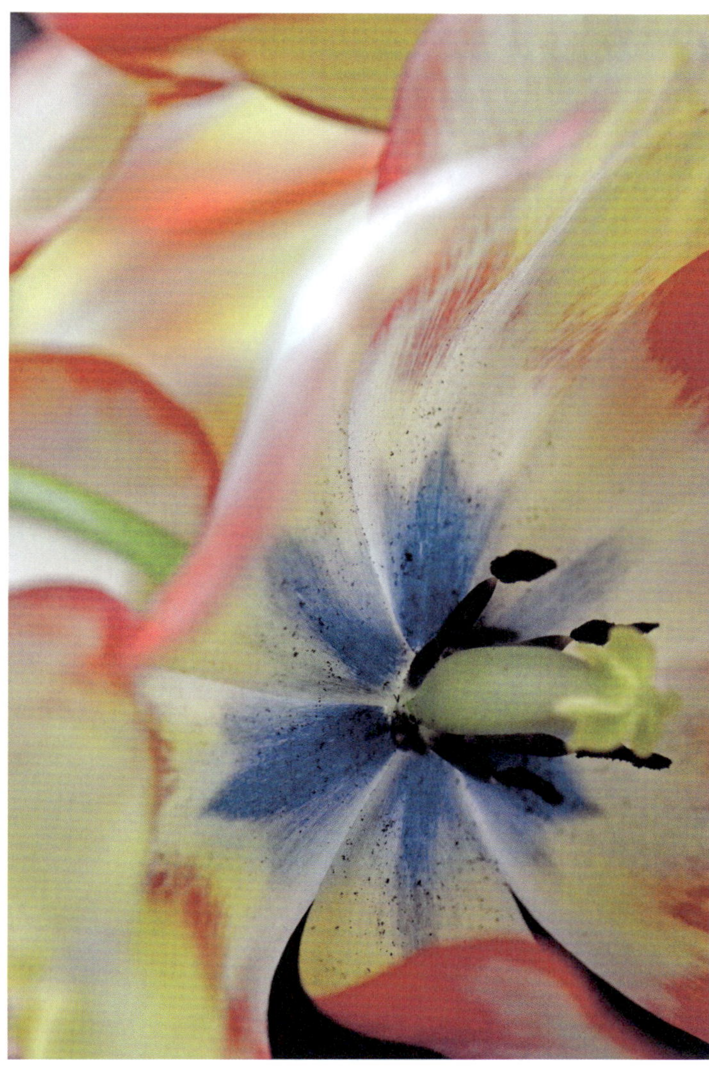

Elspeth Diederix, **Miracle2 #06**, 2019, photograph. Courtesy of Elspeth Diederix and Stigter Van Doesburg, Amsterdam.

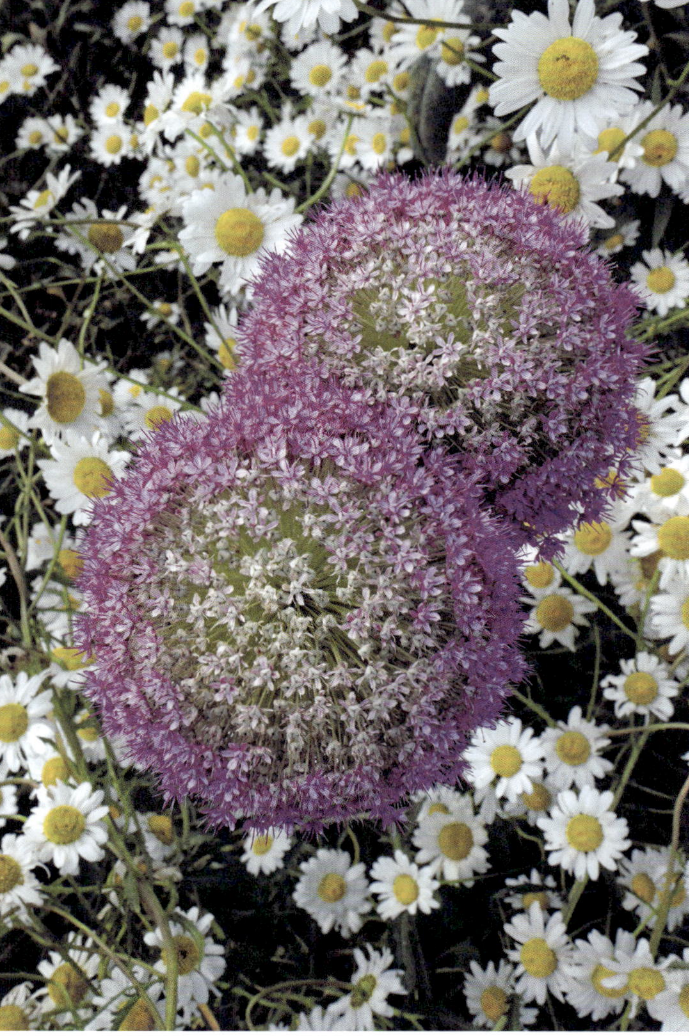

Elspeth Diederix, **Miracle2 #07**, 2019, photograph. Courtesy of Elspeth Diederix and Stigter Van Doesburg, Amsterdam.

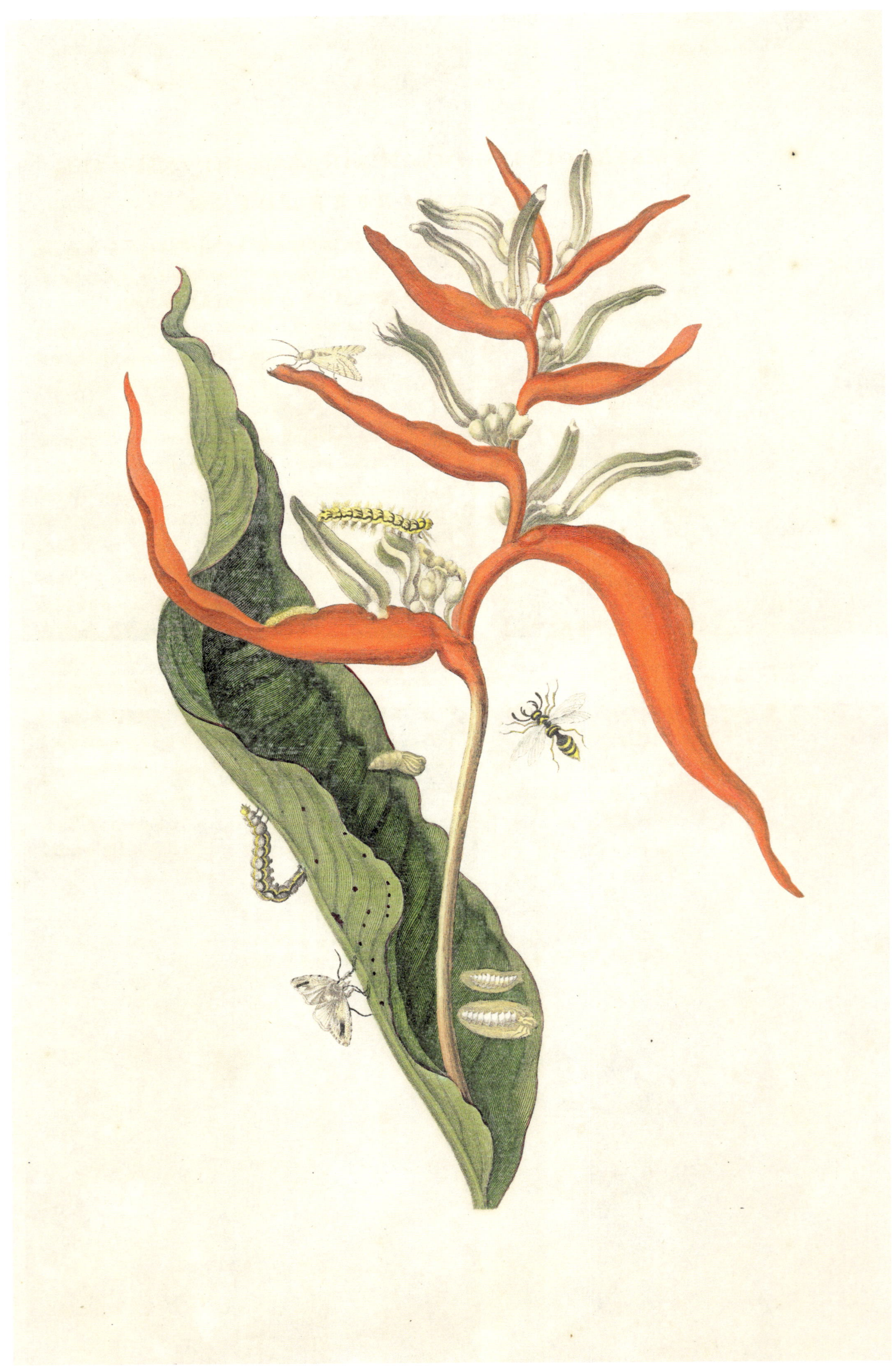

Maria Sibylla Merian, **Metamorphosis Insectorum Surinamensium**, 1705, book. Courtesy University of Utrecht.

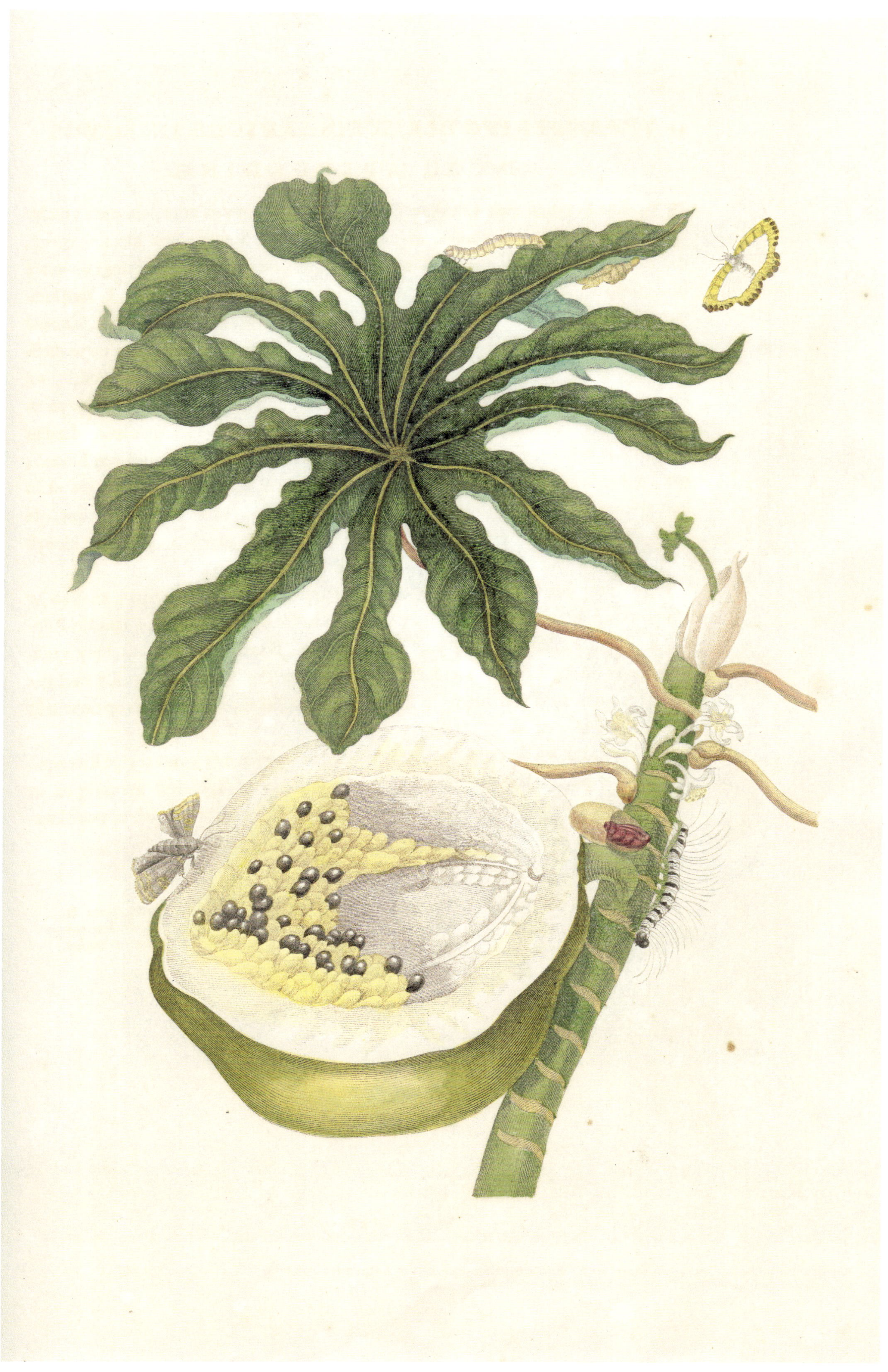

Maria Sibylla Merian, **Metamorphosis Insectorum Surinamensium**, 1705, book. Courtesy University of Utrecht.

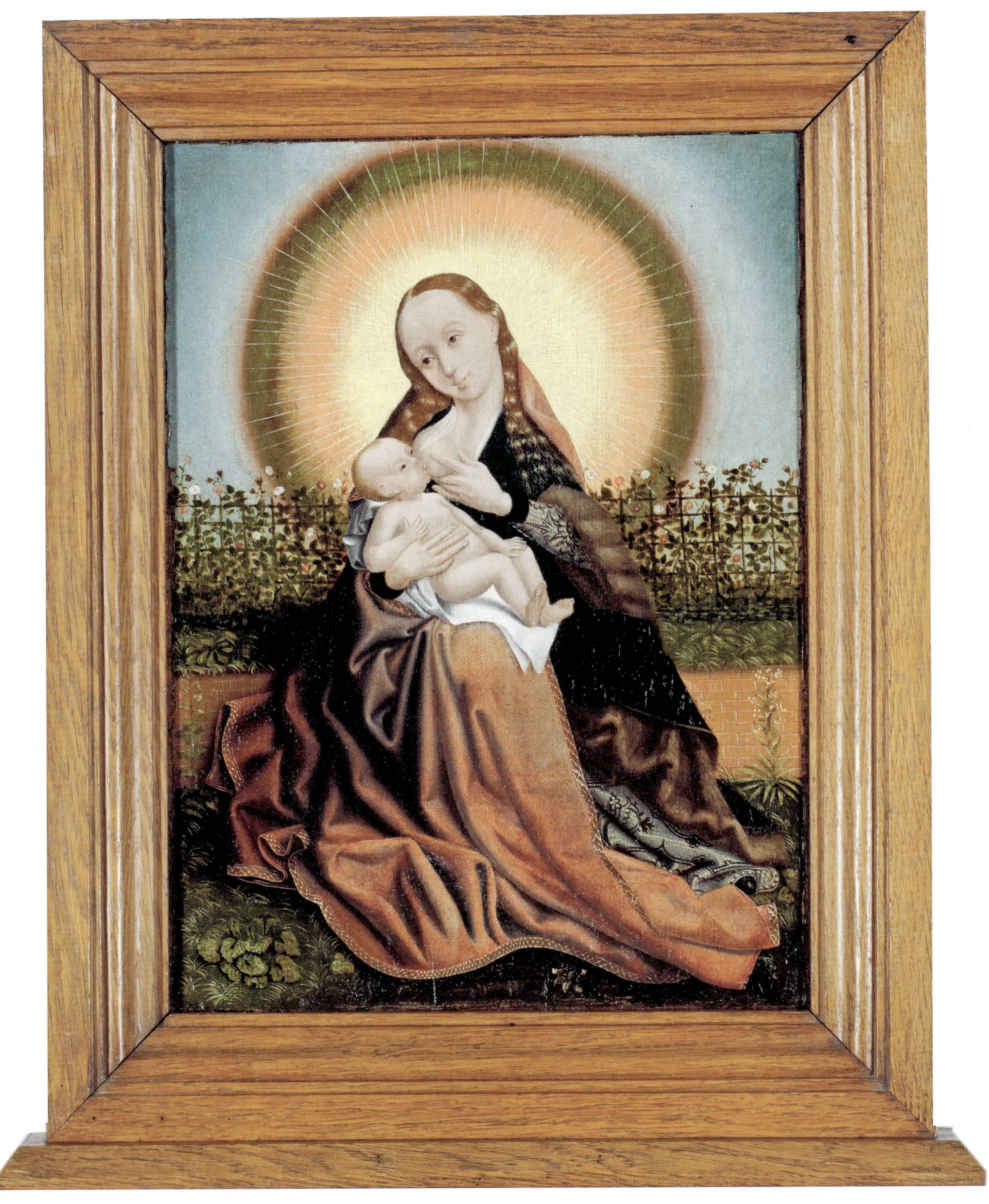

Anonymous (Northern Netherlands), **Mary with Child with Halo in Front of a Rose Hedge**, 1475-1499, oil on panel, 37 x 27 cm. Courtesy Museum Catharijneconvent, Utrecht. Photo: Ruben de Heer.

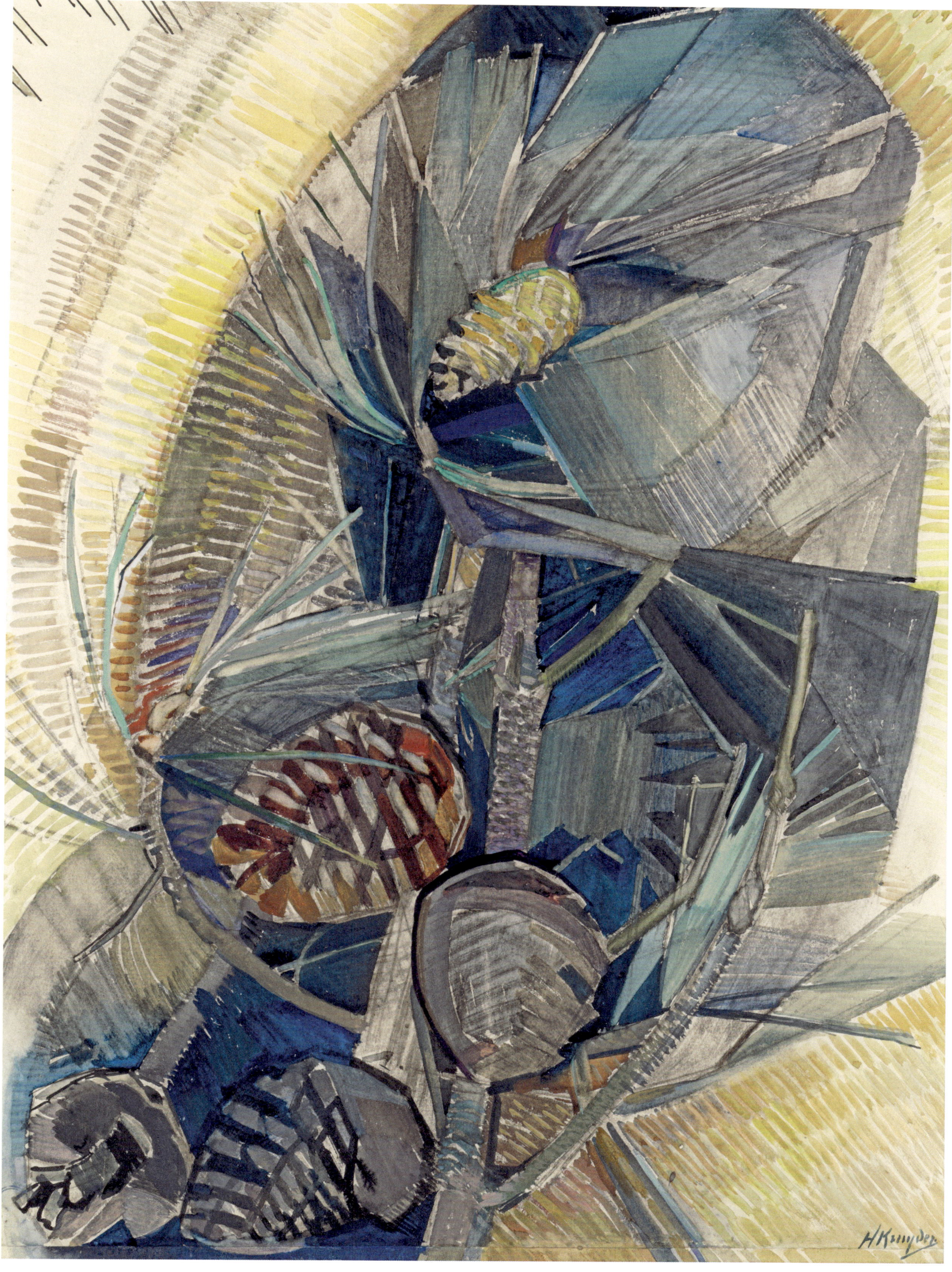

Herman Kruyder, **Maritime Pine Sprig**, 1917–1918, watercolour on paper, 65 × 48.5 cm. Courtesy Centraal Museum, Utrecht. Photo: Adriaan van Dam.

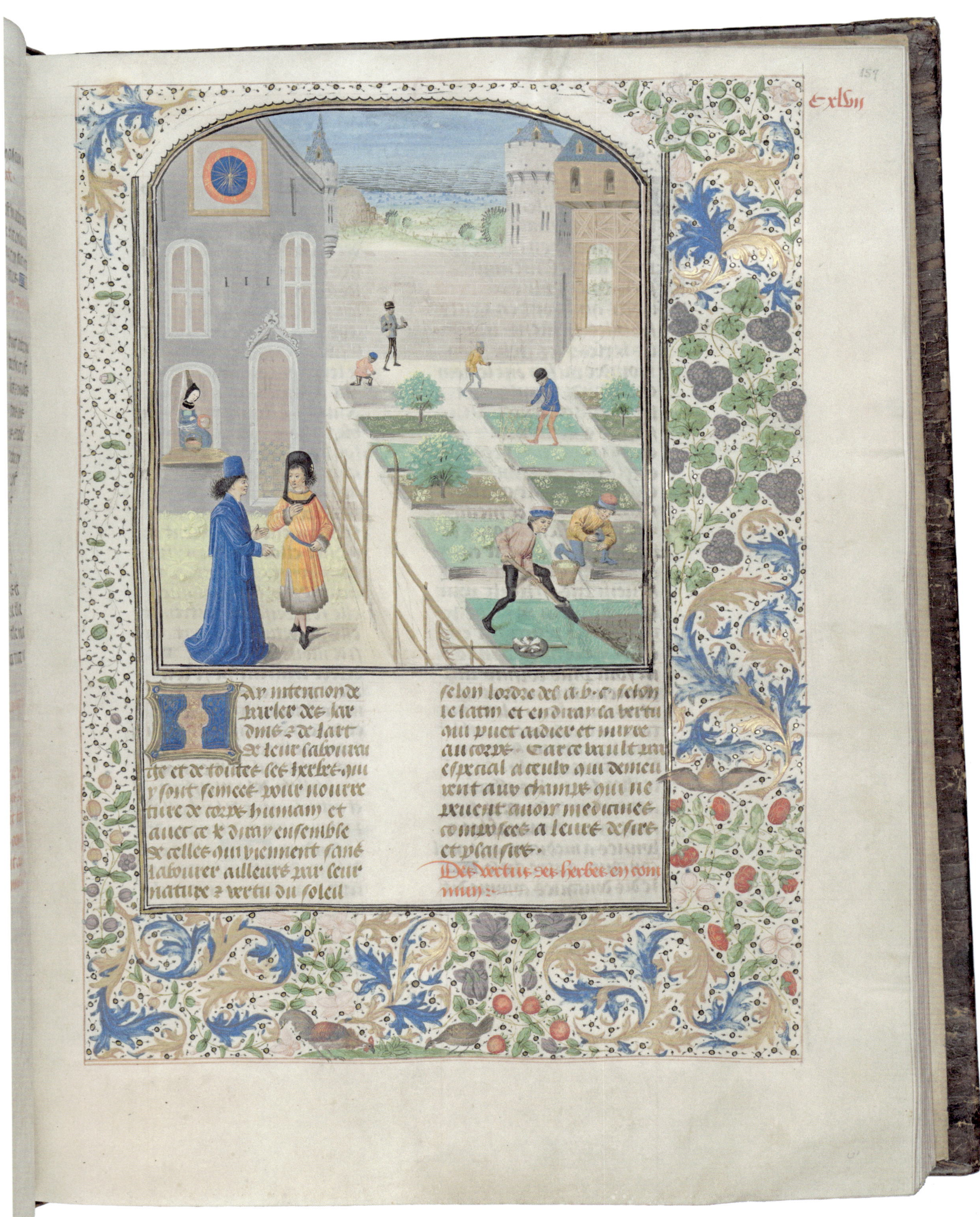

Pietro de' Crescenzi, **Le livre des prouffis champestres et ruraux**, fol. 157r., c. 1470, manuscript. Courtesy The Morgan Library & Museum, New York.

PHARMACOPOEIA

> Derek Ball came here after his 'accident', after the discovery of my seropositivity.
> Behind the facade my life is at sixes and sevens. I water the roses and wonder whether I will see them bloom. I plant my herbal garden as a panacea,
> read up on all the aches and pains that plants will cure—and know they are not going to help. The garden as pharmacopoeia has failed.
>
> Yet there is a thrill in watching the plants spring up that gives me hope. Even so, I find myself unable to record the disaster that has befallen some
> of my friends, particularly dear Howard, who I miss more than imagination.
> He wanders into my mind—as he wandered out of a stormy night eighteen months ago.
>
> Jarman, *Modern Nature*, 179.

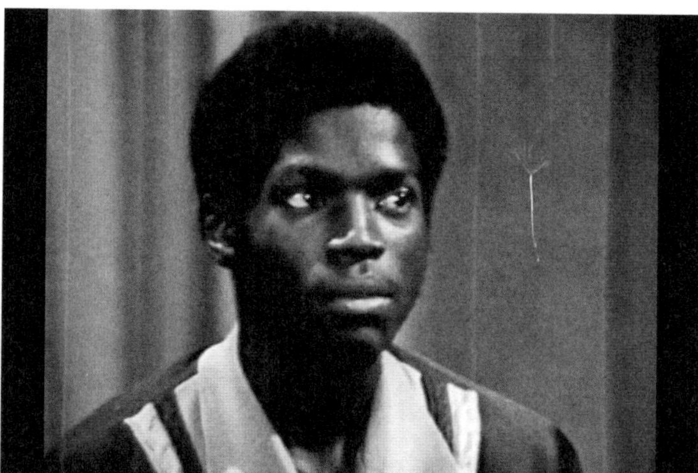

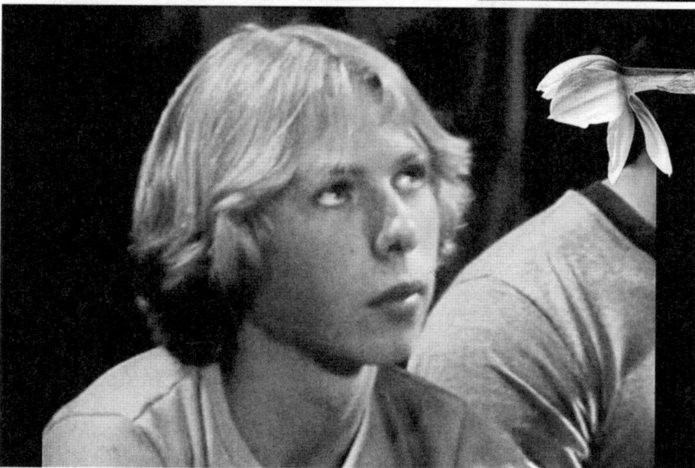

Jort van der Laan, **I AM A POLLINATOR! I AM A POLLINATOR!**, 2020, video still. Courtesy Jort van der Laan.

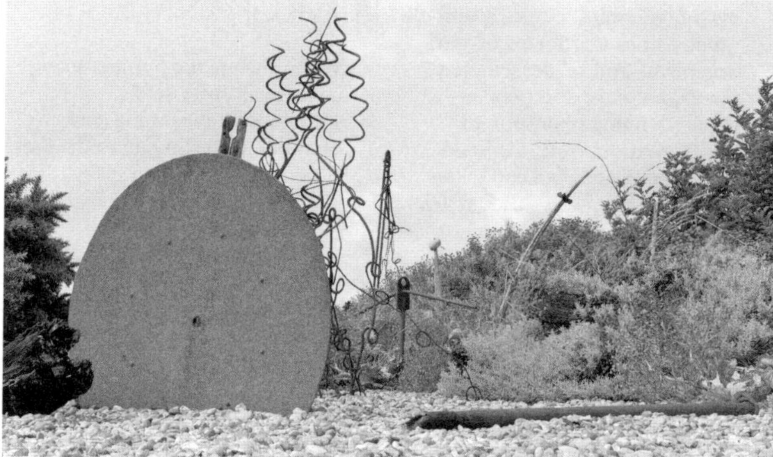

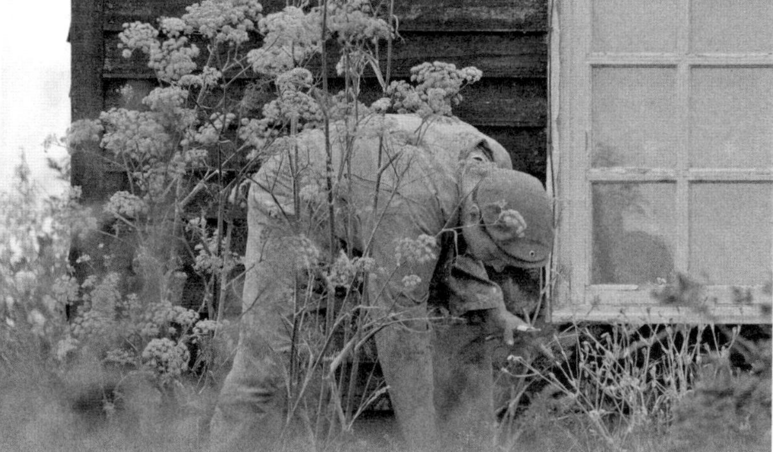

Jort van der Laan, **All-heal Fennel**, 2017, video still. Courtesy Jort van der Laan.

JORT VAN DER LAAN

Jort van der Laan's short film *All-heal Fennel* is based on a road trip to Derek Jarman's Prospect Cottage. The tightened border controls at Calais, *Guardian*-reader tourism, and traces of *Blue*—Jarman's haunting cinematic reflection on dying and living with HIV/AIDS—together form a layered political landscape. In *'I AM A POLLINATOR! I AM A POLLINATOR!'* a similar political layering takes place through a composition of contrasting images. Van der Laan juxtaposes the terrified faces of teenagers in the award-winning documentary *Scared Straight!* (1978) with a series of apparently benign flowers. Scared Straight programmes involved taking at-risk youth to visit adult prisons, where they were subjected to brutal intimidation by long-term inmates to be warned off a life of crime. The flowers in *'I AM A POLLINATOR! I AM A POLLINATOR!'* refer to alternative interventions and to a not-so-straight queer floriography, as described by Jarman in his journal *Modern Nature*. (ed.)

CPR (CHARLOTTE ROOIJACKERS)

CPR's practice views and names the world through a pharmaco-poetic lens. The ancient Greek word *pharmakon*, which means both 'remedy' and 'poison', describes in a single word how every substance can have both a healing and toxic effect on the body, depending on its dosage. Not only drugs but everything in and around us has a psychoactive effect. Everything touches us, from air to aesthetics, and thus affects how we feel and what we think. The work *Floruit, S/he Flourished* stems from that idea and is about the stomach and the healing and informative effects of bleeding. This series of works questions how we recognize and treat trauma, with a view to radical interspecies solidarity. (ed.)

PLANTATIONOCENE

> It is the notion of Plantationocene, yet another alternative to the Anthropocene, that attracts our attention (Haraway et al., 2015; Tsing, 2015). The Plantationocene points to the ongoing socioecological consequences of plantation agriculture and the permutations and persistence of the plantation across time and space. Here, we affirm the merit of the Plantationocene concept and acknowledge the importance of analyzing the spatial history of the plantation in understanding the present. However, we argue that the emerging conceptualizations of the Plantationocene are limited in several important ways. Most pointedly, their multispecies framing minimizes the role of racial politics and leads to a flattened notion of 'making kin' that is inadequate for the creation of more just ecologies in the plantation present.
>
> Davis et al., 'Anthropocene, Capitalocene, ... Plantationocene?', 2–3.

However, if we think seriously about the Plantationocene, these new kinship relations portend contentious spatializations of human and nonhuman life and the politics of embodiment. We must ask then, what purchase the plantation has in nominating the geologic epoch it concerns and what is elided or obfuscated by its current conceptualization. Thus, we consider whether and how the specificity of Black embodiment is treated in contemplating futures beyond the plantation logics that inform ongoing dispossession, environmental crisis, and white supremacy. It is only in a footnote for example, that Haraway (2015) addresses these plantation realities and even there the explication warrants interrogation.The footnote reads:

> Scholars have long understood that the slave plantation system was the model and motor for the carbon-greedy machine-based factory system that is often cited as an inflection point for the Anthropocene. Nurtured in even the harshest circumstances, slave gardens not only provided crucial human food, but also refuges for biodiverse plants, animals, fungi, and soils. Slave gardens are an underexplored world, especially compared to imperial botanical gardens, for the travels and propagations of myriad critters. Moving material semiotic generativity around the world for capital accumulation and profit—the rapid displacement and reformulation of germ

plasm, genomes, cuttings, and all other names and forms of part organisms and of deracinated plants, animals, and people—is one defining operation of the Plantationocene, Capitalocene, and Anthropocene taken together. (Haraway, 2015, p. 162).

The scholars of the plantation and slave plot that Haraway (2015) alludes to remain unnamed. We see their nameless footnoting as part of a broader failure among initial Plantationocene scholarship to seriously attend to Black spatial and ecological thought and practice. Instead, the slave garden becomes part of a narration of networked kinship that transforms the reproduction of racial oppression and resistance into a flattened multispecies ontology—where difference among and between forms of life is obscured.

Davis et al., 'Anthropocene, Capitalocene, ... Plantationocene?', 5.

PLEASURE GARDEN

While the garden has taken the visitor to both heaven and hell, it more often fuses the sacred and profane with its literary allusions and attempts at the picturesque. As far back as the medieval hortus conclusus, the garden was also a place for pleasure, a hortus deliciarum. [...] in the early fifteenth century, the original religious symbolism of the herbarium had given way to greater interest in daily life, with the garden depicted as a courtly yet secret place set amidst a rather non-threatening, idealised landscape. This breakdown of the divisions between garden and forest, sacred and profane, continued in the Renaissance.

Brougher, 'Being There', in *Enclosed and Enchanted*, ed. Brougher and Tarantino, 11.

POLITICAL ECOLOGY

The term 'political ecology', as used herein, acknowledges approaches to the environment that, although potentially divergent, nevertheless insist on environmental matters of concern as inextricable from social, political and economic forces.

Demos, *Decolonizing Nature, 7.*

Sarah Naqvi, **Shanakht (Identity)**, 2018, natural dyes on cotton, 30.5 × 90.7 cm. Collection Alain Servais, Brussels. Photo: Wytske van Keulen, 2019.

POMEGRANATE

When she ate the pomegranate,
it was as if every seed
with its wet red shining coat
of sweet flesh clinging to the dark
core
was one of nature's eyes.
Afterward,
it was nature that was blind,
and she who was wild
with vision, condemned
to see what was before her, and
behind.

Wilner, 'The Girl with Bees in Her Hair', 33.

'Because of its very numerous seeds, the pomegranate has been, through the ages a symbol of fertility in Chinese, Persian, Semitic, Greek and Roman lore. Chinese women offer it to the goddess of mercy when praying for children, especially sons [...]. The pomegranate is often credited with being the forbidden fruit of the garden of Eden, and some say that it contains one seed from the garden. It was a symbol of wealth [...]. In Turkey the bride throws a pomegranate on the ground and the number of seeds scattered when it breaks indicates the number of children she will have' (Leach and Fried 1972:880). Mother of Attis 'Nana' was a virgin 'who conceived by putting a ripe almond or a pomegranate in her bosom' (Frazer 1933:347). Pomegranates were supposed to have sprung from the blood of Dionysus, so eating pomegranate during festival of Thesmophoria was a taboo for women. (Frazer 1933:389) There are many legends like this which indicate that pomegranate was associated with 'death' as well. Persephone ate only six seeds of pomegranate and was confined every year to the nether world for six months.

Atre, 'Many Seeded Apple', 2.

POPPIES

In Flanders fields the poppies blow
Between the crosses, row on row,
That mark our place; and in the sky
The larks, still bravely singing, fly
Scarce heard amid the guns below.
We are the Dead.Short days ago
We lived, felt dawn, saw sunset glow,
Loved and were loved, and now we lie,
In Flanders fields.
Take up our quarrel with the foe:
To you from failing hands we throw
The torch; be yours to hold it high.
If ye break faith with us who die
We shall not sleep, though poppies grow
In Flanders fields.

McCrae, *In Flanders Fields and Other Poems*, 3.

PRISON GARDEN

A garden was one of the few things in prison that one could control. To plant a seed, watch it grow, to tend it and then harvest it, offered a simple but enduring satisfaction. The sense of being the custodian of this small patch of earth offered a taste of freedom.

Mandela, *Long Walk to Freedom*, 582–583.

Sonyusha, Wronke, End of May 1917

Where do you think I am writing this letter? In the garden! I have brought out a small table at which I am now seated, hidden among the shrubs. [...]

I strolled about the garden. A light breeze was blowing, and I saw a remarkable sight. The over ripe catkins on the white poplar were scattered abroad; their seed-down was carried in all directions, filling the air as if with snow-flakes, covering the ground and the whole courtyard; the silvery seed-down made everything look quite ghostlike. The white poplar blooms later than the catkin-bearing trees, and spreads far and wide thanks to this luxuriant dispersal of its seeds; the young shoots sprout like weeds from all the crannies on the wall and from between the paving stones. [...]

I shall never forget what followed. The storm had passed on; the sky had turned a thick monotonous grey; a pale, dull, spectral twilight suddenly diffused itself over the landscape, so that it seemed as if the whole prospect were under a thick grey veil. A gentle rain was falling steadily upon the leaves; sheet lightning flamed at brief intervals, tinting the leaden grey with flashes of purple, while the distant thunder could still be heard rumbling like the declining waves of a heavy sea. Then, quite abruptly, the nightingale began to sing in the sycamore in front of my window.

Despite the rain, the lightning and the thunder, the notes rang out as clear as a bell. The bird sang as if intoxicated, as if possessed, as if wishing to drown the thunder, to illuminate the twilight.

Never have I heard anything so lovely. On the background of the alternately leaden and lurid sky, the song seemed to show like shafts of silver. It was so mysterious, so incredibly beautiful, that involuntarily I murmured the last verse of Goethe's poem, 'Oh, wert thou here!'

Always yours
Rosa

Luxemburg, *Letters to Sophie Liebknecht*.

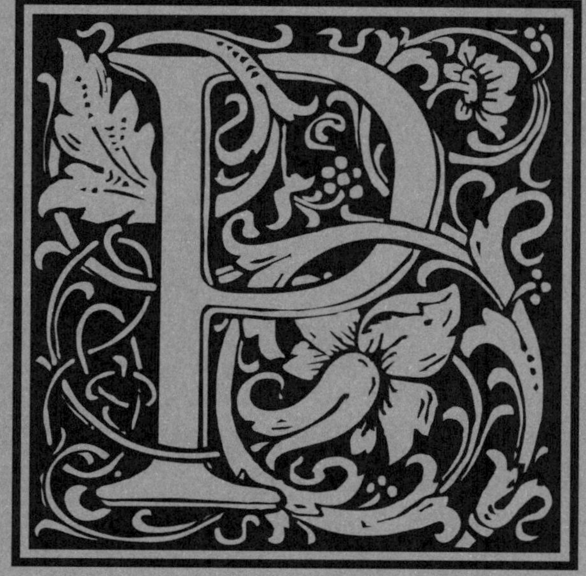

William Morris, **Letter P.**

THE GARDEN AS PHARMA-COPOEIA

Jonny Bruce

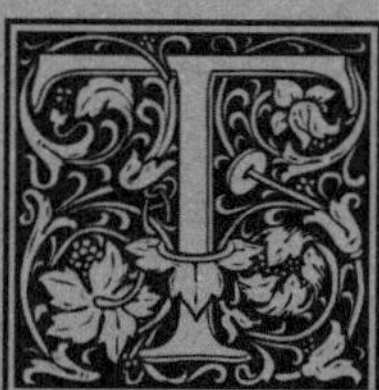he garden as pharmacopoeia plays into all expectations of what gardens should be—quiet, secluded places to heal both body and mind. It has informed historic depictions of Eden as a walled garden, a *hortus conclusus,* where Adam and Eve sheltered from the world's brutal reality. Faced with environmental catastrophe, the need to find or restore our own corner of paradise becomes ever more pressing. It is with these eyes that many approach the garden at Prospect Cottage and continue to colour the narrative around its creation. A narrative worth challenging, as Derek Jarman once wrote: 'Paradise haunts gardens'.

In the face of a positive HIV diagnosis and an antagonistic political situation, it is tempting to see Jarman's move to Dungeness as a retreat from both prejudice and disease—to create that secluded paradise on the edge of the world. While he did describe his garden as both 'therapy and pharmacopoeia', there is also a powerful magic, grounded in real-world politics, which challenges and disrupts. Perched on the shingle, Prospect Cottage is a garden without boundary; no wall or fence shelters it from the ravages of an extreme coastal environment. As he definitively wrote in *Chroma*, his poetic meditation on colour, 'No hortus conclusus, my seaside garden'.

By 1986, Jarman had lost enough friends to know the indignity of dying with AIDS. Considering this, the act of garden making takes on profound significance, both as an act of optimistic resilience and also of resistance. In a 2010 journal *Queer Ecologies*, Catriona Sandilands makes the strong argument that 'AIDS does not and cannot propel a retreat into Nature in order to find solace and harmony'. AIDS necessitates confrontation. During those last eight years of his life, this was dramatically realized through his activism, paintings, writing, and films, but also through his garden.

While he was fascinated by the idea of a physic garden and introduced many medicinal plants such as Sage, Poppy, and Wormwood, it is necessary to unpack the term pharmacopoeia and some of its misleading connotations. In its most literal sense, pharmacopoeia refers to a collection of medicines often presented in printed form as a pharmaceutical directory. This codification speaks of an Enlightenment need to rationalize— and thereby demystify—nature to provide a deeper scientific understanding of the world. This was not Jarman's mission. As an artist and thinker, he self-consciously associated with a rich heritage of dissident artists, from William Blake to Paul Nash, who saw nature as the original site of mystery. He felt a particular affinity with the Neo-Romantics of the early twentieth century who shared his occult fascination.

In his appreciation for these artists and their mystical sensibility is a certain nostalgia, a backwards glance while he grappled with his own dissatisfaction with the present. It is in light of this mysticism and nostalgic reimaging that Jarman's concept of pharmacopoeia is best understood. He may have filled his garden with medicinal plants, but there is little evidence he used them directly for his health. Rather, these plants, particularly through the lens of his beloved herbals, provided a portal to a more enchanted past. As his actor and friend Julian Sands explained, 'the plants were not merely there for decoration'.

During his time at Dungeness he saturated himself with literature about ley lines, alchemy, and occult philosophy. In particular the works of Carl Jung, who captured Jarman's frustrations in his *Man and his Symbols* (1964), in which he wrote:

> Man feels himself isolated in the cosmos, because he is no longer involved in nature and has lost his emotional 'unconscious identity' with natural phenomena… No voices speak to man from stones, plants and animals, nor does he speak to them believing they can hear. His contact with nature has gone and with it the profound emotional energy this symbolic connection supplied.

In stark contrast to the seemingly rational—yet existentially threatened—reality of Jarman's world, the writers of the past, such as the sixteenth-century herbalist John Gerard, spoke a deeper kind of truth. Described as the 'White Witch of Dungeness', Jarman channelled his magic into the garden, investing his stones with the 'power of Avebury'—just one of the many important Neolithic sites that litter Britain's countryside and so stimulated the Neo-Romantic imagination. As with the dragon teeth flints that line the beds at Prospect, charged with mystical resonance, so the plants become similarly talismanic.

Jarman's pharmacopoeia is thus better interpreted as an apothecary's garden of symbols rather than a medicine cabinet planted for its practical utility. It was the doctors and hospitals that provided his medicine and just as this garden has the potential both to heal and disrupt, so a fine line exists between medicine and poison. Nowhere is that clearer than in the reality of Jarman's own medicated experience. He described himself as 'a walking chemical laboratory' and it is important to remember how experimental many of the treatments were.

Over the pulsating colour of his film *Blue* (1993), Jarman recounts the potential side effects of DHPG, a treatment for Cytomegalovirus which was destroying his sight. This passage would be later printed in *Chroma* and is worth reproducing here in full:

> The side effects of DHPG, the drug for which I have to come into hospital to be dripped twice a day, are: low white blood cell count, increased risk of infection, low platelet count which may increase risk of bleeding, low red blood cell count (anaemia), fever, rash, abnormal liver function, chills, swelling of the body (oedema), infections, malaise, irregular heart beat, high blood pressure (hypertension), low blood pressure (hypotension), abnormal thoughts or dreams, loss of balance (ataxia), coma, confusion, dizziness, headache, nervousness, damage to nerves (paraesthesia), psychosis, sleepiness (somnolence), shaking, nausea, vomiting, loss of appetite (anorexia), diarrhoea, bleeding from the stomach or intestine (intestinal haemorrhage), abdominal pain, increased number one type of white blood cell, low blood sugar, shortness of breath, hair loss (alopecia) itching (pruritus), hives, blood in the urine, abnormal kidney function, increased blood urea, redness (inflammation), pain or irritation (phlebitis).
>
> Retinal detachments have been observed in patients both before and after initiation of therapy. The drug has caused decreased sperm production in animals and may cause infertility in humans, and birth defects in animals. Although there is no information in human studies, it should be considered a potential carcinogen since it causes tumours in animals.
>
> If you are concerned about any of the above side effects or if you would like any further information, please ask your doctor.
>
> In order to be put on the drug you have to sign a piece of paper stating you understand that all these illnesses are a possibility.

I really can't see what I am to do. I am going to sign it.

The darkness comes in with the tide.

In her persuasive article, Sandilands argues how, facing existential threats, Jarman hasthrough his garden and writing presented 'an ethical practice of remembering'. An honest act of mourning for a lost generation and environmental destruction which resonates powerfully today. One that stands in stark contrast to, as Sandilands puts it, 'the complacent bourgeois belief that modernity will "move on" from Nature'.

For while the garden is a beacon of resistance/resilience charged with disruptive myth, so too is it a site of profound grief. Even before his move to Dungeness, Jarman had developed a reputation as the 'dark magician', mischievous and charismatic; myth was drawn to and surrounded him, bleeding into the celluloid of his films and taking root in his garden. Among the stones of Prospect Cottage he planted a pharmacopoeia of symbols that continues to challenge. A place to heal, to fight, and to grieve. For while paradise may haunt gardens, 'some gardens are paradise and mine is one of them'.

I walk in this Garden
Holding the hands of dead friends,
Old age came quickly for my frosted
generation.
Cold, cold, cold
They died so silently.
Did the forgotten generations scream?
Or go full of resignation
Quietly protesting innocence?
Cold, cold, cold
They died so silently.
I have no words.
My shaking hand cannot express my fury.
Sadness is all I have, no words.
Cold, cold, cold
You died so silently.

The Garden (1990)

References

Alfrey, N. et al. *Art of the Garden – the Garden in British Art, 1800 to the Present Day,* ed. Tate, 2004.

Farthing, S and E. Webb-Ingall. *Derek Jarman's Sketchbooks*, ed. Thames & Hudson, 2013.

Jarman, Derek. *Chroma*. Vintage, 1995.

Jarman, Derek. *Derek Jarman's Garden*. Thames & Hudson, 1995.

Jarman, Derek. *Modern Nature*. Vintage, 1992.

Jarman, Derek. *Smiling in Slow Motion*. Penguin, 2018.

Jung, C. *Man and His Symbols*. Turtleback Books, 1968.

Kissane, S., and K. Rehmani-White. *Derek Jarman, Protest!*, ed. IMMA, 2020.

Sandilands, C., and B. Erickson *Queer Ecologies*, ed. Indiana University Press, 2010.

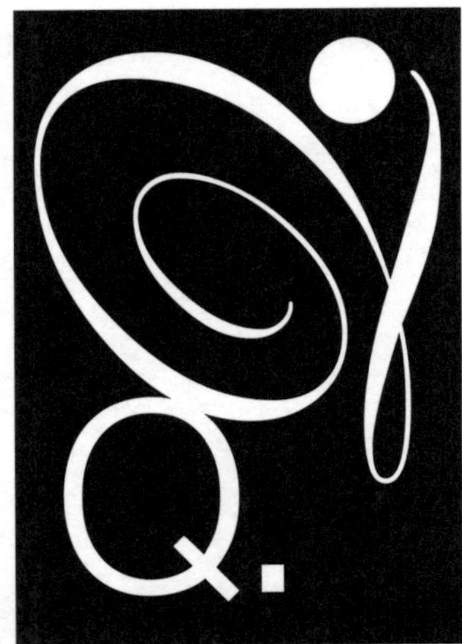

QUEER ECOLOGY

Specifically, the task of a queer ecology is to probe the intersections of sex and nature with an eye to developing a sexual politics that more clearly includes considerations of the natural world and its biosocial constitution, and an environmental politics that demonstrates an understanding of the ways in which sexual relations organize and influence both the material world of nature and our perceptions, experiences, and constitutions of that world.

Queer, then, is both noun and verb in this project: ours is an ecology that may begin in the experiences and perceptions of non-heterosexual individuals and communities, but is even more importantly one that calls into question heteronormativity itself as part of its advocacy around issues of nature and environmen— and vice versa.

Sandilands and Erickson, *Queer Ecologies*, 5.

Gardens are figures of both monumental and (in Jarman's terms) also 'modern' nature: where formal English gardens and parks speak of a sanitized, Masterpiece Theateresque nostalgia for class privilege brought to the service of ongoing paternalism, Jarman's garden deploys found objects and survivor-species (from rescued plants to recycled World War II anti-tank fencing) as a way of queering natural space, of (in O'Quinn's reading) creating a site of 'holy' queerness for the dispossessed whose history is written out of conservative national heritage-natures, and especially for those whose erotic possibilities are eradicated by homophobia and surveillance: 'Two young men holding hands on the street court ridicule, kissing they court arrest, so the worthy politicians, their collaborators, the priests, and the general public push them into corners where they can betray them in the dark. Judases in the garden of Gethsemane' (Jarman 1991, 15).

Sandilands, 'Melancholy Natures, Queer Ecologies', 350.

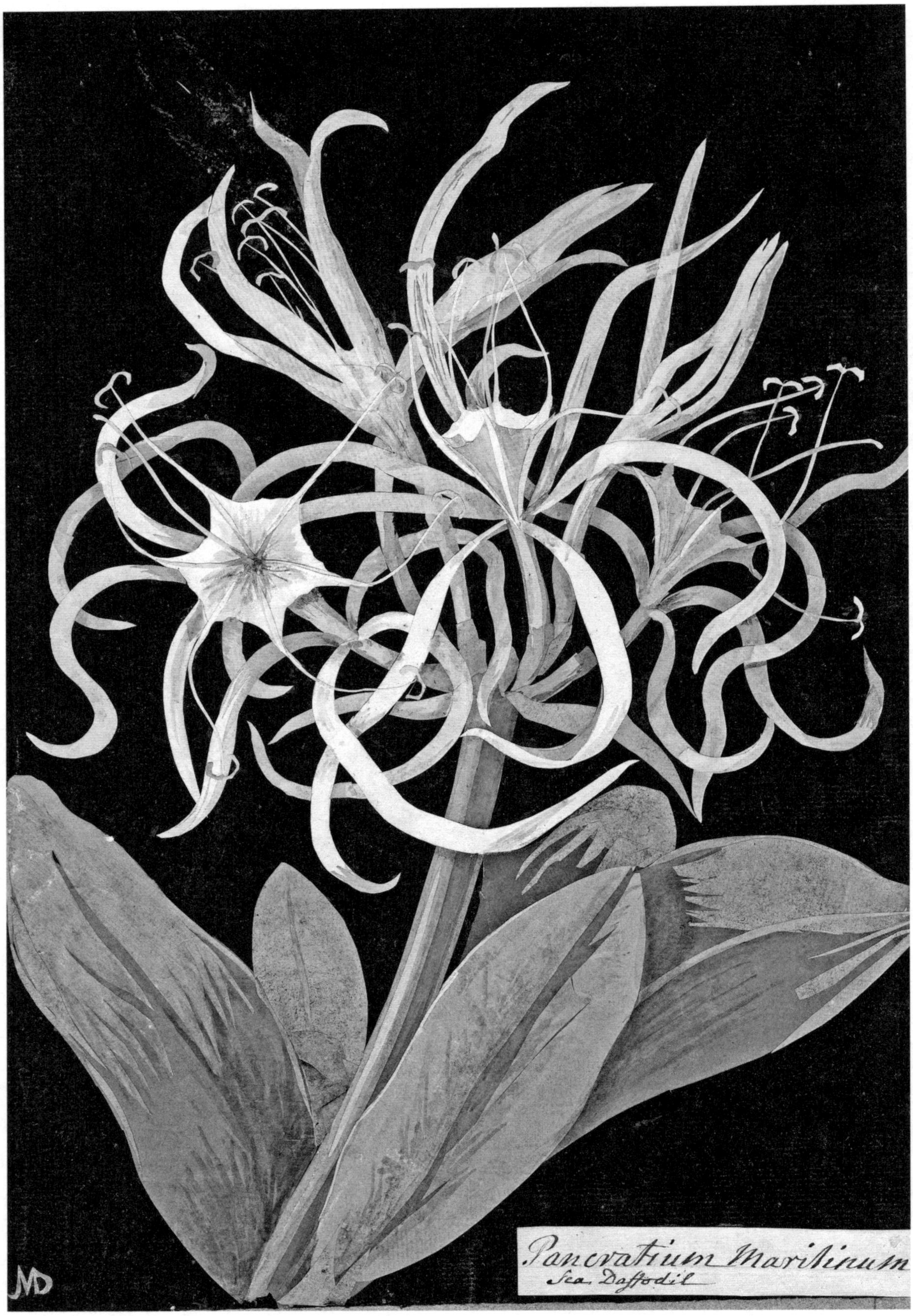

Jarman's nature is definitely queer. In the one sense, he clearly rejects any view of gardens and gardening that relies on an overarching systematization of gardening practice, be it based on application of horticultural science, quest for aesthetic harmony, or even adherence to ecological principle. His journals are a true pastiche of fragments, loosely collected into an almanac of occasionally clashing elements without movement toward resolution or ending; the journals disrupt the unity of the very idea of the garden as an element in progressivist history. But in another, even more powerful sense, Jarman's nature is also distinctly homosexual. In mixing together fragments of historical plant-knowledge, literary quotations, and gardening experiences with his own often erotically charged memories of gardens, he insists that we read each species he considers—primrose, rosemary, narcissus, dill, daffodil, bugloss—in light of its role in sexual histories as well as the botanical ones with which sex has been historically intertwined.

These sexual histories are sometimes mythical, sometimes medical, sometimes personal, and sometimes all of the above.

Sandilands, 'Melancholy Natures, Queer Ecologies', 351–352.

Mary Granville Delany, **Pancratium Maritinum (Hexandria Monogynia)**, 1778, collage, 35 × 22.2 cm. Courtesy The Trustees of the British Museum.

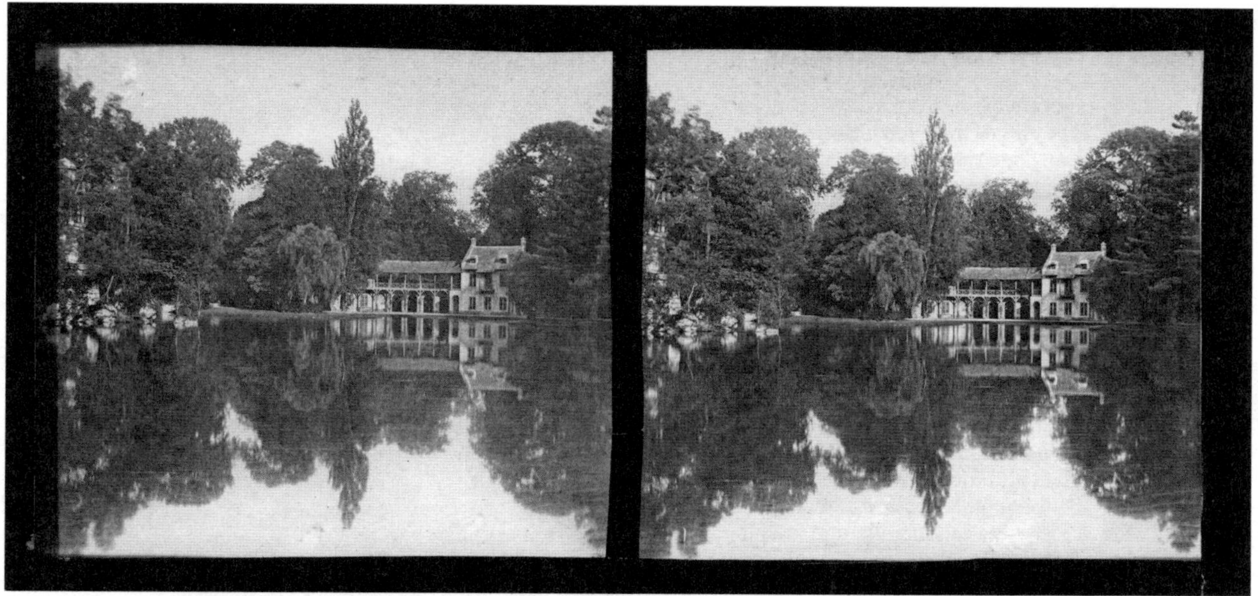

Anonymous, **View of Le Hameau de la Reine on a lake in the French garden of the Palace of Versailles**, 1860–1890, slide, 8.5 × 17.1 cm. Courtesy Rijksmuseum Amsterdam.

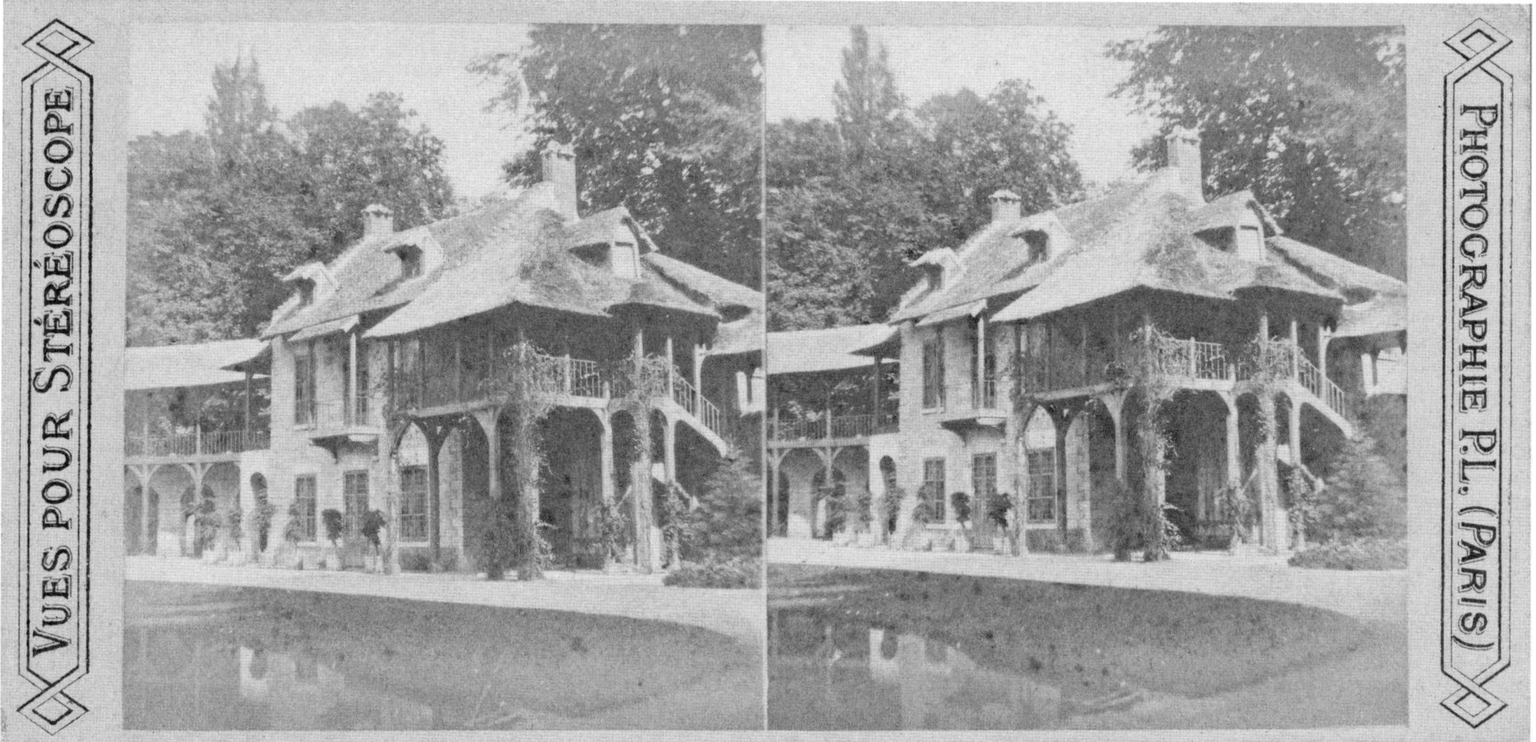

PL, **Part of Le Hameau de la Reine in the Garden of Versailles**, c. 1850–c. 1875, albumen print, 8.5 × 17 cm. Courtesy Rijksmuseum Amsterdam.

British Linnaeans such as Darwin and Delany drew on a long tradition that viewed flowers as strongly suggestive of human eroticism. The later eighteenth-century English reception of Linnaeus capitalized on this history of sexual connotation for flowers. [...] Darwin's translations of Linnaeus' Latin terms are especially anthropomorphizing, and take note of plants he calls 'inverted'. They also note those who manifest 'unallow'd desires': he speaks of certain species as 'eunuchs', others as 'feminine males', still others as 'masculine ladies'. Clearly the idea that plants mimicked human sexuality, and even human homosexuality, was part of the British cultural adaptation of Linnaeus' system.

Moore, 'Queer Gardens', 65–66.

QUEER GEORGIC

Georgic, I argue, may be understood not merely as a genre but more importantly as discursive and material practices. These practices are fundamentally concerned with articulating relations between 'man' and nature and between work and leisure, the rights of property, the founding of nations and empires, and cultivation or farming as a metaphor for civilization but also with the sexual division of labor, patriarchal lineage, and heterosexual reproduction. Georgic in its conventional forms does not merely advocate different roles for men and women. It justifies and glorifies patriarchally-organized and controlled agricultural production and heterosexual reproduction as the necessary bases for family and for national stability, peace, and prosperity. The patriarchal and heterosexual model of the good state stemming from the good family produced and reproduced by the good farm is reinforced by the traditional terms of georgic discourse: metaphors of sexual difference and of heterosexual reproduction permeate its textual and visual rhetoric. Ornamented farms both reiterated such concepts in material terms and complicated—threatening to overturn—them through the admixture of pleasure, unabashed artifice, and decoration.

Casid, 'Queer(y)ing Georgic', 304–305.

Marie-Antoinette's *Hameau* designed by the architect Richard Mique was begun in 1783 and substantially completed by 1786. Consisting of a Norman-style rustic hamlet and a farm, the *Hameau* was considered a type of *ferme ornée* or ornamented farm which combined agricultural production or utility with pleasures for the eyes and other bodily senses. Farms like these which served both as spectacle and scenario, both as visually entertaining follies within larger garden landscapes and as functioning agricultural plantations in their own right, participated in the scripting and re-scripting of georgic.

Casid, 'Queer(y)ing Georgic', 304.

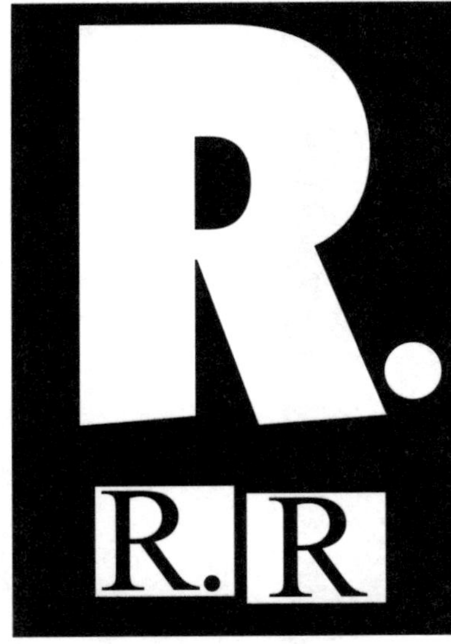

RADICANT

Let us wager that our own century's modernity will be invented precisely in opposition to all radicalism, dismissing both the bad solution of re-enrooting in identities as well as the standardization of imaginations decreed by economic globalization. For contemporary creators are already laying the foundations for a radicant art—*radicant* being a term designating an organism that grows its roots and adds new ones as it advances. To be radicant means setting one's roots in motion, staging them in heterogenous contexts and formats, denying them the power to completely define one's identity, translating ideas, transcoding images, transplanting behaviors, exchanging rather than imposing. What if twenty first-century culture were invented with those works that set themselves the task of effacing their origin in favor of a multitude of simultaneous or successive enrootings? This process of obliteration is part of the condition of the wanderer, a central figure of our precarious era, who is insistently emerging at the hear of contemporary artistic creation. This figure is accompanied by a domain of forms—the domain of the journey-form—as well as by an ethical mode: translation, whose modalities this book seeks to enumerate and whose cardinal role in contemporary culture it seeks to demonstrate.

Bourriaud, *The Radicant*, 22.

And yet the immigrant, the exile, the tourist, and the urban wanderer are the dominant figures of contemporary culture. To remain within the vocabulary of the vegetable realm, one might say that the individual of these early years of the twenty-first century resemble those plants that do not depend on a single root for their growth but advance in all directions on whatever surfaces present themselves by attaching multiple hooks to them, as ivy does. Ivy belongs to the botanical family of the Radicants, which develop their roots as they advance, unlike the radicals, whose development is determined by their being anchored in a particular soil. The stem of couch grass is radicant, as are the suckers of the strawberry plant. They grow their secondary roots alongside their primary one. The radicant develops in accord with its host soil. It confirms to the latter's twists and turns and adapts to its surfaces and geological features. It translates itself into the terms of the space in which it moves. With its at once dynamic and dialogical signification, the adjective 'radicant' captures this contemporary subject, caught between the need for a connection with its environment and the forces of uprooting, between globalization and singularity, between identity and opening to the other. It defines the subject as an object of negotiation.

Bourriaud, *The Radicant*, 51.

RADICLE

The primary root, or radicle, is the first organ to appear when a seed germinates. It grows downward into the soil, anchoring the seedling. In gymnosperms and dicotyledons (angiosperms with two seed leaves), the radicle becomes a taproot. It grows downward, and secondary roots grow laterally from it to form a taproot system. In some plants, such as carrots and turnips, the taproot also serves as food storage.

Encyclopaedia Britannica, 'Root'.

RENAISSANCE GARDEN

The first Italian Renaissance gardens, built astride Roman ruins on hillsides, were sculpture gardens, theaters, archaeological museums, alfresco botanical encyclopedias, educational academies, and amusement parks that drew on special effects to entertain the public. Their meaning was either moral or allegorical, natural or scientific, and political lessons were incorporated into their designs. [...] The Renaissance garden symbolized the Edenic, pre-Fall of Christian Man and an arcadian (Roman) time that was associated with earthly paradise, a mythical past, or a future utopian time of eternal pleasure and natural harmony. Through its arcadian associations with Paradise, the garden embodied all pleasure and was a contrast to man's worldly existence. [...] A typical Renaissance garden was first viewed and entered from a loggia at the base of a villa. The garden's overall geometric plan was seen as if in a perspectival painting or from the back of a theater looking straight at the stage. The apse was like a stage's proscenium overlooking the garden below and prepared the visitor for later close-up views of the garden's statues, flora, hidden vistas, and emblematic narrative flow.

Graham, *Rock My Religion*, 286–288.

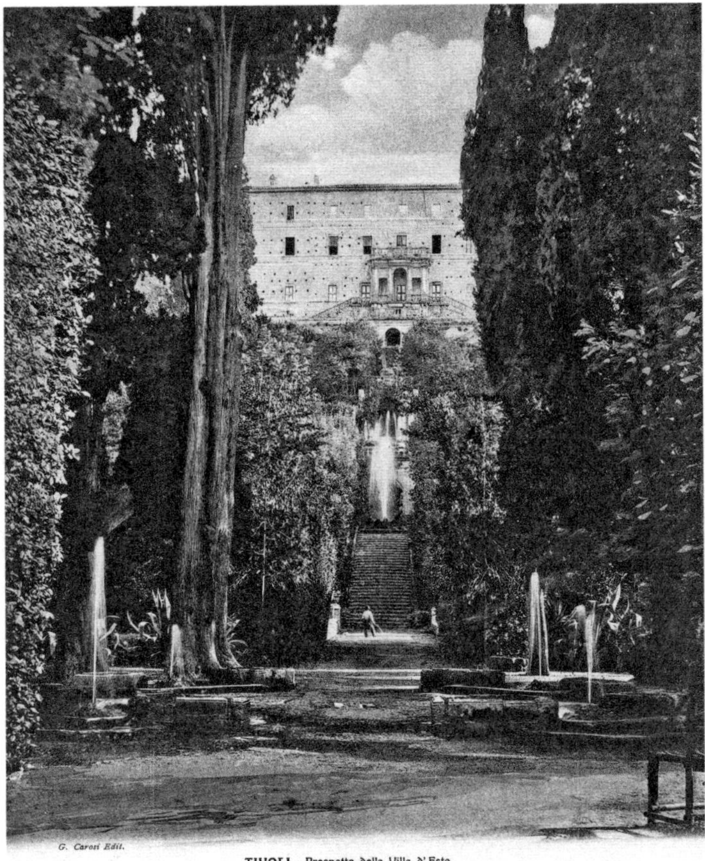

Anonymous, **Prospetto della Villa d'Este**, c. 1900, collotype on paper, 25.4 × 19.5 cm. Courtesy Rijksmuseum Amsterdam.

RHIZOME

The wisdom of the plants: even when they have roots, there is always an outside where they form a rhizome with something else—with the wind, an animal, human beings.

Deleuze and Guattari, *A Thousand Plateaus*, 12.

A system of this kind could be called a rhizome. A rhizome as subterranean stem is absolutely different from roots and radicles. Bulbs and tubers are rhizomes. Plants with roots or radicles may be rhizomorphic in other respects altogether: the question is whether plant life in its specificity is not entirely rhizomatic. Even some animals are, in their pack form. Rats are rhizomes.

Let us summarize the principal characteristics of a rhizome: unlike trees or their roots, the rhizome connects any point to any other point, and its traits are not necessarily linked to traits of the same nature; it brings into play very different regimes of signs, and even nonsign states. The rhizome is reducible neither to the One nor the multiple. It is not the One that becomes Two or even directly three, four, five, etc. It is not a multiple derived from the One, or to which One is added (n + 1). It is composed not of units but of dimensions, or rather directions in motion. It has neither beginning nor end, but always a middle (milieu) from which it grows and which it overspills. It constitutes linear multiplicities with n dimensions having neither subject nor object, which can be laid out on a plane of consistency, and from which the One is always subtracted (n – 1).

Deleuze and Guattari, *A Thousand Plateaus*, 7.

A rhizome has no beginning or end; it is always in the middle, between things, interbeing, intermezzo. The tree is filiation, but the rhizome is alliance, uniquely alliance. The tree imposes the verb 'to be' but the fabric of the rhizome is the conjunction, 'and... and... and...' This conjunction carries enough force to shake and uproot the verb 'to be'. Where are you going? Where are you coming from? What are you heading for? These are totally useless questions. Making a clean slate, starting or beginning again from ground zero, seeking a beginning or a foundation-all imply a false conception of voyage and movement (a conception that is methodical, pedagogical, initiatory, symbolic...).

Deleuze and Guattari, *A Thousand Plateaus*, 26.

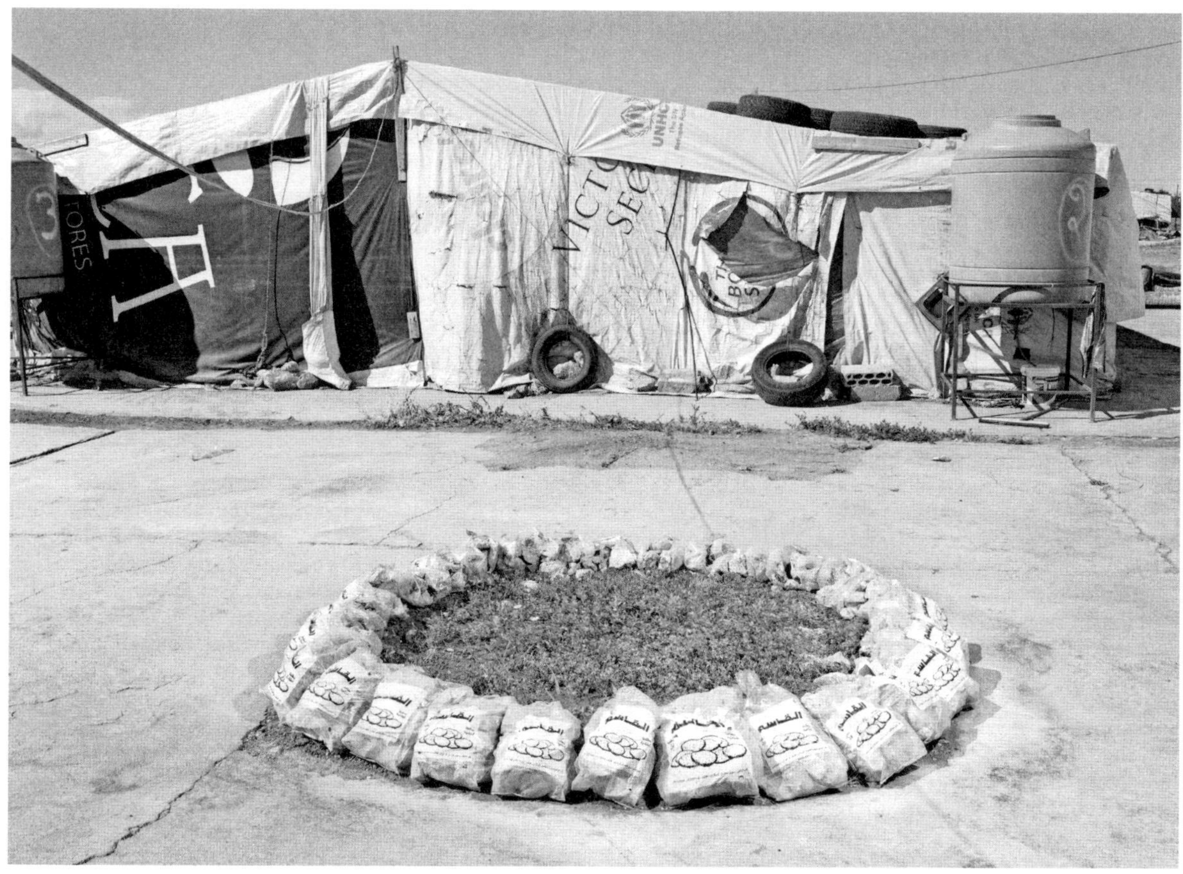

Henk Wildschut, **Baalbek, Beqaa, Lebanon-May**, 2018, photograph. Courtesy Henk Wildschut.

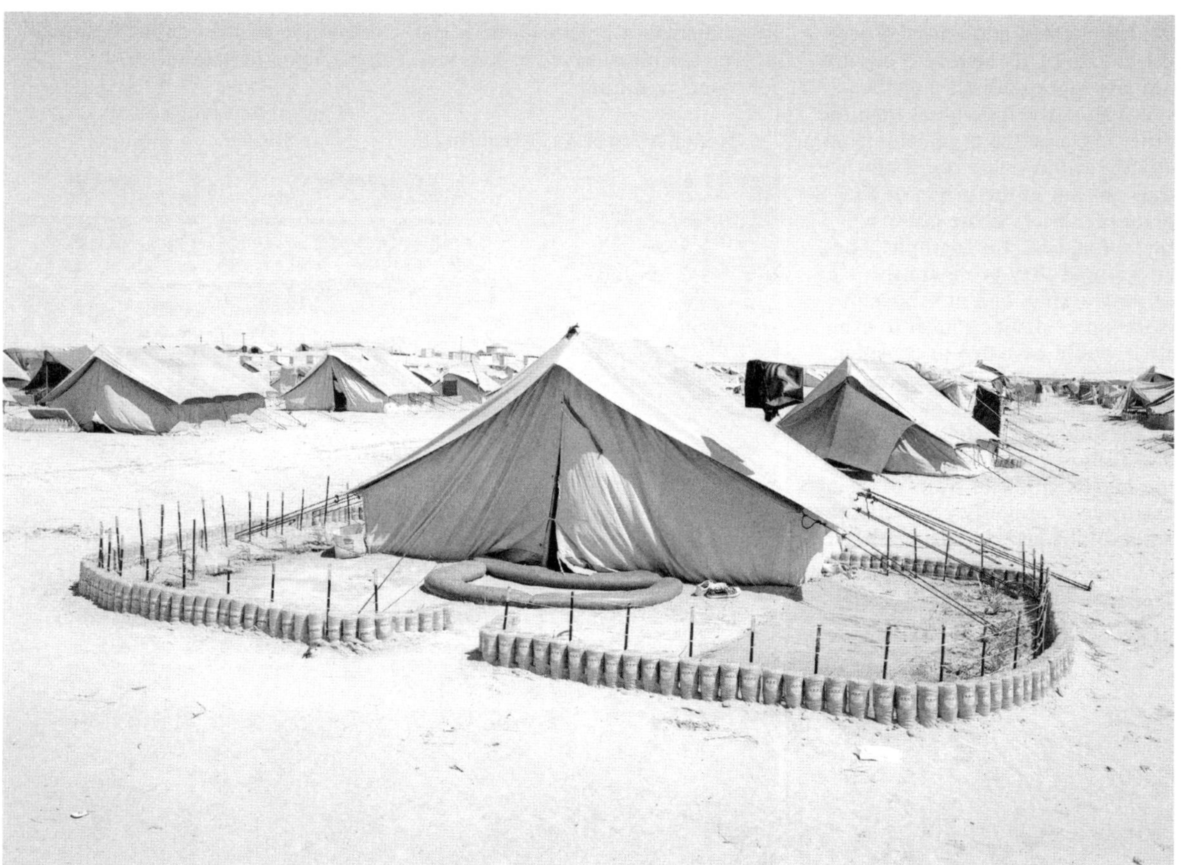

Henk Wildschut, **Choucha Camp, Tunisia-July**, 2011, photograph. Courtesy Henk Wildschut.

ROOTED

HENK WILDSCHUT

In the photographic series Rooted, Henk Wildschut records the improvised gardens of people who have been uprooted in recent years and ended up in refugee camps in Europe and the Middle East. The gardens have a clearly temporary character, as if they could be cleared away at any time. Sometimes the gardens form a demarcation around the tent or other temporary accommodation. Wildschut was struck by the fact that the refugees had planted not only vegetables, but also flowers and ornamental plants, which seem to have a primarily symbolic function: jasmine, for example, is a reminder of the homes they have left behind. In a hopeless situation, gardening and seeing plants blossom can provide comfort. (ed.)

When war broke out in Syria in 2013, Brahim and his family fled for Darwa to the Zaatari refugee camp in northern Jordan, on the Syrian border. Brahim noticed that people in the camp enjoyed being surrounded by plants and flowers. He saw a way to make money, and together with his father opened a small flower and plant shop in the camp. So far, the little shop seemed to have done well. Brahim told me the best-selling plants are trees, because they will provide shade in the future. He also sells lots of gardenias. His personal favourite is the rose, because of its lovely fragrance.

I was engaged in a reportage project in the earthquake-struck north of Pakistan in 2006 when I first noticed a newly planted micro-garden in a refugee camp. The sight of something as prosaic as that in such a chaotic situation was unexpected and moving. The existence of these tiny gardens changed my view of refugees: I began to see the residents as resilient survivors instead of as victims. It was with this outlook that I began my study of the refugee problems in Calais from 2006 onwards.

It was not until 2015 that little gardens like these started to appear outside the makeshift huts and tents in the 'Jungle'. The arrival of thousands of migrants in 2015 had provoked stringent security measures in Calais harbour. It became clear to the camp residents that their stay in the French seaport of Calais would last longer than they planned. By planting little gardens in this unwelcoming setting, the migrants in the sand dunes seemed to be striving to reconcile themselves with the situation. They used plants to create a gentler, more domestic atmosphere. The impersonality of the unofficial camp was diminished and the camp dwellers literally began to put down roots in foreign soil.

Abu Hamzi and his family fled the horrors of the war in Syria and arrived at the Zaatari refugee camp in Jordan in 2013. Abu had worked as a horticulturist in Damascus and was specialized in the shaping of shrubs. He had planted a beautiful garden with flowers and lots of succulents that do well in the dry ground around his shelter in the camp. When he feels stressed out, he goes into his garden. Its beauty relaxes him, he says, and caring for the garden is good for his soul.

A few weeks ago he discovered a peach sprouting in the back of his garden, presumably growing from a discarded pit. Abu put crates over the young sapling 'to protect it from the kids, who yank everything out of the ground if you don't watch out'. He is hoping it will grow into a nice big tree, because that will give him shade and fruit.

Wildschut, *Rooted.*

ROOTS

They are hidden and invisible to the vast majority of animal organisms, who compete for attention on the platforms of terra firma. Sunk as they are in a cryptic, cloistered world, they pass their lives without the slightest idea about the explosion of forms and events that swarm between Earth and sky. Roots are the most enigmatic forms of the plant world. Their body is often infinitely large and infinitely more complex than its aerial twin, the one that plants let appear in the light of day: the total surface of the root system of a rye plant can reach 400 square meters, that is, a surface 130 times larger than that of the plant's aerial body.

In the history of plant life, they arrived relatively late: for millions of years, plants could do without roots—in the sea as on earth. *Primum vegetari deinde radicare* [first be animated, then grow roots]: plant life would seem not to need roots in order to define itself, exist, or at least survive. The origin of roots is obscure, and it is not easy to distinguish their forms. The first fossil evidence dates back to 390 million years ago. As in all forms of life destined to last for millions of years, their origin is due to fortuitous invention and bricolage more than to methodical, conscious elaboration: the first kinds of roots were functional modifications of the trunk or horizontal rhizomes deprived of leaves. Their morphology as well as their physiology is extremely variable: their functions have changed over time and cannot be univocally attributed to them; sometimes—as is the case with mycorrhizae—they are delegated to other organisms, which enter into a symbiotic relationship with the plant. They seem to live cut off from the multiplicity of living beings, and yet it is thanks to them that plants come to be aware of what goes on around them. Plato had already compared our head, and hence reason, to a 'root': the human being, he said, is 'a plant of the sky [phuton ouranion] and not of the earth', with the roots going up—a sort of inverted plant. But the version that was to become canonical was given by Aristotle in the treatise De anima: 'up and down are not for all things what they are for the whole world: if we are to distinguish and identify organs according to their functions, the roots of plants are analogous to the head in animals'. [...]

It is through the root system, in effect, that a plant acquires the vast majority of information on its own state and that of the environment in which it is immersed; it is also through the roots that it comes into contact with other, limitrophic individuals and manages, collectively, the risks and difficulties of underground life. The roots make the soil and the subterranean world a space of spiritual communication. Thanks to them, then, the most solid part of the Earth is transformed into an enormous planetary brain through which matter circulates, along with information on the identity and state of the organisms that populate the surrounding environment. It is as if the eternal night, in which one imagines the depths of the Earth to be plunged, were anything but a long and deaf sleep. In the immense and silent horn of the underground, night is a perception without organs, without eyes and without ears, a perception that takes place through the whole body. Intelligence, thanks to roots, exists in mineral form, in a world without sun and without movement. [...]

In ordinary speech as in literature and art, roots are often the emblem and the allegory of what is most fundamental and originary, what is most obstinately solid and stable, what is necessary. They are the plant organ par excellence. And yet it would be hard to find a more ambiguous form among those that life has created and adopted over the course of its history. They are not any more necessary to the survival of the individual than the other parts of the organism; from a strictly evolutionary point of view, they are not at the origin of the plant result—as is the photosynthetic function, for example. The advantages they bring are those of networking, and not those of isolation or distinction. But, even so, it would be naive to consider them a secondary and 'decorative' appendage. Roots are not what we thought they were, but they express and embody, all the same, one of the most significant traits of plant existence: ambiguity, hybridity, their amphibious and double character.

Coccia, *The Life of Plants*, 77–81.

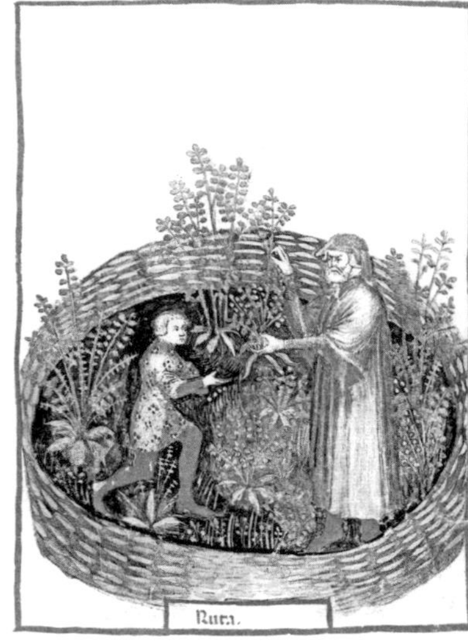

Tacuinum Sanitatis of Paris, fourteenth century, manuscript. Courtesy Science Photo Library.

RUE (RUTA GRAVEOLEN)

Here is a shadowed grove which takes its colour
From the miniature forest of glaucous rue.
Through its small leaves and short umbels which rise
Like clusters of spears it sends the wind's breath
And the sun's rays down to its roots below.
Touch it but gently and it yields a heavy
Fragrance. Many a healing power it has
Especially, they say, to combat
Hidden toxin and to expel from the bowels
The invading forces of noxious poison.

Strabo, *Hortulus*, 33.

MIEN RUYS

Mien Ruys always sought after the essence of the space and the possibilities of the plot: a simple, functional arrangement with a loose natural plantation. In the latter she differed from her colleagues of that time. They also aspired to simplicity and clearness, but considered perennial borders an unnecessary decoration. However, to Mien Ruys, it was adding the perennials that made it possible to have an experience of nature in a garden. Possibly because of this difference of opinion it was Mien Ruys who received many assignments for private gardens and in time her ideas served as a model for others to follow.

Tuinen Mien Ruys, 'Mien Ruys'.

In Britain, the Arts and Crafts garden tradition exemplified by Lawrence Johnstone's Hidcote (1907 onwards) and Harold Nicolson and Vita Sackville-West's Sissinghurst (1930 onwards) resolved a central contradiction for British gardeners, balancing their love of informal planting (mostly herbaceous perennials) with a continued hankering after formal garden features, now restricted to hedges, occasional topiary and garden structures. In the Netherlands, Mien Ruys (1904–1999) did something to achieve a modernist version of the same resolution of the conflict between formality and naturalism.

Oudolf and Kingsbury, *Planting*, 67.

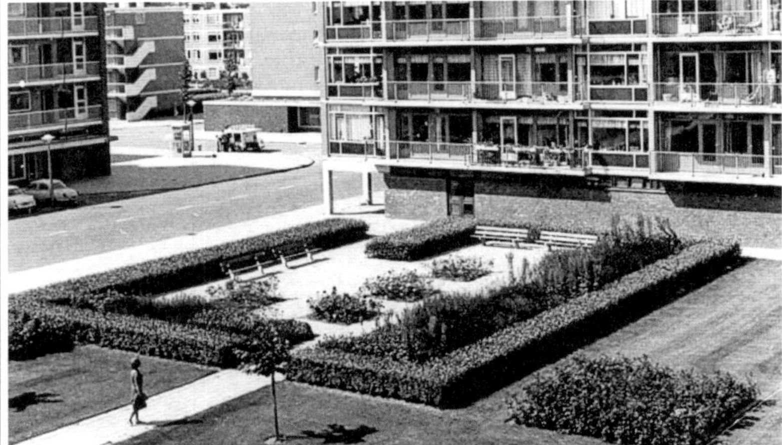

Anonymous, **Communal garden at Buitenveldert**, c. 1963, photograph. Courtesy Tuinarchitectenburo Mien Ruys Hans Veldhoen and Tuinen Mien Ruys.

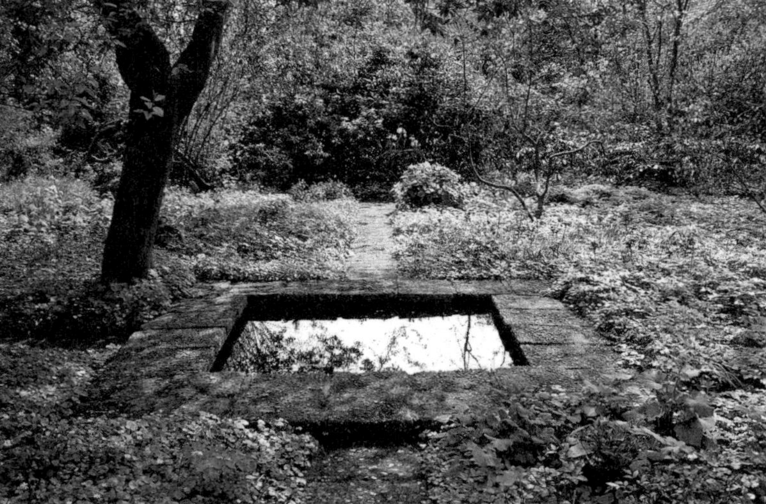

Anonymous, **Frankendael housing project, Amsterdam**, c. 1963, photograph. Courtesy Tuinarchitectenburo Mien Ruys Hans Veldhoen and Tuinen Mien Ruys.

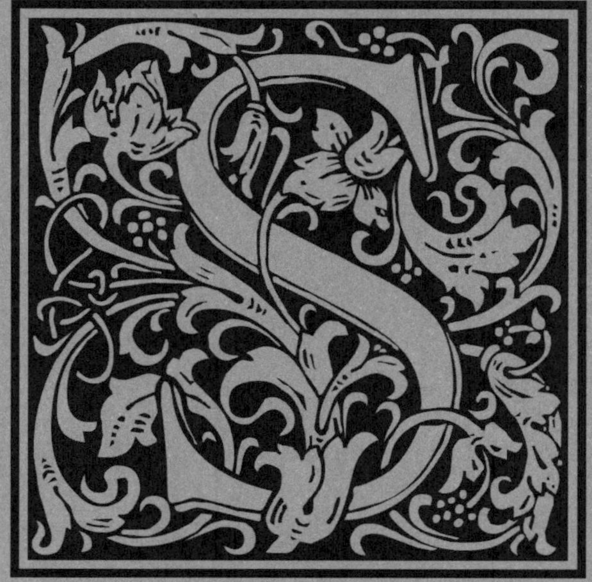

William Morris, **Letter S.**

ROELANT SAVERIJ'S GARDEN

Liesbeth M. Helmus

he advent of navigation systems such as TomTom and online map services such as Google Maps over the past two decades has brought about a decline in the use of physical maps and city plans to navigate unfamiliar terrain. The photographic precision that these systems offer was, of course, unattainable for the makers of seventeenth-century city plans. They made a schematic drawing of a city, in which the roads, waterways, and buildings are shown in bird's-eye view. They also delineated the parks and gardens, today's 'green spaces'.

fig. 1

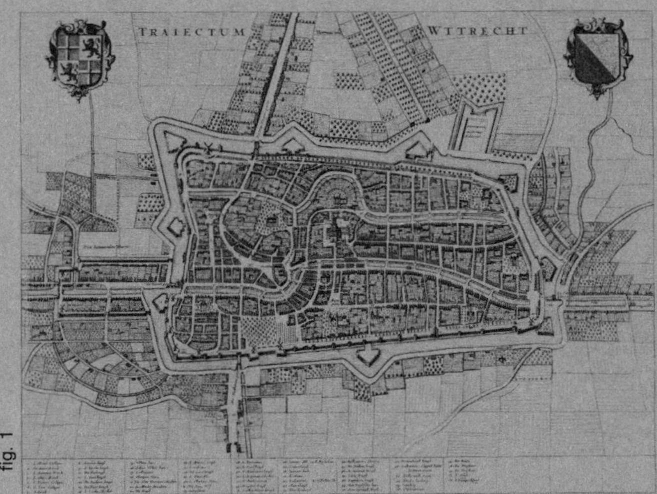

Joan Blaeu, Trajectum Wttrecht from **Toonneel der Steden van de Vereenighde Nederlanden met hare beschrijvingen**, 1649, copper engraving, 38 x 50 cm. Courtesy Het Utrechts Archief.

A hand-coloured map of Utrecht from 1649 shows how the built-up area is surrounded by city walls with bastions that protrude like arrows, encircled by a broad moat (fig. 1 — see page 205 for an image of the map in color). The city is connected to the surrounding fields and forests by bridges at the four compass points, each with a city gate: to the north the Weerdpoort, to the south the Tolsteegpoort, to the west the Catharijnepoort, and to the east the Wittevrouwenpoort. The city's two main waterways, the Oudegracht and the Nieuwegracht, flow straight through the city from north to south, their banks connected by numerous bridges. The Oudegracht (Old Canal), which flows into the Kromme Rijn and the Vaartsche Rijn in the south and into the River Vecht in the north, has no fewer than sixteen bridges. The Nieuwegracht (New Canal), which, as its name suggests, is of a later date, has six bridges.

The cathedral, or Domkerk, stands at the heart of the city. As with other early plans, the Gothic building is easily recognizable, despite its rudimentary representation. The roofs of the ecclesiastical buildings, like that of the cathedral, are distinguished by their blue colour, as are the waterways. The streets and squares are white; the houses that line them are drawn as rectangles with red pitched roofs. The parks are filled with deciduous trees and the gardens are schematically divided into flower beds. All that grows and blooms is coloured green.

If we walk west from the cathedral, turn left immediately over the Sint Maartensbrug (Saint Martin's Bridge), and then immediately right, we find ourselves in Boterstraat

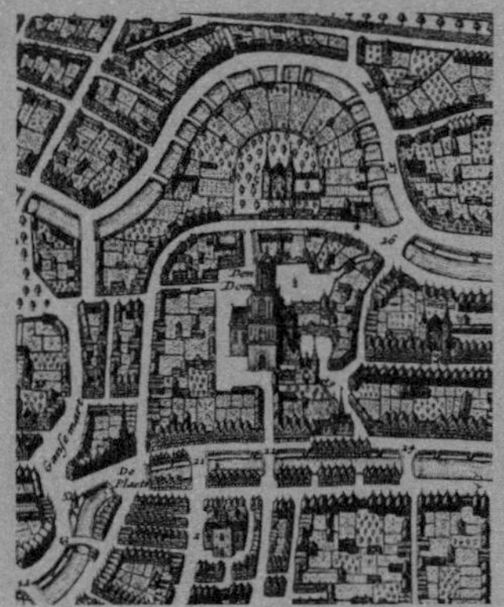
fig. 2

(Butter Street, fig. 2). Here, at the rear of what is today number twenty, was the garden of the famous painter Roelant Saverij (1576–1639). Little is known about it except that it contained flowers and plants that were of considerable value. They were sold together with the property on 30 October 1638, following Saverij's bankruptcy, to the painter Petrus Portengen (1604/12–1643). Portengen paid 5,400 guilders for the house, plus 400 guilders for some items of movable property and the contents of the garden.[1]

Saverij mainly painted landscapes with animals, but also produced twenty or so extremely beautiful flower still lifes.[2] All but one are signed and most date from the period stretching from 1603 to 1630. The *Large Flower Still Life with Crown Imperial* (1624) is the largest and most complex of his flower compositions (fig. 3). Because all the flowers and animals in the bouquet are different, it is almost like a painted inventory of a collection of 'naturalia' (natural objects), an extremely costly undertaking in the seventeenth century. The painting features no fewer than sixty-three varieties of flowers and forty-five different insects, reptiles, and birds.[3] In, under, and around the bouquet are numerous lizards, beetles, butterflies, grasshoppers, and many other insects. The large grey cockatoo, tugging with its beak at a frog's left leg, stands out for its colour and detailing. On the other side, a kingfisher sits quietly on a twig. The two birds could be intended as an antithesis between active and contemplative life, between aggression and war on the one hand, and rest and peace on the other. The whole painting can be explained in this way. All the animals, large or small, and all the flowers can be seen as symbols and ascribed a meaning.[4] In general terms, a flower arrangement such as this, like all other flower still lifes of this period, refers to the transience of earthly existence.

Saverij could never have arranged this bouquet and painted it from life. Not only is the pewter-coloured vase far too small for its enormous load, but the flowers that make up the arrangement bloom in different seasons. The spring flowers predominate, but there are also those that bloom in the summer, such as the rose. Although they have not been preserved, Saverij must have made studies of the individual flowers, which he later used to compose the bouquet he had in mind.[5] This also explains why the proportions of the flowers are not always correct in respect to each other. The romanticized image of the middle-aged painter wandering among the flowers in his own garden in preparation for his painting is an attractive one. Whether he planted his own garden or had someone else to tend it is unknown. What we do know is that the interest in growing exotic flowers skyrocketed in the seventeenth century.

Flower gardens had a different function from monastery gardens, where crops and herbs were cultivated for their medicinal properties. The flower gardens allowed the

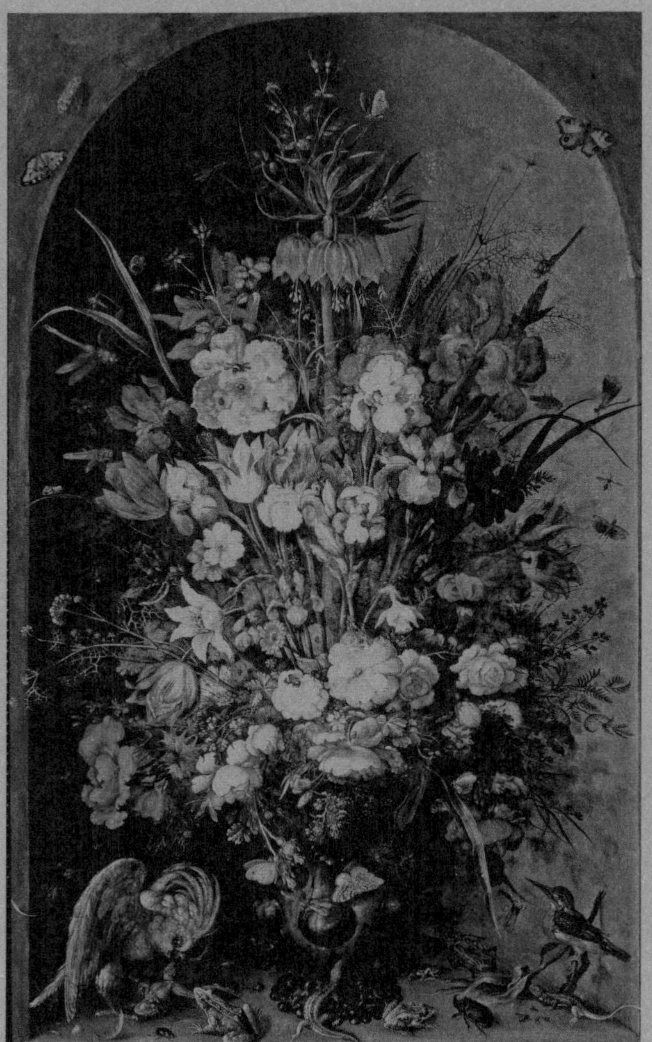
fig. 3 Roelant Saverij, **Large Flower Still Life with Crown Imperial**, 1624, oil on panel, 130 x 80 cm. Courtesy Centraal Museum, Utrecht.

1 Het Utrechts Archief, Stadsbestuur van Utrecht 1577–1795 (access no. 702), inv. no. 3218–5, Decreetboek, fol. 100–05. See S.A.C. Dudok van Heel and M.J. Bok, 'De familie van Roelant Roghman', in **De kasteeltekeningen van Roelant Roghmans**, ed. W.T. Kloek (Alphen aan den Rijn: Canaletto, 1990), vol. 2, 6–14, and Filippe de Potter and Isabelle de Jaegere, 'Het leven van een kunstenaar', in **Roelandt Saverij 1576–1639**, eds. Isabelle de Jaegere and Olga Kotková (Prague: Národní Galerie; Kortrijk: Broelmuseum, 2011), 26. According to A.F.E. Kipp in '4. Boterstraat 20', **Archeologische en Bouwhistorische Kroniek gemeente Utrecht 1988**, 49–69, 67. Portengen acquired the property in August 1638.

2 K.J. Müllenmeister, **Roelant Savery: Die Gemälde mit kritischem Oeuvre-katalog** (Freren: Luca Verlag, 1988), 165 and 361–362 identifies twenty-four flower still lifes, dating from between 1603 and 1630, of which the whereabouts of three are unknown.

3 For the identification of the flowers and animals, see Sam Segal, 'The Flower Pieces of Roelandt Saverij', **Rudolf II and His Court (Leids Kunsthistorisch Jaarboek)** (Leiden: Delftsche Uitgevers Maatschappij, 1982), 315–319, and Herbert Genten, Ekkehard Mai, and Martina Schalgenhaufen, eds., **Roelant Savery in seiner Zeit: (1576–1639)** (Cologne: Wallraf-Richartz-Museum; Utrecht: Centraal Museum, 1985–1986), 130–134.

4 See, for example, Sam Segal, 'Roelant Savery als Blumenmaler', in **Roelant Savery in seiner Zeit: (1576–1639)**, eds. Herbert Genten, Ekkehard Mai, and Martina Schalgenhaufen (Cologne: Wallraf-Richartz-Museum; Utrecht: Centraal Museum, 1985–1986), 62–63.

5 J. Spicer-Durham, **The Drawings of Roelandt Saverij**, diss. (New Haven: Yale University, 1979), 246–261, and J. Spicer in Joaneath A. Spicer and Lynn Federle Orr, eds., **Masters of Light: Dutch Painters in Utrecht during the Golden Age** (San Francisco: Museum of Fine Arts; Baltimore: The Walters Art Gallery; London: The National Gallery of Art, 1997–1998), 47.

gardener to learn about the growth and propagation of flowers and plants and to enjoy the appearances, colours, and scents of nature. Whether they belonged to the court or private individuals, flower gardens were prestige projects: most of the plants came from Southern Europe or Asia Minor and were very rare.[6] Tulips, which were imported from Turkey, commanded astronomical prices.[7] The first specimens flowered in Leiden in the spring of 1594 in the garden of the botanist Carolus Clusius (1526–1609), who also introduced the magnificent crown imperial, which had been taken from Persia via Turkey to Vienna, and to the Northern Netherlands around 1580.[8] In Saverij's painting, it is surrounded by many other exotics, including irises, tulips, roses, anemones, delphiniums, forget-me-nots, cornflowers, snake's head fritillary, poppies, and other flowers. In addition to expensive cultivars, the bouquet also contains many wildflowers. This preference for native species and non-flowering with decorative foliage, such as ferns, is typical of Saverij.[9]

ROELANT SAVERIJ

Roelant Saverij was born in 1576 in the Flemish city of Kortrijk.[10] When the city was captured by the Malcontents in 1580, his family, who were Mennonites, fled to the more liberal Holland, first to Haarlem and then to Amsterdam. Archival documents show that Saverij lived there in 1602 with his brother Jacob, who was six years his senior. On 27 August of that year, they drew up their wills together.[11] Saverij named his brother as his sole heir, but fate dealt a different hand: Jacob died of the plague a year later, after which Saverij left Amsterdam. His older brother must have been important to him, not only because he was close family and his housemate, but also because he taught him to paint.[12] None of Jacob's paintings have survived but we know from archival documents and from designs for engravings that he painted flower still lifes.[13] He may also have encouraged his brother to paint landscapes with animals. In late 1603 or early 1604, in any case following Jacob's death, Saverij moved to Prague, where he became court painter to Rudolf II (1552–1612). The emperor had a special interest in natural history and must certainly have been attracted by the highly realistic depictions of animals and flowers in which Saverij excelled. And there was no shortage of study materials at the court: Rudolf had an extensive menagerie with rare exotic animals and a famous flower garden filled with the most impressive imported specimens. Sketch sheets from the years 1606 to 1607 bear witness to a trip that Saverij made to the Tyrolean Alps.[14] Until recently, it was always assumed that, upon Rudolf's death in 1612, Saverij entered the service of his younger brother, Matthias (1557–1619), but this is now doubted.[15] In any case, in 1613 and 1615 he appears to have been back in Amsterdam to deal with family matters and by September 1618 he was registered as a resident of Utrecht. He may have chosen the city because it was home to several relatives, including his cousin Catharina and her husband, and his brother-in-law Cornelis de Bruyn, an art dealer.[16] Saverij initially settled in the Snippevlucht district in the city centre and became a member of the Guild of Saint Luke in 1619. Two years later, on 7 November 1621, he moved to the stately building on the south side of Boterstraat (now number twenty), which he named 'Het Keyzerswapen' (The Emperor's Arms), proudly referring to his time at the imperial court in Prague. The building that is now number ten, a few houses away, was home to Paulus Moreelse (1571–1638), who painted a portrait of his colleague and good friend around this time. The painting does not appear to have survived but served as the basis for an engraving made in 1647 (fig. 4).[17]

Boterstraat dates back to the thirteenth century, when it was a prestigious street and home to the city's most prominent families. The house that Saverij bought was originally a large medieval brick building with two floors and a wooden roof construction.[18]
It was sited on the north-east corner of a large lot that probably measured seventy by sixteen metres. After many radical renovations over successive centuries, it was gradually adapted to conform to seventeenth-century ideas of domestic comfort. Behind the house was the 'blomhoff', or flower garden. We know nothing about the garden's appearance, as indeed little is known about the

6 See Onno Wijnands, 'Tulpen naar Amsterdam: Plantenverkeer tussen Nederland en Turkije', in **Topkapi & Turkomanie. Turks-Nederlandse ontmoetingen sinds 1600**, eds. Hans Theunissen, Annelies Abelmann and Wim Meulenkamp (Amsterdam: Bataafsche Leeuw, 1989), 97–106.

7 For an extensive study of the tulip mania, see Anne Goldgar, **Tulipmania: Money, Honor, and Knowledge in the Dutch Golden Age** (Chicago: University of Chicago Press, 2007).

8 Wijnands, 'Tulpen naar Amsterdam', 105–106.

9 Segal, 'The Flower Pieces of Roelandt Saverij', 320.

10 For a recent account of the life of Roelant Saverij, see De Potter and De Jaegere, 'Het leven van een kunstenaar', 11–36.

11 J. Briels, **De Zuidnederlandse immigratie in Amsterdam en Haarlem omstreeks 1572–1630** (Utrecht: [s.n.], 1976), 288–289. See also De Potter and De Jaegere, 'Het leven van een kunstenaar', 20.

12 Karel van Mander, **Het Schilder-Boeck** (Haarlem 1604), fol. 260, 36–40.

13 De Potter and De Jaegere, 'Het leven van een kunstenaar', 20.

14 Joachim von Sandrart, **Teutsche Academie der edlen Bau-, Bild- und Mahlerey-Künste**, Nuremberg 1675–80, II (1675), book 3, 305.

15 De Potter and De Jaegere, 'Het leven van een kunstenaar', 23.

16 Ibid., 28.

17 Eric Domela Nieuwenhuis, **Paulus Moreelse (1571–1638)**, diss. (Leiden University, 2001), vol. 2, cat. no. GRP57-1, 415–416.

18 For the history of the construction of Boterstraat 20, see Kipp, '4. Boterstraat 20'.

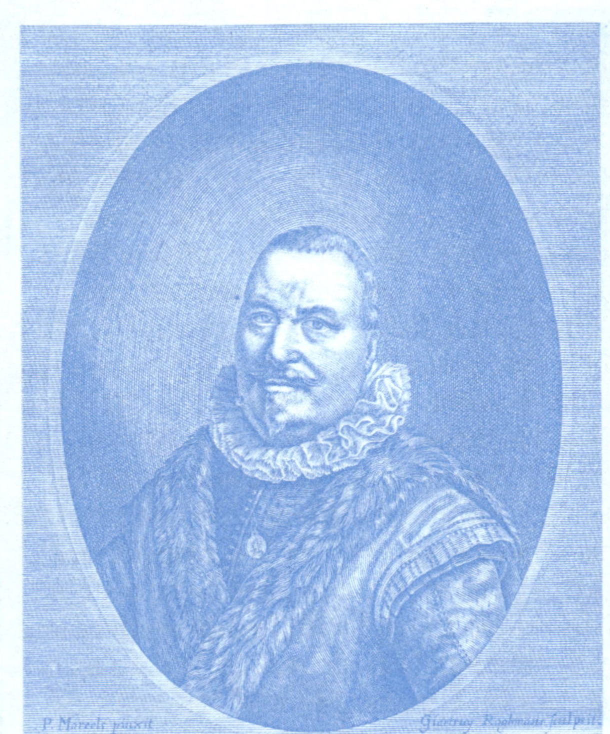

fig. 4 Geertruydt Roghman after Paulus Moreelse, **Portrait of Roelant Saverij**, 1647, engraving, 26.7 x 16.2 cm. Courtesy Rijksmuseum Amsterdam.

number and location of any of the flower gardens in Utrecht in the period spanning 1600 to 1630.[19] What we do know is that Saverij's garden was private and, therefore, probably accessible only with his permission. The painter Jacob Marrel (1613/14–1681) moved in 1632 from Frankfurt am Main to Utrecht, where he lived from 1641 to 1649 'in de Blomhof' (in the flower garden) on Bergstraat, located in what is now Wijk C.[20] Like Saverij, he specialized in flower still lifes, but worked within a different tradition, having been taught by Jan Davidszoon de Heem (1606–1684), who came from Antwerp. The 'Blomhof' on Bergstraat where Marrel lived may have been publicly accessible, but that did not mean that it was not privately owned and maintained. In such cases, theft was a constant worry since the bulbs were extremely expensive.[21]

'IN DEN BLOM-HOF' ('HORTUS FLORIDUS')

Utrecht had a great many flower lovers. Crispijn van de Passe the Younger (1574–1690) mentions twenty of them by name in his *In den Blom-Hof* of 1614, in addition to five in Amsterdam and Haarlem, and two in Leiden. He mentions the professions of only four of them: two were apothecaries, one was a surgeon, and the other was a physician, fields that have traditionally fostered an interest in plants and herbs. *In den Blom-Hof* was published in Utrecht, where Van de Passe lived and worked at that time, which may explain why the list of dedicatees in that city is far longer than those from Leiden, where the aforementioned Clusius was a professor and managed the botanical garden.

The book is made up of engravings of flowering plants, organized by blooming period, from spring to winter. The title page states that Van de Passe has 'copied them painstakingly from nature'.[22] Each of the four sections is accompanied by a text that explains how to illuminate these flowers. Since the engravings are uncoloured, the descriptions thus serve to complete the picture by giving the reader a sense of the flowers' colours—yet these descriptions also show that his manual goes much further. Van de Passe states very specifically which pigments are most suitable for colouring the flowers, making his book an expert guide for the painter of flower still lifes.

As an example, let us take the majestic plant that Saverij painted orangey red at the top of his *Large Flower Still Life with Crown Imperial*, but which also exists in a bright yellow variant. In *In den Blom-Hof*, it is number twelve of the spring flowers (fig. 5). The accompanying instructions are quite explicit: the hanging flowers are to be coloured with ochre, an earthy pigment varying from yellowy brown to red, which may be softened somewhat by the addition of orangey red lead. Stil de grain yellow, an organic pigment extracted from various plants, berries, or wood, is to be used for the highlights. A layer of indigo underneath will help to get the right shade of the brown buds of the flowers. The green copper pigment verdigris, also known as Spanish green, is recommended for colouring the stem.

Van de Passe included an example of a garden for each season. In the spring garden, the crown imperial is the centrepiece of the circular flower bed in the foreground (fig. 6). On either side are two examples of the

19 For a brief history of seventeenth-century private gardens in the Northern Netherlands, see J. Kuijlen, C.S. Oldenburger-Ebbers, and D.O. Wijnands, **Paradisus Batavus: Bibliografie van plantencatalogi van onderwijstuinen, particuliere tuinen en kwekerscollecties in de Noordelijke en Zuidelijke Nederlanden (1550–1839)** (Wageningen: Pudoc, 1983), 32–34.

20 Information from Marten Jan Bok, Utrecht.

21 Anne Marie Backer, 'Tuinkunst tijdens de opstand: Marie de Brimeu, prinses van Chimay en de "humanisering" van de bloem (1550–1605)', **Cascade bulletin voor tuinhistorie** 15, no. 2 (2006), 21.

22 'met groote moete [sic] naer het leven gheconterfeyt'.

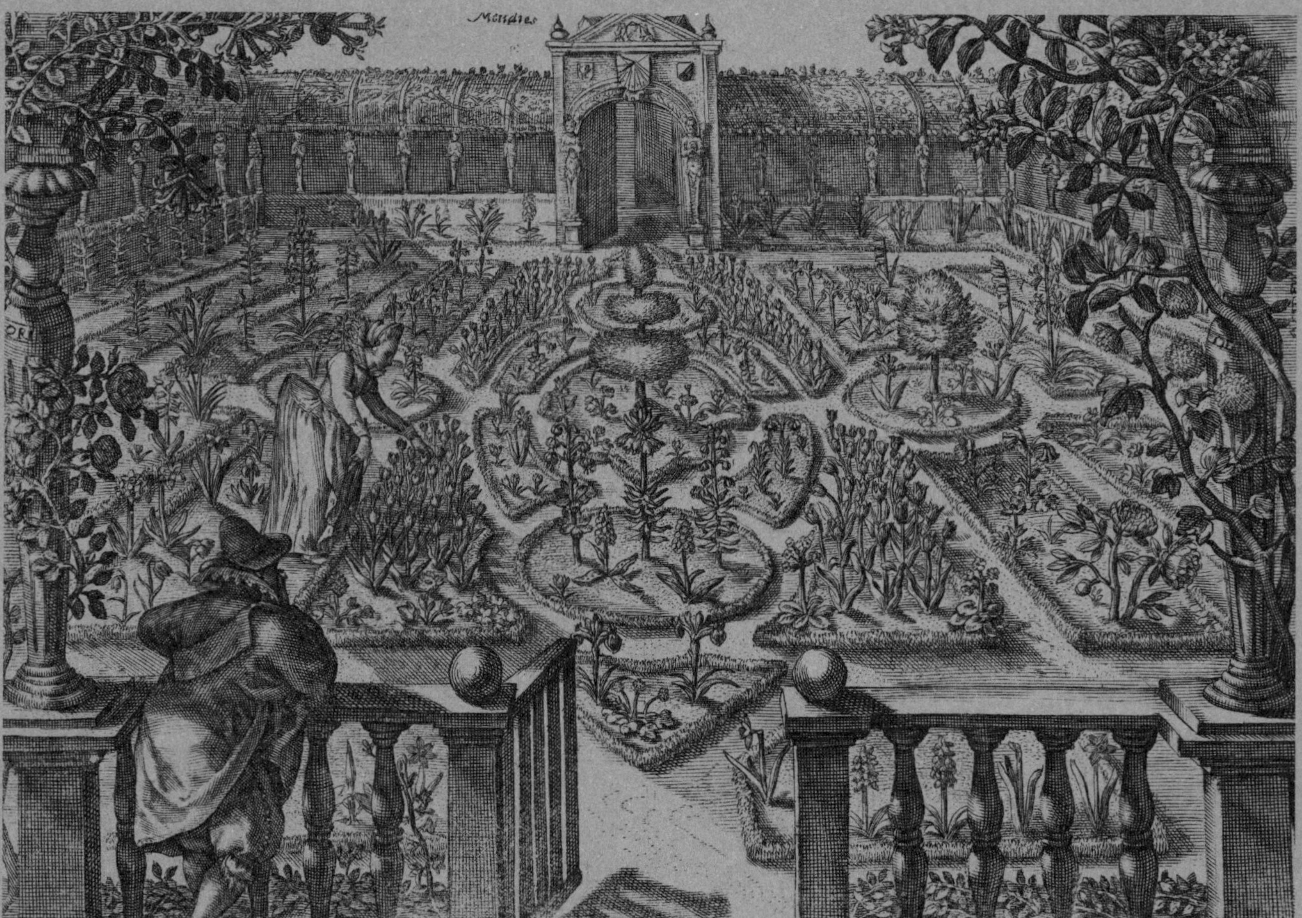

Fig. 5 Crispijn van den Passe, **Den Blom-hof**, 1615–1616, book page. Courtesy University of Utrecht.

Persian lily (no. 25: *Lilium persicum*). The plants in front of it resemble two hyacinths (no. 6: the Star Hyacinth from Guienne or the one from Spain). The crown imperial is known not only for its appearance, but also for its pungent, unpleasant odour. It is no coincidence that it is planted alongside heavily scented lilies, which come from the same family as the crown imperial, and hyacinths, which also have a rather strong fragrance. The garden also features a variety of daffodils, crocuses, irises, and anemones, but they are far outnumbered by the extremely dear tulips imported from Turkey that were so popular in the seventeenth century and which are now seen as typically Dutch.

The garden is enclosed, with a high gate to the south and a low fence to the north. To the right of the gate are the coat of arms of Utrecht. East and west are indicated on the fluted pillars, which are covered with climbing roses. The garden is divided into a geometric pattern of flower beds, in which the flowers are not 'en groupe', but are planted as individual objects in the dark earth. They are colourful jewels fostered with great care and attention by the female owner of this fictional garden. Saverij's garden may have looked similar. The site behind Boterstraat 20, as can be seen in the detail of the 1647 map (fig. 2), also had a geometric layout. This very global arrangement naturally arose from the imagination of the map-maker, but he does refer to what the draughtsman knew—that is how a private garden looked—and to make it recognizable he coloured it green.

Saverij died at the end of February 1639, less than four months after the sale of his house, fireplace, and garden at the age of sixty or sixty-one, depending on his exact date of birth, which is unknown.[23] He was utterly destitute and possibly not entirely sound of mind,[24] despite the fact that he was a celebrated and highly successful painter in his own lifetime. Somehow, he must have fallen upon hard times. According to Joachim von Sandrart (1606–1688), who visited Utrecht in 1625 and also spoke to colleagues there, Saverij painted in the morning and spent his afternoons in elegant company.[25] Paulus Moreelse, the still life painter Balthasar van der Ast (1593/94–1657), and other colleagues visited him almost daily.[26] Legal documents show that Saverij was a heavy drinker, and,

23 Dudok van Heel and Bok, 'De familie van Roelant Roghman', 10.

24 Hendrik Roghman wrote: 'Nature took his life by the dispersion of the senses' ('Natuur benam hem 't leven door verstrooinge der sinne'). De Potter and De Jaegere, 'Het leven van een kunstenaar', 28.

25 Von Sandrart, **Teutsche Academie der edlen Bau-, Bild- und Mahlerey-Künste**, II, book 3, 305. See also De Potter and De Jaegere, 'Het leven van een kunstenaar', 28.

26 De Potter and De Jaegere, 'Het leven van een kunstenaar',

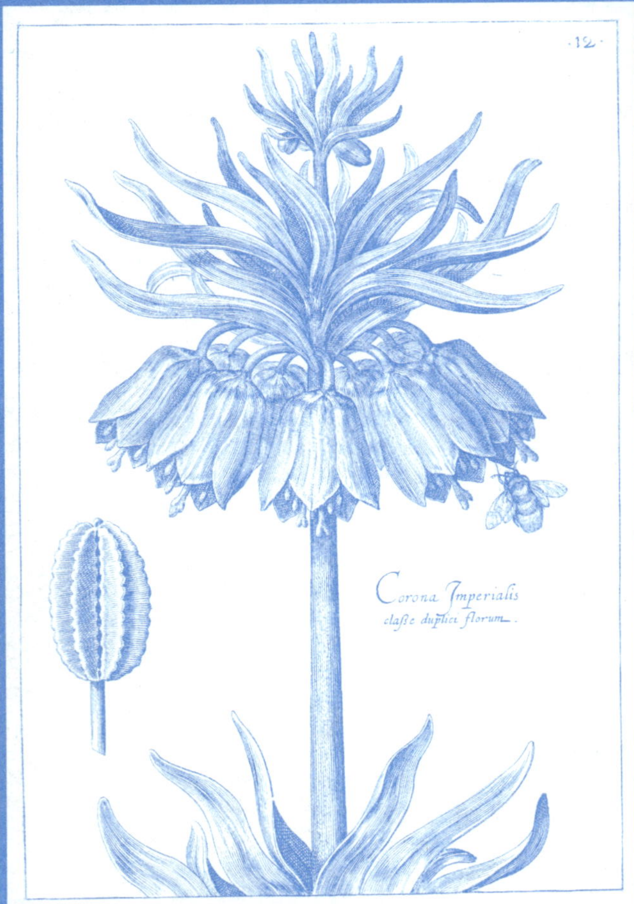

Fig. 6 Crispijn van den Passe, **Den Blom-hof**, 1615–1616, book page. Courtesy University of Utrecht.

therefore, easy prey for family members who were after his money. Indeed, he was cheated out of his money by his own niece and brother-in-law, who got him drunk and made him sign IOUs.[27] His resident maidservant Willemtgen van Angeren—Saverij was unmarried—probably never received the two-hundred guilders he had promised her in his will of 17 December 1634: 'one cannot pluck feathers from a bald chicken'.[28]

'While the world weeps, the souls laugh again in the Elysian Fields now that the Master comes, honouring their Dominion with all manner of animals, with wild Woods and with Lovely Flowers'.[29] So reads the hymn to Roelant Saverij beneath his portrait engraving (fig. 4). The blessed in the Elysean Fields rejoice, knowing that by his coming they are assured of all manner of animals, wild forests, and loving flowers. For it seems, as is stated in the first line, that he surpassed nature in depicting rocks, forests, beasts, and flowers. The Prague years at the court of Emperor Rudolf II were the most beautiful of his life.

27 Ibid., 28.

28 Dudok van Heel and Bok, 'De familie van Roelant Roghman', 10.

29 'Terwijl de werelt weent, soo lachen weer de geesten, int Elisei velt, nu dat de Meester comt. Vierende hun Rijck met allerleye beesten, met woeste Bosschen en met Lieffelijck Geblomt'.

The closure of all libraries and other research institutes as a result of the lockdown due to the COVID-19 pandemic has made it almost impossible to conduct sound scholarly research. No doubt there are publications that I have missed because of this, for which I apologize. Peter van Baaren-Grob, Lisanne Bedaux, Marten Jan Bok, and René de Kam helped me with my research, for which I would like to thank them.

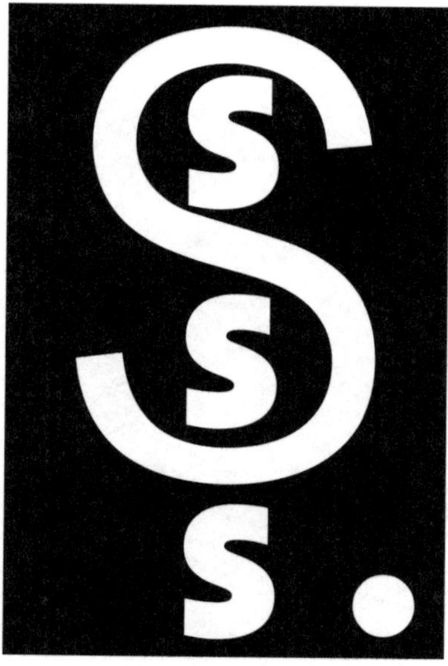

VITA SACKVILLE WEST

Small pleasures must correct great tragedies,
Therefore of gardens in the midst of war
I boldly tell. Once of the noble land
I dared to pull the organ-stops, the deep
Notes of the bass, the diapason's range
Of rich rotation, yielding crop by crop;
Of season after season as the wheel
Turned cyclic in the grooves and groves of time;
I told the classic tools, the plough, the scythe,
In husbandry's important ritual,
But now of agriculture's little brother
I touch the pretty treble, pluck the string,
Making the necklace of a gardener's year,
A gardener's job, for better or for worse
Strung all too easily in beads of verse.
No strong no ruthless plough-share cutting clods,
No harrow toothèd as the saurian jaws,
Shall tear or comb my sward of garden theme,
But smaller spade and hoe and lowly trowel
And ungloved fingers with their certain touch.

Sackville-West, *The Garden*, 13.

NIKI DE SAINT PHALLE

What Saint Phalle, who died in 2002, left behind in Tuscany is dazzling or deranged, transcendent or tawdry, depending on whom you ask. Amid peaceful olive groves and ochre fields grazed by horses and sheep sits a house-size sculpture of a sphinx, with mirrored blue hair and a bright-red crown, a flower blooming on one of her breasts and a lavender heart on the nipple of the other. The interior is covered in shards of mirror, as if a colossal disco ball had been turned inside out. (During the two decades that Saint Phalle worked on the garden, her bedroom was inside one breast, her kitchen in the other.) A sprawling, fantastical castle, with a rainbow mosaic tower, sits near a blue head some fifty feet high, sprouting a second, mirrored head crowned by a huge hand. Downhill, the Devil stands amid some shrubs, a rainbow-winged hermaphrodite with a sweet face, womanly hips, and three gold penises. It is as if a psychedelic bomb had exploded in the most picturesque part of Tuscany.

Levy, 'Beautiful Monsters'.

ROELANT SAVERIJ

This large still life by the Flemish, Utrecht-based painter Roelant Saverij features sixty-three kinds of flowers and forty-four different types of animals. He paired wildflowers with decorative petals with cultivars such as the crown imperial, the tulip, and the rose, which were costly at that time. The crown imperial had a special significance for Saverij as a reference to one of his patrons: Rudolf II, the Holy Roman Emperor (1552–1612). The artist was so proud of this patronage that he even renamed his house with a large garden on Boterstraat 'The Emperor's Arms'. Until around 1550, gardens in Europe were exclusively planted with native species, but colonial trade brought exotic species to the Netherlands, completely transforming the look of European gardens. Saverij also cultivated these new species in his garden in Utrecht.

Liesbeth M. Helmus

ROELANT SAVERIJ

This apparently casual flower arrangement is, in fact, a precisely thought-out masterpiece. In this bouquet, Saverij brought together flowers that bloom at different times of the year. Two sand lizards and a beetle crawl across the light-yellow stone plinth at the bottom. Two rare shells from Indonesia and West Africa bear witness to the Netherlands' colonial past, while the precise representation of the insects indicates the emergence of a new science: entomology. As a whole, the painting symbolizes the transience of life on earth.

Liesbeth M. Helmus

ROELANT SAVERIJ'S GARDEN

See page 163 for 'Roelant Saverij's Garden' by Liesbeth M.Helmus.

SCHREBERGÄRTEN

STAN DOUGLAS

In this series of photographs, Canadian artist Stan Douglas has documented various allotments, known in Germany as 'Schrebergärten', named after the German physician Moritz Schreber (1808–1861). Schreber believed that allotments were the antidote to emerging urbanization and the pollution of the Industrial Revolution, allowing the workers to escape the toxic fumes and mind-numbing factory labour. More than a century later, Douglas pays tribute to the great variety of ways in which individual gardeners have approached their plot of land. Although the plots are the same size, each gardener has created their own version of paradise: where one gardener plants flowers, another grows vegetables; one garden is wild and lush, the other neatly raked. (ed.)

Further encouragement for the spread of the allotment movement came from an educational association founded in the mid-nineteenth century to promote the ideas of Dr Schreber. It aimed to improve the health and education of the people through sport and play in the open air, particularly for children and adolescents. As the director of the orthopaedic home in Leipzig, Dr Schreber saw the physiological and psychological damage caused by the working conditions which even those age groups suffered at that time. He therefore recommended local authorities to create public playgrounds and organize regular games there under pedagogical supervision.

Mosser and Teysott, *The Architecture of Western Gardens*, 451.

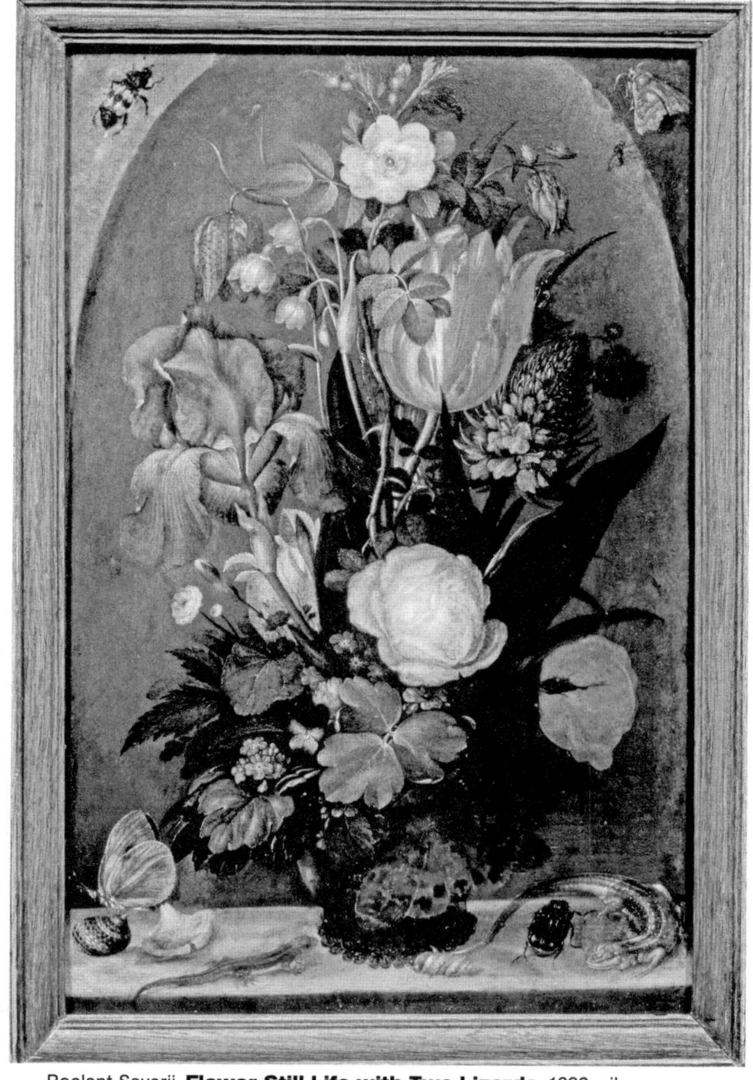

Roelant Saverij, **Flower Still Life with Two Lizards**, 1603, oil on copper, 29 x 19 cm. Courtesy Centraal Museum, Utrecht.

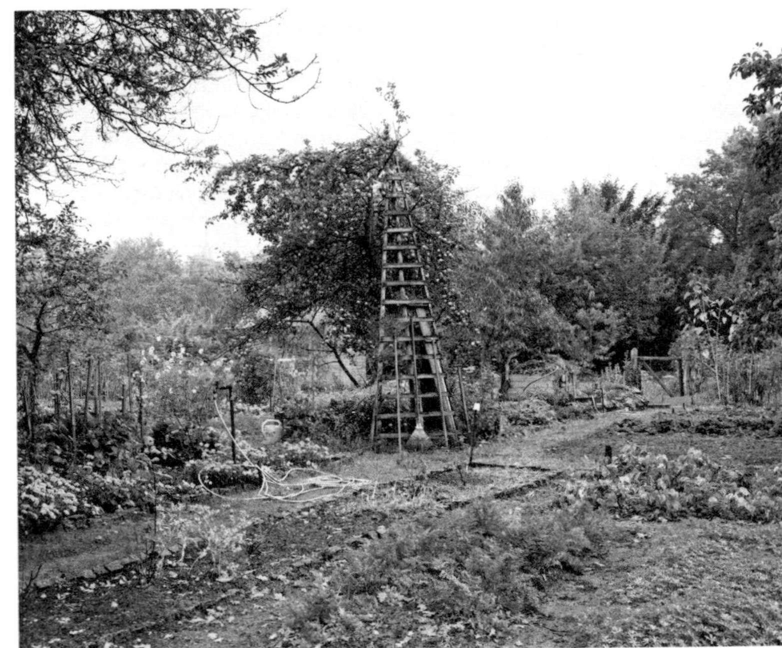

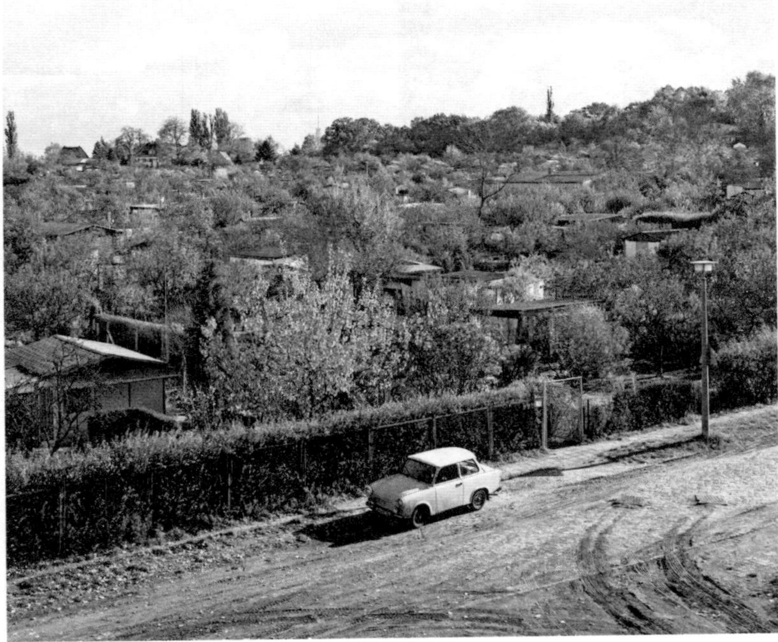

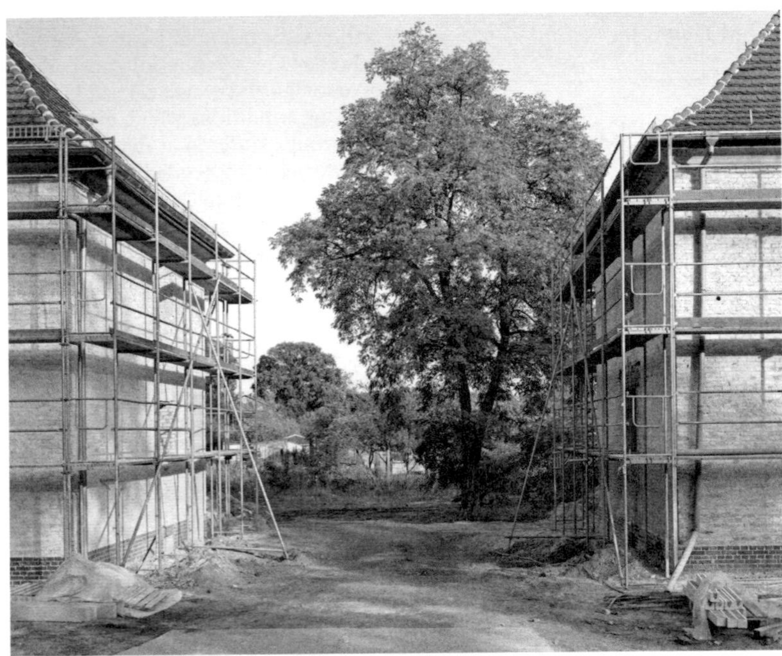

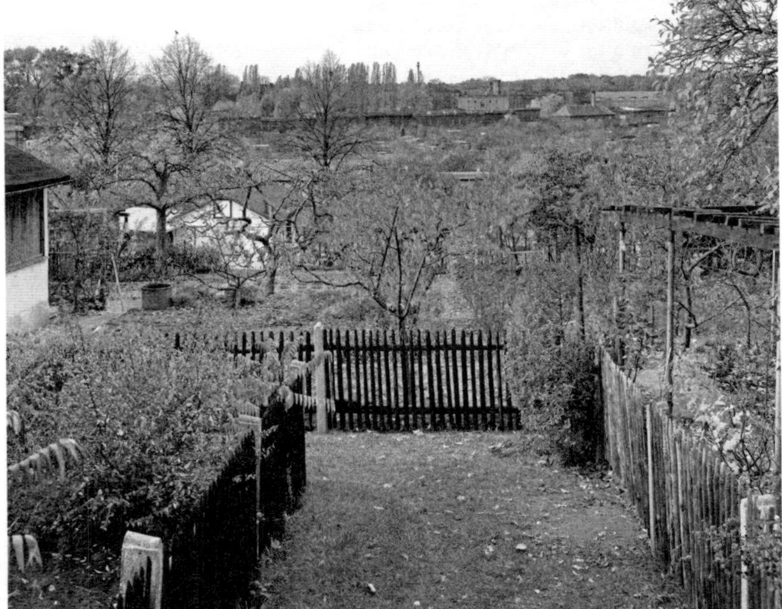

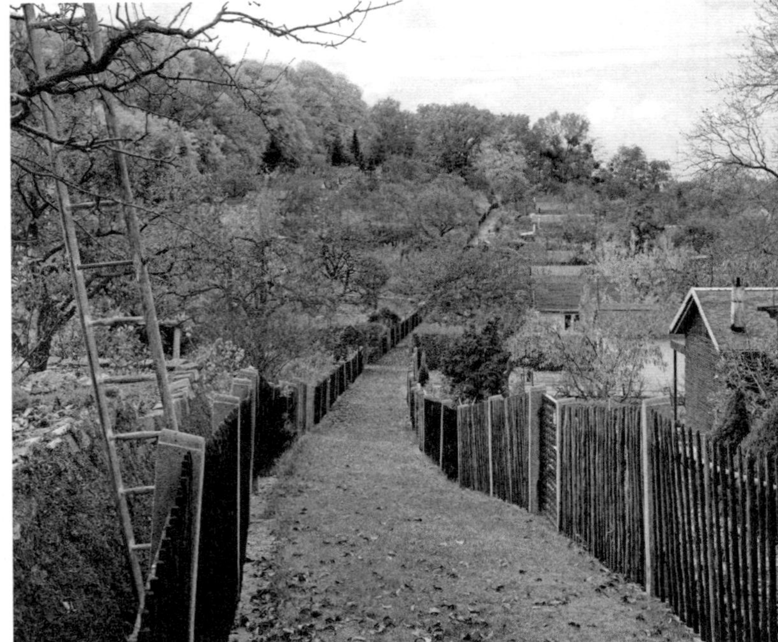

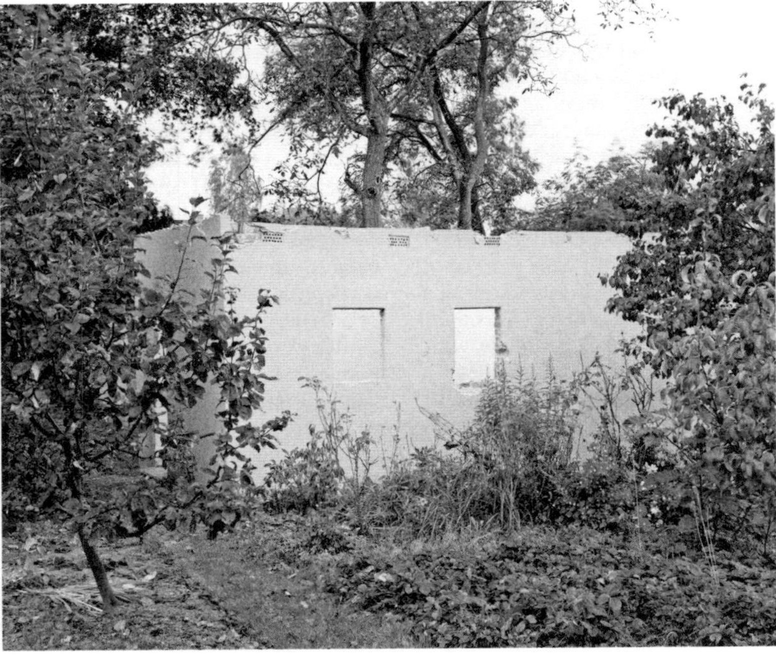

Stan Douglas, **Potsdamer Schrebergärten (Potsdam Gardens Portfolio)**, 1994–2005, fifteen chromogenic prints. Hasso Plattner Collection, © Stan Douglas. Courtesy Stan Douglas, Victoria Miro and David Zwirner.

By the end of the nineteenth century, the growth of public lawns could not keep pace with the fast, industrially influenced growth of many European towns. Daniel Gottlob Moritz Schreber, orthopedist and educationist from Leipzig, advocated in 1843 the installation of playgrounds for children, which his friend Ernst Hauschild began to realize. In 1864, he founded the Schreberverein zur Förderung des Jugendpflege, des Familielebens, der Volkserziehung und Volksgesundung (Schreber Association for the Advancement of Youth Care, Family Life, Public Education and Public Health), an organization that called for the provision of space for children's playgrounds and alter became a program for installing family gardens all over Germany. 'Schreber Gardens' promoted not only health care but also assured food in large European industrial towns. Especially during the two World Wars, the Schreber gardens, in England known as 'allotments', fulfilled these two basic functions. The importance of Scheber gardens, called community garden in the United States and Canada, has decreased because of the agricultural mass production of fruits and vegetables during the last decades, and they have developed more and more into valuable private garden paradises for townspeople who want to fulfill their desire of an own garden. Because of their oftentimes rigid regulations for cultivation, conservative arrangements, and design, Schreber gardens were regarded as an expression of narrow-mindedness for a long time, but this image is changing in many places.

Weilacher, 'Use and Reception', 96.

Daniel Gottlieb Moritz Schreber (1808–1861), the German physician and pedagogue, is well known for both his contributions as a social reformer and for the sadistic 'reforms' he exercised upon his eventually psychotic and suicidal sons. *Memoirs of My Nervous Illness* 1903, the reflections of Daniel Paul, Scheber's youngest son, was a model for Sigmund Freud's study of paranoia and schizophrenia. The case led Freud to analyze other accounts of patriarchic oppression, such as E.T.A. Hoffmann's 'Der Sandmann' (1815), a vivid tale of a child's bogeyman and the extension of its underlying pathology into adult madness—and, in retrospect, a prophecy of Teutonic horror.

Schreber is also the mind behind Schreber gardens, urban garden allotments introduced by the German government to assist the poor in the first half of the nineteenth century. In his Christian mission to improve the physical and psychological environment of working- and middle-class families, Schreber saw gardens as both therapeutic and functional.

Smith, *Down the Garden Path*, 92.

SECRET GARDEN

If you look the right way, you can see that the whole world is a garden.

Holland, *The Secret Garden*.

Historically and psychologically, gardens carry a sense of secrecy: Eden, the Garden of Eros where Psyche sneaks in, *The Secret Garden*—a classic novel and film. Secrecy is also a feature of many gardens in China and Japan. Visitors to Kyoto, for instance, are disappointed not to see anything while walking on the street. All the beautiful gardens are hidden behind high walls. It is the same in China. A garden is an extension of a private, inner space into the outer world. Like skin, a garden belongs both to the outer open space and to one's inner life. It was with the arrival of civil society that gardens became open spaces, often surrounded by fences instead of walls. Gardens in the United States and Canada are generally open. A typical garden in front of a suburban house surrounded by a low hedge or fence serves both as proof of the owner's status (that is why most of them look alike) and as the interface for communication with neighbors.

Goldberg, *The Robot in the Garden*, 205.

SEED

SEEDS
William Blathwayt, Secretary of Foreign Plantations.
Dyrham Park, 1690.

The seeds of empire arrive in envelopes:
maple, red cherry, hickory nuts,
America's bright heirlooms.

Blathwayt has them sown in beds.
They germinate out of sight,
wriggle through soil.

He sips chocolate from pots,
administers colonies from his hearth,
contemplates planting at home and abroad.

Time passes, profits grow.
He surveys his flowers.
Only the brightest are plucked.

The exotic blooms are much admired:
they stand to attention for state visitors.
But how they shiver in their delft vases.

Fowler, *Green Unpleasant Land*, 294.

Seed, the characteristic reproductive body of both angiosperms (flowering plants) and gymnosperms (e.g., conifers, cycads, and ginkgos). Essentially, a seed consists of a miniature undeveloped plant (the embryo), which, alone or in the company of stored food for its early development after germination, is surrounded by a protective coat (the testa). Frequently small in size and making negligible demands upon their environment, seeds are eminently suited to perform a wide variety of functions the relationships of which are not always obvious: multiplication, perennation (surviving seasons of stress such as winter), dormancy (a state of arrested development), and dispersal. Pollination and the 'seed habit' are considered the most important factors responsible for the overwhelming evolutionary success of the flowering plants, which number more than 300,000 species.

Encyclopaedia Britannica, 'Seed'.

SEEDLING

HANS VAN LUNTEREN
Nature is strictly controlled and managed in urban areas in the Netherlands, yet it takes over in unexpected places, for example where the municipal mower cannot reach. Hans van Lunteren is fascinated by these uncontrollable manifestations of nature, whose ultimate expression is the seedling: a young plant that has self-seeded under the right conditions. Together with Jessica van Essen and Hans van Dijk, van Lunteren has developed the project *Seedlings of the City* in which the seedling symbolizes nature's powerful potential to re-establish itself. The affection that people feel for these chance germinations is expressed in a series of interviews with local residents about their favourite seedling. Especially for the exhibition, van Lunteren and Ienke Kastelein have developed a *Seedling Walk*, a sensory tour through back alleys and hidden gardens and along the Singel canal, whereby the seedling plays the lead role. (ed.)

SOIL

Soil is a material composed of five ingredients — minerals, soil organic matter, living organisms, gas, and water. Soil minerals are divided into three size classes—clay, silt, and sand; the percentages of particles in these size classes is called soil texture. The mineralogy of soils is diverse. For example, a clay mineral called smectite can shrink and swell so much upon wetting and drying that it can knock over buildings. The most common mineral in soils is quartz; it makes beautiful crystals but it is not very reactive. Soil organic matter is plant, animal, and microbial residues in various states of decomposition; it is a critical ingredient—in fact the percentage of soil organic matter in a soil is among the best indicators of agricultural soil quality. Soil colors range from the common browns, yellows, reds, grays, whites, and blacks to rare soil colors such as greens and blues.

Needelman, 'What Are Soils?'

SOLASTALGIA

Solastalgia is a new concept developed to give greater meaning and clarity to environmentally induced distress. As opposed to nostalgia—the melancholia or homesickness experienced by individuals when separated from a loved home—solastalgia is the distress that is produced by environmental change impacting on people while they are directly connected to their home environment.

Albrecht, 'Solastalgia', 95.

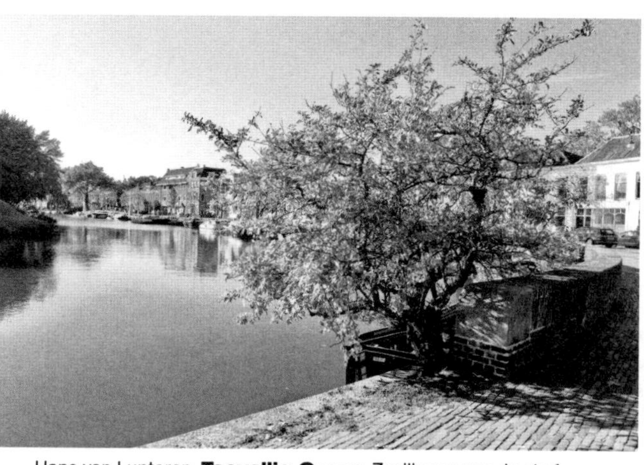

Hans van Lunteren, **Toevallig Groen**, Zaailingen van de stad.

SPECIES

The word 'species' comes from the Latin speciēs, 'a seeing'. Maybe we are losing species and languages, our joy, because we don't wish to see what we are doing.

Vicuña, 'Language is Migrant'.

The Latin term species, which means 'appearance', 'aspect', or 'vision', derives from a root signifying 'to look, to see'. This root is also found in *speculum* (mirror), *spectrum* (image, ghost), *perspicuus* (transparent, clearly seen), *speciosus* (beautiful, giving itself to be seen), *specimen* (example, sign), and *spectaculum* (spectacle). In philosophical terminology, *species* was used to translate the Greek *eidos* (as *genus* was used to translate *genos*); hence the sense the term takes on in natural science (animal or plant species) and in the language of commerce, where the term signifies 'commodities' (particularly in the sense of drugs and spices) and, later, money (*espèces*). [...]

Specious first meant 'beautiful' and only later came to mean 'untrue, apparent'. *Species* was first defined as that which makes visible and only later became the principle of classification and equivalence. 'To be special [*far specie*]' can mean 'to surprise and astonish' (in a negative sense) by not fitting into established rules, but the notion that individuals constitute a species and belong together in a homogenous class tends to be reassuring.

Nothing is more instructive than this double meaning. The species is what presents and communicates itself to the gaze, what renders visible and, at the same time, what can—and must, at all costs—be fixed in a substance and in a specific difference in order to constitute an identity. [...]

Everywhere the special must be reduced to the personal and the personal to the substantial. The transformation of the *species* into a principle of identity and classification is the original sin of our culture, its most implacable apparatus [*dispositivo*].

Agamben, *Profanations*, 56–59.

Species, like all the old and important words, is equally promiscuous, but in the visual register rather than the gustatory. The Latin *specere* is at the root of things here, with its tones of 'to look' and 'to behold'. In logic, *species* refers to a mental impression or idea, strengthening the notion that thinking and seeing are clones. Referring both to the relentlessly 'specific' or particular and to a class of individuals with the same characteristics, *species* contains its own opposite in the most promising—or special—way. Debates about whether species are earthly organic entities or taxonomic conveniences are coextensive with the discourse we call 'biology'. Species is about the dance linking kin and kind. The ability to interbreed reproductively is the rough and ready requirement for members of the same biological species; all those lateral gene exchangers such as bacteria have never made very good species. Also, biotechnologically mediated gene transfers redo kin and kind at rates and in patterns unprecedented on earth, generating messmates at table who do not know how to eat well and, in my judgment, often should not be guests together at all. Which companion species will, and should, live and die, and how, is at stake. [...]

The word *species* also structures conservation and environmental discourses, with their 'endangered species' that function simultaneously to locate value and to evoke death and extinction in ways familiar in colonial representations of the always vanishing indigene. The discursive tie between the colonized, the enslaved, the noncitizen, and the animal—all reduced to type, all Others to rational man, and all essential to his bright constitution—is at the heart of racism and flourishes, lethally, in the entrails of humanism. Woven into that tie in all the categories is 'woman's' putative self-defining responsibility to 'the species', as this singular and typological female is reduced to her reproductive function. Fecund, she lies outside the bright territory of man even as she is his conduit. The labeling of African American men in the United States as an 'endangered species' makes palpable the ongoing animalization that fuels liberal and conservative racialization alike. *Species* reeks of race and sex; and where and when species meet, that heritage must be untied and better knots of companion species attempted within and across differences. Loosening the grip of analogies that issue in the collapse of all of man's others into one another, companion species must instead learn to live intersectionally.

Haraway, *When Species Meet*, 17–18.

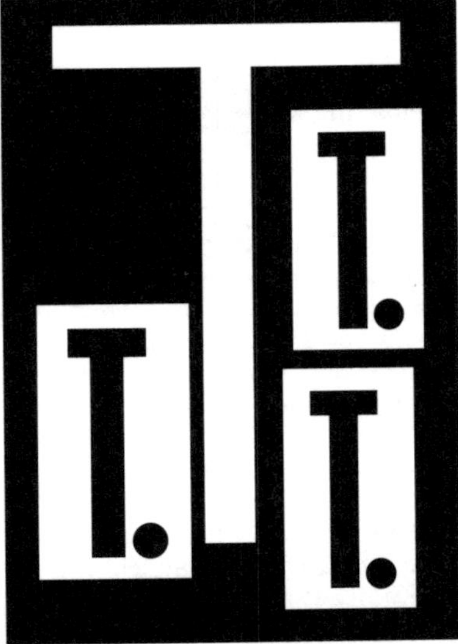

TAXONOMY

These ambiguities, redundancies and deficiencies remind us of those which doctor Franz Kuhn attributes to a certain Chinese encyclopaedia entitled *Celestial Empire of Benevolent Knowledge*. In its remote pages it is written that the animals are divided into:

(a) belonging to the emperor
(b) embalmed
(c) tame
(d) sucking pigs
(e) sirens
(f) fabulous
(g) stray dogs
(h) included in the present classification
(i) frenzied
(j) innumerable
(k) drawn with a very fine camelhair brush
(l) et cetera
(m) having just broken the water pitcher
(n) that from a long way off look like flies.

Borges, *The Analytical Language of John Wilkins*.

LEARNING FROM LINNAEUS

To choose smartly the name of a geologic epoch requires us to ask an additional question, that is, *why* should we, or, in the case of an already chosen name described above, why did we choose a particular name? My favorite example that illustrates the importance of asking this subsequent question comes from the scholarship of feminist historian of science Londa Schiebinger in her prize-winning book *Nature's Body: Gender in the Making of Modern Science* (1993), in which she asks the question, why are mammals called mammals? Throughout the book, Schiebinger shows that seventeenth- and eighteenth-century European social and political struggles influenced taxonomy and physical anthropology. Thus, natural historians of that time created a peculiar and enduring vision of nature that embodied the sexual and racial tensions of the time period. Schiebinger's chapter on the choice by renowned taxonomist Carl Linnaeus to name warm-blooded, hairy animals 'Mammalia', even though mammae are not a pronounced unifying characteristic of this group, relates to my argument. As Schiebinger points out, milk-producing mammae function only in half of these animals (the females), and only then for part of the time when they are lactating. Schiebinger reasons that Linnaeus could have chosen hair, three ear bones, or a four-chambered heart—ungulates, sloths, bats, sea cows, humans, and apes share these characteristics—as the defining feature of this group, but instead he made the female mammae the icon of the group. In doing so, he paved the way for thinking about females solely in terms of sexuality and underscored eighteenth-century women's position as nurturing caretakers.

Schiebinger asks, why did Linnaeus choose the name 'Mammalia' when he might have chosen 'Pilosa' (the hairy ones) or 'Aurecaviga' (the hollow-eared ones)? She answers that cultural forces and pressing political trends molded his view of nature. As a physician and father of seven children, Linnaeus revered the maternal breast during this time when doctors and politicians were praising the virtues of mother's milk. Linnaeus was involved in the struggle against wet nursing that emerged alongside political realignments that undermined women's public power and attached new value to women's domestic roles. Learning from Linnaeus and Schiebinger, we are right to ask, in my opinion, why choose Anthropos (Greek for human) as the namesake of a new epoch of geologic time? What do we obscure and what do we privilege with such a choice?

Schneiderman, 'The Anthropocene Controversy', 175.

TIME

The gardener digs in another time, without past or future, beginning or end. A time that does not cleave the day with rush hours, lunch breaks, the last bus home. As you walk in the garden you pass into this time—the moment of entering can never be remembered. Around you the landscape lies transfigured. Here is the Amen beyond the prayer.

Jarman, *Modern Nature*, 30.

Such consolations are nothing new. In her diary of 1939, Virginia Woolf records hearing Hitler on the radio. Her husband, Leonard, was in the garden he'd painstakingly constructed at Monk's House, their damp green cottage in Rodmell, East Sussex. 'I shan't come in', he shouted. 'I'm planting iris, and they will be flowering long after he is dead.' It was true. Gardening situates you in a different kind of time, the antithesis of the agitating present of social media. Time becomes circular, not chronological; minutes stretch into hours; some actions don't bear fruit for decades. The gardener is not immune to attrition and loss but is daily confronted by the ongoing good news of fecundity. A peony returns, alien pink shoots thrusting from bare soil. The fennel self-seeds; there is an abundance of cosmos out of nowhere.

Laing, 'The Intertwining of Art, Gardening, Filmmaking and Writing'.

TRAMPOLINE

JULIETTE BLIGHTMAN
The British artist Juliette Blightman documented the trampoline in her back garden for a whole year. During the summer, it provided hours of pleasure, but in the winter it became an abandoned plaything occupying space. Her daughter uses it in various ways: for jumping on, alone and with friends, and also as a retreat. Blightman compares the trampoline to the private space that Virginia Woolf (1882–1941) describes in her essay *A Room of One's Own* (1929), which was essential for her to be able to write. A space, she concludes, that women have seldom been allowed in the course of history. (ed.)

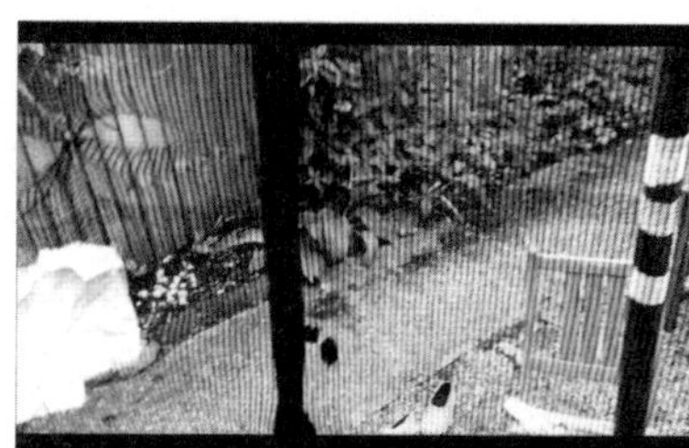

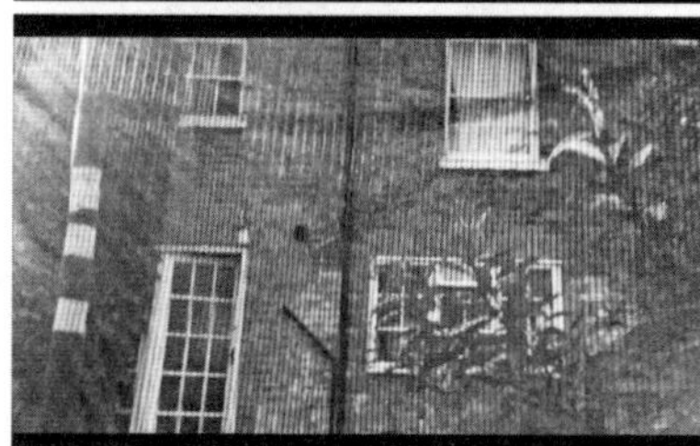

Juliette Blightman, **A Room of One's Own**, 2020, installation view. Courtesy Juliette Blightman and Galerie Fons Welters, Amsterdam. Photo: Gert Jan van Rooij.

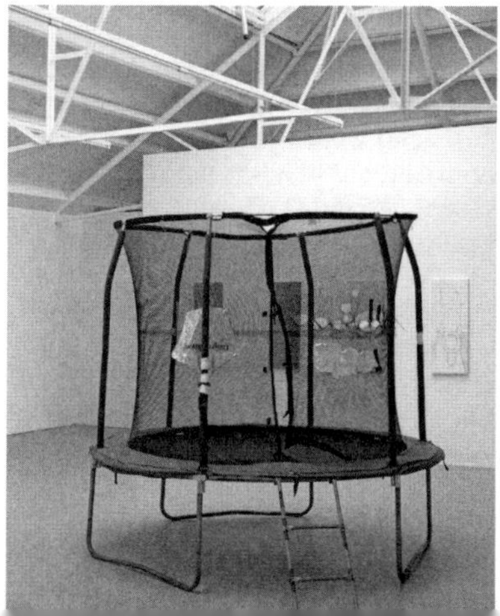

Juliette Blightman, **A Carpet For Your Somersaults**, 2020, video still. Courtesy Juliette Blightman and Galerie Fons Welters, Amsterdam.

TRELLIS

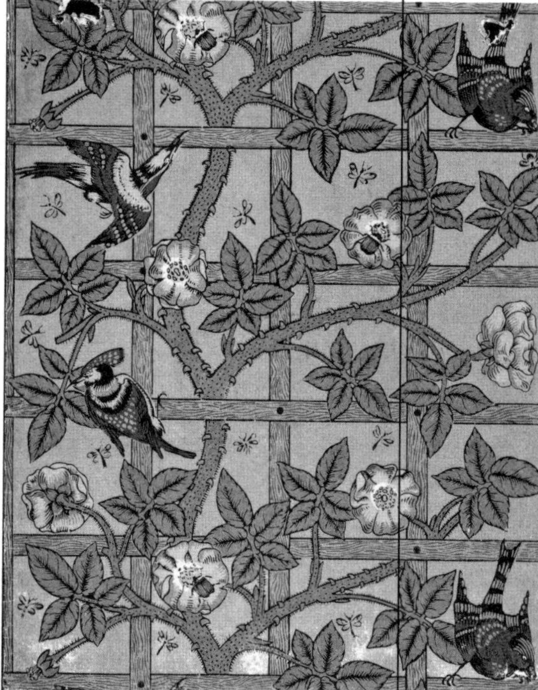

William Morris and Philip Speakman Webb, **Trellis**, 1862, block print, 68 × 52.9 cm. Courtesy Alamy/Victoria and Albert Museum, London.

TULIP

JENNIFER TEE
Jennifer Tee began making her first tulip-petal collages in 2014. The motifs derive from South Sumatran textiles called *tampan* and *palepai* that were used in ceremonies marking important moments in life. Because the textiles often depict a ship, they are also known as ship cloths. The ship symbolizes an intermediate state—travelling towards something—and contains human figures, animals, and objects. The starting point for this work is Tee's Chinese-Indonesian roots: her maternal grandfather was a tulip merchant—the tulip has become a symbol of Dutch identity—and her father came to the Netherlands from Indonesia at a young age with his family after World War II. However, the work transcends the merely autobiographical, resonating with spiritual echoes and current political connotations. (ed.)

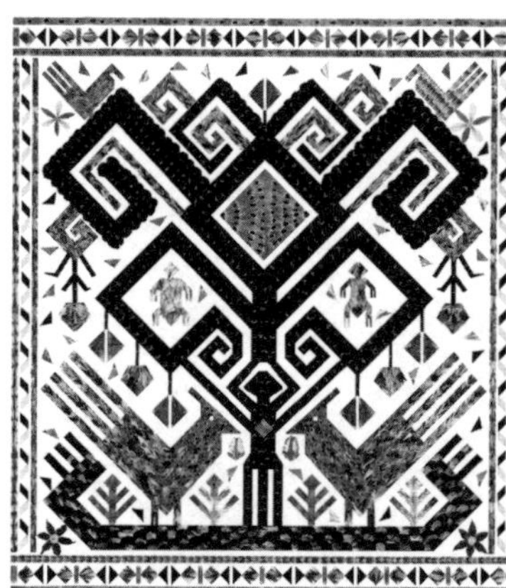

Jennifer Tee, **Tampan Tulip**, 2014–2020, collage. Courtesy Galerie Fons Welters, Amsterdam.

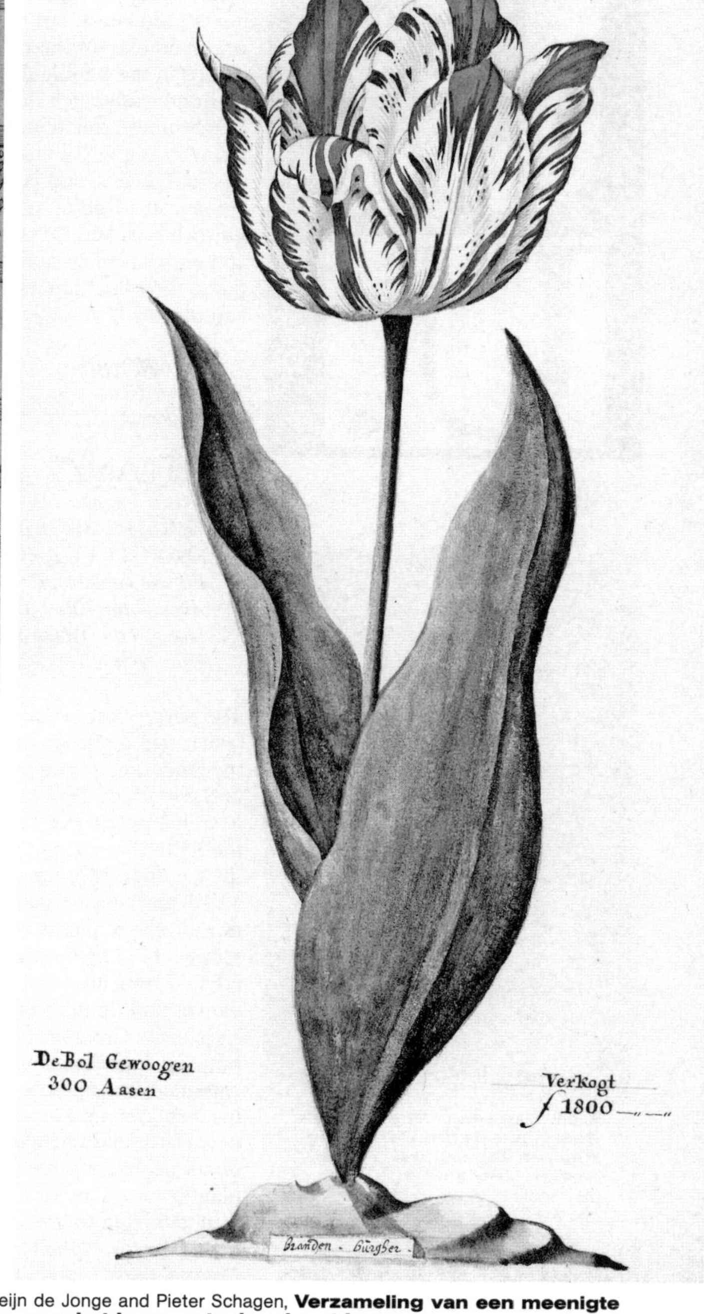

Pieter Holsteijn de Jonge and Pieter Schagen, **Verzameling van een meenigte tulipaanen, naar het leven geteekend met hunne naamen, en swaarte der bollen, zoo als die publicq verkogt zijn, te Haarlem in den jaare A. 1637, door P. Cos, bloemist te Haarlem**, 1637, gouache and watercolour on paper. Courtesy University of Wageningen.

TULIP BOOK

Until the late 1620s, the tulip was a rare, exotic flower from Asia, cultivated only in small circles. The white tulip flecked with red at the edges of the petals in Johannes Bosschaert's flower arrangement was one of the rarest and most costly specimens. At the beginning of 1637, thirty thousand guilders was offered for three bulbs of this *Semper Augustus* tulip, at a time when the most expensive houses along Amsterdam's canals, complete with garden and coach house, cost ten thousand guilders. The speculative nature of the tulip trade eventually resulted in the complete collapse of the market, with many bankruptcies. (ed.)

TURFED BENCH

A raised bench planted with grass and herbs serving as an aromatic seat.

Aben and De Wit, *The Enclosed Garden*, 250.

A garden full of flowers form the setting for *Le Roman de la Rose* and this was the ideal place for courtly love, a delightful spot shut off from the outside world. Courting but also rhetoric, philosophy, music and sport took place there against a backdrop of widely spaced trees, on turfed seats, in and around the fountain, all of these seemingly placed at random on a fresh green lawn.

Aben and De Wit, *The Enclosed Garden*, 38–39.

UNICORN

The unicorn, which is also called *rhinoceros* in Greek, has this nature: it is a little beast, not unlike a young goat, and extraordinarily swift. It has a horn in the middle of its brow, and no hunter can catch it. But it can be caught in the following fashion: a girl who is a virgin is led to the place where it dwells, and is left there alone in the forest. As soon as the unicorn sees her, it leaps into her lap and embraces her, and goes to sleep there; then the hunters capture it and display it in the king's palace.

Barber, *Bestiary*, 36.

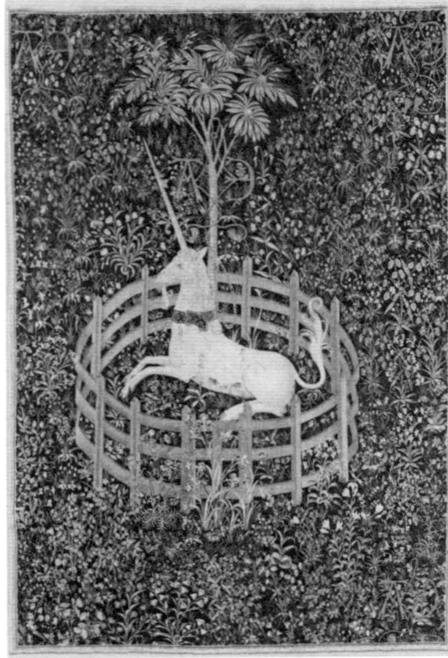

Anonymous French, **The Unicorn Rests in a Garden (from the Unicorn Tapestries)**, 1495–1505, tapestry, 368 × 251.5 cm. Courtesy The Metropolitan Museum of Art, New York and Art Resource/Scala, Florence.

URPFLANZE

PERSIJN BROERSEN & MARGIT LUKÁCS
Fix the Variable, Exclude the Accidental, Eliminate the Impure, Unravel the Tangled, Discover the Unknown, 2021

The perception of nature and the construction and manipulation of the landscape play a prominent role in the work of Persijn Broersen & Margit Lukács. For Framework, the LED screens on the façade of the Centraal Museum, they made a new work based on the collection of exotic plants assembled around 1737 by George Clifford III (1685–1760), an Amsterdam-based banker and director of the Dutch East India Company. The Swedish botanist Carl Linnaeus (1707–1778) classified these plants according to his own system. However, he did not necessarily base his classifications on an objective observation of the plants, but on an idealized version, as if referring to *urpflanze* (original plant). In the video by Broersen & Lukacs, these individual plants come to life as a fierce crowd and threaten to break free from the straitjacket imposed on them. (ed.)

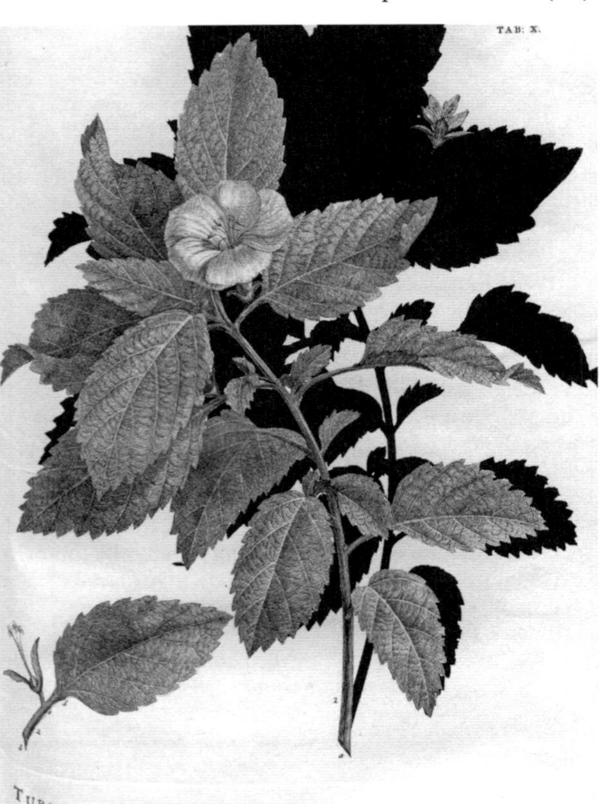

Persijn Broersen & Margit Lukács, work-in-progress **(Fix the Variable, Exclude the Accidental, Eliminate the Impure, Unravel the Tangled, Discover the Unknown)**, Turnera Hortus Cliffortianus, 2021.

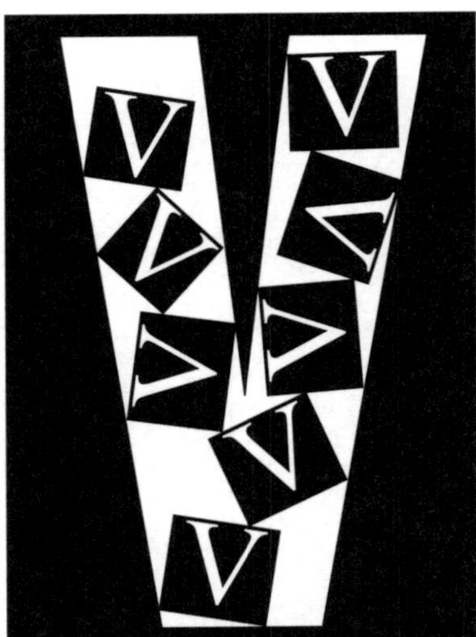

VIOLETS

The violet held a secret. Along the hedgerow that ran down to the cliffs at Hordle deep purple violets grew—perhaps no more than a dozen plants. I stumbled across them late one sunny March afternoon as I came up the cliff path from the sea. They were hidden in a small recess. I stood for some moments dazzled by them.

Day after day I returned from the dull regimental existence of an English boarding school to my secret garden—the first of many that blossomed in my dreams. It was here that I brought him, sworn to secrecy, and then watched him slip out of his grey flannel suit and lie naked in the spring sunlight. Here our hands first touched; then I pulled down my trousers and lay beside him. Bliss that he turned and lay naked on his stomach, laughing as my hand ran down his back and disappeared into the warm darkness between his thighs. He called it the lovely feeling' and returned the next day, inviting me into his bed that night.

Obsessive violets drawing the evening shadows to themselves, our fingers touching in the purple.

Term ended. I bought myself violets from the florist's and put them by my bedside. My grandmother disapproved of flowers in the bedroom, said they corrupted the air. Violets, she said, were the flower of death.

But the violet, I discovered, was third in the trinity of symbolic flowers, flower of purity,

Whose virtue neither the heat of the sun melted away,
Neither the rain has washed and driven away.

The violet, Nothing behind the best for smelling sweetly, a thousand more will provoke your content.

A new orchard and garden was mine.

That summer, when the wheat had grown waist high, we carved a secret path from the violet grove into the centre of the field, and lay there chewing the unformed seeds, rubbing ourselves all over each other's bronzed and salty bodies, such was our happy garden state.

Jarman, *Modern Nature*, 37–38.

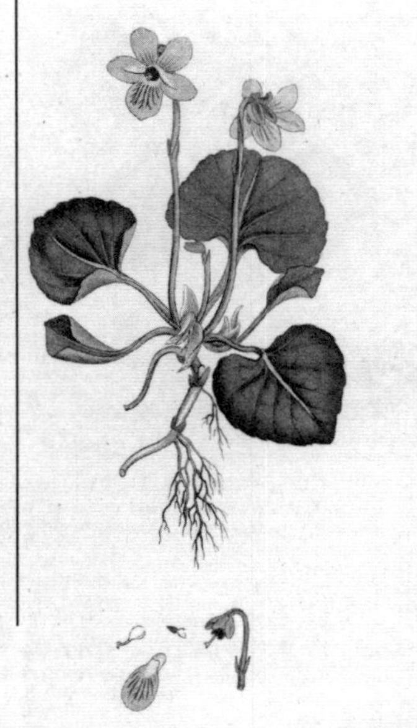

James Sowerby, **Marsh Violet (Viola palustris)**, 1798, drawing from **English Botany** 1798. Courtesy Alamy/Florilegius.

VIRIDITAS

The remarkable twelfth-century abbess Saint Hildegard of Bingen took the Benedictine teachings further. Highly respected as a composer and a theologian, as well as a medicinal herbalist, she developed her own philosophy based on the connection between the human spirit and the growth force of the earth which she called viriditas. Like the source of a river, viriditas is the font of energy on which all other life forms ultimately depend. The word combines the Latin for green and truth. Viriditas is the origin of goodness and health, in contrast to ariditas, or dryness, which Hildegard regarded… as its life-defying opposite.

The greening power of viriditas is both literal and symbolic. It refers to the flourishing of nature as well as the vibrancy of the human spirit. By placing 'greenness' at the heart of her thinking, Hildegard recognised that people can only thrive when the natural world thrives. She understood that there is an inescapable link between the health of the planet and human physical and spiritual health, which is why she is increasingly regarded as a forerunner of the modern ecological movement.

In a garden filled with light and suffused with the energy of new growth, the green pulse of life can be felt at its strongest. Whether we conceive of the natural growth force in terms of God, Mother Earth, biology, or a mixture of these, there is a living relationship at work. Gardening is an interchange through which nature gives life to our reparative wishes, be it turning waste into nutritious compost, helping pollinators thrive, or beautifying the earth. Gardening involves striving to keep pests and weeds at bay to provide nourishment in all its various forms—greenness and shade, colour and beauty and all the fruits of the earth.

Stuart-Smith, *The Well-Gardened Mind*, 12–14.

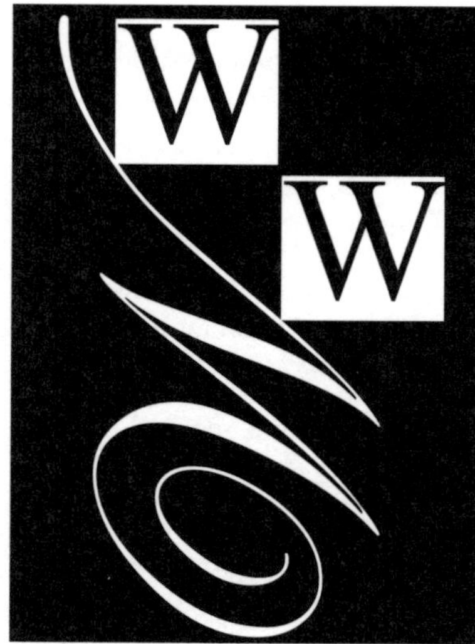

WALLFLOWER

See page 177 for 'Wallflower' by Jonny Bruce.

WEED

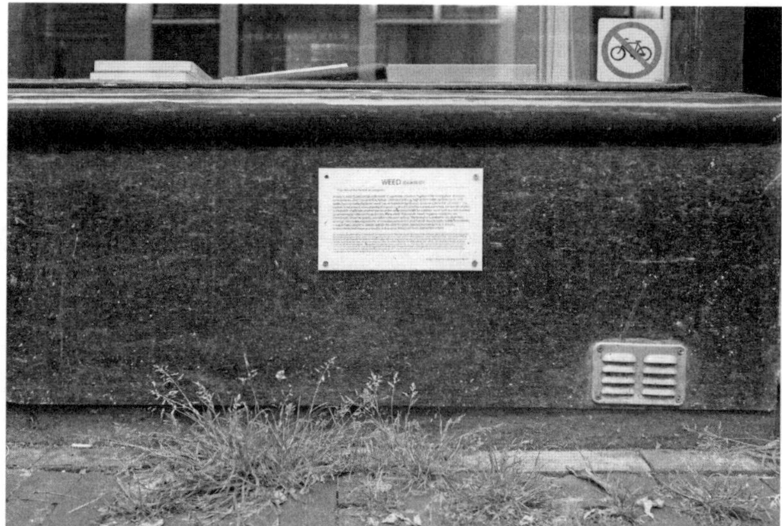

WEED (ONKRUID)

From Wikipedia, the free encyclopedia

A weed is a plant considered undesirable in a particular situation, "a plant in the wrong place". Examples commonly are plants unwanted in human-controlled settings, such as farm fields, gardens, lawns, and parks. Taxonomically, the term "weed" has no botanical significance, because a plant that is a weed in one context is not a weed when growing in a situation where it is in fact wanted, and where one species of plant is a valuable crop plant, another species in the same genus might be a serious weed, such as a wild bramble growing among cultivated loganberries. Many plants that people widely regard as weeds also are intentionally grown in gardens and other cultivated settings. The term also is applied to any plant that grows or reproduces aggressively, or is invasive outside its native habitat. More broadly "weed" occasionally is applied pejoratively to species outside the plant kingdom, species that can survive in diverse environments and reproduce quickly; in this sense it has even been applied to humans.

Rumiko Hagiwara, **Weed**, 2019, installation view at Althuis Hofland Fine Arts, Amsterdam.

WILD GARDEN

William Robinson was at the forefront of the new movement. A Scottish gardener whose prolific writing output and impassioned rhetoric set the tone for the Arts and Crafts garden movement, Robinson's influence was formed through his books and his monthly magazine *Country Life,* as well as through design commissions. In *The Wild Garden*, he poses a convincing alternative to the Victorians' showy, carpet-bedding style plantings of annual flowers, explaining methods for the naturalization of hardy northern perennial flowers in 'woods, copses, and pleasure grounds'. Where in the eighteenth-century landscape park, Kent and Brown manipulated the human gaze, extending it beyond property boundaries into the countryside, to make of the garden a landscape, Robinson physically leaps the frame with a sack of narcissus bulbs and a trowel. He blurs the boundary between 'landscape' and 'wilderness' with flowers, flowers with specific Northern European and North American cultural meanings. Long, evocative lists of flower names in Robinson's text serve as nostalgic litanies of the 'infinitely varied scenes [...] in the wilder parts of all northern and temperate regions [...]. Such beauty may be realized in every wood and copse and shrubbery that screens our "trim gardens".' (Robinson, *The Wild Garden*, 1881: 4) Robinson's plant naturalization techniques symbolically domesticated the rougher boundaries of the landscape, bringing forest, alpine, and meadow pictures into the garden purview. Where previously landscaping had addressed the representational boundary between garden and agricultural landscape, Robinson represented the uncultivated wilderness as a garden. Now Nature aspired to the condition of pre-social, Rousseauian wilds.

Robertson, *Occasional Work and Seven Walks from the Office for Soft Architecture*, 103–104.

Alfred Parsons and William Robinson, **The Wild Garden**, 1883, frontispiece. Courtesy Wellesley College Library.

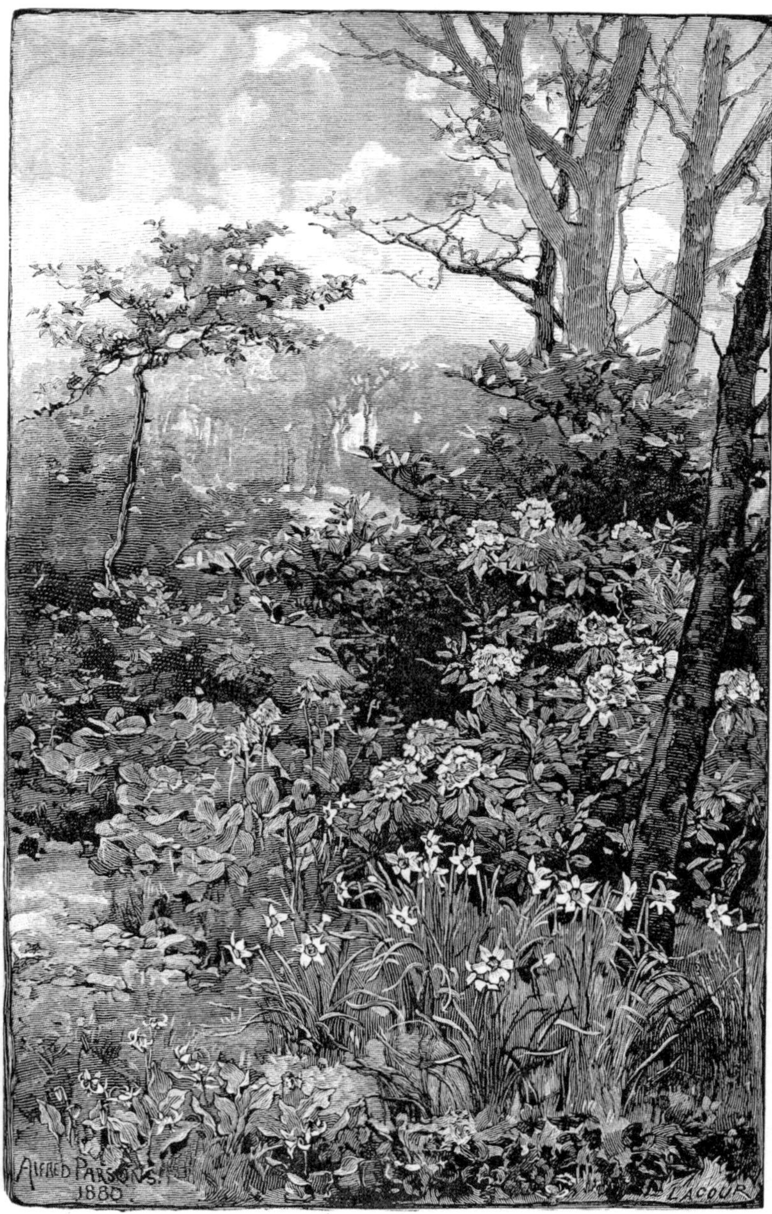

WILDERNESS

Yet shall the garden with the state of war
Aptly contrast, a miniature endeavour
To hold the graces and the courtesies
Against a horrid wilderness.

Sackville-West, *The Garden*, 14.

Monday 9, January 1989

Planted roses: Rugosa double de Coubert Harrisonii, Rosa mundi—a selection of old roses from Rassel's in Earls Court. By the time I have finished there will be over thirty scattered in clumps through the garden, disrupting its wildness as little as possible.

I arrived at dusk in the nursery set in its little square under the plane trees—it's a romantic place. Walking around in the deepening gloom through the rows of plants you are drawn into dreams of long summer days, looking at the ageing photos above each plant. Rosa mundi, rose of the world, with its crimson and blush striped flowers, an old sport from the apothecary's Rose officionalis the rose of Provins. It was brought back by a 12th century crusader and immortalised by Guillaume de Lorris in his poem the Roman de La Rose. When I took my roses to pay for them I found my old friend André manning the till. He laughed at the idea of my wilderness garden.

Jarman, *Modern Nature*, 4.

WILDNESS

I wish to speak a word for Nature, for absolute freedom and wildness, as contrasted with a freedom and culture merely civil,—to regard man as an inhabitant, or a part and parcel of Nature, rather than a member of society.

Thoreau, 'Walking', 657.

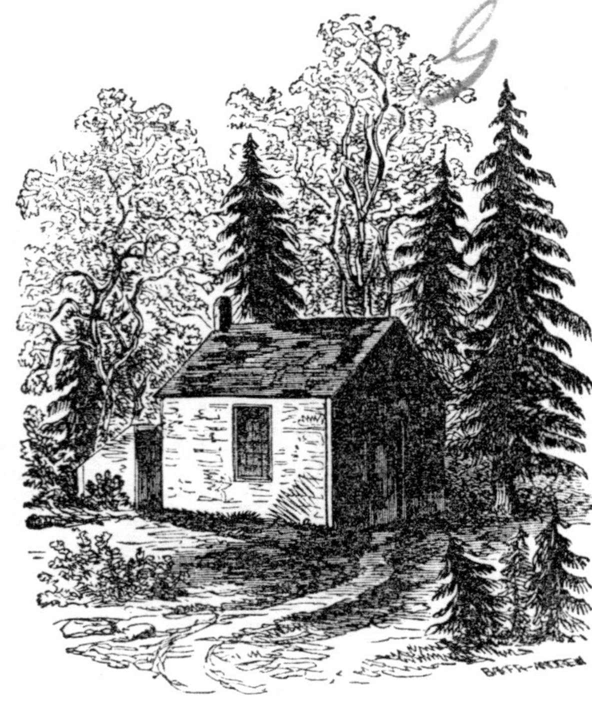

Henry David Thoreau, **Walden; or life in the woods**, 1854, frontispice. Courtesy of the Library of Congress.

[W]hat I have been preparing to say is that in Wildness is the preservation of the world. Every tree sends its fibres forth in search of the Wild. The cities import it at any price. Men plough and sail for it. From the forest and wilderness come the tonics and barks which brace mankind. [...] Give me a wildness whose glance no civilisation can endure,—as if we lived on the marrow of koodoos devoured raw.

Thoreau, 'Walking', 665.

'Wild', like 'barbaric', has been used to describe everyone who is outside of a civilizing order of things. It becomes quite difficult to repurpose 'wildness' because of the way it has been used. We may be critical of these civilizational discourses, yet there's still a romantic charisma attached to the notion of wildness. Could the term be repurposed or has it, in fact, already been repurposed? Is it part of a post-queer, post-natural understanding of illegible forms of being in a body? Queer has a rather recent provenance, whereas wild has a much longer historical arc that dates back to the medieval period and holds within it many different assemblages, people, things and animals.

Burns, 'Jack Halberstam on Wildness'.

WINTER GARDEN

The same artificial 'dream' was induced by the winter garden, which allowed exotic and tropical vegetation to be displayed even in the temperate or cold climates of northern, industrial European cities year-round. The winter garden, like the shopping arcade and Paxton's Crystal Palace at the International Exhibition in London in 1851, was a replica of a world within a world. With the appearance of the winter garden, the meditative, private garden was replaced by the public botanical garden-museum and became a place for mass education and entertainment and a temporary refuge from everyday life.

Graham, *Rock my Religion*, 292.

WOOD WIDE WEB

A tree's most important means of staying connected to other trees is a 'wood wide web' of soil fungi that connects vegetation in an intimate network that allows the sharing of an enormous amount of information and goods. Scientific research aimed at understanding the astonishing abilities of this partnership between fungi and plants has only just begun.

Wohlleben, *The Hidden Life of Trees*, viii.

A tree is not a forest. On its own, a tree cannot establish a consistent local climate. It is at the mercy of wind and weather. But together, many trees create an ecosystem that moderates extremes of heat and cold, stores a great deal of water, and generates a great deal of humidity. And in this protected environment, trees can live to be very old. To get to this point, the community must remain intact no matter what. [...] Every tree, therefore, is valuable to the community and worth keeping around for as long as possible. And that is why even sick individuals are supported and nourished until they recover. Next time, perhaps it will be the other way round, and the supporting tree might be the one in need of assistance.

Wohlleben, *The Hidden Life of Trees*, 4.

The web is so dense that there can be hundreds of kilometers of mycelium under a single footstep. And not only that, that mycelium connects different individuals in the forest, individuals not only of the same species but between species, like birch and fir, and it works kind of like the Internet.

Simard, 'How Trees Talk to Each Other'.

The biggest, darkest nodes are the busiest nodes. We call those hub trees, or more fondly, mother trees, because it turns out that those hub trees nurture their young, the ones growing in the understory. [...] Mother trees colonize their kin with bigger mycorrhizal networks. They send them more carbon below ground. They even reduce their own root competition to make elbow room for their kids. When mother trees are injured or dying, they also send messages of wisdom on to the next generation of seedlings. So we've used isotope tracing to trace carbon moving from an injured mother tree down her trunk into the mycorrhizal network and into her neighboring seedlings, not only carbon but also defense signals. And these two compounds have increased the resistance of those seedlings to future stresses. So trees talk.

Simard, 'How Trees Talk to Each Other'.

Forests aren't simply collections of trees, they're complex systems with hubs and networks that overlap and connect trees and allow them to communicate, and they provide avenues for feedbacks and adaptation, and this makes the forest resilient. That's because there are many hub trees and many overlapping networks. But they're also vulnerable, vulnerable not only to natural disturbances like bark beetles that preferentially attack big old trees but high-grade logging and clear-cut logging.

Simard, 'How Trees Talk to Each Other'.

WORLDS

See page 179 for 'Worlds' by Catriona Sandilands.

WORMS

Darwin watched English worms: many, many of them for many, many hours. He watched how they moved, where they went, and what they did, and, most of all, he watched how they made topsoil or 'vegetable mould': after digesting 'earthly matter', they would deposit the castings at the mouth of their burrows, thus continually bringing to the surface a refined layer of vegetable mold. It is, writes Darwin, 'a marvellous reflection that the whole of the [...] mould over any [...] expanse has passed, and will again pass, every few years through the bodies of worms'. But the claim with which Darwin ends his *Formation of Vegetable Mould through the Actions of Worms with Observations on Their Habits* (1881) is not about biology or agronomy but about history: 'Worms have played a more important part in the history of the world than most persons would at first assume' (Mould, 305). How do worms make history? They make it by making vegetable mold, which makes possible 'seedlings of all kinds', which makes possible an earth hospitable to humans, which makes possible the cultural artifacts, rituals, plans, and endeavors of human history (Mould, 309). Worms also 'make history' by preserving the artifacts that humans make: worms protect 'for an indefinitely long period every object, not liable to decay, which is dropped on the surface of the land, by burying it beneath their castings', a service for which 'archaeologists ought to be grateful to worms' (Mould, 308).

Bennet, *Vibrant Matter*, 95–96.

W continues on page 183.

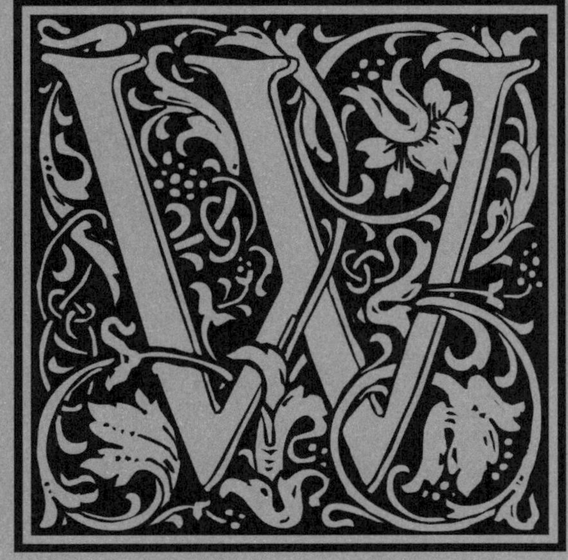

William Morris, **Letter W**.

WALLFLOWER

Jonny Bruce

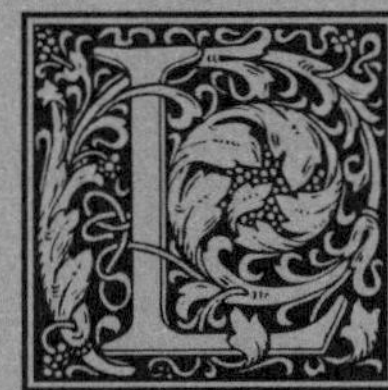

Last June, whilst clearing the cold frames that run along the side of Prospect Cottage, I discovered a cache of plant labels under the tangle of weeds, broken pots, and sun-bleached plastic. Among them was a simple white label on which, in Jarman's own unmistakable cursive, the word *wallflower* had been hurriedly scrawled. Over the years researching and working in the garden at Prospect I have handled many unique objects often inscribed with that distinctive script. However, there is something intimate about a handwritten label—an aide memoir—which tells of a process, of a seed being sown, of a cutting potted.

Even after I had sorted and stored the labels, the word *wallflower* hung in the air, catching on stray associations that surrounded my imaginings about Jarman and his garden. Turning this word revealed different strands of significance—a multifold metaphor of Jarman's own nature and the queer world he inhabited. However, before unpicking these threads, it is necessary to explain what a wallflower is.

Botanically, wallflower is one common name given to the short-lived, spring-flowering perennial, Erysimum cheiri. Hailing from Southern Europe, this gaudy member of the cabbage family has long been cultivated and has even naturalized in many parts of the British Isles. While the petals of the wild species tend towards the bright yellow of oilseed rape, selected forms have brought pink, orange, and deep, velvety reds into its spectrum. Adapted to the dry, poor soils of the Mediterranean, wallflowers thrive among the stones of Dungeness, where they liberally self-sow. Favouring the bases of walls on the leeward-side of the cottage, their generous blooms seem to deny the harshness of their environment.

While we are attracted to this floriferousness, such ostentatious display is at odds with the other common meaning of wallflower, used to describe a shy person more likely to be found at the edge of the room than the heart of the party. Thus, within this unassuming word lies an essential contradiction—a contradiction that anyone who has delved into the life and work of Derek Jarman would quickly recognize.

In the swinging London of the late nineteen-sixties and nineteen-seventies, Jarman was a vibrant part of a queer scene that included artists like David Hockney, Patrick Procktor, and Andrew Logan. Logan's *Alternative Miss World,* a satirical pageant of radical drag, is an excellent example of how comfortable Jarman was at centre stage. Having come in third at the inaugural *Miss World* in 1972, he did eventually claim the crown in 1975 as Miss Crêpe Suzette, admitting many years later, in a *Face to Face* interview with Jeremy Isaacs, that 'it was the one time in my life I really wanted to win'.

However, there was also a quieter side which distanced him from this set. He considered himself an 'edge figure', finding stability in the garden, away from London, which—having been a nomad all his life—he described as an anchor. His friend and collaborator, Neil Bartlett, captured this tension well in his introduction to *Smiling in Slow Motion*, Jarman's final set of published diaries: 'He was noisy, glittering and public...But he was also a very private man, happiest when working alone or with small bands of fellow conspirators, under the wire and off the radar'.[1]

1 Derek Jarman, **Smiling in Slow Motion**, Penguin, 2018

The introvert wallflower within the extrovert wallflower.

Showiness is often criticized as indulgent but the wallflower's tenacity speaks of hope. In an article on the 'Culture of the Wallflower' for the 1848 publication *The Floricultural Cabinet*, the horticulturalist A. Briton enthuses how the wallflower 'attaches itself to the desolate, and enlivens the ruins which time and neglect would otherwise have rendered terrible'. Jarman echoes these lines in *Modern Nature* when he describes wallflowers having 'a special place in my heart' and how it 'grows wild here on the cliffs of Folkestone. And in Somerset, where I spent much of my childhood, it covered the stone walls...shedding its tints of golden dye on which the morning sunbeams love to rest'.

Plants for Jarman were receptacles of meaning. They held stories and personal significance beyond aesthetic appearance. He loved their history and folklore and his own story is populated with flowers which 'spring up and entwine themselves like bindweed along the footpaths of my childhood'. One such flower-strewn path was his fledgling sexuality, and he recalls how as skinny nine-year-olds he and a classmate would push through the hedge to a hidden corner of the school grounds, where they lay naked on a carpet of violets exploring 'the contours of forgotten landscapes' with the 'obsessive violets drawing the evening shadows to themselves, our fingers touching in the purple'.

Tragically, it is along this same path that one can find the origins of contradiction. Betrayed to the night matron, they were caught in bed, an act for which he was beaten and publicly lectured. Unsurprisingly, he became demoralized and reclusive and enjoyed no other sexual contact for thirteen years. The frustration is palpable when reading his later accounts of his own adolescence *'corrupted by heterosexuality'*. Those innocent violets of youth so cruelly traumatized into shrinking violets and wallflowers. While not every gay man has had this exact experience, most will recognize the restrictive shame.

By the 1980s, shame had taken on new colours as the crisis of HIV/AIDS unfolded and it is hard to overstate the importance and bravery of Jarman's decision to reveal his positive diagnosis in December 1986. As one of the first public figures to be open about his status, he confronted societal prejudice and discriminatory government policy to shine a light for the beleaguered queer community, which Jarman felt had become 'a ghetto of frightened and unhappy people'. Jarman was unapologetically gay and the camp extravagance of his art was inherently political. Even today when so much ground has been gained towards social equality, homophobia and transphobia still insinuate themselves into the everyday. As the exuberant wallflowers of Prospect Cottage seem to deny the harsh conditions of Dungeness, so the irreverent flamboyance of queer culture—despite constant attempts to co-opt it—continues to exist as an act of protest.

While I would like to propose *wallflower* as symbolic of queer resistance, it feels appropriate to the intimacy of my initial discovery that the final thread left to unpick speaks of Jarman's own experience. For while 1986 saw Jarman diagnosed with HIV, it was also the year he met Keith Collins, the love of his life. Although I came to Prospect Cottage through Jarman's reputation as a filmmaker, it was Keith who welcomed and encouraged me into the garden. I was only four years old when Jarman died in 1994 and Keith would go on to care for Prospect for almost 25 years, until his own sudden death from brain cancer in August 2018. In all the time I spent with Keith, he never claimed ownership but rather explained how he would always care for this garden out of duty and remembrance for the man he loved. In the language of flowers, wallflowers connote 'true love in adversity' and it is fitting that those selfsame wallflowers, sown by Derek and tended by Keith, continue to flourish among the stones.

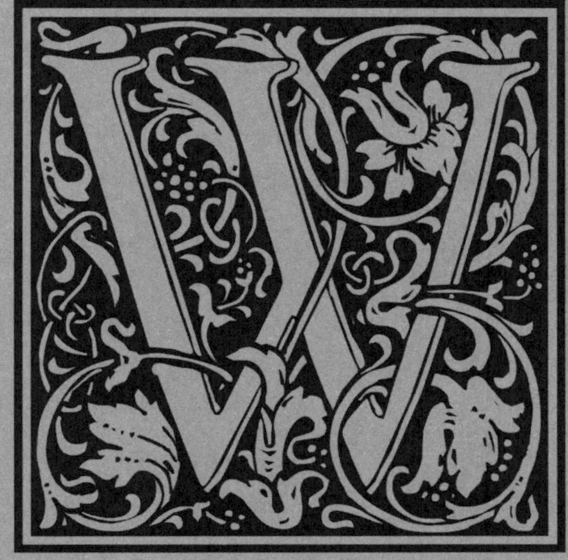

William Morris, **Letter W.**

WORLDS

Catriona Sandilands

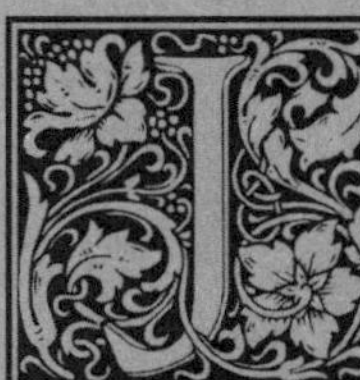

anuary. On Galiano Island, BC (Canada) where I am writing, the month is long, dark, damp, and cold. Especially in COVID isolation, it is a long stretch of hibernation. The woodstove is lit and there is a pot of bean and tomato soup on top, complete with some of the overwintering kale from the garden. Part of the annual winter ritual, the first seed catalogue also arrived in the mail yesterday. Amid my enjoyment of the January sounds, smells, and tastes, I am also called to imagine future seasons with luscious pictures of peas, beans, tomatoes, summer squash, and annual herbs, not to mention the abundant flowers I can't help but miss in these somewhat monochromatic times. Black Krim tomatoes: 'The flesh is tinted green and has a wonderful, almost salty quality'. Glorious Gleam nasturtiums: 'Large, fragrant, double and semi-double, multicoloured flowers blanket the plants … [and] spill over a low wall for a great effect'. Celebration Swiss chard: 'Thick red, yellow, rose, gold, and white stems bear slightly savoyed leaves of burgundy and green'.[1]

Seed catalogues inspire world-making. Last year, for the first time, I drew a careful grid of my vegetable garden on a sheet of paper, measuring out in miniature which plants would go where: who should and shouldn't be planted next to whom, which plants have similar needs for water and fertilizer, the timing of the peas up the lattice in relation to that of the beets growing underneath them. It was a deeply enriching experience. In my research and planning, I learned a great deal more about companion planting, and about the diverse plant-human-pollinator-soil worlds that different food gardeners envision and practice. Of course, there are the important 'three sisters' of many Indigenous nations on this continent: corn, beans, and squash, in which beans tendril up the growing corn, and squash delight in their combined shade throughout the summer and fruit in the fall (the beans also fix nitrogen for the other two, and the squash repay the collective favour by keeping weeds at bay). But there are also other worlds. Interplanting strawberries with leafy herbs and vegetables deters hungry birds, attracts important pollinators, and prompts nutrient-sharing. Planting calendula among tomatoes repels a host of predatory insects and attracts pollinator ones; including basil in the mix both amplifies predator-repellence and, I am told, improves tomato flavour (not to mention the abundant joys of the calendula and basil themselves). However, fennel is not a good idea for a small garden like mine, as its allelopathic properties inhibit the growth of many vegetables and cause others to bolt (which is a shame as I love fennel). No matter how you approach it, garden world-making involves careful attention to the needs and desires of the many beings who are essential to the world's unfolding.

However, as any gardener will tell you, even the most carefully planned world-

1 All descriptions are from the West Coast Seeds **Gardening Planning Guide 2021**.

makings may not go according to the plans of their human imaginers. Last year, despite my careful grids, some of my cherry tomatoes went unexpectedly rogue: they took up all the nutrients that I had otherwise imagined would be shared with cucumbers, basil, and summer squash, and they also refused to stay inside the caged territories I had assigned them. Although these tomatoes were supposedly all 'determinate' varieties, apparently they did not read the catalogue as they spilled abundantly and prolifically into all the spaces they possibly could, meaning that I had more (albeit delicious) tomatoes than I could have imagined but relatively few of anything else (although the calendula are still blooming at the edges of the bed deep into January, for which I am grateful). The kale and chard grew very well, as did the peas and beans, but the beets did not for reasons that I don't entirely understand as I babied them along with sensitive thinning and encouraging conversations. Perhaps too much nitrogen in the soil? Not enough phosphorous? Perhaps the soil, although I carefully prepared it before planting, was still too compacted? Should I have side-dressed before planting them? I will learn for next time.

All this is to say: world-making in the garden is not only about human desires, and many gardeners have understood this reality for a long time before me. Although there are garden traditions that *aspire* to tight control—there is no question, for example, that a determination to 'master nature' is part of some European garden cultures (including their North American 'lawn and order' offspring)—the reality faced by people who actually *work* in gardens is that these worlds are very much multispecies endeavours and, further, that they are also beholden to even more elemental actors: light, heat, cold, water, air, minerals. Gardens are as much about humble, sensitive, and agile response—and 'response-ability', in Donna Haraway's terms—as they are about even the most thoughtful human planning.[2] Even a small vegetable garden like mine is an ongoing process of complex co-creation, and an important part of the world that a garden creates, at the end of the day (on top of tomato abundance), is a greater understanding of, and respect for, the many lively desires that go into its making.

2 Donna Haraway, **Staying with the Trouble: Making Kin in the Chthulucene** (Durham: Duke University Press, 2016), 34.

Through her brilliant book *Unthinking Mastery*, Julietta Singh has helped me transform this rather banal horticultural insight into a more sustained philosophy. One of Singh's overall projects in her book is to move toward modes of inhabitation, of the world and of ourselves, that do not aspire to mastery (totalization, control, proprietorship, splitting of subject from object), but rather to a sustained practice of acknowledging shared vulnerability and 'being together in common' that is 'shaped by the intimate awareness of relations of dependency'. As she writes, this project has never been more urgent:

> Even while the discourse of modernity has disavowed [...] dependency through its desire to render the human master of everything, the fragility of the human in the wake and anticipation of so many intercultural and ecological catastrophes can no longer afford to pretend that is it not dependent materially, bodily, and psychically on others, both human and nonhuman.[3]

Not surprisingly, this project takes her into the garden. Against romantic ideas of gardens as utopian spaces of Edenic coexistence or gratifying Georgic productivity (both of which have ideas of mastery lurking not too deep in their narrative soil), Singh wants us to inhabit gardens in a way that 'cultivates discomfort'. Specifically, she asks us to consider the world of the garden as *entangled in* the fraught and often violent world at large and not as a refuge against it. Moreover, she insists we attend to the garden not only as a site of wonder and pleasure, but also as 'a space rife with uncontrollable and at times unwelcome life [whose recognition] begins to upend the stability of the gardener as [masterful] subject'.[4]

Alongside her reflections on her mother's complicated garden and her own, equally complicated experiences of summer work as a tree planter in northern Canada[5], Singh considers the garden writing of Jamaica Kincaid, and especially her extraordinary 1999 essay collection *My Garden (Book)*.

3 Julietta Singh, **Unthinking Mastery: Dehumanism and Decolonial Entanglements** (Durham: Duke University Press, 2018), 21 and 23.

4 Ibid., 170.

5 The idea of a summer job planting trees may sound idyllic and restorative to those unfamiliar with the work, but the reality is the opposite. Tree planters are hired by private companies to work in the waste spaces of often remote, industrially clear-cut forests; workers are typically paid per seedling and work through pounding sun or rain and relentless insects. The repetitive labour is brutal, and the monocultural result is decidedly not a restored forest.

Like Singh, I love this book both because of Kincaid's rich and detailed stories about working and living in her Vermont garden and, perhaps more importantly, because of the way she writes, with exceptional honesty and insight, about the fact that garden-worlds inspire what she calls *vexation* as much as satisfaction in their human participants: 'How agitated I am in the garden, and how happy I am to be so agitated. How vexed I often am when I am in the garden, and how happy I am to be so vexed'.[6] As Singh underlines, for Kincaid these moments of vexation—dissatisfaction, disappointment, failure, frustration, devastation, grief, neurosis, anxiety—are *as important for the garden-world* as any apparently satisfied and successful bloomings, fruitings, designs, profusions, and exuberances. Focusing on the garden as a site of vexation highlights the fact that the gardener's plans turn out, in the end, to be what Kincaid calls 'ordinary', and that the world that actually happens in the garden is *extraordinary*: a multispecies co-creation that both negotiates among and overflows the desires of any of the individual participants, with results that are new and unexpected. The disappointments and failures, from the point of view of the human gardener, are also humbling reminders of more-than-human involvements in world-creation: from this perspective, how happy I am, as Kincaid might say, to be so humbled.[7]

The opening essay in *My Garden (Book)*, 'Wisteria', begins with a question that gardeners often ask of themselves: 'What to do?' In Kincaid's case, the question concerns a *Wisteria floribunda* that is blooming in late July, 'instead of May, the way wisterias in general are supposed to do'.[8] You can hear her agitation: *What to do?* She also tells us, however, that she *likes* to ask this question, 'especially when I myself do not have an answer to it'.[9] When the question comes up and she cannot answer it, she still feels 'confident and secure that someone somewhere has had this same perplexing condition [...] and he or she will explain to me the phenomenon that is in front of me'.[10] However, the answer does not ever arrive; instead, there are only more questions, both hers and others': 'Should I let it go, blooming and blooming, each new bud looking authoritative but also not quite right at all, as if on a dare, a surprise even to itself, looking as if its out-of-seasonness was a *modest, tentative query*?'.[11] *What to do?* introduces her garden as a multispecies community of questioners: Kincaid, other gardeners and garden writers, two oddly-behaving wisteria, some monkshood, a fox, a baby rabbit, roses, tomatoes, a magnolia, a banana tree in a pot, and many others. Rather than a harmonious, holistic tapestry, the garden is *itself* always in a state of vexation: a weaving-together, but also a coming-apart. As she writes:

> Oh, how I like the rush of things, the thickness of things, everything condensed as it is happening, long after it has happened, so that any attempt to understand it will become like an unraveling of a large piece of cloth that has been laid flat and framed and placed as a hanging on a wall and, even then, expected to stand for something.[12]

Kincaid also insists on understanding and working her garden as forms of critical and personal engagement in, and not retreat from, larger sociopolitical worlds. Despite the intentions of some gardeners to create sheltered spaces of refuge and repose from larger-scale political and economic machinations, the reality of gardens is anything but. As spaces, as institutions, and as privileged nodes in global movements of plants and people, gardens are not only worlds but also *in* and *of* the world. Kincaid's focus on writing this engagement connects her agitation in the garden with her discomfort in the world as a whole; further, it demonstrates that gardens and gardening are not benevolent but are, instead, often implicated in inequitable and exploitive relations tied to private property, class, imperialism, and colonialism. In *My Garden (Book)*, she considers her own journey to her Vermont garden in relation to those of the plants she favours—many plants travelled similar routes to get there as enslaved people—and she also frankly describes the racism she experiences in Vermont gardener-worlds as a constituent part of her multispecies experiences of the

6 Jamaica Kincaid, **My Garden (Book)** (New York: Farrar, Strauss and Giroux, 1999), 14.

7 Of course, my enjoyment of humility in relation to a disappointing beet yield is not the same thing as despair over total crop disaster for a small farmer whose subsistence or income depends on it. Letting go of mastery also means building a more resilient network of mutual aid so that both abundance and failure can be shared. As Singh points out, there is a strong connection between mastery and private property.

8 Kincaid, **My Garden (Book)**, 11.

9 Ibid., 11.

10 Ibid., 12.

11 Ibid., my emphasis.

12 Ibid., 24.

13 Ibid., 8.

14 Ibid., 135.

15 Singh, **Unthinking Mastery**, 162.

place. She has, without really knowing why, designed beds that resemble a map of the Caribbean as an 'exercise in memory'.[13] She understands her preferences for particular species and colours as embedded in her early life in Antigua, where 'gardens' were not really part of her experience other than the imperial botanical garden in St. John's, full of plants from anywhere in the tropics but Antigua. She reflects on her personal involvement in gardens, class, colonialism, and appropriation, noting that she is now part of the 'conquering class' that moves plants around the world and ending the book with a description of a plant-collecting trip to China. And she considers the movement of specific plants in/to/ through her garden as part of their global, imperial botanical and horticultural travels, connecting her world, and the worlds of the plant catalogues, nurserymen, and flower shows that are part of it, with the lives of the botanists and imperialists—'land adventurer[s] and botany thie[ves]'—such as Christopher Columbus, Hernando Cortés, Joseph Banks, and Meriweather Lewis, whose work was so instrumental in creating the racist, colonial conditions in which these current worlds unfold.[14]

Kincaid's garden, then, is *worldly* in many senses: globalized, cosmopolitan, and interconnected, as well as grounded, earthy, and thickly immersed in the multispecies present. As Singh also emphasizes, Kincaid brings the imperialist history of gardening into her vexing, questioning, disobedient garden both to remember and to *resist*. Her 'commitment to living along with things [is] tied to colonial histories and the lessons wrought from them' because the violences inflicted by imperialism and colonialism are ongoing and manifest in her garden, and because she chooses to live with and among these violences *otherwise*.[15] Kincaid insists not on 'purifying' the space by, say, working exclusively with native plants (which would, in this view, be an attempt to erase both the garden's history and her own, another sort of mastery), but on disrupting the whole idea that gardens should be spaces of purity in the first place. Gardening self-consciously with hybrid wisteria, rhododendrons, hollyhocks, and roses—and apples, cabbages, carrots, and cucumbers—is, for Kincaid, a form of embodied immersion in a very uncomfortable world history, and her agitation is both a response to her happy lack of control over the plants in her garden, and also part of a principled resistance against the imperial, colonial fiction that gardens are places that create 'proper' landscapes—productive, rationalized, orderly—in the midst of ones that are deemed, by the colonizer, to be wild, unorganized, and under-utilized.[16]

This is a lot to think about as I eat my soup by the fire and leaf through the seed catalogues. Although I have often thought about the gardens in which I live and work as worldly sorts of worlds, I cannot help but be agitated by Singh and Kincaid.[17] *What to do?* This year, I will still plant Black Krim tomatoes (probably too many of them) and they, being 'indeterminate', will require a lot of staking and caging, as well as even more space individually than I gave the plants last year. I will try growing winter squash under my peas instead of beets: the 'Uchiki Red Kuri' look lovely and are supposed to mature nicely early. I will plant more Swiss chard than last year—they are, like the calendula, still growing colourfully in January—and I will move the potatoes to a bed of their own in order to do so (although the slugs may well quash my plans for rainbow chard abundance, especially if it is a wet spring). However, especially in these difficult and uncertain times, I know I cannot disconnect this small garden-world from the larger ones that shape it (any more than I can control the slugs, try as I might). And so the question of *what to do* must also address how to live in the larger world *otherwise*, as Kincaid demonstrates, and how to plant these questions among the flowers and vegetables. I myself do not have definitive answers, but I understand that it is important for me to live with the discomfort as part of the process of finding out. It will take more than dreaming with a seed catalogue.

16 This logic is, of course, part of the so-called Doctrine of Discovery, which claimed, as part of its rationale for occupation, that Indigenous peoples were not working the land to its full potential (or at all). See William Cronon, 'The Trouble with Wilderness: Or, Getting Back to the Wrong Nature', in **Uncommon Ground: Rethinking the Human Place in Nature**, ed. William Cronon (New York: W.W. Norton & Co., 1995, 69–90.

17 For example, Catriona Sandilands, 'I See My Garden as a Barometer of Climate Change'. **The Guardian**, 9 July 2018, theguardian.com/commentisfree/2018/jul/09/i-see-my-garden-as-a-barometer-of-climate-change.

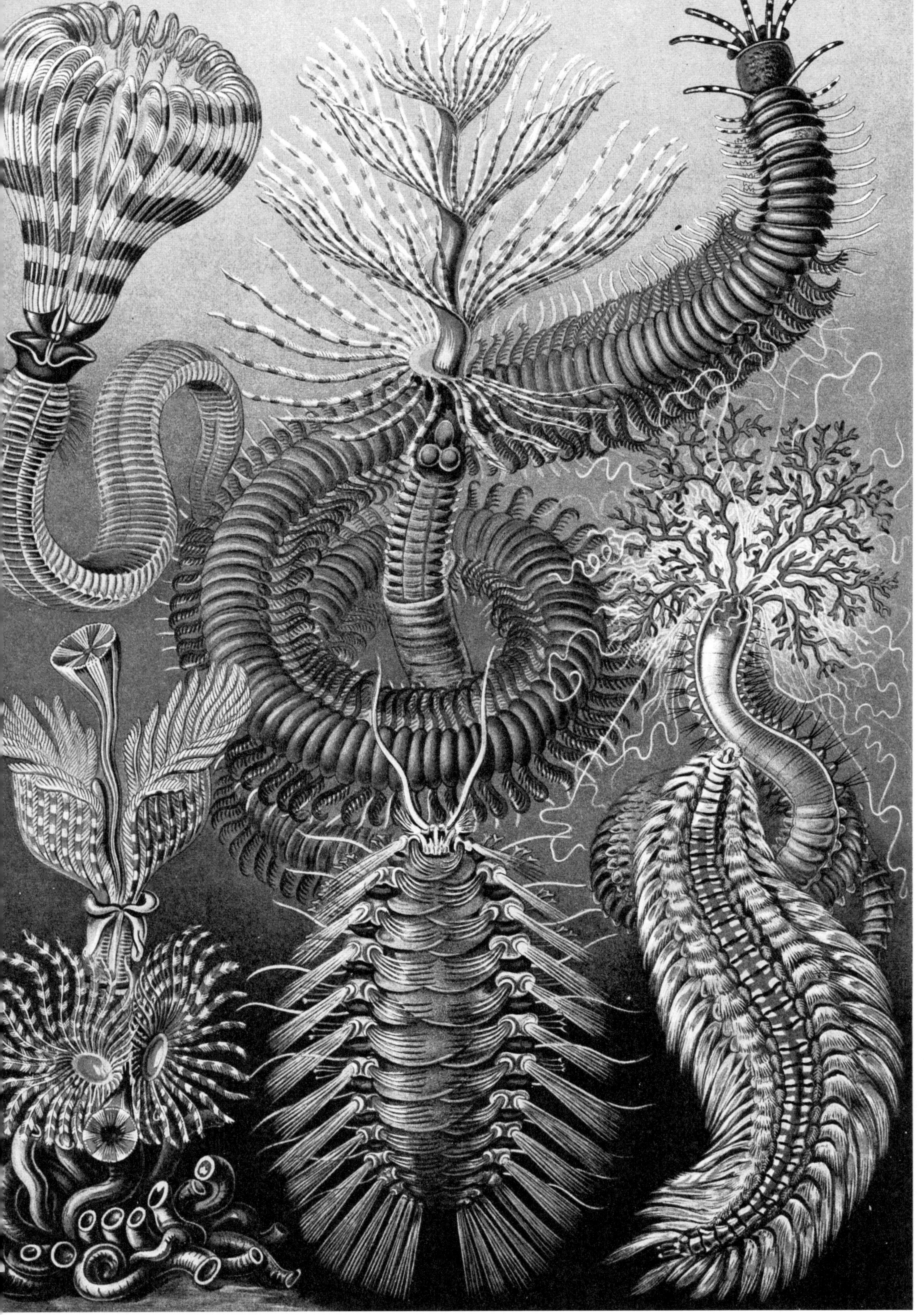

Ernst Haeckel, **Plate 4: Diatomea** from **Kunstformen der Natur**, 1904, engraving.

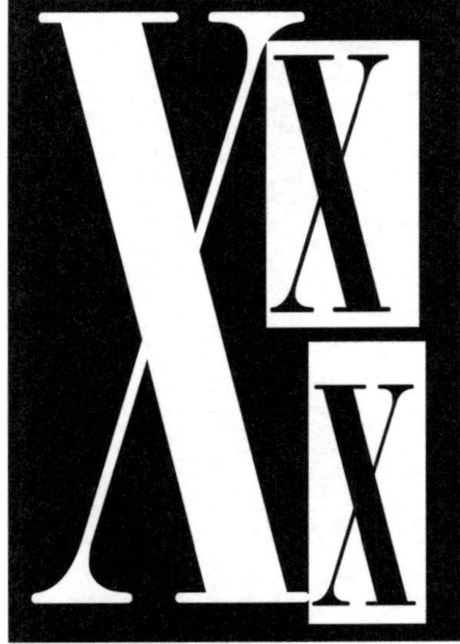

XENOPHOBIA

Over the last two decades, landscape designers have tended to avoid the use of plants that are labeled exotic, or non-native. Many professionals and laypeople who are interested in nature, landscape, and gardens assume that what they believe are indigenous, or native, plants are unquestionably better than those that are not.

> Gröning and Wolschke-Bulmahn, 'The Native Plant Enthusiasm', 75.

XERISCAPING

In Latin, *xero* means dry and *scape* means landscape or view. As an official landscaping technique, xeriscaping seems to have 'originated' in the 1980's as a result of ongoing, multi-year droughts plaguing the Western United States, but people have been planting to match their climate for centuries. [...]

Seven Principles of Xeriscaping

1. Sound landscape planning and design.
2. Limitation of turf (commonly referred to as lawn) to appropriate, functional areas.
3. Use of water efficient plants.
4. Efficient irrigation.
5. Soil amendments.
6. Use of mulches.
7. Appropriate landscape maintenance.

> Rodomsky-Bish, 'The Seven Principles of Xeriscaping'.

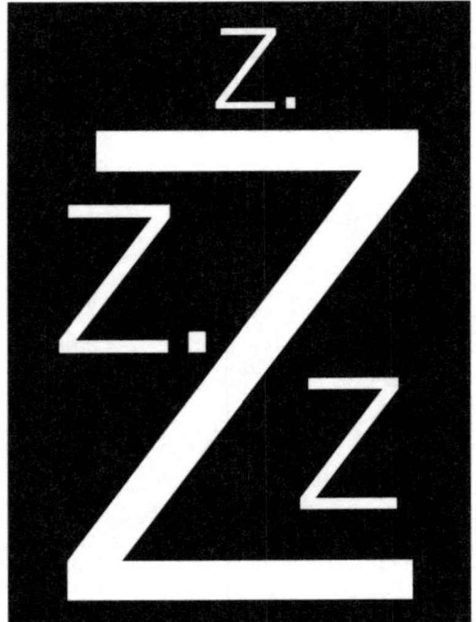

ZEN GARDEN

The rock-and-sand garden of *Ryoan-ji*, the 'Temple of the Peaceful Dragon' in north-west Kyoto, is an example of a *kare-sansui* garden in its purest form—without water, without plants, without even a tree. The garden lies on the south side of the *hojo*, the abbot's quarters, and is bounded by a low wall. It is an outstanding illustration of that enduring characteristic of the Japanese sense of beauty, namely the superimposition of natural and rectangular form.

> Nitschke, *Japanese Gardens*, 89.

The evolution of religious, artistic and social thinking in Japan is mirrored in the role assigned to rocks and plants by Japanese garden designers. This role had changed greatly over the course of history. It began as the imitation of the external forms of nature, but as the laws of nature became increasingly understood, its focus shifted to the imitation of the essence of nature and its internal mode of operation, only to move on, in modern times, to the superimposition of man's egoistic will on nature.

> Nitschke, *Japanese Gardens*, 27.

But the empty expanse of sand in front of a Buddhist temple or the blank piece of paper in Zen painting is not in itself sufficient to inspire such profound insights. It needs the sophisticated interplay of form with its non-form, of object with its space. It is here, perhaps, that we find the ultimate purpose of garden art—to provide the necessary forum for such insight. The garden of *Ryoan-ji* symbolizes neither a natural nor a mythological landscape. Indeed, it symbolizes nothing, in the sense that symbolizes not. I see in it an abstract composition of 'natural' objects in space which is intended to induce meditation. It belongs to the art of void.

> Nitschke, *Japanese Gardens*, 92.

One can make gardens according to the ancient meanings or according to the ancient shapes, but actually the person who is designing the garden and building it is from the present time and no other. The significance of the fact that we are people who live in the present is that we cannot make gardens that embody the meaning of the old times or have the shape of those times. So, in this case, we can only make a garden that is an imitation and this is meaningless.

> Shigemori, 'Shin-Sakuteiki', 292.

Cage's interest in Japanese gardens became manifest in the Ryoanji works, a series of compositions and visual art works. It is not surprising that he found a strong resonance with his own ideas in Japanese gardens. Japanese aesthetics played an important role in the emergence of modernism and in the formation of artists of Cage's generation; furthermore, Cage developed a personal interest in Japanese culture through his engagement with Zen, his friendships with Japanese artists, and his visits to Japan. The art of garden design was formed by the same historical and cultural forces that shaped the other traditional arts of Japan, with which it shares underlying aesthetic principles. Parallels between garden design and Cage's work are consequently not difficult to find.

> Whittington, 'Digging in John Cage's Garden', 12.

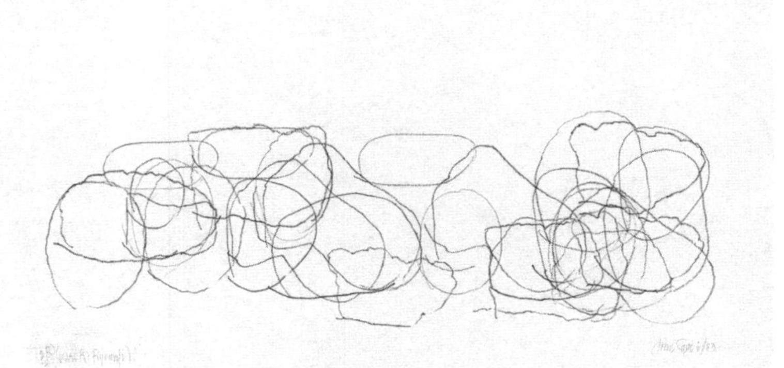

John Cage, **2R/4 Where R = Ryoanji**, 1983, drawing, 25.7 × 48.9 cm. Courtesy Pierpont Morgan Library, New York and John Cage Trust.

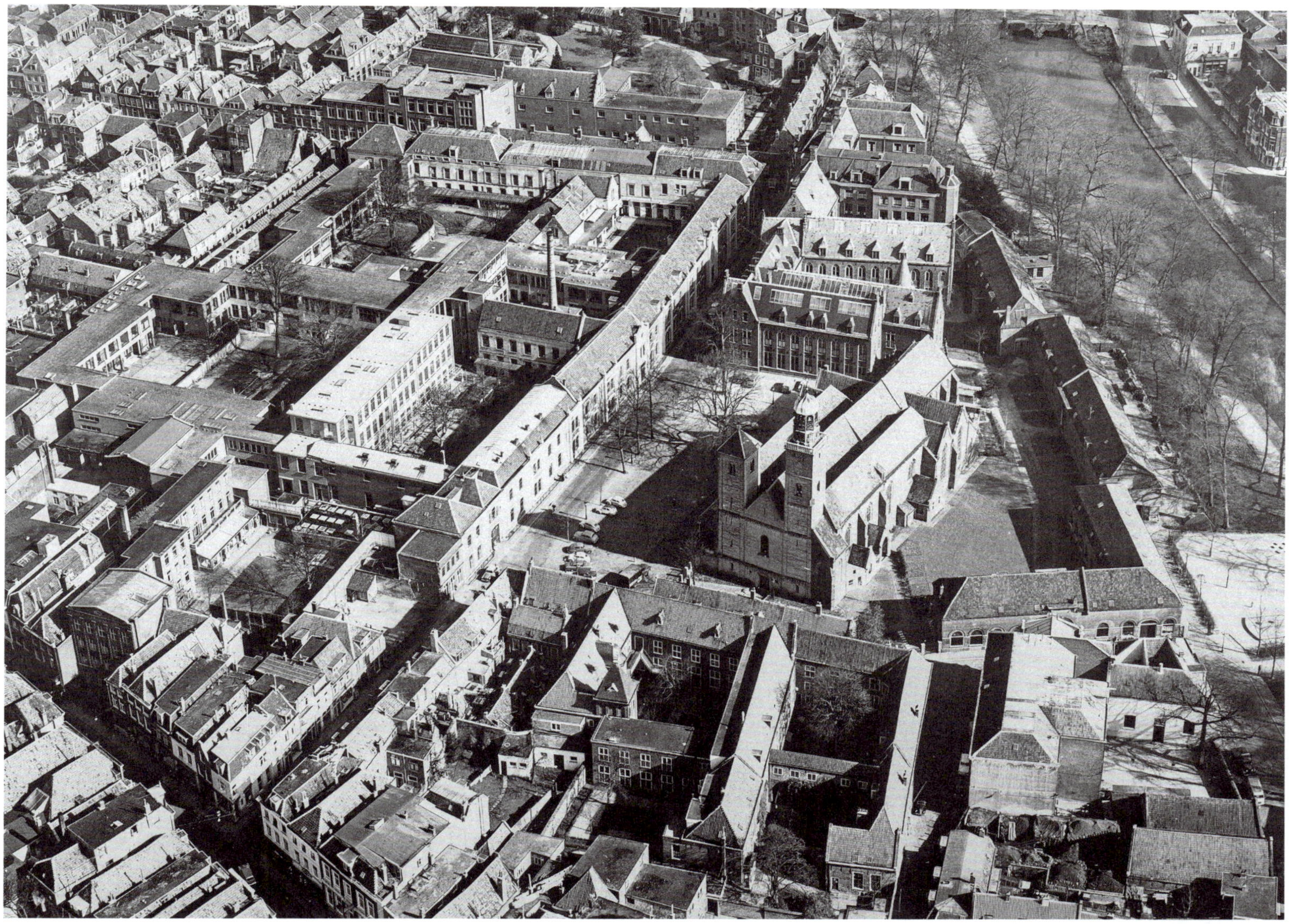

Centraal Museum Utrecht, 1960-1961, aerial photo. Photo: Centraal Museum Utrecht/KLM Aerospace.

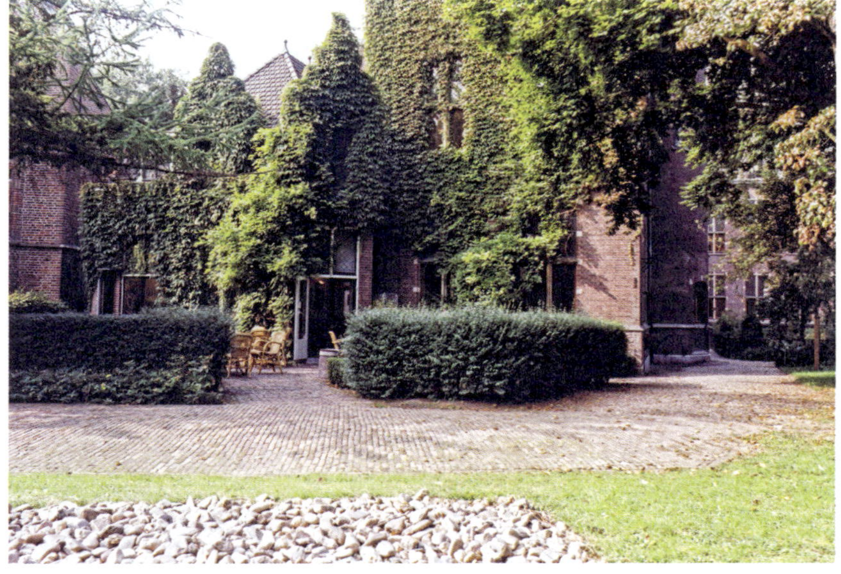

Garden Centraal Museum Utrecht, 1996. Photo: Centraal Museum Utrecht/Dea Rijper.

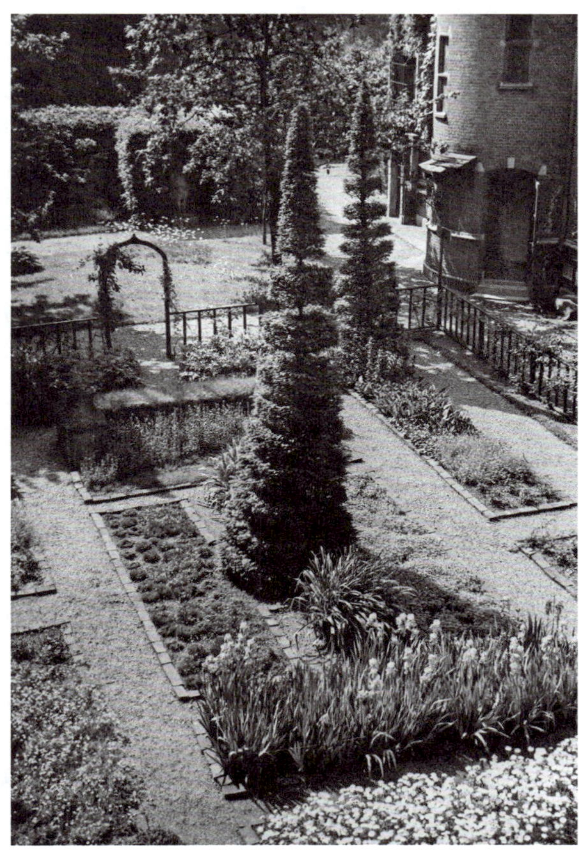

Garden Centraal Museum, 1942. Photo: Centraal Museum Utrecht/Claar Pronk.

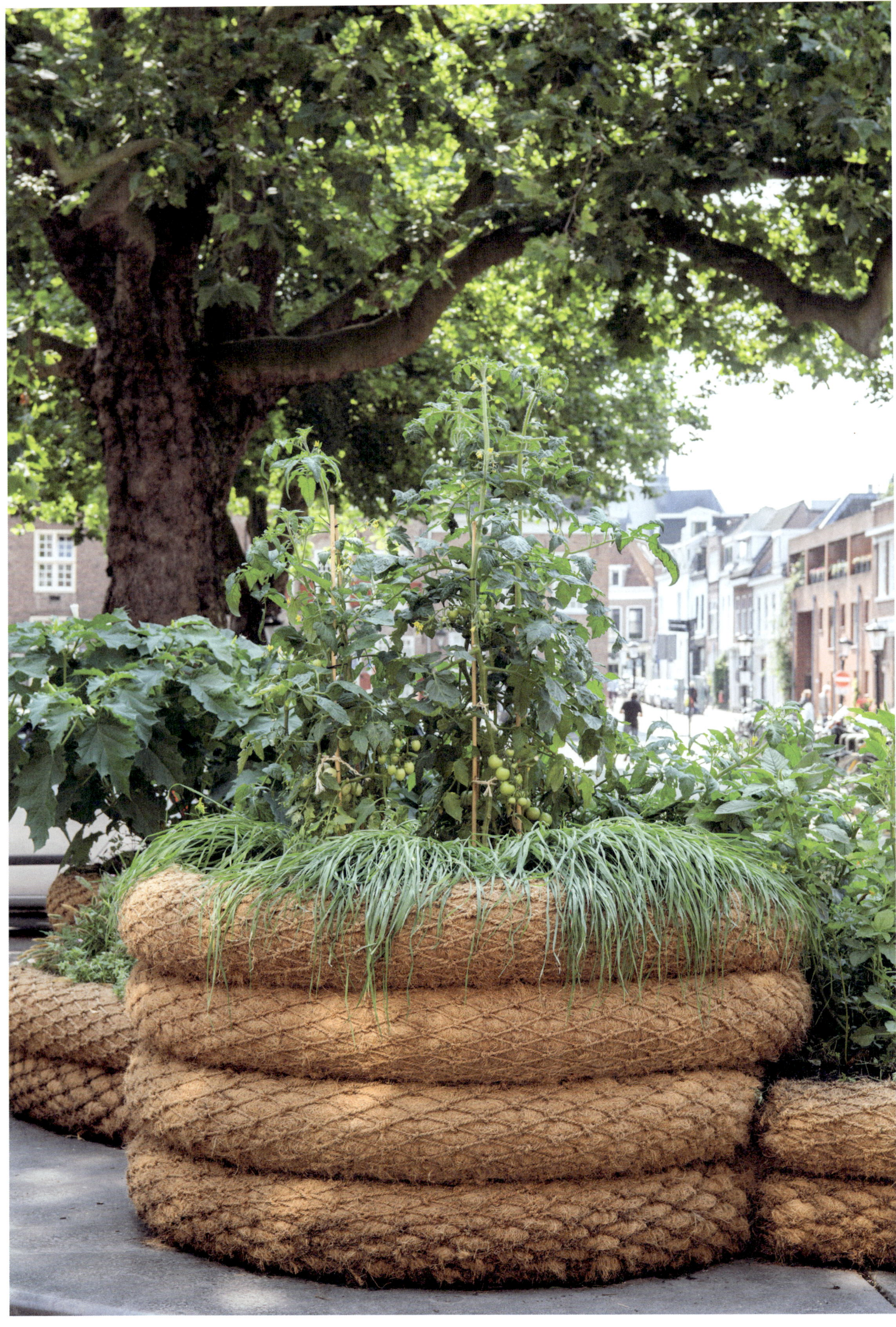

Maria Thereza Alves, **Seeds of Change: A Ballast Flora Garden (Liverpool)**, 2021, courtesy the artist and Michel Rein, Paris/Brussels. Photography Robert Oosterbroek.

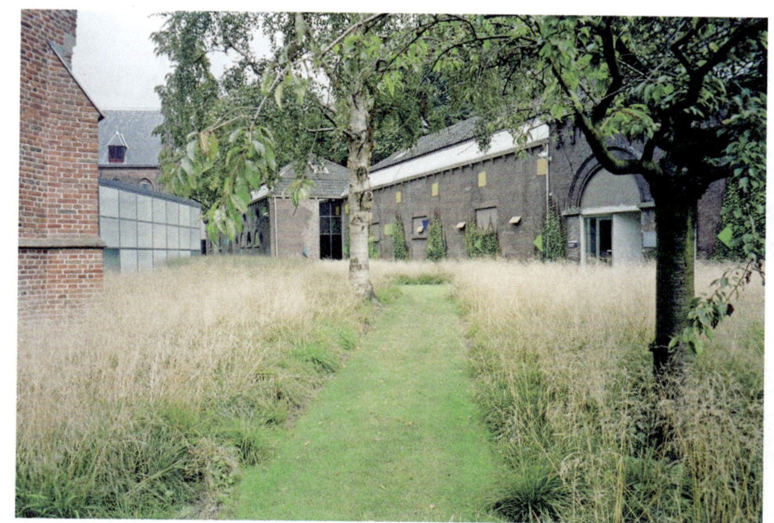

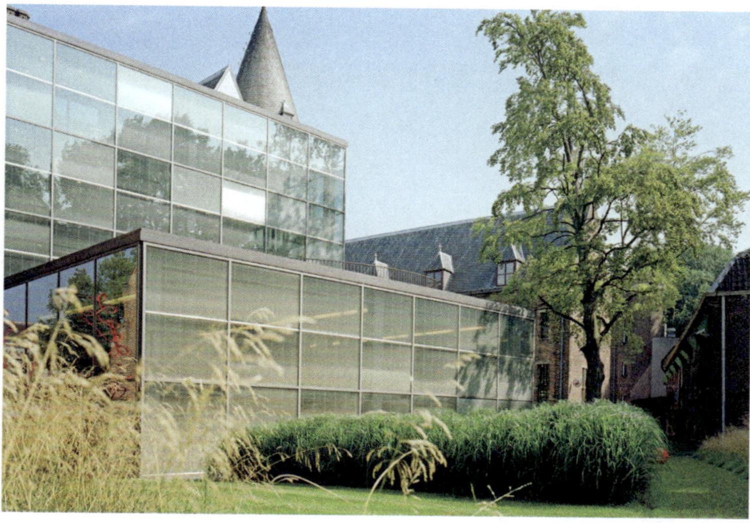

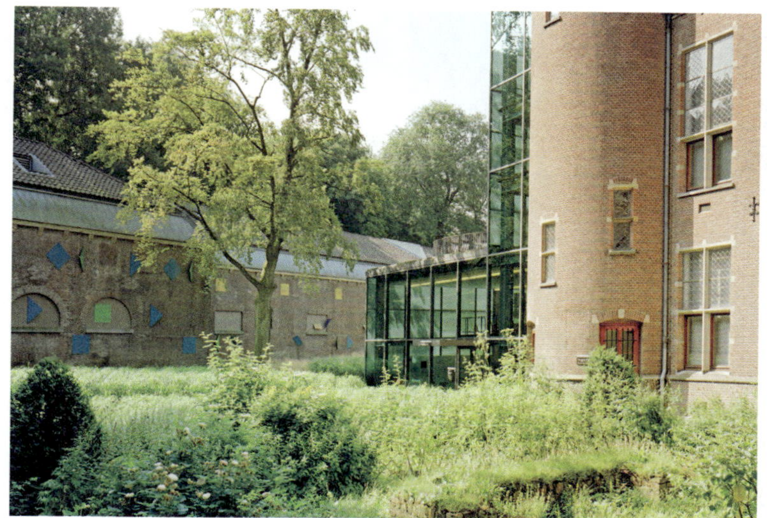

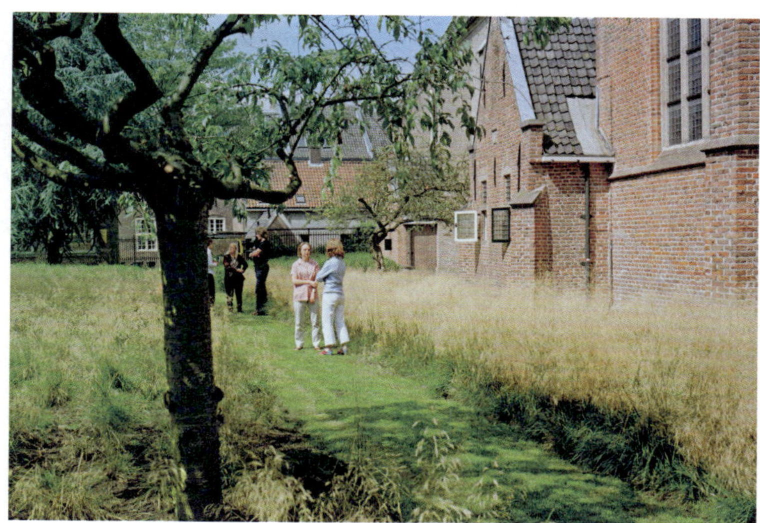

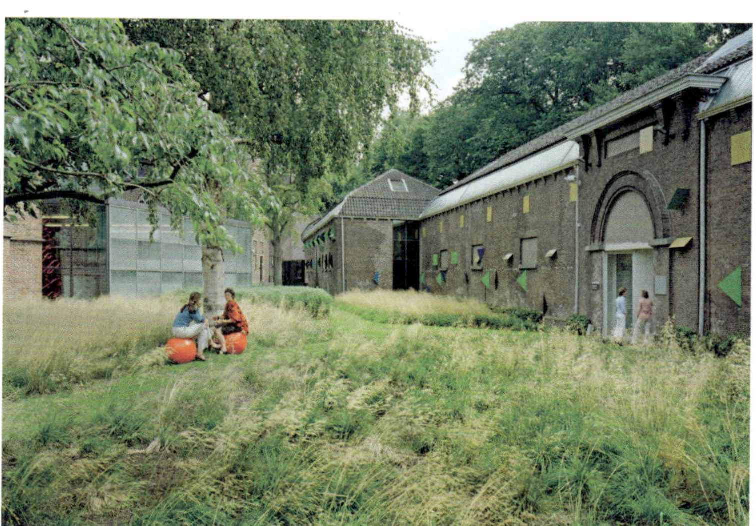

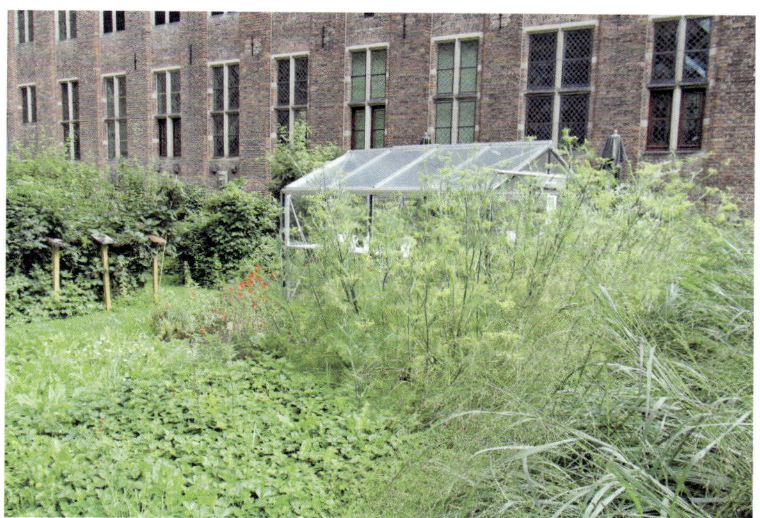

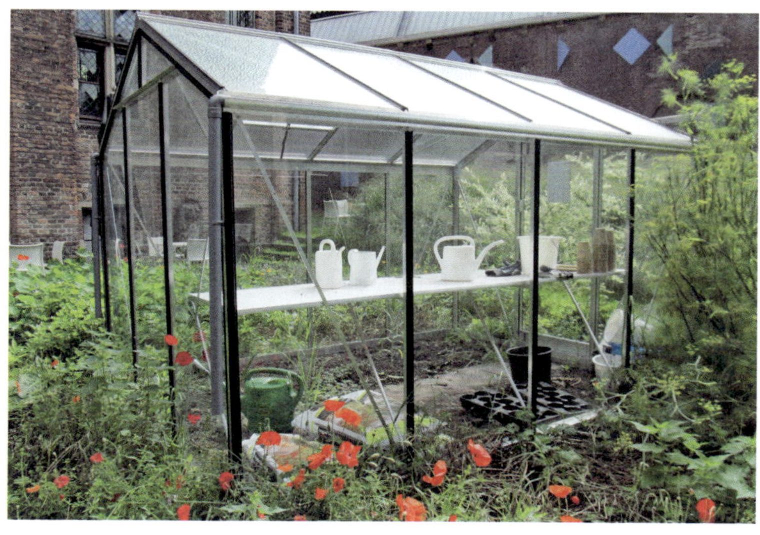

Garden Centraal Museum Utrecht, September 2002.
Photo: Centraal Museum Utrecht/Hans Wilschut.

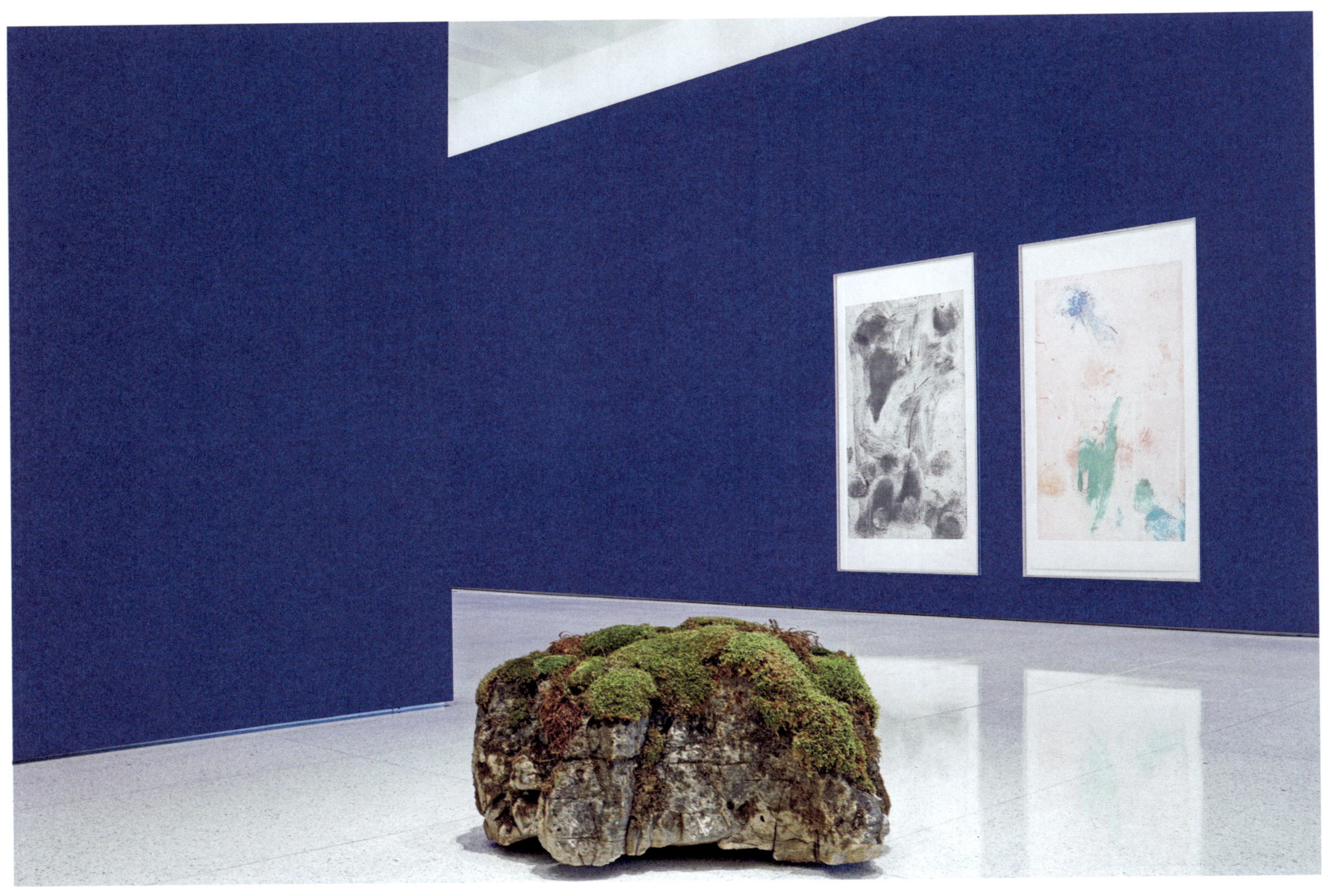

Andrea Büttner, **Limestone with Moss**, 2015, installation view at Walker Art Center, Minneapolis. Courtesy Walker Art Center, Minneapolis/Andrea Büttner/Hollybush Gardens. Photo: Gene Pittman.

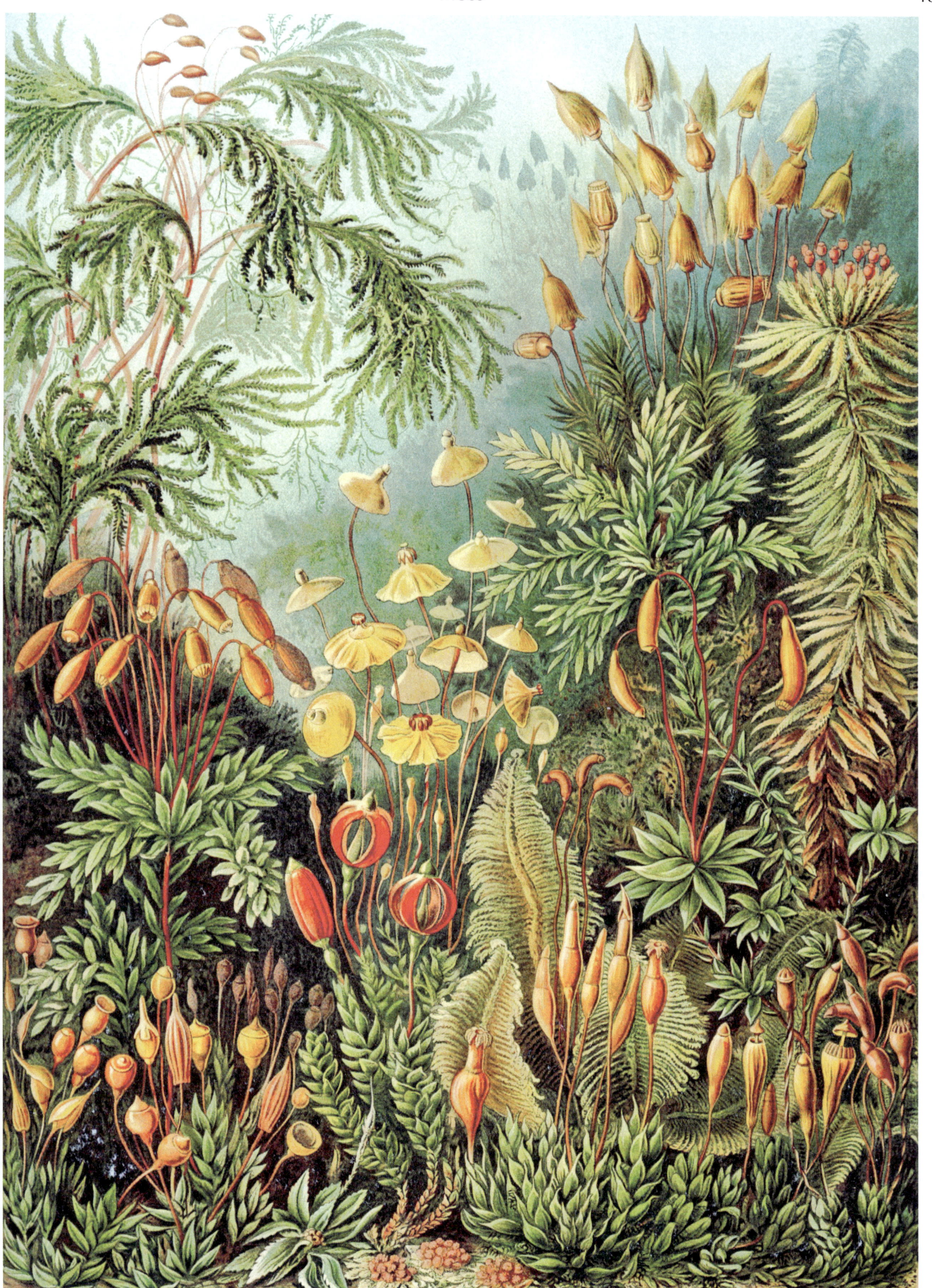

Ernst Haeckel, **Plate 72, Muscinae** from **Kunstformen der Natur**, 1904, engraving.

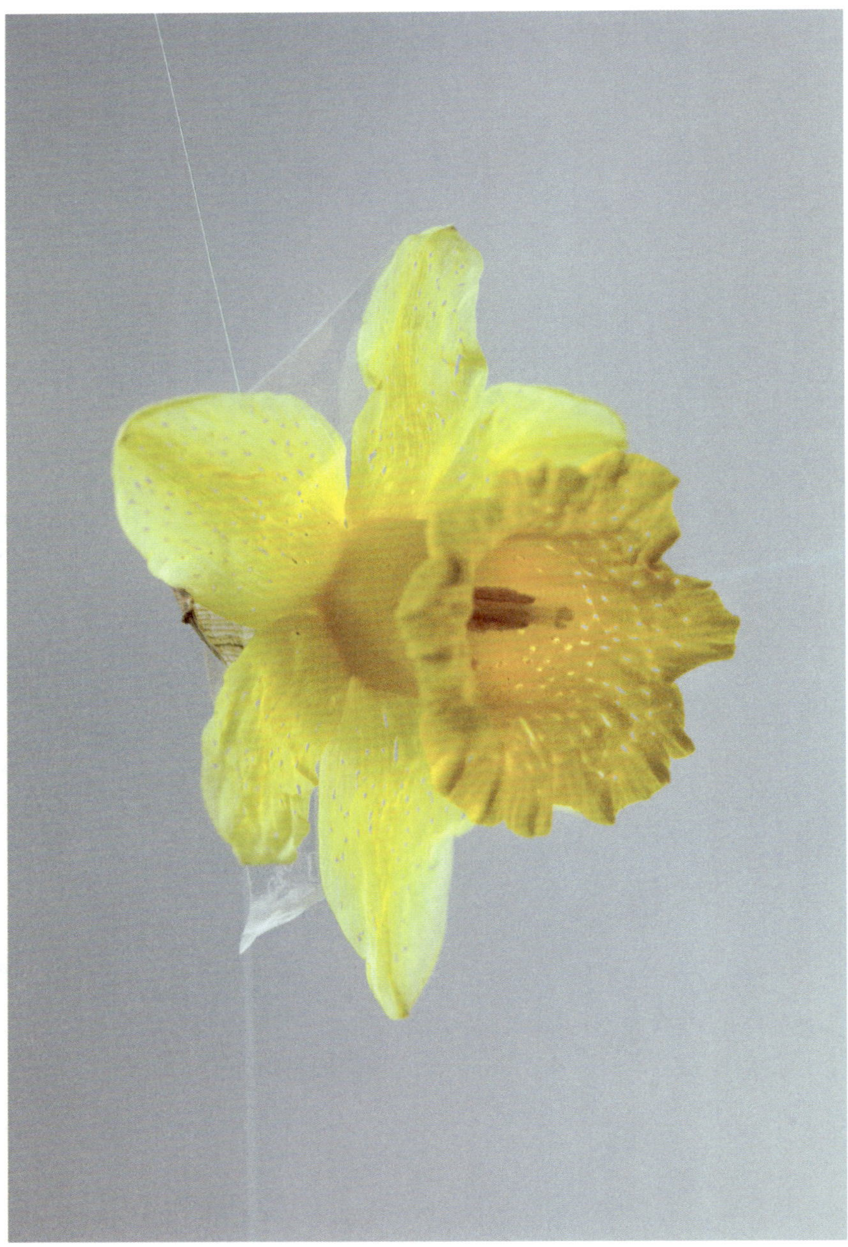

Elspeth Diederix, **Daffodil**, 2018, photograph. Courtesy Elspeth Diederix and Stigter Van Doesburg, Amsterdam.

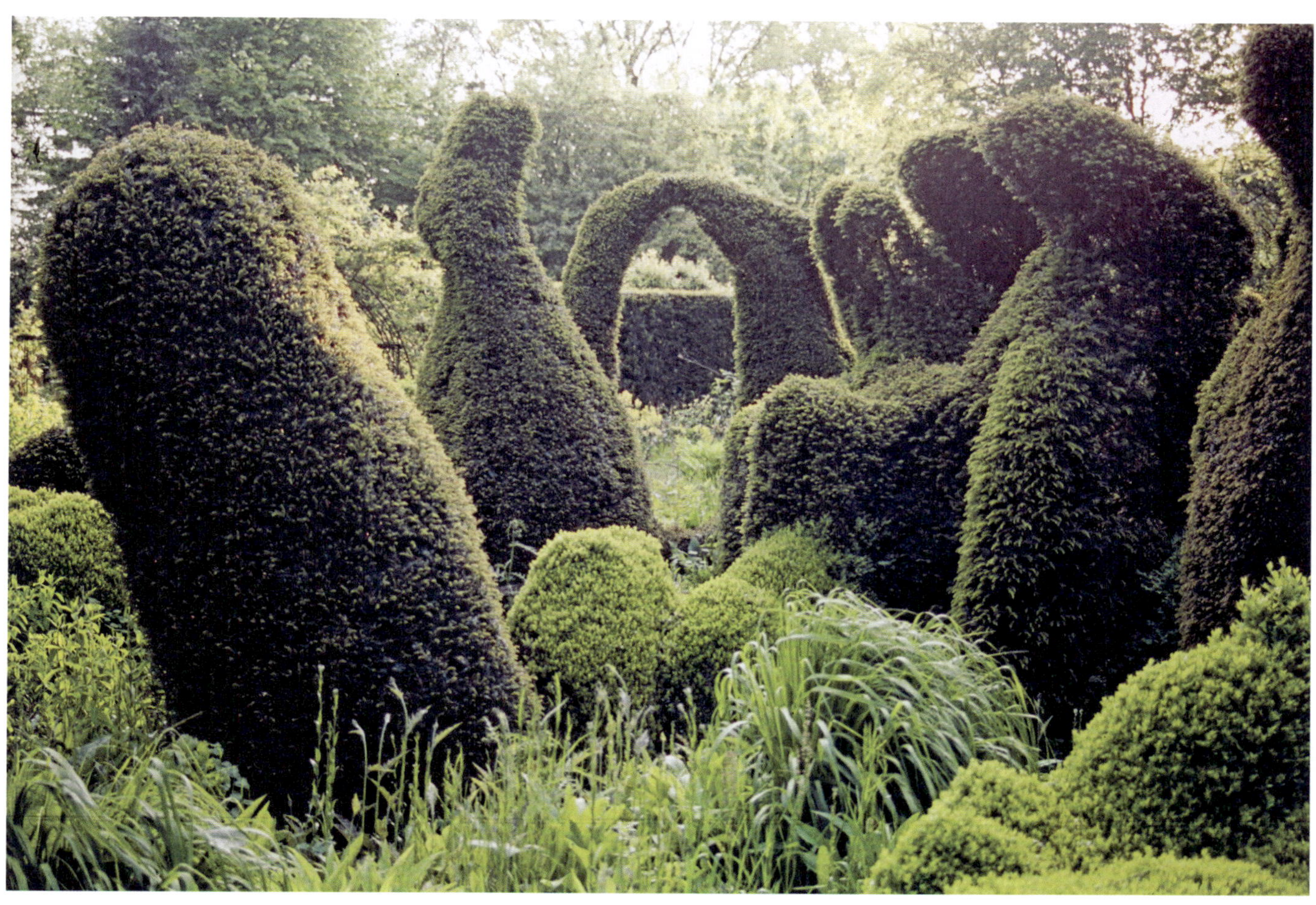

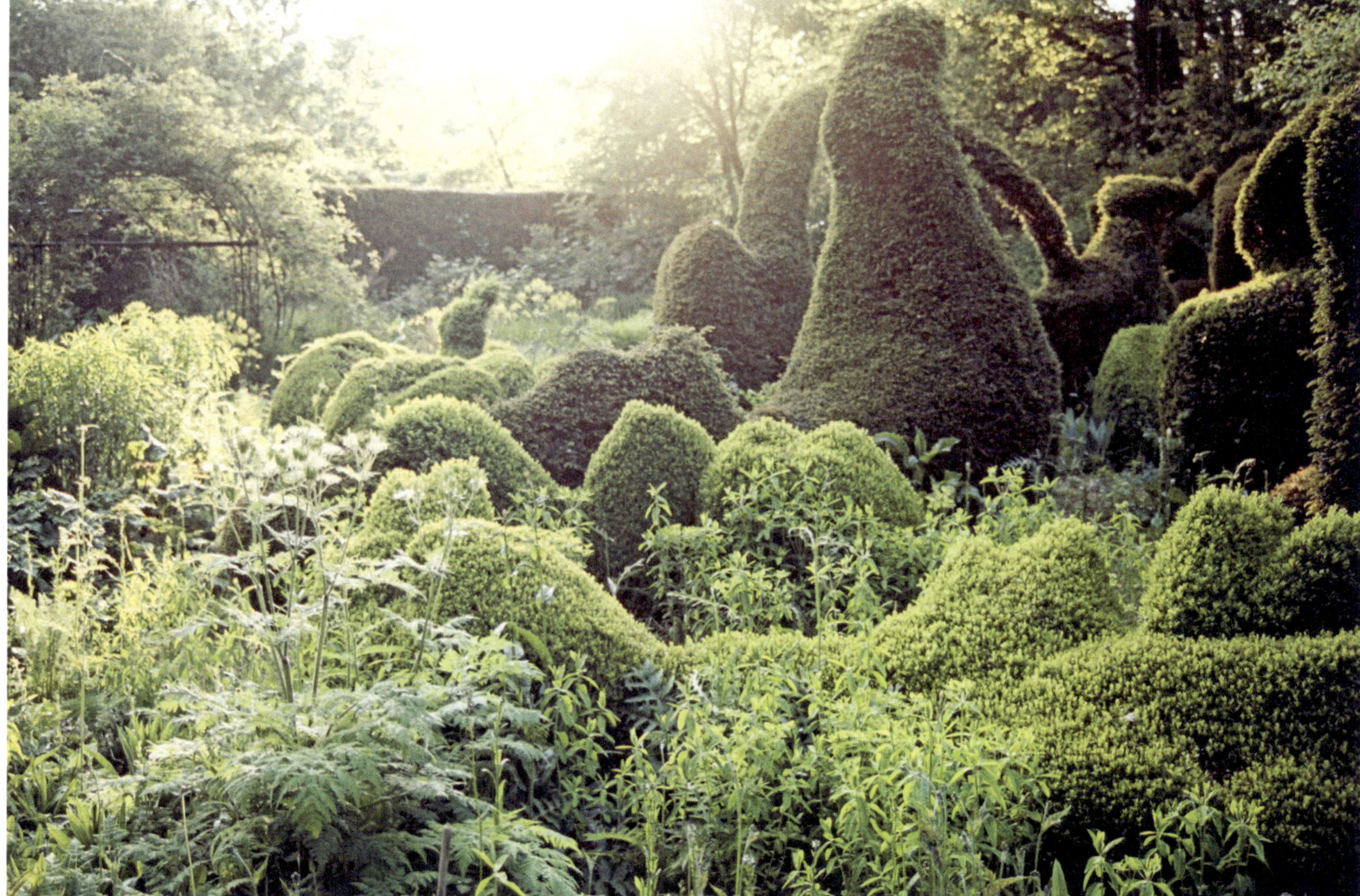

Henk Gerritsen and Anton Schlepers, **Priona Gardens**. Courtesy Priona Gardens.

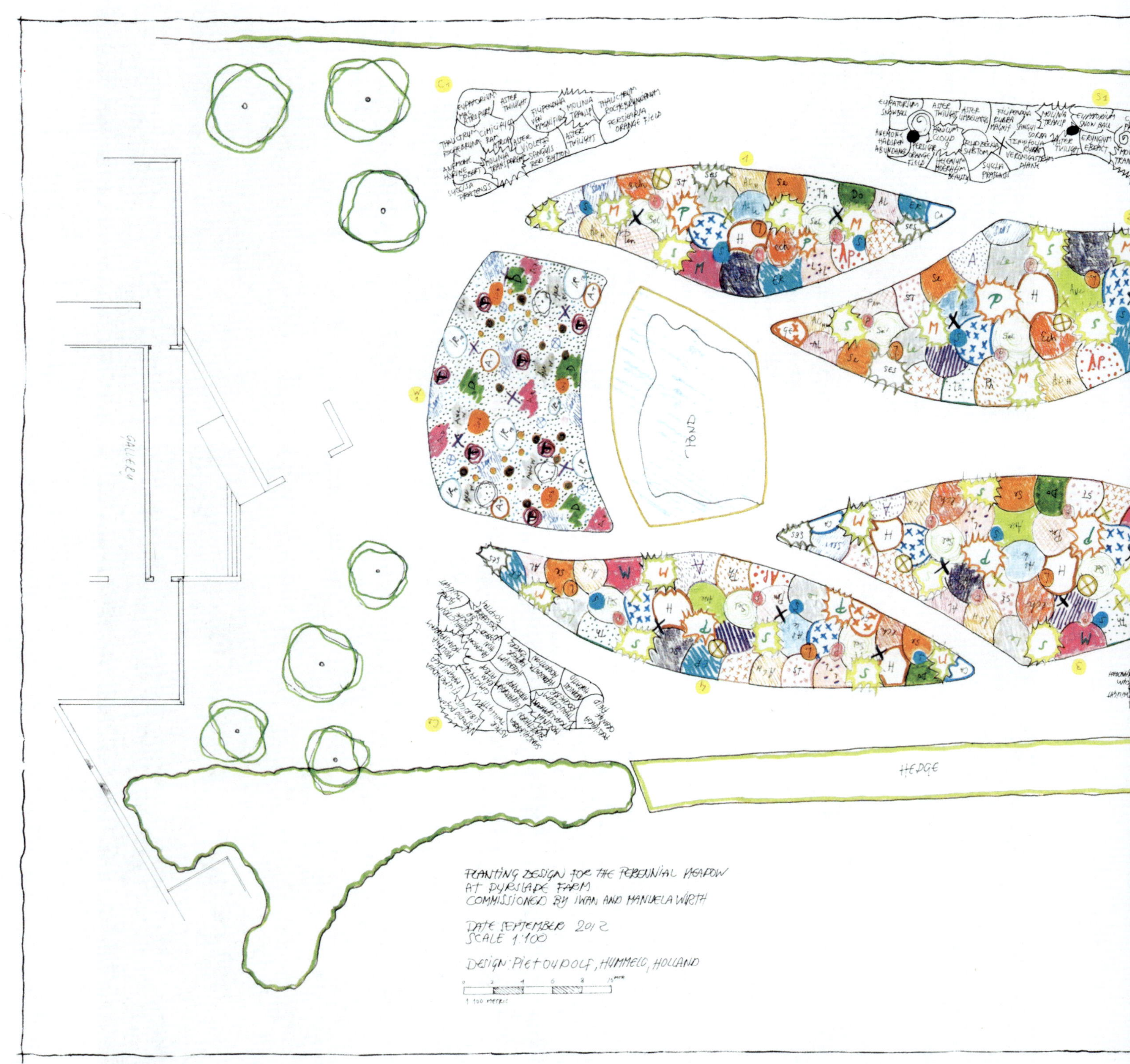

Piet Oudolf, **Planting Design for Oudolf Field, Hauser & Wirth Somerset**, 2018, drawing. Courtesy Hauser & Wirth/Piet Oudolf. Photo: Alex Delfanne.

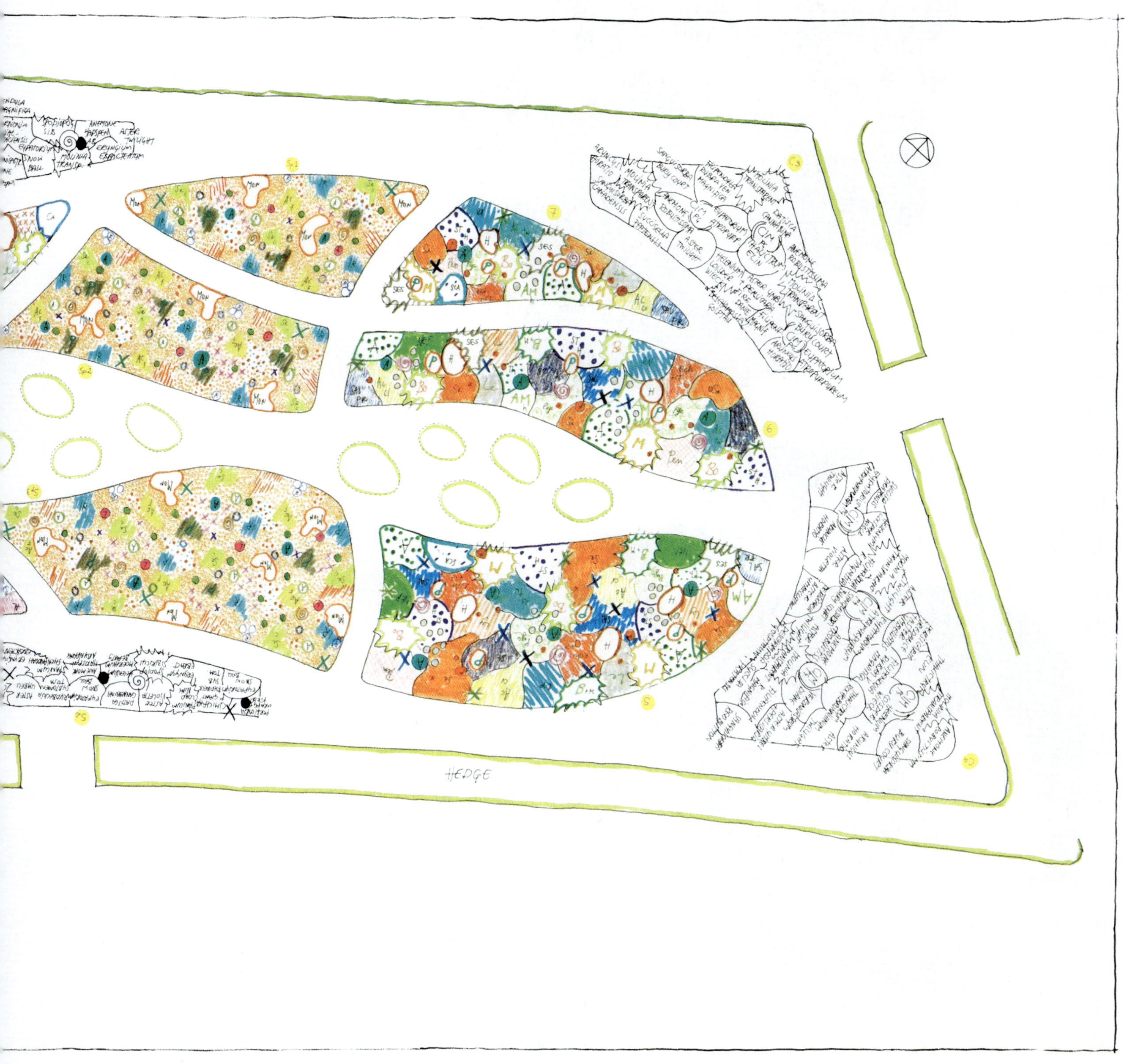
HEDGE

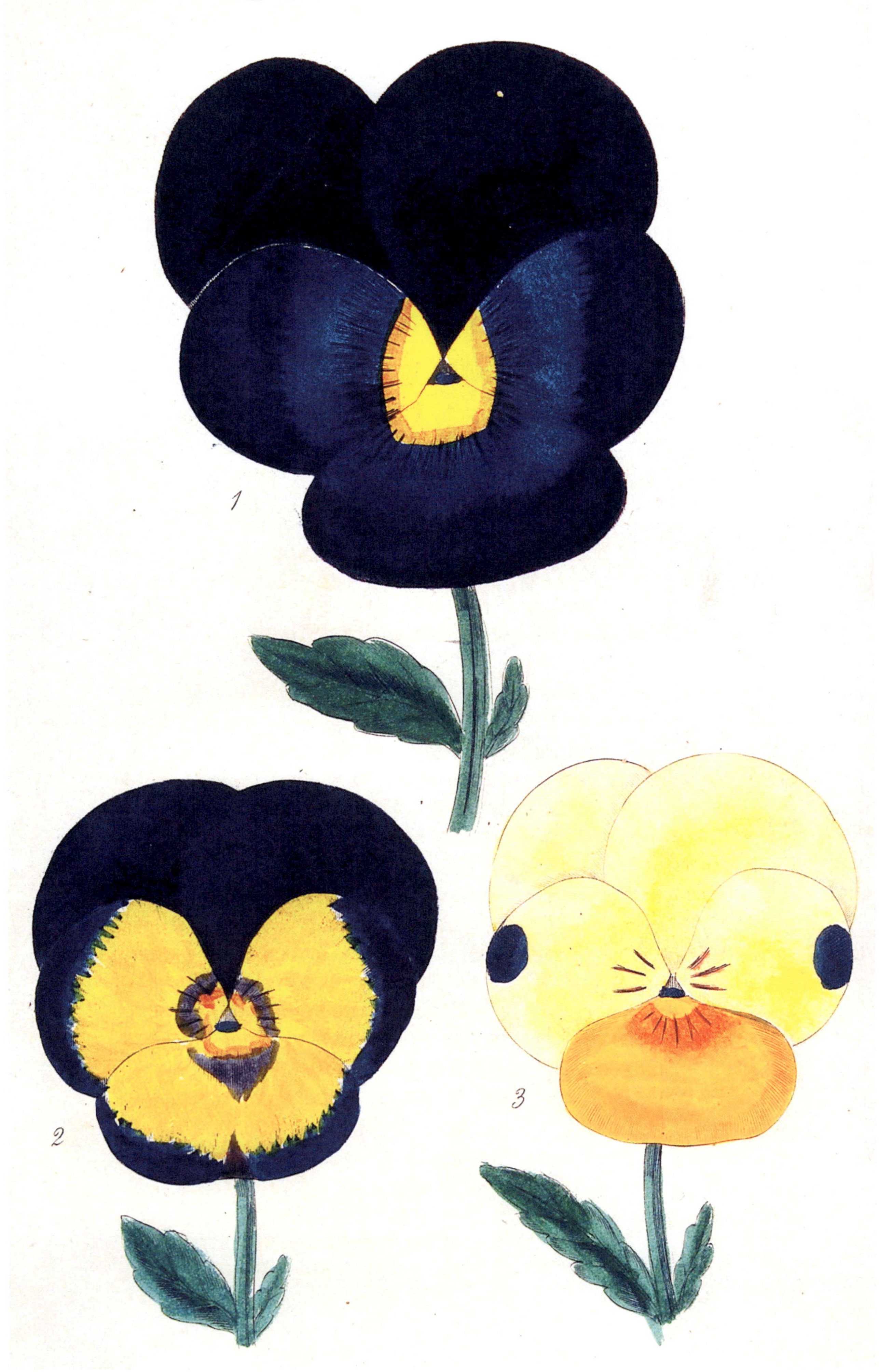

J. & J. Parkin, **Flowers of three different varieties of pansy (Viola species)**, c. 1835, engraving.
Courtesy Wellcome Collection, London.

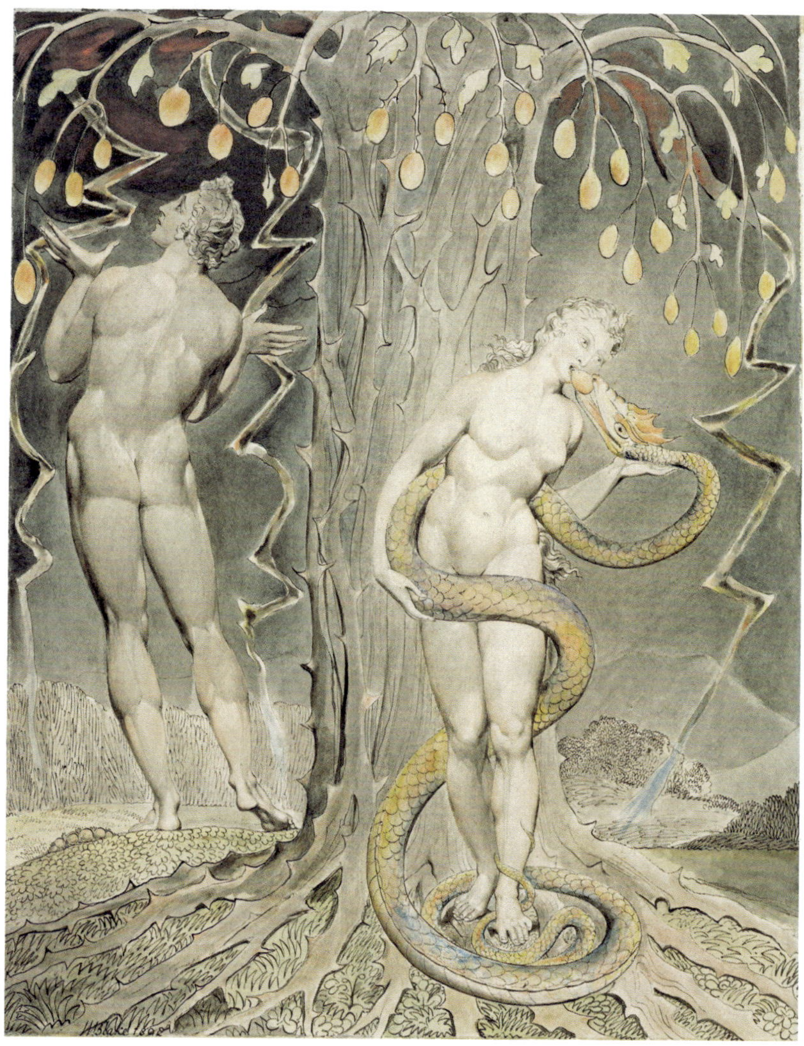

William Blake, **The Temptation and Fall of Eve (Illustration to Milton's Paradise Lost)**, 1808, watercolour on paper, 49.7 × 38.7 cm. Courtesy Museum of Fine Arts, Boston and Art Resource/Scala, Florence.

WHILE THE SPECTATORS / WHO IMAGINED THEMSELVES IN THE GARDENS OF ALCINOUS / WERE UNABLE TO TEAR THEMSELVES AWAY / THE SITE OF THE BASTILLE AND ITS DUNGEONS / WHICH HAD BEEN CONVERTED INTO GROVES / HELD OTHER CHARMS FOR THOSE WHOM THE PASSAGE OF A SINGLE YEAR HAD NOT YET ACCUSTOMED TO BELIEVE THEIR EYES · AN ARTIFICIAL WOOD / CONSISTING OF LARGE TREES / HAD BEEN PLANTED THERE · IT WAS EXTREMELY WELL LIT · IN THE MIDDLE OF THIS LAIR OF DESPOTISM / THERE HAD ALSO BEEN PLANTED A PIKE / WITH A CAP OF LIBERTY STUCK ON THE TOP · CLOSE BY HAD BEEN BURIED THE RUINS OF THE BASTILLE · AMONGST ITS IRONS AND GRATINGS COULD BE SEEN THE BAS-RELIEF REPRESENTING SLAVES IN CHAINS WHICH HAD APTLY ADORNED THE FORTRESS'S GREAT CLOCK / THE MOST SURPRISING ASPECT OF THE SIGHT PERHAPS BEING THAT THE FORTRESS COULD HAVE BEEN TOPPLED WITHOUT OVERWHELMING IN ITS FALL THE POSTERITY OF THE TYRANTS BY WHOM IT HAD BEEN RAISED / AND WHO HAD FILLED IT WITH SO MANY INNOCENT VICTIMS · THESE RUINS / AND THE MEMORIES THEY CALLED UP / WERE IN SINGULAR CONTRAST WITH THE INSCRIPTION THAT COULD BE READ AT THE ENTRANCE TO THE GROVE - A SIMPLE INSCRIPTION WHOSE PLACEMENT GAVE IT A TRULY SUBLIME BEAUTY -

ICI ON DANSE

CAMILLE DESMOULINS / PARIS / YEAR ONE OF THE AGE OF LIBERTY

Ian Hamilton Finlay, **Pastoral**, 1996, silkscreen on paper, 40 × 50 cm. Courtesy Van Abbemuseum, Eindhoven.

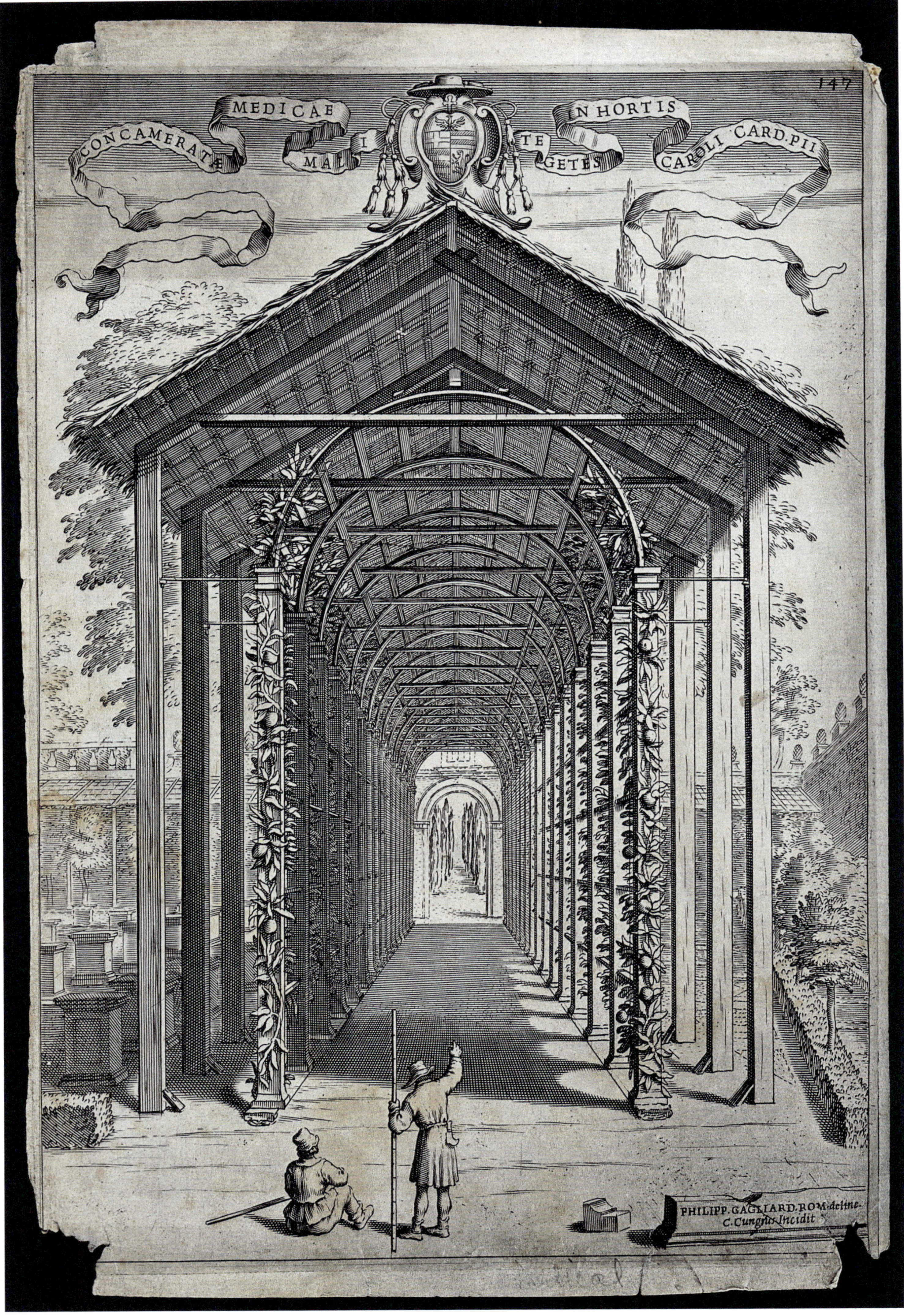

Camillo Cungi after Filippo Gagliardi, **Two men in the garden of Cardinal Carlo Pio di Savoia admiring a pergola on which citron fruits are growing**, 1600–1699, engraving, 31 × 22 cm. Courtesy Wellcome Collection, London.

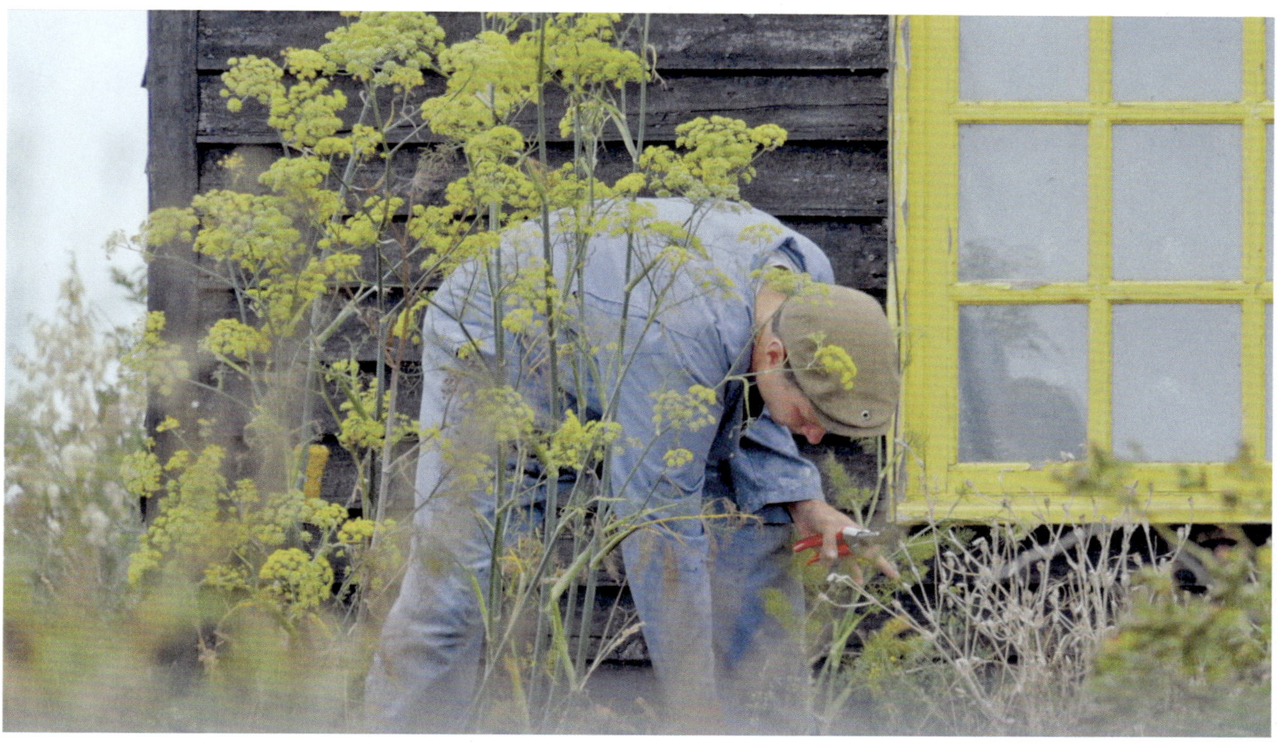

Jort van der Laan, **All-heal Fennel**, 2017, video still. Courtesy Jort van der Laan.

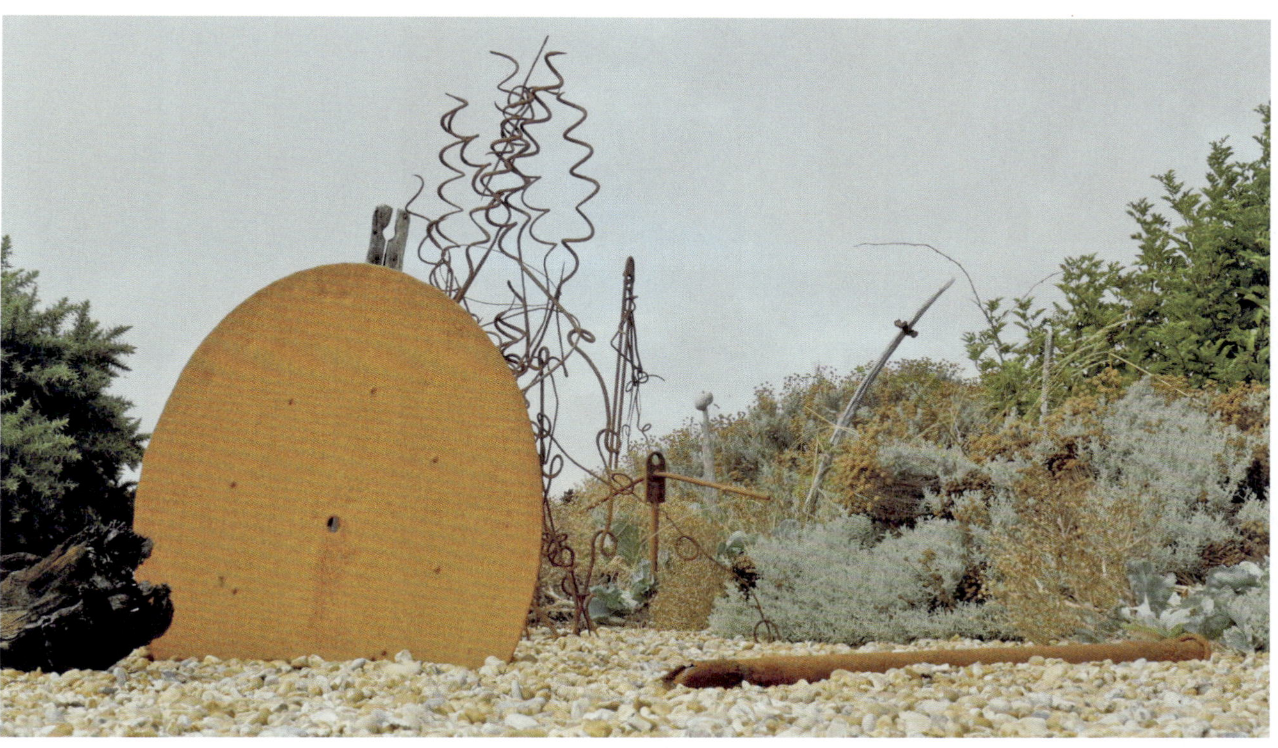

Jort van der Laan, **All-heal Fennel**, 2017, video still. Courtesy Jort van der Laan.

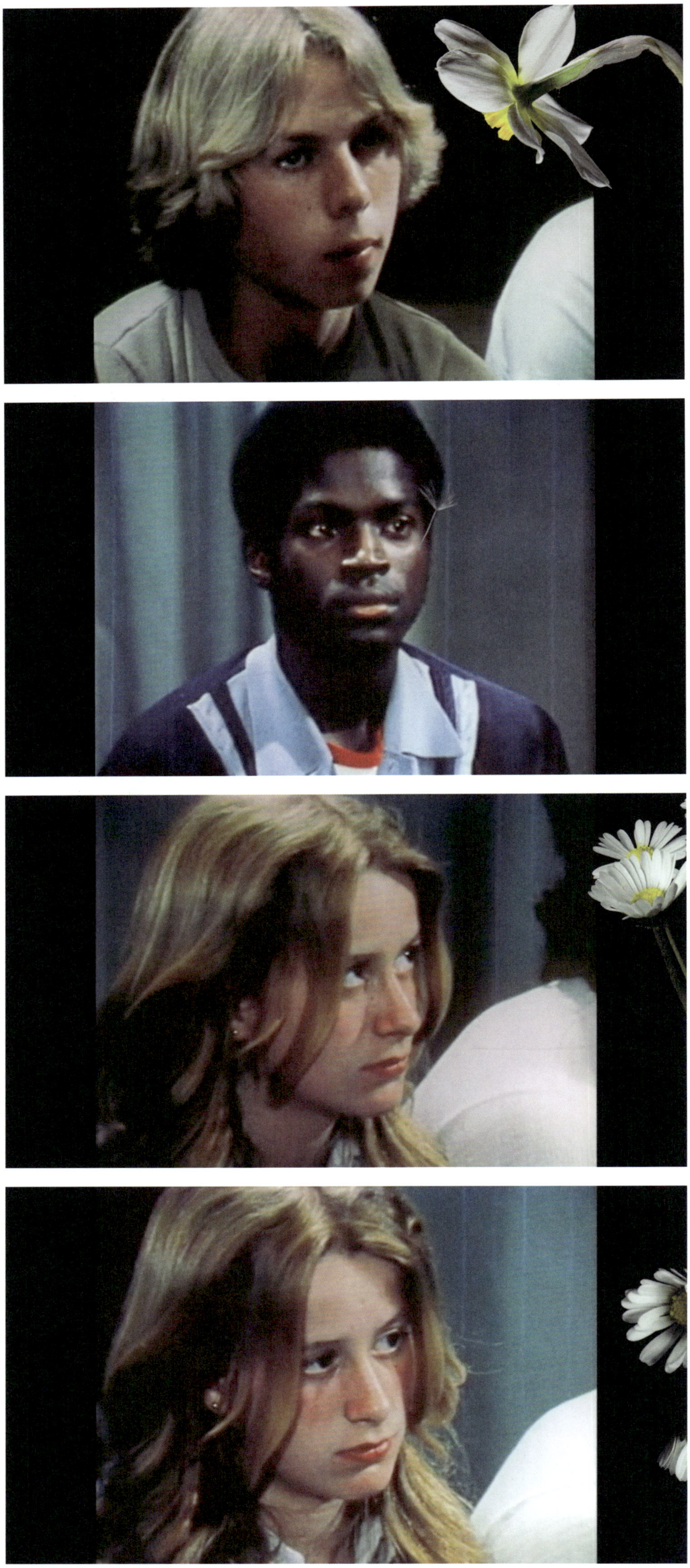

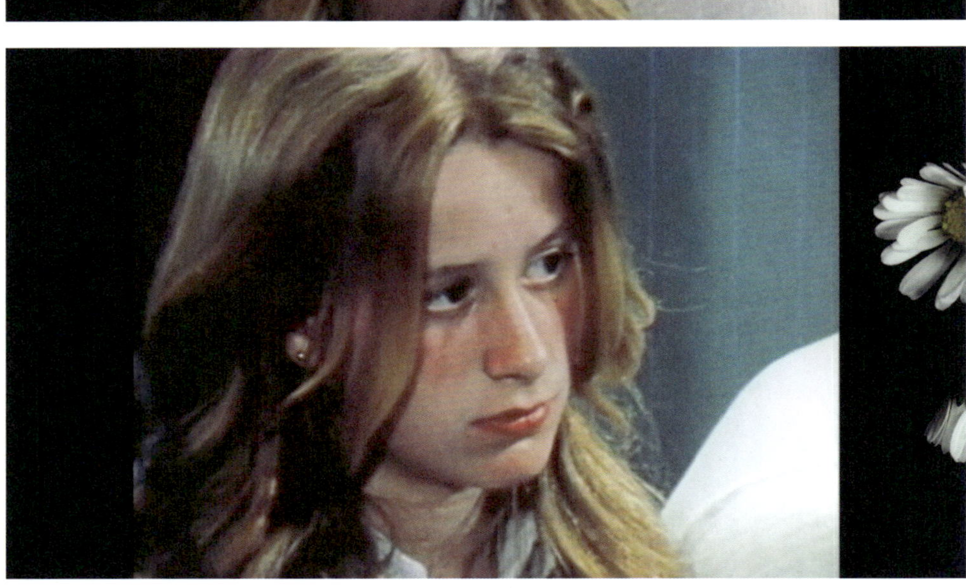

Jort van der Laan, **I AM A POLLINATOR! I AM A POLLINATOR!**, 2020, video still. Courtesy Jort van der Laan.

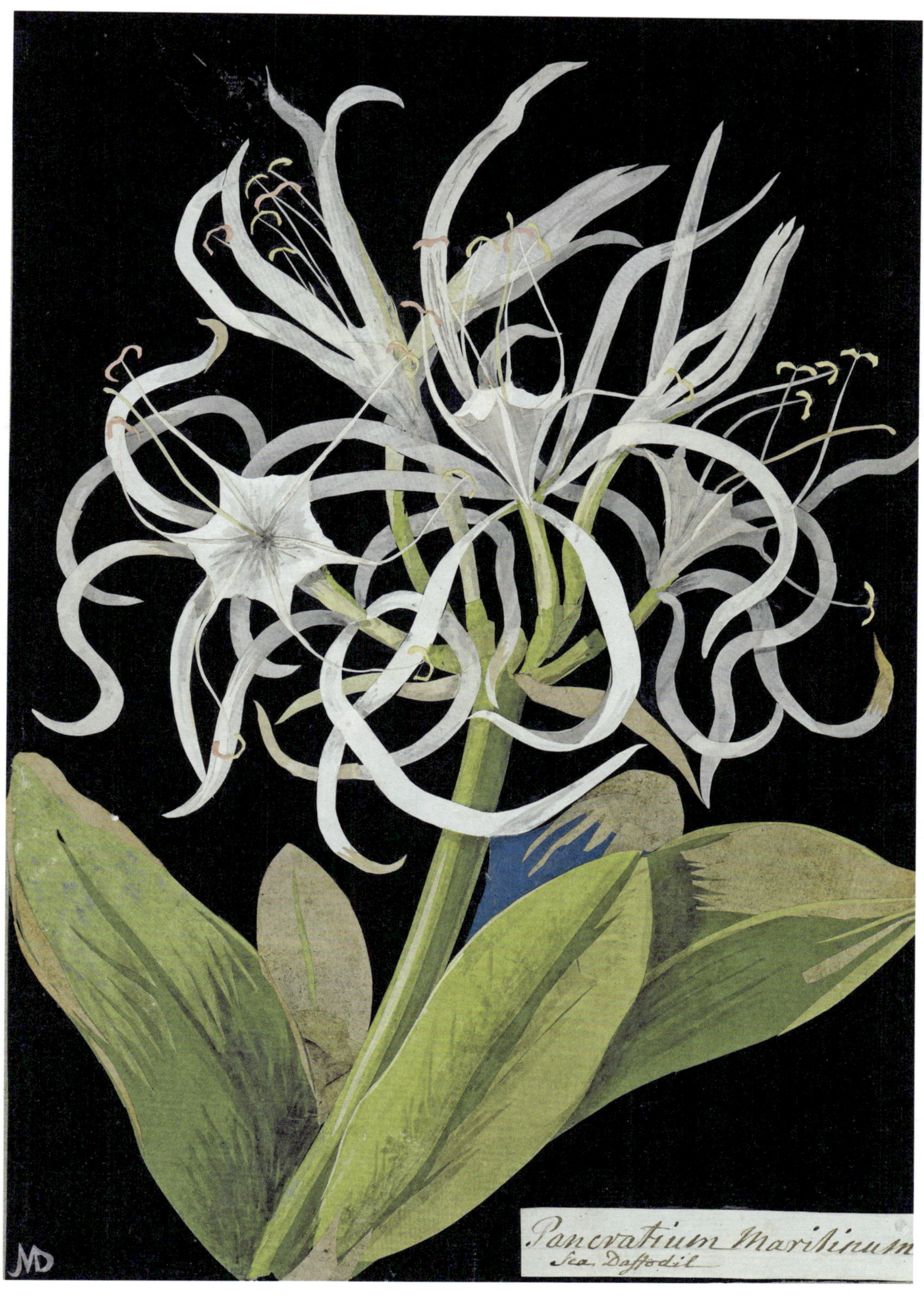

Mary Granville Delany, **Pancratium Maritinum (Hexandria Monogynia)**, 1778, collage, 35 × 22.2 cm.
Courtesy The Trustees of the British Museum.

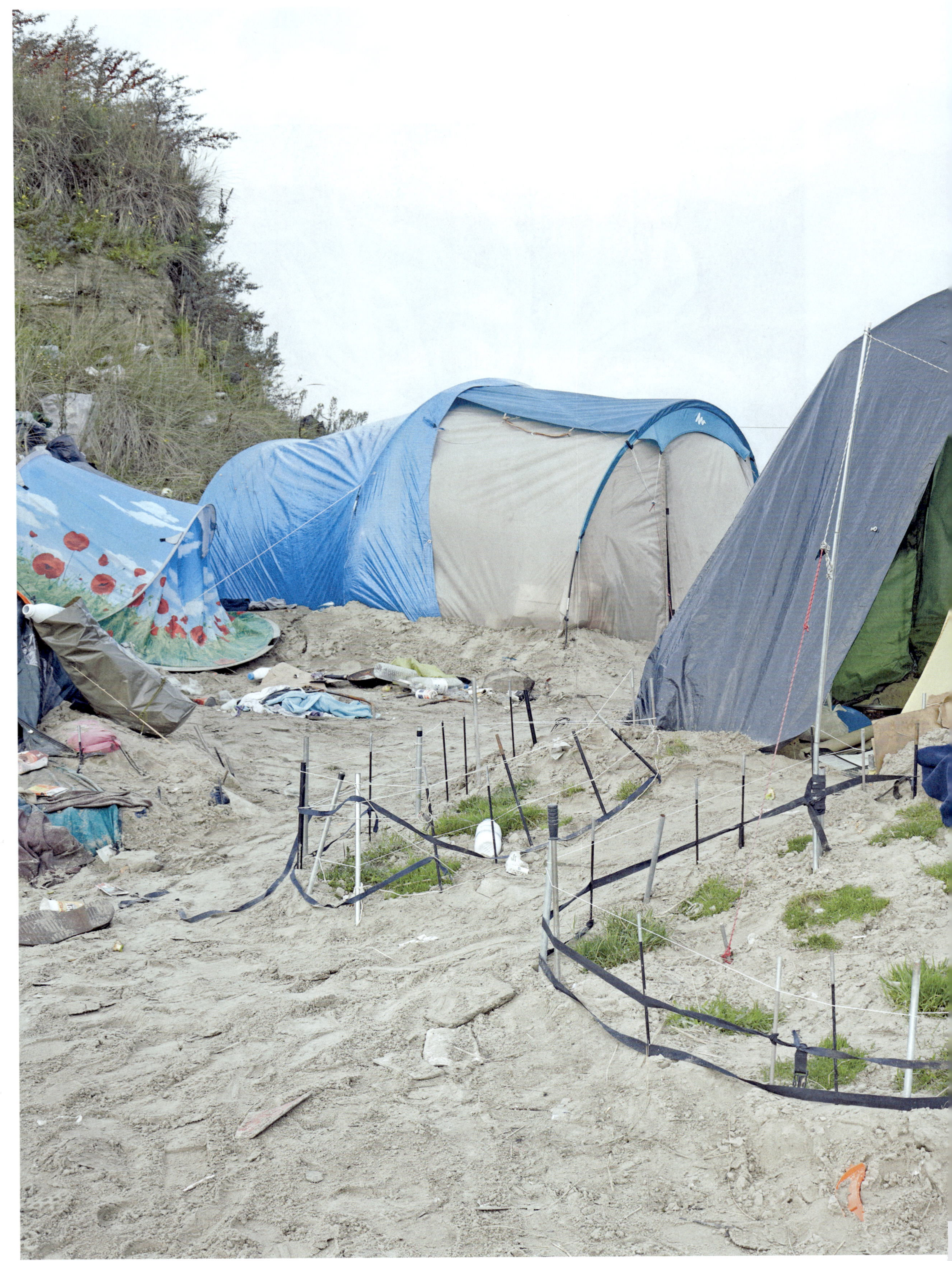

Henk Wildschut, **Calais, France-November**, 2015, photograph. Courtesy Henk Wildschut.

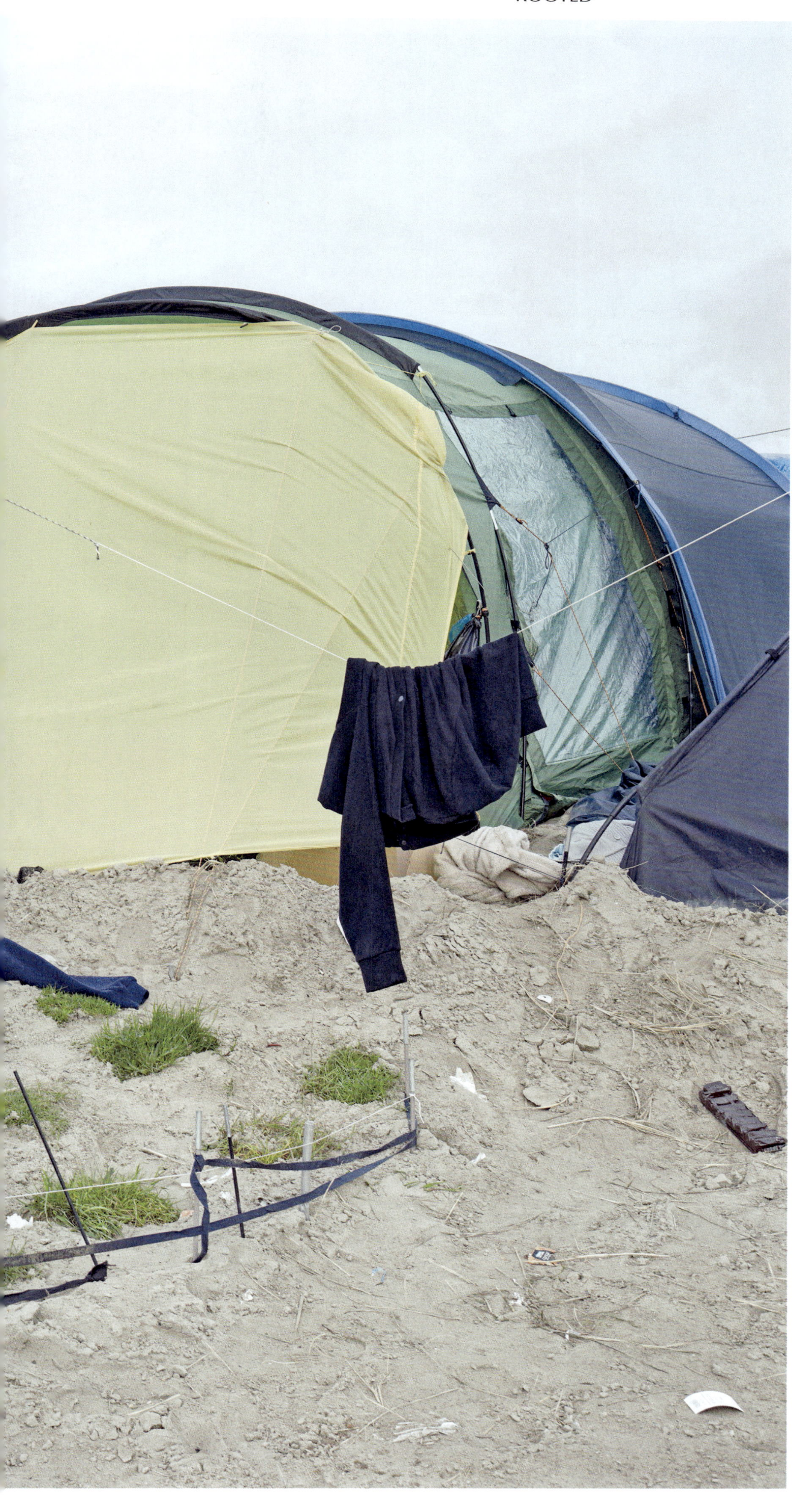

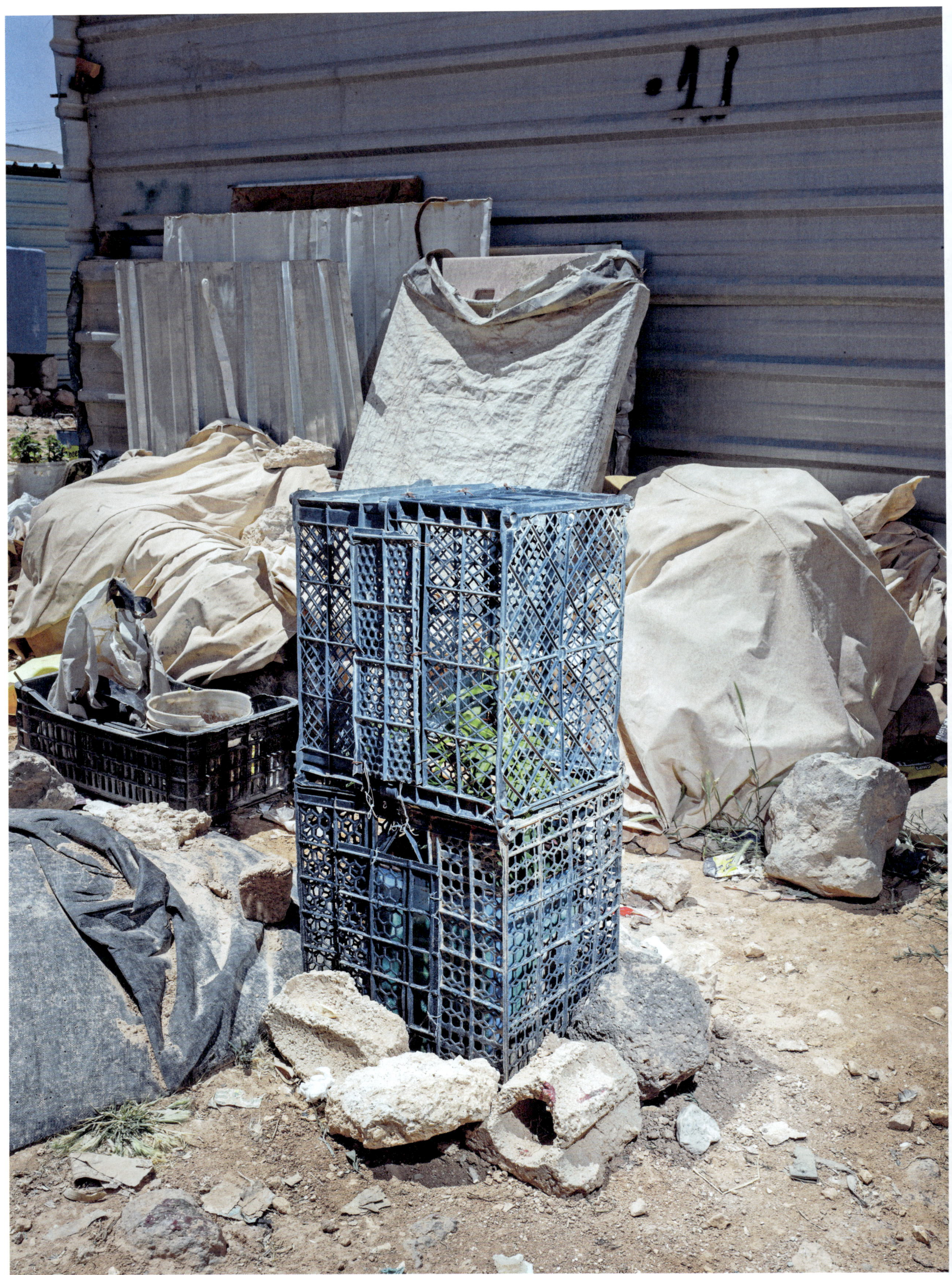

Henk Wildschut, **Zaatari Camp, Jordan-April**, 2018, photograph. Courtesy Henk Wildschut.

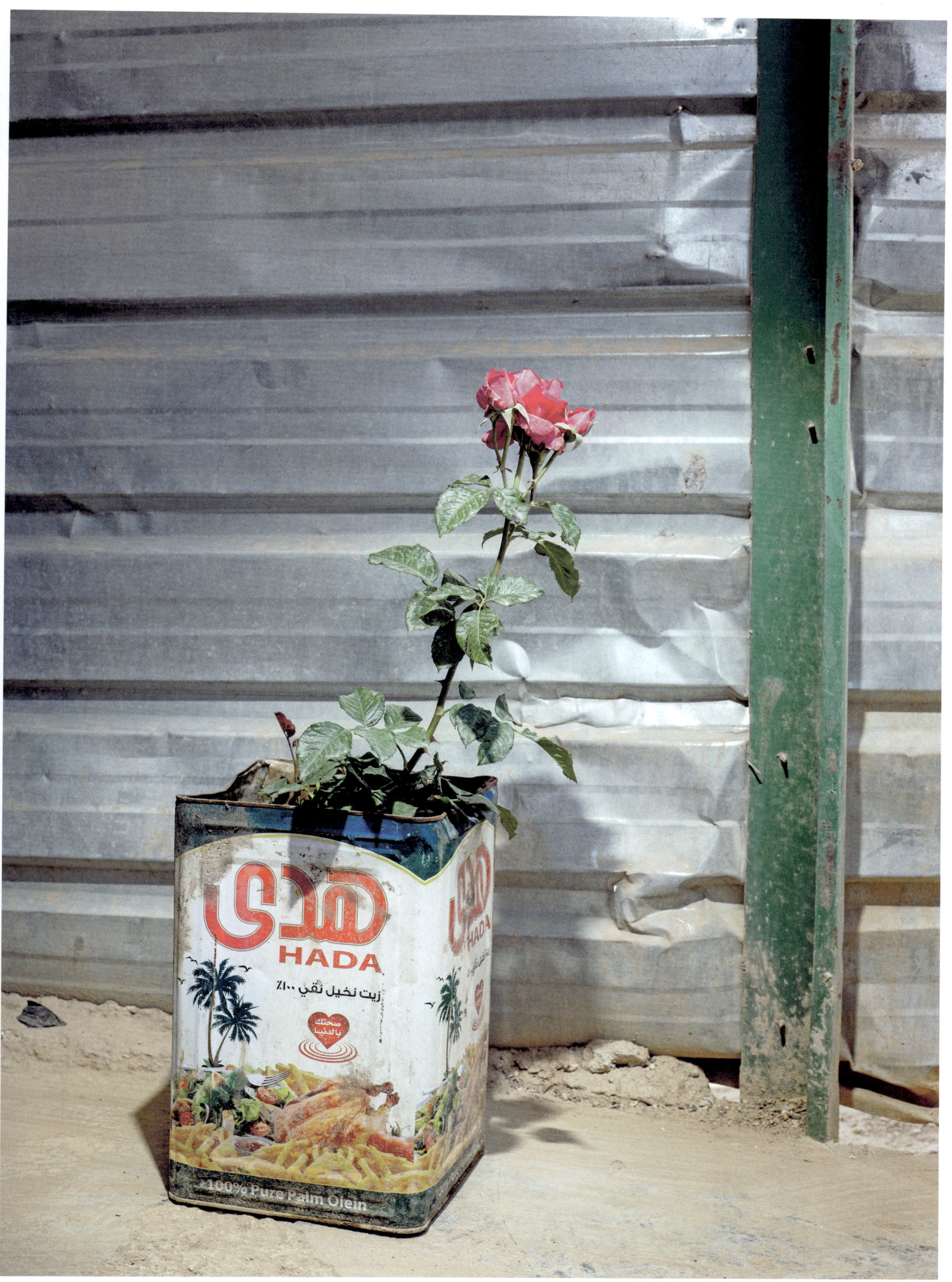

Henk Wildschut, **Zaatari Camp, Jordan-April**, 2018, photograph. Courtesy Henk Wildschut.

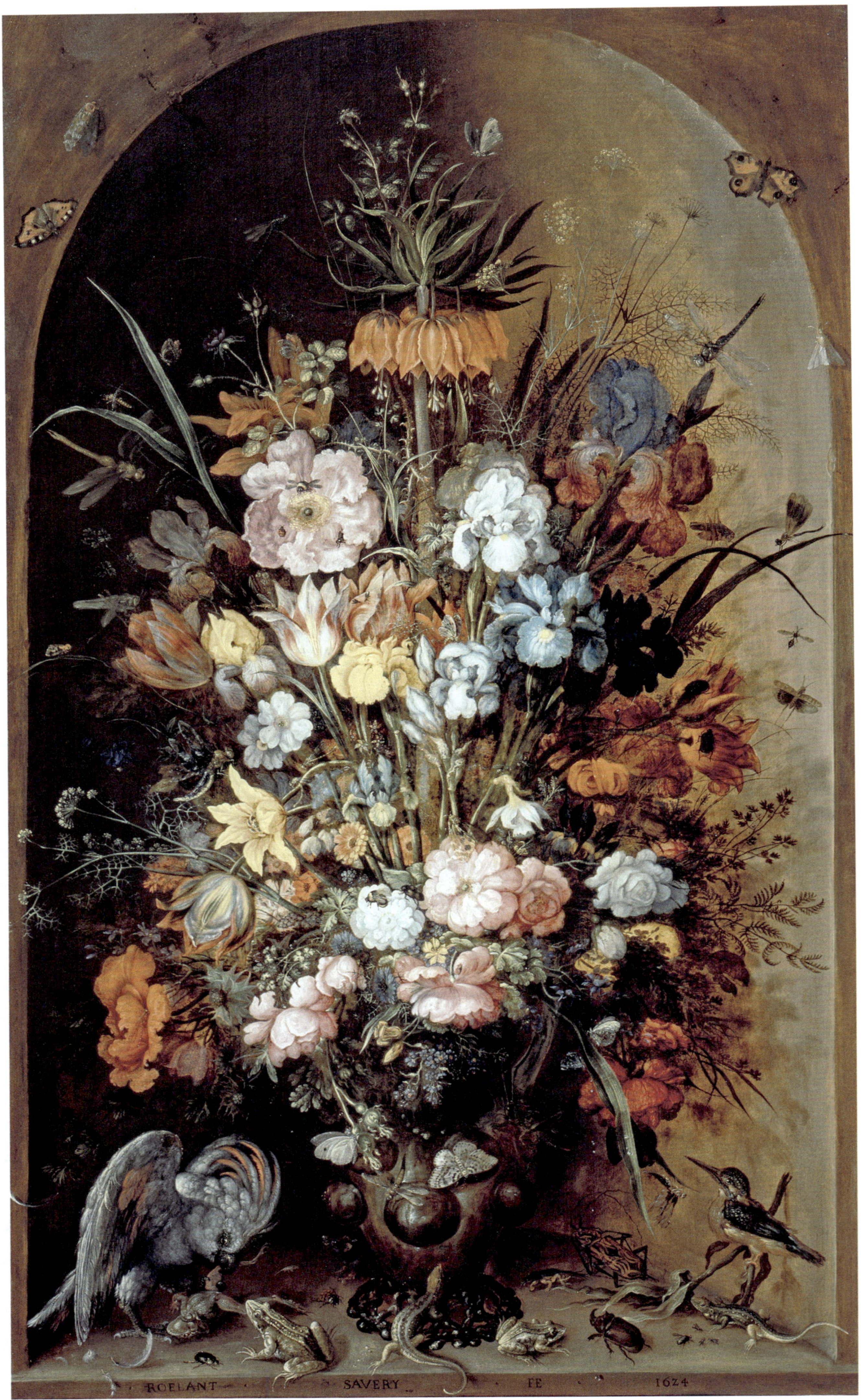

Roelant Saverij, **Large Flower Still Life with Crown Imperial**, 1624, oil on panel, 130 x 80 cm. Courtesy Centraal Museum, Utrecht.

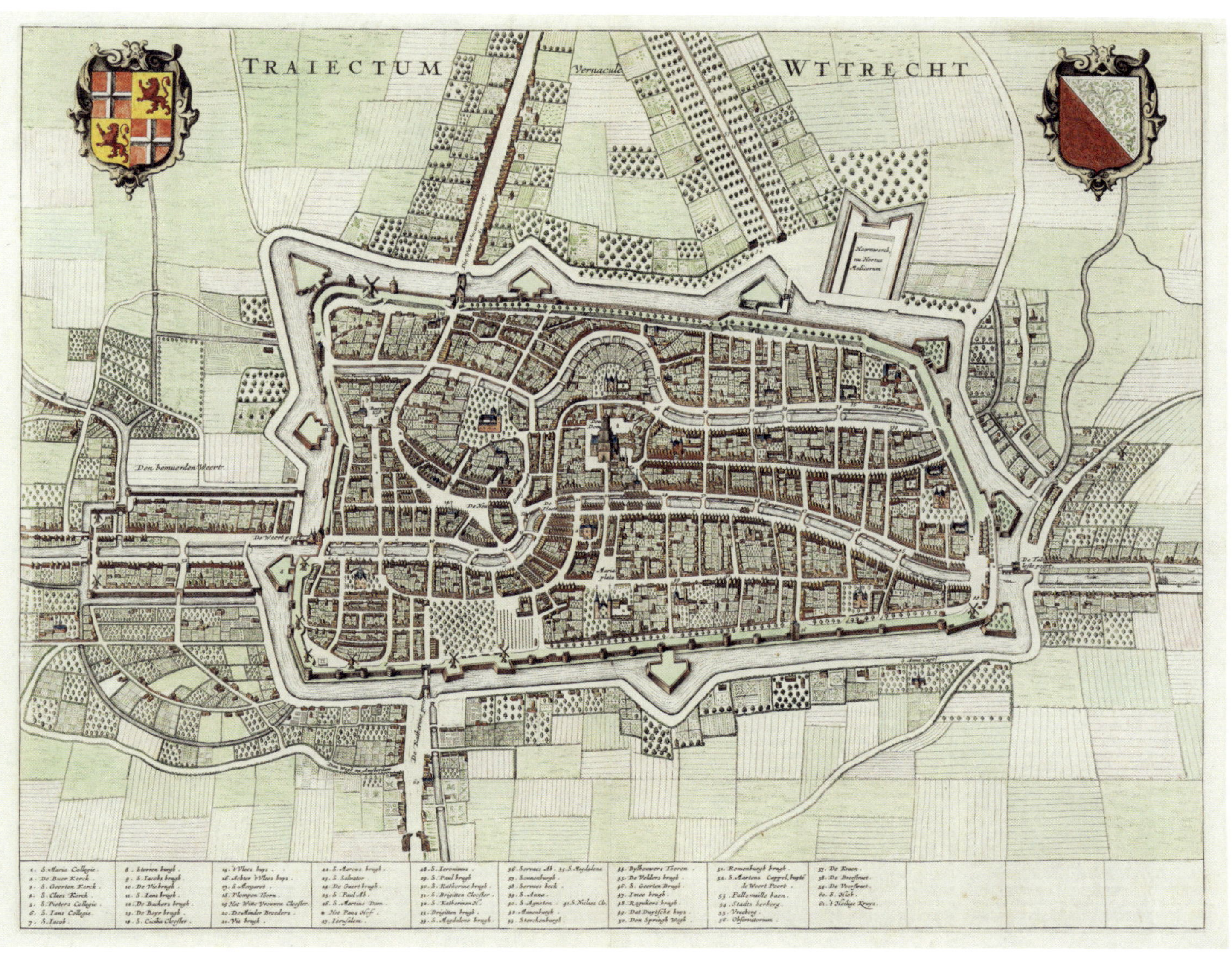

Joan Blaeu, Trajectum Wttrecht from **Toonneel der Steden van de Vereenighde Nederlanden met hare beschrijvingen**, 1649, copper engraving, 38 x 50 cm. Courtesy Het Utrechts Archief.

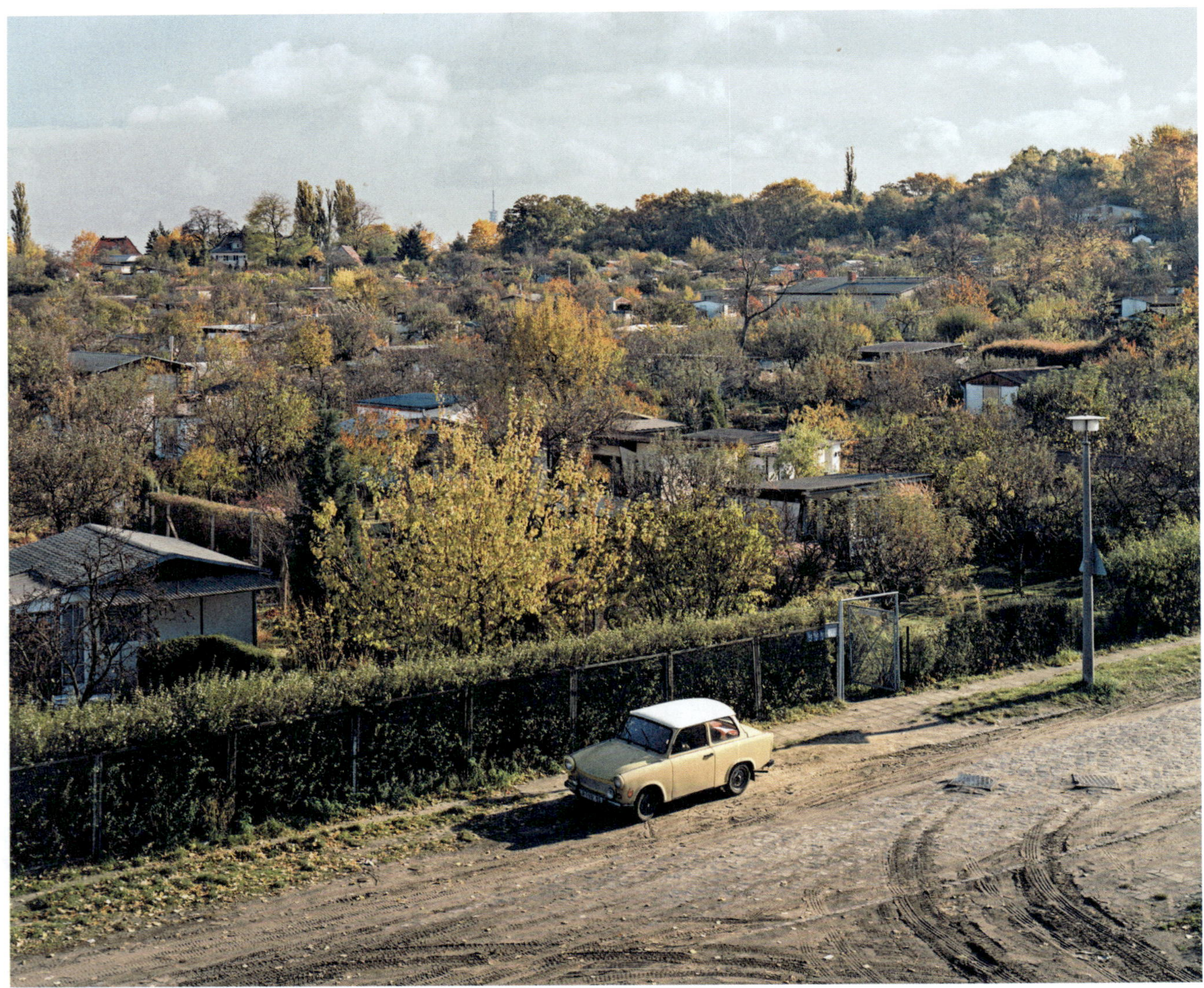

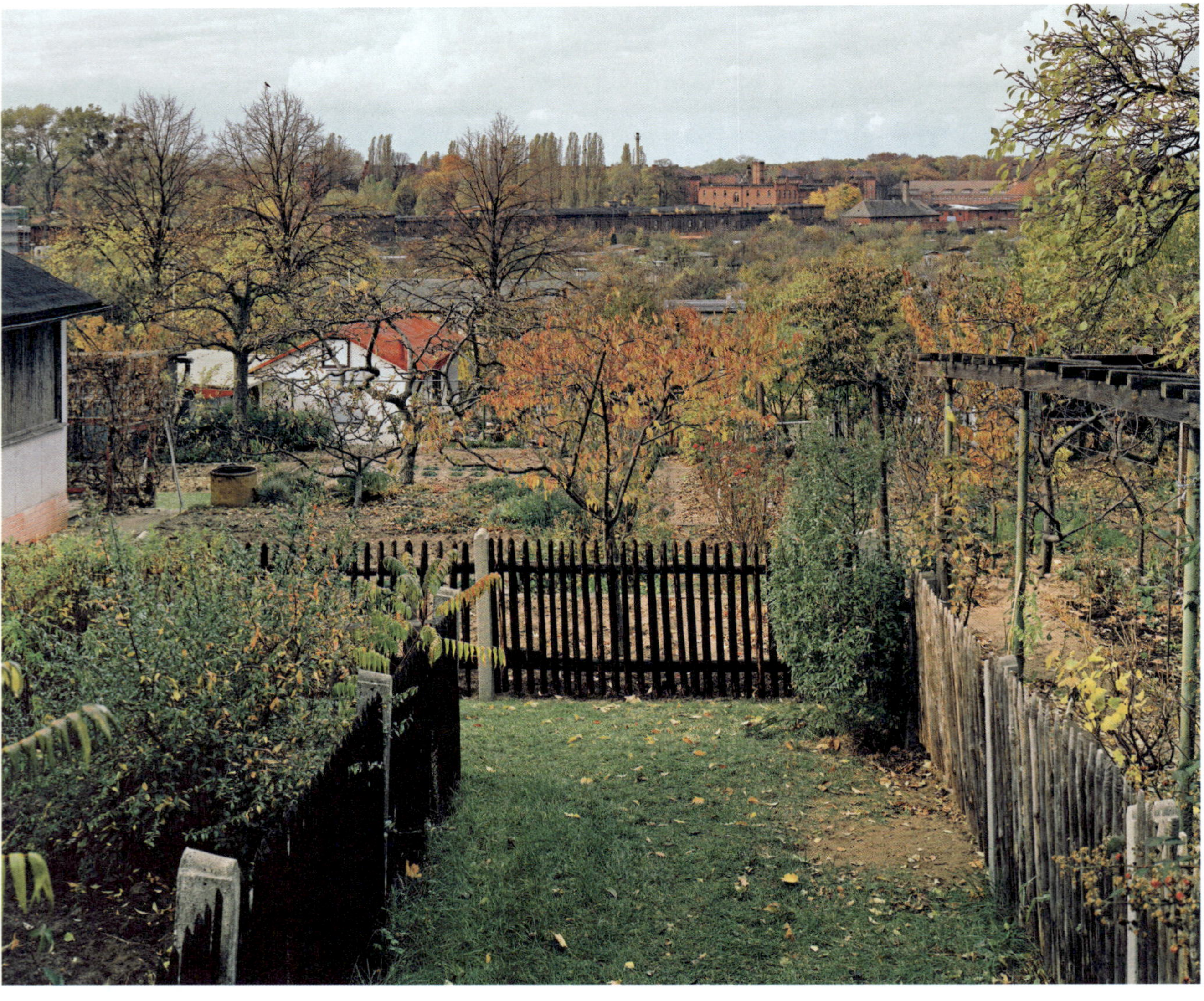

Stan Douglas, **Potsdamer Schrebergärten (Potsdam Gardens Portfolio)**, 1994–2005, fifteen chromogenic prints.
Hasso Plattner Collection, © Stan Douglas. Courtesy Stan Douglas, Victoria Miro and David Zwirner.

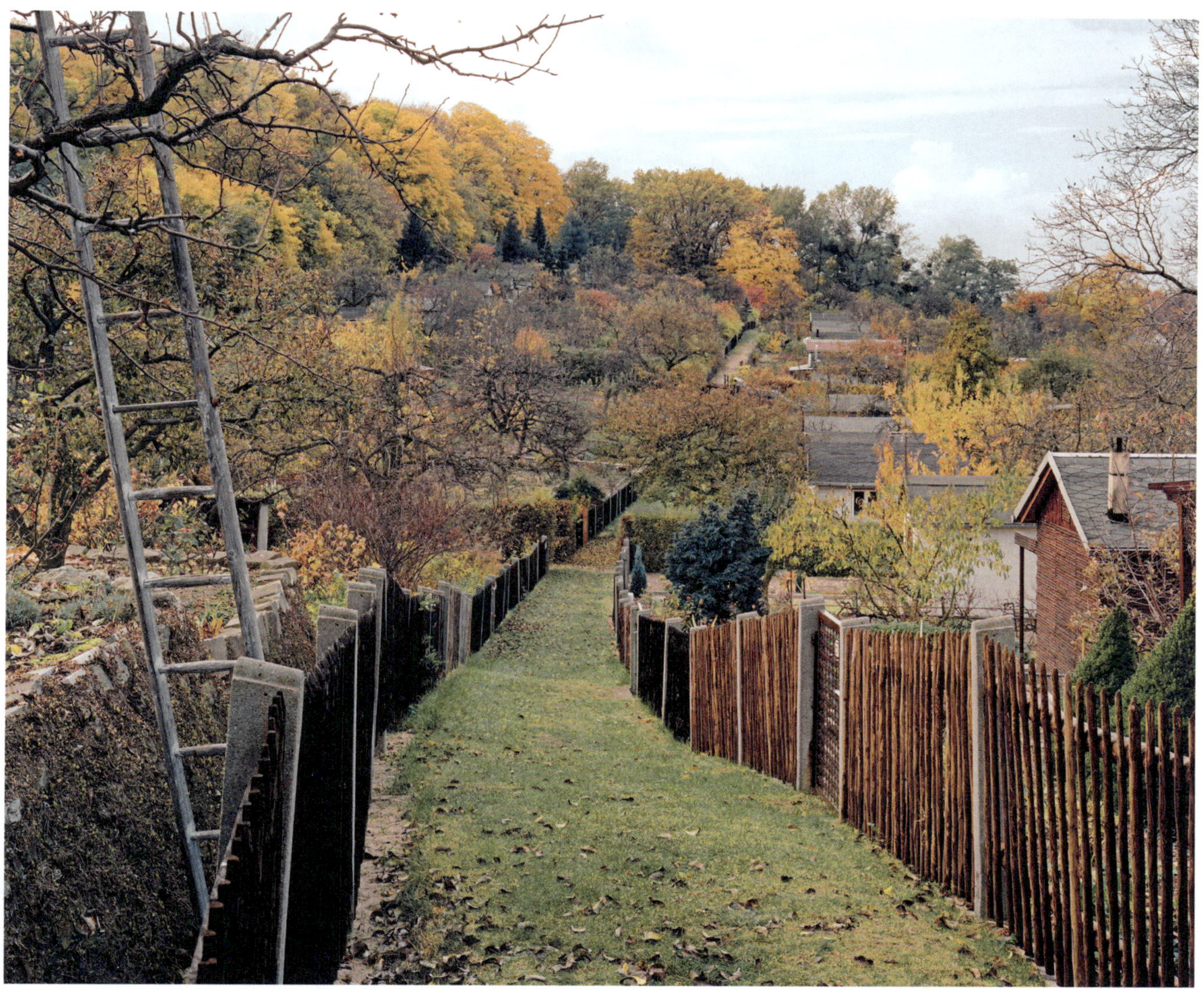

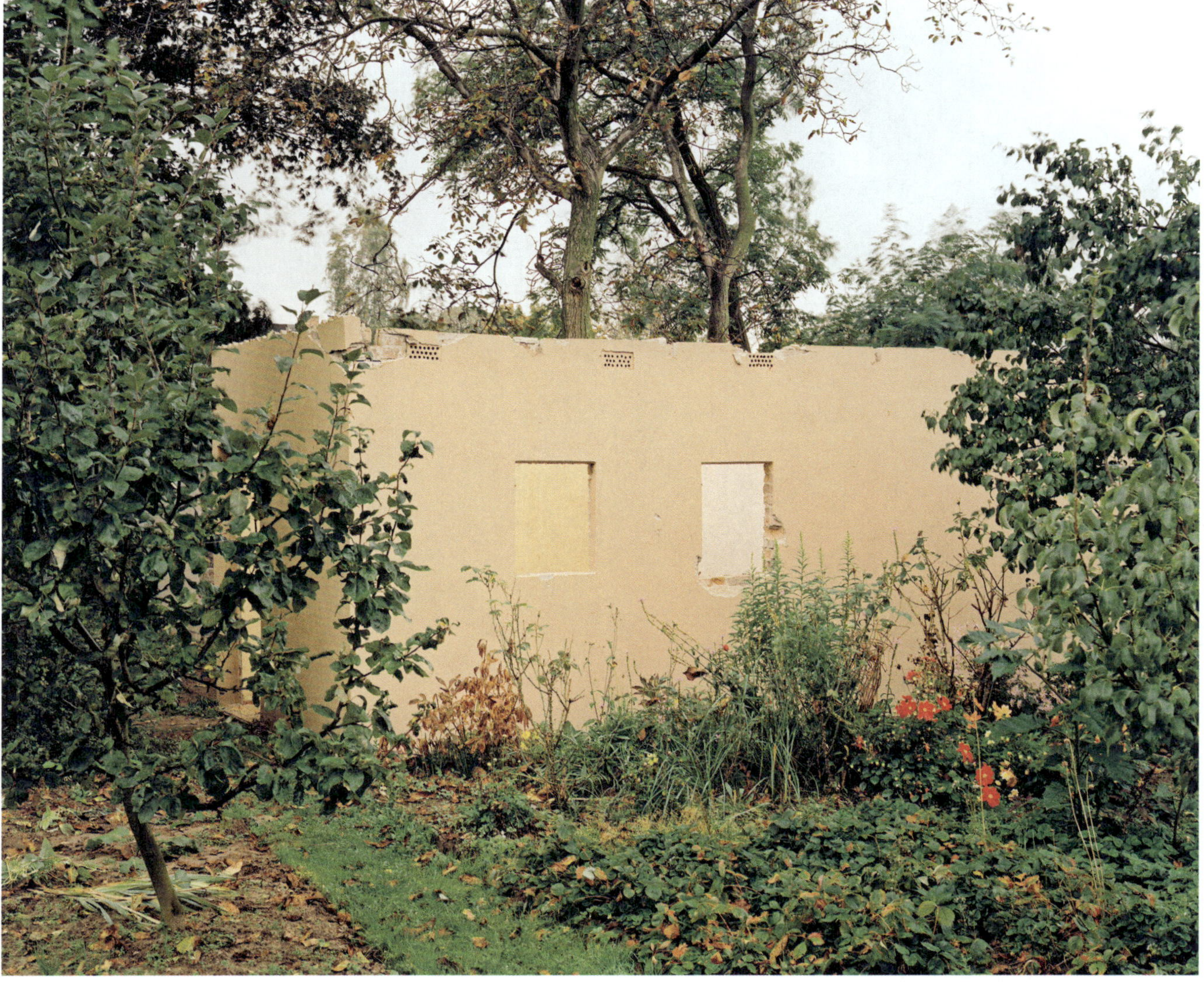

Stan Douglas, **Potsdamer Schrebergärten (Potsdam Gardens Portfolio)**, 1994–2005, fifteen chromogenic prints.
Hasso Plattner Collection, © Stan Douglas. Courtesy Stan Douglas, Victoria Miro and David Zwirner.

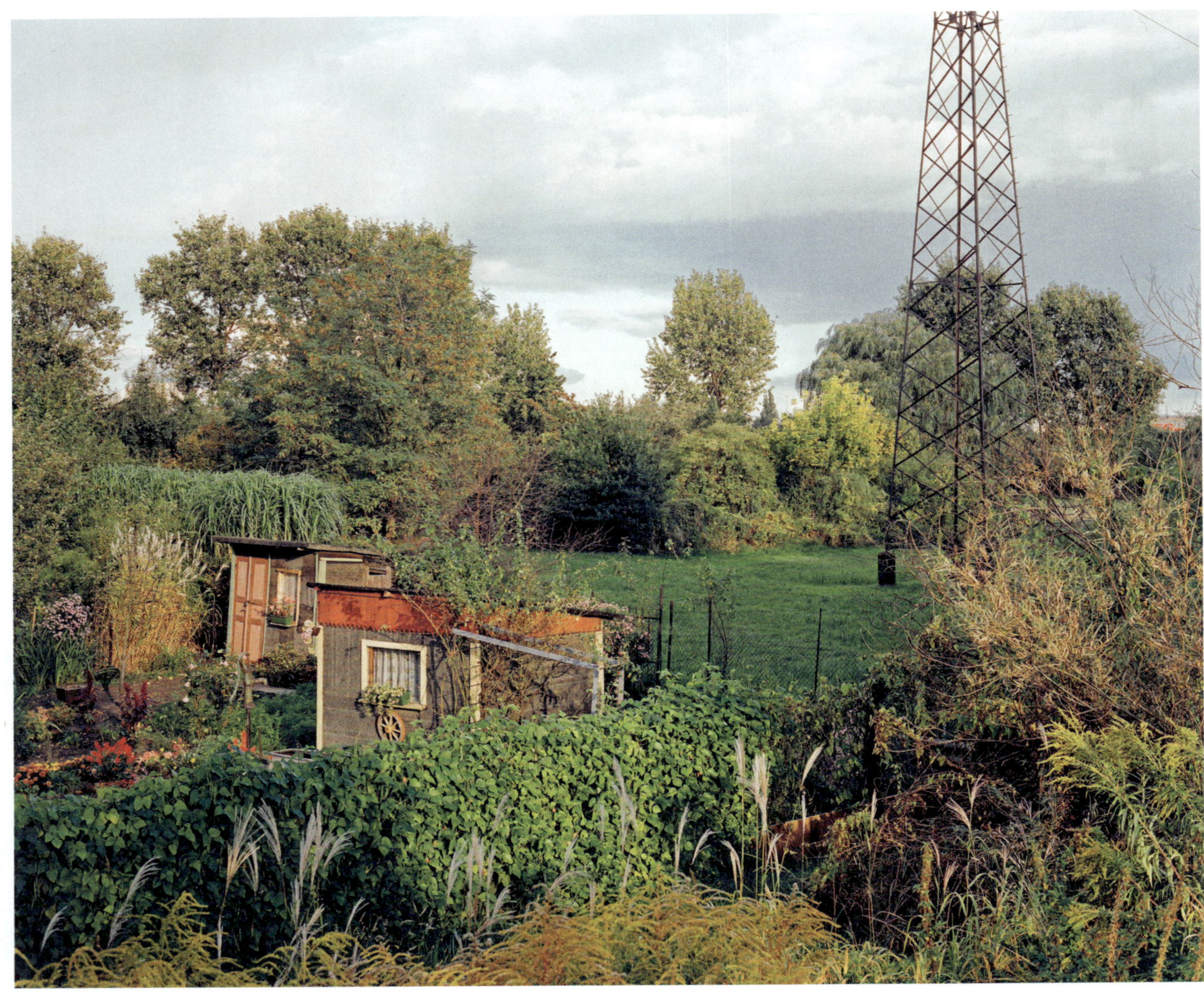

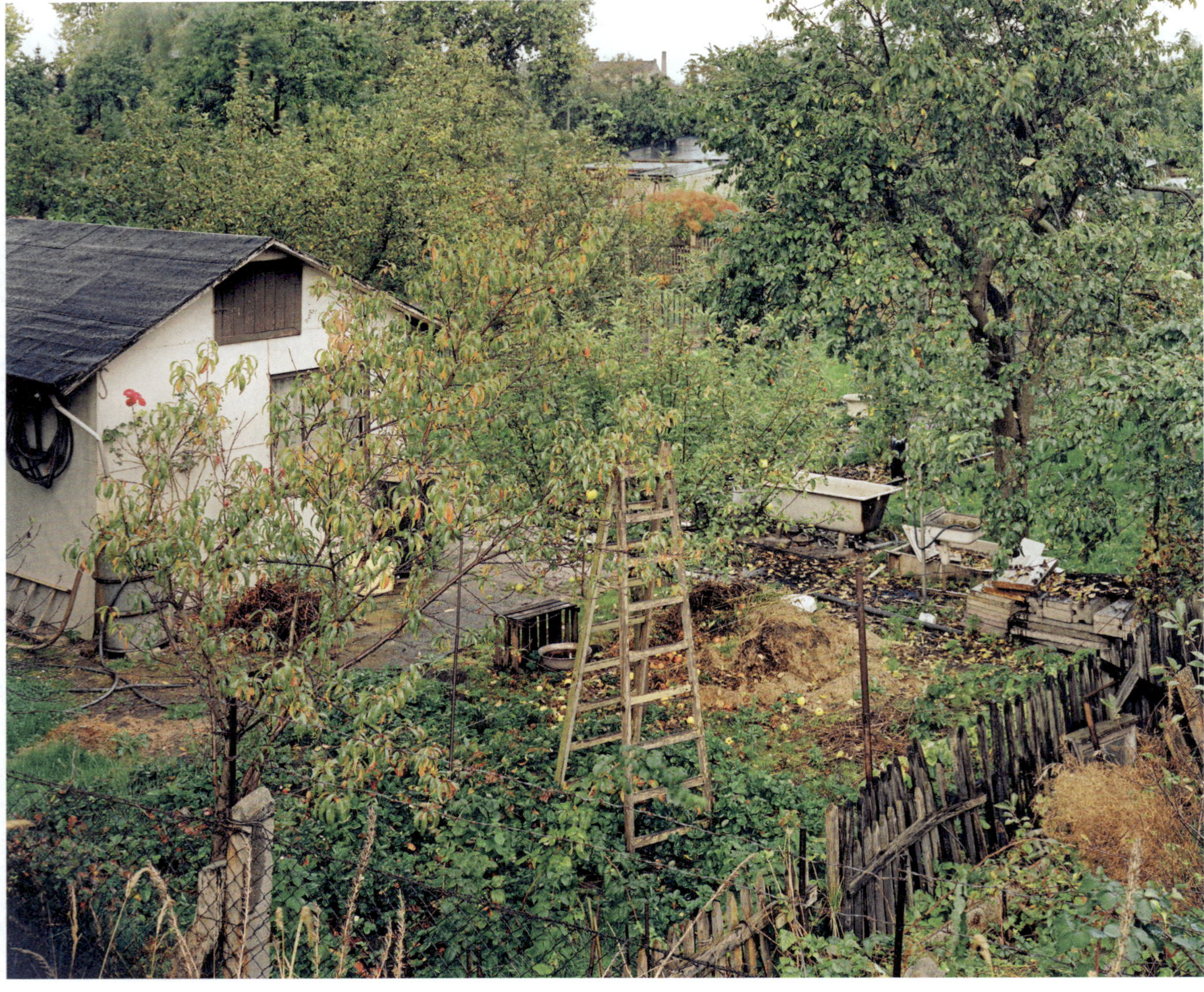

Stan Douglas, **Potsdamer Schrebergärten (Potsdam Gardens Portfolio)**, 1994–2005, fifteen chromogenic prints.
Hasso Plattner Collection, © Stan Douglas. Courtesy Stan Douglas, Victoria Miro and David Zwirner.

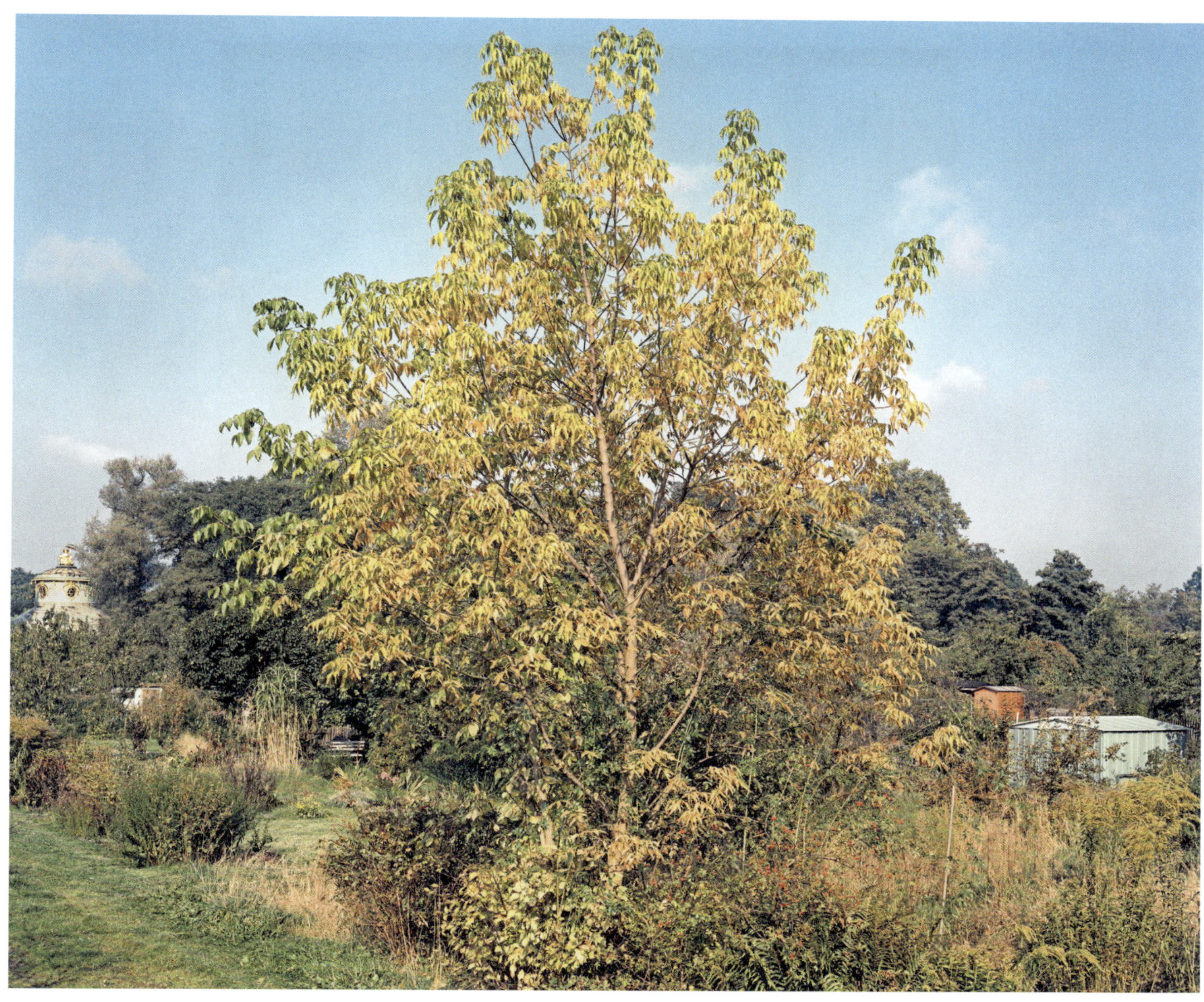

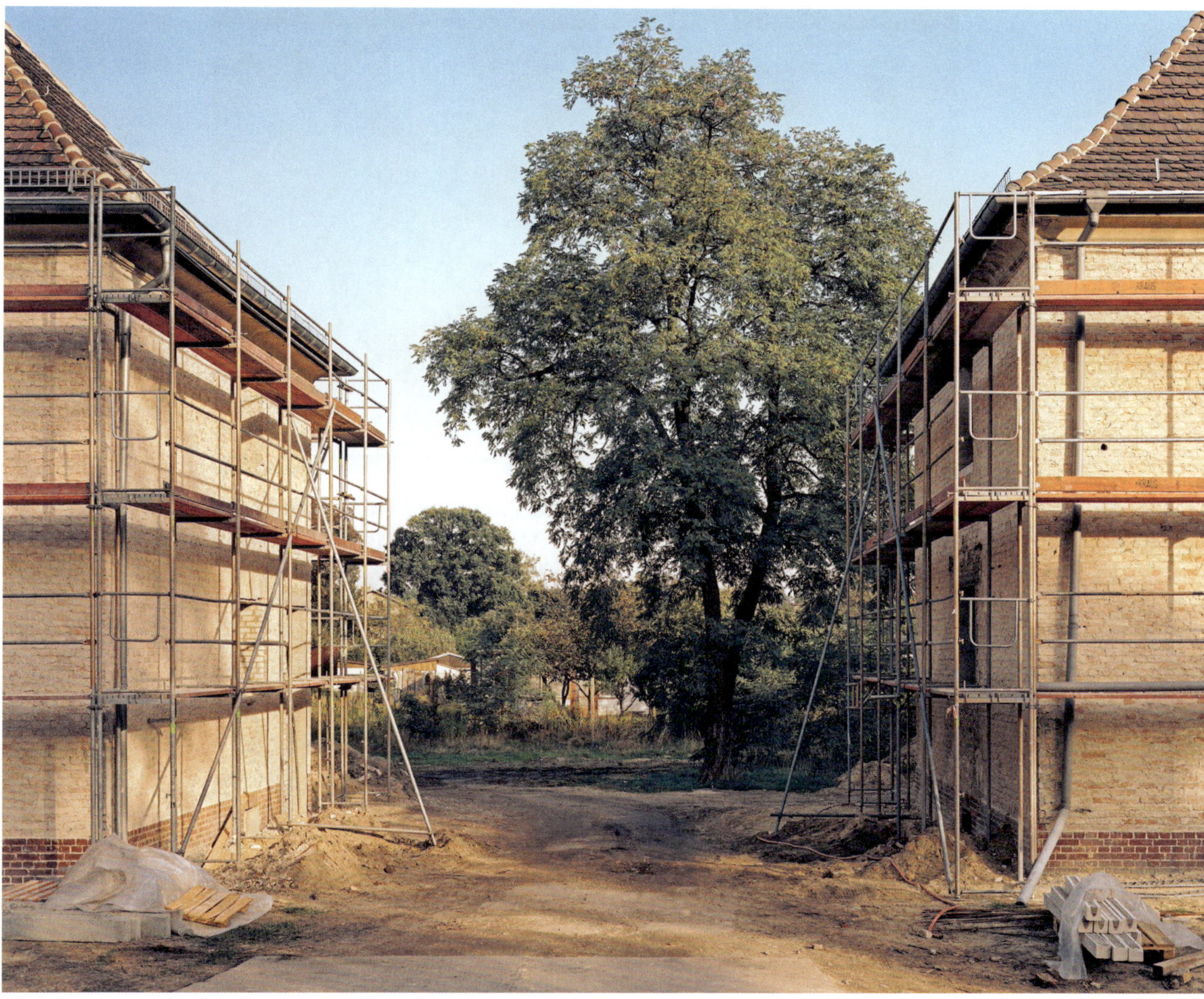

Stan Douglas, **Potsdamer Schrebergärten (Potsdam Gardens Portfolio)**, 1994–2005, fifteen chromogenic prints.
Hasso Plattner Collection, © Stan Douglas. Courtesy Stan Douglas, Victoria Miro and David Zwirner.

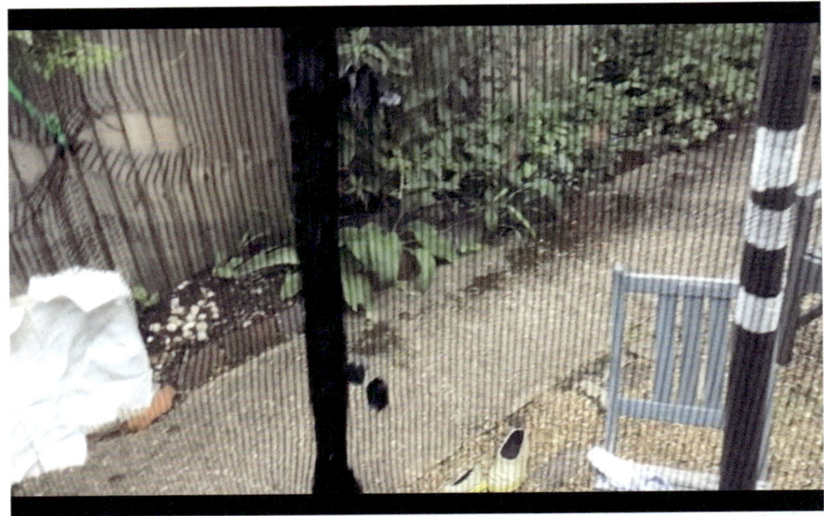

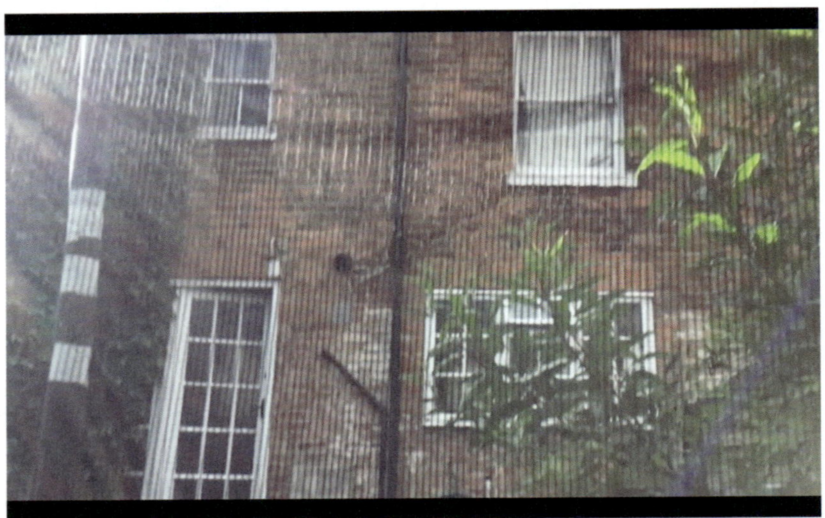

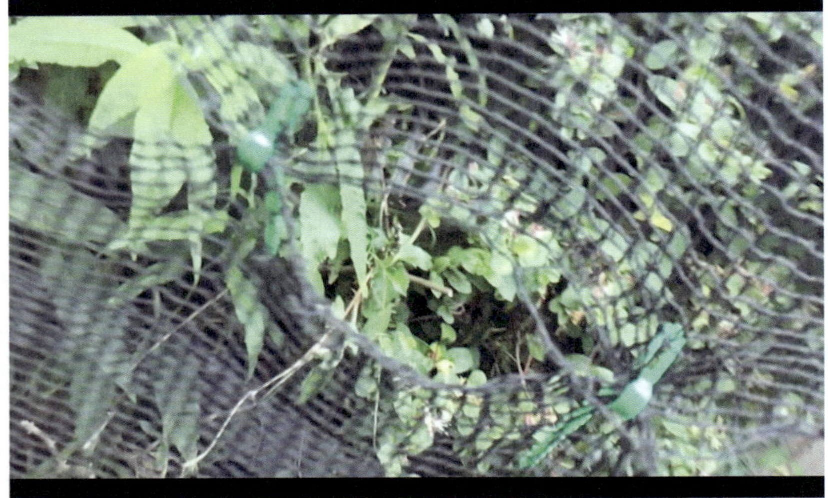

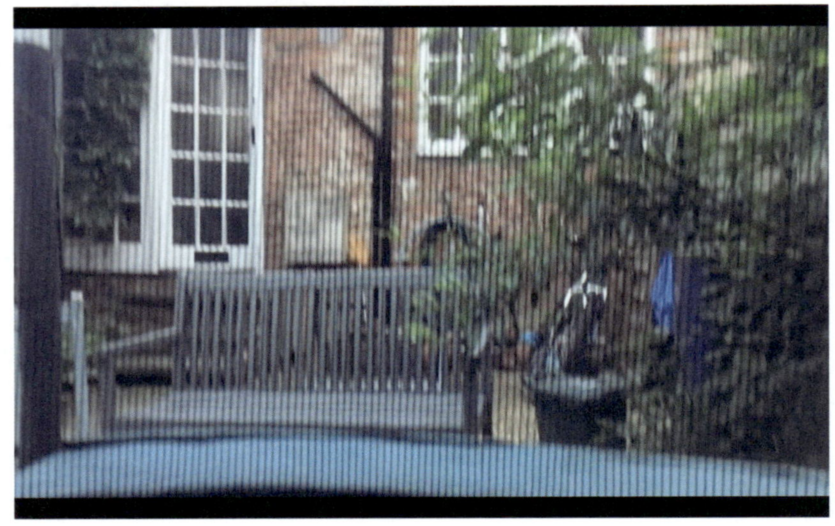

Juliette Blightman, **A Carpet For Your Somersaults**, 2020, video still. Courtesy Juliette Blightman and Galerie Fons Welters, Amsterdam.

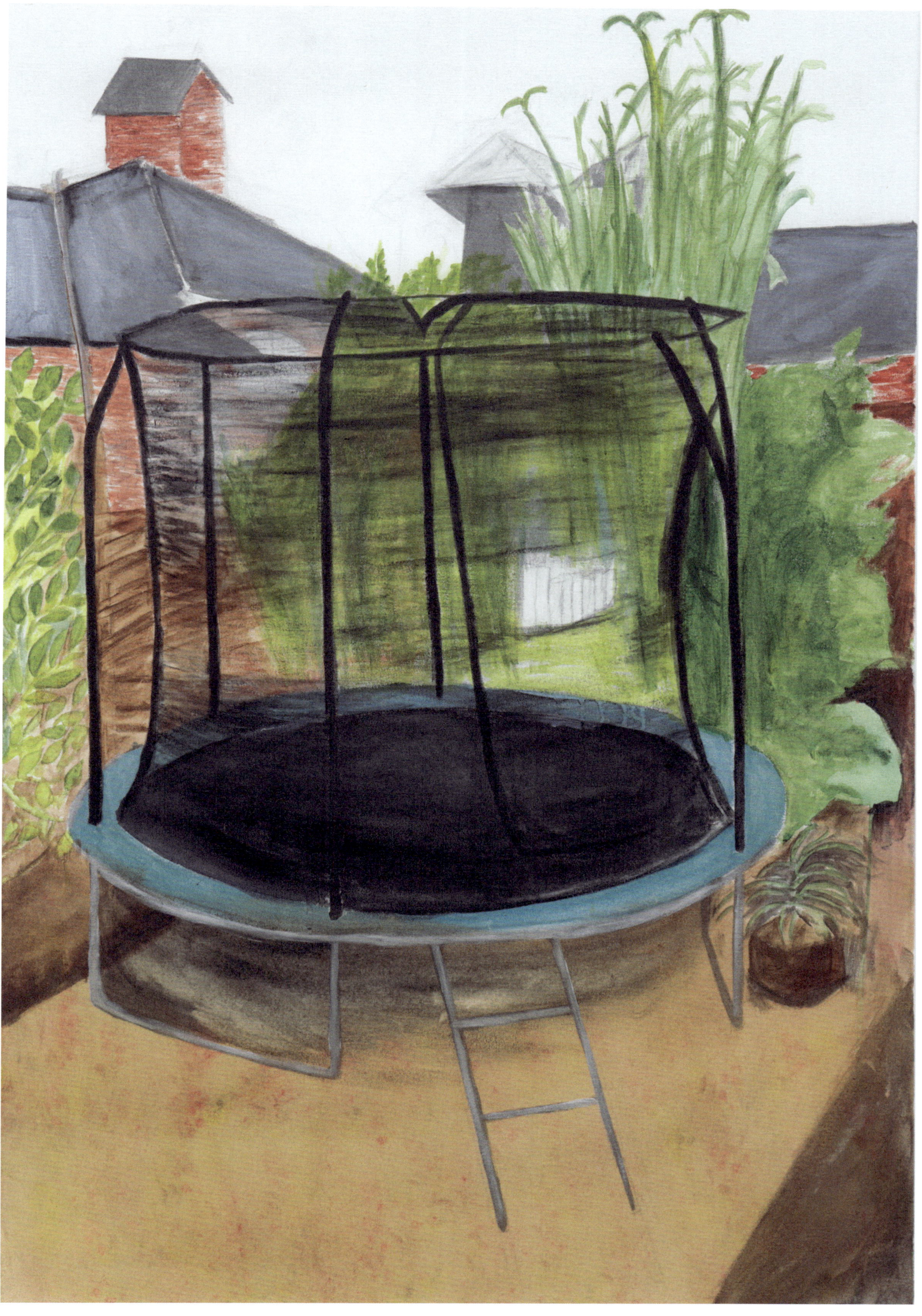

Juliette Blightman, **16th of July**, 2020, acrylic and pencil on canvas. Courtesy Juliette Blightman and Galerie Fons Welters, Amsterdam. Photo Gert Jan van Rooij.

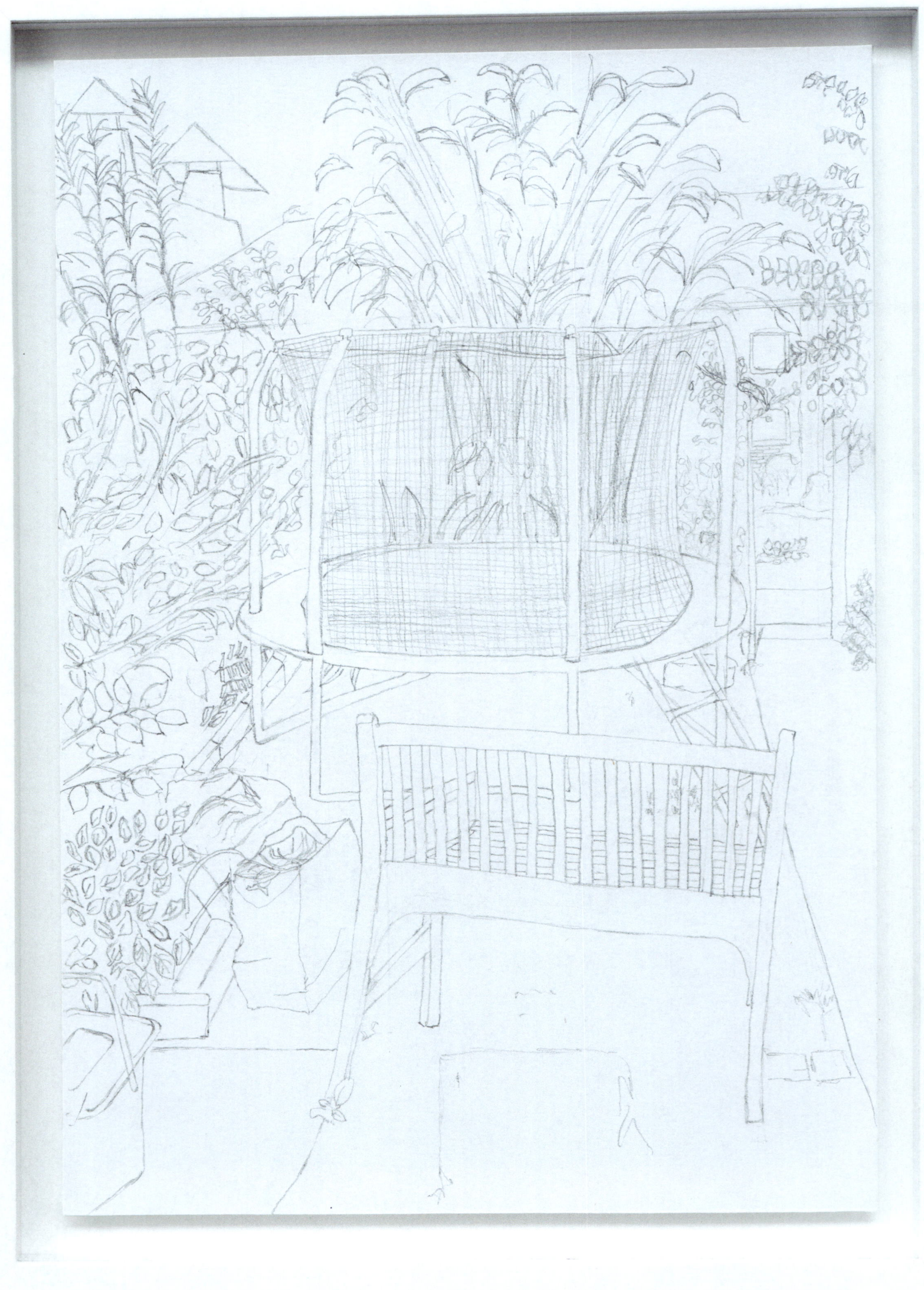

Juliette Blightman, **14th August, 2020**, 2020, drawing, 34 × 25.5 cm. Photo: Gert Jan van Rooij.

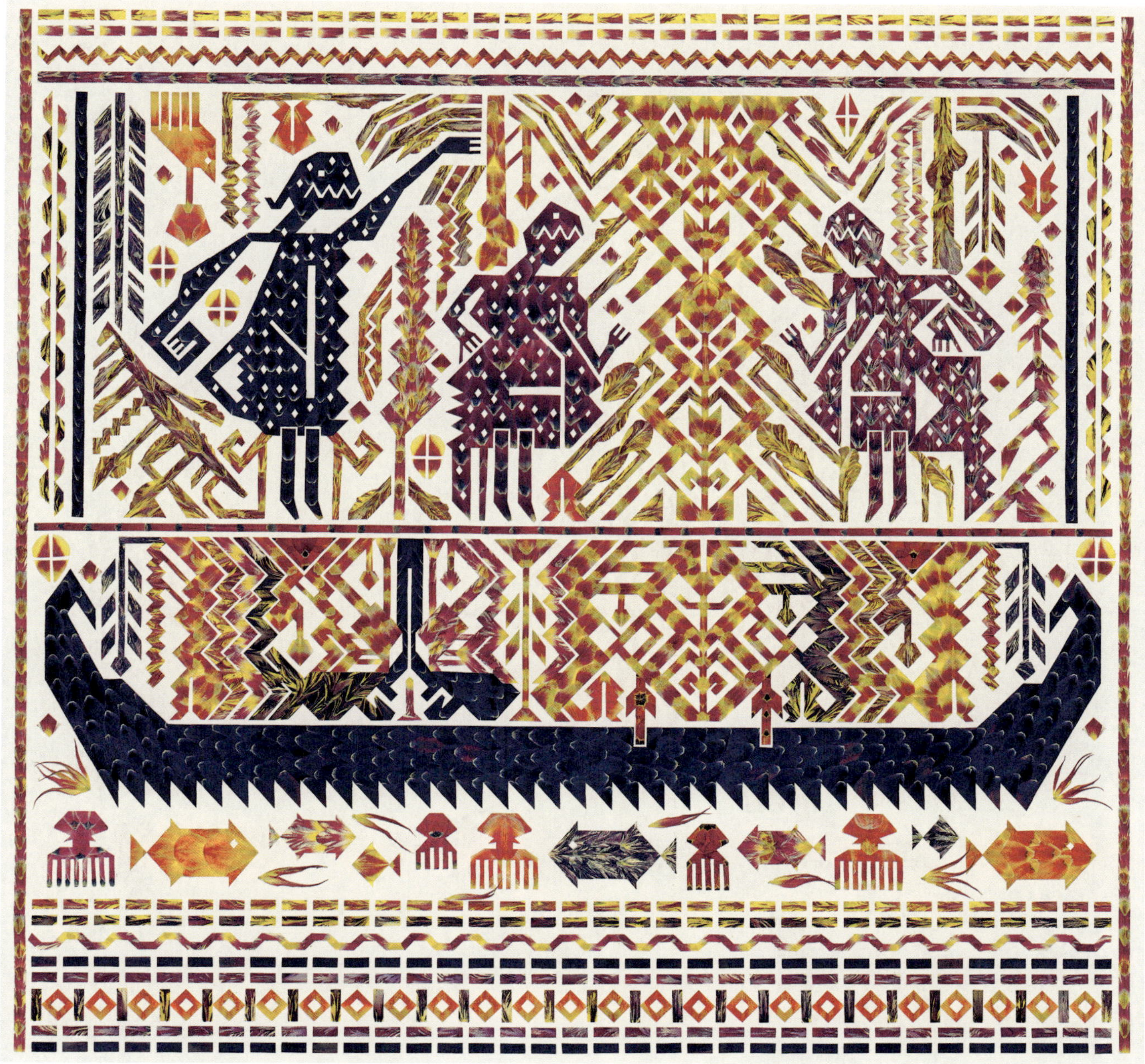

Jennifer Tee, **Tampan World Mountain, Tree of Life**, 2021, tulip petal collage on paper, 172 x 188 cm. Courtesy Galerie Fons Welters.

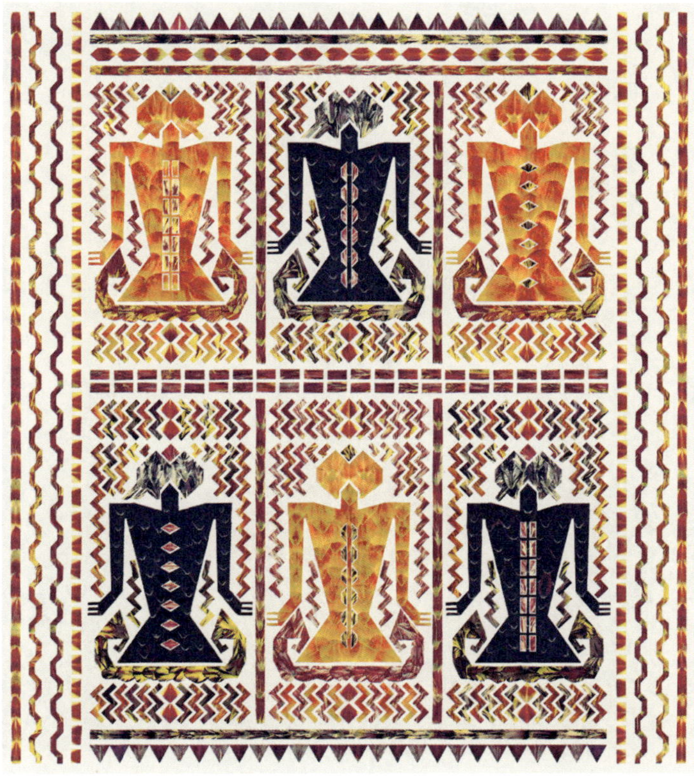

Jennifer Tee, **Tampan Six Subtle Bodies**, 2021, tulip petal collage on paper, 150 x 165 cm. Courtesy Galerie Fons Welters.

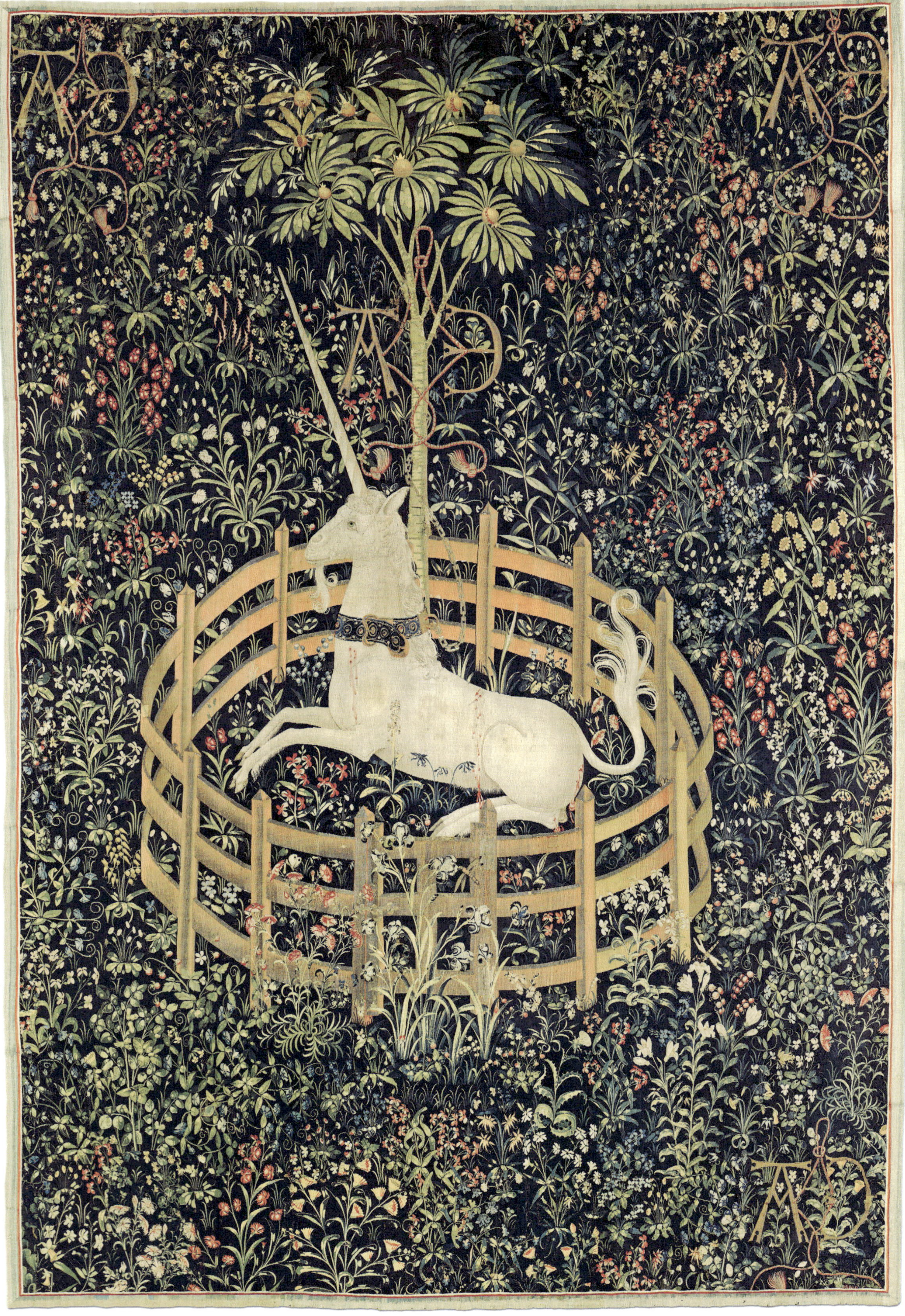

Anonymous French, **The Unicorn Rests in a Garden (from the Unicorn Tapestries)**, 1495–1505, tapestry, 368 × 251.5 cm. Courtesy The Metropolitan Museum of Art, New York and Art Resource/Scala, Florence.

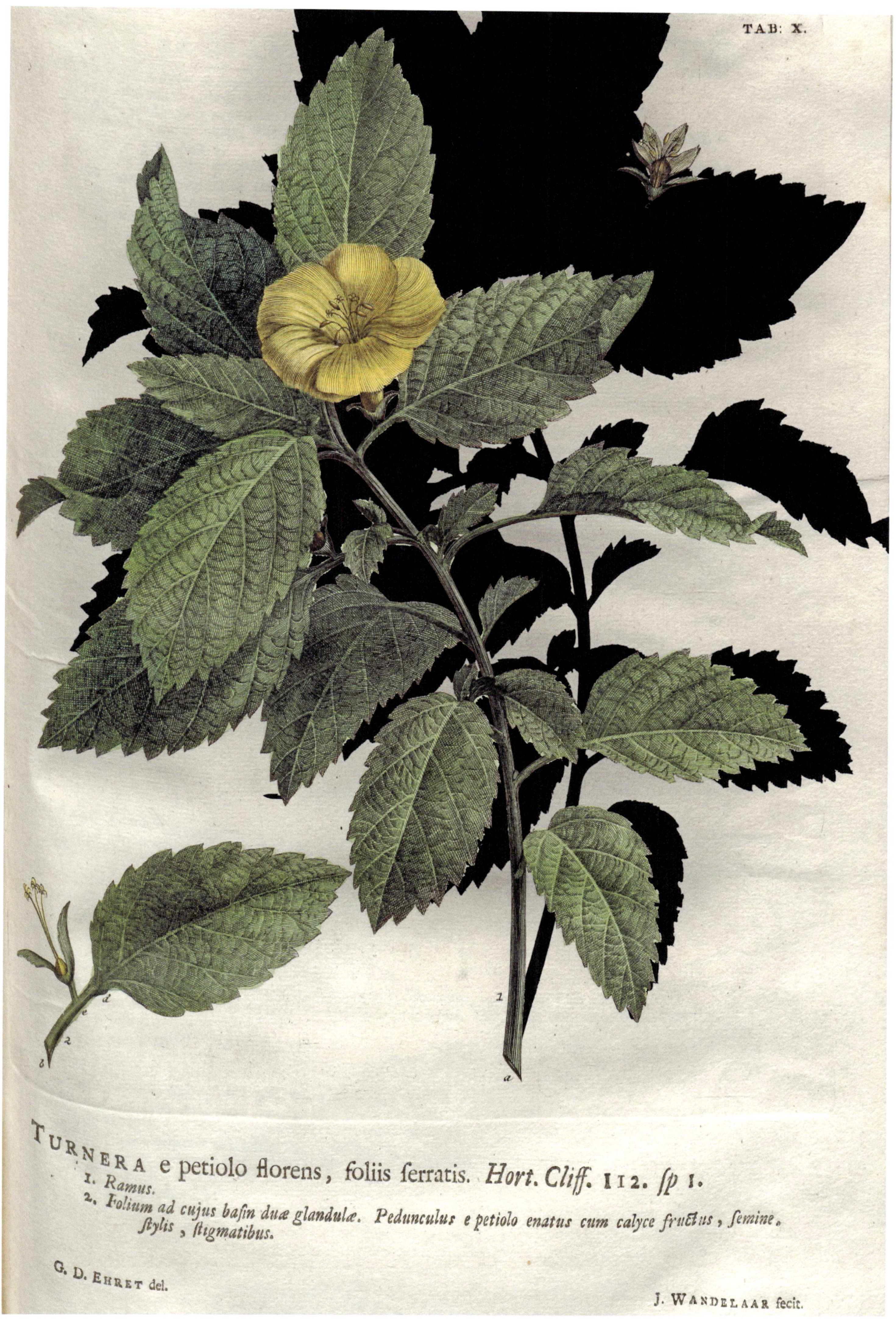

Persijn Broersen & Margit Lukács, work-in-progress **(Fix the Variable, Exclude the Accidental, Eliminate the Impure, Unravel the Tangled, Discover the Unknown)**, Turnera Hortus Cliffortianus, 2021.

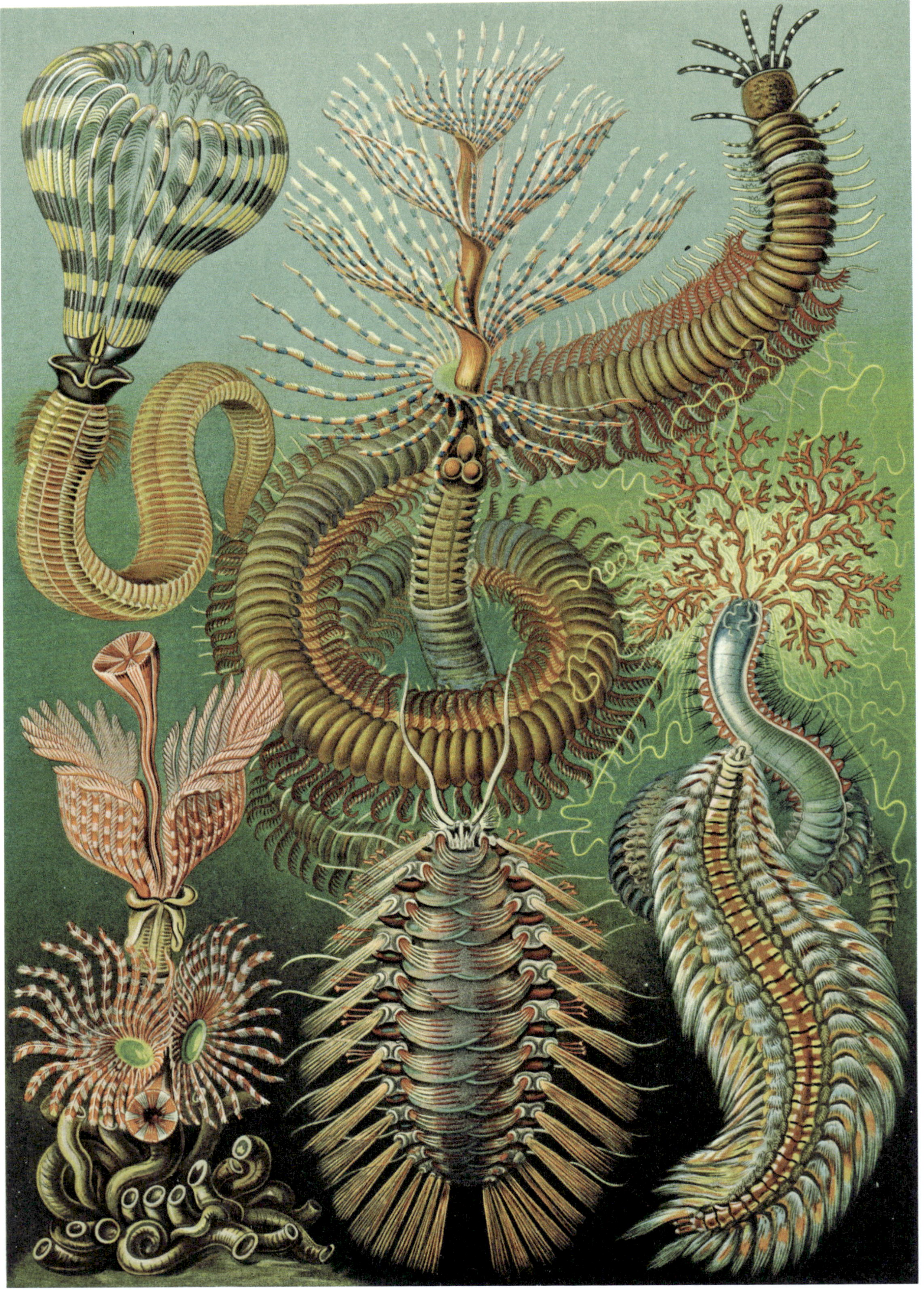

Ernst Haeckel, **Plate 4: Diatomea** from **Kunstformen der Natur**, 1904, engraving.

EPILOGUE

Bart Rutten

On 20 January 1916, the City Council of Utrecht decided that the former Convent of Saint Agnes in Agnietenstraat should be repurposed as a 'central museum' in which all the city's collections could be housed. The collections of the art society Kunstliefde, the Archiepiscopal Museum, and the Museum of Arts and Crafts were indeed brought together in this Centraal Museum in 1921. These are the roots of our broad collections, resembling today a richly planted flower bed, full of variety.

The convent, founded in 1420, had a garden at the rear, where crops could be sown and harvested, and a plot that served as a burial ground for the sisters. Life and death, past and present have always been linked in this location, home to our museum for a hundred years now. And, as you can read in this publication, in that period the garden has taken on many different guises.

From June 2021, the Centraal Museum, the oldest municipal museum in the Netherlands, is celebrating its centenary on Agnietenstraat in the remnants of the former convent and in a new building that opened in 1921. In 1987, the Centraal Museum also acquired the former stable complex on the Singel, which now forms the stage for the ambitious exhibition 'The Botanical Revolution: On the Necessity of Art and Gardening'. These buildings embraced, as it were, the medieval garden, which became increasingly central as a result of this expansion. This medieval garden thus became the hub around which the museum complex has nestled, and since the last renovation in 2016, the garden has become an even more emphatic orientation point for visitors, who are afforded views of it from the windows in the galleries.

While the appearance of the museum's garden has changed radically over the years, the collection contains a garden that, albeit modest, has remained unchanged for 350 years. The ground floor of the famous doll's house that belonged to Petronella de la Court features a beautiful garden, complete with a bench, statues on pedestals, and miniature plant pots. It is between these two gardening extremes that the exhibition and this publication navigate. The garden as a bearer of meaning. The garden as an oasis of peace and civilized nature within an urban environment. The garden as a metaphor for pleasure. And in this time, the garden as a necessary natural space to ensure our well-being.

Elsewhere in this publication, Laurie Cluitmans, the museum's Curator of Contemporary Art, writes: 'In a time of climate change, we see that artists are considering the garden as a refuge: a site for relaxation, a place to experience a different rhythm than that of the nine-to-five, where gardening is a hopeful form of labour in which, through care, plants and flowers are brought to blossom'. In this publication and in the exhibition it accompanies, she has considered the full range of meanings that the garden has in our time. I am grateful to her for the generosity with which she has put forward the research, most of which she conducted before she joined the museum, at the service of this wonderful project. With its building, its history, its collection, and programming vision, the Centraal Museum, I believe, provides the perfect soil conditions for this project to develop to its full potential.

The exhibition brings together new and existing works by contemporary artists with historical works from the collection and some special loans. An object's meaning, what or whom it represents and the type of story it tells, is dependent upon the context in which it is presented. Every generation develops new visions of the past, imbuing artworks with new meanings. Our task is to investigate the dynamics between objects and the changing geopolitical and historical contexts from a contemporary perspective, and to share these with the public. We do this in 'The Botanical Revolution' by explicitly seeking a dialogue between the art of today and the art of the past. Because although the exhibition's starting point is contemporary art—my great thanks go to those artists who have created or loaned new works for this exhibition—we also offer historical depth through a surprising use of well-known and lesser-known pieces from our own collection of modern art and art from the time of Petronella de la Court.

This selection is augmented by impressive loans from Museum Catharijneconvent, the Centre Pompidou, the Bonnefanten, the Rijksmuseum, and the Stedelijk Museum Amsterdam. I would, therefore, also like to extend my thanks to our colleagues who have loaned these works in good faith, for it is precisely the presence of these historical artworks in the exhibition that enriches the soil, allowing the art of today to blossom even more radiantly. I would also like to thank the authors who have contributed to this publication, beautifully designed by Bart de Baets, and made possible thanks to the generous support of the Stichting Jaap Harten Fonds, the Creative Industries Fund NL, dr. Hendrik Mullerfonds, and Stichting De Gijselaar-Hintzenfonds.

The exhibition has also been made possible by the Mondriaan Fund, Fund 21, Creative Industries Fund, Gemeente Utrecht, VriendenLoterij, Ministerie van OCW, MUNT Hypotheken and Van Baaren Stichting, which has enabled us to bring many beautiful works to Utrecht and to commission FormaFantasma to undertake the exhibition design, thus adding another special chapter to our steadily growing tradition of ambitious exhibition design.

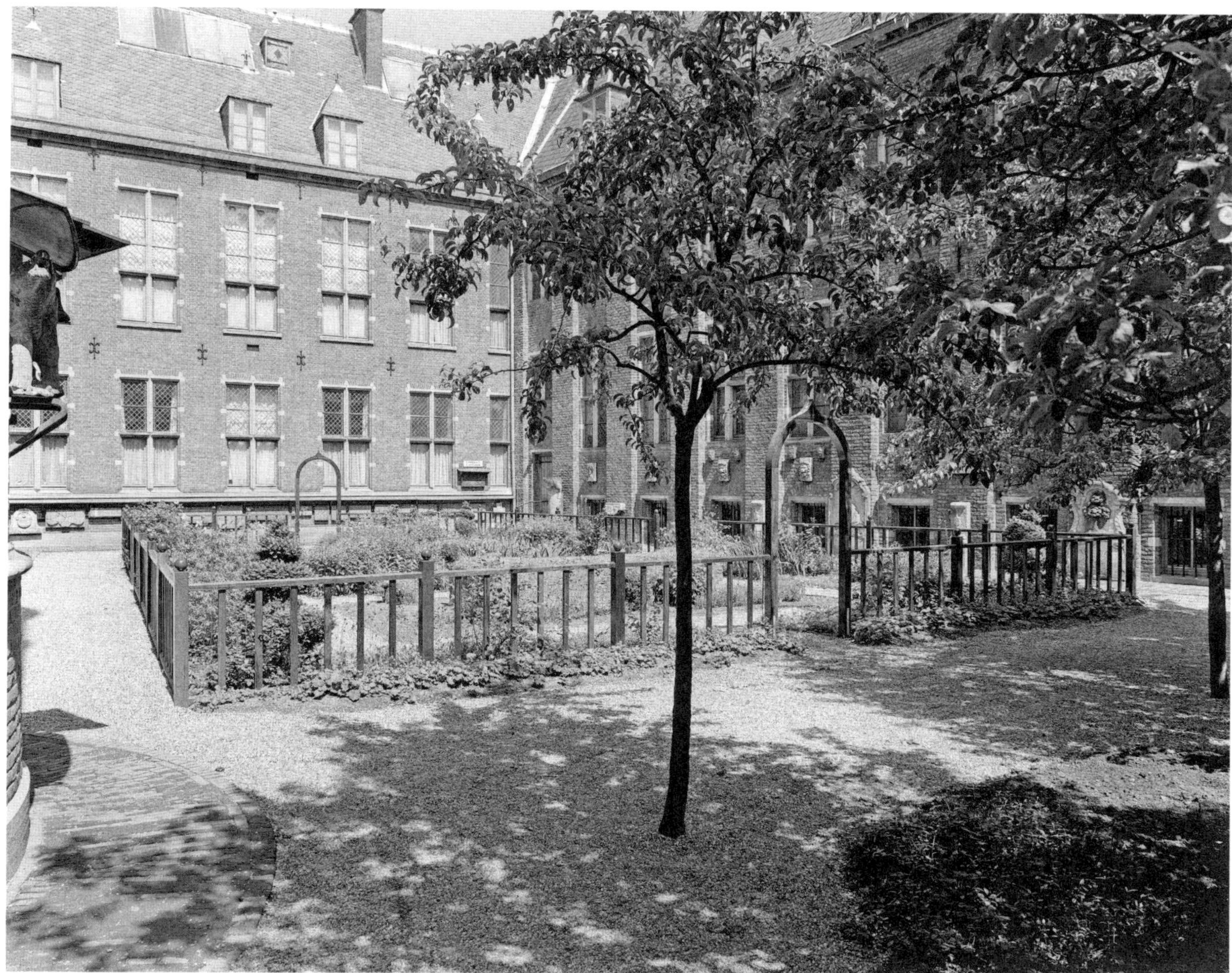
Garden Centraal Museum, 1974. © Centraal Museum Utrecht.

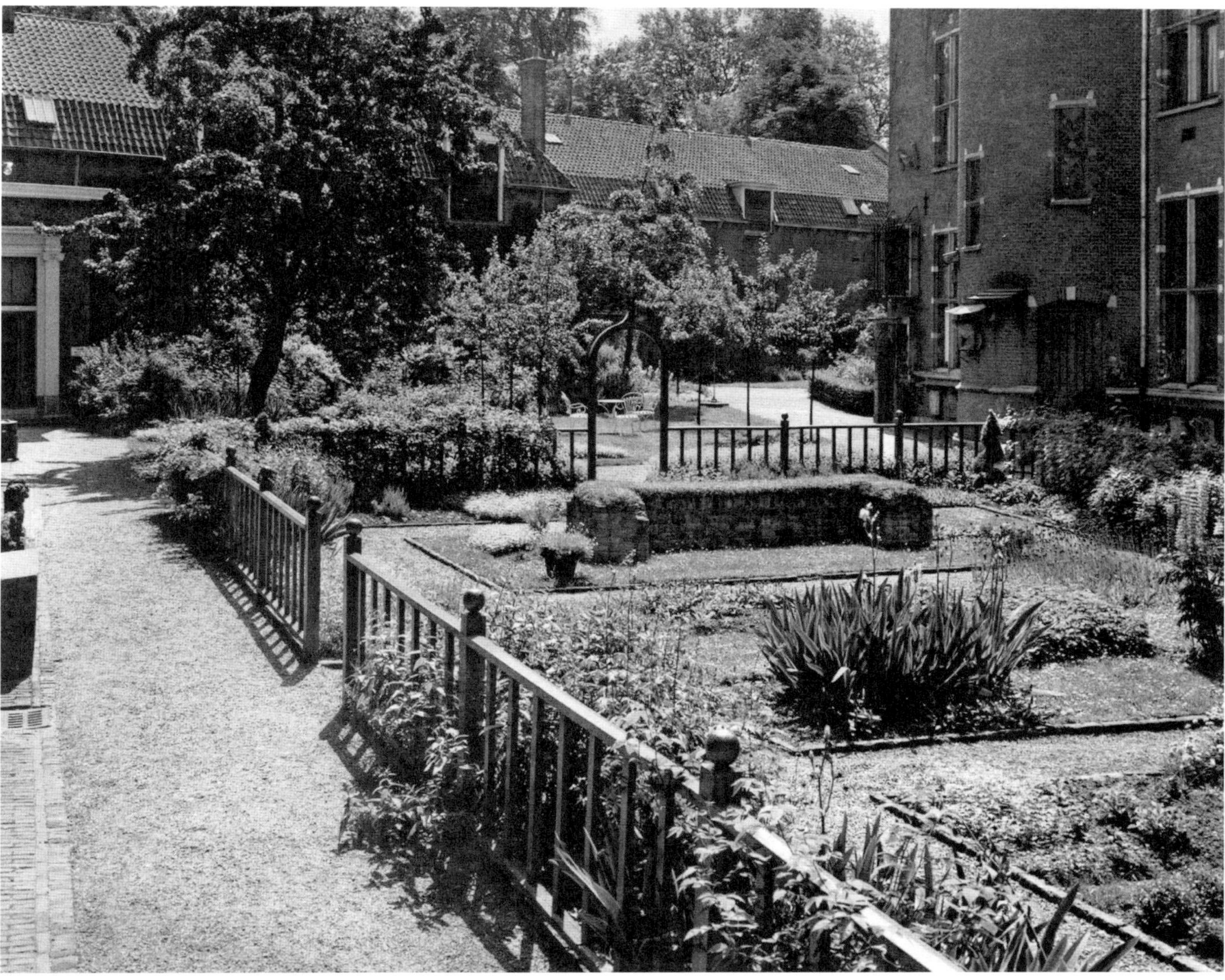
Garden Centraal Museum, 1974. © Centraal Museum Utrecht.

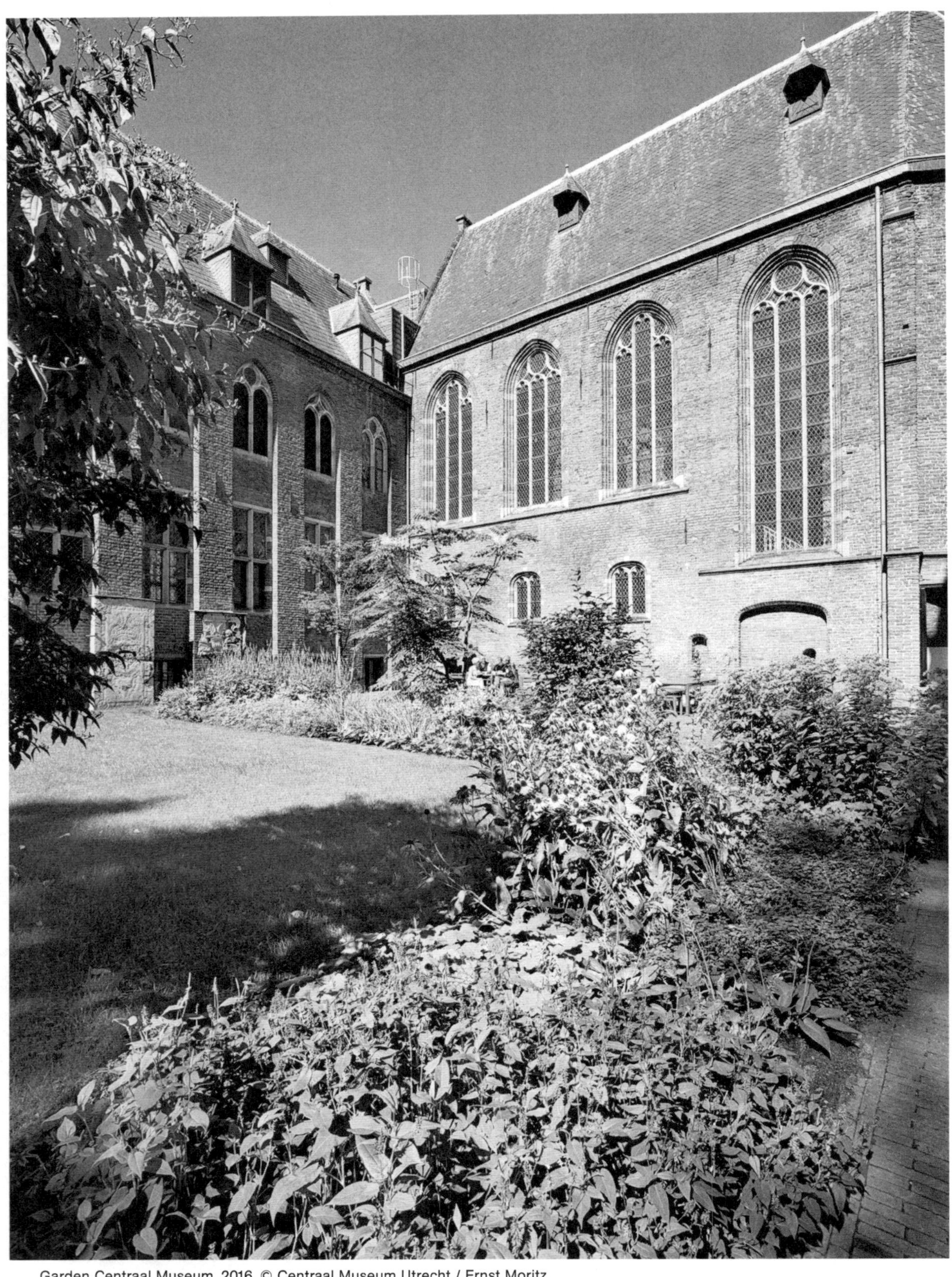

Garden Centraal Museum, 2016. © Centraal Museum Utrecht / Ernst Moritz.

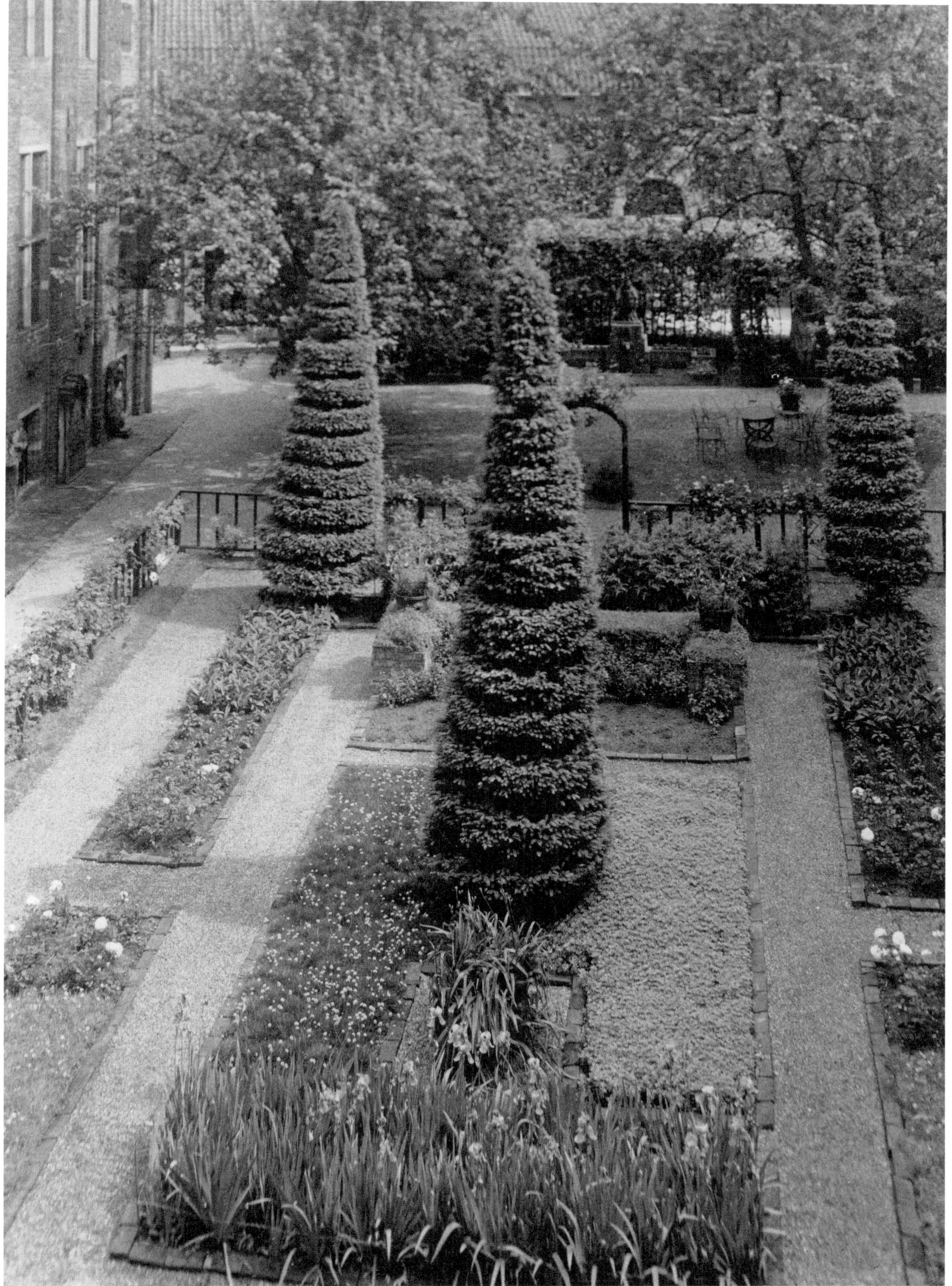

Garden Centraal Museum, 1984. © Centraal Museum Utrecht / Gerard van der Haar.

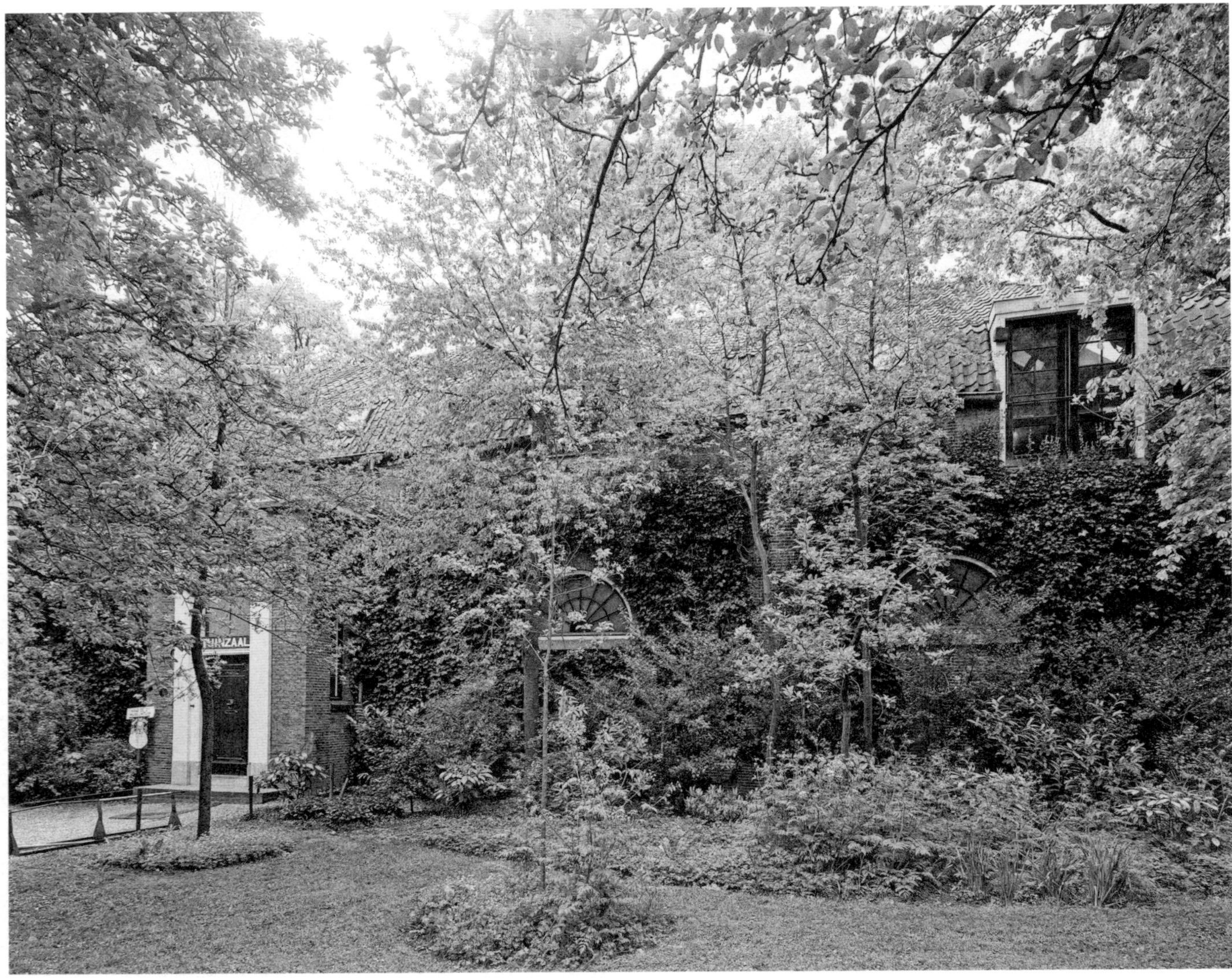

Centraal Museum, 1984. © Centraal Museum Utrecht / Gerard van der Haar.

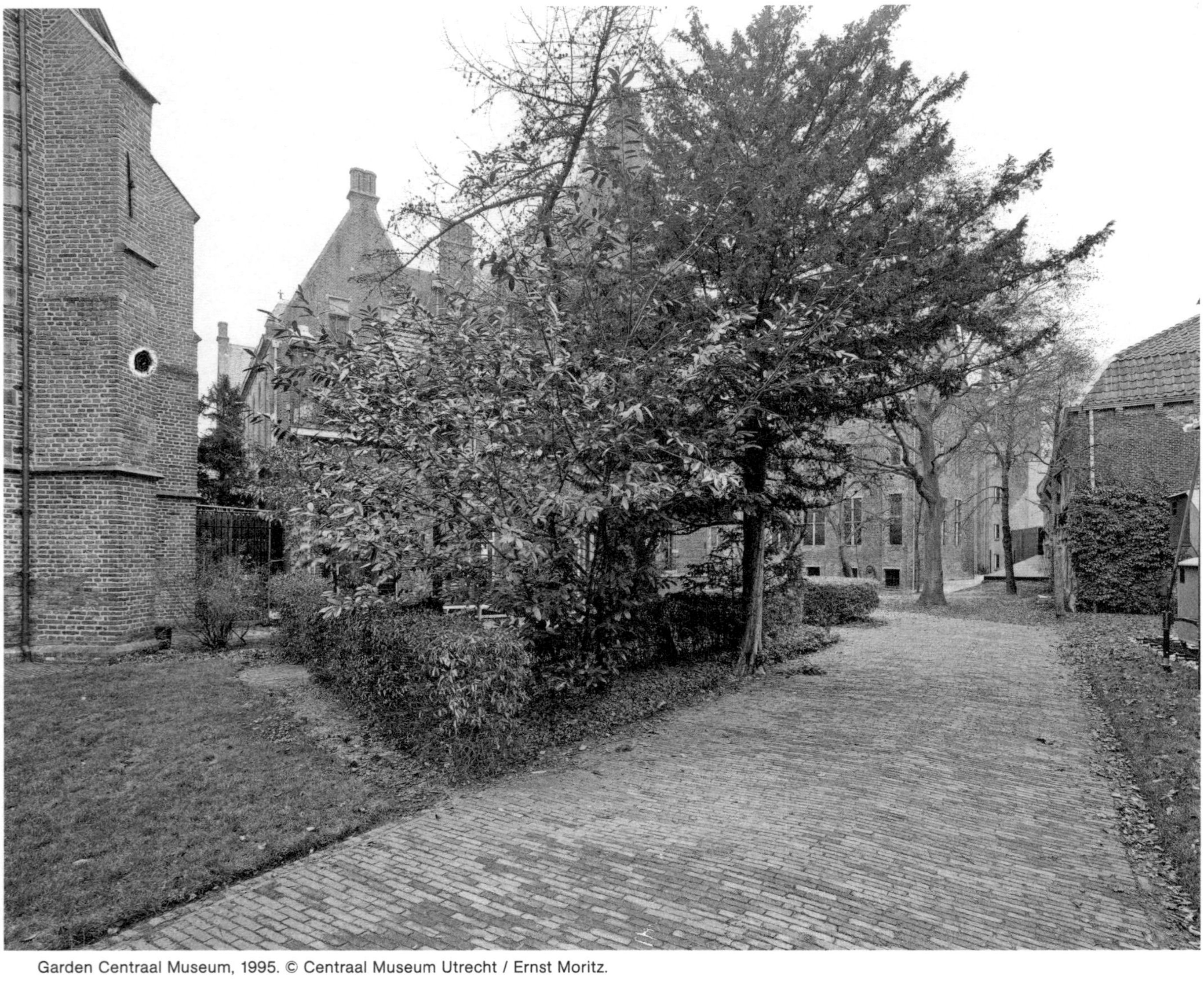

Garden Centraal Museum, 1995. © Centraal Museum Utrecht / Ernst Moritz.

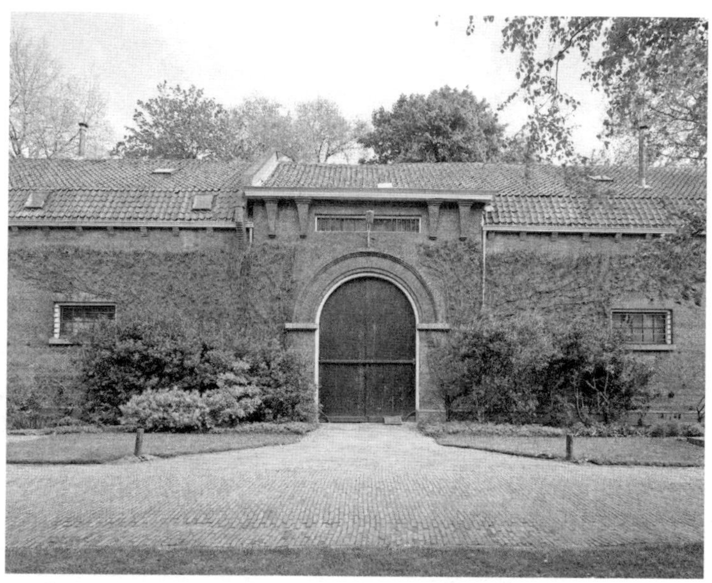

Garden Centraal Museum, 1984. © Centraal Museum Utrecht / Gerard van der Haar

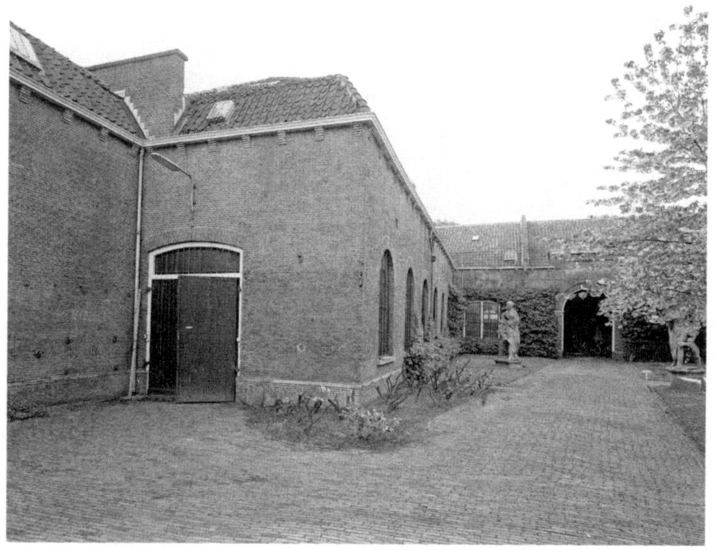

Garden Centraal Museum, 1984. © Centraal Museum Utrecht / Gerard van der Haar

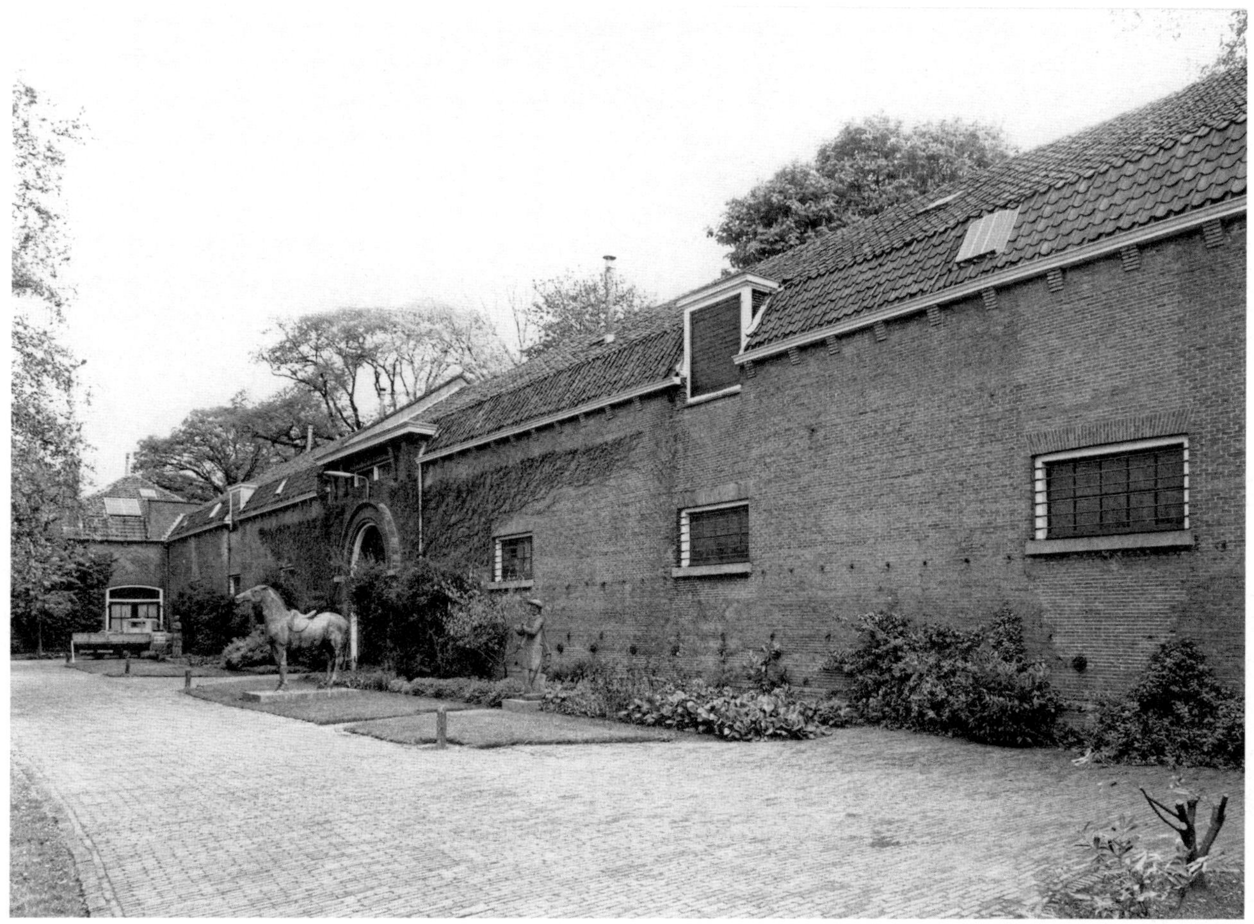

Garden Centraal Museum, 2016. © Centraal Museum Utrecht / Ernst Moritz.

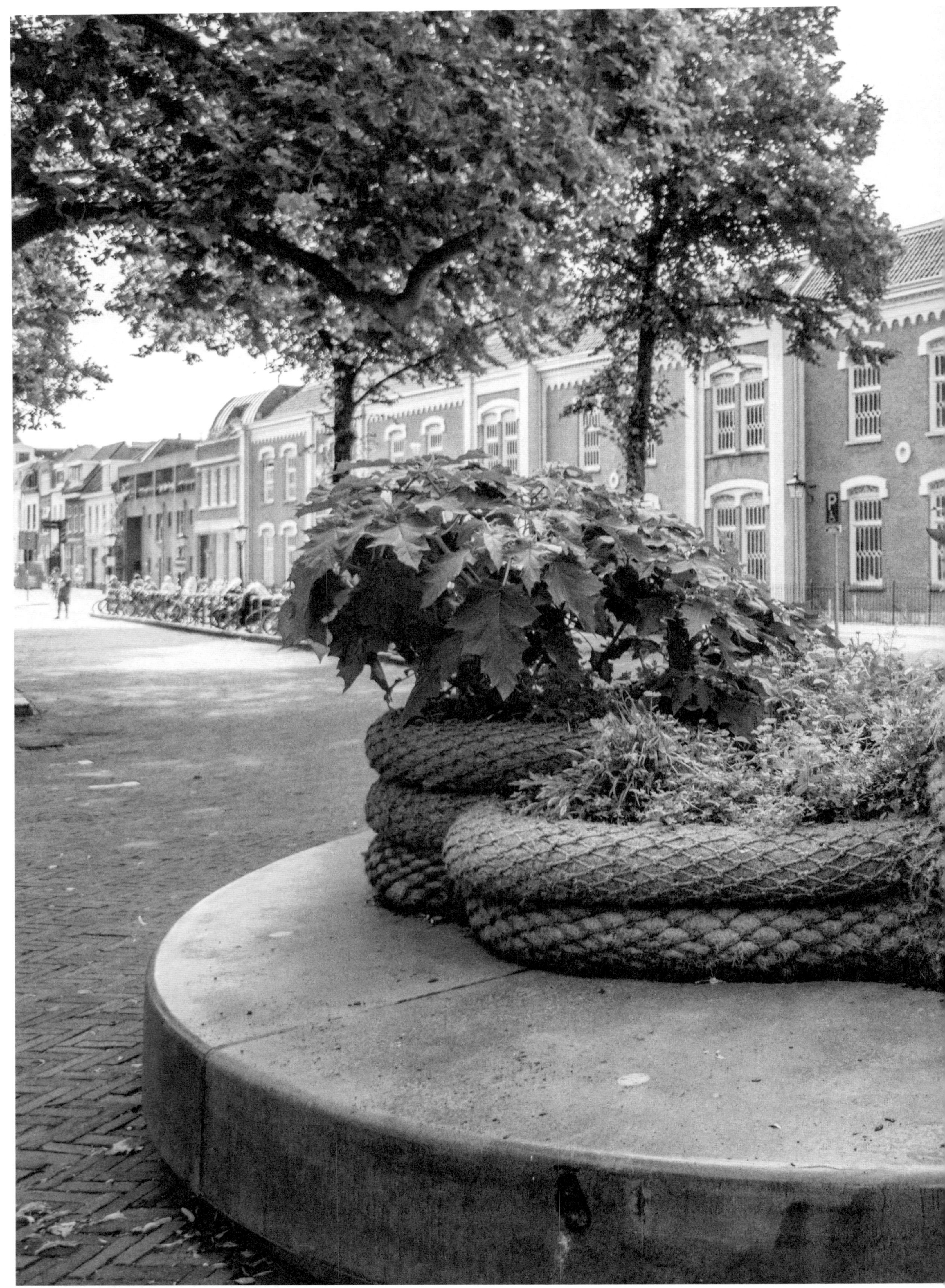

Maria Thereza Alves, **Seeds of Change: A Ballast Flora Garden (Liverpool)**, 2021, courtesy the artist and Michel Rein, Paris/Brussels. Photography Robert Oosterbroek.

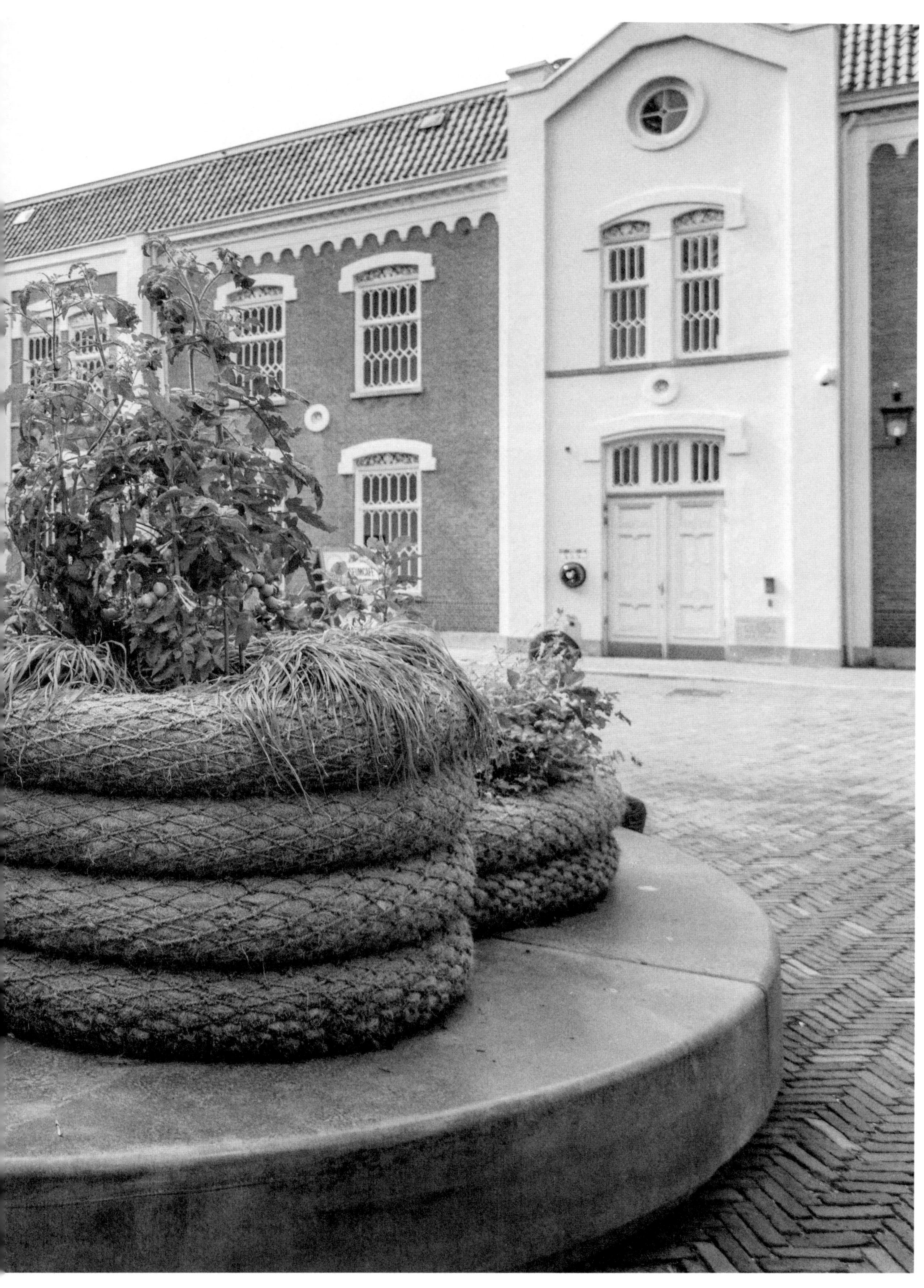

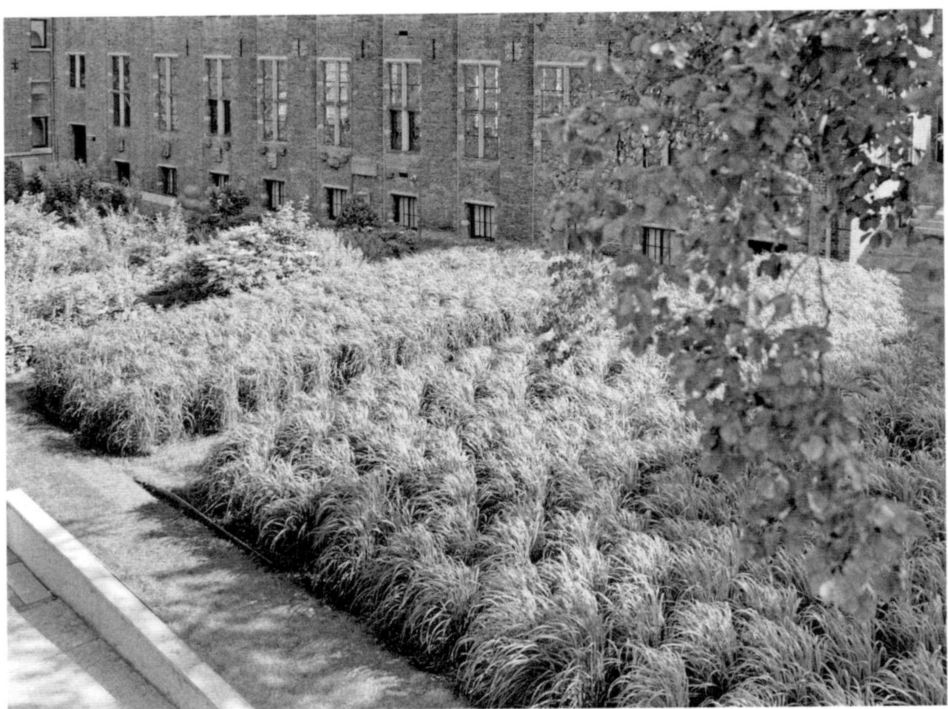

Garden Centraal Museum Utrecht, September 2002. © Centraal Museum Utrecht/Hans Wilschut.

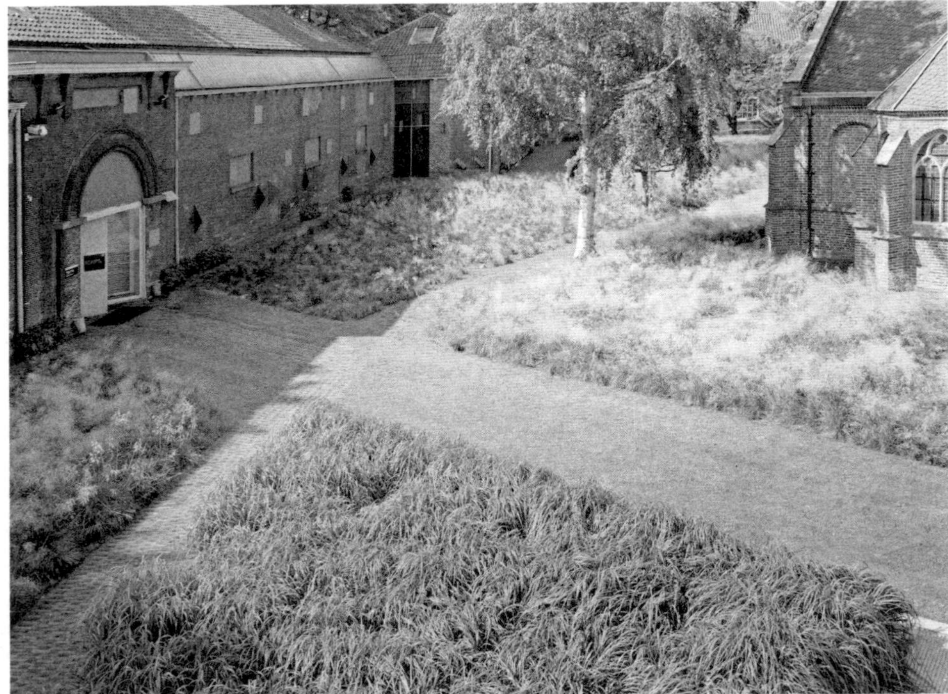

Garden Centraal Museum Utrecht, September 2002. © Centraal Museum Utrecht/Hans Wilschut.

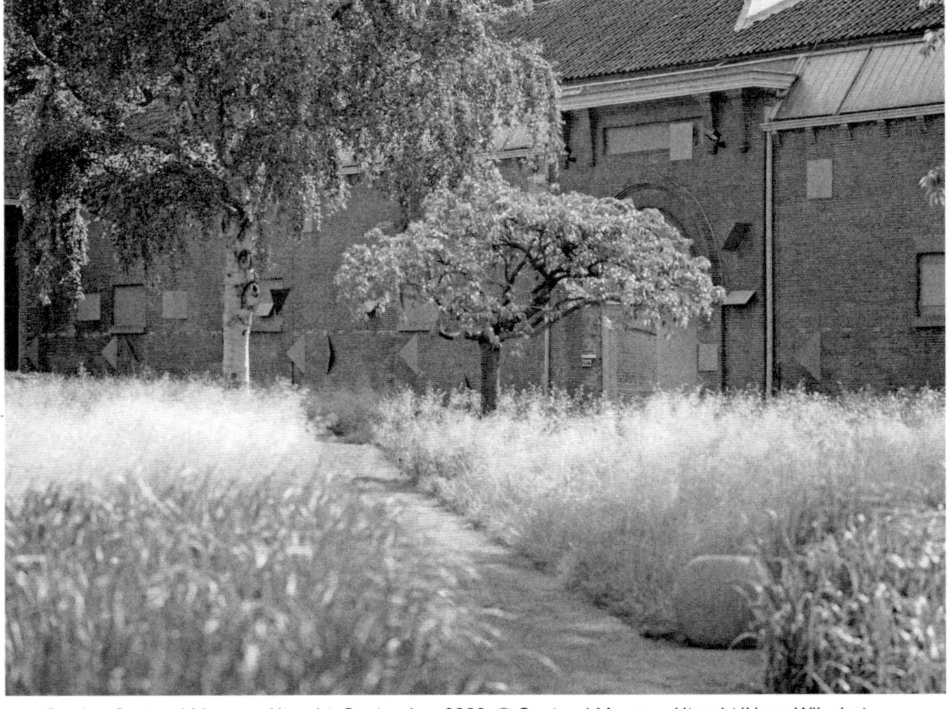

Garden Centraal Museum Utrecht, September 2002. © Centraal Museum Utrecht/Hans Wilschut.

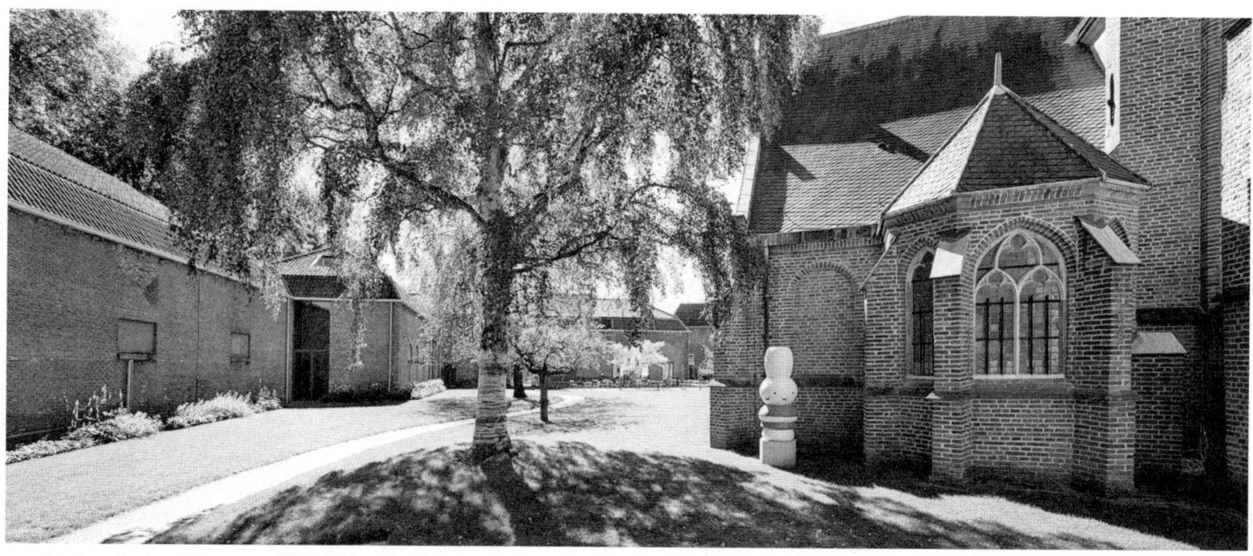

Garden Centraal Museum, 2016. © Centraal Museum Utrecht / Ernst Moritz.

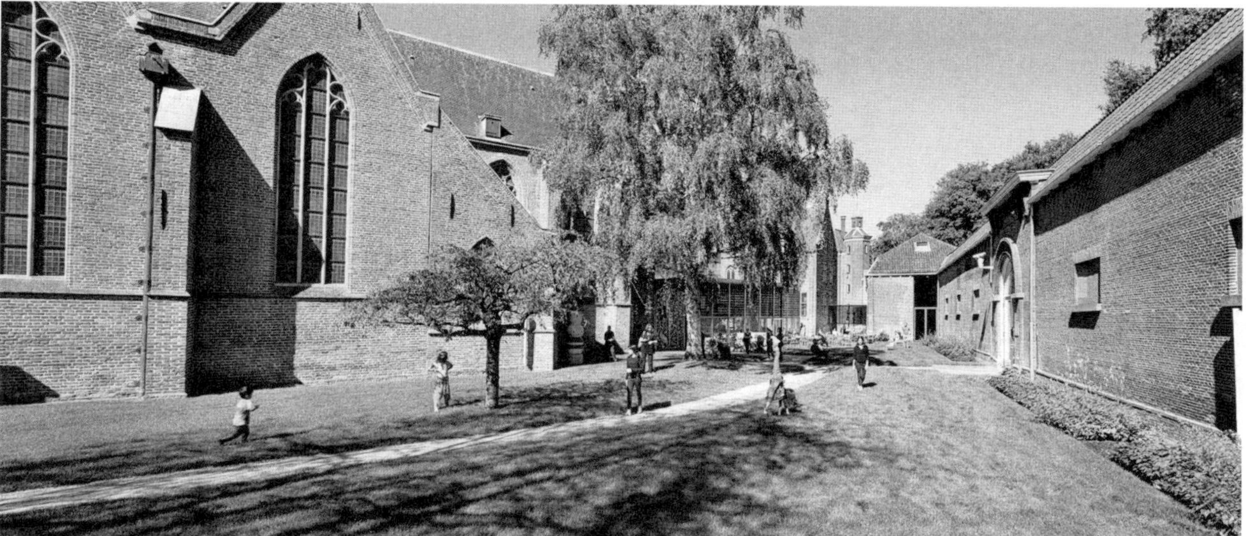

Garden Centraal Museum, 2016. © Centraal Museum Utrecht / Ernst Moritz.

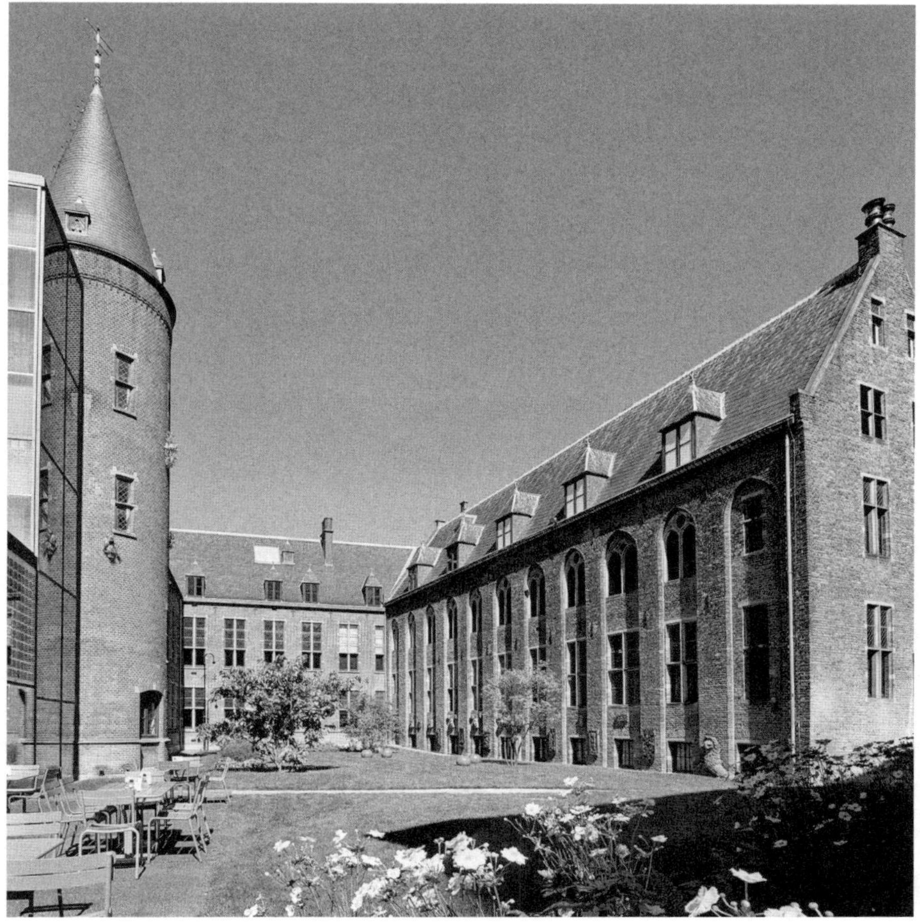

Garden Centraal Museum, 1967. © Centraal Museum.

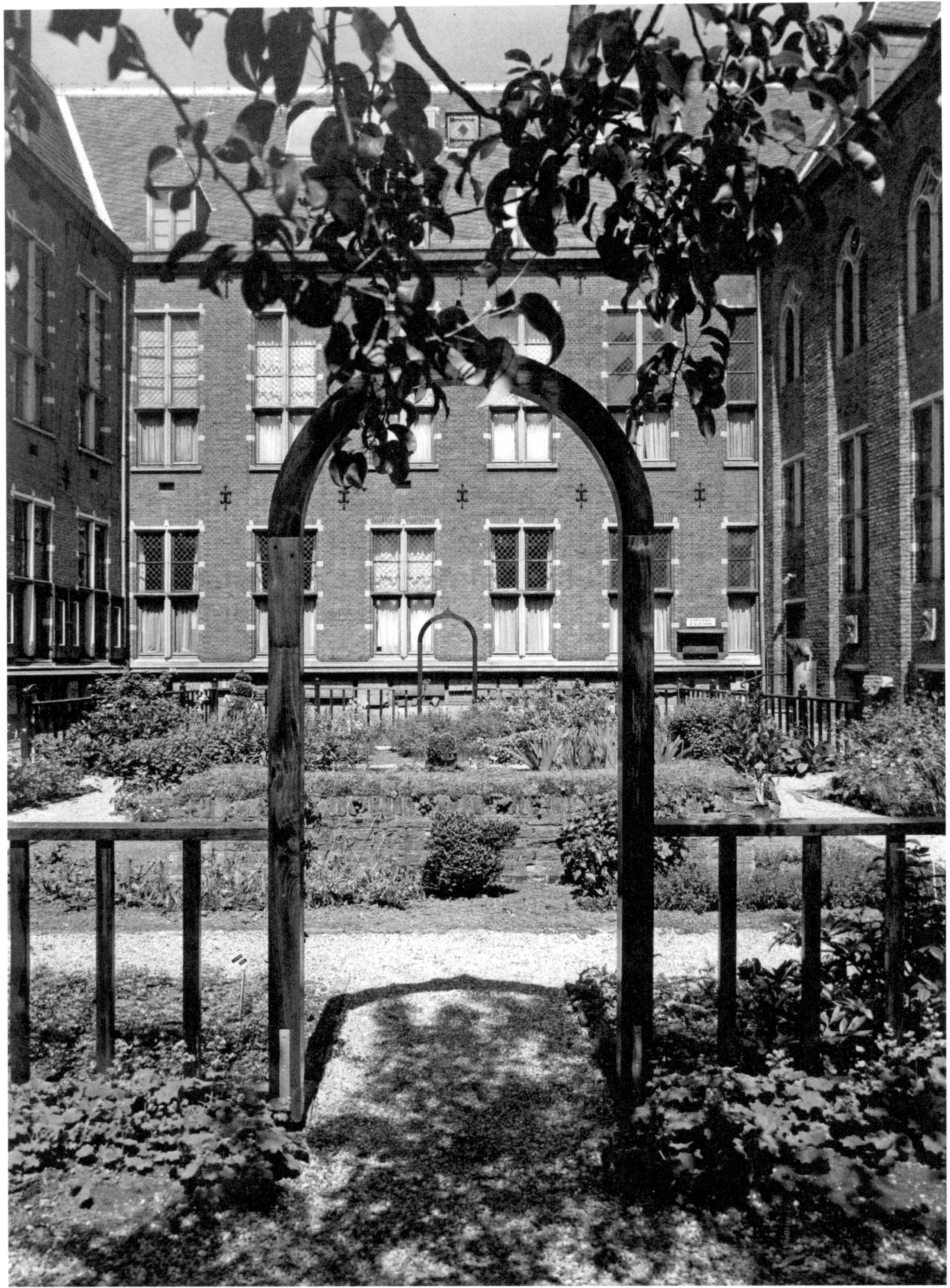

Centraal Museum, 1984. © Centraal Museum Utrecht / Gerard van der Haar.

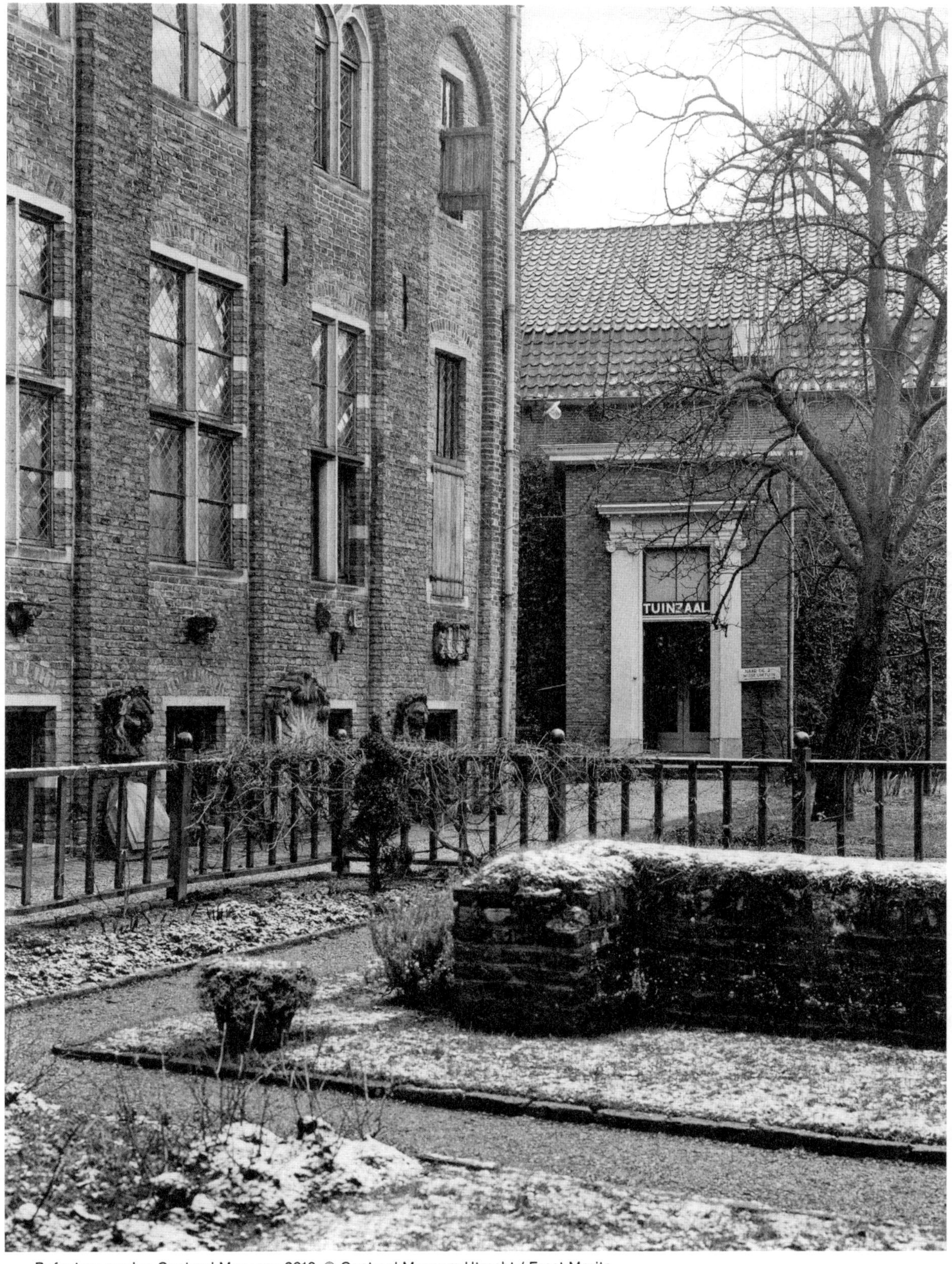

Refectory garden Centraal Museum, 2016. © Centraal Museum Utrecht / Ernst Moritz.

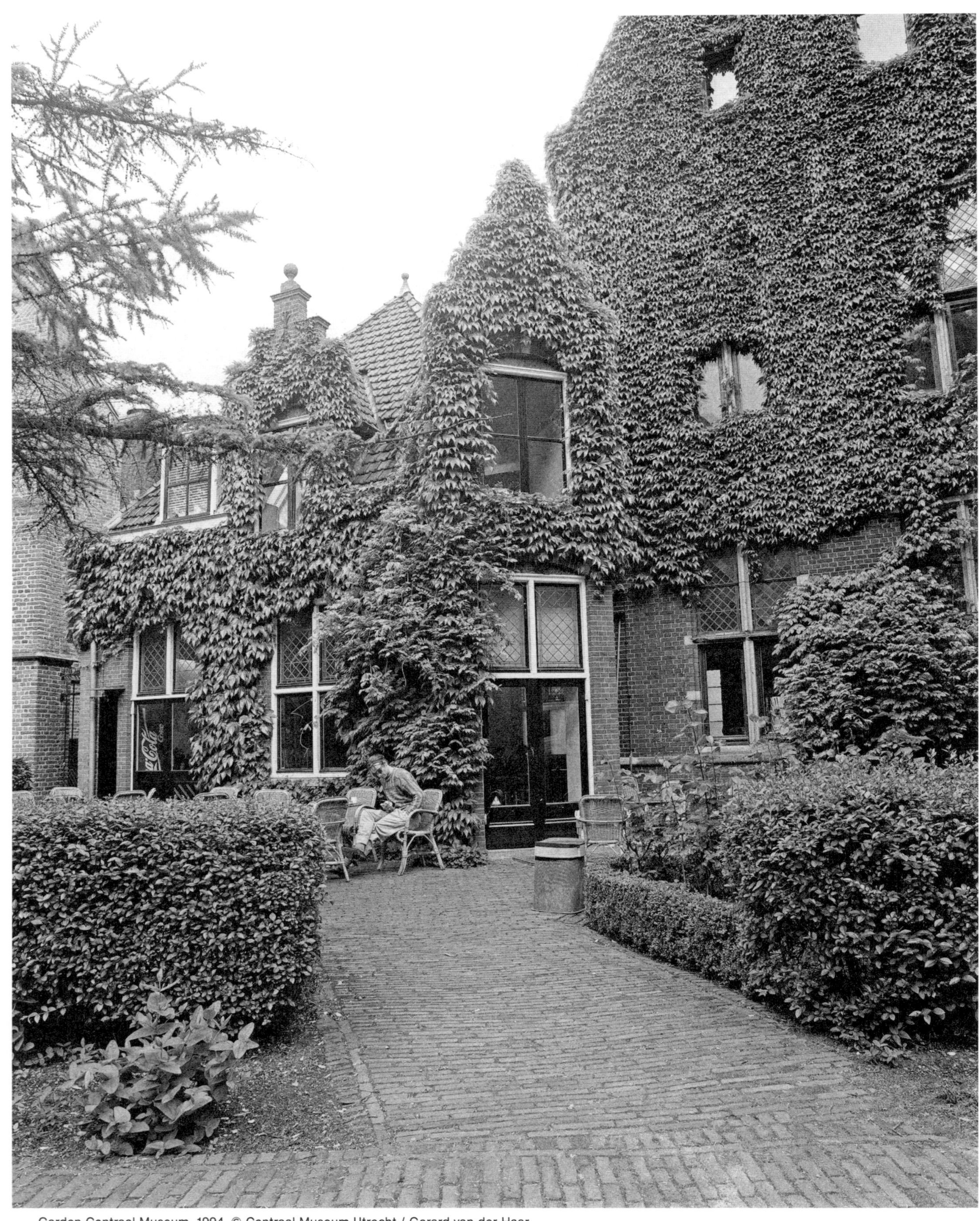

Garden Centraal Museum, 1994. © Centraal Museum Utrecht / Gerard van der Haar.

Curator's Acknow-ledgements

Laurie Cluitmans

The first ideas for this publication and the exhibition it accompanied arose in 2015. Since then, many people have offered advice and contributed to this quest for the contemporary meaning of the garden in a time of climate crisis. This project would not have been possible without the contributions, critical reflections, and new perspectives offered by numerous individuals. What began as a cautious interest has thus been able to grow into this collection of fragments brought together by artists, curators, writers, and the team at the Centraal Museum. I would like to express my profound gratitude to all of them.

In 2015, together with Maria Schnyder, Curator at the De Pont Museum in Tilburg, I undertook an initial research trip to Ian Hamilton Finlay's garden, Little Sparta, near Edinburgh, in Scotland. Although our research focused on sculpture gardens in the more classic sense of the word, Finlay demonstrated an entirely different possibility. His Little Sparta is a garden where an idiosyncratic world view is expressed in a precise relationship between sculptures and vegetation.

A year later, captivated by the idea of the artist's garden and following a collaboration with artist Jort van der Laan, along with two other artists, Derk Alberts and Charlotte Rooijackers, we visited Derek Jarman's garden at Prospect Cottage in Dungeness, on England's south coast. There we met Jonny Bruce, an art historian and gardener who at that time was volunteering in Jarman's garden. At Dungeness, a garden without walls emerged: without walls or boundaries, Jarman's garden was open to everyone.

As a result of this trip, van der Laan and I curated the exhibition 'All Heal (Valerian)' at Rongwrong in Amsterdam, a project made possible by the Amsterdam Fund for the Arts. Artists Sara Sejin Chang (Sara van der Heide), Elspeth Diederix, and Werker-Collective shared their own interpretation of the healing aspects and contemporary importance of the garden. Some of the artworks shown there are featured in the exhibition at the Centraal Museum and in this publication. The trip and encounters inspired me to write an essay for the Prize for Young Art Criticism, which I am humbled and grateful to have won. Having just started as a full-time freelance curator, the award confirmed my new direction. A grant from the Mondriaan Fund and a residency at the Center for Curatorial Studies at Bard College in Upstate New York further enabled me to continue my research. The many conversations there, especially with Galit Eilat, Alhena Katsof and Alex Kitnick, helped to broaden my perspective while sharpening the concept.

When I started as Curator of Contemporary Art at the Centraal Museum in January 2018, my research was immediately embraced by Artistic Director Bart Rutten and Business Director Marco Grob, allowing me to develop my plans further into this current exhibition and publication. The advice of Rutten and Liesbeth M. Helmus, Senior Curator of Old Masters, was decisive for the selection of modern art and old-masters. In collaboration with the museum's project group, under the sharp guidance of Lotte van Schellen, my abstract plans became concrete.

The knowledge, keen eyes, and playful ideas of the museum's collection management, marketing, and education teams—Kirsten Doornbos, Steffi Maas, Marije Meilink, Sigrid Noordijk, Pascale Pere, and Eveline Reeskamp—were essential in translating the exhibition concept for the visitor. Henk Heerink and Vladi Rapaport turned the dreams of the exhibition design into a reality. Frederik Markusse was responsible for picture editing and digitizing the photo archive of the Centraal Museum's garden. Anna Kesler and Martien van Liefland took care of the fundraising.

It goes without saying that this would not have been possible without the generous participation of the artists, and their work, perspective, and engaged conversations have helped to shape this exhibition:
Derk Alberts, Maria Thereza Alves, Yael Bartana, Jurgen Bey, Juliette Blightman, Abraham Bloemaert, Johannes Bosschaert, Ambrosius Bosschaert de Jonge, Andrea Büttner, Persijn Broersen & Margit Lukács, Sara Sejin Chang (Sara van der Heide), CPR (Charlotte Rooijackers), Meester van Delft, Jeremy Deller, Elspeth Diederix, Stan Douglas, Albrecht Dürer, Cecile Espinasse, Ian Hamilton Finlay, Vincent van Gogh, Lungiswa Gqunta, Hendrick Goltzius, Rumiko Hagiwara, Saskia Noor van Imhoff, Patricia Kaersenhout, Tetsumi Kudo, Herman Justus Kruyder, Jort van der Laan, Hans van Lunteren & Ienke Kastelein, Kerry James Marshall, Master of Paulus and Barnabas, Maria Sibylla Merian, Sarah Naqvi & Mylou Oord & Shreya de Souza, Maria Pask, Otto van Rees, Willem de Rooij, Roelant Saverij, Jennifer Tee and Henk Wildschut.

Several museums, commercial galleries, and private collectors entrusted their works to the museum's good care: Rijksmuseum, Stedelijk Museum Amsterdam, Van Abbemuseum, Frans Hals Museum, het Bonnefanten, Museum Catharijneconvent, Centre Georges Pompidou, Musée du Quai Branly, Westfälisches Landesmuseum, David Zwirner Gallery, Museum Minsk, Potsdam, Ellen de Bruijne Projects, George Kargl Fine Arts, Wenen, Universiteit Utrecht, Universiteit Wageningen, collection De Bruin-Heijn, private collection Defares, private collection Rijs.

Sophie Delfos, intern, and Eva Burgering, curator in training, conducted research that contributed to making the special loans possible. Many other colleagues offered advice regarding possible loans and additions to the abecedarium.

The Formafantasma team, consisting of Andrea Trimarchi, Simone Farresin, and Simon Ballen, delivered a beautiful exhibition design that reflects the experience of a Japanese zen garden, where industrial elements seep through. Thanks to their understated yet distinctive and sustainable modular system, the works of art can shine in their own right and tell a story together.

My thanks go to all the authors for their carefully considered contributions to this book: Maria Barnas, Jonny Bruce, Thiëmo Heilbron, Erik A. de Jong, Liesbeth M. Helmus, René de Kam, Alhena Katsof, Jamaica Kincaid, Catriona Sandilands, Patricia de Vries.

It was quite a challenge to complete the abecedarium within the time frame, but we succeeded thanks to the detective work and perseverance of Eva Burgering and Arent Boon, research intern. They also worked together on the picture editing and the rich diversity of images is, in part, thanks to them.

The publication could not have been realized without the exacting editing of Hans Schopping, the critical advice of Gerard Forde, the knowledge and support of Pia Pol from Valiz, and Bart de Baets's beautiful and playful design.

Finally, there was a certain person who was always ready to brainstorm or to distract.

I owe them all an immense debt of gratitude.

MARIA BARNAS (1973) is a poet and visual artist. Her language-based work can be found in magazines, books, sound pieces, films, and installations. She is Head of the Temporary MA Programme Approaching Language at Sandberg Institute, Amsterdam, and writes about poetry for the newspaper *NRC Handelsblad*. Barnas is also editor of the literary magazine *De Gids*.

JONNY BRUCE is a freelance gardener and writer. Since graduating from Cambridge University with a BA in Art History in 2013, he has been gardening full time, including two years at Great Dixter in East Sussex. He recently spent four years in the Netherlands at the renowned organic plant nursery De Hessenhof, near Ede. Bruce started working as the primary gardener at Prospect Cottage in 2014 when its owner, Keith Collins, died in August 2018. Having now returned to the UK, he continues his work as a gardener and writer, alongside the continued maintenance of the garden at Prospect Cottage.

LAURIE CLUITMANS (1984) is a curator and art critic. Since January 2018, she has worked as Curator of Contemporary Art at the Centraal Museum, and previously served as Gallery Director at Galerie Fons Welters in Amsterdam and as an independent curator and critic. Her recent exhibitions include 'Stuff Matters: Jessica Stockholder' and 'Eaten by Non-Humans: Janis Rafa', both at the Centraal Museum. Cluitmans has also curated exhibitions for de Appel, Amsterdam, Sculpture International, Rotterdam, and De Hallen Haarlem. In 2016, she was awarded the Prize for Young Art Criticism for her essay on the garden of Derek Jarman. This publication and eponymous exhibition are the result of her research on artists' gardens.

THIËMO HEILBRON (1986) is trained as a biologist and ecologist and graduated on the botanical heritage of the plantations of Suriname. He is the Founder and Director of the social enterprise Fawaka Ondernemersschool and Curator of Green & Sustainability at Rijksmuseum Muiderslot. Plants with origins from all over the world grow in Suriname and, on the basis of these plants and local people's stories about them, one can reconstruct the history of the country. At the Rijksmuseum Muiderslot, Heilbron is currently working on the living collection—the gardens of the Muiderslot—and unlocking the stories behind the plants. With his company Fawaka Ondernemersschool he develops educational programmes on sustainable entrepreneurship for children and teens.

LIESBETH M. HELMUS is Senior Curator of Sixteenth- and Seventeenth-Century Dutch Painting at the Centraal Museum in Utrecht, Netherlands. She obtained her PhD from the University of Amsterdam in 2010. Her recent exhibitions include 'Utrecht, Caravaggio and Europe', Centraal Museum Utrecht with the Alte Pinakothek Munich, 2018–2019, and 'Pleasure and Piety: The Art of Joachim Wtewael (1566–1638)', National Gallery of Art Washington and the Museum of Fine Arts Houston, 2015–2016. Helmus is an internationally renowned scholar who has published widely on Dutch painting, and is currently working on a book about the Utrecht painter Gerard van Honthorst.

ERIK A. DE JONG is a Professor Emeritus of Culture, Landscape and Nature at the University of Amsterdam. His PhD thesis *Nature and Art* (1993) was awarded an Erasmus study prize. He has worked in Wageningen, New York, and at Harvard, and his interests concern the relationship between man and nature and the meaning of garden, park, and landscape. He has lectured from Sweden to Japan, Switzerland to the USA, and his recent exhibitions include 'The Story of Gardening', with Kossmanndejong Amsterdam at The Newt in Somerset, 2020. As a board member, de Jong is committed to the Landje van De Boer in Bloemendaal and the learning place at the regenerative farm Bodemzicht, Nijmegen. The Swedish Dendrological Society appointed him an honorary member. At the present time, he tends to two gardens.

RENÉ DE KAM is a curator and historian and studied History at the University of Utrecht. He is Curator of Utrecht History at the Centraal Museum and previously worked in the Department of Heritage at the municipality of Utrecht. De Kam's recent publications include *The Walled City. History of Defending the City* (2020); *The History of Utrecht from a Bird's Eye View* (2017), and *The Domtoren of Utrecht. The City's Pride* (2014). De Kam has also been involved in a number of exhibitions about the history of Utrecht.

ALHENA KATSOF is a doctoral candidate in Performance Studies at the Tisch School of the Arts, New York University, and teaches at Eugene Lang College of Liberal Arts, The New School. Her numerous exhibition-based projects include 'Towards the Unknown', 2014, a travelling show of drawings, scores, and graphic notations by the musician Yusef Lateef, which she curated at White Columns in New York City. Katsof's recent essays have appeared in *Nicole Eisenman: Sturm und Drang* (2021); *Andrea Geyer: Dance in a Future with All Present* (2019); *The Artist As Curator: An Anthology* (2017); and *Solution 263: Double Agent* (2015). She lives and works in New York City.

JAMAICA KINCAID is a writer, novelist, and professor. Her works include *Annie John*, *Lucy*, *The Autobiography of My Mother*, and *Mr. Potter*, as well as her classic history of her Antigua, *A Small Place* and memoir *My Brother*. Her first book, the collection of stories *At the Bottom of the River*, won the Morton Dauwen Zabel Award from the American Academy and Institute of Arts and was nominated for the PEN/Faulkner Award for Fiction. Kincaid's last novel, *See Now Then*, was published in 2013. Professor of African and African American Studies in Residence at Harvard University, Kincaid was elected to the American Academy of Arts and Letters in 2004. She has received a Guggenheim Award, the Lannan Literary Award for Fiction, the Prix Femina Étranger, Anisfield-Wolf Book Award, the Clifton Fadiman Medal, and the Dan David Prize for Literature in 2017.

BART RUTTEN has been the Artistic Director of the Centraal Museum since May 2017. Before his appointment in Utrecht, he was Head of Collections at the Stedelijk Museum Amsterdam and as a curator coordinated exhibitions such as 'De Oase van Matisse' (2015) and 'Kazimir Malevich and the Russian Avant-Garde' (2013). Prior to that he worked at the Stedelijk Museum's-Hertogenbosch and the Netherlands Media Art Institute. Rutten presents items on exhibitions for the AvroTros' TV programme *Nu te zien*. He is a member of several advisory committees and boards in Utrecht and the Netherlands, including the Supervisory Board of the Stedelijk Museum Alkmaar, advisor to the Rembrandt Association, Musea Bekennen Kleur, and the HEM in Zaandam.

CATRIONA SANDILANDS is a Professor of Environmental Arts and Justice in the Faculty of Environmental and Urban Change at York University. She is known for her extensive writing on queer and feminist ecologies and for her current writing on plants and botanical relationships, which will be collected in the in-progress monograph Plantasmagoria: Botanical Encounters in the [M]Anthropocene. Other publications include *Queer Ecologies: Sex, Nature, Politics, Desire* (co-edited with Bruce Erickson) (2010). Sandilands has also edited a volume of creative writing on climate change, *Rising Tides*, published by Caitlin Press in 2019.

PATRICIA DE VRIES is an Assistant Professor of Philosophy at Maastricht University. She holds a PhD from the Erasmus University in Rotterdam, with her work residing at the intersection of philosophy, digital art, society, and technology. De Vries explores the artistic and social imaginaries of emerging technologies and the anxieties that often underpin our relation to them. Previously, she worked as a Research Fellow at Digital Asia Hub in Hong Kong, a think tank affiliated to the Berkman Klein Center for Internet & Society at Harvard University, and was a visiting scholar at the Chinese University of Hong Kong, as well as working as a researcher and project coordinator at the Institute of Network Cultures in Amsterdam.

VALIZ is an independent international publisher, addressing contemporary developments in art, design, architecture, and urban affairs. Their books provide critical reflection and interdisciplinary inspiration in a broad and imaginative way, often establishing a connection between cultural disciplines and socio-economic questions. Valiz is headed by Astrid Vorstermans (1960) and Pia Pol (1985).

BART DE BAETS (1979) is a graphic designer based in Amsterdam. His design for the Sandberg Institute's temporary master programme The Radical Cut Up was nominated for a Dutch Design Award. It resulted in a commission to design a series of stamps for PostNL (Summer 2021). He is currently designing the graphic identity of the Kunstverein Langenhagen and its bi-monthly *KVL Bulletin*. Commissioned by the Architecture Academy in Amsterdam, together with Sandra Kassenaar he will design the next ten issues of *Forum*, a magazine published by AetA, the Dutch architects' society. He has been teaching design at the Gerrit Rietveld academy in Amsterdam and at the Royal Academy of Arts in The Hague since 2009.

Aben, Rob, and Saskia de Wit. *The Enclosed Garden: History and Development of the Hortus Conclusus and its Reintroduction into the Present-day Urban Landscape*. Rotterdam: 010 Publishers, 1999.

Abrioux, Yves. *Ian Hamilton Finlay: A Visual Primer*. 2nd ed. London: Reaktion, 1992.

Abufarha, Nasser. 'Land of Symbols: Cactus, Poppies, Orange and Olive Trees in Palestine.' *Identities: Global Studies in Culture and Power* 15, no. 3 (2008): 343–368.

Agamben, Giorgio. *Profanations*. New York: Zone Books, 2015.

Albrecht, Glenn, et al. 'Solastalgia: The Distress Caused by Environmental Change.' *Australasian Psychiatry* 15, no. 1 (2007): 95–98.

Artis Micropia. 'Mycorrhiza: Plants and Fungi Interact.' micropia.nl/en/discover/microbiology/mycorrhiza (accessed 6 January 2021).

Atre, Shubhangana. 'Many Seeded Apple: The Fruit of Fertility.' *Bulletin of the Deccan College Post-Graduate and Research Institute* 46, no. 1 (1987): 1–7.

Atwood, Margaret. 'Rachel Carson's Silent Spring, 50 Years On.' *The Guardian*, 7 December 2012. theguardian.com/books/2012/dec/07/why-rachel-carson-is-a-saint.

Barber, Richard. *Bestiary: MS Bodley 764*. Oxford: Boydell & Brewer Ltd, 1992.

Bell, Simon, et al., eds. *Urban Allotment Gardens in Europe*. London and New York: Routledge, 2016.

Bending, Stephen. *Green Retreats: Women, Gardens and Eighteenth-Century Culture*. Cambridge: Cambridge University Press, 2013.

Bennett, Jane. 'Vibrant Matter.' *CSPA Quarterly* no. 14 (August 2016): 7–11.

Borges, Jorge Luis. *The Analytical Language of John Wilkins*. Translated by Lilia Graciela Vázquez. *Alamut: Bastion of Peace and Information*. ccrma.stanford.edu/courses/155/assignment/ex1/Borges.pdf (accessed 16 December 2020).

Bourriaud, Nicolas. *The Radicant*. Translated by James Gussen and Lili Porten. New York: Sternberg Press, 2009.

Brougher, Kerry, and Michael Tarantino, eds. *Enclosed & Enchanted*. Oxford: Museum of Modern Art, 2000.

Bruce, Jonny. 'Lichens.' *SNAKY ZINE #2 On Movement*. Self-published, edited by Romy Day Winkel and Joy Brandsma. 2020

Burns, Sean. 'Jack Halberstam on Wildness, Illegibility and the Commercialization of Desire.' *Frieze*, 15 December 2020. frieze.com/interview/jack-halberstam-wild-things-disorder-of-desire.

Canon van Nederland. '1930 Tuindorp: Nieuwe wijk op de grens met de stad Utrecht.' canonvannederland.nl/nl/utrecht/regio-noordwest/maartensdijk/tuindorp (accessed 11 January 2020).

Casid, Jill. 'Queer(y)ing Georgic: Utility, Pleasure, and Marie-Antoinette's Ornamented Farm.' *Eighteenth-Century Studies* 30, no. 3 (1997): 304–318.

Capon, Brian. *Botany for Gardeners*. Portland: Timber Press, 2010.

Carson, Rachel. *Silent Spring*. Boston and New York: Houghton Mifflin, 1962.

Chalker-Scott, Linda. 'Hugelkultur: What is it, and Should it Be Used in Home Gardens?' *Washington State University Extension*. research.wsulibs.wsu.edu:8443/xmlui/bitstream/handle/2376/12233/FS283E.pdf?sequence=1&isAllowed=y (accessed 16 December 2020).

Chandler, Raymond. *The Big Sleep*. Project Gutenberg. gutenberg.ca/ebooks/chandlerr-bigsleep/chandlerr-bigsleep-00-h.html (accessed 6 January 2021).

Chisholm, Diane. 'Biophilia and the Ecological Future of Queer Desire.' In *Queer Ecologies: Sex, Nature, Politics and Desire*. Edited by Catriona Sandilands and Bruce Erickson, 359–381. Bloomington: Indiana University Press, 2010.

Clayton, Peter, and Martin Price, eds. *The Seven Wonders of the Ancient World*. London and New York: Routledge, 1988.

Coccia, Emanuele. *The Life of Plants: A Metaphysics of Mixture*. Cambridge: Polity, 2019.

Commons Network Team. 'Art + Commons: Announcing a New Collaboration.' *Commons Network*. commonsnetwork.org/news/art-commons-announcing-a-new-collaboration/ (10 October 2019).

Crutzen, Paul. 'Geology of Mankind.' *Nature* 415 (2002): 23.

Cuomo, Chris. *Feminism and Ecological Communities: An Ethic of Flourishing*. London and New York: Routledge, 1998.

Darwin, Erasmus. *The Botanic Garden: A Poem in Two Parts*. Project Gutenberg. gutenberg.org/cache/epub/9612/pg9612.html (accessed 17 December 2020).

Davis, Janae, Alex A. Moulton, Levi Van Sant and Brian Williams. 'Anthropocene, Capitalocene, ... Plantationocene?: A Manifesto for Ecological Justice in an Age of Global Crises.' *Geography Compass* 13, no. 5 (May 2019), 1–15. doi.org/10.1111/gec3.12438.

Deleuze, Gilles, and Felix Guattari. *A Thousand Plateaus: Capitalism and Schizophrenia*. Translated by Brian Massumi. Minneapolis: University of Minnesota Press, 1987.

Demos, T.J. *Decolonizing Nature: Contemporary Art and the Politics of Ecology*. Cambridge: MIT Press, 2016.

Encyclopaedia Britannica. britannica.com (accessed 5 January 2021).

Encyclopaedia Iranica. iranicaonline.org (accessed 5 January 2021).

Finlay, Ian Hamilton. 'More Detached Sentences on Gardening in the Manner of Shenstone.' *PN Review 42* 11, no. 2 (1985), 18–20.

Foucault, Michel. 'Of Other Spaces.' Translated by Jay Miskowiec. *Diacritics* 16, no. 1 (1986), 22–27.

Fowler, Corinne. *Green Unpleasant Land: Creative Responses to Rural England's Colonial Connections*. Leeds: Peepal Tree, 2020.

Gan, Elaine, et al. 'Introduction: Haunted Landscapes of the Anthropocene.' In *Arts of Living on a Damaged Planet*. Edited by Ana Tsing et al., 1–14. Minneapolis: University of Minnesota Press, 2017.

Gleason, Kathryn L., ed. *A Cultural History of Gardens in Antiquity*. London: Bloomsbury, 2013.

Goldberg, Ken, ed. *The Robot in the Garden: Telerobotics and Telepistemology in the Age of the Internet*. Cambridge: MIT Press, 2000.

Grabar, Oleg. *The Alhambra*. Cambridge: Harvard University Press, 1978.

Graham, Dan, et al. *Rock my Religion: Writings and Projects 1965–1990*. Edited by Brian Wallis. Cambridge: MIT Press, 1993.

Grimal, Pierre, and Stephan Kershaw, ed. *A Concise Dictionary of Classical Mythology*. From the translation by A.R. Maxwell-Hyslop. Oxford: Basil Blackwell Ltd, 1990.

Gröning, Gert, and Joachim Wolschke-Bulmahn. 'The Native Plant Enthusiasm: Ecological Panacea or Xenophobia?' *Arnoldia* 62, no. 4 (2010): 75–88.

Groot, Marion de. 'Ian Hamilton Finlay: Plug In #09.' Eindhoven: Van Abbemuseum. vanabbemuseum.nl/en/programme/programme/ian-hamilton-finlay/ (accessed 6 January 2021).

Haeg, Fritz. 'Edible Estates.' fritzhaeg.com/garden/initiatives/edibleestates/about.html (accessed 11 December 2020).

Haraway, Donna. 'Anthropocene, Capitalocene, Plantationocene, Chtulucene: Making Kin.' *Environmental Humanities* 6 (2015): 159–165.
–, *Staying with the Trouble: Making Kin in the Chthulucene*. Durham and London: Duke University Press, 2016.
–, *When Species Meet*. Vol 3. Minneapolis: University of Minnesota Press, 2008.

Harrison, Robert Pogue. *Gardens: An Essay on the Human Condition*. Chicago: University of Chicago Press, 2008.

Healthy Hildegard. 'What is Hildegard's Viriditas?' healthyhildegard.com/hildegards-viriditas/ (accessed 11 January 2020).

Hickey, David, and Susan Tallman. *The Collections of Barbara Bloom*. Göttingen: Steidl Publishers, 2008.

Higgie, Jennifer. 'The Worlds of Derek Jarman's Garden.' *Frieze*, 3 September 2020.. frieze.com/article/worlds-derek-jarmans-garden: (accessed 6 January 2021)

Holland, Agnieszka. *The Secret Garden*. Los Angeles, Warner Bros., 1993.

Hunt, John Dixon. *A World of Gardens*. London: Reaktion Books, 2014.

Hyde, Elizabeth, ed. *A Cultural History of Gardens in the Renaissance*. London: Bloomsbury Publishing, 2013.

Israel, Franklin. 'AD Revisits: Georgia O'Keeffe.' *Architectural Digest*, 31 December 2011. architecturaldigest.com/story/georgia-okeeffe-artist-new-mexico-ghost-ranch-article (accessed 16 December 2020).

Jacobs, Peter. 'Types of Gardens.' In *A Cultural History of Gardens in the Modern Age*. Edited by John Dixon Hunt, 37–61. London: Bloomsbury, 2016.

Jarman, Derek. *Modern Nature*. Minnesota: University of Minnesota Press, 1992.
–, *Derek Jarman's Garden*. London: Thames & Hudson, 1995.

Jekyll, Gertrude. *Home and Garden: Notes and Thoughts, Practical and Critical, of a Worker in Both*. London: Longmans, Green and Co., 1900. archive.org/details/homegardennotest00jeky/page/n9/mode/2up.
–, *Colour Schemes for the Flower Garden*. London: Country Life, 1919.

Jong, Erik A . de. 'Arcadia Disrupted.' In *Ian Hamilton Finlay: Et in Arcadia Ego*. The Hague: Stroom HCBK, 1999.
–, Gnomenculture.' *Viewpoints: Garden History and Landscape Studies at the Bard Graduate Center* 1, no. 2 (Spring/Summer 2004), 1–4.

Kellert, Stephen, and Edward Wilson, eds. *The Biophilia Hypothesis*. Washington: Island Press, 1995.

Kimmerer, Robin Wall. *Gathering Moss: A Natural and Cultural History of Mosses*. Corvallis: Oregon State University Press, 2003.

Kincaid, Jamaica. *My Garden (Book)*. New York: Farrar, Straus and Giroux, 1999.

Laing, Olivia. 'The Intertwining of Art, Gardening, Filmmaking and Writing.' *Frieze*, 20 April 2018. frieze.com/article/inter-twining-art-gardening-filmmak-ing-and-writing (accessed 5 January 2021).

Latimer, Quinn. *Like a Woman: Essays, Readings, Poems*. Berlin: Sternberg, 2017.

Latour, Bruno. *Facing Gaia: Eight Lectures on the New Climate Regime*. Translated by Cathy Porter. Cambridge: Polity Press, 2017.

Leslie, Michael, eds. *A Cultural History of Gardens in the Medieval Age*. London: Bloomsbury, 2013.

Levy, Ariel. 'Beautiful Monsters: Art and Obsession in Tuscany.' *The New Yorker*, 11 April 2016. new-yorker.com/magazine/2016/04/18/niki-de-saint-phalles-tarot-garden.

Lightman, Bernard, eds. *A Companion to the History of Science*. Hoboken: John Wiley & Sods, 2016.

Lovelock, James. *Gaia: A New Look at Life on Earth*. Oxford: Oxford Paperbacks, 2000.
–, *The Ages of Gaia: A Biography of our Living Earth*. Oxford: Oxford University Press, 2000.

Luxemburg, Rosa. *Letters to Sophie Liebknecht*. Marxists.org. marxists.org/archive/luxemburg/1917/undated/01.htm (accessed 16 December 2020).

MacDonald, Bruce. *Practical Woody Plant Propagation for Nursery Growers, Volume I*. Portland: Timber Press, 1986.

Mandela, Nelson. *Long Walk to Freedom*. 2nd ed. London: Abacus, 2013.

McCrae, John. *In Flanders Fields and Other Poems*. New York and London: Knickerbocker Press, 1919.

McKay, George. *Radical Gardening: Politics, Idealism & Rebellion in the Garden*. London: Frances Lincoln, 2011.

Meloy, Ellen. *The Anthropology of Turquoise: Reflections on Desert, Sea, Stone and Sky*. New York: Vintage, 2003.

Metzger, Gustav, and Andrew Wilson. *Gustav Metzger: Damaged Nature, Auto-Destructive Art*. London: Coracle Press, 1996.

Milton, John Everett. *Paradise Lost*. The John Milton Reading Room. dartmouth.edu/~milton/reading_room/pl/intro/text.shtml (accessed 16 December 2020).

Moore, Jason, ed. *Anthropocene or Capitalocene? Nature, History and the Crisis of Capitalism*. Oakland: PM Press, 2016.

Moore, Lisa Lynne. 'Queer Gardens: Mary Delany's Flowers and Friendships.' *Eighteenth-Century Studies* 39, no. 1 (2005): 49–70.

Mosser, Monique, and Georges Teysott, eds. *The Architecture of Western Gardens: A Design History from the Renaissance to the Present Day*. Cambridge: MIT Press, 1991.

Needelman, Brian A. 'What Are Soils?' *The Nature Education Knowledge Project*, 2013. nature.com/scitable/knowledge/library/what-are-soils-67647639/ (accessed 16 December 2020).

Nitschke, Günter. *Japanese Gardens. Right Angle and Natural Form*. Cologne: Taschen, 2003.

Oudolf, Piet, and Noel Kingsbury. *Planting: A New Perspective*. Portland: Timber Press, 2013.
–, and Henk Gerritsen. *Planting the Natural Garden*. Edited by Noel Kingsbury. Portland: Timber Press, 2019.

Pearce, J.M.S. 'The Doctrine of Signatures.' *European Neurology* 60, no. 1 (June 2008): 51–51. doi.org/10.1159/000131714.

Perényi, Eleanor. *Green Thoughts: A Writer in the Garden*. New York: Vintage Books, 1983.

Poe, Edgar Allen. *The Works of Edgar Allan Poe. The Raven Edition: Volume II*. Project Gutenberg. gutenberg.org/files/2148/2148-h/2148-h.htm#chap2.17 (accessed 16 December 2020).

Porter, Geraldine. 'What is a Ha-Ha?' *National Trust*. national-trust.org.uk/features/what-is-a-ha-ha (accessed 16 December 2020).

Prest, John. *The Garden of Eden: The Botanic Garden and the Re-creation of Paradise*. New Haven: Yale University Press, 1981.

Reynolds, Richard. 'Guerrilla Gardening Tips.' guerrillagardening.org/ggtips.html (accessed 16 December 2020).
–, *On Guerrilla Gardening: A Handbook for Gardening without Boundaries*. London: Bloomsbury Publishing, 2014.

Robertson, Lisa. *Occasional Work and Seven Walks from the Office for Soft Architecture*. Astoria: Clear Cut Press, 2003.

Rodomsky-Bish, Becca. 'The Seven Principles of Xeriscaping.' *The Habitat Network*, 20 October 2015. content.yardmap.org/learn/the-seven-principles-of-xeriscape/.

Romakin, Helena, and Vanina Saracino. 'Humus.' *e-flux*.e-flux.com/readers/340320/humus (accessed 16 December 2020).

Sackville-West, Vita. *The Garden*. London: Michael Joseph Limited, 1946.

Sandilands, Catriona. *The Good-Natured Feminist: Ecofeminism and the Quest for Democracy*. London and Minneapolis: University of Minnesota Press, 1999.
–, 'Melancholy Natures, Queer Ecologies.' In *Queer Ecologies: Sex, Nature, Politics and Desire*. Edited by Catriona Sandilands and Bruce Erickson, 331–358. Bloomington: Indiana University Press, 2010.
–, and Bruce Erickson, eds. *Queer Ecologies: Sex, Nature, Politics and Desire*. Bloomington: Indiana University Press, 2010.

Schama, Simon. *Landscape and Memory*. New York: Vintage, 1995.

Schmitz, Oswald. *The New Ecology: Rethinking a Science for the Anthropocene*. Princeton: Princeton University Press, 2017.

Schneiderman, Jill S. 'The Anthropocene Controversy.' In *Anthropocene Feminism*. Edited by Richard Grusin, 169–198. Minneapolis: University of Minnesota Press, 2017.

Serra, Clara, and Teresa Nobre de Carvalho. *The Emperor's Flowers. From Bulb to Carpet*. Lisbon: Calouste Gulbenkian Museum, 2018.

Sheldrake, Merlin. *Entangled Life: How Fungi Make Our Worlds, Change Our Minds, and Shape Our Futures*. New York: Random House, 2020.

Shigemori, Mirei. 'Shin-Sakuteiki.' In *Shigemori Mirei Sakuhinshû: Niwa Kamigami e no Apurôchi*. Tokyo: Seibundô Shinkô Sha, 1976.

Shiva, Vandana. 'Growing Gardens of Diversity Weaving Gardens of Love.' *Jivad: The Vandana Shiva Blog*, 15 January 2020. navdanya.org/bija-refelections/2020/01/15/growing-gardens-of-diversity-weav-ing-gardens-of-love/.
–, and Maria Mies. *Ecofeminism*. London: Zed Books, 2014.

Simard, Suzanne. 'How Trees Talk to Each Other.' Filmed June 2016 at TEDSummit, Banff, Canada. Video, 18:11. ted.com/talks/suzanne_simard_how_trees_talk_to_each_other?language=mg.

Smith, Valerie, et al. *Down the Garden Path: The Artist's Garden After Modernism*. New York: Queens Museum of Art, 2006.

Spaid, Sue. *Ecovention*. Cincinnati: The Contemporary Arts Center, Eco-artspace and Greenmuseum.org, 2002.

Spencer, Tony. 'New Year Perennial Field Report: People, Plants, Places.' *The New Perennialist: Explorations in Naturalistic Planting Design*, 4 January 2018. thenewperennialist.com/new-year-perennial-field-report-peo-ple-plants-places/.

Stanford Encyclopedia of Philosophy. 'Ecology.' First published 23 December 2005. plato.stanford.edu/entries/ecology/.

Stengers, Isabelle. In *Catastrophic Times: Resisting the Coming Barbarism*. Translated by Andrew Goffey. London: Open Humanities Press, 2015.

Strabo, Walahfrid. *Hortulus*. Translated by Raef Payne. Pittsburgh: The Hunt Botanical Library, 1966.

Strathern, Marilyn. *Reproducing the Future: Essays on Anthropology, Kinship and the New Reproductive Technologies*. Manchester: Manchester University Press, 1992.

Stuart-Smith, Sue. *The Well-Gardened Mind: Rediscovering Nature in the Modern World*. London: William Collins, 2020.

Tankard, Judith B. *Gardens of the Arts & Crafts Movement*. Portland: Timber Press, 2018.

Tarantino, Michael. 'Enclosed and Enchanted: Et in Arcadia Ego.' In *Enclosed and Enchanted*. Edited by Kerry Brougher and Michael Tarantino, 19–32. Oxford: Museum of Modern Art, 2000.

Thoreau, Henry David. 'Walking.' *The Atlantic Monthly: A Magazine on Literature, Art and Politics* 9, no. 56 (1862): 657–674.

Titley, Norah M. *Plants and Gardens in Persian, Mughal and Turkish Art*. London: British Library, 1979.

Tola, Miriam. 'Composing with Gaia: Isabelle Stengers and the Feminist Politics of the Earth.' *PhænEx* 11, no. 1 (Spring/Summer 2016): 1–21.

Tsing, Ana, Heather Swanson, Elaine Gan and Nils Bubant, eds. *Arts of Living on a Damaged Planet*. Minneapolis and London: University of Minnesota Press, 2017.

Tuinen Mien Ruys. 'Mien Ruys.' tuinenmienruys.nl/en/mien-ruys-1/ (accessed 5 January 2021).

UNESCO Intangible Cultural Heritage. 'Javanese Pekarangan Homegarden System.' ich.unesco.org/en/individual-case-study-00988&id=00004 (accessed 16 December 2020).

Vicuña, Cecilia. 'Language is Migrant.' *South as a State of Mind: documenta 14* 8, no. 3 (2016). documenta14.de/en/south/904_language_is_migrant (accessed December 16, 2020).

Vidal-Castro, Francisco. 'Ibn Luyūn.' In *Encyclopaedia of Islam, THREE*. Edited by Kate Fleet et al. referenceworks.brillonline.com/entries/encyclopaedia-of-islam-3/*-COM_30643 (accessed 16 December 2020).

Vincent, Alice. *Rootbound: Rewilding a Life*. London: Canongate, 2020.

Wahmann, Birgit. 'Allotments and Schrebergarten in Germany'. In *The Architecture of Western Gardens: A Design History from the Renaissance to the Present Day*. Edited by Monique Mosser and George Teyssot, 451–453. Cambridge: MIT Press, 1991.

Walker, Sophie. *The Japanese Garden*. London: Phaidon, 2017.

Wark, McKenzie. 'Chtulucene, Capitalocene, Anthropocene.' *Public Seminar*, 8 September 2016. publicseminar.org/2016/09/chthulu/.

Weilacher, Udo. 'Use and Reception.' In *A Cultural History of Gardens in the Modern Age*. Edited by John Dixon Hunt, 93–116. London: Bloomsbury, 2016.

Weiss, Allen S. *Mirrors of Infinity: The French Formal Garden and 17th-Century Metaphysics*. New York: Princeton Architectural Press, 1995.

Whittington, Stephen. 'Digging In John Cage's Garden: Cage and Ryōanji.' *Malaysian Journal of Music* 2, no. 2 (2013): 12–21.

Wigley, Mark. 'Electric Lawn.' In *The American Lawn*. Edited by Georges Teyssot, 154–195. Princeton: Princeton Architectural Press, 1999.

Wildschut, Henk. *Rooted*. Amsterdam: Henk Wildschut, 2019.

Wilner, Eleanor. 'The Girls with Bees in Her Hair.' In *Gardens: An Essay on the Human Condition*. Edited by Robert Harrison. Chicago and London: University Press of Chicago, 2008.

Wilson, Edward. *Biophilia*. Cambridge: Harvard University Press, 1984.

Wohlleben, Peter. *The Hidden Life Of Trees: What They Feel, How They Communicate: Discoveries from a Secret World*. Vancouver and Berkeley: Greystone Books, 2015.

Wordsworth, William. *Poems Volume I*. en.wikisource.org/wiki/Poems_(Wordsworth,_1815)/Volume_1/To_the_same_Flower_(Daisy) (accessed 17 December 2020).

EDITOR
Laurie Cluitmans

ASSISTANT EDITORS
Arent Boon, Eva Burgering

CONTRIBUTIONS BY
Maria Barnas
Jonny Bruce
Bart Rutten
Laurie Cluitmans
Thiëmo Heilbron
Liesbeth M. Helmus
Erik A. de Jong
René de Kam
Alhena Katsof
Jamaica Kincaid
Catriona Sandilands
Patricia de Vries

TRANSLATION
Gerard Forde
Michele Hutchison

COPY-EDITING
Neil Fawle

INITIAL EDITING OF TEXTS CENTRAAL MUSEUM
Hans Schopping

PROOFREADING
Els Brinkman

INDEX
Nic de Jong

IMAGE RESEARCH
Arent Boon
Eva Burgering

GRAPHIC DESIGN
Bart de Baets

TYPEFACES
Times Nr. Seven MT
Optima
AG Buch BQ Regular
AG Buch Extended BQ Bold

PAPER INSIDE
Munken premium cream 1.95
Soporset 1.3

PAPER COVER
Arena White Rough

LITHOGRAPHY
Mariska Bijl

PRINTING AND BINDING
Wilco Art Books, Amersfoort

PUBLISHING PARTNERS

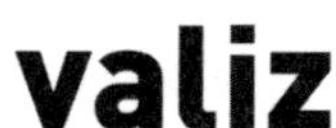

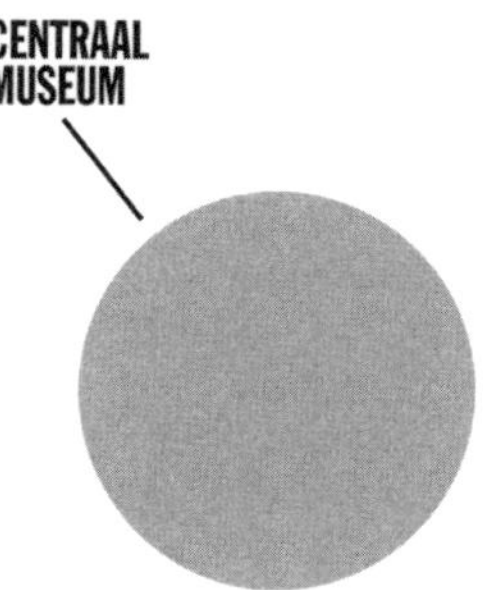

Centraal Museum, Utrecht

This publication has been printed on FSC-certified paper by an FSC-certified printer. The FSC, Forest Stewardship Council promotes environmentally appropriate, socially beneficial, and economically viable management of the world's forests. fsc.org

INTERNATIONAL DISTRIBUTION
BE/NL/LU: Centraal Boekhuis, www.centraal.boekhuis.nl
Europe/Asia (except GB/IE): Idea Books, www.ideabooks.nl
GB/IE: Anagram Books, www.anagrambooks.com
USA/Canada/Latin America: D.A.P., www.artbook.com
Australia: Perimeter Books, www.perimeterbooks.com
Individual orders: www.valiz.nl; info@valiz.nl

ISBN 978-94-93246-00-3
Printed and bound in the EU, 2021

THIS PUBLICATION WAS MADE POSSIBLE THROUGH THE GENEROUS SUPPORT OF
Creative Industries Fund
Stichting Jaap Harten Fonds
dr. Hendrik Mullerfonds
Stichting De Gijselaar-Hintzenfonds

creative industries fund NL

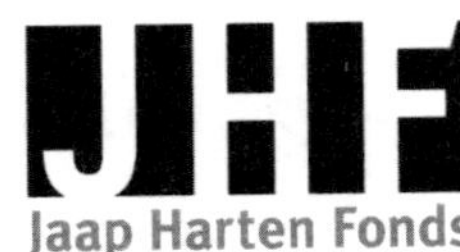

De Gijselaar-Hintzenfonds

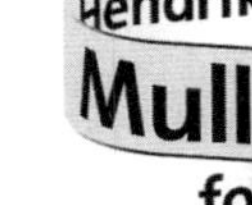

THE EXHIBITION IN THE CENTRAAL MUSEUM IS SUPPORTED BY
Fonds 21
Gemeente Utrecht
VriendenLoterij
Ministerie van OCW
Mondriaan Fonds
MUNT hypotheken
Creative Industries Fund
Van Baaren Stichting.

FONDS 21

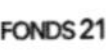

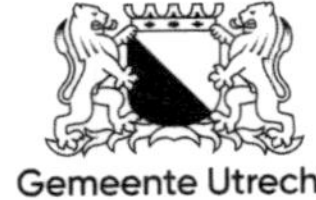

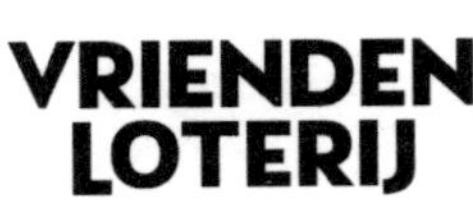

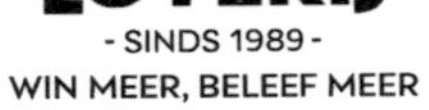

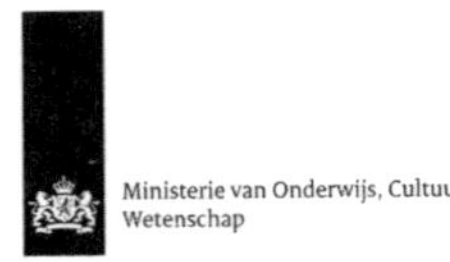

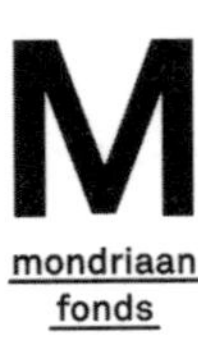

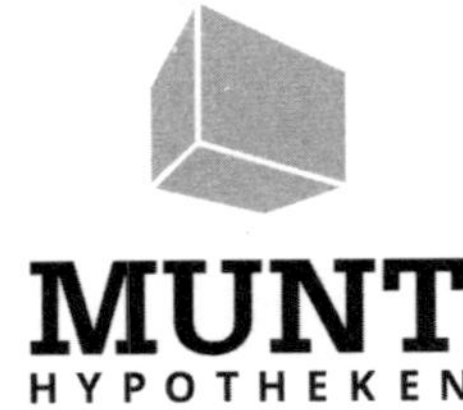

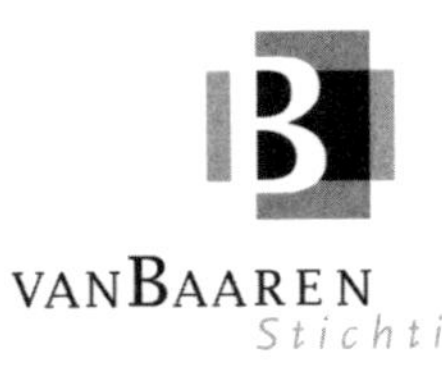